AN AID FOR
MANAGERIAL
DECISION MAKING

Management
Science

AN AID FOR MANAGERIAL DECISION MAKING

Management Science

Larry M. Austin
James R. Burns

Texas Tech University

MACMILLAN PUBLISHING COMPANY
NEW YORK

Collier Macmillan Publishers
London

Copyright © 1985, Macmillan Publishing Company, a division of
Macmillan, Inc.

Printed in the United States of America

Macmillan Publishing Company
866 Third Avenue, New York, New York 10022

Collier Macmillan Canada, Inc.

Library of Congress Cataloging in Publication Data

Austin, Larry M.
  Management science.
  Includes index.
  1. Management science. I. Burns, James R.
II. Title.
T56.A87 1985   658.4'03   84-9720
ISBN 0-02-304840-9

Printing: 1 2 3 4 5 6 7 8   Year: 5 6 7 8 9 0 1 2 3

ISBN   0-02-304840-9

PREFACE

This text is intended for use in quantitative methods courses in management science/operations research (MS/OR) as taught to business administration students. A business student needs to learn how to formulate models to enhance his or her problem-solving and decision-making abilities and is much less concerned with the mathematical details of the algorithms used to solve these models. The organization and substance of this book are geared therefore toward *problem* solution and model conceptualization — not hand solution of textbook models.

In view of the specific pedagogical needs of the future manager, we adopted the following goals and criteria for the design of this text:

1. To emphasize the development of problem solving and model formulation skills, including
   a. Recognition of how and when a particular type of model can be of value
   b. The ability to construct an appropriate model of the problem
2. To consider carefully the assumptions that underlie each model and its associated algorithm(s)
3. To discuss available commercial computer codes, including
   a. How to use them
   b. How to interpret the outputs they produce
4. To introduce the student to a variety of real-world problems and their models through the use of brief but realistic cases
5. To articulate the art and science of decision making under conditions of certainty, risk, and uncertainty/complexity
6. To employ a managerial perspective that focuses on decision making rather than on the mathematical details of solution techniques

In addition, this book places a strong emphasis on "what-if" modeling. Typically, optimization models address the issue "what's best." We attempt to show how such models can also be used to address the question "what-if." In addition, simulation models are generally believed to address the question "what-if"; however, such models can also be used to consider "what's best."

v

Criteria for deciding whether one should simulate or optimize are therefore given particular attention.

This is not a text that "forces" an analytic, quantitative approach to decision making and management. Rather, we recognize the importance of decision factors that are intuitive, subjective, judgmental, and unquantifiable as an inherent component of each realistic minicase. We illustrate how only a proper *mix* of quantitative and nonquantitative considerations can lead to a satisfactory solution strategy.

We treat decision making at all levels of the organization. The organization or firm is represented as a hierarchy of decision making in which higher-level management determines the parameters that are used for lower levels of decision making. At each level, modeling begins with an assessment of which factors or variables are within the decision maker's capacity to influence and which can only be observed. All model formulations, therefore, begin and end with a specified decision maker's perspective and perception of the problem. And there is no shunning of the complexity that usually accompanies problems in the real world.

ORGANIZATION OF THE TEXT

The text begins with a discussion of modeling as both art and science. The importance of modeling is discussed, and the notation used in the text is introduced. We characterize the model-building process in some generality and discuss the criteria by which the manager classifies his or her problem and chooses an appropriate model to represent that problem. These notions are presented in Chapter 1.

The remainder of the text is divided into the following four parts:

Decision Making Under Certainty

Decision Making Under Risk

Decision Making Under Uncertainty/Complexity

Management Science and the Future

In the following, we briefly describe each of these parts.

Chapters 2 through 6 are devoted to decision making under certainty. These chapters systematically present some deterministic mathematical programming models — linear, integer, network, and nonlinear programming. We also have included dynamic programming.

Chapters 7 through 11 describe concepts related to decision making under risk. Chapter 7 discusses the use of decision trees, the concept of expected value and opportunity loss, Bayesian analysis, and the concept of economic utility. Chapter 8 describes the use of queueing (waiting-line) models. Chapters 9 and 10 discuss discrete simulation and Markov chains, respectively. Chapter 11 describes the extension of probabilistic concepts to project scheduling and inventory management.

Chapters 12 through 15 discuss models for decision making under uncertainty and complexity. Chapter 12 covers classical decision models. Chapter 13 discusses modeling with multiple objectives and goal programming. Chapter 14 is devoted to a description of structural models for characterizing the complexity of the decision environment: DELTA charting, cross-impact matrices, and causal modeling are all given careful attention. Chapter 15 deals with continuous simulation models.

The last part is its own chapter and presents our view of the "high-tech" future of 1995.

ORGANIZATION OF EACH CHAPTER

Except for Chapter 11, each chapter discusses exactly one type of MS/OR model, and a uniform format is used throughout most of the text. This format is intended to achieve the goals mentioned above. As indicated in the table of contents, a typical chapter consists of the following sections:

a. Underlying assumptions
b. _____ Modeling
c. Solution Approaches
d. Available _____ Computer Codes
e. Developing Alternative Solutions
f. State of the Art in _____
g. Minicases
h. Summary
i. Problems
j. References and Additional Readings

Section a, as its name implies, carefully discusses underlying assumptions. Here such concepts as linearity and multistage decision making are given managerial meaning. We also describe the problem classes appropriate for this type of model.

Section b describes the models verbally and presents an intuitive description of the corresponding mathematical representations. Terms that have to do with the algorithm used to solve the model (e.g., artificial variable, pivot, entering variable, exiting variable) are omitted or deemphasized. Section b devotes particular attention to how models of this type are formulated and what the data requirements are.

Section c is an intuitive description of the algorithm(s) used to solve models of this type. In this section, the algorithms are described by analogy or by use of graphical and tabular illustrations.

Section d discusses one or more available computer codes and describes its use for the particular model type being considered. The focus is on specifying the inputs needed and on the ability to interpret properly the output produced by the program.

Section e discusses sensitivity studies and parametric analyses of model solutions that can be performed to assist in developing alternative solutions to the problem.

Section f discusses state-of-the-art topics associated with the model being considered, including computational considerations as related to problem size, potential difficulties encountered during computer implementation, and so on.

Our purpose in including these brief discussions of advanced models and techniques is to make potential and practicing managers aware that they exist — and nothing more. To discuss these approaches in detail would take us beyond the intended scope of the book. To omit them altogether would convey to students an incomplete and, therefore, erroneous impression of the dynamic nature of management science.

Section g contain "minicases" — hypothetical and actual short cases that illustrate applications of the model to realistic problems. Not all minicases report successful applications; some describe *unsuccessful* applications — and why they were unsuccessful. These minicases reflect the complexity of the real-world decision environment.

Section h summarizes the material presented in the chapter and provides a nutshell overview of the chapter contents.

Section i contains end of chapter problems that we hope will stimulate and challenge the student.

Section j is chapter references and suggestions for additional readings.

This book emphasizes the problem-definitional aspects of MS/OR usage and recognizes a need for coping with the complexity of the real-world decision environment. It treats such complexity with candor, and it presents tools for characterizing and analyzing the complexity of the real world. The book presents a managerial perspective of decision analysis that caters specifically to the epistemological needs of future managers.

Although the writing style is informal, and despite the fact that the authors indulge freely in their affinity for puns and unconventional scenarios, this is a *deadly serious book.* It is not about algorithms. It is about the difficult, complex, and frustrating process of managerial decision making. If the book has a "theme," it can be described best by the following phrase, which is repeated several times herein:

Models don't make decisions — Managers do.

SUPPORTING MATERIALS

For the convenience of adopters, we have written an *Instructor's Manual* to accompany the text. In addition to giving solutions to most of the end-of-chapter problems, the manual contains "chats with the authors" — informal discussions about the approach we took to the material in each chapter. We also decipher some of the puns for those not accustomed to such frippery. Finally, we include two sets of syllabi, exams, and handouts that we actually used in our MBA course in management science — one set for each author. The purpose of including our own teaching materials is merely to illustrate two ways that the book can be used in class since our teaching styles happen to be quite different.

A complete software package programmed by James R. Burns and an accompanying manual entitled "Management Science Models and the Micro-computer" are available from Macmillan. The manual has most of the same chapter titles as the textbook, so that the package can be used as a supplement to the text. The software is very user-friendly and an exceptionally good pedagogical tool.

ACKNOWLEDGMENTS

In preparing this book for publication, we were very fortunate to have the advice and assistance of a truly exceptional group of reviewers. Special thanks go to Jim Wetherbe of the University of Minnesota, Bob Minch of the Krannert School at Purdue University, and Mike Hanna of the University of Texas-Arlington, all of whom made invaluable suggestions — while resisting the urge to exact revenge upon their former professors!

Our sincere expression of appreciation for their most helpful comments also goes to Scott Turner at Oklahoma State, William Tinney at UT-Arlington, David Schilling at Ohio State, James Pope at Old Dominion, Dave Pentico at Virginia Commonwealth, T. H. Mattheiss at Alabama, Terry Harrison at Penn State, Guisseppi Forgionne at Cal Poly-Pomona, James Dyer at UT-Austin, Stephen Bechtold at Florida State, and Edward Baker at U. of Miami.

We would like to acknowledge the patient professionalism of our Editor, Jack Repcheck, and our Production Supervisor, Hurd Hutchins, at Macmillan — as well as the foresight and courage of Macmillan Publishing Company in deciding to try something new.

We wish to thank the Battelle Memorial Institute for the use of the following figures in Chapter 14: 14-6, 14-7, 14-8, 14-13, 14-16, 14-17, 14-21, 14-22, 14-23, and 14-24. We also wish to thank the MIT Press for the use of Figure 15-15.

For their help in typing the seemingly endless versions of the manuscript, we thank Nina Klinkenberg, Gloria Smith, and Pam Knighten. For their incisive comments on three draft versions of the book, and for the raw material for several excellent minicases, we are grateful to our MBA students — present and past. And to our dean, Carl Stem, and our colleagues at Texas Tech, we appreciate your support and encouragement.

Finally, but by no means least, we thank Jill and Marilu, who make it all worthwhile, and to whom we dedicate this book.

L.M.A.
J.R.B.

CONTENTS

||| DECISION MAKING UNDER UNCERTAINTY AND COMPLEXITY

IV MANAGERIAL DECISION MAKING: MANAGING THE FUTURE

Appendices

CHAPTER 1

Introduction: Problems, Models, Decisions, and Systems

This book is concerned with solving problems and making decisions. Among cerebral and cognitive activities, these represent some of the most fundamental undertakings in which we human beings engage, and they form the main thesis of the book: namely, that the use of management science (MS) models can make us better decision makers and problem solvers. A *model* is a paradigm, a description and an explanation of the relationship of the parts of the problem to each other, or of the problem to its environment. Models help us to understand the problem. Models enable us to evaluate the courses of action we could take in any given decision situation. Models reflect the structure of the system or decision they are intended to represent.

Each of us uses models as a basis for making decisions. An oil firm executive gathers information in the form of printed data, listens to the opinions of others, and concludes that retail gasoline prices must be raised in response to increases in the price of crude oil. An economist reads the consumer price statistics and concludes that more stringent controls on the money supply must be applied. A student keeps close track of his performance in his courses so as to determine how much effort will be required to achieve the grades he wants. In each case, a mental model is formulated as a basis for making decisions. Even our interpersonal responses stem from models; in this case, our personalities are said by psychologists to be strongly colored by our mental model of ourselves—our self-image.

Our mental concepts of a particular situation represent the model—either explicit or implicit—that we use to make decisions in both private and professional life. At times, that mental model is biased, fuzzy, incomplete, inaccurate, or just plain wrong. Obviously, the response or decision stemming from that

1

Figure 1.1   A stockbroker's mental model of the market.

mental model will probably be wrong also, and the consequences of the unscrupulous decision must be faced. The point is that all conscious decisions are made on the basis of models. So the question then is not *whether* we should use models; the question is rather one of *what kinds.*

Consider the stockbroker shown in Figure 1.1. His mental model of the stock market suggests that the market will continue to go up in the short run before dropping drastically. In light of his mental model, the stockbroker is advising his clients to sell their holdings. If the stockbroker has many colleagues who share the same view of the market, then their simultaneous advice to investors could actually cause the predicted downturn to occur. Thus, in this case, the mental model becomes self-fulfilling. Such are the hazards of forecasting models in the managerial sciences. "Gloom and doom" predictions may create the very factors responsible for drastic downward readjustments. Clearly, models influence managerial behavior, which weighs heavily upon the outcomes that accrue from the system itself. Self-image models, furthermore, tend to be consistently self-fulfilling.

This book focuses on management science (or "MS") models, and its premise is that such models are better decision aids than are mental models alone. Actually such models should be used to influence, formalize, and "concretize" the mental models on which all decisions are made. An MS model may encompass quantitative, mathematical, or graphic forms. It is to be distinguished from the verbal models that comprise much of the literature in business, economics, sociology, political science, and psychology.

It is our contention that MS models will enable better decisions to be made. Questions such as, "What form do these models take?" "How are these models formulated?" "What data are needed?" and "How are these models solved?" must be addressed. The answers to these questions constitute most of the content of this book.

PROBLEMS AND DECISIONS

Problems arise whenever there is a perceived difference between *what is desired* and *what is.* In the language of the economist, wherever expectations differ substantially from realizations, a problem occurs.

Problems serve as motivators for doing something. What is done must first begin with a decision about what to do. So problems ultimately lead to decisions as indicated in Figure 1.2. *Decision making has as its goal that of mitigating or*

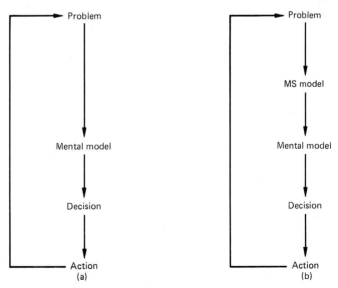

Figure 1.2 Relationships among models, problems, decisions, and systems.

alleviating perceived problems. The "problem" may be that the system is inefficient or that profits are not maximized or costs not minimized. In Figure 1.2a, a
problem leads to a decision about that problem, and then to some action — the
decision could be to do nothing for now. The decision will thereafter have an
impact upon the problem, and the problem will either diminish or be exacer-
bated. The effect upon the problem will be observed, and this will lead to further
decisions about the problem in question.

The plan and purpose of this book is to insert into the decision process the
use of MS models, as shown in Figure 1.2b. The problem is studied in the
framework of its own *system* to enable a contextual understanding of the
problem. This is the essence of the so-called *systems approach* popularized in
recent years by Churchman [1] and others. The *system* that encompasses the
problem includes all structural components that interact with the problem in
some way along with the interactions. A good problem solver should try to
develop the largest possible perspective of that problem. This is tantamount to
understanding the problem within the context of its own system.

MODEL CLASSIFICATION

Most models can be classified in a variety of different ways. For example,
purpose, perspective, degree of abstraction, and *content* represent four different
classification criteria.

Models classified according to *purpose* would require that we consider the
kinds of uses to which models can be put, as indicated in Table 1.1. We can use
models for planning, for forecasting, for training, for behavioral research, or for
some combination of these. Both planning and forecasting models improve the
decision-making acumen of managers and represent the two most widely employed purposes to which models can be put by managers. Training models, for
example, enable pilots to increase their skills in what are called flight simulations, whereas behavioral research models explain why the behavior of people,
organizations, or animals is likely to manifest itself in a certain way.

Models classified according to *perspective* fall into two basic categories:
descriptive and prescriptive. Descriptive models try to depict an existing
situation — "telling it like it is." Prescriptive models, on the other hand, attempt to prescribe an ideal situation. A company's accounting and bookkeep-

Table 1.1   Major Modeling Categories

Purpose	*Perspective*	*Degree of Abstraction*	*Content*
Planning	Descriptive	Isomorphic	Mental constructs
Forecasting	Prescriptive	Homomorphic	Physical prototypes
Training			Verbal descriptions
Behavioral			Management science
research			(MS) models

ing records, for example, represent a descriptive model of what the earnings structure actually is—for example, net earnings around 5% of gross investment. However, resident within the minds of top-level management is an "ideal" model with earnings of 8%. A plan is evolved for taking the firm's earnings, as indicated by the descriptive model, a step in the direction of the prescriptive model.

Models classified according to *degree of abstraction* are either isomorphic (one to one) or homomorphic (one to many). An isomorphic model is one in which every component in the real-world system has a corresponding component in the model. Such models are said to have components that are in one to one correspondence with components in the real world. On the other hand, a homomorphic model is one in which each component in the model may represent many components in the real-world system. As an example, it is customary to use one variable to represent the number of components of a certain type; in a way, the decision variable represents all such components. In this case the correspondence is said to be one to many. Most of the models described in this book are one to many in the sense that one component may represent more than one component in the real system.

Models are most often classified according to *content*. Four categories are recognized as indicated in Table 1.1: mental models, physical models, verbal models, and MS models.

Mental models are the basis for all human behavior. Since our mental faculties are limited, there is a limit to the number of factors we can consider simultaneously. Psychologists tell us that this limit is *7 plus or minus 2*. (The seven-digit telephone number was determined after extensive research suggested that seven digits was the maximum that could be easily remembered.) MS models serve as information input to mental models. Clearly, MS models must produce results that can be easily understood to be of any value.

Physical models are widely used in science, engineering, and architecture. Miniature models of aircraft are built and are placed in wind tunnels for the purpose of studying stability, aerodynamics, and air flow characteristics. Architectural models of planned new construction are used to enable planners to get a three-dimensional perspective of the structure and, thus, to assess the overall aesthetic effect. Flight simulators represent physical models that are used to train pilots. Dress designers fabricate physical models of dresses, which are thereafter tested for marketability.

Verbal models comprise much of the literature in business, economics, sociology, psychology, political science, and history. A classic example of a verbal model is the energy-economy-environment enigma about which so much has been written over the last ten years. A typical verbal model follows.

Americans have witnessed how an emphasis upon the environment contributed to a growing demand in the transportation sector for liquid fuels, which, at times, were in short supply. To provide sufficient fuel, America's oil import quotas have risen. To offset the balance-of-payments drain, a commensurate increase in the exportation of agricultural produce was at times encouraged.

Pollution controls applied to new automobiles caused increases in their prices. Rises in the price of imported crude oil also produced price increases that reverberated throughout the economic system. These price increases served only to fan further the fires of inflation already burning because of excessive demand and insufficient supply of goods and services.

The succession of concurrent increases in fuel prices increased the profits of oil exploration companies that, along with the banking industry, invested substantial capital in the further exploration of oil. This resulted in an overabundance of oil, which stabilized fuel prices.

The behavior of the energy-economy-environment system can be traced to the decisions that were implemented and the consequences derived from those decisions.

Oswald Spengler and Arnold Toynbee have separately espoused models of history. In *The Decline of the West* [2], Spengler in 1945 suggested that Western civilization was in the winter of its life cycle and would die by the twenty-third century. In 1954 Toynbee [3] proposed a linear evolutionary model of history, in which civilization evolves from primitive to more sophisticated forms. Civilization survives by deploying increasingly sophisticated solutions to increasingly difficult problems. Other models claim that history is shaped by the moving forces of courageous men. Such models are ostensibly verbal in terms of form and content.

The last model category listed in Table 1.1 is the MS model. The MS model may itself be further classified into ever-more specific model forms. We choose in this book to classify MS models according to the decision environments for which they are most appropriate, as indicated in Table 1.2. Decision making can occur under the conditions of certainty, risk, and uncertainty/complexity. We can classify MS models as to whether they are appropriate for decision making under each of these conditions, as shown in Table 1.2.

In Figure 1.2 we tried to depict the relation between a problem and the decision that addressed the problem. Decision making under certainty simply suggests that the system (and inputs received from the environment) in which the problem is embedded can be characterized by certainty. That is, there is perfect knowledge about the system (including its inputs). Obviously, very few systems can be known and understood perfectly. Even so, for some systems, this may be an appropriate assumption. Financial models that project corporate balance sheets and income statements are of this type. Under such conditions we refer to the problem as *deterministic*. Of particular interest are the possible future states of the environment, since these states influence the inputs from the environment. If we assume that the future is known perfectly, then we are faced with decision making under certainty.

Decision making under risk involves a problem embedded in a system whose outcomes are not known perfectly. We use probability theory to characterize our imperfect knowledge about the system and about any inputs received from the environment. The possible futures are assigned probabilities in accordance with the likelihood of their occurrence. In this case, some knowledge

**Table 1.2   Decision Environments and MS
Models Discussed In This Text**

Decision Making Under Certainty

Linear Programming Models
Integer Programming Models
Modeling with Networks
Nonlinear Programming Models
Discrete Dynamic Programming Models

Decision Making Under Risk

Bayesian Analysis and Expected Utility Models
Waiting-Line Models
Discrete Simulation Models
Markov Chain Models
Project Planning and Inventory Management Models

Decision Making Under Uncertainty and Complexity

Classical Decision Models
Models Involving Multiple Objectives
Structural Models
Continuous Simulation Models

of the system and its environment is available, but perfect knowledge is not available.

Decision making under uncertainty and complexity are treated jointly since complexity creates situations involving uncertainty. Decision making under complexity involves systems and environments that consist of a large number of components and a substantial amount of interaction among the components. Sometimes the problem being considered involves a system that is so complex that its structure is not well understood by managers. Under such circumstances, it is important that they have model-building tools that will enable them to structure models of their systems, so that they can identify gaps in understanding. The resultant *structural model* provides an overall picture of the structure of the system in terms of components and interactions. Decision making under uncertainty involves a problem embedded in a system and an associated environment about which nothing is known. Investment decisions in which the risk of certain investment alternatives are unknown fall into this category.

A moment's comparison of Table 1.2 with the table of contents of this book discloses a striking similarity. This book will introduce you to each of these model types so that you can thoroughly understand when (and how) to use them. Of course, whether you use a linear programming model or a discrete simulation model will depend on the type of problem being considered. We address this subject in the section entitled "Identification of the Problem" in this chapter.

MODEL BUILDING — AN ART AND A SCIENCE

A great many definitions of MS models are particularized to a specific class of problems. The following definition is more general than most:

> **An MS model** is a quantitative representation of a process that consists of those components that are significant for the purpose being considered.

The reference to *purpose* here is significant. All models contain information about the system; however, they contain less information than is contained within the system itself, and that information is at times organized differently. What components, and what data to include in (and what to exclude from) the model, are based exclusively upon the purposes of the model-building effort. For instance, Coyle [4] intimates that the level of detail in a structure is dependent on the manager's decision variables — if the purpose is to model the system from the vantage point of the manager who controls or influences the system.

The fact that the model contains less information than is contained within the real system is an advantage in a way, because it simplifies the situation through elimination of superfluous detail. For example Thesen [5] states that "all aspects of the real situation not relevant to the purpose of the model could be ignored." For complex systems, however, Thesen points out that *all* elements directly or indirectly seem relevant to the stated purpose. The model builder is consequently faced with the difficult problem of defining the "relative relevancy of different elements of the real situation." This is one reason why model building will always remain a mixture of both art and science.

Following Thesen, we define the *art or process of model building* as "the act of (1) identifying information relevant to a problem area and (2) creating a real or imaginary *entity* containing this information in a form suitable for the purposes of this effort." In Thesen's definition, "entity" is synonymous with "model." It follows that thorough knowledge and understanding of the system is indeed essential.

We represent the process of model building and its subsequent use by 11 steps, which we refer to as "The 11 Steps to Better Modeling and Happier Managing," as exhibited in Figure 1.3. The 11 formal steps to model building, which we will discuss, are too many for us to remember easily (recall the 7 plus or minus 2 rule). So we choose to group these together into four basic categories: scenario, problem, model, and solution (SPMS). In subsequent discussions of problems and their models, we will use these four phases. Specifically, the cases to be presented will incorporate the SPMS method of description.

In the Scenario portion of our cases, we provide a description of the purpose of the model, the values that impinge upon the modeling process, and the system. In the problem portion, we provide further explanatory details about the system and about the actual problem that motivates the analysis. In the model portion, we delineate the construction and validation of the model. And in the solution portion, we describe the algorithm that was employed, the results (in terms of a recommended strategy) produced by that algorithm, and how the

Phases	Steps for Better Modeling
Scenario	1. Statement of the purpose 2. Clarification of the values 3. Determination of the system
Problem	4. Definition of the problem
Model	5. Collection of the data 6. Formulation of the model 7. Validation of the model
Solution	8. Selection of the algorithm 9. Derivation of satisfactory policies 10. Determination of the most appropriate policy 11. Implementation of the strategy

Figure 1.3   The 11 steps to better modeling and happier managing.

actual solution to the problem might differ from the solution obtained from the model.

In what follows we discuss each of the 11 steps to successful modeling in detail.

STEP 1: STATEMENT OF THE PURPOSE

Of all the modeling approaches that are possible, the MS modeling approach is the only one that deals explicitly with characterizing reality in such a way that symbolic processing can be used to arrive at decisions that are logical and explainable. This systematic way of dealing with a necessary element in human thinking usually involves the determination and justification of a set of objectives—and purposes or goals—to be achieved by the model-building initiative. A well-defined statement of the purpose of the model-building exercise will guide the manager's determination of what should be included in the model as well as what should be omitted.

Consider a classroom. Class is in session and the room is filled with students, each busily taking notes. The instructor at the front of the classroom is utilizing a chalkboard and a transparency projector (and screen) to convey important concepts. In addition, the classroom contains the students' textbooks, the chairs the students are sitting in, the students' writing materials, and the instructor's notes and transparencies. If you were asked to model this situation, which of these components would you include in your model? Would you include the students? Probably. You might also include the textbook and the students' lecture notebooks. Left out might be such items as the fluorescent lights, the walls of the classroom, and the chairs. Why? No one has told you what the purpose of the modeling exercise is. Hence, you have no criteria for deciding what should be included and what should be omitted.

Suppose that the purpose is to study the process of learning within the framework of the classroom alone. Then you would necessarily include the students, the instructor, and the instruction taking place between these components. Of lesser importance would be such components as lecture notes and textbooks. Omitted altogether would be such objects as chairs, chalkboard, and overhead fluorescent lights. The purpose then is the yardstick by which relevance is measured—the basis of inclusion and exclusion of any artifact allied with the problem of interest.

STEP 2: CLARIFICATION OF THE VALUES

Our values are the primary standards we use for weighing various alternatives and deciding among them. Values, therefore, play a very important role in decision making. A *value* is a criterion, goal, state, or standard by which we perceive or express normative or ideal circumstances. Managers continually use values to assess, measure, or compare existing real-world conditions and performance.

In terms of modeling, the manager should ask the following: "How do my values influence my perception of the problem? Specifically, how do my values influence my perceptions of

1. *What is,*
2. *What is desired,* and
3. What to do to move from *what is* to *what is desired?"*

We sometimes refer to values relating to "what is desired" as *ends values* and values relating to "how to achieve what is desired" as *means values.* In general, we find substantial agreement over ends values but substantial disagreement over means values. It is easy, for example, to get management to agree that earnings should exceed 8% of gross investment. However, considerable controversy arises when these managers begin discussing the means by which such a goal can be achieved. The advertising manager believes it can be achieved through more extensive and aggressive advertising. The production manager believes that it can be achieved through modernization of production facilities. And so it goes.

STEP 3: DETERMINATION OF THE SYSTEM

Before we can develop an MS model, we must clearly define our system. In general, this amounts to drawing a boundary around all components that we believe to be a part of the system.

A block diagram of an abstract system is shown in Figure 1.4. The small triangles represent elements or components. In this case, only those contained within the block or rectangle are perceived to be a part of the system. Evidently, systems involve a set of elements or components and a set of relationships among the interacting elements. The word *universe* refers to all elements and entities in existence. Since, in general, a given system does not comprise the entire universe, we must treat the concept of a *boundary* in connection with the definition of a system. The boundary specifies which components are a part of the environment. The *environment* of the system, then, comprises all compo-

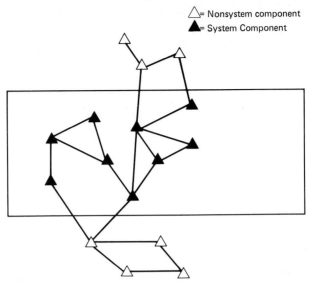

Figure 1.4   A block diagram representation of a general system.

nents that are not within the system itself. The following questions should be addressed as part of the effort to define the system:

1. From whose perspective is the system to be studied? Normally, the system should be studied from the perspective of the manager of the system.
2. What criteria should be used to select components or variables to characterize the system? Ordinarily, the analyst should choose only sufficient variables to fulfill the purpose and perspective. These are the *internal* or endogenous variables.
3. What criteria should be used to delineate the system boundary? What is the degree of separability of the system from its environment? Will the system boundary change with time?
4. What criteria should be used to select the variables that influence the system, but are not influenced by the system? These are the *input* or *exogenous* variables, or parameters.
5. What criteria should be used to choose those variables representing the outputs of the system? The *outputs* of the system are those quantities that are being (or that can be) measured. The output variables may or may not be the same as the internal variables.

The definition of the system might, therefore, consist of the following steps:

Determine the inputs or points of influence accessible to the manager.

Determine the outputs or observables measured by the manager.

Determine which components make up the system.

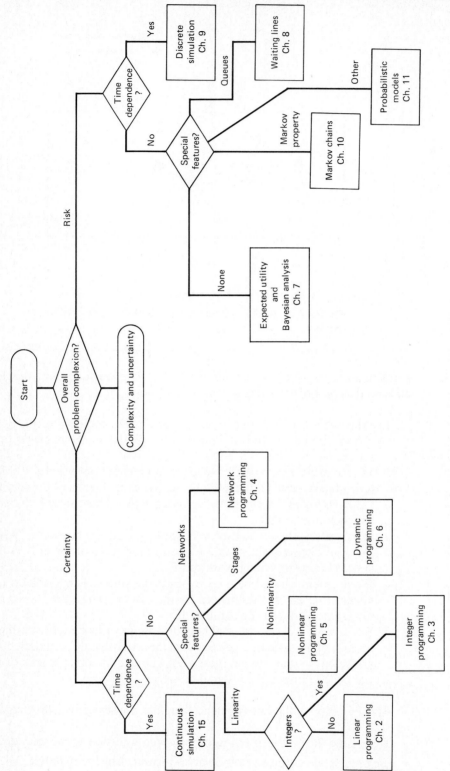

Figure 1.5a Flow chart for defining a problem and determining an appropriate model.

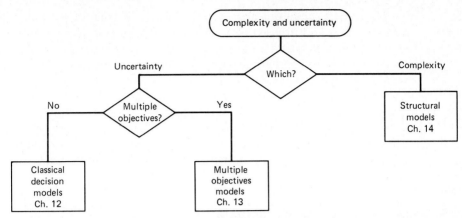

Figure 1.5b Flow chart (continued) for defining a problem and determining an appropriate model.

In deciding whether a component should be included within the boundary of the system, at least two questions should be asked:

Can the component be influenced by one of the manager's inputs?

Can the component be observed by one of the manager's outputs?

If the answer to both questions is "No," then the component does not belong within the boundary of the system. A systematic consideration of every component in this way will enable us to determine properly the system and to find its boundary.

STEP 4: IDENTIFICATION OF THE PROBLEM

Before problems can be modeled, they must first be identified and defined. Such identification begins with a consideration of the process or system that surrounds and encompasses the problem. Which of the following terms best characterizes the process: "certainty," "risk," or "uncertainty/complexity"? Next, is there an essential dependence upon time that we must take into consideration? Finally, are there special characteristics that require deliberate attention such as linearity, integer-valued decision variables, a network, or stages of decisions? The manager's responses to these questions will determine the type of model that is most appropriate.

For example, a problem that is known to be deterministic may involve a certain level of complexity, and there may be a certain time dependence that must be taken into consideration. Based upon these attributes, the manager would choose a continuous simulation model to study the problem, if Figure 1.5 is employed to determine what model type to use.

Or a manager may feel that a decision involves a certain amount of risk. The decision alternatives at the manager's disposal are first listed. Which alternative to use is largely contingent upon which "future" will occur. In a risky environment, the manager does not know with certainty which possible future will occur.

The problem definition phase is flowcharted in Figure 1.5. By responding to each question and proceeding to the next appropriate element on the flow chart, we ultimately end up at a rectangular box. This box names the type of model that is most appropriate for the problem being considered. Which model we as aspiring managers actually choose to use will depend strongly upon our perceptions of the problem at hand. The flow chart in Figure 1.5 is a simplistic guide to model choice that cannot give credence to all the factors that must be considered in actual selection. For that, you need an entire textbook of model descriptions and applications. One of the purposes of this book is to impart a kind of enlightened intuition about which model is appropriate for which situation.

STEP 5: COLLECTION OF THE DATA

This book emphasizes understanding what the data requirements are for each model that is presented. How such data can be obtained (if not already available) is treated together with how to "guesstimate" unknown and unobtainable data items. One of the benefits we get from a model-building exercise is enhanced comprehension of what data are important to the model — and thus to the decision itself.

The relationships among the MS model, the algorithm, and data are shown in Figure 1.6. In general, data collection should be performed in parallel with the actual formulation of model structure so that the model can be constructed around data that are readily available — and so that a better determination of the data requirements for the model-building exercise can be understood.

STEP 6: FORMULATION OF THE MODEL STRUCTURE

At this point, we have accomplished a definitive statement of the model's purpose, a determination of the system, and a definition of the problem. We now know what type of model to use and can begin the actual fabrication of the model structure. By *structure* we mean the relationships that will eventually characterize the model. These could be constraints, equations, or expressions — as we shall see in forthcoming chapters. Relevant variables and relationships must be identified and included.

Once formulated, the relationships will dictate what data are needed. These data requirements are then met by the data collection step. In some cases, relationships may be structured so as to take advantage of existing or available data. As previously stated, the data collection and model formulation steps should be performed in parallel.

The actual strategy for model construction will depend strongly upon the type of model that is selected. For example, suppose the problem definition step (Figs. 1.5a and b) leads to a clear determination that linear programming should be used. Then the process of model formulation for the linear program could begin. This process is, however, quite different from the process of simulation model formulation or of decision model construction. The actual details of model construction will be discussed when we discuss the model types themselves in their respective chapters.

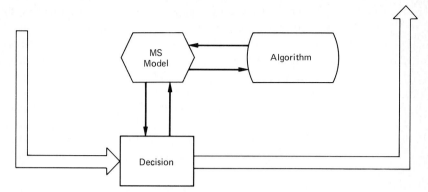

Figure 1.6   Relationships among the MS model, the associated algorithm, and data.

In general, the model construction step will involve two activities—actual formulation of the model, followed by its computer implementation.

STEP 7: VALIDATION OF THE MODEL

Validation is the exercise of comparing the model against reality to assure its authenticity and appropriateness. We use the term *verification* to denote the task of making certain that the computer implementation of the model contains no errors and that it is essentially free of "bugs." In general, a model is verified if its computer implementation does exactly what is required and conforms to the specifications for the model. If a manager uses technical specialists to perform the computer implementation, then it is the specialists' primary responsbility to ensure verification of the computer code that embodies the model. Clearly, verification represents a subtask that must be completed to validate the model.

In validation, the manager is usually interested in four areas: data validation, structure validation, behavior validation, and overall validation. In data validation, the manager does a double check on the data to determine where "softness" exists. *Soft data* are data that possess a high degree of uncertainty. The manager should instruct his or her management science specialist to perform sensitivity studies on these values so that the effect of large variations in their magnitudes, upon the results produced by the model, can be assessed. If the results are sensitive to a coefficient or parameter whose data value is "soft," then the manager may choose to measure this parameter value more accurately. Such measurement can be expensive—too expensive perhaps to be compatible with the manager's budget. In such instances, the manager must "live with" the uncertainty.

The second concern in validation is the structure of the model. Here, two types of errors can arise: errors of commission and errors of omission. An omission error occurs whenever an important relationship or variable has been omitted. Commission errors occur when relationships are included that are superfluous or are improperly formulated. We can eliminate these errors by submitting the structure to examination by others familiar with the system and its problem and by comparing the structure with other model structures developed for similar problems.

We next perform behavioral tests of validity. The term *behavioral* is used to denote the results or outputs produced by the model. Such tests usually involve inspecting the results or outputs and evaluating these for plausibility and practicality. Implausible results may suggest that the model has serious structural or data defects. In any modeling exercise, the manager starts with an incomplete understanding of both structure and behavior. By playing one against the other, the manager can increase his or her understanding of both. The end result is a better understanding of the process or problem the manager is trying to manipulate and control.

The last battery of validation tests is intended to examine the overall validity of the model. Once again the manager, assisted perhaps by an analyst, examines the model's data, structure, and outputs. At this point, all "bugs" and deficiencies in the data, structure, and behavior have been detected and corrected. The examination for overall validity is a final reality check on the compatibility and consistency of the ingredients that make up the model—the data, structure, and behavior.

STEP 8: SELECTION OF THE ALGORITHM

Solving the models espoused in this book will require the use of algorithms. An *algorithm* is a logically ordered sequence of steps required to provide a satisfactory solution to the model. The algorithm does not necessarily have to be encoded into a computer program, but this is usually the case. While it is true that all computer programs are algorithms, not all algorithms are computer programs. In particular, we can sometimes use a manual method to find the solution to the model, and this is also an algorithm. For models of any size, however, we generally use computerized algorithms because of their greatly enhanced computational efficiency. Most "real-world" models would not be solvable without the use of the computer.

In general, actual selection of the solution algorithm may occur during the "formulation of model structure" phase because codification of the model will require a prior determination of the algorithm to be used. The model to be encoded must be compatible with the solution algorithm (i.e., the specific computer package) chosen for it.

In this book, we emphasize knowing how to use the computer algorithms and packages that are available. The manager needs to know how to prepare the inputs and how to interpret the outputs from these packages. This is especially true when the manager does not hire a specialist to perform the computer implementations. The manager does not need to be an expert in the mechanics of the algorithms in the same sense that one does not need to know details about the electrical circuitry of a radio, television set, electric razor, or telephone to use these devices. However, an intuitive understanding of how each algorithm works is certainly important.

For some types of models, several algorithms could be employed in the solution. For example, one type of model (linear programming), discussed in Chapter 2, can be solved by ordinary SIMPLEX, dual SIMPLEX, or revised

SIMPLEX. In some cases the issue as to which algorithm to choose is one merely of *efficiency*—computer time required for solution; in other cases a bad choice of algorithm may lead to suboptimal results or no solution at all. It is important in some cases to be able to recognize from the characteristics of the model what algorithm is likely to be "best" in terms of an optimal result obtained with minimal computer time expenditure.

There are two basic types of algorithms employed in the solution of models in this book: heuristic and optimizing. *Heuristic algorithms* are able to produce satisfactory (but not optimal) solutions to models, whereas *optimizing algorithms* are able to produce optimal solutions to models. Searching for an optimal solution has been likened to the search for a "needle in a haystack." In view of the very considerable computation required to find optimal solutions, we sometimes defer to heuristic algorithms and satisfactory solutions that require far less computation to obtain.

STEP 9: DERIVATION OF FEASIBLE POLICIES

This step and the one that follows may be performed automatically by the algorithm or manually by the manager or his or her modeler. Optimization algorithms, for example, are capable of automatic generation of feasible policies. An *optimization algorithm* is one that searches for an optimal policy through iteration. By *optimal* we mean a policy that maximizes or minimizes a criterion representative of the manager's values. We use the word *policy* rather than decision here because the result is really a coordinated collection of decisions. Policies are *feasible* if they satisfy a manager-specified set of restrictions or constraints on acceptable policies.

While optimization algorithms have the capability automatically to generate feasible policies, this is generally not the case for simulation algorithms. This is one of the major differences between simulation and optimization. Usually, we specify manually the policies we want tested when using simulation models.

STEP 10: DETERMINATION OF THE MOST APPROPRIATE POLICY

The "most appropriate" policy is a value-laden managerial consideration based *in part* upon the information provided by MS models. The policies provided in the printed or displayed output produced by the computer must be examined carefully by the manager. For optimization models, the resultant optimal policy is usually reported. This policy is optimal only insofar as the *model* is concerned, since it rarely represents the optimal policy for the actual problem. It serves its purpose by providing us with greater insight, intuition, and understanding about the problem.

For simulation models, the most appropriate policy is generally determined through a manual process of "cut and try." First, we generate a set of policies that in some sense covers the "policy space." Then, we perform simulation runs for each policy, examine the output of these runs, and "pick a favorite." Then, we generate a second battery of policies in close proximity to the favorite one and conduct a second battery of simulation experiments. This process may be iterated as many times as desired. Finally, we arrive at a policy that appears most appropriate of those examined, and this step is completed.

There are a few instances in which an optimization algorithm is connected to a simulation model. In such cases, the optimization algorithm performs automatic generation and evaluation of policies just as it did for static optimization models.

STEP 11: IMPLEMENTATION OF THE POLICY

Once decided upon, the manager must implement his or her chosen policy. There should remain no further objections or reservations with regard to the policy in question, as these should have been resolved in earlier steps.

Implementation, once activated, must be followed up to ensure:

1. A smooth transition
2. A faithful activation that adheres to the intent of the chosen policy
3. An improved behavior or performance that is consistent with the behavior predicted by the model for this policy

These 11 steps to "better modeling and happier managing" should be taken seriously. We should agree that managers must be involved in all these steps, even though the details of accomplishing a particular step may be delegated to a management science specialist. Studies have shown that the greater the manager's involvement and participation in the model-building process, the more likely will be his or her putting to use any insights or recommendations derived from the modeling exercise. If the manager is separated by a considerable "distance" from an applicable MS model, then any conclusions, insights, or recommendations accruing from the model will be unlikely to have much of an impact. This is because the manager is unacquainted with the structural assumptions built into the model and, therefore, is unlikely to place much confidence in it. The model is said to suffer from problems of *credibility* in such cases.

In recent studies [6,7] of major models formulated to study and solve problems in the public sector, it was found that as many as two thirds of these models failed to achieve their avowed purposes in the form of actual policy intent. This represents literally millions of wasted public dollars. The reason for these failures are many and include:

1. Failure to identify a specific client, manager, or policymaker whose perspective should be used in the model formulation exercise
2. Failure to include the appropriate set of managerial inputs and outputs that would enable the manager to use the model as a policy testing instrument
3. Failure to make the structural assumptions inherent within the model comprehensible to the manager

All the alluded-to shortcomings contribute to the distance that separates the manager from the model. In this book, therefore, we will urge as much managerial involvement and participation in the modeling process as possible. Such involvement creates confidence, acceptance, and comprehension in the manager's mind. Consequently, his or her mental model begins to be framed, shaped, and influenced by the MS model until decisions begin to reflect the insight, intuition, and understanding received from the MS modeling exercise. This is the goal of all MS models and MS modeling.

Managerial involvement in the modeling process is important for other reasons. One of the primary benefits of the model comes from an exposure to the modeling process itself. The development of an MS model forces the manager to address important questions about the problem that have likely never been considered before. A model never contains as much information about the real system as must be acquired to formulate it. Modelers are rarely diligent enough to record every conceivable consideration that arose in the construction of the model. And if they were, few managers would take the time to read and understand the voluminous material that results. All such learning is by nature vicarious, whereas the understanding that accrues from participation in the model-building exercise itself is *active* learning. Thus a primary benefit to be derived from any model-building exercise may be the increased understanding that accrues from development of the model itself. To deny any manager this benefit would be counterproductive.

NOTATION

In this section, we will introduce the reader to sufficient notation (and some additional definitions) to enable a comprehension of material to follow. Mathematical notation is the language of management science. To avoid being "snowed" by management scientists, it is desirable that the manager develop at least a superficial familiarity with their mathematical jargon.

The single, most important, entity discussed in this book is the decision variable, which we shall consistently denote by x_j. The subscript j "tags" x as the jth decision variable in a collection of n such variables (most problems involve many decision variables, and it is necessary to distinguish between them). The word *variable,* as used here, is intended to connote something whose value is unknown but is to be determined by means of the model (and its associated algorithm and data). We use the term *coefficient* to denote an entity that remains constant, whose value is known from data, and that is employed in the solution of the model.

Many of the models to be discussed in this book involve linear functions and expressions. Two very prominent formulations arise in linear optimization models:

$$x_0 = c_1 x_1 + c_2 x_2 + \cdots + c_n x_n \tag{1.1}$$

and

$$a_{i1} x_1 + a_{i2} x_2 + \cdots + a_{in} x_n \le b_i \tag{1.2}$$

Here there are n decision variables x_j; the terms c_j, a_{ij}, and b_i are coefficients (constants). It is customary to write (1.1) and (1.2) as follows:

$$x_0 = \sum_{j=1}^{n} c_j x_j \tag{1.3}$$

and

$$\sum_{j=1}^{n} a_{ij} x_j \leq b_i \tag{1.4}$$

where the symbol Σ denotes summation.

In addition to these conventions, we will sometimes use function notation. For example,

$$y = f(x)$$

denotes that y is a function of a single variable x. For the case of n variables, $n > 1$, this becomes

$$y = f(x_1, x_2, \cdots, x_n)$$

Function notation is employed whenever it is not known whether the assumptions of linearity hold. In the absence of such knowledge, (1.3) and (1.4) become

$$x_0 = f(x_1, x_2, \cdots, x_n) \tag{1.5}$$

and

$$g_i(x_1, x_2, \cdots, x_n) \leq b_i \tag{1.6}$$

It is important to remark that the " $\leq$ " operator in (1.2), (1.4), or (1.6) may be replaced by an " $=$ " or a " $\geq$ " operator in these relations. Thus a particular model may involve several relations of the form (1.4) or (1.6), some having $\leq$ operators, some having $=$ operators, and some having $\geq$ operators.

Finally, we will have occasion to use a transformed variable in a model rather than the variable itself. If x_j is the variable, then x_j' (read x_j prime) is the transformed or replaced variable used in the solution. The algorithm will return a value for x_j'; it is up to the user to translate this numeric value into a value for x_j.

SOME CLASSICAL PROBLEMS IN MANAGEMENT SCIENCE

Before we delve deeply into the substance of management science, we will introduce some general problems addressed by management science. These problem descriptions should serve to impart a flavor for the power, diversity, and generality of management science methods.

RESOURCE ALLOCATION PROBLEMS

Every business manager is confronted from time to time with a rather general problem — how to get the most out of the resources available. The manager is responsible for allocating limited resources to the products and services he or she provides to the consumer or customer. Specifically, the manager wants to know how much of each product or service should be provided to maximize profits. Since resources are limited, there are constraints on the amount of product or service he or she can offer. The decision maker seeks the "product mix" that will realize the greatest net return. Depending upon the nature of the problem, the resources might be money, materials, labor, machine capacities, warehouse space, or some other factor whose availability affects the decision at hand. The problem is a recurrent one in financial planning, production scheduling, purchasing, marketing strategy, and other areas.

A typical mathematical form for such a problem that is linear is:

$$\text{MAXIMIZE } x_0 = \sum_{j=1}^{n} c_j x_j \tag{1.7}$$

$$\text{SUBJECT TO: } \sum_{j=1}^{n} a_{ij} x_j \leq b_i, \qquad i = 1, 2, \cdots, m \tag{1.8}$$

$$\text{All } x_j \geq 0$$

For a multiproduct, multiresource industry, the variable x_j would represent the amount of product j to be produced, c_j would represent the profit contribution of each unit of product j, a_{ij} would represent the amount of resource i needed by j, and b_i would represent the amount of resource i available. Our objective is to determine how much of each product to produce to maximize profit. Thus (1.7) represents a mathematical formulation of the objective or goal, and (1.8) represents the constraints imposed by limited resources upon the achievement of that objective. The symbolism $i = 1, 2, \cdots, m$ in (1.8) denotes that there are m such constraints of the form

$$\sum_{j=1}^{n} a_{ij} \leq b_i$$

As an example of a resource allocation problem, consider the following situation. We use the SPMS method of description as promised. Observe how each of the steps that comprises each phase of the SPMS method was considered and accomplished.

The Scenario: Twenty years from now, you are managing a commercial airframe manufacturing operation in which three different types of airplanes are mass produced. These aircraft share many of the same resources — including the same engines, the same avionics package, the same seats, and the same manufacturing facility. The objective is to determine how many of each type of aircraft to fabricate — to determine the product mix.

The market will buy as many of these airplanes as your facility can produce. However, there are certain constraints on the number of these aircraft that your resources and your facility impose upon the product mix. Your purpose is to maximize your return.

The Problem: The system in this case is your manufacturing facility. The environment would include the suppliers of parts and the market demand for your product. You are fortunate in that the market is "bullish" and will buy all that you can produce. You can count on your suppliers to produce and ship (on time) the requested number of parts procured. These considerations make your "decision" one involving certainty—to find that number of aircraft of each type that will maximize profit. Moreover, you obviously do not wish in any given production period to produce (and procure parts for) a fraction of an airplane, so your decision variables must be integers—a special characteristic that you must accommodate.

The Model: An appropriate model for this problem will be developed in Part I: Decision Making Under Certainty.

CAPITAL INVESTMENT DECISIONS IN RISKY ENVIRONMENTS

A manager must frequently decide whether additional capital investment will contribute to the firm's profit-making potential. This investment would expand production (or service) capacity. However, he or she is unable to determine with certainty whether market demand will be strong enough to utilize fully the additional capacity once it is in place. For example, a plastics manufacturing manager must decide whether additional plastic presses are needed in the shop. An apartment landlord must decide whether to build additional apartments. An oil drilling manager must decide whether to purchase another drilling rig.

Several important factors require consideration. First, how much additional capital outlay is required? Second, what probable return on investment can be realized? This latter question will depend upon the future strength of the marketplace, which is not known with certainty. Thus these problems are said to be characterized by risk or uncertainty. The manager's job is to weigh the risks against the profit potential of the investment.

As an example of a capital investment decision, we consider the commonplace car buying problem.

The Scenario: You are a poverty-stricken graduate student with a wife, three children, a live-in mother-in-law, two dogs, three cats, and a pet raccoon. The price of gasoline is at an all-time high and your aging auto is a ten-year-old medium-sized sport coupe that guzzles gas like a fraternity at a beer bust. Your mother-in-law is embarrassed to ride in this clunker and wonders when you will be able to afford to replace it. Your purpose is to decide what to do next.

The Problem: To bring matters to the point of a crisis, your car has finally broken down—the automatic transmission will not shift out of "park." After doing some data collection and research, you find that in the next five years fuel prices are expected to

1. Increase by 50% with probability .5
2. Increase by 100% with probability .3
3. Increase by 10% with probability .2

On the basis of this information you define your problem as one involving risk.

The Model: You begin by listing the alternatives.

1. Fix old car
2. Buy new car
3. Buy used car
4. Buy bicycle

Next you list the values that will impinge upon your selection of an alternative:

1. Comfort
2. Safety
3. Operating costs
4. Status
5. Cost of initial investment

You give consideration to the total system and environment in which your problem is embedded. An important factor in the environment of the problem is the cost of fuel for the automobile. However, this is not known with certainty.

The Solution: The solution to this problem will vary substantially from person to person. Depending upon the temperament and perspective of the decision maker, different solutions are "recommended" by the models.

A PROBLEM EMBEDDED IN A PROCESS

Occasionally, management finds itself confronted with a problem whose system is ongoing and has a definite time dependence. We shall consistently refer to such a system as a *process.* Our problem is to determine a procedure, plan, or policy for directing a process so as to meet our objectives or to achieve a desired behavior. In production planning, for example, we may wish to control the production rate to meet demand while minimizing production and inventory costs over a specified production period. This problem differs fundamentally from the airplane manufacturing problem, because demand does not exceed the production capacity of the facility. Demand is finite and known instantaneously, but it varies as a function of time. Let $x_j(t)$ represent the time-dependent inventory on hand for product j, and let $r_j(t)$ represent the rate of change of the inventory on hand. If $u_j(t)$ is the production rate of product j and $d_j(t)$ is the instantaneous demand at time t, then:

$$r_j(t) = u_j(t) - d_j(t); \quad x_j(t_0) = x_{j0}$$

Here the symbolism "(t)" denotes that r_j, u_j, and d_j are all functions of time—that is, these variables vary with time. In this expression t_0 denotes the initial or starting time and x_{j0} the initial inventory for product j.

This problem is appropriately modeled by means of simulation. As an illustration of a problem of this type, consider a company that manufactures, distributes, and sells a personal computer through a chain of retail outlets.

The Scenario: The Personal Products Division of Hacker Electronics Corporation (HEC) intends to market a personal computer in each of its 3000 company-owned, neighborhood electronics stores. All computers are manufactured in a central location and are then distributed to six major warehouses geographically dispersed throughout the country. The company-owned retail outlets receive their computers from the warehouse in closest proximity to them, and each warehouse serves 500 outlets. The company's purpose, of course, is to achieve the largest possible profit margin over the longest possible period of time. The company wishes to minimize inventory carrying costs while avoiding out-of-stock situations, both of which are "values" that relate directly to the goal of achieving the largest possible profit margin. In addition, the company is also interested in forecasting what rate of production is most appropriate.

The Problem: The system is a nationwide network for efficient manufacture, distribution and sale of personal computers. As such the system consists of a factory, six wholesale warehouses, and 3000 retail outlets. The company is concerned about inventory levels at all locations. The demand for the computer is stochastic. There is an essential time dependence that must be considered, as all major variables — inventory on hand (shelf inventory), sales, lost sales, and so on — vary with time as shown in Figure 1.7. And the time variation of these variables must be known and included in the problem formulation. For example, average carrying costs may be computed by taking the product of the per unit, per day carrying charge with the average inventory. Average inventory is determined by integrating (summing) the inventory over a certain period of time and then dividing by that time period; that is

$$\text{Average inventory} = \int_{t_0}^{t_f} \frac{\text{inventory} \ (t) \ dt}{(t_f - t_0)}$$

It is clear, therefore, that time enters into the problem in a way that forces its inclusion in a model of the problem.

The Model: HEC uses a computerized inventory control procedure that enables the company to know instantaneously its actual inventory at any outlet or warehouse. It uses two inventory control parameters — "reorder point" and "stock control level" — to adjust all inventories (used to calculate reorder quantity). Since different outlets and different warehouses experience differing levels of demand, each outlet and warehouse must essentially possess its own reorder point and stock control level.

The Solution: Finding a satisfactory inventory policy for this model is a challenging task. On the surface, there appear to be over 6000 decision variables (two for each outlet and warehouse). This is sometimes too many parameters for an optimization algorithm to juggle simultaneously in a reasonable amount of computer time. Manual approaches to generation of near-optimal policies are also impossible to achieve. A simulation model that aggregates common components of the system is one very rational approach.

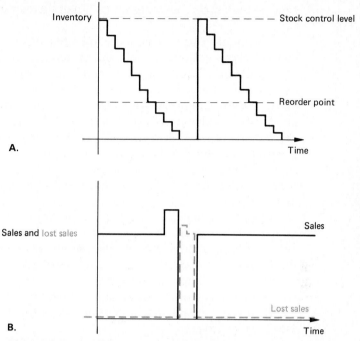

Figure 1.7 (A) Time-dependent variable "inventory" and its attendant parameters "stock control level" and "reorder point." (B) Time-dependent variables "sales" and "lost sales."

CAVEATS AND COMMENTS ON USING AND BUILDING MODELS

Management science methods do not always succeed. We can usually attribute failures to one or more of the following:

1. Insufficient managerial involvement
2. Overly optimistic expectations
3. Cost overruns
4. Fitting the problem to the technique rather than selecting the model that best fits the problem
5. Failure to use known information
6. Failure to consider the total system
7. Failure to use an unbiased, unparochial value structure with which to evaluate the results
8. Failure to use accurate data
9. Failure to recognize the difference between solution to the model and solution to the problem

Some managers believe that once they have defined the problem, it can be safely turned over to a technical analyst. Unfortunately, this practice usually results in a model that is incomprehensible to — and therefore unusable by — the manager.

At the same time managers are too often "taken in" by technical analysts who are overly optimistic about the capabilities and strengths of a particular technique. The effect of such exaggerated optimism is to build expectations in the mind of the unseasoned user that are too high and can never be achieved. Such a tendency to oversell MS models and their attendant algorithms has in some instances given management science a bad name, and some "oversold" clients and users have become sadly disillusioned as a result.

In addition, some technical analysts tend to grossly underestimate the costs associated with a given modeling study. The time requirements to complete each phase (as suggested by the analyst) should also be viewed as possibly unrealistic.

Perhaps one way in which to overcome these difficulties is to make use of *decision support systems.* These software packages can sometimes facilitate model building with or possibly without the assistance of a technical analyst. With decision support systems, the manager is better able to control the assumptions, structure, and data that go into the model. A decision support system may consist of a model base, a data base, and a user interface. Ease of use is one of the primary design considerations for these packages, which are usually interactive.

The manager should be eclectic (that is, broad based) in terms of his or her consideration of the total spectrum of possible methods and models that should be applied. In addition the manager should give ample consideration to the total system and the ultimate causes of any problem. Does the proposed solution suboptimize for a small department, or does it contribute to the goals of the entire organization? Is there any omitted relevant information? Is the perspective on the problem unbiased and nonparochial? These represent still other potential pitfalls that can make a difference between success and failure of the model.

Still another caveat relates to computers, algorithms, and software for solving models. As your *most* obedient servants, these tools do precisely what they are told to do — nothing less and nothing more. They cannot recognize faulty or erroneous input data. They cannot spot the logical flaws that resulted in a linear model for a highly nonlinear underlying problem. Computer scientists have an expression — "garbage in, garbage out" — that sums it up neatly. The orderly, impressive-looking computer printout tends for some managers to become authoritative, and they forget that the output is only as good as the input. No sausage grinder in the world can make pork sausage out of veal!

The last caveat has to do with the difference between decision making and analysis. If an analyst tears off the computer printout from a model and scurries to you with "the solution to the problem," fire him on the spot. If a computer program can make decisions, who needs you? The point, of course, is that mathematical models are important *aids* to you — the decision maker. What most analysts (and textbooks, for that matter) ignore is that, for example, typical industrial applications of linear programming computer packages deliver *the* optimum solution to the model; there will usually be thousands of other solutions with objective values within a fraction of a percent of the optimum one. This wealth of alternatives should be exploited when the decision maker considers factors exogenous to the model.

SUMMARY

Models are ubiquitous. We find we cannot even discuss models without using models. The question of whether to use models, therefore, is meaningless. The choice is really only one of alternative models.

We have, in this chapter, tried to describe management science, operations research, and the systems approach as "sister" disciplines with much overlap and having, as it were, the same parent—namely, World War II and the associated logistical and managerial problems brought on by that conflict. Each of these disciplines is concerned with models. Today the terms "management science" and "operations research" are largely synonymous—both involve the use of models that have mathematical, quantitative, or graphical forms. We call these models MS (management science) models. They are to be distinguished from mental models, physical models, and verbal models.

We suggested that MS models serve as devices for creating insight, intuition, and understanding about a problem and should, therefore, be regarded as media for guiding and enlightening the mental models of managers. As such, the final results produced by MS models should be reducible to 7 plus or minus 2 components or concepts to be assimilated into a mental model.

We found that we can classify MS models according to the type of decision environment they are most appropriate for, and according to any special characteristics they might have. In this book, for example, three such decision environments are considered: certainty, risk, and uncertainty/complexity. We discussed types of models appropriate under each category of decision environment. We also discussed model building at some length. A systems approach to modeling was described by an 11-step method organized into four phases: scenario, problem, model, and solution.

We suggested that managers would want to participate substantially in all four phases of the model-building process. Such involvement would enable decision makers to acquire the full benefit of the modeling process and would ensure that the model ultimately reflects more closely their views and perspectives of the object system.

Following this discussion, an entire section was devoted to a presentation of notation to be used in forthcoming chapters. In addition, several classic situations were introduced to impart a feeling for the kinds of problems that can be modeled. Three classical problems were considered, including a resource allocation problem, a decision problem in a risky environment, and a process problem. Finally, some caveats for model usage were presented.

In this chapter we promoted the MS modeling approach to problem solving and decision making. You may be inclined to ask, "Are there shortcomings to the MS modeling approach that I as an aspiring manager should know about?"

The basic problem with the MS modeling approach is that we are always deceived to some extent about the character of reality and that every model is wrong—sometimes even dangerously so.

Why, then, do we espouse the use of MS models? Business and bureaucratic organizations started with simple things and mechanisms, which grew or evolved into more complex things, which further evolved into the extremely complex mechanisms of today. Such growth has produced a tremendous increase in complexity. To cope with the increased complexity, more sophisticated models were required. MS models met this challenge by enabling managers to augment their cognitive capacities with constructs that enhanced understanding and comprehension of complex problems. The limitation on continued growth and competence in solving complex problems rests in part upon the MS modeling literacy of managers and prospective managers. Toward this end, let us proceed.

PROBLEMS

1. Provide at least three definitions for a "model."

2. Characterize the process of model building.

3. Define each of the following:

Algorithm	Means values
Behavior	Optimization model
Boundary	Optimizing algorithms
Coefficient	Policy
Credibility	Problem
Decision	Process
Decision support system	Simulation model
Discrete simulation	Structure
Efficiency	System
Endogenous variable	Time dependence
Ends values	Validation
Environment	Value
Exogenous variable	Variable
Feasibility	Verification
Heuristic algorithms	

4. Discuss each of the following:
    Decision making under certainty
    Decision making under risk
    Decision making under uncertainty/complexity

5. Discuss the differences and similarities between MS models and other types of models.

6. Discuss why a precise statement of the purpose of the model-building activity is critical to the success of the initiative.

7. Take a problem of interest to you through the SPMS method of description (as far as you can).

8. Describe what you would do as inventory manager to "get a handle" on HEC's inventory problem.

9. Indicate what model type you would use for each of the following situations and why.
   a. A leather wallet company is considering hiring additional leather workers to expand into the belt business. The manager has access to plenty of raw leather at reasonable prices and knows where quality buckles can be obtained inexpensively. The largest capital commitment is the requirement for additional leather workers. The company has established an esteemed reputation for its top-of-the-line wallets, which sell at well-above-average prices. However, the belt market is very competitive, and there are already many quality belt manufacturers in the business.
   b. A TV manufacturer makes five different types of television sets. The manufacturer has established a reputation for quality and reliability that is unequaled in the marketplace. The market for TV sets remains strong. The manufacturer wishes to maximize profits. The various TV sets made by this manufacturer share many of the same components that are in limited supply. How many of each TV set type to manufacture is the ultimate consideration.
   c. A large suburban bank is considering adding more teller stations to its drive-in bank facility. It knows the arrival frequency of its automobile banking customers and wishes to know how many tellers to add so that no customer will have to wait longer than 5 minutes. Currently, the average waiting time is 8 minutes during peak periods of high customer demand—Friday afternoons, for example.
   d. A large federal bureaucracy is interested in studying the future of the social security system in the United States. The work force provides revenues for the social security system, while the elderly population receives these revenues in the form of payments. As time progresses, the elderly population grows ever larger, while the work force remains stable or declines slightly during periods of recession.

10. Managerial problem solving and decision making are often conducted in group situations and as such involve consensual agreement among the members of the management team. While the objectives of management are easily agreed upon, the means by which these objectives are achieved are far more controversial. What approaches would you suggest as "strategies" for resolving conflicts relating to the means by which an agreement to a set of objectives can be reached?

11. For each description in Problem 9, determine the following:
   Purpose
   Values
   System

12. For each description in Problem 9, determine, as part of the "formulation of model structure" phase, the important
   Endogenous variables
   Inputs or exogenous variables

13. How would you settle a dispute involving a pair of managers over a particular department that both are claiming belongs to their management "system"? Is it possible that the same department could report to and receive management directives from more than one manager, as in matrix management?

14. Explain what advantages accrue from a systems approach to model building.

15. Validation involves four basic stages. What are they?

16. The decision situation faced by a manager was organized into the form of a "tree." After considering her decision alternatives, the manager decided upon three—A, B, and C—as shown. A consideration of alternative A led to the realization that only outcomes 1 or 2 could accrue from its implementation. The probabilities of these outcomes are known. If alternative B is implemented, only one outcome—outcome 3—is possible. If alternative C is implemented, outcomes 4 or 5 are possible. The probabilities of these outcomes are known. What type of decision making environment is this?

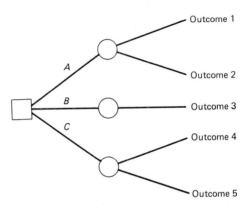

17. A simple technique for analysis of decisions is the use of a list of alternatives to characterize a "decision space." Upon completion of your degree, you will be faced with a decision involving your career. Characterize your career decision space. Analyze each alternative listed in terms of probable outcomes. As an example, consider the following:

Decision space	*Outcome*
1. Go to work for accounting firm	Modest income, but considerable job satisfaction
2. Go to work for manufacturing firm	Modest income, bad location
3. Go to work for consulting firm	Somewhat better income, less job security
4. Start own company	Bankruptcy, or tremendous wealth

18. You have a handfull of job offers on which you must make an ultimate decision. Describe what procedure you will use in evaluating the offers and deciding among them.

19. A term project is recommended in this course. Design a procedure for selecting a topic for the term project. If the professor tells you that the goal is "demonstration of a functional comprehension of the models presented in this book," does that help? Why or why not?

20. Discuss some basic differences between optimization models and simulation models.

21. Discuss how some of the reasons models fail might be mitigated.

REFERENCES

1. CHURCHMAN, C. *The Systems Approach.* New York: Dell, 1968.
2. SPENGLER, O. *The Decline of the West.* New York: Alfred A. Knopf, 1945.
3. TOYNBEE, A. *A Study of History.* New York: Oxford University Press, 1954.
4. COYLE, R. "On the Scope and Purpose of Industrial Dynamics." *International Journal of Systems Science,* Vol. 4 (1973), pp. 397–406.
5. THESEN, A, "Some Notes on Systems Models and Modelling." *International Journal of Systems Science,* Vol. 5 (1974), pp. 145–152.
6. FROMM, G., W. HAMILTON, and D. HAMILTON. *Federally Supported Mathematical Models: Survey and Analysis,* National Science Foundation—RANN publication number NSF-RA-S-74-029. Available from U.S. Government Printing Office, Washington, D.C. 20402, #038-000-00221-0 (1974).
7. *Ways to Improve Management of Federally Funded Computerized Models.* National Bureau of Standards, Number LCD-75-111 (1975).

ADDITIONAL READING

ACKOFF, R., and P. RIVETT. *A Manager's Guide to Operations Research.* New York: John Wiley & Sons, 1963.

GUPTA, J. "Management Science Implementation: Experiences of a Practising OR Manager." *Interfaces,* Vol. 7 (1977), pp. 84–90.

WOOLSEY, R. "The Measure of MS/OR Applications, or Let's Hear It for the Bean Counters," *Interfaces,* Vol. 5 (1975), pp. 74–78.

PART I

DECISION MAKING UNDER CERTAINTY

In Part I, we will consider decision-making environments in which problems can be modeled profitably by ignoring or assuming away such basic realities as the riskiness, uncertainty, and complexity inherent in "real-world" situations. In the jargon of decision theory, we will be addressing decision making under certainty (DMUC). Specifically, in the five chapters of this part, we will operate under the following assumptions:

1. Probability distributions for all parameters and decision variables needed for modeling problems are assumed to have zero variance —that is, they are represented by their means and are referred to as "deterministic."
2. The managerial problem to be modeled can be focused (for the purposes of this model) on a single objective to be optimized.

There are, of course, few if any "real-world" problems that *strictly* meet these assumptions. Why, then, should such models be included in a text that addresses potential and practicing managerial decision makers? The answer is simple and compelling. Models are not problems, and the optimal solution to a model of a problem provides nothing more than *insight* into solution of the problem. The models discussed in Part I have been used with great success in business, industry, and the public sector to provide such insight to hundreds of thousands of managerial decision makers. The key point here is that the assumptions apply to the *model,* not to the problem. The outputs from models must be recognized exactly for what they are — information based on a simplified representation of reality. Thus, conflicting objectives and probabilistic considerations must be taken into account by the decision maker in finding a viable solution to the problem. Seldom or never can *all* constraints affecting a managerial problem be included in a mathematical programming model of the problem. Issues such as social or political considerations must usually be dealt with by the decision maker external to the model. As we shall repeatedly stress, solutions generated by models constitute only one input to the decision-making process.

In what follows, we briefly discuss the major deterministic, single-objective MS models.

DETERMINISTIC OPTIMIZATION MODELS

Managerial problems that can be profitably modeled by the techniques in this section of the text tend to be operational or tactical, and the models are usually optimizing in nature. That is, they seek sets of values for decision variables that maximize profit, minimize cost, and so on. The models discussed in Part II are also single-objective models. Multiple-objective optimization models are discussed in Part III.

Mathematical Programming Models

Four of the models we will discuss in Part I — linear programming (LP), integer programming (IP), network programming (NP), and nonlinear programming (NLP) — are subsets of a modeling approach with the generic name of *mathematical programming.* The term "programming" here carries the connotation of "planning" and not "computer programming," although, as we shall see, these highly sophisticated models would be of little or no practical value without the existence of high-speed electronic computers.

All mathematical programming models fit a very general format. First, we define a mathematical function to represent the goal or objective of the problem. This function is often called the *objective function.* Next, we identify the restrictions, limitations, or *constraints* on the problem. A separate mathematical function is used to represent each such constraint. All functions are comprised of *decision variables* and *coefficients* (constants).

Linear Programming Models

The linear programming model is by far the most common form of mathematical programming model in use. Resource allocation problems, blending problems, dietary problems, and problems involving bus scheduling represent a few of the myriad problem classes to which LP is applicable. Nearly every industrial sector of the economy makes some use of LP, including the petrochemical industry, the automobile industry, the small appliance industry, and the advertising industry. At the same time, extensive use of LP is found within the various sectors of government, where such models are used to make allocation decisions. Nearly every major component of a large firm could make use of LP for such disparate applications as personnel planning, production planning, marketing planning, and product planning. Such models consist of a linear representation of the goal or objective of the system and linear representations of the restrictions or limitations imposed upon the system. We discuss LP models in Chapter 2.

Integer Programming Models

Integer programming models arise, for example, in capital budgeting situations. These models can also be used to solve managerial problems involving "go/no go" decisions or situations where the end result is either a "yes" or a "no" for each of a collection of decision variables. For example, suppose that several new products have been proposed; not all of them can be started at once. A separate decision variable is defined for each product. After solving the model, each variable will have a value of zero or one—a one meaning that the associated product is to be included in the product line and a zero meaning the opposite.

As a further example of a classical IP problem, consider the task of assigning *n* instructors to as many courses. Each instructor is to be assigned one and only one course. This problem recurs in the assignment of jobs to machines, movies to theaters, personnel to positions, and in many other assignment situations. The typical decision variable is a zero-one decision variable, which is one if an instructor should be assigned to a course and zero otherwise. The gamut of possible problems to which IP can be applied includes such classics as the problem of loading a knapsack, the problem of finding a minimum distance (or cost) tour for a traveling salesperson, and the problem of distributing fixed costs over an arbitrary number of items to produce. These and other problems are discussed in Chapter 3.

Network Programming Models

Many problems that can be modeled as IP models result in immense constraint sets and/or a very large number of decision variables. In some cases, solution of these models by IP optimization techniques is either impossible or prohibitively expensive in terms of computer time. However, some important classes of these problems can be modeled as networks (sets of "nodes" connected by "arcs"), and an optimal solution to the model can be obtained by special techniques developed for this purpose. For example, the Defense Fuel Supply Center procures 5 *billion* gallons of aviation fuel each year for the armed services. This procurement requires five bidding cycles per year to supply 300 Department of Defense installations and involves complicated bids from over 100 suppliers. An LP model of the bidding problem, with the object of minimizing total procurement and transportation cost, did not incorporate several bidding features — and required *8 hours* of computer time on an IBM 370/145 to produce a suboptimal solution! The problem was subsequently modeled as a network; we discuss this application in detail in Chapter 4. Other applications have reported successful network modeling of mathematical programming formulations with over 1 million decision variables.

Nonlinear Programming Models

There are many different types of NLP models characterized in Chapter 5. While the majority of mathematical programming applications employ linear approximations, there are some problems in which the degree of nonlinearity cannot be ignored. Such nonlinearities occur for example in product pricing, ordering with quantity discounts, and inventory control. In production systems, nonlinear relationships are empirically observed in per unit production costs, process yields, and quality characteristics. In financial circles, a classic model for portfolio design requires that the level of risk be minimized, where risk is measured by means of a quadratic function of the decision variables. NLP becomes increasingly important as models take on greater sophistication and endeavor to characterize the nonlinearities of the real world.

Recursive Optimization Models

Discrete dynamic programming (DP) is an optimization modeling technique that employs the principle of recursive optimization. Problems in this class usually require a sequence of managerial decisions (or can be modeled so that they appear to be of this form), so that the current decision depends only on the outcome of the previous one. Dynamic programming is the subject of Chapter 6.

These are the model types to be discussed in Part I. It is important to note that these models are basically static optimization models.

CHAPTER 2

Linear Programming Models

Linear programming (LP) models of economic, industrial, and social problems are all pervasive. Such models are used, for example,

By commercial airlines to schedule aircraft and flight crews

To optimize the mix of ingredients in dog and cat food

To optimize product mix in hard-goods manufacturing

By large commercial banks to manage their balance sheets

For long-range capacity planning in production facilities

To minimize trim waste in the paper industry

By investment firms to optimize portfolio selections

The list of applications is seemingly endless, and new applications are reported weekly in trade and academic journals. It is not an overstatement that — if all currently operational LP models were simultaneously destroyed — American business and industry would grind to a halt overnight.

And, yet, operational LP has been around only since 1947. A solution technique called the *SIMPLEX algorithm* was "invented" by George Dantzig [1] and was nothing more than a mathematical curiosity until the advent of the high-speed electronic computer. Applications burgeoned in the 1960s and 1970s, and today LP is a widely accepted and routinely used modeling technique.

What is the nature of this mathematical "tool" that has found its way into the board rooms and management information systems of business, industry, and public sector organizations? There are as many definitions as there are books that discuss it — and there are literally hundreds of such tomes. For the potential or practicing manager, *none* of these definitions is particularly helpful, since none succeeds in capturing the broad diversity of problems that can be profitably modeled by LP. However, in the interests of precision, an *accurate* definition of linear programming is as follows.

> **Linear programming** is a technique that seeks the extremum of an
> *n*-dimensional objective hyperplane over a polytope bounded by *n*-di-
> mensional hyperplanes.

Although accurate, this definition of LP is hardly helpful to a managerial
decision maker.

Instead of trying to describe the *model*, why not describe the aspects of
problems that lend themselves to modeling by LP? The next section does
precisely that.

UNDERLYING ASSUMPTIONS

Most managerial problems involve one or more *objectives* to be attained and
constraints under which the decision maker must operate. As noted in Chapter
1, no model will ever capture all the elements of an actual problem. However, if
the model can represent certain aspects of the problem, then the output from
the solution of the model may provide useful insights.

What kinds of problems are candidates for modeling with LP? Recalling
that our modeling environment is *deterministic* and *single objective,* it must
also possess two basic characteristics called *additivity* and *divisibility.*

ADDITIVITY

To model a problem with LP, it must be safely assumed that we can add the
individual costs, or profit contributions of the various products or processes, to
obtain an accurate total of costs or profit. Stated another way, there are no
interdependencies among the decision variables. For example, if a hand-held
calculator and a leather case are sold separately, but the case is discounted when
purchased along with the calculator, the two items can obviously not be assumed to be independent.

DIVISIBILITY

The key aspect of a problem as regards its appropriateness for modeling by LP is
divisibility. There are two considerations. First, the process to be modeled must
be operating above a level at which economies of scale are a factor and below a
level at which diminishing returns affect the outcome. In determining an efficient product mix in production planning, for example, there may be products
that — if selected for production — would involve a one-time setup cost for the
production line. Such a problem cannot be modeled as a linear program, since
cost per unit of production is different for every level of production (i.e., as
production level rises, more and more units share in the initial setup cost).
Note, however, that when the number produced grows large, the problem *at
that time* may be approximated fairly closely by LP.

Second, noninteger values of the decision variables must make managerial
sense. If a small airline, for instance, were trying to optimize its fleet mix of six

aircraft, and the LP model indicated an optimal purchase of 2.78 DC-9s and 3.22 Boeing 737s, our decision maker would hardly be overjoyed with such a result. As another example, suppose that a portfolio manager wishes the decision variable x_1 to be *one* if the common stock BOR (Borg-Warner, Inc.) should be included in the portfolio and *zero* if not. The manager's exasperation at having the LP model return the output "$x_1 = .57$" can only be imagined.

The net effect of the additivity and divisibility assumptions is that both the objective of the manager, and the constraints under which he or she must operate, must be expressible mathematically as *linear* functions. The art and science of building such models is discussed in the next section.

BUILDING LP MODELS

Some of the principles of modeling discussed in this section have already been addressed in Chapter 1. However, these principles are so critically important to successful modeling that the repetition is justified.

AN ORDERLY APPROACH TO MODEL BUILDING

In Chapter 1, the "model" phase of our SPMS methodology included three subphases: formulating the model, collecting the data, and validating the model. Since mathematical programming models (of which LP is a special case) exhibit the same mathematical pattern—an objective function that is some function of the decision variables and a set of equations or inequalities in the decision variables that constrain the objective function—much of the following can be generalized to nonlinear models as well.

Our "orderly approach to model building" in linear programming focuses on the three subphases noted in the previous paragraph: formulating the model, collecting the data, and validating the model.

Formulating The Model

Model formulation implies model selection and careful definition of decision variables before formalizing the mathematical statement of the problem. In deciding to use a linear programming model, make *certain* that your problem meets the requirements of additivity and divisibility closely enough so that no potentially misleading results emerge from the computer. Take into consideration the large amount of data required for LP modeling, and make sure that those data will be available in a timely and cost-effective manner. And above all, remember that model selection is the decision maker's responsibility, not a technical analyst's.

Why is this so? Model selection is a macro (managerial) decision because only the decision maker knows what part the analytical results from the model will play in the decision process. Thus, the relative sophistication required of those results will depend on factors exogenous to the model and of which a technical analyst will probably be unaware. For example, if factors such as labor problems, environmental pollution considerations, and financial exigencies constrain a product mix problem so heavily that all that is needed is a *feasible* mix, then it is unlikely that an LP model will provide a useful solution. Thus, managerial involvement in model selection is crucial to the success of the effort.

If an LP model is deemed appropriate, the next step is to define carefully the decision variables. We recall from Chapter 1 that a decision variable represents a *specific* entity over which a decision maker has control. For example, the "number of blue, two-door, fully equipped 1984 Z-cars to produce in the Stutz Detroit plant in June 1984" is a decision variable that the Stutz Detroit plant manager can control; "how many of the cars are sold" is not. The important point is that all decision variables must be defined precisely and unambiguously.

We are now ready to formulate the model of our problem. We have already defined our objective in previous SPMS steps. Our next task is to state the constraints under which we must operate. A useful and often insightful approach is first to state the objective and constraints verbally. Let us illustrate this point with an example problem.

Scenario: You are the chief executive officer of a commercial aircraft manufacturing company that produces three aircraft models: a two-engine model, a three-engine model, and a four-engine model. Your objective is to maximize total profit contribution generated by manufacturing the three types of aircraft.

Problem: The purchasing manager indicates that she can obtain limited numbers of engines, avionics packages, and seats each month. Furthermore, the limited supply of peripheral equipment (e.g., landing gear assemblies, cockpits) places restrictions on the numbers of each type of aircraft that can be produced. Finally, there is an overall limitation on the number of aircraft that can be produced each month due to plant capacity.

Model: It appears that we have a deterministic, single-objective problem and that additivity is present. However, a result that includes "fractions of airplanes" makes no sense, so that one aspect of the divisibility assumption does not hold. Even so, let us continue the modeling process even though the resulting model might be flawed.

The monthly decision variables are apparent: (1) how many two-engine aircraft to produce, (2) how many three-engine aircraft to produce, and (3) how many four-engine aircraft to produce. Let us now construct a verbal model of the problem.

Objective: Maximize total profit contribution.

Constraints:
1. Engine availability is limited.
2. Avionics package availability is limited.
3. Seat availability is limited.
4. There is an upper limit on production of two-engine aircraft.
5. There is an upper limit on production of three-engine aircraft.
6. There is an upper limit on production of four-engine aircraft.
7. There is an upper limit on total aircraft production.

If we are satisfied with our verbal model, the next step is to construct the mathematical version.

The formal statement of an LP model is

$$\text{OPTIMIZE } x_0 = \sum_{j=1}^{n} c_j x_j \qquad (2.1)$$

$$\text{SUBJECT TO: } \sum_{j=1}^{n} a_{ij} x_j \begin{Bmatrix} \leq \\ = \\ \geq \end{Bmatrix} b_i, \quad i = 1, \ldots, m \qquad (2.2)$$

In (2.1), "OPTIMIZE" may be either MINIMIZE or MAXIMIZE, and the objective function is a linear function of the decision variables x_j, $j = 1, \ldots, n$.

Formula (2.2) indicates that there are m linear constraints that may be equations ("$=$") or inequalities ("$\leq$" or "$\geq$").

Since our aircraft manufacturing example has three decision variables ($n = 3$) and seven constraints ($m = 7$), the general mathematical LP model is

$$\text{OPTIMIZE } x_0 = \sum_{j=1}^{3} c_j x_j$$

$$\text{SUBJECT TO: } \sum_{j=1}^{3} a_{ij} x_j \begin{Bmatrix} \leq \\ = \\ \geq \end{Bmatrix} b_i, \quad i = 1, \ldots, 7$$

Collecting The Data

In our general LP model stated in (2.1) and (2.2), there are

n cost or profit margin coefficients (c_j)

m constants on the right-hand side of the constraints (b_i)

$m \cdot n$ "technological coefficients" on the left-hand side of the constraints (a_{ij})

Thus, for a problem with 25 decision variables and 20 constraints (a modest problem in the "real world"), the decision to develop an LP model of the problem involves collecting $25 + 20 + (25 \cdot 20) = 545$ numbers. Unlike in most textbooks, these $n + m + (m \cdot n)$ numbers cannot be conveniently plucked from thin air to appear neatly assembled in a table. Depending on the nature of the problem and the decision environment, they sometimes must be forcibly extracted from the accounting department, or painstakingly sifted out of production records, or estimated from incomplete financial transaction records. If the manager's organization happens to have a sophisticated, highly integrated management information system (MIS), so much the better. But even a good MIS is no cure-all.

In our aircraft manufacturing illustration, for example, $n + m + (m \cdot n) = 3 + 7 + (7 \cdot 3) = 31$.

Once we have assembled the numbers, it is time for a healthy exercise in managerial skepticism. Remembering "garbage in, garbage out," the data should be considered "garbage" until proven otherwise. For example, decimal points are notoriously nomadic, wandering to places where they do not belong. Moreover, the level of confidence in data accuracy may vary for the various inputs to the same model. As an illustration, personnel and labor costs taken from time cards may be highly reliable, whereas numbers estimating stockout or backorder costs in the inventory system may be only "guesstimates," or at best "*scientific* guesstimates." In any case, any weaknesses in the data known to the decision maker must be recalled and taken into account when the analytical results from the model are used in the decision process.

Data for the aircraft manufacturing illustration are as supplied by the production and procurement departments:

	Aircraft Type			
	Two-Engine (x_1)	Three-Engine (x_2)	Four-Engine (x_3)	Limitation/Resource Availability
Profit Contribution/Unit	$500,000	$650,000	$900,000	—
Engines/Unit	2	3	4	60
Avionics Packages/Unit	1	1	2	35
Seats/Unit	135	175	245	3500
Number of Two-Engine	1	0	0	8
Number of Three-Engine	0	1	0	15
Number of Four-Engine	0	0	1	10
Total Aircraft	1	1	1	30

There are three decision variables ($n = 3$) and seven constraints ($m = 7$), so that the mathematical version of our verbal model would be

$$\text{MAXIMIZE } x_0 = \$500,000x_1 + \$650,000x_2 + \$900,000x_3 \qquad \text{(profit)}$$

SUBJECT TO:

1. $2x_1 + 3x_2 + 4x_3 \leq 60$ (engines)
2. $x_1 + x_2 + 2x_3 \leq 35$ (avionics)
3. $135x_1 + 175x_2 + 245x_3 \leq 3500$ (seats)
4. $x_1 \leq 8$ (two-engine)
5. $x_2 \leq 15$ (three-engine)
6. $x_3 \leq 10$ (four-engine)
7. $x_1 + x_2 + x_3 \leq 30$ (plant capacity)

Validating The Model

After we have formulated the model and have collected the data, we must take one final precautionary measure before preparing the data for computer analysis—a check for dimensional consistency. That is, we must assure that the objective function and the constraints are stated in consistent units of measurement. For example, in our aircraft production illustration, our objective is to "MAXIMIZE x_0," where x_0 is in the units "dollars of profit contribution." To check for dimensional consistency, we note that "profit contribution in dollars per unit of two-engine aircraft produced" is \$500,000 and that the dimension of decision variable x_1 is "number of two-engine aircraft produced." When we multiply \$500,000 by x_1, the resulting dimension is

$$\frac{\text{Dollars of profit contribution}}{\text{No. two-engine AC produced}} \times \text{No. two-engine AC produced} =$$

$$\text{dollars of profit contribution}$$

We get the same result for x_2 and x_3, so that the objective function is dimensionally consistent. The same procedure is used with the constraints. For example, the first constraint indicates that there is a limited supply of engines, so that the right-hand side of this constraint (60) has the dimension "No. engines." The left-hand side of the constraint has terms such as $2x_1$, whose dimensions are

$$\frac{\text{No. engines}}{\text{No. two-engine AC produced}} \times \text{No. two-engine AC produced} = \text{No. engines}$$

so that we have a consistently valid statement in terms of dimensions.

After assuring that our objective function and constraints are dimensionally consistent, we should have our technical analyst prepare the data in the form in which they will be fed to the computer for eventual analysis. As decision makers, we must *personally* make sure that all the numbers are in their proper places, and accurate. Commas in a computer-ready data set—much like decimal points—seem to have a mind of their own. One misplaced comma, or one erroneous data item, or one omitted variable or constraint is sufficient to turn the entire data set into "garbage." Once satisfied that the data are complete and accurate, the manager should have the analyst run the LP package using them as input and bring him or her the preliminary solution to the model. If the LP solution looks reasonable from a managerial perspective, the model validation phase is complete. If it does not, you should go back to the beginning and start over.

MODEL FORMULATION: TWO EXAMPLES

The minicases and problems at the end of this chapter provide a wide variety of scenarios intended to develop model formulation skills. Because of the critical importance of this phase of LP modeling and analysis, however, let us introduce our fictitious computer friend LIPS (*l*inear *i*nteractive *p*rogramming *s*ynthe-sizer), who will lead us step by step through the formulation of two small (but realistic) LP models.

LO-CAL CANDY COMPANY

LIPS: Good morning, my name is LIPS, and I am ready to assist you in formu-lating a linear model of your problem. What is your name?

PERCY: My name is Percy Sweet, and my parents, Howie and Betty, own and operate the LO-CAL Candy Company. Our company makes five lines of candy, and it takes five different kinds of ingredients to make them. I've got the production data right here — and I've also got the profit contribution per package of each product. Would you like to see these data?

LIPS: Feed them to me.

Product	Profit per Package	Ingredients (Pounds per package)				
		Dark Chocolate	Light Chocolate	Sugar	Caramel	Assorted Nuts
Nuts-a-Plenty	$1.00	.8	.2	.3	.2	.7
Bite O'Heaven	.70	.5	.1	.4	.3	.1
Chocochunk	1.10	1.0	.1	.6	.3	.9
Diet-buster	2.00	2.0	.1	1.3	.7	1.5
Goo-Chew	.60	1.1	.2	.05	.5	0

LIPS: Got it. So what's the problem?

PERCY: Well, my parents' fiftieth wedding anniversary is coming up next week, and Dad wants to take Mom to Buzzard's Roost, Montana, for a month's honeymoon — he was too busy when they were first married. The problem is that we have a bunch of perfectly good ingredients in stock, and we want to make one more production run before closing down for 30 days. The stuff will spoil if we don't use it. Mom says we have enough ingredients to make about 200 packages of each brand, for a total profit contribution of $1080. She's right, of course, and that would use up most of the light chocolate, but I think we could do better. So Dad offered to give me any profits I can generate in excess of $1080. You'd probably like to see the current inventory, so here it is.

Inventory (in pounds)

Ingredient	Amount on Hand
Dark chocolate	1411
Light chocolate	149
Sugar	815.5
Caramel	466
Nuts	1080

Lips: Got it. (Short pause) Percy, I think you came to the right place. It appears that you have a classic example of a linear product mix problem. Before we go dashing off, though, let me ask you a couple of questions. Are you sure those ingredient amounts are right for each product? Two pounds of chocolate per package of Diet-Buster seems awfully high to me, and the .05 pounds of sugar per package of Goo-Chew is an order of magnitude different from the other four products.

Percy: No, LIPS, those figures are accurate — it's the nature of the products. Anything else bother you?

Lips: Well, per unit profit contributions are always tough to estimate. Do you use a different setup for different products? Is one (or more) of the products new? Also, who took the inventory of ingredients? Are you sure it's accurate?

Percy: Not to worry, LIPS. We've been making all five products for 15 years, and the profit contributions are accurate. As for the inventory, I took it myself — and I'm certain each of the amounts is within 3% of the actual availability.

Lips: One more thing, Percy. Technically, an LP model might give answers in fractions of packages. Could you handle that?

Percy: Sure. I always take the scraps home to my German shepherd, Drucker. He loves candy.

Lips: O.K. We're going to let the five decision variables x_1, x_2, x_3, x_4, and x_5 represent the number of packages, respectively, of Nuts-a-Plenty, Bite O'Heaven, Chocochunk, Diet-Buster, and Goo-Chew to produce. Your objective appears to be maximization of total profit contribution, which is just the sum of the five individual profit contributions.

Your constraints are the amounts of the five ingredients available, and I'm also going to constrain your decision variables so that they can't take on negative values. Remember, now, when we solve this model we may not get whole packages. Ready to see the model? Here it is.

$$\text{MAXIMIZE } x_0 = x_1 + .7x_2 + 1.1x_3 + 2x_4 \quad + .6x_5 \tag{2.3}$$

$$\text{SUBJECT TO: } .8x_1 + .5x_2 + x_3 \quad + 2x_4 \quad + 1.1x_5 \le 1411 \tag{2.4}$$

$$.2x_1 + .1x_2 + .1x_3 \quad + .1x_4 \quad + .2x_5 \le 149 \tag{2.5}$$

$$.3x_1 + .4x_2 + .6x_3 \quad + 1.3x_4 + .05x_5 \le 815.5 \tag{2.6}$$

$$.2x_1 + .3x_2 + .3x_3 \quad + .7x_4 \quad + .5x_5 \le 466 \tag{2.7}$$

$$.7x_1 + .1x_2 + .9x_3 \quad + 1.5x_4 \quad \le 1080 \tag{2.8}$$

$$x_1, x_2, x_3, x_4, x_5 \ge 0 \tag{2.9}$$

Percy: That looks vaguely familiar — you said it's a linear programming model? I guess (2.3) is the objective, and the inequalities (2.4) through (2.8) stand for the constraints on dark chocolate, light chocolate, sugar, caramel, and nuts, respectively. What's the solution?

Lips: Not so fast, Percy. I've already solved the model, and I'll show you the optimal values of the decision variables in a moment to make sure my solution *appears* to make sense. But I'll warn you—you're not quite ready to use this solution to help make your decision until you absorb the rest of this chapter.

Here's my solution.

Variable	Description	Value
x_0	Profit	$1509.09
x_1	Nuts-a-Plenty	454.50 packages
x_2	Bite O'Heaven	58.78 packages
x_3	Chocochunk	0 packages
x_4	Diet-Buster	503.99 packages
x_5	Goo-Chew	9.13 packages

Does it make sense?

PERCY: I guess so, and wow! I make a cool $429.09 for myself! I'm sort of disappointed that your solution doesn't produce any Chocochunk at all— it's one of our favorites. And we *might* have a problem selling as many as 500 packages of Diet-Buster. Could you give me some other solutions that change these two products around without cutting into my profits too badly?

LIPS: You asked an interesting question, Percy. I'll see you again in Problem 5 at the end of this chapter, when you'll be able to understand my answer. This is LIPS, over and out.

TELETRONIX INDUSTRIES, INC. [3]

In this model formulation session, our decision maker is Cynthia Sizer, head of the mechanical engineering department of Teletronix Industries (TI). Cynthia is an experienced LP modeler, so her session with LIPS is conducted in the BRIEF mode. That is, LIPS dispenses with the chitchat it indulged in with Percy Sweet and gets down to business.

LIPS: Ready. Name, please.
CYNTHIA: Cynthia Sizer, CS.
LIPS: Hello, CS. Scenario, please.
CYNTHIA: My company, TI, wants to prototype a voice-driven computer communications device. The EE guys have the electronic technology just about whipped. My ME people will make the plastic case.
LIPS: Check, CS. Problem, please.
CYNTHIA: We've always used the polymer ABS for plastic cases, since its heat-deflection properties are superior—and since it also meets min standards for ultraviolet stability, strength, and shrinkage rate. ABS is expensive, however, and management is becoming more and more cost-conscious because of the increasingly competitive market. So I'm looking into the possibility of a blend of several compatible materials to try to reduce costs.

Lips: Objective is cost minimization. Decision variables are fractions of each compatible material to include in the blend. Additivity and divisibility OK?

Cynthia: Yes, LIPS. Total cost is the sum of individual material costs. No setup or integer variable problems, either.

Lips: Good. We'll work this on a per pound basis. Give me the names of the materials, their costs per pound, and a four-letter variable name for each material. We'll be using the LINDO [2] format for output. OK?

Cynthia: OK. Here goes.

Material	Cost ($ per pound)	Variable Name
Polystyrene	$.70	PSTY
Talc	.15	TALC
Glass beads	1.85	GLAS
Regrind	.10	REGR
Polypropylene	.50	PPRO
ABS plastic	1.00	ABSP

Lips: Got it. Any constraints on mix? If not, you should obviously use 100% of REGR.

Cynthia: Yes, unfortunately. TALC can't be more than 20% because of strength losses. PPRO is very unstable, so the mixture can't include more PPRO than 50% of the total of the other base plastics ABSP and PSTY. REGR has strength implications as well, but not as severely as TALC — the mixture can include up to 50% REGR. OK so far?

Lips: No problem, CS. Continue, please.

Cynthia: This one is tricky. The base plastics are ABSP, PSTY, and PPRO, as noted. Too much PSTY and/or PPRO causes problems in the extrusion mold, so that at least 60% of the total fraction of base plastics must be ABSP. Also, the three base plastics must account for a total of at least 70% of the mix.

There are two more constraints. We must limit the total of GLAS and TALC to a maximum of 25%, for cosmetic purposes. Finally, to assure sufficient mold life, we must restrict the amount of GLAS to be no more than 15% of the mix.

Lips: You missed one constraint, CS — the fractions of materials must sum to 1. Here are the objective function and constraints exactly as you described them. Check them over carefully.

$$\text{MINIMIZE } x_0 = .7 \text{ PSTY} + .15 \text{ TALC} + 1.85 \text{ GLAS} + .1 \text{ REGR} + .5 \text{ PPRO} + 1.0 \text{ ABSP} \tag{a}$$

$$\text{SUBJECT TO:} \qquad \text{TALC} \quad \leq .2 \tag{b}$$

$$\text{PPRO} \quad \leq .5 \text{ (ABSP + PSTY)} \tag{c}$$

$$\text{REGR} \quad \leq .5 \tag{d}$$

$$ABSP \geq .6 \, (PSTY + PPRO + ABSP) \qquad (e)$$

$$PSTY + PPRO + ABSP \geq .7 \qquad (f)$$

$$GLAS + TALC \qquad \leq .25 \qquad (g)$$

$$GLAS \qquad \leq .15 \qquad (h)$$

$$PSTY + TALC + GLAS + REGR$$
$$+ \, PPRO + ABSP \; = 1 \qquad (i)$$

ALL VARIABLES NON-NEGATIVE

CYNTHIA: (Short pause) Looks good, LIPS. But you can't give the model to LINDO in that form, can you? Don't all variables have to be on the left sides of the inequalities?

LIPS: Correct, CS. I have a subroutine that does exactly that, but experience tells me that decision makers like to see the mathematical model exactly as they fed it in. However, if you'd like to see what LINDO will get, here's my call to LINDO on your screen.

```
RUN LINDO
MINIMIZE      .7PS + .15TA + 1.85GL + .1RE + .5PP +   AB
SUBJECT TO:        TA                                  < .2
             −.5PS                         +   PP − .5AB < 0
                                      RE                < .5
             −.6PS                        −.6PP + .4AB > 0
                                        +  PP +   AB > .7
                  TA +     GL                          < .25
                           GL                          < .15
             PS +    TA +  GL +  RE +  PP +  AB = 1
END
GO
```

CYNTHIA: You're right, LIPS. It's harder to check for errors in formulation in this format. What's the optimal solution to my model?

LIPS: Already run. I'll convert fractions into percentages for you.

Cost per Pound   *$.599333*

Material	Percent
PSTY	4.6667
TALC	0
GLAS	0
REGR	30.0000
PPRO	23.3333
ABSP	42.0000
Check Sum	100.0000

CYNTHIA: Interesting result, LIPS. The blend costs about $.60 per pound as opposed to $1.00 using the ABS plastic alone. A cost saving of 40% will please my boss. How about sensitivity analysis?

LIPS: This is a textbook, Cynthia, so you'll have to wait until later in the chapter.

CYNTHIA: Fine. Bye.

LIPS: LIPS out.

THE SIMPLEX ALGORITHM: AN INTUITIVE DESCRIPTION

On a practical level, what goes on inside the computerized algorithm that calculates solutions to LP models is of little interest to a practicing manager. Philosophically, however, it is dangerous to know only *what* your servant does — and not *how*. Does this mean that a practicing manager should be able to solve "toy models" with pen and paper? No, but every manager needs to understand the *process* and the logic behind it.

There are several reasons for this necessity. First, as we will see in later chapters, many problems exist that can be modeled in several ways — with perhaps one model being very much more efficiently implemented than another. Moreover, one model may produce the same solution as another, but not have the capability of delivering data on the "sensitivity" of that solution to inaccuracies in the input data. Also, many optimizing algorithms work in perfectly logical fashion mathematically but produce optimal solutions with features that sometimes defy managerial common sense.

For example, the optimal solution to an LP model has the following curious property: If there are m constraints, then no more than m decision variables can have values greater than zero (in the absence of multiple optimum solutions). But constraints represent *limitations* on managerial freedom of action. Does this mean that the fewer constraints (unless $m > n$), the fewer decision variables that can be operationally positive and still give an optimal solution to the model? Yes.

For example, in the crude oil cracking problem, if a manager decided to implement the optimal solution to an LP model *as the solution to the problem,* without intervention, the number of different products would be a function of the number of constraints on production. Taken to its logical conclusion, such a manager — seeing the need (for exogenous reasons) to broaden the range of petroleum-based products produced from a given batch of crude oil — would need to look for additional constraints! Such an absurdity mandates that managers understand what is occurring in the computerized algorithm.

THE SIMPLEX ALGORITHM

The SIMPLEX algorithm for producing optimal solutions to linear programming models was "invented" by George Dantzig in 1947, and his book on this subject [1] remains the classic reference. The algorithm takes its name from the mathematical term "simplex," which in geometry is a region bounded by hyperplanes. In algebraic terms, a "simplex" is the set of all solutions to a system of linear inequalities.

The idea behind the SIMPLEX algorithm is elegantly simple. Suppose we have n decision variables and m inequality constraints, so that we are dealing with an n-dimensional "simplex." For example, a triangular pyramid would be a three-dimensional "simplex" described by $m = 4$ constraints: the three planes that intersect to form the sides and the plane that intersects with the sides to form the bottom. Since we are interested in locating a point in or on this pyramid (the feasible region) that made the value of another plane (the objective function) as large (maximization) or as small (minimization) as possible, it is logical that such a point must lie on the surface (boundary) of the pyramid, so that we can ignore the interior in our search for an optimal solution to our model.

Moreover — and this is the key to understanding how the SIMPLEX algorithm works — it can be shown that an optimal solution to a linear programming model must occur at a *vertex* of the "simplex," where a vertex is the intersection of at least n hyperplanes. In our pyramid example, there are exactly four feasible vertices — the points where each combination of three planes intersect. Instead of having to concern ourselves about the infinite number of points on the boundary of the feasible region, we therefore need only to examine the finite number of feasible vertices.

Admittedly, the number of candidate solutions may be rather large. For example, in a moderate-sized LP problem with 50 decision variables and 20 " $\geq$ " constraints, the number of vertices is approximately

$$50,980,740,270,000,000,000$$

which is roughly 50 quintillion! Surprisingly, computerized versions of the SIMPLEX algorithm routinely solve LP models hundreds of times this size in seconds (or at most minutes) on high-speed computers.

The power of the SIMPLEX method is best explained by an analogy. Let us represent the feasible vertices (most vertices, in practice, are not feasible solutions to the LP model) as footholds on a mountain and suppose that our intrepid climber wishes to reach the top (solve a maximization problem). She or he will, of course, never try to gain footing on a foothold in space (an infeasible vertex), and our climber wishes to move from one foothold to the next and thereby ascend nearer the top (increase the value of the objective function). Occasionally, our climber may be forced to move sideways to an adjacent foothold at the same distance from the top (encounter a degenerate iteration), but eventually will find a foothold that leads upward (the algorithm can be guaranteed to converge to the optimum). Thus, because of the "upward-seeking" nature of the climber (the SIMPLEX algorithm), the fact that no "sudden-death" footholds in space are considered (infeasible solutions are avoided), and the possibility of moving horizontally around the mountain to return to a previously occupied foothold is made impossible (infinite cycling cannot occur), we have a very efficient climbing strategy that uses only a very small percentage of possible footholds (iterates through a minimal number of vertices).

Mathematically speaking, the SIMPLEX algorithm does nothing more than solve sets of m equations in m unknowns — "changing out" one variable at a time until it finds the optimal set, or *basis.*

A GRAPHICAL EXAMPLE

Although dealing with "toy models" is usually not particularly insightful, in this instance a graphical illustration using a two-dimensional model is useful in understanding how the SIMPLEX algorithm works. Our "toy model" is not dignified by attaching it to a managerial scenario; rather, we present the unadorned mathematical model as follows:

Toy Model:

$$\text{MAXIMIZE } x_0 = 16x_1 + 17x_2 \tag{2.10}$$

$$\text{SUBJECT TO:} \quad 3x_1 + 5x_2 \leq 15 \tag{2.11}$$

$$8x_1 + 9x_2 \leq 36 \tag{2.12}$$

$$5x_1 + 4x_2 \leq 20 \tag{2.13}$$

$$2x_2 \leq 5 \tag{2.14}$$

$$2x_1 \leq 7 \tag{2.15}$$

$$x_1, x_2 \geq 0 \tag{2.16}$$

The feasible region is represented by the shaded area in Figure 2.1a and is the intersection of the constraints and nonnegativity restrictions on the two decision variables.

It can be demonstrated that there are theoretically 21 possible vertices for this toy model, some of which are shown as black dots in Figure 2.1a. Note, however, that only the 6 vertices labeled A, B, C, D, E, and F are *feasible;* that is, they satisfy all five formal constraints and the nonnegativity restrictions on x_1 and x_2. Note in the figure that constraint (2.12) does not play a role in outlining the feasible region; such constraints are called *redundant.*

In Figure 2.1b, the objective function is represented at three positions by the dashed lines. The SIMPLEX algorithm begins at point A (the origin) and moves first to point F ($x_1 = 0$, $x_2 = 2.5$) with an objective value of 42.5. The second iteration moves to point E ($x_1 = .83$, $x_2 = 2.5$) with an objective value of 55.8; the third and final iteration locates the optimum point D ($x_1^* = 3.08$, $x_2^* = 1.15$), with x_0^* (the maximum feasible value of the objective function) $= 68.8$.

Recalling the mountain climbing analogy, note that each successive "foothold" was indeed feasible and that our "climber" did make progress at each step until the "top" was reached. In geometric terms, observe that the objective hyperplane (a dashed line in this case) moved parallel to itself, in the direction of increasing value, until it reached the optimal vertex point. From Figure 2.1b, it is apparent that an optimal solution to an LP model must include a vertex.

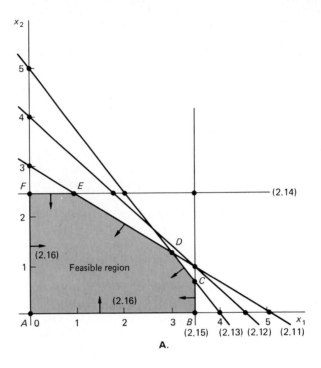

A.

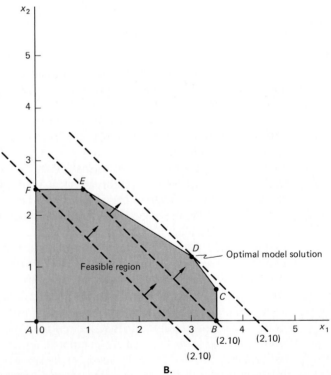

B.

Figure 2.1 (A) Feasible region for "toy model." (B) Graphical solution of "toy model."

So much for our toy model. Operational LP models may have thousands of decision variables and hundreds or even thousands of constraints, so that the graphical example just given is good only to provide insight into the operation of the SIMPLEX algorithm. Efficient computerized packages that implement the algorithm are widely available and will be discussed in the next section.

AVAILABLE LP COMPUTER CODES

There is a wide variety of available computer packages to solve LP problems. They are of two types: (1) highly efficient, tightly programmed packages for large, mainframe or "supermini" computers and (2) smaller packages, usually written in the BASIC programming language, that are intended for use on small minicomputers or microcomputers. These two types of packages will be addressed separately.

LP PACKAGES FOR MAINFRAME COMPUTERS

Installations that have IBM or "IBM look-alike" equipment such as Amdahl or National AS/6 may gain access to IBM's proprietary LP package called *Mathematical Programming System* (MPS). This package is highly efficient in both its central processing unit (CPU) time requirements and its computer storage space requirements. Not that it is critical for a manager to know, but MPS uses a device called *revised SIMPLEX* (a more computationally efficient form of the basic algorithm) and other devices like "crashing the basis" to expedite the solution. What *is* important for the manager to know is that MPS has the capability to perform *sensitivity analysis* on the LP model, and we shall talk about this in the next section. Unfortunately, many users who are not proficient computer programmers themselves find MPS difficult to use. To paraphrase Abraham Lincoln, the user documentation appears to have been written "by programmers, to programmers, and for programmers." However, once an analyst has mastered the very complex data handling procedures and learns how to access the package's sophisticated features, MPS is a very powerful and useful tool. Control Data Corporation has a similar package called APEX IV, with features very much like those in MPS.

LIPS has already made mention of another widely available LP package— LINDO (*l*inear *int*eractive *d*iscrete *o*ptimizer), authored by Linus Schrage [2]. LINDO is extremely easy to use and is interactive. This package is available from its author for a modest fee (Graduate School of Business, University of Chicago).

LP PACKAGES FOR MINI- AND MICROCOMPUTERS

As mini- and microcomputers become more and more sophisticated, they are also becoming less expensive in the sense of "dollars for a stated capability." As a result, more and more business and industrial firms are acquiring them. Most of the minicomputer manufacturers also sell software packages that operate on their own machines, and all major firms' packages include one or more LP programs. Such packages are also sold separately by firms that specialize only in producing software.

Because of the plethora of such packages, three typical ones will be discussed — and no attempt will be made to list them all (such a list would have been obsolete before this text arrived at the printer).

GSBLP

The LP program GSBLP is written in BASIC for minicomputers and is available from the Graduate School of Business at Stanford University. It will solve LP models with up to 50 decision variables and 25 constraints, with the restriction that $(n + 2) \cdot (m + 2) \le 810$. GSBLP, like MPS, uses the revised SIMPLEX method and has the capability of performing sensitivity analysis on the right-hand side values of the constraints, as well as on the objective function coefficients. This package is not fully interactive, so that complete documentation is necessary for its use.

LINPRO

LINPRO is a completely interactive LP package available from the Hewlett-Packard Users' Group. It is more limited than GSBLP in the size of model it can optimize, and it does not use advanced computational devices to expedite the solution. LINPRO is widely used by business schools as a teaching device and is an excellent vehicle for that purpose.

BLP

The LP package BLP was written by James R. Burns. BLP is completely interactive and is recommended to students and practicing managers with access only to microcomputers. Written in the Microsoft® BASIC language, BLP will "run" on the great majority of microcomputer brands. An array of sensitivity analysis tools is also available.

A "simple" version of BLP, called BSIM, is discussed and illustrated in the appendix to this chapter. The program listing of BSIM (in Microsoft BASIC) is well documented with "REMARK" statements.

DEVELOPING ALTERNATIVE SOLUTIONS

At this point, let us step back and scan the terrain over which we have traveled. In preparing to use linear programming as an aid to problem solving, a careful look was taken at the major characteristics of the problem to be certain that the LP model was appropriate. Model building was discussed — and data collection and analysis was heavily stressed. A broad discussion of the SIMPLEX algorithm for solving LP models ensued, as did a brief introduction to some computerized software packages for actually deriving solutions to the model.

Before discussing the details of developing useful information from the computer output of an optimizing LP model, it is necessary to dwell for a moment on the *nature* of solutions to LP models. For example, our toy model illustrated in Figures 2.1a and b has—as we saw—only six feasible vertex points. Thus, as theory points out, it depends only on the slope of the objective function, and whether we are minimizing or maximizing, as to which of these six points is an optimal point. Two observations are in order. First, if the objective hyperplane x_0 happens to be parallel to one of the constraints in the direction of optimization, then there will be *alternate optimal solutions.* Although having *sets* of optimal solutions to work with is highly desirable, the fact is that for most real LP models, this happenstance occurs rarely, so that in most cases, the alternate optimal solution is a mathematical oddity.

Second, note that if we do not insist on *the optimal solution to the model,* we have made a giant step in a managerial sense. Why? Because there is literally an infinite number of such solutions! For example, in our toy model, suppose that we would be willing to back off about $5\frac{1}{2}$% from the optimum value of x_0 (68.8) to a value of 65. Graphically, we have moved the objective hyperplane southwest, so that $x_1 = 3$, $x_2 = 1$ is now on the new objective hyperplane [i.e., $(3 \cdot 16) + (1 \cdot 17) = 65$]. Thus, every point in the thin polyhedron bounded by constraints 1, 3, and 5, and by the new objective function, are feasible solutions to the model, and with objective values in the range [65, 68.8]. Figure 2.2 illustrates this phenomenon.

Note in Figure 2.2 that, within the darkened area, x_1 can now range from 2.4 to 3.5 and x_2 can range from about 0.5 to 1.6 (not simultaneously, of course). One way to view this result, in a general sense, is that we have traded off some possible profit contribution for *managerial flexibility in decision making.* This

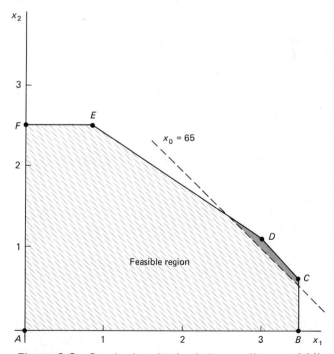

Figure 2.2 Good suboptimal solutions to "toy model."

is one of our goals — throughout this chapter and the rest of the text. And, of course, *it should be your goal* as a potential or practicing manager.

STANDARD COMPUTER OUTPUT

Table 2.1 is a reproduction of the actual computer input and output of the LINDO solution to our toy problem. Let us examine the printout from this package.

Table 2.1   LINDO Solution of Example Problem

```
MAX        16 X1 + 17 X2
SUBJECT TO
    2)     3 X1 + 5 X2 <=     15
    3)     8 X1 + 9 X2 <=     36
    4)     5 X1 + 4 X2 <=     20
    5)     2 X2 <=      5
    6)     2 X1 <=      7
END

    LP OPTIMUM FOUND   AT STEP       3

           OBJECTIVE FUNCTION VALUE

  1)          68.8461533

VARIABLE           VALUE           REDUCED COST
        X1         3.076923            0.000000
        X2         1.153846            0.000000


ROW           SLACK OR SURPLUS      DUAL PRICES
    2)            0.000000            1.615384
    3)            1.000000            0.000000
    4)            0.000000            2.230769
    5)            2.692308            0.000000
    6)            0.846154            0.000000

NO. ITERATIONS=          3

    RANGES IN WHICH THE BASIS IS UNCHANGED

                        OBJ COEFFICIENT RANGES
VARIABLE            CURRENT        ALLOWABLE        ALLOWABLE
                   COEF           INCREASE         DECREASE
        X1         16.000000       5.250000         5.800000
        X2         17.000000       9.666667         4.199999

                        RIGHTHAND SIDE RANGES
    ROW            CURRENT        ALLOWABLE        ALLOWABLE
                   RHS            INCREASE         DECREASE
    2              15.000000       1.000000         1.375000
    3              36.000000       INFINITY         1.000000
    4              20.000000       1.000000         5.833333
    5              5.000000        INFINITY         2.692308
    6              7.000000        INFINITY         0.846154
```

The first item in Table 2.1 is our toy model exactly as it was input to LINDO. The remark "LP OPTIMUM FOUND AT STEP 3" means that three iterations of the SIMPLEX algorithm were required to locate the optimal model solution—and this verifies our earlier graphical analysis. The optimal objective function value is given next, followed by the optimal values of the decision variables. The column entitled "SLACK OR SURPLUS" requires clarification.

As hinted at previously, the SIMPLEX algorithm cannot deal with systems of inequalities—it must have systems of equations on which to operate. By the simple device of adding nonnegative variables that "take up the slack" between the left-hand and right-hand sides of " $\leq$ " constraints, this condition is met. In our original toy model, therefore, the actual problem that LINDO saw was as follows:

$$\text{MAXIMIZE } x_0 = 16x_1 + 17x_2 \qquad\qquad\qquad\qquad (2.17)$$

$$\text{SUBJECT TO: } \quad 3x_1 + 5x_2 + x_3 \qquad\qquad\quad = 15 \qquad (2.18)$$

$$8x_1 + 9x_2 \qquad + x_4 \qquad\qquad = 36 \qquad (2.19)$$

$$5x_1 + 4x_2 \qquad\qquad + x_5 \qquad\quad = 20 \qquad (2.20)$$

$$2x_2 \qquad\qquad\qquad + x_6 \quad = 5 \qquad (2.21)$$

$$2x_1 \qquad\qquad\qquad\qquad\quad + x_7 = 7 \qquad (2.22)$$

$$x_j \geq 0, \quad j = 1, \ldots, 7 \qquad\qquad\qquad\qquad (2.23)$$

Handily, the program itself puts in the slack variables.

The values of the slack variables constitute important information for the decision maker. If a particular slack variable has a positive value, then—at optimality for the model—that constraint is said to be *nonbinding*. That is, if the solution to the model *happens* to be a viable solution to the problem, that constraint is really not a managerial constraint at all. On the other hand, if the slack variable has a value of zero, then the limitation represented by the constraint is said to be *binding*—and represents a very real limitation to managerial alternatives. In other words, if the constraint represents, say, a required raw material, then the limited supply available directly affects the level of profit contribution that can be attained.

The columns in the LINDO output labeled "REDUCED COST" and "DUAL PRICES" contain important information for the decision maker. Reduced costs are associated with the decision variables $x_j, j = 1, \ldots, n$. All x_j that have positive values in the optimal model solution have reduced costs of zero. If there are no alternate optimal solutions to the model, then all other x_j have positive reduced costs. The size of the reduced cost for a particular variable gives an indication of how close that variable is to being a "contender." For example, suppose that the profit contribution coefficient $c_4 = \$10$ for x_4 and that the reduced cost associated with x_4 at optimality is \$.75. This means that if c_4 had been *greater* than $\$10 + \$.75 = \$10.75$ originally, then x_4 would have had a positive value in the optimal solution. In our toy model, the reduced costs of both variables are zero, and therefore both have positive values in the optimal model solution.

The "dual prices" associated with the constraints in an LP solution are called, variously; shadow prices; or Lagrange multipliers; or marginal utilities. The middle term in the foregoing derives from a mathematical formalism attributed to a French mathematician; the first term has an intriguing cast reminiscent of the maneuvering of international spy rings, so we choose it in favor of "marginal utilities."

Importance of Shadow Prices

There is a shadow price associated with each slack variable—and therefore with each constraint. In our LINDO printout of the solution to our toy model, these are the values exhibited under the heading "DUAL PRICES." The shadow price indicates the change in total profit contribution that would occur, *given a unit change in the availability of resources represented by that constraint.* For example, the shadow price for the first constraint is approximately 1.62. This means that if the right-hand side of the first constraint had been 16 rather than 15, our total profit contribution would have been 1.62 units higher. Within certain bounds that we shall discuss later, shadow prices may be considered *rates of change,* so that if the right-hand side of the first constraint had been 17 instead of 15, the total profit contribution would have been higher by $2 \cdot (1.62)$ and so on (assuming that the current set of nonzero variables remains the same).

Note in the printout that the shadow prices of the second, fourth, and fifth constraints are all zero—which means that increased availability of the associated resources would have no effect whatsoever on total profit contribution. This comes as no surprise, since the values of the slack variables associated with these constraints (x_4, x_6, and x_7) are positive. Obviously, if our optimal model solution did not use up all these resources, additional increments certainly would not be of any value to us.

One might observe at this point: "What good is there in knowing shadow prices? We had only 15 units of the resources represented by the first constraint, after all—that's why it's a constraint!"

Good question. And the answer is in two parts. First, the value "15" may be anything from a "guesstimate" to a precisely computed quantity. It is here that the decision maker should heed the previous imprecation to recall any weaknesses in, or uncertainties about, the input data. If 15 was a "soft" number, then the entire analysis is no better than *it* is. A quick calculation for the toy model reveals that a 7% error in this number would mean approximately a 2.5% error in total profit contribution. The resource represented by the third constraint (x_5 is the slack variable) is also critical. With a shadow price of about 2.2, a 5% change in the value 20 (the right-hand side of the constraint) would result in a 3.3% error in total profit contribution. Managerial common sense tells us that one reaction might be to go back and try to obtain more reliable estimates of these critical data items—if at all possible. On the other hand, looking at the values of the slack variables for the nonbinding constraints (x_4, x_6, and x_7), we see that we have "cushions" in these three resources of 2.8%, 53.8%, and 12.1%, respectively. The margin for the second constraint may be somewhat too close for comfort, but the other two are probably not significant factors in this particular decision process.

Second, and most important, is the fact that the LP solution has focused managerial attention on the "bottlenecks" in our toy model. In general, if such analysis does nothing more than this, it will have made a most significant contribution to the decision maker. After all, the 15 units available in the first constraint, and the 20 units in the third, were not chiseled on stone tablets and handed down from on high. Those resource limitations were undoubtedly the result of *managerial decisions.* Can the surplus resources represented by the other three constraints somehow be traded off for additional units of the two binding resources? Does the increased profit contribution exceed the cost of acquiring additional units? In other words, the model has done its job; it is now time for the decision maker to do hers or his.

RANGING ANALYSIS

The LINDO package also performed something called *ranging analysis* on the optimal solution to the model, and the information is displayed in Table 2.1 under the heading, "RANGES IN WHICH THE BASIS IS UNCHANGED." The *mathematical* process by which this analysis is done is of no particular managerial interest; what is important for a decision maker is to be able to interpret the results.

Analysis of Resource Availability

The b_i, $i = 1, \ldots, m$, on the right-hand sides of the constraints usually represent limitations on resource availability and, thus, are critical inputs to the model and the decision process. One simple type of ranging analysis is to compute — one at a time, and holding the other values fixed — the ranges over which the values of these parameters may vary, without changing the current set of variables (both decision variables and slacks) that are nonzero in the optimal model solution. The LINDO computer output for this operation on our toy model has been rearranged as follows.

Right-Hand Side Ranges

		Current b_i
b_1:	$13.625 \le b_1 \le 16$	15
b_2:	$35 \quad\quad \le b_2$	36
b_3:	$14.167 \le b_3 \le 21$	20
b_4:	$2.308 \le b_4$	5
b_5:	$6.154 \le b_5$	7

These results help to give the manager additional insight into the possible effect of data inaccuracies as well as focus managerial attention on critical resources. For example, as long as the right-hand side of the first constraint (b_1) remains between 13.625 and 16, all else being equal, the current optimal model solution set remains unchanged. As we observed earlier, b_2, b_4, and b_5 can increase indefinitely without affecting the current solution set. In models of real problems, this is critically important information for decision makers.

Analysis of Objective Coefficients

In many LP models of problems, the most difficult numbers to estimate are the coefficients in the objective function ($c_j, j = 1, \ldots, n$). If the objective happens to be cost minimization, the task is somewhat easier than is the converse — maximization of total profit contribution. The reason for this is that "profit contribution" includes *both* net profit (the "bottom line") and contribution to overhead expenses not directly related to the decision variable. For this reason, the overhead contribution must be estimated using some assumed range of activity level for the variables. As we have previously noted, a production line situation in which there is a possibility of incurring a one-time setup cost for one or more items cannot accurately be modeled with linear programming. For these reasons, ranging analysis on the objective coefficients is critically important.

The LINDO computer output for this operation on our "toy model" has been rearranged as follows:

Objective Function Ranges

		Current c_i
c_1:	$10.20 \leq c_1 \leq 21.25$	16
c_2:	$12.80 \leq c_2 \leq 26.67$	17

In this example, there appears to be a relatively wide range of c_j values for which the current mix is still optimal, and the decision maker would not have the need for extreme accuracy in estimating these coefficients. As an illustration, in our toy model, the values of c_1 and c_2 would have to have "high-side" errors of about 33% and 57%, respectively, or "low-side" errors of about 36% and 25%, respectively, for the current solution to be nonoptimal. In the majority of models of real-world problems, however, ranges on the objective coefficients tend to be very narrow—which means that the accuracy of our estimates of these coefficients is critical.

It is also possible to perform ranging analysis on the constraint coefficients, and some sophisticated packages have this capability. Since the analysis is similar to the two cases just discussed, this topic will not be addressed further here. For an excellent discussion of this subject, see Wagner [4] or Hillier and Lieberman [5].

A CAVEAT FOR DECISION MAKERS

At this point, you might be saying to yourself, "There's nothing to LP modeling and analysis—it'll be a snap to use." If so, beware! You are on the verge of being afflicted with the deadly "toy model syndrome." Think ahead for a moment, and imagine that your technical analyst has just solved your 200-variable, 100-constraint LP model, using a standard computer package. Recall that you had directed the analyst to run the program for optimality, and then to run it again at 1%, 2%, and 5% below optimality. Naturally, you also ordered a complete (simple) sensitivity analysis on each run. Your input consisted of 20,300 neatly arrayed numbers. Your output consists of *243,600* numbers and weighs roughly 5 pounds! Devoting 1 second of your attention to each number would require 67.5 hours. The point is, that pile of paper is not *information* (which is what you need for decision making); it is *secondary data.*

The solution to this dilemma is simple. Almost all operational LP models are run with an auxiliary program that scans the results produced by the optimization model. Using parameters that you supply (e.g., all input elements within 5% of their upper or lower sensitivity ranges; binding constraints with shadow prices larger than the unit cost of the resources represented), the auxiliary program separates the wheat from the chaff and presents you with potentially valuable information. Is there a cookbook of such parameters? No. Every decision maker faces unique problems, and the elements of those problems may differ widely. The key is to thoroughly understand what the LP model is doing, what indicators it can provide, and what those indicators mean in the context of your decision environment. If you know what you need, and if you know what it means after you have gotten it, your technical analyst will see that you get it.

We now return to the session between LIPS and Cynthia Sizer to complete the analysis of the Teletronix Industries' plastic blending problem.

LIPS: Ready to continue, CS?

CYNTHIA: Right. Full LINDO output display, please (Table 2.2).

LIPS: Note that I only used the first two letters of the variable names, since they are unique.

CYNTHIA: Right. The reduced cost of GL is $1.75 per pound. I guess I should have eliminated that variable from the analysis based on common sense. The other material not used in the mix is TA, with a reduced cost of $.05, but the per pound cost is only $.15. Does that mean that if the cost of TA was less than $.10 per pound, the mix would include some?

LIPS: Correct, CS.

CYNTHIA: OK, the binding constraints were the ones LINDO has labeled (3), (5), (6), and (9), so that the other four constraints had no effect on this model solution. That's interesting — constraints (3), (5), and (6) are constraints on the base plastics, and (9) just assures that the mix totals 100%. It appears to me that the base plastics PS, PP, and AB are "driving" my problem.

LIPS: I agree, CS. Note in the "DUAL PRICES" column that the shadow prices for (3), (5), and (6) are .133333, $-.300000$, and $-.713333$, respectively. Recall that LINDO presents shadow prices for " $\leq$ " constraints as positive numbers and for " $\geq$ " and " $=$ " constraints as negative numbers — for the convenience of the user.

CYNTHIA: Got it, LIPS. But what do the shadow prices mean in the model like this one? There aren't any "scarce resources" as there are in a product mix problem.

LIPS: Good question. Look at the right-hand side ranging analysis on (6). Since b_5 had a value of .70, then — all else remaining the same — you would get the same materials in the optimal model mix for $.50 \leq b_5 \leq 1$. Recalling that the shadow price for this constraint is $-.713333$, and noting that a *decrease*

Table 2.2   LINDO Output for Teletronix Model

```
MIN      0.7 PS + 0.15 TA + 1.85 GL + 0.1 RE + 0.5 PP +   AB
SUBJECT TO
    2)      TA <=    0.2
    3)   - 0.5 PS +  PP - 0.5 AB <=    0
    4)      RE <=    0.5
    5)   - 0.6 PS - 0.6 PP + 0.4 AB >=    0
    6)      PS +  PP +  AB >=   0.7
    7)      TA +  GL <=    0.25
    8)      GL <=    0.15
    9)      PS +  TA +  GL +  RE +  PP +  AB =     1
END
    LP OPTIMUM FOUND  AT STEP      4

         OBJECTIVE FUNCTION VALUE
   1)        0.599333346

VARIABLE          VALUE            REDUCED COST
       PS         0.046667          0.000000
       TA         0.000000          0.050000
       GL         0.000000          1.750000
       RE         0.300000          0.000000
       PP         0.233333          0.000000
       AB         0.420000          0.000000


ROW         SLACK OR SURPLUS       DUAL PRICES
    2)         0.200000             0.000000
    3)         0.000000             0.133333
    4)         0.200000             0.000000
    5)         0.000000            -0.300000
    6)         0.000000            -0.713333
    7)         0.250000             0.000000
    8)         0.150000             0.000000
    9)         0.000000            -0.100000
```

RANGES IN WHICH THE BASIS IS UNCHANGED

OBJ COEFFICIENT RANGES

VARIABLE	CURRENT COEF	ALLOWABLE INCREASE	ALLOWABLE DECREASE
PS	0.700000	0.300000	0.200000
TA	0.150000	INFINITY	0.050000
GL	1.850000	INFINITY	1.750000
RE	0.100000	0.050000	INFINITY
PP	0.500000	0.200000	2.140000
AB	1.000000	INFINITY	0.300000

RIGHTHAND SIDE RANGES

ROW	CURRENT RHS	ALLOWABLE INCREASE	ALLOWABLE DECREASE
2	0.200000	INFINITY	0.200000
3	0.000000	0.070000	0.350000
4	0.500000	INFINITY	0.200000
5	0.000000	0.046667	0.420000
6	0.700000	0.300000	0.200000
7	0.250000	INFINITY	0.250000
8	0.150000	INFINITY	0.150000
9	1.000000	0.200000	0.300000

in b_5 loosens this " $\geq$ " constraint and therefore *reduces* the cost of the mix, for $b_5 = .5$; $x_0^* = .59333 + (.20)(-.713333) = .450666$.

CYNTHIA: I see. If I could get by with only 50% base plastics in the mix, I could lower the per pound price from about \$.60 to about \$.45. I think I'll have Polly Myrrh recheck her lab analysis on that requirement.

Another thing, LIPS. In the mechanical engineering business, there's an old saying—simple is better. What kind of price per pound would result if we stuck to just the base plastics PS, PP, and AB? If you have to solve another model, just give me the cost and the mix—I don't need to see the full LINDO output.

LIPS: I do have to solve another model, CS. Your question can't be answered easily from the printout in Table 2.2. (Short pause) Here's your solution.

```
COST PER POUND:              $.800000
   PERCENT:           PS =    0
                      PP =   40.000000
                     ABS =   60.000000
              CHECK TOTAL   100.000000
```

CYNTHIA: Eureka—that's it, LIPS! We'll convert immediately to the 40/60 mix of PP/ABS at a saving of 20%—there is no retooling needed to make that change. Then when Polly Myrrh rechecks her analysis, we'll reconsider the original optimal model mix and perhaps pick up additional savings. Thanks—you've been a big help.

LIPS: Just doing my job, ma'am. LIPS out.

EXTENSIONS OF THE SIMPLEX METHOD

In this section, we pick up the bits and pieces that were purposely avoided earlier in the interest of clarity. We then discuss some of the more sophisticated extensions of LP modeling and analysis that are useful in practice.

SOME BITS AND PIECES

All is not quite as simple as it appeared in our toy model, and certain other possibilities must be addressed.

" $\geq$ " or " $=$ " Constraints

In the case of a " $\geq$ " constraint, we must *subtract* a nonnegative "surplus variable" from the left-hand side to turn it into an equality. The shadow price for a surplus variable has the reverse connotation as the shadow price for a slack variable. Think of it this way. Increasing the b_i for a " $\leq$ " constraint in effect loosens the constraints on the model and permits the possibility of improving the value of our objective function. The reverse is true for a " $\geq$ " constraint, since increasing b_i tightens the constraining force on the problem. Therefore, the shadow price is interpreted conversely in the two cases.

How about a natural "$=$" constraint? No slack or surplus variable is needed to transform it into an equality, so how do we find a shadow price if our computerized LP package does not automatically do it for us? The simplest way to handle this situation is to write the "$=$" constraint as *two* constraints, as follows:

$$\sum_{j=1}^{n} a_{ij}x_j = b_i \tag{2.24}$$

is equivalent to:

$$\sum_{j=1}^{n} a_{ij}x_j \leq b_i$$

and $\tag{2.25}$

$$\sum_{j=1}^{n} a_{ij}x_j \geq b_i$$

One then interprets the shadow price for either the slack variable or the surplus variable in (2.25) in the usual way.

Variables with Unrestricted Signs

In some situations, it makes sense for certain decision variables to take on negative values in an optimal solution. However, one of the computational requirements of the SIMPLEX algorithm is that all variables must be nonnegative. This problem is solved easily by the addition of a single "dummy" variable z as follows. Suppose that the first k decision variables in an LP model of stock portfolio selection carry the option of buying the stock (x_j positive) or selling the stock short (x_j negative). We replace these k variables with the following transformation:

$$x_j = z - x'_j, \quad j = 1, \ldots, k \tag{2.26}$$

$$z, x'_j \geq 0 \tag{2.27}$$

Note that if it is preferable to buy stock j, then the algorithm will emerge with a value of $z > x'_j$. If a short sale is indicated, then the model generates a value of $x'_j > z$. The remarkable thing about this transformation is that it only takes *one* variable z to unconstrain *many* decision variables x_j, $j = 1, \ldots, k$.

Unbounded and Infeasible Solutions

Instead of pages of numbers, the computer will sometimes return a single page with the cryptic comments "unbounded solution" or "no feasible solution." In the former case, it means that some variable or variables can increase (decrease) without limit, so that we can make the objective function as large (small) as we wish. This, of course, is a mathematical possibility, but an operational silliness.

It means that you have made an error in modeling the problem or assembling the data. Consider yourself extremely lucky if you get back an indication of "unbounded solution" — the SIMPLEX algorithm has discovered for you that you have made an error.

The "no feasible solution" result is an entirely different matter. This *may,* of course, have come about because of modeling or data errors, in which case you are again fortunate. More likely, however, is the possibility that the LP model of your problem is *actually overconstrained.* What you have uncovered, if this is the case, is an incipient managerial disaster. For example, you may have over-committed the production line with an operationally impossible mix of ad-vance orders. Or you may have adopted an investment strategy that cannot meet SEC requirements. Or you may have targeted for a market share that your present advertising budget cannot achieve. To be absolutely candid, if *all* possi-ble constraints could be explicitly included in optimization models, *most* such models would return the output as "no feasible solution." Models that allow for the attempt to attain multiple objectives are one answer to this problem and are discussed in Chapter 13.

Duality Theory

To the MS technician, something called "duality theory" is one of the most important theoretical constructs in all of mathematical programming. For example, it forms the basis for the theoretical underpinnings that explain the meaning of shadow prices. Duality theory and its implications have led to major algorithmic developments in nonlinear programming (Chapter 5) and network modeling (Chapter 4) as well. We would insist that our technical analysts be well versed in this topic — we might even do a little name dropping in this regard before we hire them.

There is a potentially useful *computational* device based on duality theory, with which the practicing manager should be familiar. Consider the LP prob-lem P that follows.

P:

$$\text{MAXIMIZE } x_0 = \sum_{j=1}^{n} c_j x_j \tag{2.28}$$

$$\text{SUBJECT TO: } \sum_{j=1}^{n} a_{ij} x_j \leq b_i, \quad i = 1, \ldots, m \tag{2.29}$$

$$x_j \geq 0, \quad j = 1, \ldots, n \tag{2.30}$$

Duality theory demonstrates that the following problem D, which is closely associated with P, can be solved merely by inspecting the optimal solution to P:

D:

$$\text{MINIMIZE } y_0 = \sum_{i=1}^{m} b_i y_i \tag{2.31}$$

$$\text{SUBJECT TO: } \sum_{i=1}^{m} a_{ji} y_i \geq c_j, \quad j = 1, \ldots, n \qquad (2.32)$$

$$y_i \geq 0, \quad i = 1, \ldots, m \qquad (2.33)$$

Note that D is just P with the objective function coefficients and constraint right-hand sides changing places, and with the constraint coefficients transposed. It can be shown that $x_0 = y_0$ at optimality and that the optimal y_i are the shadow prices for P.

Admittedly, the managerial utility of the foregoing is not immediately obvious. However, it is a fact that computational effort with the SIMPLEX algorithm is largely a function of the number of constraints — and much less so with regard to the number of variables. Consider, therefore, the "semitoy model" D with 10 decision variables and 20 $\geq$ constraints. There will be 20 surplus variables and 20 artificial variables (SIMPLEX uses artificial variables to generate a feasible starting vertex), for a total of 50 model variables. For this small problem, there are about 47,129,212,240,000 vertices — which is a little over 47 *trillion.*

Now consider the corresponding problem P, which has 20 decision variables and 10 $\leq$ constraints. We must, of course, add 10 slack variables (but not artificial variables), for a total of 30 model variables. In this case, our problem has 30,045,015 vertices — about 30 *million* — which is less than one ten-thousandths of 1 percent of the number of vertices in D! Since we can obtain the solution for D by inspecting the optimal solution for P, the computational advantage of solving P instead of D is obvious. Moreover, some real-world LP models are so large that they will not even fit in the computer available to solve them. If the dual problem will fit, then we have breached a computational chasm with this modeling device. Finally, some sophisticated computer LP codes incorporate something called DUAL SIMPLEX, which solves the dual problem directly. Although the discussion is rather mathematical, the classic book by Dantzig covers this topic thoroughly [1].

This small peek under the immense tent of duality theory is similar to viewing one frame of the movie *Gone with the Wind.* If any of you readers stray from the world of managerial decision making into the technical briar patch of OR/MS, you will unquestionably see the entire movie — several times.

SOME ADVANCED TOPICS

Most texts of this nature avoid some or all of the following topics because of their mathematical complexity. Since we are not concerned with mastering algorithmic details — and since these topics are important modeling tools — we discuss them briefly.

Lower-Bounded Variables

Many LP models contain constraints that express lower bounds on some or all of the decision variables. For example, if the variables x_j, $j = 1, \ldots, n$, represent production levels for n products, and the marketing department had already accepted advance orders for the products in the amounts L_j, then there would be n constraints of the form $x_j \geq L_j$, $j = 1, \ldots, n$. As noted previously, the number of constraints largely determines computational complexity in the SIMPLEX method, so it is always advantageous to delete constraints whenever possible (without changing the nature of the model).

We can eliminate explicit lower-bound constraints by a simple transformation. For every decision variable with a lower bound, we make the substitution

$$x_j = x_j' + L_j, \quad j = 1, \ldots, n \tag{2.34}$$

$$x_j' \geq 0 \tag{2.35}$$

After the model has been optimized, we reverse the transformation to recover the optimal values of the original decision variables.

Upper-Bounded Variables

Consider the problem of scheduling part-time nurses in a large hospital. Among the many constraints that must be taken into consideration, suppose that state laws require payment of retirement and other benefits to nurses who work more than 20 hours in any week. We wish, therefore, to impose constraints to assure that all our part-timers work no more than 20 hours in any week. Let x_{ij} be the decision variables representing the number of hours that part-timer i works in week j, and assume that there are n part-timers. If our planning horizon is 13 weeks, then these upper-bound constraints would appear in the model as follows:

$$x_{ij} \leq 20, \quad i = 1, \ldots, n; \quad j = 1, \ldots, 13 \tag{2.36}$$

Some readers might be thinking, "There is probably a transformation like (2.34) that lets us do away with the upper-bound constraints (2.36). Let's see — that would be — $x_{ij} = 20 - x_{ij}'$." Sorry, but it won't work. Such a transformation certainly limits x_{ij} to an upper bound of 20, but what if the SIMPLEX algorithm set some $x_{ij}' = 30$? Poor nurse i would have to come in on week j and *unwork* 10 hours, a result so foolish that it deserves no further comment.

However, many sophisticated LP packages do have a feature called "implicit upper bounding." This feature is usually not automatic, however, and must be explicitly summoned by the analyst. As before, implicit upper bounding greatly expedites the solution process and allows solution of some large problems with many upper-bounded variables that otherwise would not even fit in the computer.

Transformation to Linearity

Consider the production planning problem over n future periods, where the objective is to minimize total costs. One of the costs involved is that of changing the daily rate of production between successive periods. If x_i is the number of units produced in d_i production days in period i, then x_i/d_i represents the daily production rate in that period. Suppose that it cost \$$R$ to change the daily rate by 1 unit. Then the cost of changing the rate of production between period i and period $i + 1$ is

$$R \cdot \left| \frac{x_{i+1}}{d_{i+1}} - \frac{x_i}{d_i} \right| \qquad (2.37)$$

where the symbol $| \cdot |$ means *absolute value*. Unfortunately, (2.37) is nonlinear, and cannot appear in the objective function in its present form. However, let us make use of two "dummy" variables u_i and v_i, where $u_i \geq 0$ and $v_i \geq 0$, and make the transformation:

$$\frac{x_{i+1}}{d_{i+1}} - \frac{x_i}{d_i} = u_i - v_i \qquad (2.38)$$

We then include all expressions like (2.38) — there is one between each pair of adjacent periods — as constraints in the model and replace (2.37) in the objective function by

$$R_i \cdot (u_i + v_i) \qquad (2.39)$$

Since we are trying to minimize the objective function, the algorithm will make u_i and v_i as small as possible; in fact, one of the two will always be zero. Thus, if we *increase* our production rate from period i to period $i + 1$, then u_i is the change in rate from (2.38) and picks up a cost of $R_i \cdot u_i$ in (2.39) — since $v_i = 0$. On the other hand, if the rate *decreases,* then v_i is the (negative) change in rate from (2.38) and picks up a cost of $R_i \cdot v_i$ in (2.39) — since $u_i = 0$. Thus, by adding dummy variables and constraints, we have used the SIMPLEX algorithm to solve a nonlinear problem. We shall see other examples of modeling devices like this in subsequent chapters.

Dantzig-Wolfe Decomposition

There is a class of very large LP models that technical specialists call *block diagonal* (BD) models. Other authors refer to the underlying problem as *multi-divisional* or *multiple time period* in nature. For example, an LP model with three such "blocks," "divisions," or "periods" would have the appearance of the schematic in Figure 2.3.

For the sake of clarity, let us discuss this BD problem in terms of a realistic example. Suppose that BD is the aggregate LP model for a product mix problem, for a modest-sized manufacturing firm with three semiautonomous plants that produce different products. The plant managers are vice-presidents of the firm and have historically been given profit center responsibility.

The objective function (2.40) represents the total profit contribution of the three plants, and — naturally — the chief executive officer (CEO) of the company wishes to maximize profit contribution. Constraints (2.41) represent scarce resources that will be allocated to the plants and might involve restrictions on capital investment, corporate MIS availability, trained quality control inspectors, and so on.

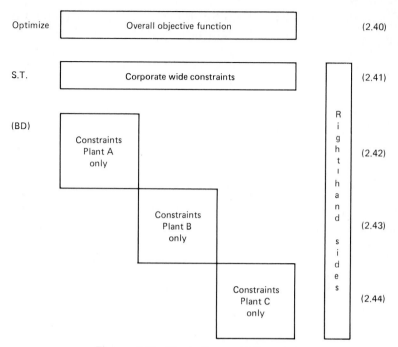

Figure 2.3 Block diagonal LP model.

Constraints (2.42), (2.43), and (2.44) pertain specifically to the internal constraints within each of the three plants, and we note that these constraint sets do not overlap each other (thus the term "block diagonal"). Therefore, if it were not for the existence of corporatewide constraints (2.41), the three plant managers could separately optimize their own individual models and report the results separately to the CEO. However, the corporatewide constraints (2.41) *do* exist — and they may represent overriding considerations that must be accounted for. The task of the CEO, then, is to divide these resources among the three plants in such a way that the overall corporate profit contribution is optimized.

You might observe — from an analytical point of view, and assuming that the corporate computer is large enough — that there is not much of a problem here. All the CEO needs to do is to request the data in (2.42), (2.43), and (2.44) from the three plant managers, run the overall model BD and analyze the results, and send back the optimal values of each set of decision variables to the appropriate plant manager. What's the point?

Models don't make decisions — Managers do.

Although corporate headquarters could certainly obtain the required data from the plants, decision makers at corporate level are most likely unfamiliar with the day-to-day operation of the plants. The decision environment no doubt differs widely from plant to plant, and the plant managers are paid to know those environments and make good decisions based on that knowledge.

A product mix handed down to a plant manager from "on high" might not even be feasible because of considerations exogenous to the model. Besides, if corporate headquarters is going to make detailed decisions such as these, who needs a plant manager with the rank of vice-president? The answer to this rhetorical question is obvious to anyone familiar with the workings of business and industry.

We now turn to the Dantzig-Wolfe decomposition approach to the multidivisional LP model but avoid the mathematical details. The approach is an iterative one—and one of the most clever optimization devices in all of management science. Basically, corporate headquarters makes an initial allocation of resources represented by the b_i in (2.41) and asks the plants to return their results. Based on these results and the shadow prices that accompany them, headquarters revises its resource allocation in such a way that overall profit contribution will increase. This process is iterated until the shadow prices eventually stabilize at their optimal values. This is a highly oversimplified description of what is happening, but it is adequate for our purposes.

In addition to the multidivisional application, note the purely computational aspects of this technique. If we have a very large LP model that will not fit on our computer, but has a block diagonal structure, we can solve it iteratively using Dantzig-Wolfe decomposition by breaking it down into smaller, more manageable pieces. As we must realize, it is a great deal more difficult to solve one 1000×1000 model than it is to solve ten 100×100 models, even considering the multiple solutions required in the iterations of the Dantzig-Wolfe technique.

Wiseacre [6]

The Scenario: Jackson Browne Mize, a retired physician, has taken up large-scale gardening as a form of relaxation, in a rectangular plot of land 150 by 200 feet that he owns. Dr. Mize is already in the highest income tax bracket, so he gives away some of the produce to his friends each year. Even so, the 30,000-square-foot plot yields so much that over half of the vegetables go to waste. Because gardening is excellent exercise as well as enjoyable, however, Dr. Mize still wishes to plant the entire plot.

The Problem: Dr. Mize's son, an MBA student at a nearby university, suggested that his father donate the excess produce to churches in the less affluent part of town. The churches could sell the vegetables through a "co-op" at reduced prices and give Dr. Mize a receipt for their value. He could then claim his donation as a deduction on his income tax return.

The good doctor liked the idea, and decided to plant beans, corn, cucumbers, onions, squash, and tomatoes. Within certain constraints, he wished to determine the optimal mix of crops that would maximize his tax deduction. Some considerations that had to be taken into account were as follows.

1. The 200-foot side of the plot runs north and south. Crops should be planted with the rows running east-west so that the prevailing wind will pass down the rows instead of hitting the crops broadside.
2. Corn is wind-pollinated, so that at least four rows must be planted to get maximum yields.
3. Dr. Mize wished to plant at least 10%, but not more than 30%, of his plot in each of the five vegetables other than cucumbers. Because cucumbers tend to be high yielding, he wished to restrict their planting to no more than 15% of the plot.

Table 2.3   Parameters for Wiseacre Case

	Vegetables					
	Beans	*Corn*	*Cucumbers*	*Onions*	*Squash*	*Tomatoes*
Spacing						
Feet between plants (in rows)	3.0	1.0	1.0	.33	2.0	2.0
Feet between rows	3.5	2.5	5.0	1.0	3.0	3.0
Yields per plant						
Good year	2 lb	6 ears	30	.6 lb	18	6.5 lb
Average year	1.5 lb	5 ears	25	.5 lb	16	5.5 lb
Bad year	1 lb	4 ears	22	.45 lb	14	4 lb
Wholesale prices	$.39/lb	$.05/ea.	$.09 ea.	$.15/lb	$.17/ea.	$.29/lb

4. From a gardening guide [7], Dr. Mize's son found the space requirements for the six vegetables and obtained yield estimates (per plant)
from a local farmer, who gave separate estimates for "good,"
"average," and "bad" growing years. A local vegetable "co-op"
supplied estimates of wholesale prices. Table 2.3 exhibits these
parameters.

The Model: Dr. Mize's son recognized his father's problem as one that
could be modeled and analyzed by linear programming and chose the decision variables $x_j, j = 1, \ldots, 6$, as the *number of rows of vegetable j to plant*
(x_j's in alphabetical order by kind of vegetable). In actuality, there were three
LP models — one each for yields in good, average, and bad growing years.
The objective function coefficients c_j are the revenues per row for each
vegetable. For example, the per row revenue for beans (c_1) was computed
as follows:

$$\text{Good year:} \quad c_1 = \frac{150 \text{ ft/row}}{3 \text{ ft/plant}} \times 2 \text{ lb/plant} \times \$.39 \text{ revenue/lb}$$

$$= \$39 \text{ revenue/row}$$

$$\text{Average year:} \quad c_1 = (50) \cdot (1.5)(\$.39) = \$29.25 \text{ revenue/row}$$

$$\text{Bad year:} \quad c_1 = (50) \cdot (1.0)(\$.39) = \$19.50 \text{ revenue/row, and so forth}$$

Table 2.4   Objective Coefficients for Wiseacre Case

	Beans	Corn	Cucumbers	Onions	Squash	Tomatoes
Good year	$39.00	$45.00	$405.00	$40.50	$299.50	$141.38
Average year	$29.25	$37.50	$337.50	$33.75	$204.00	$119.63
Bad year	$19.50	$30.00	$297.00	$30.38	$178.50	$87.00

The objective function coefficients are summarized in Table 2.4. The model
for a "good year" is as follows.

$$\text{MAXIMIZE } x_0 = 39x_1 + 45x_2 + 405x_3 + 40.5x_4 + 229.5x_5 + 141.38x_6 \tag{2.45}$$

$$\text{SUBJECT TO: } 3.5x_1 \qquad\qquad \leq 60 \tag{2.46}$$

$$2.5x_2 \qquad\qquad \leq 60 \tag{2.47}$$

$$5x_3 \qquad\qquad \leq 30 \tag{2.48}$$

$$x_4 \qquad\qquad \leq 60 \tag{2.49}$$

$$3x_5 \qquad \leq 60 \tag{2.50}$$

$$3x_6 \leq 60 \tag{2.51}$$

$$x_2 \qquad\qquad \geq 4 \tag{2.52}$$

$$3.5x_1 \qquad\qquad \geq 20 \tag{2.53}$$

$$2.5x_2 \qquad\qquad \geq 20 \tag{2.54}$$

$$5x_3 \qquad\qquad \geq 20 \tag{2.55}$$

$$x_4 \qquad\qquad \geq 20 \tag{2.56}$$

$$3x_5 \qquad \geq 20 \tag{2.57}$$

$$3x_6 \geq 20 \quad (2.58)$$
$$3.5x_1 + 2.5x_2 + 5x_3 + x_4 + 3x_5 + 3x_6 \leq 200 \quad (2.59)$$
$$x_j \geq 0, \quad j = 1, \ldots, 6 \quad (2.60)$$

Constraints (2.46) through (2.51) are the upper bounds (15% for cucumbers, 30% for others) on space for each vegetable; constraint (2.52) imposes the requirement that at least four rows of corn be planted; and (2.59) limits the size of the total crop to be 200 feet north-south.

The model can easily be solved by BLP or LINDO in its present form. However, it was noted that constraint (2.52) is nonbinding, since (2.53) will assure that at least four rows of corn are planted. Furthermore, the constraints (2.53) through (2.58) are merely lower bounds on the variables. If we let

$$x_j = \frac{x_j' + 20}{\text{No. feet between rows}}, \quad j = 1, \ldots, n \quad (2.61)$$

and make this transformation in the model, we have the much smaller (but equivalent) LP model:

MAXIMIZE $x_0 = 11.143x_1' + 18x_2' + 81x_3' + 40.5x_4' + 76.5x_5' + 47.127x_6' + \$5485.39$ (2.62)

SUBJECT TO:	x_1'					≤ 40 (2.63)
	x_2'					≤ 40 (2.64)
		x_3'				≤ 10 (2.65)
			x_4'			≤ 40 (2.66)
				x_5'		≤ 40 (2.67)
					x_6'	≤ 40 (2.68)
$x_1' +$	$x_2' +$	$x_3' +$	$x_4' +$	$x_5' +$	x_6'	≤ 80 (2.69)
		$x_j' \geq 0,$	$j = 1, \ldots, 6$			(2.70)

Solution to the Model: This optimal solution to the original model is identical for all three objective functions (good, average, bad) and is given as follows:

Variable Values

			Revenue		
Variable	Vegetables	Number of Rows	Good	Average	Bad
x_1	Beans	5.7143	$ 222.85	$ 167.14	$ 111.43
x_2	Corn	8	360.00	300.00	240.00
x_3	Cucumbers	6	2,430.00	2025.00	1782.00
x_4	Onions	20	810.00	675.00	607.60
x_5	Squash	20	4,590.00	4080.00	3570.00
x_6	Tomatoes	16.6667	2,356.33	1993.83	1450.00
Totals		76.3810	$10,769.18	$9240.97	$7761.03

Constraint	Type	Shadow Prices
Beans	Lower bound	$29.77
Corn	Lower bound	23.12
Cucumbers	Upper bound	2.38
Onions	Lower bound	3.95
Squash	Upper bound	29.02
Tomatoes	Both	—
Available Land	Upper bound	37.70

Solution to the Problem: To simplify planting, 6 rows of beans and 16 rows of tomatoes (rather than fractional rows) were decided upon. This reduced the total revenue by about $83 (for a good year), but it made working the plot much easier for Doctor Mize and still resulted in a feasible solution.

The doctor was surprised at the high shadow price associated with an additional 150-foot row (e.g., $37.70 per row for a good year). However, his son pointed out that Dr. Mize's insistence upon at least 10% of the crop being planted in beans and 10% in corn, and that no more than 30% be planted in squash, was significantly reducing the total tax deduction that could be generated on the present plot.

Finally, Dr. Mize—impressed with his son's resourcefulness—asked him: "Son, what if we hadn't known about linear programming, and I had decided to plant one sixth of the plot with each kind of vegetable. What sort of tax deduction would I have gotten, say, in a good year?"

"Good question, Dad," replied the son, "and I knew you were going to ask it. First of all, that would violate your constraint of not planting more than 15% in cucumbers. If we ignore that constraint and plant 25 row-feet in each vegetable, the total write-off would be about $6857 in a good year, so that LP would have made you about $3912 in additional deductions."

"Son," chuckled Dr. Mize, "I'm impressed."

Billy Hill's Still

The Scenario: J. William "Billy" Hill III is the CEO, chairman of the board, and production manager for Billy Hill's Still, Inc. (BHS), a company located in the Tennessee mountains. The firm produces and distributes a line of beverages popular in the region. BHS manufactures three basic product lines—Rotgut, Harvest Moon, and White Lightning—but each line comes in either light or dark (depending on what type of corn is used) and high or low potency (depending on cooking time). Therefore, BHS essentially manufactures 12 distinct products.

The market for all three product lines is excellent, with demand always exceeding supply. Distribution is handled by Billy's cousin Zack, who drives a modified "Daytona 500" racing automobile. The distribution channel is currently at capacity, which is the reason BHS cannot increase production.

The Problem: One cloudy Sunday afternoon, the firm's industrial intelligence network learned that several gentlemen representing the federal Internal Revenue Service were planning what they hoped to be a surprise visit to the BHS distillery and were scheduled to arrive in 72 hours. Mr. Hill concluded that good business practice dictated the temporary dismantling of the distilling equipment, but the 72-hour warning would allow him to make another run from his on-hand inventory of corn (150 bushels of light and 225 bushels of dark). Cooking time, corn requirements, and profit contribution per 10-gallon batch of each brand are given in Table 2.5.

In addition to the limited supply of corn and brewing time, there are other factors that complicate Billy's problem.

1. BHS's marketing department (Billy's brother Zeke) has already accepted orders for 50 gallons (five batches) of Rotgut light, but the customer will take either low- or high-potency product.
2. To keep the still from clogging on long production runs, at least one third of the batches must be made with dark corn.
3. Sales records indicate that about 40% of previous sales have been

Table 2.5   Parameters for Billy Hill's Still

Brand		Bushels of Corn (per 10-gal batch)		Cooking Time (in minutes per 10-gal batch)	Profit Contribution (in $ per 10-gal batch)
		White	Dark		
Rotgut	LL*	3		60	17
	LH	5		85	25
	DL		2	45	16
	DH		3	95	28
Harvest Moon	LL	4		80	28
	LH	6		120	40
	DL		3	85	24
	DH		5	130	36
White Lightning	LL	5		115	43
	LH	8		125	48
	DL		6	145	44
	DH		7	180	52

* LL = light corn, low potency; LH = light corn, high potency; DL = dark corn, low potency; DH = dark corn, high potency.

high-potency products, so Billy wishes to produce at least this amount.

The Model: Billy's older sister Daisy Hill, who completed junior high school and serves as the company's management science analyst, observes that the problem could be modeled by LP—except that the number of batches cannot be fractional. Since BHS's microcomputer does not have an integer LP package, she decides to model the problem as a linear program anyway to see what happens.

The object is obviously to maximize total profit contribution, and the decisions involve the number of batches of each of the 12 products to run. She lets x_{ij} = number of batches of the ith brand and the jth type to produce, $i = 1, \ldots, 3$, $j = 1, \ldots, 4$. (For example, x_{23} would represent Harvest Moon, dark, low potency.) The LP model is

$$\text{MAXIMIZE } x_0 = \begin{array}{l} 17x_{11} + 25x_{12} + 16x_{13} + 28x_{14} + 28x_{21} + 40x_{22} \\ + 24x_{23} + 36x_{24} + 43x_{31} + 48x_{32} + 44x_{33} + 52x_{34} \end{array} \quad (2.71)$$

SUBJECT TO:
$$3x_{11} + 5x_{12} \qquad\qquad + 4x_{21} + 6x_{22} \\ + 5x_{31} + 8x_{32} \qquad\qquad \leq 150 \quad (2.72)$$

$$2x_{13} + 3x_{14} \\ + 3x_{23} + 5x_{24} \qquad\qquad + 6x_{33} + 7x_{34} \leq 225 \quad (2.73)$$

$$60x_{11} + 85x_{12} + 45x_{13} + 95x_{14} + 80x_{21} + 120x_{22} \\ + 85x_{23} + 130x_{24} + 115x_{31} + 125x_{32} + 145x_{33} + 180x_{34} \leq 4320 \quad (2.74)$$

$$x_{11} + x_{12} \qquad\qquad \geq 5 \quad (2.75)$$

$$\begin{array}{l} -x_{11} - x_{12} + 2x_{13} + 2x_{14} - x_{21} - x_{22} \\ + 2x_{23} + 2x_{24} - x_{31} - x_{32} + 2x_{33} + 2x_{34} \geq 0 \end{array} \quad (2.76)$$

$$\begin{array}{l} -x_{11} + 1.5x_{12} - x_{13} + 1.5x_{14} - x_{21} + 1.5x_{22} \\ -x_{23} + 1.5x_{24} - x_{31} + 1.5x_{32} - x_{33} + 1.5x_{34} \geq 0 \end{array} \quad (2.77)$$

$$x_{ij} \geq 0, \quad i = 1, \ldots, 3, \quad j = 1, \ldots, 4 \quad (2.78)$$

Constraints (2.72) and (2.73) are the limits on available light and dark corn, respectively, and (2.74) represents the 72 hours (4320 minutes) remaining until the "revenuers" arrive. Constraint (2.75) guarantees that Zeke's advance order will be filled, and (2.76) and (2.77) impose the desired restrictions on runs with dark corn and runs of high-potency product, respectively.

Solution to the Model: The optimal solution to the model emerged from the computer as follows.

Variable	Description	Optimal Model Values
x_{12}	Rotgut, light-high	5 batches
x_{13}	Rotgut, dark-low	36.0115 batches
x_{14}	Rotgut, dark-high	3.3827 batches
x_{32}	White Lightning, light-high	15.6250 batches
s_2	Dark corn unused	142.8290 bushels
s_5	Surplus on dark corn usage restriction	58.1634 bushels

All other variables and slacks have the value zero.

Profit contribution: $1545.90

Constraint	Shadow Price
Supply of light corn	$1.30 per bushel
Time remaining	.32 per minute
Advance orders, lower bound	6.30 per batch
High potency, lower bound	1.60 per batch

Solution to the Problem: Since the model solution was obviously not implementable because it involved fractional batches, and since BHS had no ILP computer code, Daisy experimented a bit with rounding to produce the following feasible solution to the problem.

Variable	Values	Variable	Values
x_{12}	5 batches	s_1	5 bushels
x_{13}	36 batches	s_2	141 bushels
x_{14}	4 batches	s_3	16 minutes
x_{32}	15 batches	s_4	0 excess
		s_5	60 excess
		s_6	0 excess

Profit contribution: $1533

In addition, Daisy recommended to Billy that the Rotgut, dark, low potency (x_{13}), run be scheduled *last*, since it produced the lowest-profit batches and could be cut short if more than the 16 minutes of "getaway time" (s_3) seemed desirable.

When Daisy presented Billy with the results of her analysis, he was pleased—and decided to implement her recommended product mix. He was also intrigued by the shadow prices in the original LP solution. It was obvious that Zeke's accepting advance orders of Rotgut, light cost additional profits, since the associated shadow price was $6.30 per batch. Moreover, the light corn supply shortage cost BHS $1.30 per bushel in profits, even though there was an astonishing overage of more than 140 bushels of dark corn. There was obviously an inventory management problem that needed attending to when the company resumed operations.

Finally, there was a problem with the pricing strategy for Harvest Moon products, since none ended up in an optimal solution. Billy made a mental note to look into the advisability of repricing (or perhaps discontinuing) this product line after the "dust had settled" from the "revenuers" visit.

IPP [8]

The Scenario: Mike Rowe, the CEO and founder of Arizona Silicon Products (ASP), Inc., pored thoughtfully over the sales forecasts by ASP's three sales regions for next fiscal year. Total projected profit for the company's five computer component products was $5.139 million based on sales estimates, an increase of 28% over the current year. This was typical of the explosive growth experienced by ASP in the three years since Mike started the company.

The Problem: When Mike compared sales forecasts with the output from ASP's LP program that optimized product mix, the same aggravating situation cropped up again: ASP had the capacity to produce more of certain products than its three regional sales divisions were able (or willing?) to sell. Mike's problem is illustrated in the following.

Profit/Production Capacity Analysis

Product	Optimal Production (units)	Forecast Sales (units)	Profit Potential	Profit from Forecast Sales	Difference
RAM	1,000,000	1,000,000	$1,435,000	$1,435,000	—
ROM	3,612,000	2,000,000	1,191,960	660,000	$531,960
Linear	1,000,000	1,000,000	630,000	630,000	—
IC	3,000,000	3,000,000	264,000	264,000	—
MP	1,215,000	1,000,000	2,612,250	2,150,000	462,250
Totals	9,827,000	8,000,000	$6,133,210	$5,139,000	$994,210

If ASP's sales organizations could sell everything the company could produce in the ROM and MP lines, almost a million additional dollars could be added to the bottom line. Mike called in Mal Inger, his vice-president of marketing, and laid out the numbers. But Mal insisted as he always did that ASP's sales people were overworked and underpaid and would have to strain mightily just to make the forecast sales figures — much less sell additional units of ROM and MP.

After Mike disgustedly dismissed Mal Inger, he turned his attention back to the numbers — when in a flash came the realization that the additional profit potential in the table was considerably *understated!* The profit contribution figures for the 8,000,000 units of forecast sales included all overhead and fixed costs; a higher level of sales would in effect reduce per unit costs and result in even higher overall profits. Something had to be done.

Mike called in ASP's resident behavioral and psychiatric consultant. She listened carefully to his narrative, paused thoughtfully before replying, and spoke as follows:

"Mr. Rowe," she said, "your mistake was allowing the vice-president of marketing to set sales quotas before you knew what production potential would be. People are so very predictable — once they "lock onto" a particular quantitative goal or objective, it immediately becomes an *upper bound* on their capabilities—regardless of their actual performance potential. However, if you try to unilaterally raise sales quotas at this point, you'll only make matters worse. Would you like for me to suggest an alternative?''

"You bet,'' responded Mike. ''I need all of the help I can get.''

She continued. ''I'm no economist, of course, but I do understand that per unit profit contribution increases as sales volume increases—as long as that volume doesn't approach the level of diminishing returns. Why don't you consider something like an incremental profit program (IPP) that allows the sales regions to *compete* for higher sales quotas in return for bonus commissions on incremental sales? If you work it right, ASP could receive the *current* level of profit contribution for the additional sales, and the sales people could earn the *incremental* difference.''

The Model: Mike decided to concentrate first on the MP line, since the high profit contribution ($2.15) meant that fewer incremental sales would be needed for good results than would be the case for ROM ($.33 profit contribution). He called up the marketing budget for MP on his terminal, as follows.

Fiscal Year Marketing Budget: MP

Expense Item	Per Unit Marketing Expense			Budget
	Region I	Region II	Region III	
Personnel	$.095	$.100	$.100	$100,000
Travel	.018	.020	.025	25,000
Promotion	.010	.010	.010	15,000
Totals	$.123	$.130	$.135	$140,000
FY sales quotas (units)	200,000	400,000	400,000	Expense $130,600

Mike's first thought upon seeing the cost data on MP was to model his problem as an LP model. He let x_1, x_2, and x_3 represent the sales quotas for regions I, II, and III, respectively, with the idea of maximizing total sales. There were six constraints: remain within the total personnel, travel, and promotion budgets, and assign at least the current sales quotas to each region. He entered the following model into his LP SIMPLEX package.

$$\text{MAXIMIZE } x_0 = \quad x_1 + \quad x_2 + \quad x_3$$
$$\text{SUBJECT TO:} \quad .095x_1 + .100x_2 + .100x_3 \leq 100,000$$
$$.018x_1 + .020x_2 + .025x_3 \leq \ 25,000$$
$$.010x_1 + .010x_2 + .010x_3 \leq \ 15,000$$
$$x_1 \qquad\qquad\qquad \geq 200,000$$
$$x_2 \qquad\qquad \geq 400,000$$
$$x_3 \geq 400,000$$
$$x_1, x_2, x_3 \geq 0$$

After checking his input data, Mike stared at his LP model uneasily. Something was wrong — and he couldn't put his finger on it.

Solution to the Model: Mike invoked his SIMPLEX algorithm, and the instant he saw the following solution — he realized his modeling error.

Optimal $x_0 = 1{,}010{,}526.316$

Variables	Values	Reduced Costs
x_1	210,526.316	0
x_2	400,000	0
x_3	400,000	0

Row	Slack or Surplus	Dual Prices
1	0	.1053
2	3,210.527	0
3	4,894.737	0
4	10,526.316	0
5	0	.000053
6	0	.000053

He had considered the subconstraint on the personnel budget for MP to be binding, which meant that there was about $3,210 excess budget available for travel and about $4,895 excess for promotion. He grinned sheepishly — glad that he was alone in his office.

Solution to the Problem: Turning off the computer console, Mike picked up a scratch pad and a pencil. "Let's see," he vocalized, "there is a total unbudgeted expense for MP of $140,000 − $130,600 = $9,400. Since region I has the most efficient per unit marketing cost of $.123, there is enough budget money for them to sell $9,400/$.123 $\doteq$ 76,423 units, for an additional profit at the *current* margin of ($2.15) · (76,423) $\doteq$ $164,309. As a rule of thumb, that increment would generate *actual* profit contribution of about $2.35, or about $8\frac{1}{2}$% above current margin."

Getting Mal Inger back into his office, Mike Rowe announced the IPP — and instructed Mal to offer region I an additional quota of 76,000 units of MP at an 8% bonus. If they took it, the other (less efficient) regions were to be given the opportunity to bid on some or all units — but at lower bonuses that reflected their higher marketing costs.

"And Mal," warned Mike, "I want the IPP to be run with *vigor and enthusiasm*. If you can't do it that way, I'll find someone who can."

The moral in this minicase is: Don't let MS models *get in the way* of solving problems.

SUMMARY

This chapter has introduced you to the widely used optimization modeling technique called linear programming. You should now be able to recognize problems that can be modeled by LP and build those models. You should also realize that you know just enough about the technical details of the SIMPLEX algorithm to appreciate its dependability, but not nearly as much as a technically trained analyst.

This chapter has also introduced you to the assumptions of linear programming — additivity and divisibility. This chapter has diligently deliberated the very important issues of LP model construction involving model selection, data collection and analysis, and model validation. Examples of LP model formulation were presented with meticulous care and attention using interactive dialogue with LIPS. Then an intuitive description of the SIMPLEX algorithm was presented and a graphical example was described. Algorithms for solution of LP models were characterized in terms of the computers they execute on — mainframes, minis, or micros. A typical LP solution printout (LINDO) was described in terms of the information content it contained beyond mere presentation of the optimal solution. Terms like "shadow price" (or its synonym "DUAL PRICE"), "REDUCED COST," and "SLACK OR SURPLUS" were given meaning and the managerial significance of the numbers whose columns are labeled with these terms was explained. The information that followed "RANGES IN WHICH THE BASIS IS UNCHANGED" was also described in detail. While other programs may use somewhat different formats and terms, you will find that comprehension across formats and programs is retained once a specific data format (such as LINDO) is understood. Ranging data, for example, is always understood to apply to ranges over which right-hand sides and objective function coefficients can be varied without causing the current optimal set of decision variables to change.

The chapter then discusses extensions of LP modeling and analysis that are useful in practice. Such issues as how shadow prices for "≥" and "=" constraints are interpreted, how variables that can legitimately take on negative as well as positive values are handled, what has gone wrong when the computer reports that the SOLUTION IS UNBOUNDED or that the SOLUTION IS INFEASIBLE, are also treated. The chapter then treats with equal candor and care such topics as duality theory, lower-bounded variables, upper-bounded variables, transformation to linearity, and Dantzig-Wolfe decomposition.

The three minicases serve to reinforce the concepts of the chapter — including model formulation, interpretation of the solution printouts, and the synthesis of plans for investigation of the perceived problems.

In Chapter 3, we will relax one of the requirements of divisibility and consider integer (otherwise linear) programming models. As we shall see, this seemingly innocuous change leads to an order of magnitude increase in solution difficulty. Nevertheless, integer (otherwise linear) modeling is extremely important in practice.

PROBLEMS

1.   *The Scenario:*   The Daley Paper Co. manufactures heavy-duty wrapping paper in large rolls, which are a standard 200 feet long and 150 inches wide. These large rolls are then cut to custom widths, on order, by huge slitting machines. These machines have many cutters that can be spaced differently for every run, if necessary.

The Problem: The profit margins in this highly competitive industry tend to be narrow, and the problem of trim waste is a serious one. For example, suppose that Lotta Papel, the production supervisor, received the following orders from the sales department for today's production run.

Width (inches)	Number of Rolls
16	300
24	400
48	200
60	100

We see that one run of 100 rolls might involve setting one cutter at 60 in. (one 60-in. roll), one at 108 in. (one 48-in. roll), one at 132 in. (one 24-in. roll), and one at 148 in. (one 16-in. roll), satisfying 400 of the orders and incurring 2-in. of trim waste. But is this the best strategy?

The Model: Can this problem be profitably modeled as a linear program? If so, what are the decision variables? What is the objective function? What are the constraints? (*Hint:* There are 24 feasible ways in which to set the cutters to produce the required widths without having trim waste as large as 16 in. per roll.)

2.   *The Scenario:*   The Hyperbole Advertising Agency has been retained by a regional food company to handle the introduction of its new candy bar, which is made from glandless cottonseed. A medium-sized town has been selected as a trial market, and three advertising media are available: television, radio, and local newspaper. Advertising rates for radio and television vary widely depending on length of the "spot," time of day and day of week, and so on, and the same is true of the size and placement of newspaper ads. Hyperbole in this case is operating with a fixed advertising budget.

The Problem: Since a fixed budget is involved, the account executive must decide on an efficient media mix. She has available a complete set of rate books for all three media, as well as market research data on exposure levels of the various subcategories (size and placement of newspaper ads, ratings for specific shows, etc.).

The Model: Can this problem be modeled effectively as a linear program? Why or why not?

3.   *The Scenario:*   Herzbrennen, Inc., is a highly integrated regional fast-food chain that owns its own beef processing plants, warehouses, delivery truck fleet, retail outlets, and clinics specializing in gastrointestinal disorders. There are ten beef processing plants, which make deliveries to six warehouses, which in turn supply 100 fast-food restaurants. Since the restaurants serve only cheeseburgers and Pepsi's (registered trademark), the hamburger patty is used as the basic planning unit.

The Problem: As the cost of gasoline skyrocketed, the company discovered that profits were literally going up in smoke—from the exhaust pipes of their delivery vehicles. Tommy Hertz, the distribution manager for the company, found himself under increasing pressure from the CEO to cut costs while not degrading service level. The present delivery schedule was put together by Fran Shipman, based on her 20 years of experience, using "rules of thumb" that had always served her well. Demand information from the restaurants, production information from the beef processing plants, capacities of the warehouses, and shipping and production costs per 100 pounds of beef patties were kept up to date in the company's management information system.

The Model:
a. Can this problem be modeled accurately as a linear program?
b. Using summation notation, write the LP model for this problem using the following definitions.
   Let

   x_{ij} = no. units shipped from plant i to warehouse j

   y_{jk} = no. units shipped from warehouse j to restaurant k

   P_i = production capacity of plant i

   W_j = warehouse capacity of warehouse j

   D_k = daily demand by restaurant k

   c_{ij} = unit cost of shipping from plant i to warehouse j

   s_{jk} = unit of cost of shipping from warehouse j to restaurant k

   Your model should end up with 660 variables and 122 constraints.
c. Apologies for (b). This problem is called a *transshipment* problem and can be solved much more efficiently as a network model. We'll see it again in Chapter 4.

4.   ***The Scenario:*** The College of Business Administration at a large public university wished to build a faculty with overall excellence in teaching, scholarly research, and service to the profession and its various publics. One way to do this is to demand and expect excellence in all three areas from every faculty member, which is obviously unrealistic. Another way would be to expect certain basic levels of competence in all three areas but to allow each faculty member to excel in the area in which he or she is most competent.

The Problem: One incentive to faculty members is the annual pay raise based on performance during the past year (sometimes referred to as a "merit raise"). In an attempt to quantify the relative importance of each category (and two subcategories of teaching and service), and to stimulate a basic level of competence in each, the faculty voted the following percentages as appropriate in each category and subcategory.

Each year, a five-member dean's Merit Advisory Committee meets many long hours to analyze faculty annual reports. Using a complex rating scheme, the committee eventually arrives at five lists of faculty members in rank order—from least productive to most—in each of the four subcategories (student evaluation; teaching, other; institutional service; and service, other) and in research. The problem, then, is to use those rankings to generate an overall "order of merit" that satisfactorily reflects the twofold policy of the college: that each faculty member should attempt to achieve a minimum level of performance in all three broad categories, and that each faculty member should be rewarded for achieving excellence in his or her strongest suit.

	Academic Rank*		
Category	Professor	Associate Professor	Assistant Professor
Teaching			
Student evaluation	5–25%	5–25%	5–25%
Other	15–35	15–35	15–35
Overall	30–60	30–60	30–60
Research	10–60	15–60	20–60
Service			
Institutional	5–20	5–20	5–20
Other	0–40	0–35	0–30
Overall	5–50	5–45	5–40

* The reasons for distinctions by academic rank in the research and service categories are not important in the context of this discussion.

The Model:
a. Recognizing that we are dealing with highly subjective assessments that have been transformed into ordinal rankings, can this problem be modeled as a linear program? Why or why not?
b. Numbering each faculty member randomly, and letting s_{ij} be the ranking (in reverse order of competence) by faculty member i on subcategory j, write an LP model that maximizes each faculty member's overall "merit score" in relation to all other faculty members.
c. Comment of the efficacy of using an approach similar to this in determining pay raises for your present or potential employees in business or industry. What are the advantages? What are the potential pitfalls?

5.   **The Scenario:** We return to the LO-CAL Candy Company discussion in the previous section entitled "Model Formulation: Two Examples."

    The Problem: Recall that Percy Sweet, our young entrepreneur, wished to solve an optimal product mix problem that had arisen in his parents' firm, the LO-CAL Candy Company.

    The Model: With the assistance of LIPS (linear interactive programming synthesizer), Percy had built and "checked out" a linear programming model of his problem.

    Solution to the Model: LIPS had already displayed the solution of the LP model to Percy, but it had shown him only the optimal model values of the objective function and the five decision variables. We have queried LIPS, who is ready now to reveal the full solution in LINDO format, as exhibited in Table 2.6.

Solution to the Problem:
a. Recalling Percy's disappointment that no production of Chocochunk (x_3) was included in the model solution, and noting that the "reduced cost" for x_3 was $.0087 at optimality (compared with a per unit profit contribution of $1.10) what do you think would happen to total profit contribution if we had our analyst "force" x_3 into the solution?
b. Note the very high shadow price ("dual price" in LINDO terminology) of $2.497 per pound for light chocolate. Depending on the purchase price per pound, might it behoove Percy to invest some of his *own* money to buy more before running the batch?

Table 2.6: LINDO Solution of LO-CAL Model.

```
MAX        X1 + 0.7 X2 + 1.1 X3 + 2 X4 + 0.6 X5
SUBJECT TO
   2)      0.8 X1 + 0.5 X2 +   X3 + 2 X4 + 1.1 X5 <=     1411
   3)      0.2 X1 + 0.1 X2 + 0.1 X3 + 0.1 X4 + 0.2 X5 <=      149
   4)      0.3 X1 + 0.4 X2 + 0.6 X3 + 1.3 X4 + 0.05 X5 <=     815.5
   5)      0.2 X1 + 0.3 X2 + 0.3 X3 + 0.7 X4 + 0.5 X5 <=      466
   6)      0.7 X1 + 0.1 X2 + 0.9 X3 + 1.5 X4 <=    1080
END
```

```
    LP OPTIMUM FOUND  AT STEP       4

        OBJECTIVE FUNCTION VALUE

  1)          1509.08728
```

VARIABLE	VALUE	REDUCED COST
X1	454.483276	0.000000
X2	58.781662	0.000000
X3	0.000000	0.008737
X4	503.989014	0.000000
X5	9.131340	0.000000

ROW	SLACK OR SURPLUS	DUAL PRICES
2)	0.000000	0.045432
3)	0.000000	2.497254
4)	0.000000	1.011483
5)	0.110855	0.000000
6)	0.000000	0.229656

```
NO. ITERATIONS=         4

    RANGES IN WHICH THE BASIS IS UNCHANGED
```

		OBJ COEFFICIENT RANGES	
VARIABLE	CURRENT COEF	ALLOWABLE INCREASE	ALLOWABLE DECREASE
X1	1.000000	0.052299	0.019488
X2	0.700000	0.043961	0.345734
X3	1.100000	0.008737	INFINITY
X4	2.000000	0.956405	0.021902
X5	0.600000	0.100574	0.039565

		RIGHTHAND SIDE RANGES	
ROW	CURRENT RHS	ALLOWABLE INCREASE	ALLOWABLE DECREASE
2	1411.000000	0.262462	7.952207
3	149.000000	1.042452	11.868917
4	815.500000	0.392301	20.092094
5	466.000000	INFINITY	0.110855
6	1080.000000	16.043924	0.318113

c. Recall that Percy was uncertain about LO-CAL's ability to sell more than 500 packages of Diet-Buster (x_4). What would happen if we added the constraint "$x_4 \leq u_4$," where u_4 represents the maximum sales of Diet-Buster that Percy believes can be attained? If you have a computerized LP package available, run this model for $u_4 = 200$, 300, and 400.

d. Examine the ranges for which the objective function coefficients remain unchanged. If Percy had any doubts about the accuracy of per unit profit contributions (c_j) for each of the five products, which c_j value is the *most* questionable? The *least?*

e. Recall that Percy was certain that the inventory figures for the five ingredients were within 3% of his estimates. By examining the right-hand side (b_i) ranging analysis, could this small error result in a different optimal product mix from the current optimal one?

f. If you have access to LINDO, perform the following analysis. Enter the model as in Table 2.6, but add the following constraint:

$$x_1 + .7x_2 + 1.1x_3 + 2x_4 + .6x_5 \leq 1500$$

This constraint is referred to as an "objective cut" and has the effect of reducing the total profit contribution from $1509.08 to $1500—less than 1%. Note the solution to this new model, and check to see whether x_3 (Chocochunk) has a positive value. If not, give LINDO the command "PIVOT x_3" and then "TABLEAU." What will happen is that x_3 will take on a nonzero value, and the resulting model solution will have an objective value of $1500. This exercise parallels our earlier toy model discussion illustrated in Figure 2.2.

6.   ***The Scenario:***   Ice Train, Inc. (ITI), is a discount store that specializes in television sets. The firm stocks four models: a small portable, an economy model (12-in. screen), a standard model (19-in. screen), and a deluxe model (25-in. screen). The Christmas holidays are just around the corner, and the store manager Cara Lott is preparing to place her annual order.

The Problem: ITI's warehouse will accommodate only 120,000 cu. ft of boxed television sets, but demand for the portable, economy, and standard models is believed to be very strong this year. Sales for the deluxe model, however, have never exceeded 5000 units, and Cara would not wish to stock more than this number. Layaway orders have already been received as follows: portable, 1000; economy, 1500; standard, 1200, and deluxe, 500. Cara will, of course, have her order include at least these amounts.

The profit contributions for each model, and their per unit volume in cubic feet, are as follows:

	Model			
	Portable	Economy	Standard	Deluxe
Profit Contribution ($)	40	55	125	200
Volume (ft³)	2	3	6	9

This year, ITI is offering a special. Customers who purchase a deluxe model can get a special deal on a portable television if they wish. The profit contribution for this "package deal" is $220.

The Model:

a. Can this problem be modeled and analyzed by using linear programming? Why or why not? (Hint: Consider the assumption of additivity.)

b. Ignore the effect of the "special" and model the remaining problem as an LP model. Note that the lower-bound constraints can be removed from the model by employing the transformations "$x_j = x_j' + L_j, j = 1, \ldots, 4$," where the L_j are the number of layaway orders for each of the four models. Thus, there are only two operational constraints: the limitation on warehouse space and the upper bound on the "deluxe" model.

Solution to the Model: Letting x_j = number of each model to order, $j = 1, \ldots,$ 4, in increasing order of size, verify that the optimal model solution is as follows.

Variable	Description	Value
x_0	Profit	$2,549,583.33
x_1	Portable	1,000
x_2	Economy	1,500
x_3	Standard	11,416.67
x_4	Deluxe	5,000

Shadow Prices	
Warehouse space	$20.83 per ft³
Upper bound on deluxe	$12.50 per unit

The "reduced costs" for variables x_1 and x_2 at optimality are $1.67 and $7.50, respectively.

Solution to the Problem:

a. Note that variables x_1 (portable) and x_2 (economy) are at their lower bounds and that x_4 (deluxe) is at its upper bound, at optimality. What does this fact suggest about the effect of taking advance layaway orders for the cheaper models, and about the effect of limited demand for the deluxe models, on total profit contribution?

b. The reduced cost at optimality for x_2 (economy) is $7.50, which means that the profit contribution would have to increase by at least that much for it to be profitable to order more than the lower bound of 1500 units. What managerial implications does this have for the firm's pricing and product line strategy?

c. The foregoing solution ignores the "special" that combines certain joint sales of portable and deluxe models. Consider the following possible ways of incorporating this feature into the LP model, and determine whether either is satisfactory.

   (1) Introduce a fifth product consisting of one portable and one deluxe, with a profit contribution of $220 and a volume of $9 + 2 = 11$ cu. ft.

   (2) Assume that every customer who buys a deluxe (other than the 500 already in layaway) will purchase a portable at the special price, and set the transformed variable x_1' equal to the transformed variable x_4'.

d. Note that the shadow price for storage space is $20.83, which is [125/6 contribution for x_3/per unit volume for x_3.] Explain why this is the case.

e. Suppose that orders for the four models can be placed only in lots of 144 (1 gross) because of shipping policies adopted by the supplier. Do we still have a problem that can be modeled and analyzed profitably by linear programming? Why or why not? (*Hint:* Consider the assumption of divisibility.)

7.   ***The Scenario [9]:***   Blitzen Development, International (BDI), a company headquartered in Bonn, Federal Republic of Germany, has acquired undeveloped commercial property in such typical American cities as Berlin, Texas; Pottsdam, New York; and
Wittenberg, Ohio. BDI's current project is developing a complex in suburban Stuttgart,
Arkansas that will contain a variety of stores, offices, and apartments.

The Problem: BDI's vice-president of planning has learned through market surveys
that the development patterns for different U.S. cities must be tailored to the peculiar
tastes and preferences of the local populace. In Stuttgart, Arkansas for example, stores
and shops must be located on the ground floor, offices may be located only on the lower
two floors, and apartments can be rented only if they are less than four stories above the
ground.

Further, Stuttgarters express strong preference for a complex that includes some of
all three types of units (apartments, stores, and offices)—some of the merchants and
office workers preferring to live and shop where they work to avoid the long drive in
heavy traffic to the downtown business district.

BDI's management scientist has analyzed survey responses from Stuttgarters and
recommends to the vice-president that the following upper-bound constraints on type of
unit must be maintained.

Type of Unit	Level	Maximum Percentage
Apartment	First floor	10%
	Second floor	50
	Third floor	100
Office	First floor	60
	Second floor	75
Store	First floor	50

Another consideration is that units of different quality are possible (e.g., sound-
proofing, interior finishing), with three categories for apartments and two categories of
offices, but only one category for stores. Rental charges in deutschemarks per square
foot per year; initial construction costs (in DM/ft^2, exclusive of land costs) are given in
the following tables.

Annual Rentals (in DM/ft^2/yr)

Type of Unit	Level	Quality Categories 1 (Highest)	2 (Medium)	3 (Lowest)
Apartment	First floor	DM 3.00	DM 2.50	N/A
	Second floor	DM 3.00	DM 2.50	N/A
	Third floor	DM 2.50	DM 2.00	N/A
Office	First floor	DM 4.50	DM 4.00	DM 3.50
	Second floor	DM 4.00	DM 3.50	DM 3.00
Store	First floor	DM 3.25	N/A	N/A

N/A—Not applicable

Construction Costs (in DM/ft²)

Type of Unit	Level	Quality Class		
		1 (Highest)	2 (Medium)	3 (Lowest)
Apartment	First floor	DM 18.00	DM 16.00	N/A
	Second floor	DM 17.00	DM 15.00	N/A
	Third floor	DM 16.00	DM 14.00	N/A
Office	First floor	DM 19.00	DM 17.00	DM 13.00
	Second floor	DM 18.00	DM 15.00	DM 14.00
Store	First floor	DM 11.00	N/A	N/A

N/A—Not applicable

The commercial lot on which the complex is to be built was formerly owned by Joanie Mitchell Enterprises and is a very large, beautiful, heavily wooded bird sanctuary — a veritable paradise. Since abundant land is available, there is no constraint on space—the land not occupied by the building itself will be paved over for a parking lot. However, only 4 million deutschemarks are allocated to the project. The vice-president of planning wishes to maximize total rent income.

The Model:
a. Let x_{ijk} be the decision variables that represent the number of square feet of unit type i (apartment, office, store) to be built on level j (first, second, or third floors) of quality class k (highest, medium, lowest). Can this problem be modeled as a linear program?
b. If the answer to (a) is "yes," write the LP model. Be sure to include constraints that force the square footage of the three floors to be the same.

Solution to the Model: Use an LP computer package to solve your model.

Solution to the Problem:
a. By forcing the square footage of all three floors to be the same, we in effect force construction of a three-story complex. Can this problem be modeled in such a way that only two stories can be built if it is more profitable to do so?
b. Impose the lower-bound constraints that force at least 25% of the floor space to be allocated to each type of unit (apartment, office, store). How does this affect total rental income?

8. In the Wiseacre case, ignore Dr. Mize's restriction of planting no more than 15% of the crop in cucumbers and solve the new model with a computerized SIMPLEX package. Analyze the resulting optimal model solution and explain why it is so markedly different from the original solution.

9. a. Consider these two toy models:

P1:
$$\text{MAXIMIZE } x_0 = 3x_1 + 4x_2 + 6x_3$$
$$\text{SUBJECT TO:} \quad 4x_1 + 3x_2 + 5x_3 \leq 40$$
$$3x_1 + 2x_2 + 6x_3 \geq 89$$
$$x_1, x_2, x_3 \geq 0$$

P2:
$$\text{MINIMIZE } x_0 = 2x_1 - x_2 + x_3$$
$$\text{SUBJECT TO:} \quad x_1 - x_2 + 3x_3 \leq 18$$
$$2x_1 + 2x_2 + 4x_3 \geq 12$$
$$x_1, x_2, x_3 \geq 0$$

Solve (P1) and (P2) using a SIMPLEX computer package.

b. Oops! The right-hand side of the second constraint in (P1) should have been 39 rather than 89 (misread the advance order quantity), and the objective coefficient of x_2 in (P2) should have been $+1$ rather than -1 (typographical error). Make these changes and try it again.

c. Write the dual models (D1) and (D2) of the *original* (P1) and (P2), and solve them with a computerized SIMPLEX package. (Note: First change the " $\le$ " constraints by multiplying both sides by -1.)

10. In the Billy Hill's Still case, renege on Zeke's advance order by discarding (2.75) and rerun the model using a computerized SIMPLEX package. Analyze the results carefully.

APPENDIX: BSIM—A Simple SIMPLEX Code

This appendix contains a listing of the Microsoft BASIC® source code for a simple SIMPLEX algorithm called BSIM, a program listing of which has been placed at the end of the appendix. Some of the features of BSIM are

1. It will solve only LP maximization models with " $\le$ " constraints.
2. It is dynamically dimensioned, so there is no limit on model size. However, BSIM is an inefficient way of solving large models.
3. The code interactively prompts the user for model data—one element at a time—and allows the option of having the interim SIMPLEX matrices (tableaux) displayed on the screen or printed. The program automatically inserts slack variables to create a system of m equations in $m + n$ variables.
4. Output includes the optimal value of the objective function, the optimal values of the decision and slack variables, and the shadow prices. BSIM does not have the capability of performing ranging analyses.

BSIM is extensively documented internally, with 68 of the 182 lines of code being "REMARK" statements. These statements explain the operation of the SIMPLEX algorithm using a minimum of mathematical terminology. Thus, by discarding the "REMARK" statements, BSIM can be implemented by entering only 114 lines of BASIC code.

We illustrate the operation of BSIM with two example modeling and solution sessions.

Our illustrations include a 2-variable, 4-constraint motel room configuration problem and a 16-variable, 6-constraint portfolio selection problem.

A Motel Room Configuration Problem

The Scenario: A motel manager rents single and double rooms on a nightly basis to people who want overnight lodging. The manager is interested in maximizing the revenue potential of the facility, which consists of 200 units—some of which are single rooms (one double bed), with the remainder being double rooms (two double beds).

The Problem: The manager must decide how many of the total number of rooms should be singles and how many should be doubles. Each single unit rents for $35 per night and each double unit rents for $50 per night. Units come in three sizes: standard, large, and extra large. There are 75 standard units, 50 large units, and 75 extra large units. For obvious reasons, the manager prefers not to rent extra large units as singles. Also the standard units are too crowded when two double beds are placed in them. Finally, the manager has at his disposal only 350 double beds.

The Model: The problem appears to be appropriately modeled by LP, except that the decision variables x_1 (number of single rooms) and x_2 (number of double rooms) are integer valued. Ignoring this fact for the moment, the LP model is as follows:

$$
\begin{aligned}
\text{MAXIMIZE } x_0 = 35x_1 + 50x_2 \qquad & \text{(total revenue)} \\
x_1 + \quad x_2 \le 200 \qquad & \text{(rooms available} \\
x_1 + 2x_2 \le 350 \qquad & \text{(beds available)} \\
x_2 \le 125 \qquad & \text{(no doubles in standard rooms)} \\
x_1 \qquad\quad \le 125 \qquad & \text{(no extra-large rooms as singles)} \\
x_1, x_2 \ge 0 &
\end{aligned}
$$

Solution to the Model: The dialogue with BSIM output is displayed in Figure 1. Note that the user requested that the SIMPLEX matrices (tableaux) be printed for each iteration. Also note that the solution to this model is naturally integer.

Figure 1   Sample BSIM dialogue.

```
WELCOME TO BSIM. I CAN SOLVE LP MODELS
WITH MAXIMIZATION OBJECTIVE FUNCTIONS
AND WITH <= CONSTRAINTS.

HOW MANY DECISION VARIABLES DO YOU HAVE
IN YOUR LP MAXIMIZATION MODEL?
?2
HOW MANY <= CONSTRAINTS ARE THERE?
?4

COEFFICIENT OF VARIABLE 1 IN CONSTRAINT 1 IS: 1
COEFFICIENT OF VARIABLE 2 IN CONSTRAINT 1 IS: 1
COEFFICIENT OF VARIABLE 1 IN CONSTRAINT 2 IS: 1
COEFFICIENT OF VARIABLE 2 IN CONSTRAINT 2 IS: 2
COEFFICIENT OF VARIABLE 1 IN CONSTRAINT 3 IS: 0
COEFFICIENT OF VARIABLE 2 IN CONSTRAINT 3 IS: 1
COEFFICIENT OF VARIABLE 1 IN CONSTRAINT 4 IS: 1
COEFFICIENT OF VARIABLE 2 IN CONSTRAINT 4 IS: 0

AMOUNT OF RESOURCES IN CONSTRAINT 1 IS: 200
AMOUNT OF RESOURCES IN CONSTRAINT 2 IS: 350
AMOUNT OF RESOURCES IN CONSTRAINT 3 IS: 125
AMOUNT OF RESOURCES IN CONSTRAINT 4 IS: 125

WHAT IS THE COEFFICIENT ASSOC. WITH VARIABLE 1 IN THE OBJECTIVE FUNCTION? 35
WHAT IS THE COEFFICIENT ASSOC. WITH VARIABLE 2 IN THE OBJECTIVE FUNCTION? 50

THANK YOU. I HAVE ADDED 4 SLACK VARIABLES TO YOUR <= CONSTRAINTS, SO
THAT THERE ARE NOW 4 EQUATIONS IN 6 VARIABLES. I WILL DISPLAY THESE
EQUATIONS AS A MATRIX OF COEFFICIENTS CALLED A TABLEAU.
THE OBJECTIVE FUNCTION IS THE FIRST ROW ( ROW 0).

ROW 0: 35 50 0 0 0 0    0

ROW 1: 1   1   1 0 0 0   200
ROW 2: 1   2   0 1 0 0   350
ROW 3: 0   1   0 0 1 0   125
ROW 4  1   0   0 0 0 1   125

PLEASE CHECK THIS TABLEAU TO MAKE SURE THE NUMBERS ARE CORRECT.
NOTE THAT THE SLACK VARIABLES I ADDED ALL HAVE THE COEFFICIENT "1"
IN THE APPROPRIATE ROW.
IF EVERYTHING ELSE IS ALL RIGHT, TYPE OK. OTHERWISE, HIT "RETURN"
AND WE'LL START OVER AGAIN.
?ok
WOULD YOU WOULD YOU LIKE TO SEE EACH TABLEAU AS THE SIMPLEX ALGORITHM
PROCEEDS? IF SO, TYPE "YES". OTHERWISE, HIT "RETURN" AND BSIM WILL
DISPLAY ONLY THE OPTIMAL MODEL SOLUTION.
?yes

ROW 0:   -35.  0  0  0  50.  0     6250.

ROW 1:    1.  0  1. 0  -1.  0       75.
ROW 2:    1.  0  0  1. -2   0      100.
```

```
ROW 3:      0   1. 0  0    1.   0      125.
ROW 4:      1.  0  0  0    0    1.     125.

ROW 0:      0   0 35. 0   15.   0     8875.

ROW 1:      1.  0  1. 0   -1.   0       75.
ROW 2:      0   0 -1. 1.  -1.   0       25.
ROW 3:      0   1. 0  0    1.   0      125.
ROW 4:      0   0 -1. 0    1.   1.      50.
```

OPTIMAL VALUE OF THE OBJECTIVE FUNCTION IS   8875.

OPTIMAL VALUE FOR VARIABLE 1 IS   75.
OPTIMAL VALUE FOR VARIABLE 2 IS 125.

SHADOW PRICES ARE AS FOLLOWS

CONSTRAINT   SHADOW PRICE

```
    1            35.
    2             0
    3            15.
    4             0
```

HIT RETURN TO END
?<return>

A Portfolio Selection Problem

The Scenario: A stockbroker has been asked by a client to invest a sizeable sum of money in a portfolio of common stocks. The overall objective is to maximize the growth of capital. However, the portfolio is not to exceed a prescribed degree of risk. Also, the portfolio must provide at least enough income to pay for taxes and other expenses.

The Problem: The stockbroker has available information on a large number of companies, broken down into various industry groups. Each company is rated on a scale of 0 to 9 for its growth and risk potential, where 0 indicates no growth or no risk and 9 indicates highest growth or highest risk. No more than 35 percent of the portfolio is to be invested in any one industry group. The total risk factor cannot exceed 10. The information about the companies is given in Table 1.

The Model: Let x_j represent the fraction of the portfolio to be invested in company j. Then the model can be formulated in accordance with the remarks supplied as follows:

Table 1   Portfolio Selection Model Data

Industry	A	B	C	D
Company #	1 2 3 4	5 6 7 8	9 10 11 12	13 14 15 16
Growth	7 2 8 9	3 6 7 8	6 4 3 4	8 8 8 9
Risk	3 6 5 8	1 3 7 2	1 4 5 6	9 7 8 7

MAXIMIZE $x_0 = 7x_1 + 2x_2 + 8x_3 + 9x_4 + 3x_5 + 6x_6 + 7x_7 + 8x_8 + 6x_9 + 4x_{10}$
$$+ 3x_{11} + 4x_{12} + 8x_{13} + 8x_{14} + 8x_{15} + 9x_{16} \quad \text{(growth of capital)}$$
SUBJECT TO: $3x_1 + 6x_2 + 5x_3 + 8x_4 + x_5 + 3x_6 + 7x_7 + 2x_8 + x_9 + 4x_{10}$
$$+ 5x_{11} + 6x_{12} + 9x_{13} + 7x_{14} + 8x_{15} + 7x_{16} \leq 10 \quad \text{(risk)}$$
$$x_1 + x_2 + x_3 + x_4 + x_5 + x_6 + x_7 + x_8 + x_9 + x_{10} + x_{11}$$
$$+ x_{12} + x_{13} + x_{14} + x_{15} + x_{16} \leq 1 \quad \text{(fraction)}$$
$$x_1 + x_2 + x_3 + x_4 \leq .35 \quad \text{(industry A)}$$

$$x_5 + x_6 + x_7 + x_8 \le .35 \quad \text{(industry B)}$$
$$x_9 + x_{10} + x_{11} + x_{12} \le .35 \quad \text{(industry C)}$$
$$x_{13} + x_{14} + x_{15} + x_{16} \le .35 \quad \text{(industry D)}$$
$$x_j \ge 0 \text{ for } j = 1, ..., 16$$

Solution to the Model: The dialogue with BSIM output and the optimal model results are displayed in Figure 2.

Note that entering the model data for this problem required 120 separate queries by BSIM, which illustrates our earlier observation that this simple code is tedious to use in solving large problems.

Figure 2   Sample BSIM dialogue.

```
WELCOME TO BSIM. I CAN SOLVE LP MODELS
WITH MAXIMIZATION OBJECTIVE FUNCTIONS
AND WITH <= CONSTRAINTS.

HOW MANY DECISION VARIABLES DO YOU HAVE
IN YOUR LP MAXIMIZATION MODEL?
16

HOW MANY <= CONSTRAINTS ARE THERE?
?6

COEFFICIENT OF VARIABLE 1 IN CONSTRAINT 1 IS: 3

COEFFICIENT OF VARIABLE 2 IN CONSTRAINT 1 IS: 6
                          .
                          .
                          .
COEFFICIENT OF VARIABLE 16 IN CONSTRAINT 6 IS: 1

AMOUNT OF RESOURCES IN CONSTRAINT 1 IS: 1
                          .
                          .
                          .
AMOUNT OF RESOURCES IN CONSTRAINT 6 IS: .35

WHAT IS THE COEFFICIENT ASSOCIATED WITH VARIABLE 1 IN THE OBJECTIVE FUNCTION? 7
                          .
                          .
                          .
WHAT IS THE COEFFICIENT ASSOCIATED WITH VARIABLE 16 IN THE OBJECTIVE FUNCTION?97

THANK YOU. I HAVE ADDED 6 SLACK VARIABLES TO YOUR <= CONSTRAINTS, SO
THAT THERE ARE NOW 6 EQUATIONS IN 22 VARIABLES. I WILL DISPLAY THESE
EQUATIONS AS A MATRIX OF COEFFICIENTS CALLED A TABLEAU.
THE OBJECTIVE FUNCTION IS THE FIRST ROW ( ROW 0).

ROW 0:  7 2 8 9 3 6 7 8 6 4 3 4 8 8 8 9 0 0 0 0 0 0    0

ROW 1:  3 6 5 8 1 3 7 2 1 4 5 6 9 7 8 7 1 0 0 0 0 0   10
ROW 2:  1 1 1 1 1 1 1 1 1 1 1 1 1 1 1 1 0 1 0 0 0 0    1
ROW 3:  1 1 1 1 0 0 0 0 0 0 0 0 0 0 0 0 0 0 1 0 0 0   .35
ROW 4:  0 0 0 0 1 1 1 1 0 0 0 0 0 0 0 0 0 0 0 1 0 0   .35
ROW 5:  0 0 0 0 0 0 0 0 1 1 1 1 0 0 0 0 0 0 0 0 1 0   .35
ROW 6:  0 0 0 0 0 0 0 0 0 0 0 0 1 1 1 1 0 0 0 0 0 1   .35

PLEASE CHECK THIS TABLEAU TO MAKE SURE THE NUMBERS ARE CORRECT.
NOTE THAT THE SLACK VARIABLES I ADDED ALL HAVE THE COEFFICIENT "1"
IN THE APPROPRIATE ROW.
IF EVERYTHING ELSE IS ALL RIGHT, TYPE "OK". OTHERWISE, HIT "RETURN"
AND WE'LL START OVER AGAIN.
?ok
WOULD YOU LIKE TO SEE EACH TABLEAU AS THE SIMPLEX ALGORITHM
PROCEEDS? IF SO, TYPE "YES". OTHERWISE, HIT "RETURN" AND BSIM WILL
DISPLAY ONLY THE OPTIMAL MODEL SOLUTION.
?<return>

OPTIMAL VALUE OF THE OBJECTIVE FUNCTION IS  8.7

OPTIMAL VALUE FOR VARIABLE  4 IS .35
OPTIMAL VALUE FOR VARIABLE  8 IS .3
OPTIMAL VALUE FOR VARIABLE 16 IS .35
```

OTHER VARIABLES HAVE A VALUE OF ZERO.

SHADOW PRICES ARE AS FOLLOWS

CONSTRAINT   SHADOW PRICE

1	0
2	8
3	1
4	0
5	0
6	1

HIT "RETURN" TO END
?<return>

Figure 3 Program listing for BSIM.

```
1010   REM * ————————————————————————————————————————————*
1020   REM *   BSIM: A SIMPLEX CODE WRITTEN                        *
1030   REM *   BY JAMES R. BURNS IN THE MICRO-SOFT                 *
1040   REM *   BASIC PROGRAMMING LANGUAGE.  IT WILL                *
1050   REM *   SOLVE LP MODELS WITH A MAXIMIZATION                 *
1060   REM *   OBJECTIVE FUNCTION AND < = CONSTRAINTS.             *
1070   REM *   IT WILL NOT SOLVE LP MODELS WITH A                  *
1080   REM *   MINIMIZATION OBJECTIVE FUNCTION OR WITH             *
1090   REM *   > = or = CONSTRAINTS.                               *
1100   REM * ————————————————————————————————————————————*
1110   PRINT   "WELCOME TO BSIM.  I CAN SOLVE LP MODELS"
1120   PRINT   "WITH MAXIMIZATION OBJECTIVE FUNCTIONS"
1130   PRINT   "AND WITH < = CONSTRAINTS."
1140   PRINT
1150   REM * ————————————————————————————————————————————*
1160   REM *   THE NEXT SECTION ALLOWS THE USER TO INPUT          *
1170   REM *   COEFFICIENTS AND PARAMETERS OF AN LP               *
1180   REM *   MODEL, INTERACTIVELY.                              *
1190   REM * ————————————————————————————————————————————*
1200   PRINT   "HOW MANY DECISION VARIABLES DO YOU HAVE"
1210   INPUT   "IN YOUR LP MAXIMIZATION MODEL?"; N
1220   INPUT   "HOW MANY < = CONSTRAINTS ARE THERE?"; M
1230   E=1
1240   L=M + E
1250   K=N + L
1260   DIM TA(L, K), RA(M)
1270   PRINT
1280   FOR I=E TO M
1290       PRINT
1300       FOR J=E TO N
1310           PRINT"COEFFICIENT OF VARIABLE"; J;"IN CONSTRAINT"; I;
1320           INPUT "IS"; TA(I, J)
1330           NEXT J
1340       PRINT"AMOUNT OF RESOURCES IN CONSTRAINT"; I;
1350       INPUT" IS";TA(I, K)
1360       TA(I, N+I)=E
1370       NEXT I
1380   PRINT
1390   FOR J=E TO N
1400       PRINT"WHAT IS THE COEFFICIENT ASSOCIATED WITH VARIABLE"; J; " IN THE"
1410       INPUT"OBJECTIVE FUNCTION"; TA(L, J)
1420       TA(L, J)=-TA(L, J)
1430       NEXT J
1440   PRINT "THANK YOU.  I HAVE ADDED"; M; "SLACK"
1450   PRINT "VARIABLES TO YOUR <= CONSTRAINTS, SO"
1460   PRINT "THAT THERE ARE NOW"; M; "EQUATIONS"
1470   PRINT "IN"; N+M;" VARIABLES.  I WILL DISPLAY THESE"
1480   PRINT "EQUATIONS AS A MATRIX OF COEFFICIENTS"
1490   PRINT "CALLED A TABLEAU.  THE OBJECTIVE FUNCTION"
1500   PRINT "IS THE FIRST ROW."
1510   GOSUB 2710
1520   PRINT
1530   PRINT "PLEASE CHECK THIS TABLEAU TO MAKE SURE"
1540   PRINT "THE NUMBERS ARE CORRECT.  NOTE THAT THE"
1550   PRINT "SLACK VARIABLES I ADDED ALL HAVE THE"
1560   PRINT "COEFFICIENT '1' IN THE APPROPRIATE ROW."
1570   PRINT "IF EVERYTHING IS ALL RIGHT, TYPE OK."
1580   PRINT "OTHERWISE, HIT 'RETURN' AND WE'LL START"
1590   PRINT "OVER AGAIN."
1600   INPUT   Q $
1610   IF Q* <> "OK" THEN 1200
1620   REM * ————————————————————————————————————————————*
1630   REM * THE NEXT SECTION BEGINS OPERATION OF THE             *
1640   REM * SIMPLEX ALGORITHM.  THE INITIAL SOLUTION IS          *
1650   REM * THE UNIQUE SOLUTION OF THE M x M SYSTEM              *
1660   REM * OF LINEAR EQUATIONS WITH THE SLACK VARIABLES         *
```

```
1670   REM * SET EQUAL TO THE RIGHT HAND SIDES OF THE             *
1680   REM * CONSTRAINTS, AND WITH THE DECISION VARIABLES         *
1690   REM * SET EQUAL TO ZERO.   THE FIRST STEP IN EACH          *
1700   REM * ITERATION IS TO DETERMINE WHETHER SOME               *
1710   REM * VARIABLE WHOSE VALUE IS CURRENTLY ZERO CAN           *
1720   REM * BE INCREASED TO A POSITIVE VALUE, AND THEREBY        *
1730   REM * INCREASE THE VALUE OF THE OBJECTIVE FUNCTION.        *
1740   REM * IF THERE IS SUCH A VARIABLE, THEN SIMPLEX            *
1750   REM * GOES TO THE NEXT STEP.  IF NOT, THE OPTIMAL          *
1760   REM * MODEL SOLUTION HAS BEEN FOUND.                       *
1770   REM * THIS SECTION ALSO PERMITS THE USER TO HAVE           *
1780   REM * THE MATRIX (TABLEAU) FOR EACH ITERATION APPEAR ON THE *
1790   REM * MONITOR, IF DESIRED.                                 *
1794   REM * ───────────────────────────────────────────────────*
1798   PRINT
1800   PRINT "WOULD YOU LIKE TO SEE EACH TABLEAUX AS THE"
1810   PRINT "SIMPLEX ALGORITHM PROCEEDS? IF SO, TYPE YES."
1820   PRINT "OTHERWISE, HIT RETURN AND BSIM WILL DISPLAY"
1830   PRINT "ONLY THE OPTIMAL MODEL SOLUTION."
1840   PRINT
1850   INPUT T
1860   IF LEFT$(T, 1)="Y" OR LEFT$(T$, 1)="Y" THEN GOSUB 2710
1870   MI=1E35
1880   FOR Q=E TO N+M
1890       IF MI<=TA(L, Q) THEN 1920
1900       MI=TA(L, Q)
1910       IN=Q
1920       NEXT Q
1930   IF MI>=0 THEN 2470
1940   REM * ───────────────────────────────────────────────────*
1950   REM * THE PREVIOUS STEP HAS FOUND THAT SOME VARIABLE CAN   *
1960   REM * BE INCREASED FROM A VALUE OF ZERO TO A POSITIVE      *
1970   REM * VALUE AND THERE BY INCREASE THE OBJECTIVE VALUE.     *
1980   REM * SINCE THE SIMPLEX ALGORITHM SOLVES SEQUENCES OF      *
1990   REM * SYSTEMS OF M EQUATIONS IN M VARIABLES, THIS NEXT     *
2000   REM * STEP DETERMINES WHICH VARIABLE IS REPLACED BY        *
2010   REM * THE INCOMING VARIABLE.  THE LEAVING VARIABLE IS      *
2020   REM * SELECTED IN SUCH A WAY THAT THE SOLUTION TO THE      *
2030   REM * NEW SYSTEM OF EQUATIONS IS ALWAYS FEASIBLE; THAT     *
2040   REM * IS, ALL VARIABLES HAVE NON-NEGATIVE VALUES.          *
2050   REM * ───────────────────────────────────────────────────*
2060   MI=1E35
2070   OT=100
2080   FOR I=E TO M
2090       IF TA(I, IN) <= 0 THEN 2140
2100       RA(I) = TA(I, K) / TA(I, IN)
2110       IF RA(I) >= MI OR RA(I) < 0 THEN 2140
2120       MI=RA(I)
2130       OT=I
2140       NEXT I
2150   IF OT=100 THEN PRINT "SOLUTION UNBOUNDED": END
2160   REM * ───────────────────────────────────────────────────*
2170   REM * IN THE NEXT STEP, BSIM SOLVES THE NEW SYSTEM         *
2180   REM * OF M EQUATIONS IN M UNKNOWNS USING A TECHNIQUE       *
2190   REM * FROM ELEMENTARY ALGEBRA CALLED GAUSSIAN              *
2200   REM * ELIMINATION.  AFTER COMPLETING THE SOLUTION, BSIM    *
2210   REM * RETURNS TO LINE 1870 TO LOOK FOR ANOTHER VARIABLE    *
2220   REM * WHOSE CURRENT VALUE IS ZERO, AND THAT                *
2230   REM * WILL INCREASE THE VALUE OF THE OBJECTIVE             *
2240   REM * FUNCTION IF IT TAKES ON A POSITIVE VALUE.  IF        *
2250   REM * THERE IS SUCH A VARIABLE, THAN BSIM COMPLETES        *
2260   REM * ANOTHER SIMPLEX ITERATION.  IF NOT, THE OPTIMAL      *
2270   REM * LP MODEL SOLUTION HAS BEEN FOUND.                    *
2280   REM * ───────────────────────────────────────────────────*
2290   DI = TA(OT,IN)
2300   FOR I=E TO K
2310       TA(OT, I) = TA(OT, I)/DI
2320       NEXT I
```

```
2330   FOR A=E TO L
2340       IF A=OT THEN 2390
2350       MU=TA(A, IN)
2360       FOR I=E TO K
2370            TA(A, I)=TA(A, I)-MU*TA(OT, I)
2380            NEXT I
2390       NEXT A
2400   IF LEFT$(T$, 1)="Y" OK LEFT$(T$,1)="Y"THEN GOSUB 2710 REM PRINT TABLEAU
2410   GOTO 1870
2420   REM * ————————————————————————————————————————————————————————*
2430   REM * BSIM PRINTS THE MODEL SOLUTION IN THE NEXT                *
2440   REM * SECTION, TO INCLUDE THE SHADOW PRICES FOR THE             *
2450   REM * CONSTRAINTS.                                              *
2460   REM * ————————————————————————————————————————————————————————*
2470   PRINT "OPTIMAL VALUE OF THE OBJECTIVE FUNCITON IS"; TA(L,K)
2480   FOR J = E to N
2490       IF TA(L, J) > 0 THEN 2550
2500       FOR I = E TO M
2510   IF TA(I, J) < .999 OR TA(I,J)>1.001 THEN 2540
2520   PRINT "OPTIMAL VALUE FOR VARIABLE ";J; "IS"; TA(I,K)
2530   GOTO 2550
2540       NEXT I
2550     NEXT J
2560   PRINT
2570   PRINT
2580   PRINT "SHADOW PRICES ARE AS FOLLOWS."
2590   PRINT
2600   PRINT "CONSTRAINT"; TAB(18) "SHADOW PRICE"
2610   PRINT
2620   FOR I=E TO M
2630       PRINT TAB(3) I; TAB(23) TA(L, N+I)
2640       NEXT I
2650   INPUT"HIT ENTER TO END";XX
2660   END
2670   REM * ————————————————————————————————————————————————————————*
2680   REM * THE LAST SECTION OF BSIM PRINTS THE SIMPLEX TABLEAU       *
2690   REM * IF REQUESTED IN LINE 1850, AND THE INITIAL TABLEAU.       *
2700   REM * ————————————————————————————————————————————————————————*
2710   FOR U = E TO L
2720     PRINT "ROW"; U; STRING$(1, 1240)
2730     FOR V = E TO K
2740         PRINT TA(U,V)
2750         NEXT V
2760   PRINT
2770     NEXT U
2780   INPUT "HIT RETURN TO CONTINUE "; XX
2790   RETURN
```

REFERENCES

1. DANTZIG, G. *Linear Programming and Extensions.* Princeton, N.J.: Princeton University Press, 1963.
2. SCHRAGE, L. *User's Manual for LINDO.* Palo Alto, Calif.: Scientific Press, 1982.
3. MARKER, R. Adapted from an unpublished MBA term project report, College of Business Administration, Texas Tech University (1981).
4. WAGNER, H. *Principles of Operations Research,* 2nd ed. Englewood Cliffs, N.J.: Prentice-Hall, 1975.
5. HILLIER, F., and G. LIEBERMAN, *Operations Research,* 2nd ed. San Francisco: Holden-Day, 1974.
6. BUDDINGH, D. Adapted from an unpublished MBA term project report, College of Business Administration, Texas Tech University (1981).
7. CALKINS, C. *Reader's Digest Illustrated Guide to Gardening.* Pleasantville, N.Y.: Reader's Digest, 1978.
8. GOODELL, P. Adapted from an unpublished term project report, College of Business Administration, Texas Tech University (1983). Mr. Goodell is a doctoral student in marketing, as of September 1983.
9. BARRETT, M. Adapted from an unpublished MBA term project report, College of Business Administration, Texas Tech University (1983).
10. DAVIS, P. Adapted from an unpublished MBA term project report, College of Business Administration, Texas Tech University (1983).

ADDITIONAL READING

EPPEN, G., and F. GOULD, *Quantitative Concepts for Management.* Englewood Cliffs, N.J.: Prentice-Hall, 1979.
GASS, S. *Linear Programming: Methods and Extensions,* 3rd ed. New York: McGraw-Hill, 1969.

CHAPTER 3

Integer (Linear) Programming Models

If we insist that some or all of our decision variables in a linear programming model be integer valued, the resulting model is referred to as an integer (linear) programming (ILP) model. Such models are widely used in business, industry, and public sector organizations, and they serve as important aids to decision makers in a variety of applications.

There are two different scenarios in which ILP models are useful. First, and most obvious, fractional values for the decision variables may make no sense. For example, consider the managerial consequences of assigning 2.7 vacuum cleaner salesmen to a given territory or 3.2 professors to a committee. As another illustration, many items are bought or sold in round lots. Your LP model may indicate the purchase of 15.6 eggs, but the supermarkets will un-doubtedly refuse to take 4 eggs out of a dozen-egg carton — much less break one of them and sell you 60% of it. On the other hand, if the values of the decision variables are moderately large, no one would object to rounding nonintegral values to the next largest or next smallest integer, to obtain a useful solution. No rational manager would lose much sleep over deciding to order 950 ferndocks rather than 950.6253.

The second — and much more important — role for ILP models is in using the ILP algorithm for solving certain models of nonlinear problems. We will discuss this approach in detail in the second section of this chapter.

UNDERLYING ASSUMPTIONS

The underlying assumption of linearity applies to ILP models as it does to LP models — except that some or all of the decision variables are required to take on integer variables in the solution to the model. That is, we relax the second part of the divisibility assumption. If *all* decision variables must meet the integrality requirement, we refer to the model as a *pure* ILP problem; otherwise, the term *mixed* ILP model is used. We shall see examples of both.

A word of caution. If you can get usable results without having to insist on integral values of your variables, do so. If solution techniques can be compared with flora, then the SIMPLEX algorithm is the White House lawn, and ILP algorithms are the South American jungle.

INTEGER MODELING

As noted before, ILP models are useful in two quite different contexts: when there are natural integer-valued variables and when integers are used to incorporate other nonlinear features.

NATURAL INTEGER-VALUED VARIABLES

Consider the strategic capacity planning problems faced by managers in manufacturing firms. Large, special-purpose equipment like five-axis milling machines are incredibly expensive, and the decision to purchase two or three of these complex items (to replace less sophisticated equipment, perhaps) represents a capital outlay of several million dollars.

Imagine for a moment that we are hiding in the office closet of Buck Stopps, the tough, experienced vice-president of finance for Monolithic Manufacturing, Inc. Bitsy Bytes, a technical computer analyst, knocks timidly on the office door and enters clutching a ream of computer output.

"Whaddayawant, little lady — I'm busy," growls Buck through a blackened cigar stub.

"Mr. Stopps," says Bitsy, "I've got a solution to that capacity planning problem you've been working on. Let's see (referring to the computer print-out), it's $x_1 = 1.72358$ and $x_2 = 3.25987$, for a total cost of $11,360,482.17694."

"What in blazes is an x_1 and an x_2?" Buck demands.

"Oh," she replies, "x_1 stands for the number of five-axis milling machines we should purchase, and . . . "

The point is obvious. *If it makes a difference* in the solution of a managerial problem, then an ILP model should be used instead of an LP model. On the other hand, if the model solution can be rounded to integer values to produce useful information, then the time and expense required for solution of an ILP model should be avoided.

MODELING WITH SURROGATE INTEGER VARIABLES

As noted previously, the most important function of ILP is in incorporating features of problems that lead to nonlinearities in models of those problems. We will discuss quite a few such approaches in what follows, and you should be forewarned that some of them "come and go" in terms of our being able to grasp how they work. All have one thing in common, however, and that is the trade-off between increased problem size (both in numbers of variables as well as constraints) and the reduction of nonlinear considerations to manageable modeling and solution approaches.

Fixed Charge Problems

So-called "fixed charge" problems are commonplace in managerial decision making, and examples abound. The decision whether to include a new product in our line most probably involves a setup cost for the production facility, as well as a per unit cost to manufacture the item. For instance, if the setup cost is $100,000 and the variable cost per unit is $50, then the admittedly foolish decision to produce exactly one item would mean a per unit cost of $100,050. The average cost for two items would be $50,050, and so on. The point, of course, is that the decision *not* to manufacture the new product generates no cost whatsoever, so that the objective function is nonlinear. Mathematically, and in general, this term would be as follows:

$$c_j = \begin{cases} F_j + (V_j \cdot x_j) & \text{if } x_j > 0 \\ 0, \text{ otherwise} \end{cases} \tag{3.1}$$

where F_j is the fixed-charge or setup cost, V_j is the variable per unit cost to produce the new item, and x_j is the number of units produced.

To model this problem as a mathematical program, we introduce a variable y_j, which is allowed to take on only integer values. We then model the problem as follows.

$$\text{MINIMIZE: } x_0 = (V_j \cdot x_j) + (F_j \cdot y_j) + \text{everything else} \tag{3.2}$$

$$\text{SUBJECT TO: } \quad 0 \le x_j \le M \cdot y_j \tag{3.3}$$

$$0 \le y_j \le 1 \text{ and integer} \tag{3.4}$$

where M is a very large number.

If our ILP optimizing algorithm finds that the new product symbolized by x_j should be produced, it will set $y_j = 1$ and pick up the fixed charge F_j in the objective function. The constraint (3.3) becomes "$x_j \le M$," and since we selected M to be a very large number, the constraint has no effect. On the other hand, if the algorithm determines that the new item should *not* be produced, it will set $y_j = 0$ and not incur the cost F_j in (3.2). Note in (3.3), therefore, that $x_j = 0$, so that the variable cost V_j in (3.2) is likewise not incurred. Thus, we have successfully incorporated the nonlinear fixed charge.

Either-Or Situations

Consider the problem faced by Prometheus Energy, Inc., in choosing a site for its experimental solar energy facility. Two sites that average over 300 days of sunshine per year—Phoenix, Arizona, and Lubbock, Texas—are deemed leading candidates, but key attributes such as labor supply, local taxes, cost of living, and so on, vary widely between the two cities. Linear constraints that model these features for Phoenix are as follows:

$$\sum_{j=1}^{n} a_{ij}x_j \leq b_i, \quad i = 1, \ldots, m_1 \tag{3.5}$$

Analogous constraints for Lubbock are

$$\sum_{j=1}^{n} a_{ij}x_j \leq b_i, \quad i = m_1 + 1, \ldots, m \tag{3.6}$$

Obviously, the LP model shouldn't include *both* sets of constraints, since Prometheus wishes to choose only one site — and including the constraints for a nonselected site could overconstrain the problem. What we need is a way to have *either* (3.5) *or* (3.6) hold, but not both.

We can accomplish the desired goal by introducing a zero-one variable y_j, as follows. We replace (3.5) and (3.6) by

$$\sum_{j=1}^{n} a_{ij}x_j \leq b_i + y_j \cdot M, \quad i = 1, \ldots, m_1 \tag{3.7}$$

$$\sum_{j=1}^{n} a_{ij}x_j \leq b_i + (1 - y_j) \cdot M, \quad i = m_1 + 1, \ldots, m \tag{3.8}$$

$$0 \leq y_j \leq 1, \text{ and integer} \tag{3.9}$$

where M is again a huge number.

If our ILP computer algorithm emerges with $y_j = 1$, then the constraints (3.8) are binding, and those in (3.7) are not (since the right-hand sides are very large). Conversely, if $y_j = 0$, the constraints (3.7) are binding and (3.8) are not.

Specified Integer Values

In many operational problems, the value of a decision variable may be limited to a small set of feasible values. For example, it is well known that all-units price discounts for volume purchases lead to exactly $k + 1$ candidates for the optimal order quantity, where k is the number of quantities at which price breaks are offered (e.g., \$2.00 per unit if the order is between 0 and 999 units; \$1.95 per unit if the order is between 1000 and 1999 units).

Suppose that x_j can only take on values $V_1, V_2, \ldots, V_k$. Let $y_1, y_2, \ldots, y_k$ be zero-one variables, and substitute the following expression for x_j wherever it appears in the model:

$$x_j = \sum_{i=1}^{k} V_i \cdot y_i \tag{3.10}$$

We then add the constraints

$$\sum_{i=1}^{k} y_i = 1 \tag{3.11}$$

$$0 \leq y_i \leq 1 \text{ and integer}, \quad i = 1, \ldots, k \qquad (3.12)$$

Since each y_i can only be zero or one, and since the sum of the y_i values must *equal* one, only one of the y_i values can be nonzero. We have limited the values of x_j to be one of the k allowable values V_i.

Values in Specified Intervals

An extension of the concept of specified integer values for a decision variable is that a variable must either have the value zero or take on a value in one or more specified intervals. As an illustration, consider the problem faced by a commercial airline in deciding whether to "open up" a certain FAA-approved route, and — if opened — how large an aircraft to assign. Let L_1 and L_2 be the smallest economical passenger loads for the DC-9 and B-727, respectively, and let U_1 and U_2 be their respective capacities. The following modeling device accomplishes our goal. Let y_1 and y_2 be zero-one variables.

$$(L_1 \cdot y_1) + (L_2 \cdot y_2) \leq x_j \leq (U_1 \cdot y_1) + (U_2 \cdot y_2) \qquad (3.13)$$

$$y_1 + y_2 \leq 1 \qquad (3.14)$$

$$0 \leq y_1, y_2 \leq 1 \text{ and integer} \qquad (3.15)$$

Note that, if the algorithm determines that the route should not be opened, it will set $y_1 = y_2 = 0$ and, therefore, force x_j to be zero in (3.13). Because of (3.14), at most one of the y variables can take on a value of one, with the other having a value of zero. We see that (3.13) assures that *either* $L_1 \leq x_j \leq U_1$ or $L_2 \leq x_j \leq U_2$—but not both.

Enforcing Subsets of Constraints

Vera Tuft, a hard-hitting corporate chief executive officer, is considering adopting a formal management by objectives system for her firm.

With the help of her staff, Vera builds a large corporate LP model, with constraints that operationalize her objectives for the coming year. For example, she wishes to achieve a return on investment of 18%, to reduce inventory by 20%, to eliminate the use of overtime, to reduce short-term borrowing by 30%, to expand the product line by 10%, and so on. She dutifully checks and rechecks the data for accuracy, and orders the analyst to "run it through the computer." He does so, but returns apprehensively, holding a single sheet of paper with the cryptic pronouncement:

NO FEASIBLE SOLUTION

Vera is furious at first, but then pauses to reflect that it might be overly ambitious to expect to attain all ten of her goals. "I wonder," she muses, "if it would be possible to attain at least six of them?"

In general, let there be k constraints ($k = 10$ in the example), of which at least r constraints ($r = 6$ in the example) must be binding. To model this feature we need k zero-one variables y_i, $i = 1, \ldots, k$. We now replace all k constraints by

$$\sum_{j=1}^{n} a_{ij}x_j \le b_i y_i + [(1 - y_i) \cdot M], \quad i = 1, \ldots, k \quad (3.16)$$

$$\sum_{i=1}^{k} y_i \ge r \quad (3.17)$$

$$0 \le y_i \le 1 \text{ and integer}, \quad i = 1, \ldots, k$$

and where M is our familiar large number.

Suppose that a particular $y_i = 1$. We see in (3.16) that the original constraint is preserved in this case. If some $y_i = 0$, however, the right-hand side of its associated constraint is the very large number and is not binding. The expression in (3.17) assures that at least r of the original constraints are enforced.

In a sense, this modeling device gives us a limited capability to incorporate multiple criteria in our optimization model. We shall see other, more structured approaches with this capability in Chapter 13.

MODELING WITH ZERO-ONE DECISION VARIABLES

Many "real-world" problems can be modeled profitably with decision variables that themselves take on only the values zero or one. Some of the more useful are discussed in the paragraphs that follow.

Go/No Go Models

There are several modeling devices that come under the "go/no go" heading. For example, suppose that the decision variables $x_j, j = 1, \ldots, n$, represent possible investments in a portfolio, so that the result "$x_3 = 1$" would mean that the investment represented by x_3 would be included, while the result "$x_3 = 0$" would not include the associated stock or bond. To limit the *number* of different investments to, say, k out of n, we merely include the constraint

$$\sum_{j=1}^{n} x_j \le k \quad (3.18)$$

As another example, suppose that we wish to include an investment represented by x_2 only if the investment represented by x_1 is purchased. As an illustration, suppose that x_2 represents Mesa Petroleum Trust shares and x_1 represents Mesa's common stock; we might wish to link the two investments without eliminating the option of buying the common stock and not the trust shares. The following constraint accomplishes the result.

$$-x_1 + x_2 \le 0 \quad (3.19)$$

Note that x_2 can be one only if $x_1 = 1$ but that x_1 can take on values of zero or one regardless of the values of x_2.

In a third situation, we may want the selection of a particular stock, say, x_3, only if either x_1 or x_2 is selected—and x_1 and x_2 are mutually exclusive (we do not want both selected). Perhaps x_3 is a low-risk investment that could be selected to counterbalance high-risk stocks x_1 and x_2, and x_1 and x_2 are so risky that we wish to exclude the possibility of purchasing them both. This takes two constraints, as follows.

$$x_1 + x_2 \leq 1 \tag{3.20}$$

$$-x_1 - x_2 + x_3 \leq 0 \tag{3.21}$$

In (3.20), we limit the selection to either x_1 or x_2 (or neither), and in (3.21) we assure that if $x_1 = x_2 = 0$, then x_3 must be zero as well.

Traveling Salesman Model

The so-called "traveling salesman problem" is a prototype model that is applicable to a great many practical problems. The salesman allegory is as follows. Colin Kard, an ad salesman for *Plowboy* magazine (an agribusiness journal), must visit each of his 20 major clients in the Southeast. Since he is paid a straight commission, he must pay his own travel expenses, and gasoline prices are "eating his lunch." If he can find the shortest route that visits each of the 20 towns and returns home, he can save a lot of money. "Let's see," he thinks, "why don't I just lay out all possible routes, figure the cost of each one, and use the cheapest." Good thinking, Colin, except that there are 20! (20 factorial) possibilities—that's approximately two and one half *quintillion*. Back to the drawing board.

If we let $x_{ij} = 1$ if the tour should include the leg from town i to town j (and zero if not), and let c_{ij} be the associated cost, then the problem may be modeled as follows:

$$\text{MINIMIZE } x_0 = \sum_{i=1}^{n} \sum_{j=1}^{n} c_{ij} x_{ij} \tag{3.22}$$

$$\text{SUBJECT TO: } \sum_{j=1}^{n} x_{ij} = 1, \quad i = 1, \ldots, n \tag{3.23}$$

$$\sum_{i=1}^{n} x_{ij} = 1, \quad j = 1, \ldots, n \tag{3.24}$$

$$u_i - u_j + (n \cdot x_{ij}) \leq n - 1, \quad i, j = 2, \ldots, n, \quad \text{and } i \neq j \tag{3.25}$$

$$x_{ij} \geq 0 \text{ and integer for all } i, j$$

This no doubt requires explanation. Equation (3.22) is the objective function that sums up costs for the n legs of the tour (in Colin's case, $n = 20$). Constraints (3.23) and (3.24) merely assure that each site is a departure point and an arrival point *exactly once*. This makes sense. But what are constraints (3.25), and where did the u variables come from? As we have seen before, computers and their associated optimizing algorithms are most obedient—but unbelievably dumb. If constraints (3.25) are not included, we may get back a "solution" that contains *subtours*. This is illustrated in Figure 3.1. Note that our salesman begins by going from home to town 1 and thence to towns 2 and 3, and

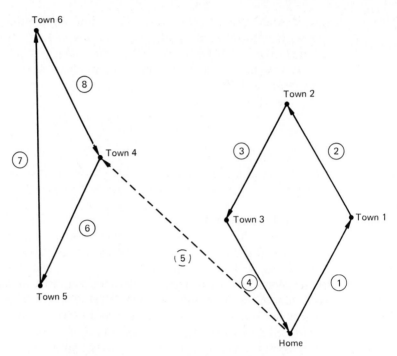

Figure 3.1 Subtours in a traveling salesman model.

then *back to home.* The fellow is then expected to somehow miraculously appear out of thin air in town 4 to continue the tour! Note that such a pattern does indeed satisfy constraints (3.23) and (3.24); that is, every town is a departure point and an arrival point exactly once (the magical translocation from home to town 4 doesn't count).

Now let us see how the ingenious device (3.25), invented by Harvey Wagner [1], prevents such an eventuality. For example, in the model illustrated by Figure 3.1, we see that $x_{12} = x_{23} = x_{31} = 1$, since these legs are included, and that all *other* $x_{ij} = 0$. Writing out the constraints associated with this subtour, we have

$$u_1 - u_2 + 6x_{12} \le 5 \tag{3.26}$$

$$u_2 - u_3 + 6x_{23} \le 5 \tag{3.27}$$

$$u_3 - u_1 + 6x_{31} \le 5 \tag{3.28}$$

But this cannot be! Note that if we add the three inequalities, we get, after rearrangement,

$$(u_1 - u_1 + u_2 - u_2 + u_3 - u_3) + [6 \cdot (x_{12} + x_{23} + x_{31})] \le 15 \tag{3.29}$$

We note that the u's cancel each other, so that — if such a subtour were allowed — (3.29) would reduce to the contradiction: $18 \le 15$. Thus addition of constraints (3.25) prevents subtours from appearing in the solution.

So, in our example, Colin would not have to enumerate all two and a half quintillion possible tours. He would merely need to set up and solve an ILP model with 440 variables and 420 constraints.

Are you becoming suspicious at this point? If not, you should be. As we shall shortly learn, an ILP model of this size is *very* difficult to solve with existing techniques. And yet good solutions to traveling salesman models involving a hundred or more "stops" can be easily obtained with heuristic methods. This is yet another example of a "model looking for a problem." Traveling salesman models can be solved for their optimal solutions by the dynamic programming techniques discussed in Chapter 6. The truth is, however, that good (but perhaps not optimal) solutions can be obtained easily by heuristic (nonoptimizing) algorithms invented expressly for that purpose.

Knapsack Model

Another ILP model with a colorful name is the *knapsack model.* Imagine that our hardy backpacker is preparing to fill a knapsack for a long trek and has several dozen items strewn about on the floor. It soon becomes obvious that everything will not fit into the knapsack, and—even if it could—it would weigh far too much to be carried. The backpacker's problem, then, is to fill the knapsack with items of a manageable total weight and at the same time give priority to the items in terms of their importance during the trek.

As a much more significant example, consider the problem of provisioning a Polaris submarine, armed with nuclear missles, for a six-month (totally submerged) tour of alert duty. Obviously, there must be enough food and supplies to sustain the crew, but what kind and how many spare parts should be carried? A failure of a part that cannot be repaired on board, and for which no spare is available, could abort the mission—and presumably threaten national security. Like the knapsack example, there is limited volume and weight capacity in the submarine.

The mathematical formulation of the knapsack problem is as follows.

$$\text{MAXIMIZE } x_0 = \sum_{j=1}^{n} c_j x_j \tag{3.30}$$

$$\text{SUBJECT TO: } \sum_{j=1}^{n} v_j x_j \le V \tag{3.31}$$

$$\sum_{j=1}^{n} w_j x_j \le W \tag{3.32}$$

$$x_j \ge 0 \text{ and integer}$$

In (3.30), the c_j are coefficients representing the level of priority or importance of the items x_j, which are zero-one integer variables (i.e., if $x_j = 1$, then item j is included). In (3.31), the v_j are the individual volumes of the items, and V is the maximum allowable volume. Likewise, in (3.32), the w_j are item weights and W is the maximum allowable weight. Obviously, there could be other constraints, such as height or width restrictions, shape, and so on.

There are other models such as those just described, and the applications of zero-one modeling are limited only by our cleverness and imagination. We discuss computational considerations in the next section.

SOLUTION APPROACHES: AN INTUITIVE DESCRIPTION

Harvey Wagner [1] uses such terms as "quest for a philosopher's stone"[1] and "the search of a lifetime" to characterize research into efficient ways to find optimal solutions to ILP models. That is, researchers have for years sought a well-behaved, dependable, and efficient method, like the SIMPLEX algorithm, which would "civilize" ILP models. Wagner's terms first appeared in print in 1971. We are not much nearer to the solution now than we were then. Why is this so?

Consider the following "first cousin" of the toy model from Chapter 2.

$$\text{MAXIMIZE } x_0 = x_1 + x_2 \tag{3.33}$$

$$\text{SUBJECT TO:} \quad -29x_1 + 42x_2 \le 147 \tag{3.34}$$

$$5x_1 - 2x_2 \le 7 \tag{3.35}$$

$$-5x_1 + 7x_2 \ge 21 \tag{3.36}$$

$$x_1, x_2 \ge 0 \text{ and integer} \tag{3.37}$$

As can be seen in Figure 3.2, the solution to the "relaxed" LP problem (without integer restrictions in (3.37)) is $x_0^* = 10.04$; $x_1^* = 3.87$, $x_2^* = 6.17$. Why not round off the LP solution to get the ILP solution? You might wish to try this on the problem some boring rainy afternoon. After all, since $x_0^* = 10.04$, neither x_1 or x_2 can be larger than 10, so that there are only $11 \cdot 11 = 121$ (remember zero) possible combinations of (x_1, x_2) pairs. If you do the enumeration, you will find that the solution is $x_0^* = 5$; $x_1^* = 1$; $x_2^* = 4$. Got the point? So much for rounding *when we must have an integral solution to an ILP model.*

Let us now briefly discuss three general solution approaches that have been pursued by ILP researchers.

BRANCH AND BOUND

Branch and bound (B&B) is a technique for solving ILP models that was introduced by Land and Doig [2] in the early 1960s and was later improved upon by Dakin [3]. Also called a "tree search," B&B is a method for *partially enumerating* solutions to combinatorial problems, in an efficient way. Although we will avoid the mathematical details, the approach is simple and logical, and we will illustrate B&B with an allegory.

---

[1] Ancient alchemists believed in the existence of a substance that could turn "base metal" like lead into gold. In recent years, government officials appear to have discovered a way to reverse this process.

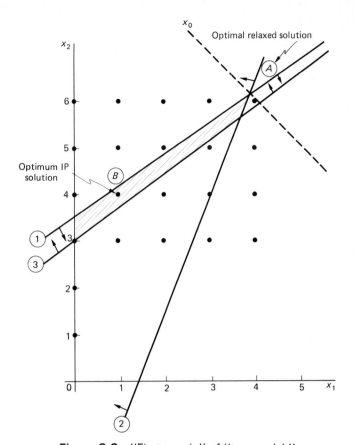

Figure 3.2 "First cousin" of "toy model."

Ernie Badges, a scoutmaster, decides to lead his young charges in Troop 66 on an overnight camping expedition in Fathombranch State Park. The heavily forested park has 30 campsites with trails connecting them in the curiously orderly way depicted in Figure 3.3. One must enter the park at the circle labeled "zero" and may then proceed into the park, always remaining on the trails. The numbered circles represent campsites.

Being a highly conscientious and devoted leader, Ernie decided that nothing but the best will do for his charges, and he is determined to locate the very best campsite in the park for their expedition. He is concerned about the amount of time it would take to investigate all 30 sites, but he is optimistic that "something will turn up" to help them avoid that eventuality. Therefore, kerchiefs in place and packs bulging, the troop stands at the entrance. For lack of a better way to start, Ernie flips a coin, and the entourage proceeds down the path to campsite 1.

Ernie's luck is with him when the troop happens upon a forest ranger at campsite 1. It seems that stinging ants have invaded the entire west side of the park, so that camping on any of those 15 sites would be unacceptable at best. Ernie notes that his problem has been cut in half at one fell swoop and leads the troop back to the entrance and thence down the path to campsite 2.

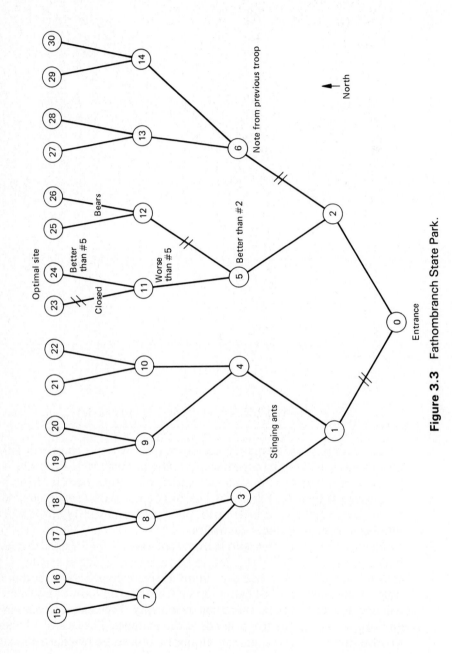

Figure 3.3 Fathombranch State Park.

Campsite 2 is acceptable, but Ernie wants the best. From afar, campsite 6 looks more promising than campsite 5, so the troop makes its way there. Again, they are in luck. A note written by a previous visiting troop, and pinned to a tree, states, "This is a better campsite than any of those to the north." But Ernie has judged campsite 2 to be better than campsite 6, so it must also be better than the other six to the north. Again, Ernie is most pleased. Seven additional sites have been eliminated, leaving only eight to go.

At campsite 5, the troop agrees that it is better than campsite 2, so only seven candidates remain. Site 11 looks more promising than site 12 from afar, but it turns out to be worse than site 5. However, a "temporarily closed" sign on the trail to campsite 23 eliminates it, and a trip to campsite 24 reveals that it is better than site 5. Thus all sites except 12, 24, 25, and 26 have been eliminated.

When the troop arrives at site 12, they spot a family of bears just to the north. Deciding that caution is the better part of valor, they return to campsite 24 and have a great night of ghost stories and fried Spam. Thus, the troop has found the best available campsite of the 30 by actually visiting only 6.

Rather than particularizing B&B to ILP problems at this point, let us discuss its "jargon" in more general terms. The information from the forest ranger allowed Ernie to *fathom* the entire branch emanating from campsite 1. Since campsite 2 was acceptable, Ernie now had a *lower bound* for the quality of the best campsite. The troop then *branched* to the set of campsites emanating from campsite 6 but found that campsite 6 *dominated* the campsites beyond it and that it was worse than the previous *incumbent,* campsite 2. The troop then *backtracked* to campsite 5, since the branch emanating from campsite 6 had been fathomed.

The troop then branched at campsite 5, again at campsite 11, and found the new incumbent to be campsite 24. One last backtrack to campsite 12 did not replace the present incumbent and allowed only an infeasible branching. So we see that the optimal campsite had been found at campsite 24, but it took a backtrack and one more branching attempt to verify that fact.

B&B and ILP

To solve an ILP problem with B&B, we first solve the associated LP problem with the SIMPLEX algorithm. If all variables are integer valued, then we are done — it *must* be the solution to the associated ILP problem.

If one or more variables are fractional, the algorithm selects one (which one is not important for our purposes) and solves two more LP problems — one with an additional constraint that limits the variable to be less than or equal to its *rounded down* value and the other with a constraint that limits the variable to be greater than or equal to its *rounded up* value (it *must,* of course, be one or the other). If we get "no feasible solution" to one of the problems, then we have fathomed an entire branch. Otherwise, we proceed to branch and backtrack, recording integer solutions as they occur, but retaining only the incumbent as a lower bound. Thus we can "cut off" (or fathom) branches in two ways: by finding them infeasible or by finding that our current incumbent is better than any solution on that branch.

Computational Difficulties with B&B

As Charlie Brown might observe, "Sigh, things are never as simple as they seem." And as usual, Charlie is right. For example, we know what an integer is—it is recognizable instantly and without question by the dullest first grader. But how about our Super-Byte Geewhiz Model PU-5000 electronic computer that cost us $3 million? If through almost unavoidable round-off error in the LP solution, the computer determines that $x_1 = 3.99999999$, it will possibly "cut off" the solution, $x_1 = 4$, leaving 3 as the integral result in x_1. We can use something called *double precision* in the computer to alleviate this difficulty, but nothing will completely eliminate it.

Another serious difficulty with B&B algorithms is that they are entirely unpredictable. That is, on one problem they might locate the optimum solution very quickly because of the nature of the problem and the type of rules used for branching. On other problems, the rules may choose the wrong path many times and end up having to enumerate a high percentage of possibilities. For example, if all our n variables are zero-one variables, then there are 2^n possible combinations. If there are 332 such variables, for example, there are about 8.75 humptillion combinations. (*Note:* A humptillion is 10 to the ninety-ninth power, and 8.75 humptillion is the largest number that our hand-held computer can handle). Problems have been constructed with special structures that would lead a B&B algorithm with specific features to enumerate *every possible combination* of variables. And 332 variables is not very many when we are modeling "real-world" problems.

However, things are not as bleak as they have just been portrayed. B&B algorithms are considered the computational "champs" at the present time, as compared with the other approach discussed next. Many operational models are indeed solved successfully by available commercial codes (to be discussed later), and you should not abandon integer modeling because solution techniques are less than perfectly dependable.

CUTTING PLANES

The logic behind B&B is simple and obvious—we merely enumerate *some* of the possible solutions while implicitly discarding most. The all-integer *cutting plane* approach, on the other hand, is not so simple to understand, in the sense of a nontechnically trained decision maker. We discuss it here, however, because of recent advances in research that make cutting plane algorithms better computational contenders.

Let us try to get a feeling for the mathematically elegant and intuitively appealing cutting plane. A cutting plane is nothing more than an additional constraint derived from the regular model constraints. It is incorporated into the associated LP model by adding it to the constraint set and performing iterations with the SIMPLEX algorithm. In effect, it "cuts off" parts of the LP feasible region without eliminating an optimal integer point.

As an illustration, let us retrieve our toy model from Chapter 2 and take a look at Figure 3.4. Note that there are ten feasible integer (sometimes called *lattice*) points, and they are represented by the black dots. The dark lines connecting eight of these points describe what is called the *integer hull* of the

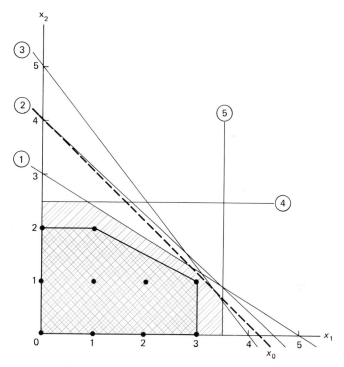

Figure 3.4 Example problem revisited.

feasible region. By the same intuition we evoked to understand why an optimal LP solution must include a vertex, it is obvious that any solution to the associated ILP problem must be a lattice point on the convex hull of the feasible region.

You are probably thinking: "If we had the three constraints (plus the non-negativity constraints, of course) that describe the convex hull, we could solve the ILP problem using ordinary SIMPLEX, since the vertices would all be integers." That's precisely what cutting plane algorithms attempt to do—to derive additional constraints called *cuts* from the original model constraints. These cuts remove pieces of the original constraint set in an effort to define as much of the integer hull as needed to form a vertex at the optimal lattice point. Since we are using the ordinary SIMPLEX technique, it will recognize the optimal solution when this vertex is found. In our "model," we see that moving the objective function parallel to itself toward the origin encounters the first lattice point at $x_1 = 3$ and $x_2 = 1$. This, then, is the optimal solution to the ILP model.

Types of Cutting Plane Algorithms

An in-depth discussion of the mechanics of cutting plane algorithms is inappropriate in this text. Briefly, then, cutting planes may be *fractional* or *all integer*. The fractional technique of Gomory [4] begins at the optimal solution to the relaxed LP model and cuts off slivers of the feasible region until it locates the optimal lattice point. This technique never locates a feasible lattice point until it locates the optimal one, so no usable solution is available until it does so. This method suffers from computer round-off error just as B&B techniques do.

All-integer cutting plane algorithms require that all model parameters be integer valued from the start. This is not particularly a problem, since most input data are rational numbers and can be converted into integers quite easily. These algorithms generate "cuts" in such a way that each simplex iteration produces yet another all-integer solution. Three basic approaches have been taken to constructing all-integer cutting plane algorithms: primal, dual, and hybrid (combination of primal and dual). All that managers need to know about this very technical subject is that primal approaches such as Young's *simplified primal algorithm* [5] do not work well in practice. Dual algorithms such as Austin and Hanna's *bounded descent algorithm* [6] and Hanna's *advanced start algorithm* [7] have shown promising results, but the jury is still out at this writing. The *constructive primal-dual algorithm* of Ghandforoush and Austin [8] is a hybrid technique and appears to work well on highly *degenerate* models (i.e., there are many zeroes in the objective function and the right-hand side of the constraints). The fixed charge problem discussed earlier is an example of such models.

Computational Efficiency

All-integer cutting plane algorithms have one very important advantage — they do not suffer from the round-off error inherent in B&B and fractional cutting plane techniques. We merely *tell* our Super-Byte computer that everything it sees is an integer, and it proceeds to solve the model for us.

However, regardless of their advantages, the truth (at least, at this writing) is that cutting plane algorithms have not performed as efficiently as B&B algorithms have on "real-world" problems. In fact, until a recent flurry of research activity into all-integer cutting planes, researchers had given them up for dead. This recent research has revived hope that efficient algorithms can be constructed using this elegant approach, but only time will tell.

ZERO-ONE MODELS

As is true throughout this text, special techniques have been developed to analyze models with special structures. For ILP models whose variables are all zero-one, Balas [9] invented a technique called the *additive algorithm.* Referred to in the literature as a *partial enumeration* scheme, the additive algorithm works in a way that is very similar to B&B — taking advantage of the special nature of the integer variables. The technique is very efficient and does not suffer from computer round-off error.

AVAILABLE ILP COMPUTER CODES

We will discuss three available ILP codes: one for mainframe machines and two for micro- and minicomputers.

IBM's MPSX

If you have an IBM or "IBM look-alike" machine, an ILP package called *MPSX* is available on a rental basis. This is basically a B&B code that is programmed very efficiently and incorporates certain technical features to speed the solution. The package is fairly expensive, and—like its LP cousin, MPS—is complicated to use. Despite its efficiency, if you give it a large, dense (few zeroes among the parameter values) model to solve, be prepared for a long wait and a large computer bill.

INTLP

INTLP is a branch and bound code available to organizations with Hewlett-Packard minicomputers like the HP-3000. It is written in BASIC and is only partially interactive. Therefore, complete documentation must be available. It will accept only small problems (20×20) and, therefore, is of limited value in a "real-world" decision-making environment. INTLP is used chiefly as a teaching medium.

PCUT 1 AND PCUT 2

PCUT 1 and PCUT 2 are two all-integer cutting plane algorithms coded by James R. Burns and Larry M. Austin. PCUT 1 is basically the *advanced dual algorithm* of Austin and Ghandforoush [10]. PCUT 2 is essentially the constructive primal-dual algorithm of Ghandforoush and Austin [8].

Both codes are completely interactive and, therefore, very user oriented. Operable on the most popular microcomputers, these codes are capable of solving many "real-world" models. Again, however, be prepared for a wait. Microcomputers are notoriously slow in "crunching" optimization models such as these. In fact, these codes store and print the interim solutions every hundred iterations—just in case the computer loses power for an instant and "forgets" everything it has done up to that point.

DEVELOPING ALTERNATIVE SOLUTIONS

Everything that was said in the section on developing alternatives in Chapter 2 is true for ILP as well. Unfortunately, the analysis is not as tidy for ILP as it was for LP. If we recall the extensive discussion on shadow prices in Chapter 2, it is unfortunate that there are no such things for ILP models. The reason is that the divisibility assumption in LP resulted in linear—and therefore continuous—constraints and objective function. Since we are dealing in ILP with a set of discrete lattice points, all bets are off in trying to determine rates of change or shadow prices. Does this mean that a decision maker must accept the initial solution to the ILP model as her or his only input? Of course not.

ALTERNATIVES WITH BRANCH AND BOUND

If your analysis is being done with a B&B code, have your analyst modify the algorithm to print out every feasible integer solution obtained along the way. Alternatively, some computer B&B codes have a "kth best solution" feature, which will find the k (whatever k you wish) solutions having the best objective values.

ALTERNATIVES WITH CUTTING PLANES

As with branch and bound, if we are using a primal code like Young's SPA or a primal-dual code like PCUT 2, we can have our programmer save every feasible solution found along the way to attaining optimality. For dual algorithms like PCUT 1, unfortunately, no feasible solutions are found prior to reaching optimality, so this device is of no value in this regard.

However, cutting plane algorithms do lend themselves to the development of suboptimal (but very good) solutions to maximization problems by the use of an interesting device called the *objective cut*. Suppose that we have obtained the optimal solution to the model, x_0^*. By the simple device of adding a constraint,

$$\sum_{j=1}^{n} c_j x_j \le x_0^* - 1 \tag{3.38}$$

and continuing the iteration with a dual algorithm like PCUT 1, we will eventually derive a feasible solution with a value of "$x_0^* - 1$" *or less*. Although we are not interested here in the technical details regarding how the cut is derived, it is intuitively appealing that such a cut "works" in practice. Obviously, such a constraint could also be added to the original LP relaxation in a branch and bound algorithm, but — unlike the case when using a cutting plane technique — the B&B code must be restarted from "scratch."

SENSITIVITY ANALYSIS IN ILP

Since we do not have shadow prices in ILP to guide our sensitivity analysis of the solution to our models, we must resort to ad hoc procedures to check the effects of data inaccuracies on our solution to the model. For example, the "stepsister" of our toy model from Chapter 2 is given here and is graphed in Figure 3.5.

$$\text{MAXIMIZE } x_0 = -2x_1 + 7x_2 \tag{3.39}$$

$$\text{SUBJECT TO: } 2x_1 + x_2 \le 12 \tag{3.40}$$

$$-7x_1 + 6x_2 \le 18 \tag{3.41}$$

$$-3x_1 + 7x_2 \le 28 \tag{3.42}$$

$$x_1, x_2 \ge 0 \text{ and integer} \tag{3.43}$$

The optimal values of the relaxed LP solution, the optimal values of the ILP solution, and the values of the "next-best" ILP solution are

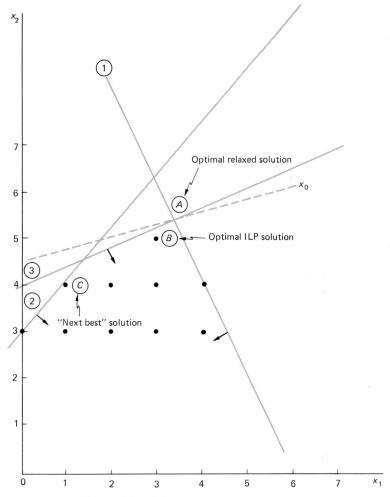

Figure 3.5 "Stepsister" of "toy model."

	Relaxed Solution	Optimal ILP Solution	"Next-Best" ILP Solution
x_0	31.29	29	26
x_1	3.29	3	1
x_2	5.41	5	4
s_1	0	1	6
s_2	8.59	9	1
s_3	0	2	3

Note from the relaxed solution and from the optimal ILP solution that we might conclude that the resource represented by constraint 2 is not particularly a problem, since in both cases the "slack" is rather large. Since the reverse is true for the first and third constraints, we would be tempted to ignore possible inaccuracies related to constraint 2 and concentrate our attention on constraints 1 and 3. However, if we proceed to find the "next-best" ILP solution to develop alternatives, we find that — although this solution has a value only about 10% away from the optimal solution — the resource represented by the second constraint is uncomfortably close to depletion, while the first and third are less so. This "herky-jerky" behavior of ILP models illustrates the difficulty of performing an orderly, dependable sensitivity analysis. This erratic behavior is especially troublesome when our model contains many zero-one variables.

What's the "bottom line" to this discussion? It's this: The manager who uses ILP models as an aid to decision making must be acutely aware of the limitations to analysis of the output and must account for those limitations when using that output. That is, it is not a matter of *whether* — but *how*.

EXTENSIONS OF ILP MODELING

In a previous section of this chapter, we looked at some modeling devices commonly used in ILP modeling. Most were straightforward and fairly easy to grasp. In this section, we will discuss some more sophisticated — but still useful — ILP modeling devices.

REDUCTION TO ZERO-ONE MODELS

As we noted previously, the so-called *additive algorithm* of Balas is a highly efficient technique for solving ILP models with only zero-one variables. What if we could reduce *any* all-integer ILP model to one that has only zero-one variables? If so, we could take advantage of the power of Balas's technique and avoid having to resort to B&B or cutting plane techniques.

Suppose in an all-integer ILP model we have available upper bounds u_j for each variable x_j (either explicitly stated or derivable implicitly from the problem constraints). For each variable x_j, we can derive an equivalent expression in terms of the weighted sum of zero-one variables y_{ij} as follows.

$$x_j = \sum_{i=0}^{K} 2^i y_{ij} \tag{3.44}$$

where

$$2^K \le u_j \le 2^{K+1} \tag{3.45}$$

The relationships in (3.44) and (3.45) are called a *binary representation* of x_j and are best explained by an example.

Suppose that the upper bound is $u_j = 9$ for x_j, so that x_j must be allowed to take on only the integral values $x_j = 0, 1, 2, \ldots, 9$. Then (3.44) becomes

$$x_j = y_{ij} + 2y_{2j} + 4y_{3j} + 8y_{4j}$$

since in (3.45), $2^3(= 8) \leq u_j(= 9) \leq 2^4(= 16)$, so that $K = 3$. To obtain the ten allowable values of x_j, the y_{ij} values would be set by the algorithm as follows:

x_j	y_{1j}	y_{2j}	y_{3j}	y_{4j}
0	0	0	0	0
1	1	0	0	0
2	0	1	0	0
3	1	1	0	0
4	0	0	1	0
5	1	0	1	0
6	0	1	1	0
7	1	1	1	0
8	0	0	0	1
9	1	0	0	1

If the upper bound "$x_j \leq 9$" is *implicit* from the other constraints, we need go no farther. If it is an *explicit* upper bound, we merely replace the constraint "$x_j \leq 9$" with "$y_{1j} + 2y_{2j} + 4y_{3j} + 8y_{4j} \leq 9$."

"But," you may be thinking, "what if I have a small ILP model with only 50 integer variables and the upper bounds are in the neighborhood of 100. Let's see, for $u_j = 100$, K would be 6—which means that I'd end up with about 350 zero-one variables rather than 50 ordinary integer variables." If you are skeptical in this regard, you should recall that as the variable values get larger and larger, we as decision makers become more and more comfortable with rounding the values of the associated relaxed LP model to get "reasonable" solutions to the ILP model. Thus the binary transformation is useful in those cases in which *small* upper bounds are involved (e.g., when we are dealing with numbers of airplanes or five-axis milling machines or other high-cost, low-volume entities).

TRANSFORMATION OF NONLINEAR TERMS

Suppose that we are dealing with a zero-one ILP model whose objective function or constraints contain nonlinear products of powers of the decision variables. For example, suppose that

$$\text{MAXIMIZE } x_0 = x_2^3 \cdot x_4 \cdot x_6^4 + \text{other terms} \qquad (3.46)$$

is our objective function, and we wish to eliminate the nonlinear term to solve the model with Balas's additive algorithm. Since the x's are all zero-one variables, common sense tells us that the nonlinear term has a value of "one" only if $x_2 = x_4 = x_6 = 1$. Otherwise, if any one of the $x_j = 0$, the term itself has a zero value.

A simple transformation and the addition of two constraints does the job, as follows.

Let

$$y = x_2^3 \cdot x_4 \cdot x_6^4 \tag{3.47}$$

We now replace (3.46) with

$$\text{MAXIMIZE } x_0 = y + \text{other terms} \tag{3.48}$$

where $y = 0$ or 1 and add the two constraints

$$x_2 + x_4 + x_6 - y \leq 2 \tag{3.49}$$
$$-x_2 - x_4 - x_6 + 3y \leq 0 \tag{3.50}$$

How does this transformation work? If $x_2 = x_4 = x_6 = 1$, then from (3.49), $y = 1$ to satisfy this constraint, and the objective function picks up the value $y = 1$. On the other hand, if x_2 or x_4 or $x_6 = 0$ in (3.50), the only way this constraint can be satisfied is for y to equal zero, and the objective function picks up the value $y = 0$. (Actually, this transformation will work *without* requiring that y be a zero-one variable; you may take this on faith or try it yourself, requiring only that y must be nonnegative.)

Disk-o-Tech

The Scenario: Disk-o-Tech, Inc., is a manufacturer of drum-disk memory units that are compatible with several popular minicomputers. The drums are modularized, each having 100 megabytes of memory, and can be wired together to make units of two, three, or four memory packs. The ''hook-up'' must be performed at one of the Disk-o-Tech plants before being shipped to order.

The company has three plants—in Ramville, Remberg, and Romtown — with production capacities of 20, 14, and 28 modules per week, respectively. The current week's orders are as follows:

1. Twelve two-module packs to Tuscaloosa, Alabama
2. Nine three-module packs to Tempe, Arizona
3. Four four-module packs to Toledo, Ohio

The Problem: The memory packs are very fragile and require expensive packaging prior to shipment. They also require special handling during shipment, which adds additional cost; the shipping and handling cost *per module* is given in Table 3.1. (*Note:* The cost per *pack* of *n* modules is merely *n* times the cost per module.)

The computer memory supply business is highly competitive, and Disk-o-Tech's profit margins have become razor thin. Seymour Prophet, the firm's CEO, has turned his attention to cost control as a possible way to retain Disk-o-Tech's market share, and the high transportation outlay caught his eye.

Entering the office of Hugh Ristick, the company's director of distribution, Mr. Prophet queries: ''Ristick, can't you do any better on the shipping costs? I just got your figures for next week, and the charges come to almost $55,000. That'll put us in the red.''

''Boss,'' replies Hugh, ''here's the schedule I worked out (see Table 3.2). I know the costs seem high, but you've got to understand what I'm up against. When I put the problem in the computer, the LP package keeps

Table 3.1 Disk-o-Tech Shipping Costs

		To		
		Tuscaloosa	Tempe	Toledo
From	Ramville	$600	$ 900	$600
	Remburg	800	800	700
	Romtown	500	1200	600

Note: Costs are per module.

Table 3.2 Hugh Ristick's Shipping Schedule

	To			
	Tuscaloosa	Tempe	Toledo	Capacity
Ramville	8(4)	3(1)	8(2)	20
Remburg	6(3)	3(1)	4(1)	14
Romtown	10(5)	21(7)	4(1)	38

Requirements: 24(12)   27(9)   16(4)

Note: Shipments are stated in modules (packs).

giving me nonsense answers. For example, the last run said to ship 13 modules from the Ramville plant to Toledo, but Toledo wants 4-module packs, and I can get only 3 packs out of 13 modules. What do I do with the extra one? I even tried putting in some extra LP constraints to get it to come out right, but then the computer started giving me answers in fractions of modules. If you want my honest opinion, this LP stuff isn't all it's cracked up to be."

The Model: With the help of a management science consultant, the Disk-o-Tech problem was modeled by IP. The key was in recognizing that the decision variables, representing shipments from the three plants to the three customers, must take on *specified integer values.*

Let x_{ij} = the number of modules shipped from plant i to customer j ($i = 1, 2, 3$ and $j = 1, 2, 3$, in the order listed in Table 3.1). Then, for example, x_{11}, x_{21}, and x_{31} represent shipments to Tuscaloosa and must take on values that are multiples of *two*. Likewise, the variables representing shipments to Tempe and Toledo must take on values that are multiples of *three* and *four,* respectively. Mathematically, the model is formulated as follows.

Let y_{ijk} be zero-one variables and let m_j be the module multiples (i.e., $m_1 = 2, m_2 = 3, m_3 = 4$). Let T_{ij} be the integer part of $\text{MIN}(S_i, R_j)/m_j$, where S_i is the capacity of the ith plant and R_j is the requirement for the jth customer.

For example, T_{22} = integer part of $\text{MIN}(14, 27)/3 = 4$. We then make the following substitutions for the x_{ij}:

$$x_{ij} = \sum_{k=1}^{T_{ij}} k \cdot m_j \cdot y_{ijk}, \quad i, j = 1, 2, 3 \tag{3.51}$$

For example,

$$x_{22} = \sum_{k=1}^{4} k \cdot 3 \cdot y_{ijk} = 3y_{221} + 6y_{222} + 9y_{223} + 12y_{224} \tag{3.52}$$

Then, by adding constraints such as

$$\sum_{k=1}^{4} y_{22k} \leq 1 \tag{3.53}$$

we force x_{22} to take on only the values 0, 3, 6, 9, or 12 (since the y variables are zero-one). Before making the substitutions for the x_{ij}, the model appears as follows:

$$\text{MINIMIZE } x_0 = 600x_{11} + 900x_{12} + 600x_{13} + 800x_{21} + 800x_{22}$$

$$+ 700x_{23} + 500x_{31} + 1200x_{32} + 600x_{33} \qquad (3.54)$$

$$\text{SUBJECT TO:} \quad x_{11} + x_{12} + x_{13} \le 20 \qquad (3.55)$$

$$x_{21} + x_{22} + x_{23} \le 14 \qquad (3.56)$$

$$x_{31} + x_{32} + x_{33} \le 38 \qquad (3.57)$$

$$x_{11} + x_{21} + x_{31} = 24 \qquad (3.58)$$

$$x_{12} + x_{22} + x_{32} = 27 \qquad (3.59)$$

$$x_{13} + x_{23} + x_{33} = 16 \qquad (3.60)$$

$$x_{ij} \ge 0, \quad i, j = 1, 2, 3 \qquad (3.61)$$

In the model, we are attempting to minimize total transportation cost in (3.54). Constraints (3.55) through (3.57) ensure that the plants do not ship more than they are capable of producing, and constraints (3.58) through (3.60) ensure that the customer's orders are filled.

After transforming the model using the substitution in (3.51), we have a model with

1. 59 zero-one variables
2. 6 original constraints of the form (3.55) through (3.60)
3. 9 constraints of the form (3.53)

Solution to the Model: The optimal solution to the model is given in Table 3.3 and yields a total shipping cost of $44,700. This shipping schedule would cost over $10,000 less than the schedule in Table 3.2 generated by Disk-o-Tech's former director of distribution.

Solution to the Problem: After inspecting the model solution carefully, Seymour Prophet decided to implement the plan without alteration. As it turned out, the excess modules were spread rather evenly among the three plants, so that if final inspection before shipment discovered a faulty

Table 3.3 Optimal Disk-o-Tech Model Solution

		To			
		Tuscaloosa	Tempe	Toledo	Not Shipped
From	Ramville		15(5)	4(1)	1
	Remburg		12(4)		2
	Romtown	24(12)		12(3)	2

Note: Shipments are stated in modules (packs).

module in a pack, at least one spare would be available at every plant. Furthermore, the smallest plant (Remburg) would ship its total output to Tempe and would be concerned only with assembling three-module packs.

The IP computer package (based on Balas's additive algorithm) provided by the consultant was used routinely thereafter by Disk-o-Tech in analyzing its shipping schedule, and Mr. Prophet considered the consultant's fee to be money well spent.

BLL, Inc.

The Scenario: Business Learning Laboratories, Inc. (BLL), is a firm that conducts noncredit professional courses for administrators, secretaries, executives, financial and marketing analysts, and others wishing to update and sharpen their technical and administrative skills. The courses vary in length from a day to two weeks and run the gamut from "Interpersonal Skills for File Clerks" to "International Macromarketing for CEOs." The majority of the seminars are taught by professors from colleges and universities in the vicinity of the course locations in over 40 cities across the country. BLL does employ some full-time seminar leaders, however.

The professional development seminar business is lucrative but highly cash flow intensive. That is, during busy season, a large amount of cash must be available to pay for "up-front" expenses such as preparation of program materials, room reservations, and so on. Except for advance deposits required for certain high-cost programs, revenues tend to lag expenses by two to six weeks.

The Problem: During the off season, BLL had followed the practice of letting cash build up in its operational accounts as activity slowed and revenue came in from busy-season programs. One of the professors who taught a program (on cash management) for the company found out about this practice. He suggested that BLL look into short-term (30-day) commercial "paper" as a means of putting idle cash to work during the slow season. The CEO of BLL liked the idea and instructed her brokers to propose appropriate investments. The following 30-day instruments were recommended.

30-Day Instruments

Instrument	Denomination	Annual Interest Rate	Risk Classification
U.S. Treasury bills	$100,000	12%	Negligible
Industrial notes	150,000	14	Low
Second mortgages	250,000	15	Moderate
Venture capital loans	500,000	18	High

In the current period, she estimated that BLL had $5,370,000 in excess cash to invest. Her brokers recommended buying 10 units of the venture capital loans for maximum return and filling out the portfolio with two industrial notes. The "high-risk" classification of the venture loans bothered her, however, and she placed the following managerial restrictions on the composition of the portfolio.

1. At least 10% of the total investment should be devoted to each of the three types of instruments other than venture capital loans.
2. No more than 50% of the total investment should be placed in industrial notes and venture capital loans, taken together.
3. No more than 20% of the total investment should be made in second mortgages.

One other consideration is that a surety fee of $10,000 must be paid for the privilege of investing in venture capital loans. Naturally, if BLL does not choose to invest in this instrument, it would not pay the fee. The fee is the same regardless of how large the investment is (other than zero).

The Model: This portfolio problem was modeled as an all-integer programming model that included a "fixed charge" feature to account for the surety fee. Note that the four instruments can be purchased only in integer multiples of their respective denominations, so that fractional purchases are not possible. The model is as follows.

Let x_j = number of the jth instrument to purchase in the given denomination, $j = 1, \ldots, 4$ (in the order given):

$$y = \begin{cases} 1, & \text{if } x_4 > 0 \\ 0, & \text{otherwise} \end{cases}$$

MAXIMIZE $x_0 = 1000x_1 + 1750x_2 + 3125x_3 + 7500x_4 - 10,000y$	(3.62)
SUBJECT TO: $100,000x_1 + 150,000x_2 + 250,000x_3 + 500,000x_4 \leq 5,370,000$	(3.63)
$100,000x_1 \qquad\qquad\qquad \geq 537,000$	(3.64)
$150,000x_2 \qquad\qquad \geq 537,000$	(3.65)
$250,000x_3 \qquad \geq 537,000$	(3.66)
$150,000x_2 \qquad + 500,000x_4 \leq 2,685,000$	(3.67)
$250,000x_3 \qquad\qquad \leq 1,074,000$	(3.68)
$x_4 - 100y \leq 0$	(3.69)
$y \leq 1$	(3.70)
$x_1, x_2, x_3, x_4, y \geq 0$	(3.71)

The objective function coefficients in (3.62) are the one-month proceeds at the stated interest rates. For example, on Treasury bills, $c_1 = (.12) \cdot (100,000)/12 = 1000$. The y term incorporates the surety fee as a "fixed charge." Note in (3.69) that if optimal $x_4 = 0$, then $y = 0$ as well, so that no investment in venture capital loans occurs and no surety fee is paid. On the other hand, if it is optimal to purchase some of this instrument, x_4 will be greater than zero, forcing $y = 1$ and picking up the $10,000 fee in (3.62).

Constraints (3.63) through (3.68) incorporate the restrictions placed on the portfolio by the CEO. The model could be decreased in size, if necessary, by using a transformation to delete the three lower-bound constraints (3.64) through (3.66).

Solution to the Model: The optimal solution to the model, as stated, is as follows.

Instrument	Number to Purchase	Amount Invested	Return
Treasury bills	18	$1,800,000	$18,000
Industrial notes	17	2,550,000	29,750
Second mortgages	4	1,000,000	12,500
Venture loans	—	—	—
Total	39	$5,350,000	$60,250

Solution to the Problem: Although shadow prices for the constraints are not computable for solutions to IP models, the CEO and her staff noted several interesting features of the "optimal" portfolio. Venture capital loans, the highest-yielding (and riskiest) instrument, were not included in the mix — even though none of the lower-bound constraints on the other three were even remotely close to being binding. As an experiment, she had her analyst rerun the model, changing from 50% to 70% the restriction on total investment in industrial notes and venture loans. The solution to the new model intrigued her.

Instrument	Number to Purchase	Amount Invested	Return
Treasury bills	7	$ 700,000	$ 7,000
Industrial notes	1	150,000	1,750
Second mortgages	4	1,000,000	12,500
Venture loans	7	3,500,000	42,500
Total	19	$5,350,000	$63,750

It was apparent that loosening the restrictions allowed the high-risk venture loans to enter at a high enough level to make the $10,000 surety fee worth paying — but the net effect was to increase substantially the level of risk in the portfolio, at only a 5.8% increase in return. The message to her as a manager was clear: High-risk investments are for "high rollers." The 13.5% (annualized) rate of return seemed reasonable for the original portfolio and its low-to-moderate overall riskiness, and she decided to go with the original optimal model solution.

SUMMARY

In this chapter, we relaxed the LP assumption of divisibility (at least partially) and discussed the highly utilitarian integer linear programming (ILP) model that resulted.

We noted that ILP models are useful in two distinct contexts: (1) when some or all of the decision variables must take on integer values for a model to be appropriate as an aid to decision making and (2) as devices to model effectively such nonlinear features as fixed charges, "either-or" constraints, alternate constraint sets, and so on. We also ventured into modeling with zero-one variables and discovered a rich variety of applications of such devices.

Next, we briefly touched on some approaches that have been used to solve ILP models and concentrated our attention on branch and bound (B&B) and cutting planes. We got a feeling for the difficulty encountered in solving ILP models in general as well as an appreciation of the unpredictability of current solution approaches. Some of the computer codes available on mainframe and micro- and minicomputers were also identified.

Our discussion of developing alternative solutions for, and performing sensitivity analysis on, ILP models revealed a greatly decreased capability in this regard, as compared with LP models. The fact that shadow prices in ILP have no precise meaning (as they do in LP) was the key shortcoming here. We then briefly discussed some advanced modeling techniques and mixed integer programming.

In the next chapter, we delve into a subset of ILP models that can be modeled as networks, taking advantage of their special structure to utilize specialized, highly efficient solution techniques.

PROBLEMS

1. *The Scenario:* The Rio de Oro Medical Clinic, which is located at 24 Carrot Street in Aspen, Colorado, is doing a booming business in setting broken limbs, peforming physical exams, and tending to various other outpatient services for regular and walk-in customers. In fact, business is so good that the head nurse, Angela Mersey, has suggested to the managing physician that the clinic begin opening on Wednesday afternoons and Saturdays during golf season — a suggestion that he promptly squelches.

    The Problem: Due to the demand for its services, the clinic is currently operating at capacity, and waiting lines form almost daily. Bill Dunn, the business manager, expresses his concern to Nurse Mersey, noting that the exclusive nature of the clinic's clientele makes it unwise to subject such people to the indignities of lolling about in the waiting room, regardless of how plush it may be.

    Dunn suggests that the physicians' lounge could be converted into another examination room, another physician and nurse could be hired to staff it, and the clinic's level of service could thereby be expanded to meet the demand. An alternative would be to hire a "rookie" M.D. and a nurse to staff the regular facility on an overtime basis, after the regular 10 A.M.–3 P.M. clinic hours (10 A.M. to 12 noon on Wednesday). There is even an outside chance that an ambitious young physician might be persuaded to see patients on

Wednesday afternoons and Saturdays during golf season — but the premium in pay would be considerable.

"Opening another examination room would cost a bundle," observes Nurse Mersey, "but so would operating the clinic after normal operating hours. Bill, which would be best?"

The Model:

a. Assuming that the objective of the Rio de Oro clinic is to maximize total profit contribution, and that the constraints on the model can be expressed as linear relationships, can this problem be modeled as an ILP model? What integer modeling device could be used to differentiate between the cost of opening another examination room and the marginal cost of overtime operation?

b. Note from a managerial viewpoint that opening another examination room represents a one-time capital outlay that — once made — cannot be recovered. On the other hand, the use of overtime gives Angela a great deal of flexibility in case the forecast patient demand does not materialize. Is there any way to include this feature in a formal ILP model of the problem? If so, how? If not, how can this possibility be accounted for?

The Solution: The problem was indeed modeled as a "fixed charge" ILP model, and the optimal solution to the model indicated that hiring a "rookie" M.D. and a nurse to staff the clinic on Wednesday afternoons and Saturdays was the desired solution. However, the forecast demand on Wednesdays and Saturdays did not materialize. The clinic was saddled with the additional expense of an overtime physician and nurse who spent most of their time playing backgammon, while the demand on the clinic during regular clinic hours continued to grow.

a. What could have caused this phenomenon?

b. Why did the ILP model fail so miserably in this instance?

2.   ***The Scenario:*** Marijane Moss is a student at Humus State University, majoring in horticulture. A last semester senior, she has completed all required courses and must enroll in at least 15 elective hours (but no more than 21) to graduate. The electives are not totally free; they must be selected from a list of courses totaling 36 hours.

The Problem: Marijane's problem is twofold: First, she must have a cumulative grade-point average (GPA) of 2.0 (C) to graduate, and she has precisely that at the moment; second, and more important, she is heavily involved in interviewing for a managerial position in the agribusiness industry and finding the right position will take time and effort during the coming semester.

Luckily, some of her sorority sisters have compiled a list of senior elective courses and have rated them on two dimensions: difficulty (from 1 to 10 in increasing order of difficulty) and time commitment required (in hours per week). This list, along with the semester credit hours for each course, is shown at top of the next page.

The Model:

a. Can Marijane's problem be modeled as an ILP model? If so, what is the objective function? What are the constraints? Do the variables have any special structure?

b. Does the ILP model in (a), if appropriate, have any special structure that, if recognized, might allow for an efficient solution technique? If so, what special solution technique might be appropriate?

Solution to the Model: We might conclude that this problem can be modeled as a *knapsack* model. That is, Marijane wishes to fill her class schedule (knapsack) with items

Number	Title	Credit Hours	Difficulty	Time Required
1. SHO 4108	Creative Fertilizing	1	4	8
2. SHO 4309	Houseplant Watering Techniques	3	2	12
3. GEO 4312	The Plains of New Mexico	3	6	6
4. GEO 4215	Agricultural History of Alaska	2	5	4
5. HEC 4421	Hibiscus in the Home	4	1	7
6. ENG 4335	Farmers' Almanac Revisited	3	8	5
7. BIO 4241	Pests of North America	2	9	3
8. SOC 4154	House Plants and Rock and Roll Music	1	3	9
9. PSY 4363	Dealing with Vegetables	3	7	6
10. ENV 4578	Air Pollution and Your Turnips	5	10	15
11. AGR 4285	Control of Noxious Grasses	2	6	8
12. LAW 4293	Plants and Their Rights	5	9	13
13. REC 4226	Touring Mesquite Country	2	3	6
Total credit hours available		36		
Total time required				102

(courses) in such a way that capacity (21 semester credit hours) is not exceeded and that minimum capacity (15 semester credit hours) is attained. However, what is an appropriate objective function?

Note that all 13 courses total to a time requirement of only 102 hours per week, so if it were not for the 21 semester credit hour limit, a student could conceivably take all of them and still get about 9 hours of sleep per night. However, in Marijane's case, free time is critical—she needs every hour she can free up to interview with company recruiters. On the other hand, if she selects a set of courses that is too difficult overall, she may not graduate.

One approach to this problem is to model it in two ways: first, *minimize the total difficulty* of the courses, ignoring the time requirement; next, *minimize total time requirement,* ignoring difficulty.

Let

$$x_j = \begin{cases} 1, \text{ if class } j \text{ is included} \\ 0, \text{ otherwise} \end{cases}$$

s_j = semester credit hours for course j

d_j = level of difficulty for course j

t_j = time required for course j

Then model 1 (M1), minimizing total difficulty, becomes

M1: $\qquad \text{MINIMIZE } x_0 = \sum_{j=1}^{13} d_j x_j$ $\qquad\qquad$ (3.72)

$\qquad\qquad \text{SUBJECT TO: } 15 \le \sum_{j=1}^{13} s_j x_j \le 21$ $\qquad\qquad$ (3.73)

$\qquad\qquad\qquad x_j = 0, 1, \quad j = 1, \ldots, 13$ $\qquad\qquad$ (3.74)

Likewise model 2 (M2), minimizing total time requirement, becomes

M2: $\qquad\qquad \text{MINIMIZE } x_0 = \sum_{j=1}^{13} t_j x_j$ $\qquad\qquad$ (3.75)

$$\text{SUBJECT TO:} \quad 15 \le \sum_{j=1}^{13} s_j x_j \le 21 \tag{3.76}$$

$$x_j = 0, 1, \quad j = 1, \dots, 13 \tag{3.77}$$

The solutions to these two models are as follows (we used Balas's additive algorithm to solve them).

For M1,

	Course No.							
	1	2	4	5	8	11	13	Total
Credit hours	1	3	2	4	1	2	2	15
Difficulty	4	2	5	1	3	6	3	24 (MIN)
Time required	8	12	4	7	9	8	6	54

For M2,

	Course No.					
	3	5	6	7	9	Total
Credit hours	3	4	3	2	3	15
Difficulty	6	1	8	9	7	31
Time required	6	7	5	3	6	27 (MIN)

Solution to the Problem:

a. We note that course 5, HEC 4421, is the only course that appears in the solutions to both (M1) and (M2). What might we conclude from this "coincidence"?

b. What exogenous factors might she take into consideration when making her final decision? How does Marijane proceed from here?

c. If there were some way numerically to prioritize the two objectives "minimize total difficulty" and "minimize total time requirements," and assign a numerical weight to each (e.g., the latter is twice as important as the former), how might Marijane incorporate this feature into the model? (*Note:* More about this in Chapter 13.)

3.   *The Scenario:*   A. Judy Cates and Susan Wynns are partners in a small law firm that specializes in defending their clients against misdemeanor charges (e.g., jaywalking, littering, speeding). Early each Monday morning, they meet to schedule their caseload for the week. Each case is characterized by two parameters: the time required by either Judy or Susan to prepare each case for court and the due date (docket schedule) set by the court for each case. The individual cases are independent of each other, so there is no case-dependent sequence to bother with.

The Problem: The two young attorneys must make two basic decisions each Monday morning: which attorney will take which of the cases and in what order the cases will be addressed. There is no particular advantage in having a case prepared *before* the time of the docket schedule; however, if the docket schedule is not met for a particular case, court charges are levied on a per hour tardy basis. Therefore, Judy and Susan decide to set up a schedule that *minimizes total tardiness* of cases for the week.

The Model:

a. Can this problem be modeled as an ILP problem? If you think so, let

    n = number of cases for the week

p_j = preparation time for case j, $j = 1, 2, \ldots, n$

d_j = due date (in hours from 7 A.M. Monday) for case j, $j = 1, 2, \ldots, n$

$x_{ijk} = \begin{cases} 1, & \text{if attorney } i \text{ processes case } j \text{ in the } k\text{th order} \\ 0, & \text{otherwise} \end{cases}$

$i = 1, 2; \quad j, k = 1, 2, \ldots, n$

Write the zero-one ILP model for this problem.

b. In your model, suppose that there are 50 cases in the hopper for a given week. How many decision variables x_{ijk} are there?

c. Suppose there are 20 attorneys in a large firm and the caseload averages 500 cases per week. How many decision variables are there in this model?

Solution to the Model: This problem is referred to in the literature as the "n-job, two-machine tardiness model." The terminology comes from a job shop environment in which two machines (attorneys, in our scenario) are available to process (prepare cases on) n jobs (cases) with known processing times (preparation times) and due dates (docket schedules). Minimization of total tardiness is a widely used objective in such situations.

The answer to the question "Is this a viable modeling technique for the tardiness problem?" is a decided "No." Researchers have worked at finding an efficient optimizing solution technique for this model for years—without success. There are, however, heuristic methods that yield "good" solutions in a reasonable amount of computer time, and these techniques are widespread in use.

If your curiosity is piqued by this problem, think about the following analogy. Consider a *pair* of traveling salesmen who must jointly visit n customers with whom they have set appointments. The time required by each of the two salesmen to travel and conduct business with each customer varies because of personalities, sales techniques, and so on. Is the "n-job, two-machine tardiness model" nothing more than an extension of the traveling salesman problem?

4. **The Scenario:** Treetops World Airlines (TWA), a small regional air carrier that operates in the Southeast, has received approval to service 12 small cities in Tennessee, Mississippi, and Alabama and to purchase at least ten passenger aircraft for this purpose.

The Problem: Al Aaron, the CEO of TWA, has narrowed his choices to four aircraft models, and some data on these aircraft are as follows:

	Aircraft Models			
	Zinger	Clunker	Ramp Queen	Banger
Unit cost	$150,000	$215,000	$260,000	$400,000
Passenger capacity	12	16	20	30
Maximum range (miles)	300	400	500	1000
Operating cost ($ per mile)	$1.50	$2.50	$3.00	$4.00

Al would like to minimize the average operating cost per mile of the aircraft purchased. TWA has a capital budget of $2,500,000 for this procurement. Two additional considerations are as follows. At least six of the aircraft must have a range of 400 miles or more to cover approved routes. Also, Al would like a total passenger capacity of at least 200 seats for the fleet.

The Model: Note at the outset that the TWA problem is *nonlinear,* since the objective function (minimize the *average* operating cost per mile) can be written

$$\text{MINIMIZE } x_0 = \frac{1.5x_1 + 2.5x_2 + 3x_3 + 4x_4}{x_1 + x_2 + x_3 + x_4} \tag{3.78}$$

This is called a *fractional programming* problem, and we will discover how to transform such problems into linear programming models in Chapter 5.

However, a more basic difficulty with modeling this problem as an integer (otherwise linear) programming model is that it has *no feasible solution* (you might try solving the associated LP model, using any objective function you choose, and verify this fact).

Solution to the Model:

a. Investigate the constraints in an attempt to understand why this problem (as stated) has no feasible solution.

b. If the availability of capital is raised to $2.6 million (from $2.5 million), the model has feasible solutions. Use *weighted operating cost* as the criterion to be minimized (i.e., $x_0 = 1.5x_1 + 2.5x_2 + 3x_3 + 4x_4$), and solve the model as a linear program (initially ignore integer requirements). You should get the following model solution; we also solved the LP version of the fractional programming model, and this solution is also given.

Criterion		Variables			
	x_0	x_1	x_2	x_3	x_4
Weighted operating cost	$27.33	4.44	—	3.33	2.67
Average operating cost	1.91	8.73	6	—	—

Note that we get very different model solutions with the two different criteria.

Solution to the Problem:

a. The LP solutions are obviously useless to Al Aaron in their present form, since purchasing .44 or .73 of an aircraft is absurd. Experiment with rounding to see if you can find a feasible integer solution to the model, and compute the objective value generated by your solution using both criteria.

b. The optimal integer solution to the *weighted operating cost* model is as follows.

Variable	Description	Value
x_0	Cost	$28 per mile
x_1	Zinger	6 aircraft
x_2	Clunker	0 aircraft
x_3	Ramp Queen	5 aircraft
x_4	Banger	1 aircraft

Note the radical difference between the integer solution and the LP solution — although the weighted operating costs vary by only $.67 per mile. Was your "rounded" solution close?

c. Comment on possible solution approaches to this problem for a large international airline that wishes to order 400 large passenger jets and that has a budget of $3.5

billion. Assuming that there were only three or four aircraft models under consideration, would solving the LP model perhaps give a usable solution without having to
resort to IP algorithms? Why or why not?

d. One way of modeling and solving problems of this type is by transforming them into
equivalent "zero-one" IP models that can be solved by Balas's very efficient additive
algorithm. Note that, since only $2.6 million is available, the upper bounds on the
four decision variables are as follows.

$$u_1 = \$2,600,000/150,000 = 17 \text{ (rounded)}$$

$$u_2 = \$2,600,000/215,000 = 12 \text{ (rounded)}$$

$$u_3 = \$2,600,000/260,000 = 10$$

$$u_4 = \$2,600,000/400,000 = 6 \text{ (rounded)}$$

Thus, we would need five variables for x_1; four variables for x_2; four variables for x_3;
and three variables for x_4. Write the equivalent "zero-one" IP model using the
weighted operating cost criterion.

5. Consider the following toy model in integer programming.

$$\text{MAXIMIZE } x_0 = x_1 + 4x_2 \qquad (3.79)$$

$$\text{SUBJECT TO:} \qquad 5x_1 + 12x_2 \leq 840 \qquad (3.80)$$

$$x_1 + x_2 \leq 90 \qquad (3.81)$$

$$-11x_1 + 7x_2 \leq 65 \qquad (3.82)$$

$$x_1, x_2 \geq 0 \text{ and integer} \qquad (3.83)$$

a. Ignore the integer restrictions and solve the model with a computer LP package.
Your solution should be as follows (approximately).

Variable	Value	Slack Variable	Value
x_0	259.64	s_1	0
x_1	30.54	s_2	2.19
x_2	57.28	s_3	0

b. Add the following constraints to the model in (a), and solve the model with a computer LP package.

$$2x_1 + 5x_2 \leq 347 \qquad (3.84)$$

$$-x_1 + x_2 \leq 26 \qquad (3.85)$$

Your solution should be as follows (exactly):

Variable	Value	Slack Variable	Value
x_0	259	s_1	1
x_1	31	s_2	2
x_2	57	s_3	7
		s_4 (new)	0
		s_5 (new)	0

c. As you may have guessed, the solution in (b) is the optimal solution to the original IP model. The two additional constraints are "cuts" that slice off noninteger portions of the feasible region and create a vertex at the optimal lattice point. Thus, given these "cuts," we could solve IP problems using the ordinary simplex algorithm. How might we go about generating such constraints?

6.   ***The Scenario [11]:***   Reconsider the Blitzen Development, Inc., problem (Problem 7) in Chapter 2. Assume that each unit (whether it be an office, a store, or an apartment) contains a fixed amount of floor space, as prescribed by the following:

Unit Type	Floor Space (in square feet)
First floor	
Offices, quality 1	800
Offices, quality 2	700
Offices, quality 3	600
Stores, quality 1	1000
Apartments, quality 1	750
Apartments, quality 2	650
Second floor	
Offices, quality 1	800
Offices, quality 2	700
Offices, quality 3	600
Apartments, quality 1	750
Apartments, quality 2	650
Third floor	
Apartments, quality 1	750
Apartments, quality 2	650

The Problem: Clearly, this is an integer programming situation. Are decision variables of the zero-one variety or simply nonnegative integers?

The Model: Define decision variables as follows. Let x_j be the number of units of a particular type to be constructed on a particular floor. Write an objective function based upon total annual rents received from each type of unit. For example, according to the problem statement in Problem 7, Chapter 2, each square foot of floor space on the first floor of office quality 1 yields $4.50 rent. Therefore, each unit would yield 800×4.5 or $3600. Similar computations must be performed to find objective functions coefficients for the remaining 12 units. The constraints are formulated in a way analogous to the LP model. Consider the final constraint—the market survey constraint that requires that no more than 10% of the total building floor area can be of the office quality 1 type. Let T, total building floor area, be given by

$$T = 800x_1 + 700x_2 + 600x_3 + 1000x_4 + 750x_5$$
$$+ \, 650x_6 + 800x_7 + 700x_8 + 600x_9 + 750x_{10}$$
$$+ \, 650x_{11} + 750x_{12} + 650x_{13}$$

Assume that x_1 and x_7 represent the number of units of office quality type 1 on the first and second floors, respectively. Then the fraction of the total floor area for office quality 1 is $(800x_1 + 800x_7)/T$ so that

$$\frac{800x_1 + 800x_7}{800x_1 + 700x_2 + 600x_3 + 1000x_4 + \cdots + 750x_{12} + 650x_{13}} \leq .1$$

By multiplying both sides of the inequality by the denominator and combining common terms, this expression reduces to the following linear inequality:

$$720x_1 - 70x_2 - 60x_3 - 100x_4 - 75x_5 - 65x_6 + 720x_7 - 70x_8$$
$$- 60x_9 - 75x_{10} - 65x_{11} - 75x_{12} - 65x_{13} \leq 0$$

Formulate the remaining constraints.

Solution to the Model: If an integer programming algorithm is available, use it to solve this model.

Solution to the Problem: How would actual solution of the problem differ from the ILP solution? What extraneous factors would likely change the ILP solution? To what extent is the final solution influenced by the ILP solution?

REFERENCES

1. WAGNER, H. *Principles of Operations Research,* 2nd ed. Englewood Cliffs, N.J.: Prentice-Hall, 1975.
2. LAND, A., and A. DOIG. "An Automatic Method for Solving Discrete Programming Problems." *Econometrica,* Vol. 28, (1960), pp. 497–520.
3. DAKIN, R. "A Tree-Search Algorithm for Mixed Integer Programming Problems." *Computational Journal,* Vol. 8 (1965), pp. 250–255.
4. GOMORY, R. "An Algorithm for Integer Solutions to Linear Problems." In *Recent Advances in Mathematical Programming,* R. L. Graves and P. Wolfe, eds., pp. 269–302. New York: McGraw-Hill, 1963.
5. YOUNG, R. "A Simplified Primal (All-Integer) Integer Programming Algorithm." *Operations Research,* Vol. 16 (1968), pp. 750–782.
6. AUSTIN, L., and M. HANNA. "The Bounded Descent Algorithm for All-Integer Programming." *Naval Research Logistics Quarterly,* Vol. 30 (1983), pp. 271–281.
7. HANNA, M., "An All-Integer Cutting Plane Algorithm with an Advanced Start." Unpublished DBA dissertation, College of Business Administration, Texas Tech University (1981).
8. GHANDFOROUSH, P., and L. AUSTIN. "A Primal-Dual Cutting Plane Algorithm for All-Integer Programming." *Naval Research Logistics Quarterly,* Vol. 28 (1981), pp. 559–567.
9. BALAS, E. "An Additive Algorithm for Solving Linear Programs with Zero-One Variables." *Operations Research,* Vol. 13 (1965), pp. 517–546.
10. AUSTIN, L., and P. GHANDFOROUSH. "An Advanced Dual Algorithm with Constraint Relaxation for All-Integer Programming." *Naval Research Logistics Quarterly,* Vol. 30 (1983), pp. 133–143.
11. BARRETT, M. Adapted from an unpublished MBA term project, College of Business Administration, Texas Tech University (1983).

ADDITIONAL READING

GARFINKEL, R., and G. NEMHAUSER. *Integer Programming.* Toronto: John Wiley & Sons, 1972.

TAHA, H. *Integer Programming: Theory, Applications, and Computations.* New York: Academic Press, 1975.

ZIONTS, S. *Linear and Integer Programming.* Englewood Cliffs, N.J.: Prentice-Hall, 1974.

CHAPTER 4

Modeling with Networks

All of us encounter *networks* evey day of our lives. We drive to work or school or to appointments on networks of roads or streets. We switch on the television and activate a stream of electrons through the circuits of the set, magically plucking reruns of "MASH" from the air. The "rumor mill" in the office or the university is a network, as is the complex system of routes flown by commercial airlines. Since networks are ubiquitous in daily life, it seems reasonable to suppose that many business, industrial, and social problems can be modeled and analyzed using such a framework.

What is a network? We will begin with a cryptic definition.

A **network** is a set of nodes connected by arcs.

If we only knew what *nodes* and *arcs* were, and precisely what "connected" meant, we would instantly understand the definition of *network*. We will create a working definition by analogy and example.

Figure 4.1 is a network that Harry Driver, a CPA, faces each weekday morning. Harry and his family live in the peaceful suburb of Sourceburg, and Harry must commute each morning by automobile to his office in the busy metropolis of Sink City. The circles in Figure 4.1 represent major road intersections (nodes) and the lines connecting them represent major thoroughfares (arcs). Arrows at the end of arcs represent allowable directions of travel, so that arcs G–F and L–J, for instance, represent one-way streets or roads, and the darkened arcs with arrows at both ends (e.g., A–M, or Kamikaze Freeway) represent two-way streets or roads.

There obviously are many routes that Harry can take to or from work. For example,

Home to work: Sourceburg–D–H–G–F–I–O–Sink City
or   Sourceburg–A–M–Q–R–O–Sink City

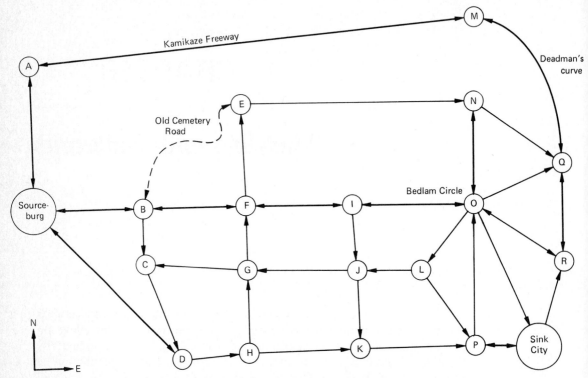

Figure 4.1 A commuter network.

Work to home: Sink City – P – O – L – J – G – C – D – Sourceburg
or   Sink City – R – Q – M – A – Sourceburg

Note in Figure 4.1 that Harry *cannot* proceed directly from C to F or from L to Sink City, since these nodes are not *connected* by arcs. Note also the wide differences among nodes in terms of access and egress. For example, there is only one way to access node H (from D) and only two nodes that are directly accessible from H (nodes G and K). On the other hand, node O (Bedlam Circle) must be very busy during rush hour, with access available from *four* nodes and egress available to *six* nodes. In our example, Harry Driver may wish to select a route to work and perhaps a different one by which to return home, based on one of several criteria. One criterion might be to minimize total distance traveled, in which case he has the problem of finding the *shortest route* through a network. Another reasonable criterion might be minimization of total travel time to and from work, which is known as a *minimum cost* (i.e., minimum time in Harry's case) *route* through a network. There are other possibilities as well, such as "minimize danger to life and limb," which would probably involve a route that avoids high-speed, heavily traveled streets or roads (Sourceburg – B – C – D – H – G – F – I – J – K – P – Sink City might qualify).

As we shall shortly see, these scenarios do not begin to exhaust the possibilities of modeling problems as networks. But what advantage do we gain by using this approach? If we recall ILP models from Chapter 3, we used zero-one variables to model situations in which a particular attribute or object is *active* in an optimal solution ($x_{ij} = 1$) or inactive ($x_{ij} = 0$). We can easily verify that Figure 4.1 contains 47 distinct arcs (note that two-way arcs must be considered to be two *separate* arcs), so that 47 zero-one variables may be used to represent the inclusion or exclusion of each arc from the desired route. If we add constraints that assure that the resulting solution is a *path* (an unbroken chain of arcs from *source* to *sink*), then minimizing some *weighted sum* of these variables (e.g., total distance, total travel time) results in a zero-one ILP model, which can be solved with Balas's additive algorithm.

But we already know the answer to the question: Network models take advantage of *special problem structures* to develop special, highly efficient algorithms, some of which we will discuss later in this chapter. But in the case of network models, there is another important advantage in a managerial sense, in that networks can be represented graphically in such a way that our understanding of the underlying problem is considerably enhanced. As an illustration, modeling Harry's "drive-to-work" problem in Figure 4.1 as a zero-one ILP model would involve 47 variables and 600 constraints. Very little managerial insight would be gained by poring over the resulting mathematical symbols; on the other hand, we immediately grasp the nature of the problem when presented with the graphical representation in Figure 4.1.

UNDERLYING ASSUMPTIONS

Since network models are all special cases of zero-one ILP models, we see that, at a minimum, they must conform to the basic assumptions discussed in Chapter 3. But while all network problems can be modeled as zero-one ILP models, the converse is *not* true. As an illustration, let us return to Figure 4.1 and suppose that Harry Driver is attempting to minimize his driving time from Sink City to Sourceburg. Let us impose one, seemingly innocuous, additional condition that no left turn is allowed at F by cars traveling northbound from G. Note that this does *not* remove arc F–B as a viable route for cars coming from I — only for those coming from G. This restriction is called a *side condition* and effectively prevents us from modeling this problem as a network. Note that an ILP model easily accommodates this side condition by use of an "if-then" constraint (see Chapter 3); that is, we impose the restriction "if $x_{GF} = 1$, then $x_{FB} = 0$." Unfortunately, there is no way of representing such a restriction in the network itself.

The basic underlying assumption that permits modeling a problem as a network is that the problem has what is sometimes called the "semi-Markov property." This impressive-sounding label means only *that there are no relationships between arcs other than those defined by associated nodes* and that nodes must define the *same* relationships for each incoming and outgoing arc. This concept will become clearer as we explore various network models.

NETWORK MODELING AND ALGORITHMS

In this section, we will discuss four basic and very useful network models:

1. Shortest route
2. Longest route
3. Minimal spanning tree
4. Optimal flow

Since we will be dealing with four *distinct* network models, we will discuss each model and its optimizing algorithm together rather than separating the modeling and algorithm treatments as we did in the previous chapters.

SHORTEST ROUTE THROUGH A NETWORK

We have already seen an example of a shortest-route model—the network in Figure 4.1 representing Harry Driver's commuting problem. It is worth noting at this point that "shortest" does not necessarily refer to physical distance. Perhaps a more descriptive title might be "Least Cost Route Through a Network," where the total "cost" to be minimized might be distance, time, expense, traffic density, exposure to speedtraps, and so on. At any rate, the shortest-route model involves identifying a "cost" c_{ij} for each arc (noting that c_{ij} *may* not be equal to c_{ji}), and the solution entails finding a path from Source (origin) to Sink (destination) that minimizes the sum of "costs" on the traversed arcs.

Before discussing an example, we must first address a subtle but important point regarding network configurations. If all "costs" for each arc are *nonnegative,* then we may proceed to find the shortest route (least cost path) through the network without further complication. However, if some or all of the costs are *negative,* then we must be concerned with whether we are dealing with an *acyclic* or a *cyclic* network. Stated simply, an acyclic network is one in which it is impossible to leave a node and traverse a path that returns to the same node. For example, the network in Figure 4.1 is *not* acyclic, since we can proceed from I to J to G to F and back to I. Note that if the sum of "costs" on this closed loop happened to be negative, then our minimizing algorithm would cycle through the loop over and over—decreasing the value of the objective function with each tour. Obviously, if the sum of "costs" were positive, the algorithm would not behave in this unusual way. For now, we will assume that all "costs" on arcs are nonnegative and thus avoid the problem of cycling. When we address "longest-route" problems in the next section, however, we will deal with this problem directly.

Shortest-Route Model — An Example
Rollin Stone, the big-time rock-'n-roll promoter, manages 20 rock groups who tour the United States and average 40 concerts each year. Some of the fastest-rising and most sought-after groups (e.g., Freddie and the Ear-Plugs, the Dull Roars, Ichabod and the Headless Horsemen) are in Rollin's "stable," and his

organization is responsible for contracting play dates, scheduling trips, and handling all the other complex logistics involved.

In an idle moment in his office, Rollin does some quick calculations on the back of an envelope. "Let's see," he muses to himself, "there are about 6 performers on the average in each group, and each group travels about 40 times a year. If airline tickets average out at about $200 a copy, that's — wow — like almost a million bucks a year! If I could cut that down a few hundred thou, it would be pure gravy."

Glancing at his wall map of the United States, Rollin notes that his bookings usually include over 150 cities in a given year, so that there are $150 \cdot 149 = 22{,}350$ combinations in which a group can play in one city and travel to the next. The matter is complicated further by the fact that the great majority of these combinations are not connected by direct flights; that is, two or more "legs" are required to go from one city to another. Finally, by taking advantage of various airline "specials," making flight reservations for the groups could be done in such a way as to minimize total air fares.

This scenario describes a problem that can be modeled profitably as a network. The nodes are, of course, the locations in which the 20 rock groups have play dates *and* other cities that provide airline links between these locations. Rollin's objective can be stated rigorously as follows: Find the path between each pair of cities in which play dates are scheduled that minimizes the per person airline fare. If there are n such cities, then there are $n(n-1)$ models for shortest routes through a network. (*Note:* Because of airline "specials" and other factors, the fare from city A to city B is not necessarily the same as from city B to city A. If the fares *are* identical in every case, then there are only $n(n-1)/2$ shortest-route models to contend with.)

Although this problem appears to be difficult to solve for large n, we shall see later that there are highly efficient algorithms that can solve problems of the magnitude of Rollin's in a few seconds on a high-speed computer.

Shortest-Route Algorithms

Highly efficient algorithms for finding the shortest route through networks have been around for many years. Basically, these algorithms *implicitly* perform SIMPLEX-like operations directly on the arc distances (or other criteria) and use shadow prices — and duality theory — to construct minimal paths. The most useful techniques automatically discover the shortest route from every node to every other node in the network, so that our rock promoter Rollin Stone would be able to solve his travel cost minimization problem quickly and efficiently. In fact, massive problems with hundreds of thousands of arcs have been solved in seconds (or at worst minutes) on modern, high-speed computers.

LONGEST ROUTE THROUGH A NETWORK

Other than the special case of a New York cabbie who takes tourists from Kennedy Airport to their downtown Manhattan hotels, why would anyone be interested in finding the *longest* path through a network? If we use our imagination, many such situations come to mind. For example, if arcs in a network represent graduate courses, the arrangement of nodes and arcs represents the prerequisite structure of our set of courses, and we can attach a weight to each course to indicate its relative importance, then the longest route through the network wold represent in some sense the *best feasible curriculum attainable.* A more recreational example might be to model the network of ski trails at Vail, Colorado, and to ski the mountain in such a way that the maximum total distance is traversed on the way to the bottom. The best known and most widely used application of the longest-route model, however, is finding the "critical path" through a network representing the activities that constitute a major project. More about this later. First, however, we must settle the "cyclic" versus "acyclic" network question.

Node Labeling in Networks

In Figure 4.1, which has a total of 20 nodes and 47 connecting arcs, it is a simple matter to inspect the network diagram visually and discover the cycles that exist. However, in large network models of real problems, the network diagram (if we actually hired a draftsman to draw it) might cover the playing field in a football stadium! Our "eyeball algorithm" would obviously be useless in such a situation.

As a small illustration, consider the 19-node, 39-arc network in Figure 4.2. Can you find a cycle in this small network by visual inspection? Perhaps you can — there are several (e.g., $16 - 12 - 14 - 17 - 16$). With 500 nodes and several thousand arcs, however, the task becomes too difficult to do by inspection, and we must have an organized method for doing two things:

1. Discovering whether a given network is cyclic
2. If the network is acyclic, numbering the nodes in such a way that *no node can be reached with a path beginning at a higher numbered node*

Such a technique, called the *node-labeling algorithm,* is incorporated into the shortest/longest — route computer codes discussed subsequently.

The Critical Path Model (CPM)

Consider the contract just signed by Ray Wray, chief executive officer of Ray's Raze and Raise, Inc. (RRR), to demolish a 200-year-old art gallery in downtown Philadelphia and subsequently to build a 20-story discotheque, a fast-food restaurant, and a parking garage in its place. We can imagine the thousands of individual activities that comprise such a massive project — as well as the complex set of *precedences* that exist between and among these activities. As a rather obvious example, RRR would certainly want to evacuate the immediate environs before setting off the dynamite to demolish the old gallery!

From experience, RRR can estimate the time required to perform each of the many individual activities, but the critical item of managerial information needed is the time to complete the entire *project.* If we model the activities as arcs in a network, and view the associated nodes as *events* in time (completion of one or more activities; beginning of other activities), we can model the problem in such a way that precedence relationships are maintained in the resulting acyclic network. The *longest route* through this project network will

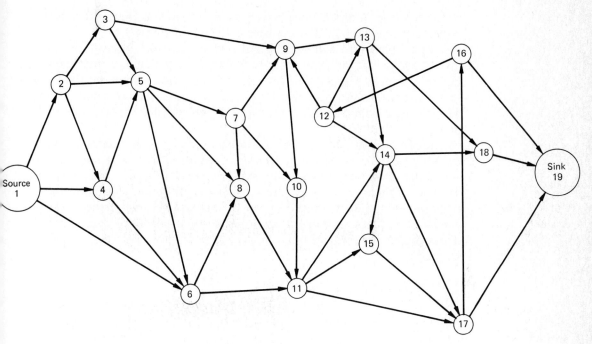

Figure 4.2 Cyclic network.

give the manager an indication of the total time required to complete this project.

In applications, project networks are usually constructed by first setting up a "macro network" consisting of large-scale activities. In the RRR illustration, suppose this network consists of the following 13 macro activities.

Activity	Description	Predecessor Activities	Expected Number of Days Required
A	Set TNT charges	—	5
B	Evacuate environs	—	4
C	Assemble dump-truck fleet	—	3
D	Detonate TNT	A, B	1
E	Clean up rubble	C, D	7
F	Excavate basement	E	12
G	Erect steel superstructure	E	15
H	Pour concrete foundation	F	10
I	Install electric/plumbing	F, G	8
J	Install flooring	I	15
K	Hang walls	I	20
L	Install elevators	I	7
M	Do finishing work	H, J, K, L	14

Note that certain activities may be pursued simultaneously (e.g., activities A, B, and C), whereas others cannot be begun until their predecessors have been completed (e.g., A and B must be completed before D is begun). The macro project network for the RRR example is given in Figure 4.3.

Some explanation is in order with regard to Figure 4.3. Note, for instance, that the activity arc for E emanates from node 4 — and that the activity arcs for C and D terminate in node 4. This means that the *earliest* time activity E can start is the *later* of the times that C or D can be completed. This makes sense, when we note from the activity descriptions that activities C and D are predecessors of activity E.

But what about the unlabeled dashed line connecting nodes 2 and 3? Couldn't we have connected nodes 1 and 3 with *two* activity arcs A and B to assure that these activities are completed before D is begun? The answer is, "Yes, we could have." However, in deference to the limited capabilities of our electronic computer, we must use an extra node and a *dummy activity* to avoid confusion. Here's why. When we assemble the input data for computer analysis of our project network, we must describe each activity with three unique descriptors:

1. Node number at the tail of the arc
2. Node number at the head of the arc
3. Activity time of the arc

If more than one arc had the same nodes as heads and tails, the computer would become hopelessly confused. Thus, it is necessary to use additional nodes and dummy arcs (with activity times of zero) to define uniquely the project network for purposes of computer analysis. We see in Figure 4.3 that this device was also used to indicate that both F and G are predecessors of I and that J, K, and L are all predecessors of M.

If you are concerned at this point that constructing a network for a large project might be an extremely complicated and time-consuming chore, please do not be. As we will see later, there are computer packages that construct an *algebraic* representation of the project network directly from the activity table, so that the actual network (as in Figure 4.3) does not need to be constructed. However, a visual representation of the project is often a valuable managerial tool as well as a helpful device in assisting us to understand project relationships.

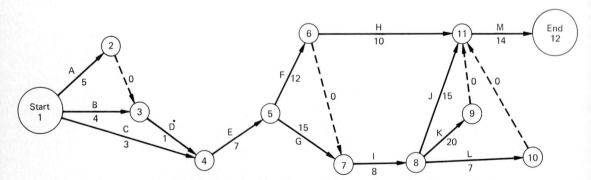

Figure 4.3 RRR macro project network.

The longest path through the network in Figure 4.3 requires a total of 70 days. Usually called the *critical path* for obvious reasons, in our example this path traverses nodes $1-2-3-4-5-7-8-9-11-12$, so that the *critical activities* are A, D, E, G, I, K, and M. Thus if any one of these critical activities is delayed, the entire project will be delayed as well.

Longest-Route Algorithms

For the general longest-route network model, an optimal solution can be generated by the simple device of reversing the algebraic signs of the "distances" and employing a shortest-route algorithm. In the special case of a project scheduling network, we are interested in knowing the earliest and latest starting times for each activity — as well as the critical path (longest route) through the network. Special algorithms called "two-pass" procedures have been developed for such models, but the basic approach remains the same.

MINIMAL SPANNING TREE MODEL

The basic purpose of spanning trees is to connect the nodes in such a way that every node can be reached from every other node by traversing designated arcs. A *minimal* spanning tree consists of a set of $n - 1$ arcs (there are n nodes) such that all nodes are "spanned" or connected and the total cost or distance is as small as possible. To illustrate the minimal spanning tree model, consider the following problem of installing a sprinkler system in a golf course.

Anita Parr, a former women's golf pro, is now the operations manager for the R. G. Bunker Country Club in Scottsdale, Arizona. Her report that the putting greens are in bad shape has elicited action from the board of directors — and Anita has the funds available to install a much needed sprinkler system. However, she is well aware that the cost of installing the system of waterpipes depends on the total length of pipe in the system, and she wishes to plan the system in such a way that each of the 18 greens has a sprinkler, that water is pumped from a single source near the club house, and that total pipe length is minimized. As a side benefit, she realizes that water pressure is inversely related to total system pipe footage.

Anita's problem — and a multitude of related problems — can be modeled as a network in which nodes represent sites to be serviced (e.g., putting greens) and arcs represent access mechanisms (e.g., waterpipes). Other illustrations include providing telephone or cable television service to a set of rural communities, scheduling regional airline service, establishing battlefield communications among combat units, providing road service among scenic areas in a large national park, and so on. Such problems can be profitably modeled using specialized networks called *minimal spanning trees*.

The Minimal Spanning Tree Algorithm

The minimal spanning tree algorithm is one of the simplest and most elegant optimizing techniques in all of MS. It is one of the very few algorithms in which "greedy" behavior is rewarded with an optimal result. For example, in the transportation problem, we might consider using a greedy approach. That is, we could find the arc with the smallest cost and ship as much as possible on that arc.

After reducing the supply and demand parameters by the amount shipped, we could repeat this process with the next lowest cost, and so on, until we had a feasible solution. Unfortunately, this greedy behavior usually leads to a suboptimal — and sometimes very poor — solution.

Although we promised earlier in the text not to belabor you with algorithmic details, the minimum spanning tree technique is so easy to understand and use that we cannot resist sharing it in its glorious simplicity.

Minimal Spanning Tree Algorithm

Step 1: Choose any node and include the arc for the node closest to it in the spanning tree. Go to step 2.

Step 2: Scan all nodes currently connected by an arc in the spanning tree, and locate the unconnected node that is closest to a connected node. Include this arc in the spanning tree and go to step 3.

Step 3: If all nodes are connected, stop; the minimal spanning tree has been found. Otherwise, go to step 2.

That's all there is to it! If there are n nodes, there will be exactly $(n - 1)$ arcs in the minimal spanning tree, so that computational effort depends only on the number of nodes — and not on the number of arcs. If you wish to try out this algorithm, an example computer network model is depicted in Figure 4.4. The minimal spanning tree is denoted by the darkened arcs. If you are still skeptical, you might choose different starting nodes in step 1 and confirm that you always get the same answer, with a total spanning distance of 106 units.

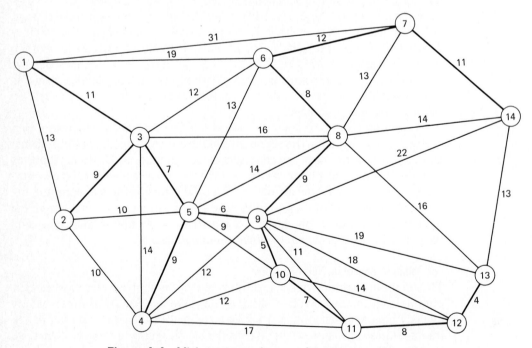

Figure 4.4   Minimum spanning tree for computer network.

OPTIMAL NETWORK FLOW MODEL

Perhaps the most widely used network representation is the optimal network flow model. As an illustration, let us view the commuter network in Figure 4.1 in a different way.

Carl Poole is the commissioner for roads and streets in Noah County—in which both Sourceburg and Sink City are located. As suburban Sourceburg grows, Carl is concerned that the traffic system leading to Sink City will become saturated, and he wishes to pinpoint bottleneck streets and roads for possible widening. Using standard criteria such as number of traffic lanes, speed limit, street or road conditions, and so on, Carl estimates the *maximum traffic flow in vehicles per hour* for each street segment (arc) between each major intersection (node). His results are depicted graphically in Figure 4.5, with flow capacities annotated on the arcs. (*Note:* On two-way streets, differential flows in each direction are separated by a slashmark.) If Carl can compute the *maximum flow* through this network, then streets or roads that are *at capacity* would be candidates for managerial attention.

Taking this illustration one step farther, consider the possibility of developing engineering estimates of the maximum *possible* traffic flows on each road segment resulting from widening the segment, changing the speed limit, and so on. If the cost of road improvements can be estimated in dollars per unit of increased flow, then we have a classical *minimum cost flow* model.

There are several special cases of the network flow model, and these special

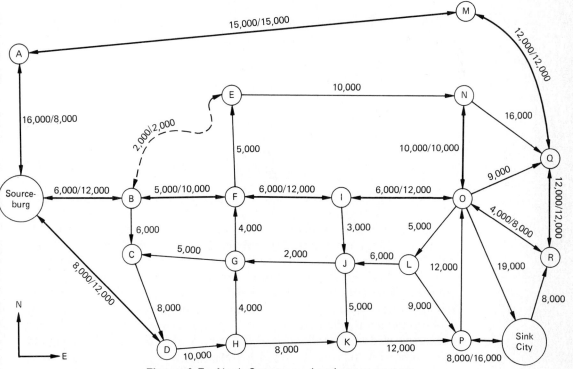

Figure 4.5 Noah County road and street system.

situations are employed so widely in practice that they have their own descriptive titles — the transportation model, the assignment model, and the transshipment model. We discuss each of these special cases.

The Transportation Model

Scarborough Condiments, Inc. (SCI), is a national distributor of spices, supplying 25 supermarket chains with "house brands" that they package and label themselves. Rosemary Thyme, who is SCI's vice-president of production, introduced the concept of a basic production unit, which is a 100-pound bale of assorted spices, and the company's 12 plants process and ship these units to advance orders from 200 supermarket supply points. Production costs vary at each of the 12 plants, as do shipping costs from the plants to the supermarket supply points. Parsley Sage, who is Rosemary's assistant vice-president, is responsible for assigning monthly production quotas to the plants as well as determining shipping patterns.

A bit of reflection reveals that SCI's problem can be modeled as a linear program. Let

x_{ij} = number of bales shipped from plant i to destination j

c_{ij} = production cost at plant i, plus shipping cost from plant i to destination j

S_i = production capacity of plant i

D_j = demand at destination j

Then the cost minimization LP model for the SCI problem may be written as

$$\text{MINIMIZE } x_0 = \sum_{i=1}^{12} \sum_{j=1}^{200} c_{ij}x_{ij} \qquad (4.1)$$

$$\text{SUBJECT TO: } \sum_{i=1}^{12} x_{ij} = D_j, \quad j = 1, \ldots, 200 \qquad (4.2)$$

$$\sum_{j=1}^{200} x_{ij} \le S_i, \quad i = 1, \ldots, 12 \qquad (4.3)$$

$$x_{ij} \ge 0; \quad i = 1, \ldots, 12, \quad j = 1, \ldots, 200 \qquad (4.4)$$

As we have seen, *modeling* a problem in a certain way, and *solving* the resulting model, are two quite different matters. For instance, the LP model has only 212 constraints: 200 in (4.2) that assure that the demands are satisfied and 12 in (4.3) that limit shipments from each plant to no more than its capacity. However, there are *2400 variables!* If SCI has access only to a microcomputer, it is highly unlikely that the LP model will even fit in the computer's memory.

Fortunately, problems such as SCI's can be modeled as special kinds of networks called *transportation models*. Figure 4.6 portrays a small transportation model with three *origins* (supply points) A, B, and C, and four *destinations* (demand points) 1, 2, 3, and 4. The nodes labeled "Source" and "Sink" are

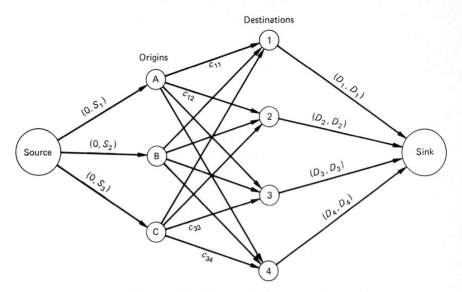

Figure 4.6 Transportation network.

added to represent the system as a network flow model. The numbers in parentheses represent minimum flow and maximum flow, respectively, through the associated arc.

Note how cleverly the network represents the associated LP model. Flow restrictions on the arcs from the "Source" to the "Supply" nodes allow no more than the production capacity for each plant to "flow into the plant," so that by something called *conservation of flow,* each plant can ship no more than its capacity. The arcs from origins to destinations are essentially uncapacitated — except that negative flow is not allowed. The arcs from the destination nodes to the "Sink" node must allow flows representing the actual demands (since both upper and lower bounds are set at the same level), so that — again because of conservation of flow — the demands are met exactly on the arcs between origin and destination nodes. The optimizing algorithm (to be discussed later) generates a flow pattern that minimizes the sum of total costs.

Some additional modeling features need to be addressed. If the total supply is greater than the total demand, there is no problem — total flow in the network can never exceed total demand. However, if total demand exceeds total supply, we *do* indeed have a problem. Some texts advise the modeler merely to add a "dummy" plant with production capacity sufficient to meet the unfilled demand — with a production and shipping cost of zero for these make-believe units. To a mathematician, this is a logical and elegant procedure; to a managerial decision maker, it is foolishness. We illustrate this observation with the following vignette.

"Boss," complains Quigley Sackett to the processing center supervisor for Callihan's Kosher Delicatessens, "the SCI shipment just came in, and they shorted us 75 bales on our order. When I called Parsley Sage, he mumbled something about having to use dummy supplies to make his algorithm work."

"After being steady customers for 15 years, we get dummies from SCI?" the supervisor exclaims. "Fine. Send them a dummy check and a sympathy card for their algorithm. And switch our spice account over to Acme."

The point, of course, is that a network model — or *any* analytical device for that matter — ignores such niceties as customer goodwill and other exogenous considerations. It is the *manager's* job to use logic, experience, and common sense to resolve difficulties such as those just noted.

Other constraints can be dealt with directly in the transportation network. For example, if limited shipping facilities are available between some origins and destinations, then upper bounds can be placed on the appropriate arcs to reflect this situation. Moreover, suppose that we are concerned with economies of scale at the production facilities represented by origins. We merely place appropriate lower bounds on the arcs from "Source" to the origin nodes. Finally, if we wish to maximize profit contribution (or some other criterion) in a transportation network, we minimize the total "cost" by using the *negatives* of the c_{ij}'s.

The Assignment Model

The *assignment model* is a special case of the transportation model, in which all supplies $S_i = 1$ and all demands $D_j = 1$. As an example, consider the problem faced daily by Juliet Romeo, chief consultant for the Capulet & Montague Computer Dating Service. Based on the analysis of questionnaires, a computer program rates each female subscriber for compatibility with each male subscriber, on a scale of 1 (instant hostility) to 20 (total empathy). Juliet's problem is to arrange n dates — n being the smaller of the numbers of women and men subscribers — so as to maximize the overall compatibility of that evening's trysts. We see that if we designate the larger group as "origins" and the other as "destinations," we have a simplified transportation problem. If we reversed this designation, we would be back in the awkward position of having to use "dummy" subscribers to make the algorithm work — a situation that Juliet would wish to assiduously avoid.

This example should not mask the importance of assignment models. They are used thousands of times each day to schedule personnel, assign aircraft to routes, route jobs onto machines, and for dozens of other purposes.

The Transshipment Model

In its original form, the transshipment model was described as a transportation network with a set of intermediate nodes between the origins and destinations. For example, in our Scarborough Condiments, Inc., problem, suppose that the plants shipped their output to a set of six warehouses and that the spice bales were then supplied to supermarket supply points from the warehouses. Although it may not be immediately obvious, this model *cannot* be solved optimally by first optimizing the shipment between plants and warehouses and then solving a separate transportation problem for warehouses and destinations. This procedure will almost always result in a *suboptimal* solution to the overall model. Happily, the intermediate nodes can be inserted into the network, appropriate arcs constructed and bounded, and a network flow model results.

As a modeling device, however, transshipment networks are *not* limited to a single set of intermediate nodes (e.g., warehouses). That is, *several* stages of transshipment can easily be included. An interesting "real-world" application of this technique was applied to the U.S. Air Force's undergraduate flying training program.

COMMENTS ON NETWORK MODELING

As we remarked at the beginning of this chapter, network models are special cases of ILP models. We also noted that the *visual* nature of networks is important in two respects: It gives insight to the underlying problem that mathematical notation cannot give; and it makes network modeling much easier to explain to unsophisticated colleagues. We shall see shortly that specialized network algorithms have been constructed and that these techniques are significantly more efficient (in computer implementation) than are ILP or even LP algorithms in solving network models.

But how do we recognize problems that can be modeled as networks? In many cases—such as critical path or spanning tree or transportation-type problems—it will be obvious. In other cases, a network formulation may be far from obvious. For example, consider the "overhaul or replace" problem for expensive equipment such as an injection molding machine. Suppose that we have just purchased one of these behemoths for $\$P_1$ and we must plan to either overhaul the current machine or purchase a new one, each year for five years into the future. Let

P_i = replacement cost at beginning of year i, $i = 1, \ldots, 5$

O_j = overhaul cost after j consecutive overhauls, $j = 0, \ldots, 4$

There is obviously a "best" strategy to follow, since we will assume that replacement costs rise with inflation and that overhaul costs escalate both because of inflation and due to rising costs associated with overhauling aging equipment (i.e., it costs more to overhaul a three-year-old injection molding machine than it does a one-year-old one). This problem can obviously be modeled as an IP problem, since it is a "go/no go" problem. However, it can also be modeled as a network, as in Figure 4.7. Note that the nodes represent the beginning of years 1, 2, . . . , 6. The 21 arcs represent decisions with respect to "overhaul or replace," and any path through the network corresponds to a strategy. For example, the path "1 – 3 – 4 – 6" would involve overhauling the machine in year 2, buying new machines in years 3 and 4, and overhauling the new machine in year 5. The total cost of this strategy would be

$$c_{13} + c_{34} + c_{46} = (P_1 + O_1) + P_3 + (P_4 + O_1) \tag{4.5}$$

It is now apparent that if we compute each of the costs c_{ij} and place them on the network, we have a simple shortest-route model to solve.

The point is this: Network modeling is an *art*, and its usefulness in many cases depends on the insight and experience of the modeler.

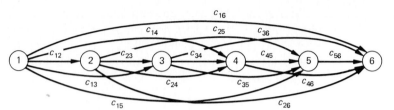

Figure 4.7 Overhaul or replace model.

Network Flow Algorithms

Since problems that can be represented as network flow models are so important in real-world applications, a great deal of research has been done in developing efficient optimizing algorithms for such models. Until very recently, the colorfully titled "out-of-kilter" algorithm of Ford and Fulkerson [2] was thought to be the most efficient computational technique possible. This approach, as is true for so many others, relies on results from LP duality theory for its power and effectiveness. Briefly, it uses parameters called "kilter numbers" to characterize network arcs—and the nature of these kilter numbers indicates whether the flow restrictions are violated, or whether current flow in an arc should be increased or decreased to improve the value of the objective function. This approach is still widely used in practice.

However, in recent years, highly efficient algorithms have been developed and tested by Bradley et al. [3] and Barr et al. [4] that outperform "out-of-kilter" codes. The basic approach of these new techniques is to take advantage of the specialized structure of so-called *generalized networks* to increase greatly computational efficiency. The technical details of these techniques are too complex for our purposes, but we note that many very large network models that were essentially intractable before can now be solved in a reasonable amount of computer time.

AVAILABLE NETWORK COMPUTER CODES

We first discuss available network optimization codes for implementation on large mainframe computers, and then we describe network packages for mini- and microcomputers. We note here that the minimal spanning tree algorithm is so simple to implement on a computer that an undergraduate business student could program the technique in an hour; therefore, we omit such codes in our coverage.

NETWORK CODES FOR MAINFRAME COMPUTERS

The shortest-route model (or the general longest-route model) can be solved efficiently by an algorithm developed by Spira [5]. This technique, with highly efficient data manipulation techniques and certain modifications, is available as one of the packages in the International Mathematical Software Library (IMSL). IMSL also includes a critical path method (CPM) code for analyzing large-scale project networks. This code also analyzes the *stochastic* version of CPM, referred to as PERT (*p*rogram *e*valuation and *r*eview *t*echnique), which we discuss in Chapter 11.

The highly efficient code GNET is available from Gordon H. Bradley at the Naval Postgraduate School in Monterey, California; a similar (perhaps more efficient) code PNET can be obtained from Darwin Klingman at the University of Texas in Austin. Both codes have been tested successfully on immense transportation, transshipment, assignment, and network flow models, and both show marked improvement over previous approaches. Versions of the original "out-of-kilter" code abound, but they have been shown to be less efficient than the GNET and PNET codes discussed here.

NETWORK CODES FOR MINI- AND MICROCOMPUTERS

Managers with access to Hewlett-Packard machines can acquire the program GCPATH, which is a longest-route algorithm. Shortest-route models can be solved by entering the negatives of the "distances." The BASIC program TRANSP solves transportation and assignment problems using a variant of the original transportation algorithm by Hitchcock [6]. The code is not very efficient and is used mainly as a pedagogical device in business schools. TRANSP is only partially interactive, so complete documentation is required for its use.

The BASIC code PATH, developed by James R. Burns, solves both shortest- and longest-route models. PATH is completely interactive, allowing the user to select one of the two objectives (shortest or longest route) and guiding the input step by step. Another program developed by the same author, called NETOK, is also available. NETOK implements the "out-of-kilter" algorithm for network flow models and is completely interactive.

With regard to the program PATH, we might note that a node-labeling algorithm is built into the code. Thus, if you are dealing with a longest-route model that happens to be a cyclic network (probably due to a modeling error), PATH will discover that fact and notify you. Moreover, to use either PATH or NETOK, it is *not* necessary to draw the actual network involved.

DEVELOPING ALTERNATIVE SOLUTIONS

As usual, we stress that using the output from quantitative models to develop alternative solutions to underlying problems is a critically important managerial activity. In the previous chapters on LP and ILP, you will recall that we were dealing solely with *optimizing* models (i.e., models that sought the best solutions available). Our task, then, was to generate *good* alternative model solutions that afforded managerial flexibility in finding a solution to the problem we were addressing. Some network models—minimal spanning tree, shortest route, minimum cost flow—are also optimizing. Others—finding the critical path in a project network, finding the maximum flow in a capacitated network—are essentially *descriptive*. We deal with these two types separately in the following.

DESCRIPTIVE NETWORK MODELS

Consider, first, the project scheduling problem and the critical path through the project network. How can a decision maker use the output from, say, PATH, to develop managerial strategies? (*Note:* There are no "alternative solutions" in the usual sense for a descriptive model.) Let us examine the output from PATH for the RRR problem depicted in Figure 4.3:

Critical Path Analysis

Critical path: A−D−E−G−I−K−M
Project completion time: 70 days

Noncritical Activity	Total Slack	Free Slack
B	1	1
C	3	3
F	3	0
H	21	21
J	5	5
L	13	13

First and most obvious, we would want to take a close look at our estimates of completion times for activities on the critical path. Every day we underestimate these times represents a day added to project completion time, and we want our estimates for the critical activities to be as good as possible.

Next we turn to noncritical activities. The column labeled "Total Slack" refers to the number of days these activities can slip or stretch out — *all immediate successor activities starting as late as possible* — without affecting project completion time. In the example, our only serious prospective problem might be with activity B — evacuating people from the vicinity of the old building. We have estimated that this activity will require four days, but we have only one day of "slack" to play with.

The column labeled "Free Slack" gives us an indication of how the noncritical activities interact. In the RRR problem, only activity F — excavation of the basement — has no free slack. The reason for this is that activity H can start as early as the day 25; if this occurs, then activity F *must* start at day 13 and end at day 25 — leaving no slack whatsoever.

Finally, the output from a CPM model can be used to assist managers in making resource allocation decisions. For example, in the absence of highly restrictive trade union agreements, fewer workers could be assigned to activity H (pouring the concrete foundation), effectively lengthening the completion time for this noncritical activity. The resources thus saved could be applied to critical activities such as G, I, or J to shorten their activity times, and thus shorten project completion time.

Another purely descriptive network model involves finding the maximum flow pattern through a capacitated network. In our earlier example, Carl Poole of Noah County used such a model to identify potential "bottlenecks" in the road and street system. An analysis very similar to the CPM discussion can be used to develop alternative strategies in this type of decision-making situation.

OPTIMIZING NETWORK MODELS

In modeling a problem as a shortest-route network model, we are seeking a path from each node in a set of nodes to each node in another (possibly nonexclusive) set. Two different managerial approaches are possible in performing sensitivity analysis on such models. First, analogous to the critical path discussion, the optimizing algorithm has (in a different sense) identified a set of critical arcs that constitute the *shortest* path through the network. We might wish to recheck our estimates carefully for the "distances" on these arcs to assure that they are accurate enough for our purposes. Second, as we discussed in LP and ILP models, there are efficient algorithms (e.g., Shier [7]) that generate the k best solutions to the model and thereby generate good, suboptimal solutions that serve as viable alternatives for the decision maker. In this way, if environmental considerations for some reason make the shortest route nonviable, the manager has good substitutes at hand.

When using minimum-cost flow networks as modeling devices, we are in luck regarding the availability of sensitivity analysis tools. We recall from our previous discussion that the special structure of network models (and especially network flow models) means that their ILP formulation-can be solved directly with the simplex algorithm — assuming that the right-hand sides of the constraints are integers. Since modern, efficient algorithms for solving these problems are based on LP theory, shadow prices are also available to aid us in our sensitivity analysis. Thus, our discussion on developing alternative solutions in Chapter 2, carries over directly for minimum cost flow network models.

STATE OF THE ART IN NETWORK MODELING

The literature dealing with modeling and solution approaches in networks is rich and varied. In this section, we will briefly discuss a few advanced topics and specialized models to get a flavor of this variety, but we must understand that our coverage is far from exhaustive. To accomplish this, we would need an entire text of this size!

THE CHINESE POSTMAN MODEL

Recall from Chapter 3 that the traveling salesman model involves a network with n nodes and with arcs connecting every node to every other node. The object is to visit every node exactly once and return to the starting node in such a way that total distance traveled (or cost incurred, etc.) is a minimum. The well-known "Chinese postman problem," named after its formulator M. Kwan [8], is a variant of the traveling salesman problem in that not all the nodes are connected to others by arcs. The object is to travel each arc at least once, and return to the original starting point, in such a way that the total distance traveled is minimum. This is precisely the problem faced by a postman — and hence the name (Kwan, as you may have guessed, is a Chinese mathematician). Other real-world problems can also be modeled in this way, for example, routing of street cleaners, snow removal crews, sanitary engineering teams (once known as garbage collectors), political canvassers, and forest fire control teams. At the present writing, however, there exists no efficient optimizing algorithm for solving the large models of this type encountered in practice. Good heuristic approaches are available, however, and as a practical matter yield solutions good enough to be helpful to decision makers.

MULTICOMMODITY NETWORK FLOWS

In transportation, transshipment, and assignment models, we dealt with minimizing the total production and transportation cost of supplying a *single* product to several destinations from several sources — perhaps with one or more intermediate stages as in the transshipment model. What if we wish to model and solve such a problem involving *several different* products? This expanded model is called *the multicommodity network flow* model, and finding efficient solution techniques for such models is on the frontier of current research efforts. The underlying problem is that each of the different products or commodities must be kept track of separately. To date, it has been shown that it is impossible to transform the general multicommodity problem into a single-commodity problem and that — even though all supplies and demands are integer valued — the optimal flow may not be integer.

IMBEDDED NETWORKS

Many large-scale models of complex problems are not themselves networks — but one or more network subproblems may be imbedded within the larger model (e.g., linear programming). For example, recall that we discussed block diagonal LP models and the use of Dantzig-Wolfe decomposition to "break them apart" for computational or operational reasons. If the submodels happen to be networks, such as transportation models, then highly efficient network optimizing algorithms can be used rather than resorting to the SIMPLEX algorithm. A surprisingly large number of such real-world problems can be modeled in this way, and a sharp-eyed decision maker should always be "on the lookout" for such situations.

THE MIN-CUT/MAX-FLOW THEOREM

We include the result we are about to discuss because it is interesting and intuitively appealing. It is called the *min-cut/max-flow theorem* and was discovered and proved by Ford and Fulkerson [2]. It goes as follows:

> The maximum flow through a capacitated network is equal to the sum of flows through the minimum cut-set, where a cut-set is defined as any set of arcs that, if severed or "cut," halts all flow from Source to Sink.

In lay terms, then, the value of the maximum possible flow through a capacitated network is equal to the sum of flow capacities of the cut-set with the lowest such sum. For example, in the Noah County network in Figure 4.4, arcs Source–A, Source–B, and Source–C form a cut-set with a total outbound flow capacity of $16,000 + 12,000 + 12,000 = 40,000$ vehicles per hour. However, the cut-set O–Sink City and P–Sink City has a total inbound flow capacity of $19,000 + 16,000 = 35,000$ vehicles per hour, so that the first cut-set is not a minimum cut-set. You might wish to verify that the latter cut-set is indeed the minimum one, so that maximum flow through the network is 35,000 vehicles per hour.

Unfortunately, applying the elegant min-cut/max-flow theorem directly has not been successful in practice. To pique your curiosity, however—and to reinforce a point from Chapter 2—this theorem amounts to a *dual* formulation of the associated LP problem.

POLKA [9]

The Scenario: The Department of Defense, through its Defense Fuel Supply Center (DFSC), annually procures about 5 billion gallons of aviation fuel for the armed services. Three types of fuel are involved, but one particular type — JP-4 — dominates the procurement process, with requirements of 4 billion gallons per year.

JP-4 is purchased through a competitive bidding process that occurs twice each year. Invitations for bid (IFBs) for a cycle normally involve supplying over 300 military installations, and bids are usually received from over 100 suppliers. Federal regulations require that bids be awarded to the lowest bidders (in an aggregate sense), based on "laid-down" cost (fuel plus transportation cost). When the analysis described here was first performed in 1973, the total annual cost involved was about $2 billion. In 1984, the same level of requirements would entail a total cost in excess of $5 billion.

The Problem: On the surface, it appeared that the bid award process could be modeled as a simple transshipment model or as a transshipment network. However, there were a wide variety of bidding options available to the suppliers, which greatly complicated the problem. Some of the more vexing of these options (from a modeling point of view) were as follows:

1. Five modes of transportation (truck, barge, railroad tank car, pipeline, and tanker) were available, but some shippers and receivers were limited in their access to one or more modes.
2. There were 53 government transshipment points available for routing and storage purposes.
3. Many of the 100-plus bidders had several shipping points, each with limited shipping facilities and fuel supplies. Thus, a particular company could submit bids totaling less than the sum of fuel available at its shipping points.
4. Bidders could submit either "destination" bids, which included shipping costs, or "origin" bids, in which the government had to determine the optimal shipping pattern and bear the resulting shipping cost.
5. Price breaks on different quantities were common.
6. "Tie-in" bids, in which one supplier made its maximum offer contingent upon the award of another (associated) supplier, were common.
7. Suppliers had the option of specifying a "minimum acceptable quantity" (MAQ) for one or more shipping points, preferring no bid award at all to an award of less than the stated MAQ.

The Model: Since the mid-1960s, DFSC had been using an LP model to generate tentative solutions to the basic bid award problem. A network model was not used because several of the bidding options could not be modeled by such a procedure (e.g., price discounts, "tie-in" bids). Moreover, the LP model did not incorporate the MAQ bids, since such bids lead to nonlinear constraints. Consequently, the LP algorithm was run initially with MAQ bids ignored. If they were not violated by the resulting model solution, then DFSC managers used the computer output as a basis for developing the bid awards; if some MAQ bids were violated, they were disqualified, and the LP model was rerun without them. This process was repeated until a feasible solution was obtained.

As MAQ bids became more and more common, DFSC managers became increasingly concerned that their suboptimal model was producing poorer and poorer solutions. In addition, each run on the agency's IBM 370/145 required *8 hours,* so that repeated runs were becoming a real problem — both as regards cost as well as machine access.

Solution to the Model: At the request of DFSC, the USAF Procurement Research Office, located at the Air Force Academy in Colorado, agreed to act as a consultant to investigate more sophisticated modeling approaches in the bid award problem. The model that finally emerged was dubbed POLKA (for *p*etroleum *o*il and *l*ubricants out-of-*k*ilter *a*lgorithm)[1] and consisted of a large minimum cost flow model imbedded within a larger model that accounted for the problem features that could not be accommodated in the network itself. POLKA ran in about *20 minutes* on the DFSC computer and produced an optimal solution. For comparison purposes, POLKA was run for two previous JP-4 bidding cycles, and it produced solutions that would have resulted in modest savings as a percentage of total cost (in absolute terms, this means that savings of $1 to $2 million dollars per cycle would have been realized). The computer program was completely debugged, a special program was written to build the data base for the model, and POLKA was operational early in 1973.

Solution to the Problem: For those with a wry sense of humor, recall that the "Arab oil embargo" occurred in 1973 — a few months after POLKA was installed. The first JP-4 bidding cycle thereafter produced bids for only *60%* of the total requirement. As sophisticated as POLKA was, even *it* couldn't produce 800 million gallons of aviation fuel! The National Security Act was invoked, however, and the armed services' requirements were met. Happily, as supplies subsequently increased and bidding again caused supply to exceed demand, POLKA was used — and (as of May 1984) is still being used in the aviation fuel procurement process.

---

[1] The original name for the optimization algorithm was POLOOKA, but the clients were not amused.

Meter Readers [10]

The Scenario: Eclectic Electric Energy, Inc. (EEE), provides electric power to a region that includes a large portion of West Texas and eastern New Mexico. In its local office in Armadillo, a city of approximately 160,000 people, the department responsible for reading electric meters is headed by Meg Watts. Meg is a recent graduate of the MBA program at a large state university and concentrated her elective courses in personnel management/organizational behavior.

Meg's office consists of a secretary, a file clerk, and eight meter readers. Her predecessor had divided the city into 20 zones, with each zone containing 8 subzones, so that the team of meter readers completed a zone every workday. Each month, therefore, the team read every electric meter in the city. In an attempt to alleviate boredom, the previous supervisor had a policy of rotating the eight readers among the 8 subzones in each zone.

The Problem: Although there had been no turnover among the meter readers for a year, Meg shortly discovered that all was not well in her department. First, upon inspecting the time cards of her readers for the past year, she discovered that the work load among the 20 zones was severely unbalanced. For zones with lower work loads, the extra time of the readers had been employed to recheck meters that are difficult to read, to reread meters as a result of customer complaints, and so on. For high-workload zones, overtime was routinely used. Meg found that some of the readers did not mind overtime and liked the extra pay; others resented taking the time away from their families. At any rate, Meg recognized that a restructuring of the zones would involve modeling and solving a very large "Chinese postman" problem and would take a great deal of time and effort on her part.

A more immediate problem was the structure of the subzones within each zone. One particularly troublesome zone seemed to be zone 7 (Ocean View Manor). Since the readers were routinely rotated among the subzones, she collected time-card data for the past six months for zone 7 and arranged them in a matrix (Table 4.1).

The average times for the readers across all subzones varied from 307 minutes for Rajesh (who was known to jog between meters) to 397 minutes for Olga (who was meticulous and had not misread a single meter all year). Meg was not concerned about this variance, which was well within the acceptable range of performance standards. What did concern her was the wide variance in times for subzones across readers—with a low of 274 minutes in zone 7-4 to a high of 424 in zone 7-8. Obviously, reallocating zone 7 to new subzones (a smaller "Chinese postman" problem) at this point would be wasted motion, since she intended to reconfigure the 20 major zones in the future.

Still, morale was deteriorating, and overall performance of her unit was unsatisfactory by Meg's standards. She felt that *something* must be done in the short term. Since the crew was scheduled to work zone 7 on Monday of the following week, she found her predecessor's scheduling book and noted that the first day of next week's schedule was to be as follows.

Table 4.1 Meter Reading Times for Zone 7

Subzones

Reader	1	2	3	4	5	6	7	8	Average
Ramon	375	360	255	285	270	360	345	405	332
Sean	345	285	225	255	240	330	290	420	311
Meiko	405	420	255	270	285	375	315	390	339
Olga	510	405	330	315	345	390	435	450	397
Chen	480	420	315	270	300	360	450	465	383
Rajesh	270	375	255	240	270	315	360	375	307
Babbette	450	390	330	285	270	405	465	435	379
Joe Don	330	315	255	270	240	345	300	450	313
Average	396	371	278	274	277	360	383	424	345

Note: Times are in minutes per day, to the nearest 15 minutes.

	Reader							
	Ramon	Sean	Meiko	Olga	Chen	Rajesh	Babbette	Joe Don
Subzone	4	6	2	1	3	5	7	8
Time	285	330	420	510	315	270	465	450

Total time: 3045 minutes, or 50.75 worker-hours

The Model: Meg Watts recognized that her short-term problem could be modeled as a special network model called the assignment model. The nodes were merely the meter readers and the subzones, and the arcs represented the assignment of readers to subzones. Since any reader could be assigned to any zone, her model would have 16 nodes and 64 arcs. She carefully checked her input data and gave it to the company's systems analyst to run.

Solution to the Model: The analyst used the NETOK computer package Meg had installed on EEE's minicomputer to generate a solution to her model. The resulting assignment is

	Reader							
	Ramon	Sean	Meiko	Olga	Chen	Rajesh	Babbette	Joe Don
Subzone	3	2	8	6	4	1	5	7
Time	255	285	390	390	270	270	270	300

Total time: 2430 minutes, or 40.5 worker-hours

Solution to the Problem: Even Meg, who had earned her MBA, was surprised at the difference of over 10 worker-hours between the original schedule and the model-generated assignment—a decrease of over 20%. She rechecked her input data once again, but found no errors. Out of curiosity, she then subtracted every entry in the "reader versus subzone" matrix from 510 (the largest entry) and had the model rerun to compute the *maximum* time. Sure enough, the model solution turned out to be the previous schedule! Meg reasoned, therefore, that using the assignment model would result in an average personnel saving of about 10%, as compared with randomly generated schedules.

The *problem,* of course, was still not solved. By demonstrating to her meter readers that Meg's assignment for zone 7 would more evenly distribute the work load and allow each reader to work the same subzone each month, she convinced them of the advantages of applying her approach to all 20 zones. Her announcement that she was reworking the 20 large zones to even out the daily variation in work load was also received positively (if a bit skeptically).

CPD [11]

The Scenario: The Center for Professional Development (CPD) at a southwestern university is an integral part of the business school, and its mission is to design, market, develop, staff, and administer seminars, conferences, and workshops of a nonacademic credit nature. The offerings of the CPD range from one-day short courses to formal, week-long schools and are attended each year by over 19,000 people in eight southwestern states. The basic objective of the CPD is to deliver the highest possible quality at a reasonable price and to be totally self-supporting financially.

The Problem: Early in 1981, a decision was made to offer a "management series" of 14 programs for middle and upper-middle managers in each of 14 southwestern cities. Each of the one-day seminars (e.g., "Women in the Work Force: A Manager's Role," "Effective Time Management") was to be offered in each city at least once in the fiscal year and two or three times in certain cities—so that a total of 284 individual seminars had to be scheduled and conducted. Since this new series was in addition to the CPD's normal complement of programs, the center's staff was faced with a significant management challenge.

The Model: Ms. Jay Lutz, the associate director of the CPD, was also a part-time MBA student at the university. The critical path network model had been discussed in class, and she recognized her problem as being amenable to analysis by this technique. (*Note:* She actually used the stochastic version of the critical path network called program evaluation and review technique, but we limit this discussion to the deterministic version.)

She first identified 17 mutually exclusive and collectively exhaustive activities involved in scheduling the series of programs and used her judg-

Table 4.2 CPD Scheduling Problem Activities

Activity	Description	Predecessor Activities	Expected Number of Weeks Required
A	Select seminars	—	2
B	Determine locations and dates	A	7
C	Confirm speakers	A	7
D	Select and order mailing lists	A	5
E	Confirm locations	B	5
F	Design brochures	C, E	3
G	Typeset brochure copy	F	3
H	Print brochures	G	4
I	Send labels to printer/mailer	D	1
J	Mail brochures	H, I	3
K	Conduct registration process	J	5
L	Reconfirm sites/facilities/setups	J	1
M	Order/ship course materials	K	3.5
N	Prepare on-site materials	K	2
O	Ship on-site materials	L, N	1
P	Conduct seminars	M, O	0.2
Q	Final reconciliation of accounts	P	5

ment and staff input to estimate completion times for each. This information is summarized in Table 4.2, and Figure 4.8 displays the associated network.

Solution to the Model: As indicated in Figure 4.8, the program PATH was used to determine the longest route through the network, and this

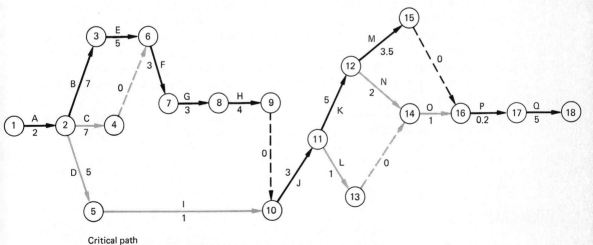

Critical path
Nodes: 1-2-3-6-7-8-9-10-11-12-15-16-17-18
Arcs: A-B-E-F-G-H-dummy-J-K-M-dummy-P-Q

Figure 4.8 CPD critical path network.

critical path is highlighted. Eleven of the 17 activities appear on the critical path, and the model indicates that the seminar scheduling project will take about 40.7 weeks to complete.

Solution to the Problem: As usual, modeling this problem as a critical path network gave Ms. Lutz insight into her complex scheduling problem, but it did not provide a "canned" solution. Activities D and I have a combined slack of 16 weeks, so that these tasks can be safely delayed to concentrate staff effort on critical activities A, B, E, F, G, and H. On the other hand, activities N and O—while not on the critical path—are very nearly so, with combined slack of only half a week. Finally, activity L could be postponed up to six weeks without affecting total completion, and activity C has free slack of five weeks.

The CPD used the results of this analysis for planning purposes and monitored its progress against the estimated mileposts generated by the critical path network. This application proved to be so useful that Ms. Lutz planned subsequently to incorporate all CPD program scheduling and operation into a larger, more complex network.

SUMMARY

In this chapter, we surveyed a special class of ILP models that can be posed and analyzed efficiently as networks. We noted that these special cases have natural integer solutions whenever the input parameters are all integers.

We first discussed four widely used network models: shortest route, longest route, minimal spanning tree, and optimal flow. As a special case of a longest-route model, we introduced the very useful application of project scheduling with the critical path method. Transportation, assignment, and transshipment models were covered as special cases of the optimal network flow case.

After discussing available computer codes, we addressed postoptimality analysis for two classes of network models: descriptive and optimizing. We ended our trek through the topic of network modeling with some advanced topics such as the "Chinese postman" model and multicommodity flow models.

In the next chapter—on nonlinear programming—we relax the additivity restriction in Chapter 2, and we shall see that the road gets considerably rockier as a result.

PROBLEMS

1.   *The Scenario:*   The Careful Intrigue Agency (CIA) maintains a system of worldwide "operatives" in 400 foreign cities. Because of the highly sensitive nature of the agency's responsibilities, all electronic communication with these operatives must be via special

secure voice networks that "scramble" the message at one end and "unscramble" it at the other. Volume of message traffic is high, and certain "all-ears" messages that must be transmitted to each and every operative arise several times daily. Harry Matta, the current director of operations, is inordinately proud of the existing communication system (that he was responsible for installing). The system involves transmitting messages from CIA headquarters in Virginia, directly and individually to each operative, and only two "all-ears" transmissions have been compromised in the past five years.

The Problem: In a cost-cutting mood, Congress has passed next fiscal year's budget that includes a 20% decrease in CIA's operating funds. Harry and his staff go to work immediately to identify areas for cost savings. He briefly considers, but ultimately abandons, the idea of withdrawing operatives from Tierra del Fuego and Nova Scotia. A tentative suggestion from a department head that Harry get rid of his personal chef, valet, and chauffeur meets with stony silence. However, Harry is stunned to learn that the CIA's long-distance telephone charges are running $23 million per year and are escalating rapidly. Perhaps there is some way to reduce telephone expenditures without sacrificing operational effectiveness.

The Model: The current practice is to transmit "all-ears" messages directly from headquarters. Since each operative has the capability of contacting other operatives, why couldn't headquarters contact a few directly and have them pass on the message to nearby operatives, continuing the "relay" until all parties had been contacted? There would still be 400 telephone calls, but many would obviously be much less expensive than a direct call from headquarters. Harry asks his operations research analyst to calculate long-distance charges per minute between all 400 cities and headquarters and recommend a call relay system that minimizes costs.

The Solution:
a. Does this appear to be a problem that can be modeled as a network? If so, what are the nodes and arcs?
b. Assuming that a call from city A to city B may *not* cost the same as from B to A, how many arcs does this network have?
c. Can a solution to the network model be expressed in terms of a minimal spanning tree? If so, how does the CIA problem differ from "normal" problems that can be modeled as networks of this type?

2.   **The Scenario:** Tom Laundry, the affable, congenial head coach of the Dallas Dudes professional football team, is preparing to select his starting players for the upcoming season. The team's training camp is located in Dragon's Den, Arizona, and the combination of "three-a-day" workouts and the 110-degree heat has already discouraged most of the aspiring rookies (and a few of the veterans as well). The offensive team is set, as are the defensive line and linebackers. Only the four defensive secondary positions are still "up for grabs."

The Problem: Eight players remain in contention for starting positions at strong safety (SS), weak safety (WS), right corner (RC), and left corner (LC). Two additional players are needed as substitutes, so that two of the eight candidates will get a pink slip and a one-way airline ticket home. Coach Laundry wishes, of course, to select the four starters in such a way that the strongest possible secondary results and to choose the two substitutes so that defensive capability is not seriously degraded if one of the starters is injured.

The Model: The head coach instructs his defensive coaches to schedule scrimmages so that each of the eight candidates plays each of the four positions and rate each candidate in each position on a scale of 1 (terminally inept) to 10 (exceptionally talented). The ratings that resulted are as follows:

Player	Position				Sum of Scores
	SS	WS	RC	LC	
Aloysius	6	5	7	8	26
Bertram	3	10	1	10	24
Chauncey	8	8	2	9	27
Dunsinane	10	9	1	2	22
Egbert	9	8	3	7	27
Fauntelroy	3	2	10	9	24
Gherkin	7	6	8	5	26
Helmer	10	5	3	5	23

a. How many different ways can Coach Laundry assign players to the four positions, neglecting for a moment the necessity of selecting two remaining players as substitutes?
b. Can this assignment problem be modeled as a network? If so, how many nodes and arcs are there?
c. What is the nature of an appropriate objective function for this model?
d. What do you think of the "additivity" assumption inherent in network modeling, as it applies to this problem? That is, do you think player performance at a position is independent of the other players in the defensive strategy? .

Solution to the Model: Billy Bob Bruce, the Dallas Dudes' OR analyst, was instructed to solve the model, which he proceeded to do using the NETOK algorithm on the club's minicomputer. Not knowing quite how to handle the selection of substitutes, he first solved the assignment problem by maximizing the sum of scores, with the following results.

Defensive Secondary

Position	Player	Score
Strong safety	Helmer	10
Weak safety	Dunsinane	9
Right corner	Fauntelroy	10
Left corner	Bertram	10
Total score		39

Noting that the total score for this assignment is the highest possible (since it is impossible to include all four of the "10's"), Billy Bob smugly turned to the problem of choosing the two substitutes. Since the individual scores for both Chauncey and Egbert sum to 27 across the four positions, as compared with 26 each for Aloysius and Gherkin, he decided to recommend that the former be retained as substitutes and—to demonstrate his efficiency—ordered one-way airline tickets for Aloysius and Gherkin.

Solution to the Problem: Upon receiving the "solution" from Billy Bob, Coach Laundry glanced briefly over the results. Several items came to his attention. First, if total scores across the four positions give any indication of overall athletic ability, the four players recommended as starting players were the poorest of the eight. Second, if Billy Bob's plan were implemented and Fauntelroy was subsequently injured in a game,

Chauncey and Egbert both performed very poorly at right corner during the scrimmages—and would probably be poor substitutes. Third, Fauntelroy performed well at *both* corner positions, as did Dunsinane at *both* safety positions. On this basis, Coach Laundry decided on Dunsinane and Fauntelroy as substitutes. Before firing Billy Bob, the coach had him run the algorithm once again with the other six players, with the following result.

Defensive Secondary

Position	Player	Score
Strong safety	Helmer	10
Weak safety	Bertram	10
Right corner	Gherkin	8
Left corner	Chauncey	9
Total score		37

Finding no additional exogenous factors that affected this problem, Coach Laundry decided to implement the foregoing solution and sent poor Aloysius and Egbert packing.

3.   *The Scenario:*   The accounting firm of Upp and Cummings, CPAs, is in the process of planning its auditing schedule for next month. The main office is located in Gaapville, and the firm's three other offices are in Tenkay, Greenshade, and Sasburg. For each of the ten clients whose audits are due, the managing partner Juan Upp has estimated how many auditors will be needed. These requirements, as well as the numbers of auditors available at each of the four offices, are as follows:

	Customer No.										
	1	2	3	4	5	6	7	8	9	10	Total
Auditors needed	4	9	2	12	7	6	9	3	18	5	75

	Office				
	Gaapville	Tenkay	Greenshade	Sasburg	Total
Auditors available	35	20	25	10	90

The Problem: Since the firm's audit staff among the four offices varies widely in experience, and since the difficulty of audits differs from one client to the next, assigning an auditor from a particular office to a given firm involves a considerable setup cost in terms of preparation time. A poor assignment pattern could cost the firm dearly in terms of inefficient use of its personnel resources. Furthermore, there are additional complications. First, none of the auditors stationed in Sasburg have experience in oil and gas accounting, so auditors from the other offices must be assigned to clients 2 and 9. Second, because of company policy, no audit is ever conducted for a given client with all auditors from the same office. And, finally, the 15 available auditors not assigned to audits will be sent to the same office for required professional training in Bayesian discriminant analysis.

The Model: Juan has his staff estimate the costs in hours c_{ij} for training each auditor from the ith office to audit the jth firm. For $i = 4$ (Sasburg), he is careful to make c_{42} and c_{49} artificially large numbers, in effect taking care of the first complication. Although he recognizes his problem as being similar to a transportation problem, he is not quite sure how to incorporate the second complication — no single-office audits of a client — so he ignores it for the moment. The third complication, he realizes, isn't really a problem — since his supply of auditors exceeds the client requirement.

The following is a matrix showing the c_{ij}, requirements, and supplies:

Auditor Training Costs (worker-hours per auditor)

		Client										Training	Supply
		1	2	3	4	5	6	7	8	9	10		
Office	Gaapville	8	21	15	13	9	17	8	7	26	9	0	35
	Tenkay	14	18	17	19	12	6	0	15	24	13	0	20
	Greenshade	9	15	18	16	16	15	11	13	21	19	0	25
	Sasburg	11	M*	14	7	23	9	6	18	M*	7	0	10
	Requirement	4	9	2	12	7	6	9	3	18	5	15	90

* M is a very large number.

The Solution: As Juan had suspected, the solution that emerged from the computer violated the "single-office" audit policy for eight of the ten clients. This solution is

Upp and Cummings Model Solution: Auditor Assignment

Office	Client										Training
	1	2	3	4	5	6	7	8	9	10	
Gaapville	4	0	2	2	7	0	9	3	0	5	3
Tenkay	0	0	0	0	0	6	0	0	2	0	12
Greenshade	0	9	0	0	0	0	0	0	16	0	0
Sasburg	0	0	0	10	0	0	0	0	0	0	0

Total cost: 914 worker-hours

By "fiddling" with the model solution, Juan is able to generate the following *feasible* assignment.

Upp and Cummings Feasible Solution: Auditor Assignment

Office	Client										Training
	1	2	3	4	5	6	7	8	9	10	
Gaapville	3	0	1	3	6	1	7	2	2	4	6
Tenkay	0	1	1	0	1	5	2	1	0	0	9
Greenshade	1	8	0	0	0	0	0	0	16	0	0
Sasburg	0	0	0	9	0	0	0	0	0	1	0

Total cost: 954 worker-hours

a. Noting that Juan's "fiddled solution" is about 4.4% more expensive than the optimal (but infeasible) solution, should Juan—in your opinion—go to the additional expense of modeling the problem as an ILP model? Why or why not?

b. The following represents the *worst* possible solution to the transportation network model.

Upp and Cummings Worst Model Solution: Auditor Assignment

					Client						
Office	1	2	3	4	5	6	7	8	9	10	Training
Gaapville	0	9	0	0	0	6	0	0	18	0	2
Tenkay	4	0	0	12	0	0	0	0	0	0	4
Greenshade	0	0	2	0	0	0	9	0	0	5	9
Sasburg	0	0	0	0	7	0	0	3	0	0	0

Total cost: 1488 worker-hours

Given your estimate of the cost of trained auditor manhours, do you think that the time and expense of modeling this problem and solving the model was justified? Why or why not?

4. There is a curious property associated with transportation networks, called the "more for less" phenomenon. Consider the following toy model displayed in a classical transportation tableau (still used in many MS/OR texts).

Supply Points

		A	B	C	D	Demand
	1	11 ¹	⁶	9 ³	⁵	20
Demand Points	2	⁷	2 ³	8 ¹	⁶	10
	3	⁹	11 ⁴	⁵	14 ⁴	25
	Supply	11	13	17	14	

In the transportation tableau, the small numbers in the upper-right corner of each cell are the c_{ij}'s—the unit transportation cost from demand point i to supply point j. The other numbers in the illustration represent an optimal solution to the model, and you can easily verify that the minimum total cost is $152.

Suppose, after the model had been solved, that demand point 2 increased its order by 5 units (from 10 to 15) and supply point A indicated that it could meet this additional demand by using overtime (producing 16 units rather than 11). Thus, our total shipment has increased by 5 units (from 55 to 60), or about 9%. The optimal solution to this new model is

Supply Points

Demand Points	A	B	C	D	Demand
1	*1* 16	*6*	*3* 4	*5*	20
2	*7*	*3* 2	*1* 13	*6*	15
3	*9*	*4* 11	*5*	*4* 14	25
Supply	16	13	17	14	

You may wish to verify that the total cost of this new shipping pattern is \$147—which is \$5 (about 3%) *less* than the original.

a. Is the result counterintuitive from your perspective? That is, does the fact that we *decreased* costs 3% by *increasing* shipping volume 9% seem paradoxical? If so, compare the two tableaus and their respective solutions. Can you see that the additional 5 units of demand and supply allowed us to ship more cheaply from C-2 and A-1 while decreasing the shipment from the higher-cost route C-1?

b. By how many more units could we increase demand at 2 and supply at A before cost savings ceased?

c. In the *original* model, would *decreasing* demand by 2 actually increase costs? Why or why not? (*Hint: Increasing* managerial options can *never* result in poorer performance in a technical sense.)

5. One interesting way of finding the shortest route through a network (given that all arc distances are nonnegative) is to build an *analog* model of the network. Pieces of string are used to represent the arcs, and their lengths are proportional to the distances they represent. The strings are then tied together, and the knots represent the network nodes. To "solve the model," one merely grasps the starting node with one hand and the destination node with the other and pulls the string network taut. The length of the resulting line is the shortest distance between the two selected nodes, and the arcs that are taut represent the arcs that make up the shortest route.

a. From a managerial standpoint, would this analog model conceivably have any practical value? Answer as though you were a consultant for a metropolitan emergency ambulance company with units stationed throughout the city and you were dealing with the owner Sy Rheen, who came up "through the ranks" as an ambulance driver.

b. Could our string model be adapted somehow to find the critical path (longest "distance") through an activity scheduling network? If so, what would be the relationship between an activity's duration and the length of the corresponding piece of string? How would you handle "dummy" activities? How would you determine slack time for noncritical activities?

6. Consider the following LP formulation of the maximum network flow model.
Let

x_F = total flow through the network

x_{ij} = flow on arc (i, j) from node i to node j

u_{ij} = flow capacity on arc (i, j)

$$\text{MAXIMIZE } x_0 = x_F \tag{4.6}$$

$$\text{SUBJECT TO:} \quad \sum_{(1,\,j \text{ in network})} x_{1j} = x_F \tag{4.7}$$

$$\sum_{(k,\,j \text{ in network})} x_{kj} = \sum_{(i,\,k \text{ in network})} x_{ik} \tag{4.8}$$

$$\sum_{(i,\,n \text{ in network})} x_{in} = x_F \tag{4.9}$$

$$x_{ij} \leq u_{ij} \text{ for all } i, j \text{ in network} \tag{4.10}$$

Node 1 is the starting node (Source), and node n is the ending node (Sink). Constraints (4.7) and (4.9) assure that the flow from Source and to Sink are the same. Constraints (4.8) are called "conservation of flow" equations and guarantee that the flow in and out of each node is equal. The constraints in (4.10) limit the flow on each arc to be less than or equal to its capacity.

As an illustration, consider the following simple network flow diagram and its LP formulation. The numbers on the arcs are flow capacities.

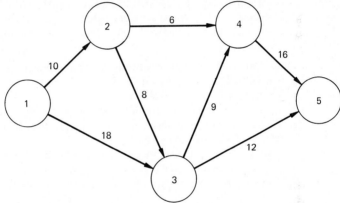

$$\text{MAXIMIZE } x_0 \qquad\qquad\qquad -x_F = 0 \tag{4.11}$$

$$\text{SUBJECT TO:} \quad x_{12} + x_{13} \qquad\qquad\qquad -x_F = 0 \tag{4.12}$$

$$x_{12} \qquad - x_{23} - x_{24} \qquad\qquad = 0 \tag{4.13}$$

$$x_{13} + x_{23} \qquad - x_{34} - x_{35} \qquad = 0 \tag{4.14}$$

$$x_{24} + x_{34} \qquad - x_{45} \qquad = 0 \tag{4.15}$$

$$x_{35} + x_{45} - x_F = 0 \tag{4.16}$$

$$x_{12} \qquad\qquad\qquad\qquad \leq 10 \tag{4.17}$$

$$x_{13} \qquad\qquad\qquad \leq 18 \tag{4.18}$$

$$x_{23} \qquad\qquad\qquad \leq 8 \tag{4.19}$$

$$x_{24} \qquad\qquad\qquad \leq 6 \tag{4.20}$$

$$x_{34} \qquad\qquad \leq 9 \tag{4.21}$$

$$x_{35} \qquad\qquad \leq 12 \tag{4.22}$$

$$x_{45} \leq 16 \tag{4.23}$$

In optimizing algorithms, a special modeling device is used to take care of the upper-bound constraints, so that the resulting constraint matrix has the "semi-Markov property" mentioned earlier.

a. You may wish to verify that the maximum flow through this network is 27 units, as follows:

$$x_{12} = 10 \quad x_{23} = 4 \quad x_{34} = 9 \quad x_{45} = 15$$
$$x_{13} = 17 \quad x_{24} = 6 \quad x_{35} = 12 \quad x_F = 27$$

Check the solution to see if the conservation of flow conditions are met. Do you see that the minimum cut-set consists of arcs (2, 4), (3, 4), and (3, 5)?

b. What would be the effect if the upper-bound constraint on arc (3, 4) were increased by one unit (from 9 to 10)?

c. If the network represented part of the proposed circuit design for a hand-held computer, and the "flow capacities" represented current limitations, what could you conclude about the design parameter (capacity) of arc (2, 3)?

d. The illustration has five nodes and seven arcs, and its LP formulation involves eight variables and 12 constraints. Certain "real-world" network flow models may have thousands of nodes and tens of thousands of arcs. In addition to this complication of sheer size, the LP formulation results in so-called "highly degenerate models"— those with many zeroes in both the objective function and the right-hand sides of the constraints—and are difficult to solve efficiently. Does this illustration help you to understand the importance of specialized, highly efficient algorithms like NETOK and PNET, that take advantage of the network structure?

7. Think about the following entities in terms of modeling and analysis with networks.
   a. The electric power system of a city
   b. The U.S. decennial census
   c. The curriculum structure of a multipurpose business school
   d. The flow of raw materials and finished goods through an assembly line
   e. "Word-of-mouth" advertising
   f. A vertically integrated company that sells fast-food franchises
   g. Assigning graduate assistants to professors
   h. Planning the intricate process of a kidney transplant operation

REFERENCES

1. GLOVER, F., J. HULTZ, D. KLINGMAN, and J. STUTZ. "Generalized Networks: A Fundamental Computer-Based Planning Tool." *Management Science,* Vol. 24 (1978), pp. 1209–1220.

2. FORD, L., JR., and D. FULKERSON. *Flows in Networks.* Princeton, N.J.: Princeton University Press, 1962.

3. BRADLEY, G., G. BROWN, and G. GRAVES. "GNET, A Primal Capacitated Network Program." Monterey, Calif.: Naval Postgraduate School, Copyright 1975, 1977.

4. BARR, R., F. GLOVER, and D. KLINGMAN. "A New Alternating Basis Algorithm for Semi-Assignment Networks," Report No. 77-3. Management Science Report Series, University of Colorado, Boulder, Colo., 1977.

5. SPIRA, P. "A New Algorithm for Finding All Shortest Paths in a Graph of Positive Arcs in Average Time 0 $(n^2 \log^2 n)$." *SIAM Journal of Computing,* Vol. 21 (1973), pp. 28–32.

6. HITCHCOCK, F. "The Distribution of a Product from Several Sources to Numerous Localities." *Journal of Mathematics and Physics,* Vol. 20 (1941), pp. 224–230.

7. SHIER, D. "Iterative Methods for Determining the k Shortest Paths in a Network." *Networks,* Vol. 6 (1976), pp. 205–230.

8. KWAN, M. "Graphic Programming Using Odd or Even Points." *Chinese Mathematics,* Vol. 1 (1962), pp. 273–277.

9. AUSTIN, L. and W. HOGAN. "Optimizing the Procurement of Aviation Fuels." *Management Science,* Vol. 22 (1976), pp. 515–527.

10. BAIRD, B. Adapted from an unpublished MBA term project report, College of Business Administration, Texas Tech University (1981).

11. LUTZ, J. Adapted from an unpublished MBA term project report, College of Business Administration, Texas Tech University (1982).

ADDITIONAL READING

MINIEKA, E. *Optimization Algorithms for Networks and Graphs.* New York: Marcel Dekker, 1978.

WAGNER, H. *Principles of Operations Research,* 2nd ed., Englewood Cliffs, N.J.: Prentice-Hall, 1975.

CHAPTER 5

Nonlinear Programming Models

"Nothing stays linear for very long," or so an old adage would have it. And to our way of thinking nothing could be closer to the truth. As we have noted before, society—and along with it, business, commerce, and industry—is becoming increasingly complex. The problems of declining productivity, increasingly scarce resources, stiffer international competition, and higher interest rates all dictate that we employ more sophisticated models to help alleviate these "messes." One form these sophisticated models can take belongs to the class we call nonlinear programming (NLP) models.

Chapters on NLP models in introductory management science texts are rare. The inclusion of such a chapter in this text will, we hope, achieve the following goals:

To instill an understanding of the role NLP plays within decision making under certainty

To impart an appreciation for how nonlinearities arise in deterministic optimization models and what NLP applications are commonplace

To survey the algorithms and solution techniques utilized to solve NLP models

To characterize the importance of the SIMPLEX algorithm and variants of it in solution of NLP models

To enable you to recognize nonlinear situations and cope with them in a general sense.

As methods of conducting business become increasingly complicated, more and more firms are forced to relax overly stringent assumptions of linearity in their optimization models to accommodate better the nonlinearities of the real world. A typical example of the increased complexity of business is in the pricing of products and services. Products that previously were sold separately are now being priced together at a discount. At the same time, volume discounts represent a popular form of pricing that introduces nonlinearities into the pricing problem. A retailer must now consider complicated price schedules when replenishing depleted inventories. Such pricing strategies have a significant effect upon sales, so that gross revenue ends up being a nonlinear function of price.

Another frequent situation where nonlinearities arise is in the blending of ingredients to produce a product. Blends of dog food, gasoline, and metallic alloys all represent situations where the "whole may not be equal to the sum of its parts." Nonlinearities arise chiefly because some product properties, such as octane number and vapor pressure in gasoline, are nonlinear functions of the amounts and properties of each component in the blend.

To give you some idea how frequently nonlinear phenomena occur in reality, let us follow through the regular working day of a young marketing manager named Nona Lanier. Nona begins her day early; following the usual get-ready chores, she begins to get herself breakfast. She discovers in the process that she is low on milk, butter, and eggs, so she decides to make a trip to the grocery store on her way home from work. While eating breakfast, she thinks about that new 30-watt stereo system she has had her eye on. After taking a vitamin pill, Nona begins the trek across town in her small European sports car. There are several stops on the way to work, and each stop requires "solution" of a nonlinear problem involving distances and speeds. Her driving skills handle this very nicely.

Upon arrival at her office, Ms. Lanier begins her regular work day. Her company is in the computer software business, and her job involves (among other things) pricing the individual programs so as to maximize total revenues for her company. The problem is nonlinear since gross revenues are a function of price and sales volume (which *itself* is a function of price!). Nona is forced to think nonlinearly throughout the day.

At the end of her workday, she is ready to go shopping. She goes first to the Good Vibrations Sound Center where she listens to several stereo systems and discovers that the less expensive units do not always produce "linear" sound. The salesclerk points out that if she purchases an entire system (consisting of receiver, turntable, and speakers), it will be sold to her at a discount. *Again* she is forced to think nonlinearly, but she decides to postpone this purchasing decision for another day.

From the Sound Center she motors to Food City. Here again she is confronted with nonlinear decision situations — how much milk, butter, and eggs to buy so she will have enough until next week, considering that trips to the grocery store also cost time and money.

When she arrives home, she is exhausted. (No wonder, with all the nonlinearities!) So ends a typical nonlinear day in the life of Nona Lanier, and thus ends our tale.

NLP models have been around a long time, and classical methods for solving some of these models date back to the eighteenth century. As a modeling and optimization technique, NLP is much older than LP, which got its start during World War II.

Until recently, most NLP models belonged to the realms of physics and engineering. Today, the use of NLP in business is growing rapidly, or so the literature on business models would suggest. In this chapter, we will look at some typical nonlinear business models and investigate how such models are solved by NLP algorithms. Even though NLP has traditionally enjoyed a much greater breadth of application to engineering than to business, we will confine our attention to the NLP models of business and industrial problems.

UNDERLYING ASSUMPTIONS

In the introduction to this part of the text, recall that we defined something called a *mathematical program* or — in terminology more germane for our purpose — a *mathematical programming model.* This model is repeated for convenience:

$$\text{OPTIMIZE} \quad x_0 = f(x_1, x_2, \ldots, x_n) \tag{5.1}$$

$$\text{SUBJECT TO:} \quad g_i(x_1, x_2, \ldots, x_n) \left\{ \begin{array}{c} \leq \\ = \\ \geq \end{array} \right\} b_i, \quad i = 1, \ldots, m \tag{5.2}$$

In Chapter 2, the objective function f and the m constraints g_i were linear functions (because of additivity and divisibility assumptions in the underlying problem), and we explored model analysis and development of the resulting linear program. Obviously, if certain mathematical programs are linear, then all others must be nonlinear (the logic is inescapable!). However, we avoided this dichotomy temporarily by looking at models that are linear except for the requirement that some or all of their decision values must be integer valued — and thus integer (linear) programs emerged in Chapter 3. Chapter 4 dealt with a special case of ILP models called network models. In this chapter, then, we are ready to "bite the bullet" and discuss nonlinear programming directly. In terms that an Australian would understand immediately, we are about to depart the modern, orderly confines of Sydney and launch into the wild, uncharted vistas of the "outback."

What assumptions must be met for us to model managerial problems as nonlinear programs? At first glance, it seems simple enough: Some decision variable, or some relationship between or among decision variables, must not satisfy either the divisibility or additivity assumptions — or both. However, "first glances" are often notoriously deceiving — and this is particulary true in the case of NLP modeling. As we will see later in this chapter, there is no general NLP algorithm that can solve all nonlinear models — and most probably there never will be. Therefore, our challenge as managerial decision makers in modeling nonlinear problems is to attempt to model them in certain ways that lead to computationally tractable forms. Since each of these forms has its own unique set of underlying assumptions, it is not very profitable to attempt to discuss general assumptions.

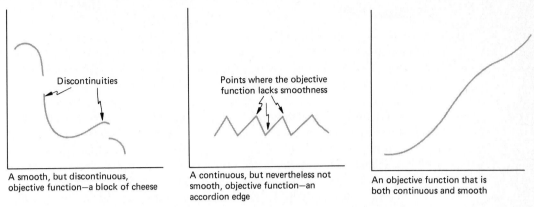

A smooth, but discontinuous, objective function—a block of cheese

A continuous, but nevertheless not smooth, objective function—an accordion edge

An objective function that is both continuous and smooth

Figure 5.1   Appearance of objective functions that may be discontinuous or lacking in smoothness.

However, before we plunge into specialized NLP modeling and analysis, we can make certain broad observations about this large and very complex subject. First, the functions in (5.1) and (5.2) must be reasonably *well behaved*. For example, it is highly advantageous from a computational standpoint if the feasible set of points described by the constraints in (5.2) is *convex;* that is, if we draw a line between *any two points* in the feasible region, every point on the line is also in the feasible region. A football is convex; a doughnut is not.

Second, it is convenient if both our objective function and feasible set are *smooth and continuous:* A block of Swiss cheese is smooth but not continuous, and an accordion is continuous but not smooth. Examples of these are shown in Figure 5.1. There are other features that we will discuss in connection with specific modeling approaches, but the "story" on NLP should be beginning to come into focus. An appropriate analogy is that, of the thousands of species of wild beasts on the planet, human beings have been able to domesticate (or even tame) a relative few. We now discuss a handful of the "docile" varieties of NLP models.

NONLINEAR MODELING

At this point in our trek through the nonlinear "outback," we face a dichotomy of some significant proportions. Should we approach nonlinear modeling in the usual way — by investigating the various mathematical forms that such models can take? Or should we discuss several *examples* of nonlinear modeling from business and industry (letting them evolve into whatever mathematical form is appropriate), and hope they turn out to be computationally tractable? There is something to be said for both approaches — but let us proceed with the latter. From a managerial point of view, a good model of a problem — regardless of its ease or difficulty of analysis — is very much preferable to one that is formulated by "mashing" the problem so that it fits a convenient mold.

A PRICING MODEL

Never Mower, Inc., manufactures a popular line of lawn mowers for the residential market. The "Chopper," a gas-powered, hand-propelled mower with a 14″ cut and no frills (it's even painted Army olive drab), has always been the company's "bread and butter" product. However, Ed Poe, the company's new vice-president of engineering, is disdainful of the mundane Chopper and has had his staff design a new mower tentatively entitled the "Zipper," which is the pride and joy of the Engineering Department. Resting on a six-wheel chassis with floating suspension, the Zipper is electric powered, self-starting, self-propelled and has an 18″ cut. Plans include its availability in eight decorator colors, with rustproof paint, racing stripes, and chrome trim as standard features.

Poe and T. Raven, who is the company's pricing specialist, are having a "head-knocking" session over the Zipper with Moe Delaune, the CEO of Never Mower, Inc.

"Chief," argues Ed Poe, "the Zipper is just what the doctor ordered. We need to add a little pizzazz to our image—the Chopper is as dull as a Sunday drive in West Texas. Get Raven here to put it in his LP model, and I'll bet the Zipper will come out a winner."

"Mr. Delaune," replies Raven, "We sell the Chopper for $99.95 and get a consistent 15% return on our investment. Besides (nodding toward Poe), the problem isn't linear. The relationship of selling price to sales volume is linear (Figure 5.2a), and the variable cost is a linear function of the number of units produced (Figure 5.2b), but profit contribution is a *quadratic* function of selling price (Figure 5.2c). In fact, here's a summary of my analysis (Table 5.1). As you can see, the optimal selling price turns out to be about $166, which we estimate will generate sales of about 7200 mowers. Production estimates the variable cost of production at $125 per copy, with a line setup cost of $250,000. That means that the estimated first-year profit contribution of the Zipper would be around $45,000, on a capital outlay of about $1.15 million—and that's a return on investment of less than 4%. I think the Zipper is a poor investment."

"Gentlemen," said Moe Delaune, "thank you for your input—I'll make a decision on the Zipper by Thursday. Before you leave, though, I'm trying to take a more personal interest in my staff. What's the most important thing in your lives right now?"

"That's easy, boss," retorts Poe, "it's my girl friend Lenore."

Quoth T. Raven, "Never Mower."

Our vignette is a small allegory of the product pricing problem. If we expand our horizons to encompass multiple products, and include a set of linear constraints on scarce resources, we have a *quadratic programming model.*

AN INVENTORY CONTROL MODEL

Maintaining adequate stocks of inventory is a classic example of nonlinear modeling. The inventory situation could be large, as in maintenance of sufficient refined liquid fuel reserves to sustain demand for an entire country, or small, as in maintaining enough milk in the refrigerator to accommodate antic-

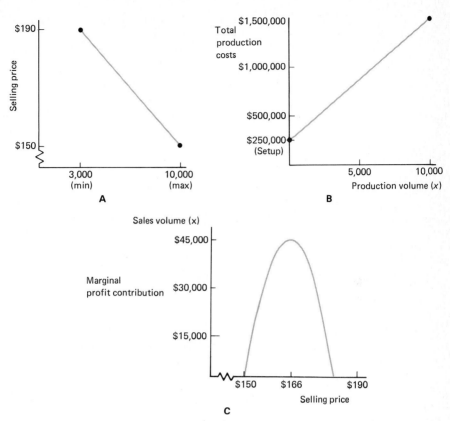

Figure 5.2 (a) Selling price to volume. (b) Production costs to volume. (c) Profit to selling price.

ipated demand for a family of four between trips to the grocery store. The objective in every case is straightforward minimization of the costs associated with the inventory.

The simplest inventory model involves only two types of costs: the cost of *ordering* items and the cost of *holding* them. Ordering costs include such items as clerical time, forms, postage, and supervisory review of purchase orders. Holding costs cover such things as storage and handling, insurance, obsolescence, and opportunity cost of the capital resources involved. This model requires some underlying assumptions that in many cases are frankly nonsensical from a realistic managerial point of view but can be relaxed (and will be in Chapter 11) to create more useful analytical tools. These assumptions are

1. Demand for each product is constant and is known with certainty.
2. Per unit cost for each product is constant, and price discounts are not available.
3. Ordering cost for each product can be expressed as a constant dollar amount per order.
4. Holding cost for each product can be stated as a percentage of the average value of the inventory.

Table 5.1   Profitability Analysis of "Zipper"

Price/Volume Analysis

x = unit sales
$P(x)$ = unit price as a function of sales
　　　Minimum price = $150 (sales of 10,000)
　　　Maximum price = $190 (sales of 3,000)

$$P(x) = \frac{145,000 - 4x}{700}$$

Cost/Volume Analysis

Setup cost = $250,000
Unit variable cost = $125
$C(x)$ = total cost as a function of sales
　　　= 250,000 + 125x

Profit/Price Analysis

$R(x)$ = total revenue
　　　= $x \cdot P(x)$
$PC(x)$ = total price contribution
　　　= $R(x) - C(x)$

$$PC(x) = \frac{-40x^2 + 575,000x}{7000} - 250,000$$

Optimal Model Solution

$P^*(x^*) = \$166.07 \quad x^* = 7187.50 \quad PC^*(x^*) = \$45,200.89$

With these restrictive assumptions in mind, let us develop the so-called economic order quantity (EOQ) model (sometimes called the "Wilson model") for n items.

Let

d_j = annual demand in units for the jth item

c_j = per order ordering cost of the jth item

h_j = holding cost as a fraction of the average on-hand value of the jth item

p_j = per unit purchase price for the jth item

q_j = quantity of the jth item ordered each time an order is placed

Since we order q_j items each time we order, the number of orders per year is d_j/q_j, so that the annual ordering cost is $(c_j \cdot d_j)/q_j$ for the jth item.

The average on-hand inventory for the jth item is merely $q_j/2$, as can be seen from Figure 5.3. Here $q/2$ is the average number of units of inventory because half the time there are more than $q/2$ units in inventory and half the time there are less than $q/2$ units in inventory. Hence, the average value of the inventory is $(p_j \cdot q_j)/2$. The annual holding cost is therefore $(h_j \cdot p_j \cdot q_j)/2$.

Our total inventory cost T_j for item j is the sum of ordering and holding costs, and the cost of ordering and holding all items is then T, where

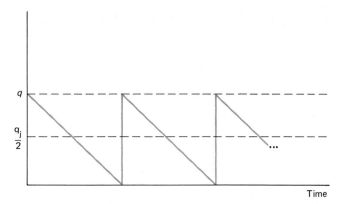

Figure 5.3 Graph of inventory variation over time for a particular product j.

$$T = \sum_{j=1}^{n} T_j = \sum_{j=1}^{n} [(c_j \cdot d_j)/q_j + (h_j \cdot p_j \cdot q_j/2)] \tag{5.3}$$

Since (5.3) includes nonlinear terms that express ordering costs, it is a nonlinear function. In our inventory problem, we would wish to minimize T—subject perhaps to constraints on capital availability, total storage space at our disposal, and so on. Thus our object would be to find optimal order quantities q_j^* that satisfied whatever constraints were present and that minimized total ordering and holding costs. The model, therefore, turns out to be a nonlinear programming model. If there were no constraints, we could solve for optimal ordering quantities for each product separately.

A SCRAP MINIMIZATION MODEL

In many manufacturing and fabrication industries, profits are literally "driven" by the level of scrap materials. For example, plants that manufacture industrial equipment such as heavy-duty generators, pumps, and the like usually cut flat components with special dies, and the amount of scrap can be carefully controlled through placement of the cutting machines on the sheet metal, ordering sheet metal in appropriate sizes, and so on.

Consider the case of a die-cutting subcontractor who wishes to combine orders in such a way that the percentage of sheet metal scrap (as a fraction of total stock) is minimized. If each of n die-cut orders results in s_j pounds of scrap for each cut, and requires a basic weight of w_j pounds of sheet metal (including scrap) for each cut of the jth product, then — letting x_j be the number of plates of the jth type to produce — an appropriate model might be as follows:

$$\text{MINIMIZE } x_0 = \frac{\displaystyle\sum_{j=1}^{n} s_j \cdot x_j}{\displaystyle\sum_{j=1}^{n} w_j \cdot x_j} \tag{5.4}$$

SUBJECT TO: Constraints on advance orders, scarce raw materials,
                        product mix, limited machine time, and so on   (5.5)

The objective function (5.4) is decidedly nonlinear — being the ratio of two linear functions (total scrap weight and total stock weight). If the constraints in (5.5) happen to be linear, then the resulting model is called a *fractional programming model.* As we will see later, a mathematical transformation will convert such models into equivalent linear programs.

A CONTAINER COST MINIMIZATION PROBLEM

Among others, the chemical industry faces many problems — both technical and economic — that are amenable to modeling and analysis using nonlinear programming models (we noted the nonlinear gasoline blending model earlier). One interesting application involves designing containers for storage and/or shipment of toxic or otherwise dangerous chemicals. Let us assume that containers must have rectangular tops, sides, and bottoms for convenience in shipping via railroad boxcar, and let l, w, and h, respectively, represent their length, width, and height.

The bottoms must be constructed of specially coated, heavy-load-bearing alloys. The sides must also be constructed with coated alloys to resist chemical erosion but do not have to bear as heavy a load as the bottoms. Finally, the tops must be fume resistant, but they do not require load-bearing or erosion-resistant material. Let

V = required volume of the container
a = cost per square foot of material for bottoms
b = cost per square foot of material for sides
c = cost per square foot of material for tops

Our basic cost minimization model would look like

MINIMIZE $x_0 = (a \cdot l \cdot w) + 2(b \cdot h \cdot w) + 2(b \cdot l \cdot w) + (c \cdot l \cdot w)$ (5.6)

SUBJECT TO: $l \cdot h \cdot w \geq V,$ (5.7)

                        other constraints such as railroad boxcar dimensions,
                        load-bearing capacity of materials, and so on   (5.8)

The resulting model is most certainly nonlinear, since every term contains products of some or all of the three decision variables. Such models are called *geometric programming models* and — as we will discover — can be solved rather easily with special techniques.

GENESIS OF NLP MODELS

The NLP models just discussed developed naturally from underlying physical or economic principles. There is another entire family of NLP models that arise *empirically.* For example, a particular cost or profit or constraint function may result from fitting curves (or equations) to historical data. One such example with which we are all familiar is the least squares technique used to develop regression models. If a good fit can be obtained only by the use of nonlinear functions, then our resulting optimization model will be nonlinear as well.

The foregoing has attempted to capture the flavor and almost infinite variety of nonlinear modeling, and we have not scratched the surface of this immense and complex subject. Next, we take a very shallow dive into a deep and turbulent ocean — that of solution techniques for NLP models.

NLP SOLUTION APPROACHES: AN INTUITIVE DESCRIPTION

Unlike the situation with LP models, there is no single, general algorithm for solving NLP models. Researchers in this highly technical area have developed a variety of approaches, and these approaches can be classified into four categories: indirect methods, direct methods, linearization, and miscellaneous methods. Some examples of each are indicated in Table 5.2.

We will not try to cover all the specific techniques listed in Table 5.2, in detail. Rather, we will attempt to grasp the rationale behind each general approach and illustrate it with an example or two.

INDIRECT METHODS

For NLP models with certain "nice" properties, we can use theoretical results from the calculus to find optimal solutions. For example, in our inventory model from the previous section, if we happen to have equality constraints, we can use something called *Lagrange multipliers* to transform our model into an *unconstrained* model and use differential calculus to find the optimal ordering quantities. The "Kuhn-Tucker conditions" referred to in Table 5.2 are theoretical results that use this device in an extended sense to derive *necessary conditions* for an optimal solution. We should realize that the Lagrange multiplier technique is important in a theoretical sense (i.e., in developing algorithms).

DIRECT METHODS

The most general approaches available for solving NLP models are the so-called *direct methods.* Such techniques basically consist of searching the feasible region in an organized way in an attempt to methodically improve the value of the objective function. As a parallel to the mountain-climbing analogy in our discussion of the simplex algorithm, consider the following vexing analogy to using direct methods in NLP.

Imagine that you are lost in a remote mountain range. Your goal is to climb to the highest peak (or descend to the lowest valley) so you can be found. To make matters even worse, you are blindfolded and cannot see the terrain around you! You can only sense whether you are walking uphill (or downhill). Occasionally, you encounter cliffs, and at other times deep valleys. You continue to walk up (or down) until there is no direction that will take you higher

Table 5.2   Nonlinear Programming Approaches

1. Indirect methods
     Differential calculus
     Kuhn-Tucker necessary conditions
2. Direct methods
     Univariate methods
     Multivariate methods
     Penalty function methods
     Grid search methods
     Generalized reduced gradient methods (GRG)
3. Linearization
     Quadratic programming
     Separable programming
     Approximation programming
     Successive linear programming methods (SLP)
     Successive linear constrained programming methods (SLCP)
     Fractional programming
4. Miscellaneous methods
     Geometric programming
     Dynamic programming

(or lower). At this point you have reached a peak (valley), but—unfortunately —there is no way of knowing whether it is the highest peak (or the lowest valley).

This is exactly what we ask our computer to do when we use direct methods to solve an NLP problem. Essentially, these methods use recursive algorithms to conduct a search for a solution. Like a blindfolded hiker, these methods are able to sense only the local "terrain" and thus converge to a local optimum only. While these methods are "blind" in the sense that they are unable to provide a complete picture or description of the shape of the mountain range, they are nevertheless popular methods for solving small to moderate-sized (200 or less variables) NLP models with extensive nonlinearities.

One interesting direct method is the *sequential unconstrained minimization technique (SUMT)* of Fiacco and McCormick [1]. This algorithm, which is one of the so-called "barrier" or "penalty" approaches, uses a special function to formulate the model so that a "barrier" is erected inside the feasible region in such a way that the search for better and better values of the objective function can never stray outside that region. If you could build a SUMT-like fence to contain a vicious dog, the fence would get higher and higher as the animal got closer and closer!

Gradient search methods such as Lasdon's GRG2 [2] are the most popular direct-type algorithms in practice, and there is a variety of such approaches. We will discuss GRG2 and similar available computer codes in the next section.

LINEARIZATION

We have already seen two examples of NLP models for which *linearization* is useful: the fractional programming model we developed for the scrap minimization problem and the quadratic programming model of an inventory system. Before we briefly discuss these and other specific models, let us look at the philosophy that underpins the solution approach of linearization.

Consider for a moment the communication problem between man and his obedient servant, the electronic computer. Most modern civilizations have adopted the decimal number system (i.e., base 10), so that practically everybody knows, for example, that $1 + 1 = 2$. Not so the computer. Since it basically operates with the *binary* number system, it cannot recognize the symbol "2"—since there is no such thing in this system—and insists that $1 + 1 =$ "10." What we need to do, therefore, is to translate our numbers into a language that the computer can understand, tell the computer to "do its own thing" in the binary "language," and have its results translated back into our "language" so that we can understand them. This translation process is analogous to what linearization accomplishes for some NLP models. We know how to solve LP problems very efficiently, so—if certain NLP problems can be translated (transformed) into LP problems—we can solve the equivalent LP models and reverse the transformation to recover the NLP model solutions. Let's get down to particulars.

Fractional Programming Models

As discussed earlier, the fractional programming model is as follows.

$$\text{OPTIMIZE}^1 \; x_0 = \frac{\sum_{j=1}^{n} s_j \cdot x_j}{\sum_{j=1}^{n} w_j \cdot x_j} \tag{5.9}$$

$$\text{SUBJECT TO:} \quad \sum_{j=1}^{n} a_{ij} \cdot x_j \left\{ \begin{matrix} \leq \\ = \\ \geq \end{matrix} \right\} b_i, \quad i = 1, \ldots, m \tag{5.10}$$

Let us define $v > 0$ as

$$v = \frac{1}{\sum_{j=1}^{n} w_j \cdot x_j} \tag{5.11}$$

If we substitute (5.11) into (5.9), we have

$$\text{OPTIMIZE} \; x_0 = \sum_{j=1}^{n} s_j \cdot (v \cdot x_j) \tag{5.12}$$

This eliminates the linear expression in the denominator of (5.9) all right, but we are left with a nonlinear function (5.12) in which there are *products* of

---

[1] We must insist that the denominator not be zero for any feasible values of x_j, so as to have a meaningful model.

variables. What if we multiplied both sides of the constraints (5.10) by v and cross-multiplied the new expression (5.11)? The result would be (after a bit of algebraic simplification)

$$\text{OPTIMIZE } x_0 = \sum_{j=1}^{n} s_j \cdot (v \cdot x_j) \tag{5.12}$$

$$\text{SUBJECT TO: } \sum_{j=1}^{n} a_{ij} \cdot (v \cdot x_j) \begin{Bmatrix} \leq \\ = \\ \geq \end{Bmatrix} v \cdot b_i, \quad i = 1, \ldots, m \tag{5.13}$$

$$\sum_{j=1}^{n} w_j \cdot (v \cdot x_j) = 1 \tag{5.14}$$

$$\text{All } x_j \text{ and } v \geq 0$$

The resulting model is *still* nonlinear of course, but we now perform the crucial transformation.

Let

$$y_j = v \cdot x_j, \quad j = 1, \ldots, n \tag{5.15}$$

and substitute this expression into (5.12), (5.13), and (5.14) to get

$$\text{OPTIMIZE } x_0 = \sum_{j=1}^{n} s_j \cdot y_j \tag{5.16}$$

$$\text{SUBJECT TO: } \sum_{j=1}^{n} (a_{ij} \cdot y_j) - (b_i \cdot v) \begin{Bmatrix} \leq \\ = \\ \geq \end{Bmatrix} 0, \quad i = 1, \ldots, m \tag{5.17}$$

$$\sum_{j=1}^{n} w_j \cdot y_j = 1 \tag{5.18}$$

And now we have the LP (5.16) through (5.18) whose decision variables are y_j, $j = 1, \ldots, n$ and v. After solving this LP model with a SIMPLEX code, we recover the desired solution by reversing the transformation (5.15):

$$x_j = \frac{y_j}{v}, \quad j = 1, \ldots, n \tag{5.19}$$

Thus, by adding one variable v and one constraint (5.18), we have transformed an NLP model into an LP model.

Quadratic Programming Models

Quadratic programming models are those that can be formulated as follows:

$$\text{OPTIMIZE } x_0 = \sum_{j=1}^{n} \sum_{k=1}^{n} (c_{jk} \cdot x_j \cdot x_k) + \sum_{j=1}^{n} d_j x_j \tag{5.20}$$

$$\text{SUBJECT TO:} \quad \sum_{j=1}^{n} a_{ij}x_j \left\{ \begin{matrix} \leq \\ = \\ \geq \end{matrix} \right\} b_i, \quad i = 1, \ldots, m \quad (5.21)$$

As we can see, quadratic programming models involve an objective function that is a quadratic function of the decision variables and a set of linear constraints. In addition to the pricing problem we looked at earlier, such models arise naturally in such diverse applications as portfolio management and personnel assignment.

There are several approaches that have been developed to solve quadratic programming models, but one of the more interesting is the Frank-Wolfe *quadratic programming algorithm* [3]. We will not go into the details here, but this technique converts the nonlinear model into an equivalent aggregated LP model consisting of a primal model and its associated dual model. The SIMPLEX algorithm must be altered slightly to include something called "restricted basis entry" but the transformation from an NLP to an LP model is the essence of the approach.

Linear Approximation Models

If our nonlinear objective and/or constraint functions are "well behaved" in a certain mathematical sense, we can *approximate* these functions by successive linear segments. For example, the highly nonlinear function $f(x)$ in Figure 5.4 has been approximated by six line segments. Obviously, we could have obtained a better "fit" by using 12 or even 24 line segments, but — as is usually the case in life — there is no "free lunch" in linear approximation techniques. Each of the line segments represents a *variable*[2] in the resulting linear model, so that there is a direct trade-off between the *accuracy* of the approximation and the *size* of the resulting LP model. As was the case with quadratic programming, we must alter the SIMPLEX algorithm slightly to make sure we get a meaningful solution to the LP model.

How "well behaved" does an NLP objective or constraint function have to be to be a candidate for approximation by linear segments? One class of such models is *separable* NLP models, which have the following configuration.

$$\text{OPTIMIZE } x_0 = \sum_{j=1}^{n} f_j(x_j) \quad (5.22)$$

$$\text{SUBJECT TO:} \quad \sum_{j=1}^{n} g_i(x_j) \left\{ \begin{matrix} \leq \\ = \\ \geq \end{matrix} \right\} b_i, \quad i = 1, \ldots, m \quad (5.23)$$

Note that each term in the objective function and constraints is a function of exactly one decision variable — although the functions themselves can assume highly nonlinear forms. Separable models can be approximated easily by linear

---

[2] The approximating line segments are merely convex linear combinations of extreme points, and the resulting variables w_k are the convex weights.

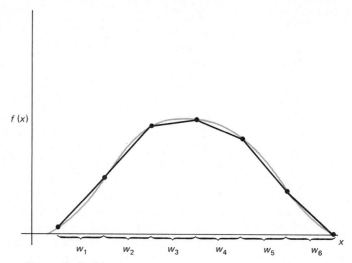

Figure 5.4   Linear approximation of a nonlinear function.

functions and — within the capability of our computer to grapple with large LP models — can be solved to any desired degree of accuracy.

Other Linearization Techniques

There is a wide variety of other approaches such as successive linear programming, direct linearization of MINIMAX objective functions, and so on that have been developed to "tame" certain NLP models. These, as well as those just discussed, all take essentially the same approach — they transform NLP models that we cannot solve directly into equivalent LP models that can be solved with the SIMPLEX algorithm (with modifications, perhaps). Such approaches are on the frontier of current research into solution techniques in nonlinear programming.

MISCELLANEOUS METHODS

The geometric programming model that evolved in our previous look at optimizing the dimensions of chemical shipping containers is one example of NLP models that can be solved with specialized techniques that do not fit neatly into one of the first three categories. The solution technique called *geometric programming* solves models whose objective function and constraints consist of expressions called *posynomials* (sums of terms that are products of powers of the decision variables). We observe here that the technique is based on the theory of duality.

Another "miscellaneous" method used to solve nonlinear models is the so-called *dynamic programming* technique. This approach is so useful, important, and versatile that we will discuss it separately in the next chapter.

AVAILABLE NLP COMPUTER CODES

We first take a look at NLP computer codes that may be available in your computer center. We then discuss some other "mainframe codes" available for solution of large models. Finally, we will consider codes available for solution of small problems on small computers. By and large, the mainframe computer codes will not run on small computers and conversely. Mainframe computer codes are written primarily in FORTRAN and are not readily adaptable to small computers because they are designed to solve large models. The codes written for small computers employ BASIC as their source language, and the dialects of BASIC are so diverse that it is not likely that such codes will execute on mainframe computers without extensive modification.

COMMERCIAL MAINFRAME COMPUTER CODES

Some of the NLP codes that are available in most computer installations, particularly if the installation uses IBM software, are included in the IBM Scientific Subroutine Package (SSP) and the IMSL (International Mathematics and Statistics Library).

The IBM-SSP
This package contains two subroutines for function minimization—FMCG and FMFP, standing for function-minimization-conjugate-gradient and function-minimization-Fletcher-Powell, respectively. The documentation for the package describes how to use these routines.

IMSL
The IMSL library has several codes that are useful in solving NLP models. The subroutines run the gamut from a program to find the minimum of a unimodal one-dimensional function (ZXGSN) to a complex multivariate gradient search code (ZXCGR). The IMSL package isn't easy for a nonprogrammer to use, but then that's what computer analysts are for.

OTHER MAINFRAME COMPUTER CODES

We now discuss other mainframe NLP codes that your installation is unlikely to have on hand but that can be obtained from their owners and/or "inventors."

NAG Library
The NAG (National Algorithms Group) library is available from Dr. Walter Murray, Division of Numerical Analysis Computing, National Physical Laboratory, Teddington, Middlesex TW11 OLW, England. It includes 8 unconstrained minimization codes, 12 codes for NLP models with linear constraints, and 4 codes for NLP models with nonlinear constraints. All programs are written in standard FORTRAN.

Harwell Library

This library includes codes for unconstrained minimization, quadratic programming, and NLP models with linear constraints. The major routine for nonlinearly constrained models is an "augmented Lagrangian" method known as VFOIA/AD. The library is available from Harwell Program Library, AERE, Harwell, Didcot, Oxfordshire, England OX11 ORA.

OPTIMA Library:

This library contains a code for unconstrained minimization, one for nonlinear least squares, three for nonlinearly constrained minimization, one that utilizes penalty functions, one that uses an "augmented Lagrangian," and a recursive quadratic programming code called OPRQP. This library is available from the Numerical Optimisation Centre, The Hatfield Polytechnic, Hatfield, Hertfordshire, England.

Survey of Available Codes:

In their excellent survey papers [4,5], Lasdon and Waren present an in-depth exposition of both NLP applications and available NLP codes. Lasdon's code GRG2, which is a direct method in our terminology, is available for a nominal fee from the Graduate School of Business, University of Texas at Austin. This code is tightly programmed and works well on a wide variety of models.

NLP CODES FOR SMALL COMPUTERS

NONLP, a package created by James R. Burns, is a set of NLP computer codes written in BASIC and incorporated into a single package. These computer codes are *partially* interactive—that is, some coding is required to enter the objective function and the constraints. Using NONLP, it is possible to perform timing and accuracy tests on the various algorithms that make up the package and to compare them. The package is very useful for solving small NLP models and includes the following algorithms:

One-dimensional minimization
  Cubic interpolation
  Fibonacci search

Multidimensional minimization
  Fletcher-Powell algorithm [6]
  Powell algorithm [7]

The multidimensional search routines are capable of using the one-dimensional search algorithm to perform line searches. The package requires roughly 16K (kilobytes) of RAM (random access memory) to load and will execute very satisfactorily on personal computers with 64K (or more) of RAM.

In addition, the Hewlett-Packard library contains a nonlinear code LINQUP that will solve either linear or quadratic programming models. The code is not very efficient in an operational sense, but it is an effective pedagogical device.

DEVELOPING ALTERNATIVE SOLUTIONS

Structured approaches to developing alternative solutions to NLP models form a mixed bag, at best. For methods that employ Lagrange multipliers to incorporate constraints into the objective functions, the values of these multiplier variables for the optimal model solution behave exactly like shadow prices in LP. That is, they are *marginal utilities* for the resources represented by the associated constraints.

Most NLP algorithms generate better and better solutions along the way, and these good (but suboptimal) solutions can easily be recorded and used to provide managerial flexibility in the decision-making process. One obvious exception is the class of so-called "outer" methods that produce only infeasible solutions until the optimal model solution is found. Also, a caveat is in order here. As we noted earlier, indirect methods (as well as most direct methods) sometimes locate a *local* optimum that is not the global optimum we are looking for. Figure 5.5 depicts such a situation. In such cases, the algorithm can sometimes be "re-started" at several different initial points in an effort to locate the global optimum.

On the surface, it would appear that models that are solved by linearization approaches (i.e., transformed into LP models and solved by the SIMPLEX algorithm) are amenable to "postoptimality" or "sensitivity analysis" by the techniques in Chapter 2. This is true to a certain extent, but we must keep in mind that we are dealing with LP models that are *transformations* of NLP models, so that we must be very careful how we interpret shadow prices and other LP indicators. Such analyses are indeed possible but, unfortunately, are beyond the scope of this text.

To summarize, generating alternative solutions and performing sensitivity analyses in the nonlinear "outback" are ill-structured undertakings at best—except in a few special cases.

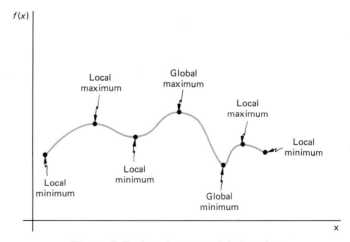

Figure 5.5   Local versus global optima.

STATE OF THE ART IN NLP

Large-scale nonlinear programming is becoming increasingly important in the refinery and petrochemical industries. As mentioned earlier, corporate and industrial mathematical models have gradually evolved from LP models to NLP models. In some cases the computer codes used to solve these models have also evolved to ever more elaborate variations of the SIMPLEX algorithm. Following Lasdon [5], we describe a few such codes being used in the oil and gas industry. A successive linear programming (SLP) code for solving NLPs arising from refinery optimization is used at Shell Oil. This program has been used to solve problems with up to 30 nonlinear variables and 100 nonlinear constraints.

It is also reported that Gulf Oil used an SLP package consisting of revised SIMPLEX and conjugate gradient methods. A more sophisticated SLP package was used by the Kuwait Oil Company. The largest problem solved to date had 2336 constraints, 4392 linear variables, 400 nonlinear variables, and a SIMPLEX matrix containing 20,000 nonzero elements.

Marathon Oil uses a nonlinear refinery model to perform its refinery optimization. The model is a hierarchical structure with the first level consisting of 20 major FORTRAN simulation submodels for the refinery process. These submodels provide input data for an LP system that coordinates the operations of the submodels.

These are a few of the major NLP methods and models in use by the refinery and petrochemical industries. Similar models and computer codes are in use by Chevron, Standard Oil of California, Union Carbide, and others [5]. Problems ranging from product blending, refinery unit optimization, design of multiplant production, and distribution planning are discussed in the literature.

The literature suggests many other areas of application of large-scale NLP models. Two important ones are networks and economic planning. Nonlinear network topics include electric power dispatch, hydroelectric reservoir management, and problems involving traffic flow in urban transportation networks. Economic planning applications include large dynamic econometric models as well as a variety of static equilibrium models and submodels of larger planning systems.

In our discussion so far, we have left out a great deal more than we have included on the subject of nonlinear programming. And we should not be surprised that this is the case. Numerous brilliant and highly trained mathematicians and operations researchers have devoted their professional lives to investigating small corners of the nonlinear "outback," and much more remains to be discovered than is currently known.

Colossus of Roads

The Scenario: Colossus of Roads, Inc. (COR), is a major manufacturer of earth-moving, grading, and street-paving equipment. Their premier products are the Zeus and Pharos (medium and large earth movers, respectively), the Babylon and Mausolus (narrow- and wide-track road graders, respectively), and the Pyramid (a large street-paving machine). The products are assembled and shipped from COR's plant in Gomorrah, Pennsylvania. There has been a rising demand for COR's products in the past 12 months, and the plant is currently operating at capacity.

The Problem: Artemis "Art" Temple, the company's head of production, has been using a linear programming procedure to help him make product mix decisions each quarter and has found the computer analysis to be most useful. He has always been puzzled by one aspect of the model solution, however. When the LP model indicates that a relatively small number of a given piece of equipment should be produced, the profit contributions are consistently overstated; for relatively large numbers, profit contributions are understated. In the past, he had used a "rule of thumb" that partially accounted for this phenomenon, but with production at full capacity, he was increasingly uncomfortable with this procedure. He suspects that the objective function was nonlinear, but he does not know what to do about it.

The LP model Art used had four constraints: work force availability, space availability in the plant's assembly area, supply of oversized tires (common to all five machines), and a company policy that dictated the assembly of at least as many graders as earth movers. He had already received the data for next quarter and had constructed the LP model as follows. (*Note:* The variables $x_1, \ldots, x_5$ represent numbers of Zeus, Pharos, Babylon, Mausolus, and Pyramid machines to assemble, respectively.)

Profit
contribution MAXIMIZE $x_0 = 3.5x_1 + 4x_2 + 2.5x_3 + 3x_4 + 5.25x_5$ (5.24)
($000s)

Work force SUBJECT TO: $90x_1 + 100x_2 + 75x_3 + 80x_4 + 125x_5 \leq 17{,}000$ (5.25)
(hours)

Space $4x_1 + 5x_2 + 2x_3 + 3x_4 + 8x_5 \leq 740$ (5.26)
(100 ft^2)

Tires $16x_1 + 24x_2 + 12x_3 + 12x_4 + 36x_5 \leq 3000$ (5.27)
(number)

Mix $x_1 + x_2 - x_3 - x_4 \leq 0$ (5.28)

$$x_j \geq 0, \quad j = 1, \ldots, 5 \qquad (5.29)$$

After the analyst ran the LP package and Art rounded the solution, he compared the "optimal" mix with the maximum capacities of the individual machines as follows:

Variable	Product	Optimal LP Solution	Actual Optimal ILP Solution	Art's Rounded LP Solution	Maximum Capacity
x_1	Zeus	90.458	87	90	185
x_2	Pharos	—	1	—	125
x_3	Babylon	—	—	—	226
x_4	Mausolus	90.458	93	90	212
x_5	Pyramid	12.977	13	13	83
Objective value:		$656,107	$655,750	$653,250	

The indicated numbers of Zeus and Mausolus machines did not bother Art, since they were fairly close to the midpoints of their production ranges. The Babylon and Pharos were not produced at all, so they were no problem. The Pyramid, however, was at the extreme low end of its production range, and as a result, the total profit could be considerably overstated by this production mix.

The Model: As a last resort, Art called corporate headquarters in Carthage, New York, to request assistance, and Polly Gnomeal, COR's chief MS/OR analyst, was in his office the next day. After explaining the situation and expressing his concerns, Polly went to work. A week later, she was ready to brief Art on the results of her investigation.

By plotting past profit contribution data, it appeared to Polly that the profit contribution functions for all five products could be approximated by a classical S-curve (Figure 5.6). The general equation for the curve she developed is as follows.

$$P(x_j) = \frac{3(T \cdot x_j^2)}{M_j^2} - \frac{2(T \cdot x_j^3)}{M_j^3} \tag{5.30}$$

where M_j is the maximum number of the jth machine that can be produced in the plant and T is total maximum profit contribution associated with producing M_j units (or $c_j \cdot M_j$, where c_j is Art's estimate of per unit profit contribution used in his LP model). When Polly showed Art the graph of the S curve, Art nodded affirmatively—that's precisely the effect he had suspected (profit overstated for small quantities and understated for large ones).

Plugging in the appropriate numbers and simplifying the objective function, we have the following nonlinear objective function:

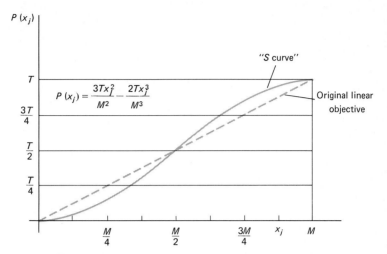

Figure 5.6 Profit function for Colossus of Roads.

MAXIMIZE $x_0 = 0.0568x_1^2 - 0.0002x_1^3 + 0.0960x_2^2 - 0.0005x_2^3 + 0.0332x_3^2$
$- 0.0001x_3^3 + 0.0425x_4^2 - 0.0001x_4^3 + 0.1898x_5^2$
$- 0.0015x_5^3$ (5.31)

The constraints, of course, remain the same, so that (5.31) and (5.25) through (5.29) represent a nonlinear programming model.

   Solution to the Model: Art was impressed with Ms. Gnomeal's NLP model, but he was quick to observe that he had no NLP code on his minicomputer—and he *certainly* had no intention of trying to solve the model by hand! Polly reassured him, noting that Art's model turned out to be *separable* in the decision variables and could thus be approximated by linearization. She judged that Art's minicomputer should be able to handle about 400 variables with its LP code and recommended setting up a grid in steps of three units. For example, the substitution for x_1 would be as follows.

$$x_1 = \sum_{i=1}^{62} 3 \cdot (i \cdot w_{i1})$$ (5.32)

or

$$x_1 = 3w_{11} + 6w_{21} + 9w_{31} + \cdots + 183w_{61,1} + 186w_{62,1}$$ (5.33)

since the maximum value for x_1 is 185. In all, the linearized model would have 383 variables. Before leaving for Carthage, Polly briefed Art's computer analyst on modifying the LP code so that none of the new w variables could take on positive values unless one of its "neighbors" was also positive (i.e., after the first w_{ij} for some j had initially become positive).

   The model was constructed, and—although the minicomputer "crunched" for quite a while—an optimal model solution was obtained. This solution, along with the original LP solution for comparison purposes, is given here.

Variable	Product	Nonlinear Solution	LP Solution
x_1	Zeus	100	90.458
x_2	Pharos	—	—
x_3	Babylon	—	—
x_4	Mausolus	100	90.458
x_5	Pyramid	—	12.977
Objective value:	$654,067		

Solution to the Problem: When he saw the nonlinear solution, Art Temple leaned back thoughtfully in his chair. It appeared that the company policy dictating the assembly of at least as many graders as earth movers was "driving" the problem. As an experiment, he discarded this policy constraint (5.28) and reran his original LP model. To his surprise, he got two alternative optimal *integer* solutions:

Solution to Revised Model

Variable	Product	Solution 1	Solution 2
x_1	Zeus	164	144
x_2	Pharos	—	10
x_3	Babylon	—	—
x_4	Mausolus	28	38
x_5	Pyramid	—	—
Objective value:	$658,000		

Substituting both solutions into the nonlinear objective function (5.31) produced profit contributions of $654,716 (1) and $629,252 (2). Thus it appeared that the original nonlinear solution that indicated the production of 100 each Zeus and Mausolus machines was about the best COR could do and that the policy constraint actually had little effect on total profit contribution. Equally important, the ILP model gave solutions so close to the NLP solution that Art decided to abandon Polly Gnomeal's elegant model, since the additional expense involved did not appear to justify its use.

Beau-Kay, Inc.

The Scenario: Beau-Kay, Inc. (BKI), is a regional firm in the Southwest that produces fertilizer for the home gardening market. The company's most successful product is Meadow Muffin, which is blended from two basic ingredients: a nitrate compound and a natural compound obtained from cattle feedlots in the area. Both ingredients are in plentiful supply, and BKI is at full production capacity to meet the high demand for this product.

The Problem: Beau Vines, the co-owner of BKI, was reviewing production planning with his partner Kay Monton, and they were studying the results of a linear programming model that had been installed by a management science consultant several years ago. The input data were as follows.

	Ingredients		Requirements
	Nitrate	Feedlot	(pounds per bag)
Nitrous oxide	25%	40%	At least 30
Lime	10	6	At least 7
Potash	4	5	No more than 5
Nictic acid	8	10	No more than 10
Phosphate	10	8	No more than 10
Inert ingredients	43	31	—
Cost per pound	$.15	$.18	

The model solution had indicated the minimum cost at $15 per 90-pound bag consisting of 40 pounds of nitrate and 50 pounds of feedlot, for an average cost per pound of $.166667. As he was studying the model, it occurred to Beau that the 90-pound mix was purely arbitrary, being the smallest weight that would meet all of the blending constraints. "I wonder," he remarked to Kay, "whether we could lower our per pound cost by producing a heavier standard bag?"

The Model: Kay, recalling dimly the management science course from her MBA program at the Hereford Business School, replied, "Beau, I think you're right. What we want is a mix that will minimize our average *per pound* cost — and not the total cost of a bag of Meadow Muffin. Let's see — the model would be as follows — with x_1 and x_2 being the number of pounds of nitrate and feedlot, respectively, per bag."

$$\text{MINIMIZE } x_0 = \frac{.15x_1 + .18x_2}{x_1 + x_2} \tag{5.34}$$

$$\text{SUBJECT TO: } .25x_1 + .40x_2 \geq 30 \tag{5.35}$$

$$.10x_1 + .06x_2 \geq 7 \tag{5.36}$$

$$.04x_1 + .05x_2 \leq 5 \tag{5.37}$$

$$.08x_1 + .10x_2 \leq 10 \tag{5.38}$$

$$.10x_1 + .08x_2 \leq 10 \tag{5.39}$$

$$x_1, x_2 \geq 0 \tag{5.40}$$

"By George, I think you've got it, Kay," exclaimed Beau, "but there's one small problem. That's a nonlinear objective function, and all we've got on our Mini-Mite computer is an LP package. I guess we'll have to get that consultant back out here."

Solution to the Model: "Not so fast, Beau," retorted Kay, "what we've got here is called a fractional programming model. There is a device we can use to transform it into an LP model, solve the LP formulation, and reverse the transformation to get our solution."

Let

$$v = \frac{1}{x_1 + x_2}; \quad y_1 = v \cdot x_1; \quad y_2 = v \cdot x_2$$

MINIMIZE $x_0' = .15y_1 + .18y_2$		(5.41)
SUBJECT TO: $.25y_1 + .40y_2 - 30v \geq 0$		(5.42)
$.10y_1 + .06y_2 - 7v \geq 0$		(5.43)
$.04y_1 + .05y_2 - 5v \leq 0$		(5.44)
$.08y_1 + .10y_2 - 10v \leq 0$		(5.45)
$.10y_1 + .08y_2 - 10v \leq 0$		(5.46)
$y_1 + y_2 = 1$		(5.47)
$y_1, y_2, v \geq 0$		(5.48)

The LP solution to (5.41) through (5.48) emerged from the computer as follows:

$$x_0 = 0.157143 \quad y_1 = 0.761905 \quad y_2 = 0.238095 \quad v = 0.00952381$$

Reversing the transformation yielded

$$x_1 = \frac{y_1}{v} \doteq 80 \text{ pounds of nitrate}$$

$$x_2 = \frac{y_2}{v} \doteq 25 \text{ pounds of feedlot}$$

Checking this solution in the original LP formulation yielded:

$s_1 = 0$:   nitrous oxide constraint exactly met
$s_2 = 2.5\text{lb}$:   lime constraint more than met
$s_3 = .55\text{lb}$:   potash constraint more than met
$s_4 = .10\text{lb}$:   nictic acid constraint more than met
$s_5 = 0$:   phosphate constraint exactly met

Solution to the Problem: "That's amazing," remarked Beau upon examining the solution. "The new mix is only 15 pounds more per bag than our current formula, but the proportion of the ingredients is drastically different. And notice the difference in costs per pound—$.157143 versus our current $.166667—or $.009524. If we sell 2 million pounds of Meadow Muffin this year as we did last year, that's a total cost saving of over $19,000. Let's order a supply of 105-pound bags right now."

"Hold your horses, Beau," cautioned Kay, "we're the decision makers here—not that fractional programming model. Our ingredient cost for our present 90-pound bag of Meadow Muffin is $15.00 and our one-third markup to the $20.00 selling price covers our overhead and other costs and gets us about $2 profit per bag. With this new mixture, the ingredients in the 105-pound bag would cost us $16.50 per bag, so a one-third markup would increase the selling price to $22 per bag. What will our customers say?''

"They'll be pleased as punch," Beau answered. "They'll be getting 16.7% more fertilizer at only a 10% increase in price. Of course, we will sell about 14.3% fewer bags to meet the same demand level in pounds, but our profit margin per bag will go up by 25% to $2.50 per bag. That means our overall profit will rise a little over 7%. See — there's something in it for everybody.''

"Yep," observed Kay, "except for our feedlot supplier. He won't be happy when we cut our order in half. On the other hand our nitrate supplier will be delighted when we double our order. They've got so much of that stuff they don't know what to do with it.''

SUMMARY

In the foregoing, we saw that nonlinear programming models come in a wide variety of forms, and that — unlike the case with LP models — the underlying assumptions are associated with different model forms rather than with one general NLP model. The art of nonlinear modeling was illustrated with several examples. Typical applications of NLP arise in price bundling and discounting, product blending, inventory control, and scrap minimization.

Four different solutions approaches were described — direct methods, indirect methods, linearization, and miscellaneous methods — and each approach was illustrated with one or two specific examples. A variety of available computer codes that implement these solution approaches were also discussed.

We then saw that generating alternative solutions from NLP models, and performing sensitivity analyses on them, is tricky at best.

If you are left with an uneasy feeling about NLP models — as opposed to their docile, well-behaved LP cousins from Chapter 2 — then this chapter has done its job well.

While NLP models are difficult, they are not unsolvable, in that many solution approaches to NLP utilize the SIMPLEX algorithm in some way. Certainly this is true of large-scale NLP applications, but it is true of fractional programming and quadratic programming as well.

In Chapters 2 through 5, we have surveyed the terrain of deterministic optimization models from the "catbird's seat" of mathematical programming. In Chapter 6, we will look at a totally different approach to modeling certain managerial problems, called *multistage modeling.*

PROBLEMS

1. Linear regression is a widely used technique for analyzing data sets, and almost every undergraduate business student is exposed to it as a freshman or sophomore (if not sooner, in high school). In simple regression, a straight line is constructed in such a way that the sum of *squared* distances between the line and the values of the dependent variable is minimized. In the multivariate case, a hyperplane performs this function.

One difficulty with minimizing *squared* sums of distances is that "outliners" in the data set can sometimes completely dominate the results. That is, squaring distances tends to "wash out" the effects of all but abnormally large (or small) data values. For example, consider the following time series representing the selling price of BOR on the New York Stock Exchange at the close on eight consecutive Fridays:

x_1	Week No.	1	2	3	4	5	6	7	8
y_1	Price	$24\frac{3}{8}$	$25\frac{7}{8}$	$25\frac{1}{2}$	$26\frac{3}{4}$	$27\frac{1}{2}$	$27\frac{3}{4}$	$28\frac{1}{8}$	$25\frac{1}{2}$

The dark line in Figure 5.7 is the least squares regression line for this data set. Note how the outlier (week 8) "bent" the line toward itself and away from the other seven points.

Another way of describing linear relationships among points in a data set is *mean absolute deviation* (MAD) regression. That is, we might wish to have a regression function that minimized the sum (or equivalently the average) of *absolute* deviations from the points in the data set. Mathematically, this is stated as follows.

$$\text{MINIMIZE } x_0 = \sum_{i=1}^{n} |ax_i + b - y_i| \tag{5.49}$$

Unfortunately, the absolute value function is not differentiable, so we cannot use calculus to find the optimal values of (a) and (b)—as we do in least square regression.

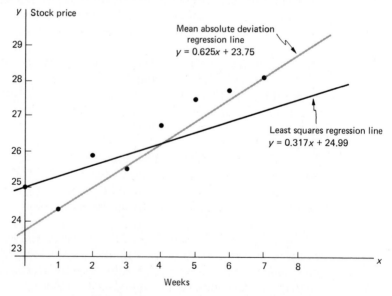

Figure 5.7 Regression on stock prices.

Also, from a mathematical programming point of view, (5.49) is nonlinear—so we cannot directly apply LP solution techniques.

a. Consider the following LP model

$$\text{MINIMIZE } x_0 = \sum_{i=1}^{n} u_i + \sum_{i=1}^{n} v_i \tag{5.50}$$

$$\text{SUBJECT TO:} \quad ax_i + b - u_i + v_i = y_i,$$
$$i = 1, \ldots, n \tag{5.51}$$

$$u_i, v_i \geq 0 \text{ for all } i \tag{5.52}$$

$$a, b \text{ unconstrained in sign} \tag{5.53}$$

where the (x_i, y_i) are the coordinates of the n points in our data set and the u_i and v_i are a set of "accounting variables."

Do you see that solving the ordinary LP model (5.50) through (5.53) yields the optimal values of the regression parameters a and b in $y = ax + b$? (*Hint:* What we have done is to set each of the absolute value expressions in (5.49) equal to the difference between two nonnegative variables.)

b. The MAD regression line for the BOR stock price data is shown as the light line in Figure 5.7. Note that this line "discounts" point 8 and has a higher slope and smaller intercept than the least squares regression line.

If you were comfortable with using time as the independent variable for forecasting purposes, which of the two regression lines would you place more confidence in—all else being equal?

c. Note that MAD regression can also be used to fit *nonlinear* functions to a data set. In this case, however, the resulting mathematical program has a linear objective function and *nonlinear* constraints. Depending on the nature of the nonlinear function, what solution approaches discussed in this chapter might be used to find the optimal regression parameters?

d. As noted in this chapter, many nonlinear programming models arise *empirically*. That is, historical data are fit to a curve of some kind, and the resulting function is used, perhaps, as the objective function in a nonlinear programming model. Do you think MAD regression might be more suitable for this purpose than least squares regression? Why or why not?

2.   *The Scenario:*   Hurley Byrd, a former military paramedic and private pilot, is considering establishing a helicopter ambulance service in the sparsely populated north-central plains states. Figure 5.8 exhibits the cities or towns he would want to serve, along with their populations. He has also marked off a mileage grid of the 25,000-square-mile area that contains the 15 cities in which the 45,000 people live.

The Problem: Hurley wishes to establish a base for his helicopter ambulance service in such a way that he maximizes the overall service level he provides and at the same time minimizes total miles flown—and thus minimizes gasoline consumption.

Having attended the U.S. Army's three-day short course on mechanical engineering, Hurley recognizes his problem as one similar to that of finding the *weighted center of gravity*. That is, if he obtains the grid coordinates (x_i, y_i) of each of the 15 towns and lets the weights w_i be the towns' populations, the weighted center of gravity model is as follows.

$$\text{MINIMIZE } x_0 = \frac{\sum_{i=1}^{15} w_i[(x - x_i)^2 + (y - y_i)^2]}{\sum_{i=1}^{15} w_i} \tag{5.54}$$

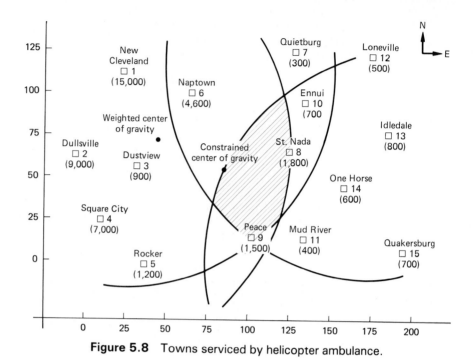

Figure 5.8 Towns serviced by helicopter ambulance.

He digs out the formulas for finding (x^*, y^*), the weighted center of gravity, as follows.

$$x^* = \frac{\sum_{i=1}^{15} w_i x_i}{\sum_{i=1}^{15} w_i}; \qquad y^* = \frac{\sum_{i=1}^{15} w_i y_i}{\sum_{i=1}^{15} w_i} \qquad (5.55)$$

Plugging in the numbers, he obtains $x^* = 45.32$; $y^* = 71.83$, which is about 20 miles northeast of Dustview. To his chagrin, this "optimal" location is 170 miles away from Quakersburg, and the range of his converted helicopter ambulance is only 125 miles. He also notes that Loneville and Idledale would also be outside his helicopter's range.

Hurley's problem is known in engineering as a *constrained center of gravity problem* and in the MS/OR literature as a *facility location problem*. Think for a moment about how we could express the constraints that, along with the objective function (5.54), would result in a nonlinear programming model of this problem. Note that a circle of radius 125 miles, with Loneville (12) as its center, includes all towns but the five western-most ones and that a similar circle centered on Dullsville (2) includes these five towns. Constructing similar circles around New Cleveland (1) and Quakersburg (15) produces the odd-shaped shaded area in Figure 5.8. You might wish to verify that every town is within 125 miles of every point in this shaded area. This, then, is the feasible region. The model is formulated mathematically as follows.

$$\text{MINIMIZE } x_0 = \frac{\sum_{i=1}^{15} w_i[(x - x_i)^2 + (y - y_i)^2]}{\sum_{i=1}^{15} w_i} \qquad (5.56)$$

SUBJECT TO: (Loneville) $(x - 175)^2 + (y - 115)^2 \leq (125)^2$ (5.57)

(Dullsville) $(x - 0)^2 + (y - 65)^2 \leq (125)^2$ (5.58)

(New Cleveland) $(x - 25)^2 + (y - 110)^2 \leq (125)^2$ (5.59)

(Quakersburg) $(x - 200)^2 + (y - 0)^2 \leq (125)^2$ (5.60)

Solution to the Model: The model exhibited is a nonlinear programming model that could probably best be solved formally with an algorithm such as GRG2 or—since all of the functions are separable—linearized and solved with an LP package.

a. Study Figure 5.8 and consider the following. The *unconstrained* minimum point is at coordinates (45.32, 71.83), which is outside the feasible region. Does it seem intuitive that we would like the optimal *constrained* point to be as close to (45.32, 71.83) as possible? If this conjecture is correct, we can solve this model graphically by finding (with a compass) the point at which a circle drawn around the point (45.32, 71.83) touches the boundary of the feasible region. By inspection, this point lies on the circle drawn around Quakersburg and has coordinates of approximately (85, 55). Do you believe this point to be the optimal constrained center of gravity? Why or why not?

Solution to the Problem: As is usually the case, modeling the problem and solving the model resulted in nothing more than managerial insight. The "optimal" constrained point in this case ended up 38 miles from the nearest town, in the middle of a deserted lignite mine! Notice that—if Hurley wanted to locate his firm in inhabited surroundings—only the small towns of St. Nada and Peace lie within the feasible region.

a. Suppose Hurley Byrd regretfully abandoned the possibility of providing helicopter ambulance service to the small towns of Loneville, Idledale, and Quakersburg, whose total population of 2000 is only 4% of the population of the area. What would happen to the unconstrained center of gravity? Would all remaining towns be within a 125-mile radius of the new location?

b. If you were acting as a consultant to Hurley on this problem, how would you go about investigating the sensitivity of the solution to the range of his helicopter?

c. Suppose, instead of sparsely settled countryside and helicopter ambulance service, we were discussing normal automotive ambulance service in a large city. Would the center of gravity model be appropriate in this case (assuming a rectangular pattern of streets)? Do you see that we would need an *absolute value* minimization objective rather than a "sum-of-squares" objective?

3.   *The Scenario:* Barbara Seville is a management science consultant to Hairy Story, Inc. (HSI), a chain of hair styling salons; she assists the company in selecting locations for new salons and in configuring them. HSI does not build its own shops; rather, the company leases vacant space in what it considers to be good locations. Business is booming, and Barbara is essentially working full time for HSI.

The Problem: Since leased space varies widely in size from one location to the next, each salon is configured somewhat differently. There are six basic "stations" that can be included (e.g., washing, cutting, drying), and each has a certain "utility." However, the utility of *additional* stations of a certain type diminishes monotonically as the number increases. Each salon must, of course, include at least one of the six types of station, but there is obviously an upper limit on the numbers of station types desirable in a particular salon—regardless of how much floor space is available. Barbara would like to build a general model that would suggest an "optimal" configuration based on floor space available.

The Model: In talking to Lucinda Cutter, the company's CEO, Barbara is able to formalize two key aspects of the problem: the maximum number allowable for each type of station and the approximate shapes of the six "utility functions" for each type of station. These curves appear to be roughly parabolic, so she adopts the following basic utility curve.

Let

M_i = maximum number of type i stations allowed

V_i = utility for M_i stations

x_i = number of stations of type i included

y_i = utility of x_i stations

Mathematically, the quadratic function for station i is

$$y_i(x_i) = \frac{-V_i \cdot x_i^2}{M_i^2} + \frac{2V_i \cdot x_i}{M_i} \tag{5.61}$$

This general utility function is graphed in Figure 5.9.

The parameters for each station type, to include their floor space requirements in square feet, are

	Station Type					
	1	2	3	4	5	6
Maximum no. (M_i)	2	3	5	6	6	7
Maximum utility (V_i)	10	10	9	8	6	5
Floor space (ft²)	30	27	21	18	19	15

If we let F be the total square footage available for a particular location, our mathematical optimization model is

$$\text{MAXIMIZE } x_0 = \left(\frac{-10 \cdot x_1^2}{4} + \frac{20x_1}{2} \right) + \left(\frac{-10x_2^2}{9} + \frac{20x_2}{3} \right) + \left(\frac{-9x_3^2}{25} + \frac{18x_3}{5} \right)$$
$$+ \left(\frac{-8x_4^2}{36} + \frac{16x_4}{6} \right) + \left(\frac{-6x_5^2}{36} + \frac{12x_5}{6} \right) + \left(\frac{-5x_6^2}{49} + \frac{10x_6}{7} \right) \tag{5.62}$$

SUBJECT TO:
$$x_i \geq 1,$$
$$i = 1, \ldots, 6 \tag{5.63}$$
$$30x_1 + 27x_2 + 21x_3 + 18x_4 + 19x_5 + 15x_6 \leq F \tag{5.64}$$
$$x_1 \leq 2 \tag{5.65}$$
$$x_2 \leq 3 \tag{5.66}$$
$$x_3 \leq 5 \tag{5.67}$$
$$x_4 \leq 6 \tag{5.68}$$
$$x_5 \leq 6 \tag{5.69}$$
$$x_6 \leq 7 \tag{5.70}$$

a. Is the model (5.62) through (5.70) a classical quadratic programming model? Are the nonlinearities separable?

b. The model is known as a *constrained quadratic knapsack model*—you met the simpler *linear* knapsack model in Chapter 3. Do you see that this is actually

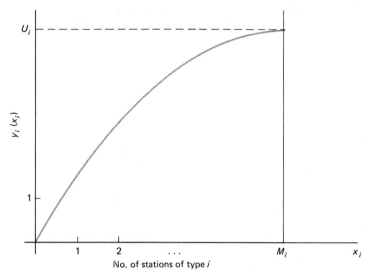

Figure 5.9 General utility function for Hairy Story, Inc.

a nonlinear IP model in that "fractions of stations" is an absurdity, practically speaking?

Solution to the Model: Before feeding the model to a computer, Barbara leaned back in her chair and studied it thoughtfully. The model (given appropriate values of F, the total floor space available) could be solved easily by the Frank-Wolfe quadratic programming algorithm available in HSI's computer package. She realized that she would probably get noninteger solutions, but perhaps some useful insights could be obtained anyway. Analyzing the model a bit more carefully, she realized that the lower-bound constraints (5.63) could be removed by making the simple transformation: $x_j = y_j + 1$; that would cut down the size of the problem and make it easier to solve. Then — in a flash of insight — she realized that the upper-bound constraints (5.65) through (5.70) were, for practical problems, nonbinding as well! The reason for this phenomenon is that, the way the utility functions were constructed, each parabola took on its maximum value at M_i — the maximum number of type i stations allowed. The optimizing model would never allow x_i to be greater than M_i, therefore, since this would result in a *decrease* in total utility! Making the lower-bound transformation, simplifying (5.62) and discarding the upper-bound constraints produced the following equivalent model:

$$\text{MAXIMIZE } x_0 = \frac{-5y_1^2}{2} + 5y_1 - \frac{10y_2^2}{9} + \frac{40y_2}{9} - \frac{9y_3^2}{25} + \frac{72y_3}{25}$$

$$- \frac{2y_4^2}{9} + \frac{20y_4}{9} - \frac{1y_5^2}{6} + \frac{5y_5}{3} - \frac{5y_6^2}{49} + \frac{60y_6}{49} + \frac{80,482}{3,675} \quad (5.71)$$

SUBJECT TO: $30y_1 + 27y_2 + 21y_3 + 18y_4 + 19y_5 + 15y_6 \le F - 130 \quad (5.72)$

$\qquad\qquad\quad y_i \ge 0$ and integer, $i = 1, \ldots, 6 \quad (5.73)$

The Frank-Wolfe quadratic programming algorithm gave the following model solutions (after reversing the transformations) for $F = 430$ square feet:

Variables	Optimal Model Values	M_i	Rounded Model Values	Feasible Model Values
x_1	1.7874	2	2	2
x_2	2.5694	3	3	3
x_3	3.9963	5	4	3
x_4	4.5647	6	5	5
x_5	3.9800	6	4	4
x_6	4.3952	7	4	4

Maximum utility = 45.4881

Shadow price for floor space at $F = 430 ft^2 = .035439$

Barbara noted that the "rounded" model solution is infeasible, requiring 451 ft² instead of 430. Since station 3 requires exactly 21 ft² of space, letting $x_3 = 3$ instead of $x_3 = 4$ produces a feasible integer solution, and the resulting total "utility" is 44.75 — or 98.4% of the theoretical maximum.

Solution to the Problem: Before briefing Lucinda Cutter on the results of her model, Barbara noted that a bare minimum salon (one of each station) would require 130 ft² and the largest possible salon (M_i of each station) would require 573 ft². She reran the model for F values of $130 + 25k$, $k = 0, 1, . . . , 16$, and 573, and "fiddled" with the noninteger solutions to produce "good" feasible solutions for each value of F. She also computed the total "utility" for each configuration, noting that it ranged from a low of about 21.9 for $F = 130$ to 48 for $F = 573$.

Linda reviewed Barbara's results with a practiced eye, mentally checking some of the configurations for "reasonableness" based on her long experience in the "hair game." Two or three of the configurations seemed a bit unbalanced in the low end of the square footage range, and she asked Barbara to analyze the effects of an arbitrary change in configuration for these cases. Finally, she nodded her approval of the analysis in general.

"Barbara, that's a fine job — as usual," Lucinda said, "but I'm going to use your results in a slightly different way from what you intended. I'm going to have our market research guys estimate the type and volume of business we can expect in a given location. When I have those data, I'll come up with a configuration that will satisfy the demand and use your model to identify the amount of square footage we need to lease for the new salon. That will simplify our location problem immensely."

Barbara replied. "It's just like they told us in my MBA program: Models don't make decisions — managers do."

a. Based on the results of the nonlinear optimization model Barbara used, and her rounding to obtain feasible *integer* solutions, would you recommend that Hairy Story, Inc., try to obtain an integer quadratic programming algorithm to solve the configuration model? Why or why not?

b. Consider the following alternative. Each of the quadratic functions for the six variables in the model could be approximated by piecewise linear functions in such a way that the endpoints were at *integer* values of x_1. For example, $M_2 = 3$, so that the utility function for x_2 could be approximated by three line segments with endpoints at $x_2 = 0, 1, 2$, and 3. You can easily verify that a total of 29 such segments would be needed to approximate the six utility functions. The weighting variables could then be treated as zero-one variables, and the model could be optimized using Balas's additive algorithm (see Chapter 3). Therefore, it would produce integer solutions. Would this approach work (in a technical sense)? Would such an approach be advisable in this case (in a managerial sense)?

c. In the configuration model, what is the significance of the shadow price for floor space?

d. As you will learn in Chapter 6, this problem can be also modeled, and the model can be solved efficiently, as a *dynamic programming model.*

REFERENCES

1. FIACCO, A. V., and G. McCORMICK. *Nonlinear Programming: Sequential Unconstrained Minimization Techniques.* New York: John Wiley & Sons, 1968.
2. LASDON, L., A. WAREN, A. JAIN, and M. RATNER. "Design and Testing of Generalized Reduced Gradient Code for Nonlinear Programming." *ACM Trans. Math. Software,* Vol. 4 (1978), pp. 34–50.
3. FRANK, M., and P. WOLFE. "An Algorithm for Quadratic Programming." *Naval Research Logistics Quarterly,* Vol. 3 (1956), pp. 95–110.
4. WAREN, A., and L. LASDON. "The Status of Nonlinear Programming Software." *Operations Research,* Vol. 27 (1979), pp. 431–456.
5. LASDON, L., and A. WAREN. "Survey of Nonlinear Programming Applications." *Operations Research,* Vol. 28 (1980), pp. 1029–1073.
6. FLETCHER, R., and M. POWELL. "A Rapidly Convergent Descent Method for Minimization." *Computer Journal,* Vol. 6 (1963), pp. 163–168.
7. POWELL, M. "An Efficient Method for Finding the Minimum of a Function of Several Variables Without Calculating Derivatives." *Computer Journal,* Vol. 7 (1964), pp. 155–162.

CHAPTER 6

Discrete Dynamic Programming Models

Most people have heard the story about the three blind men who were asked to describe an elephant by touching it. The man who felt the beast's leg compared it to a tree, the one who examined the tail concluded that an elephant is a variety of snake, and so forth. The point is that our view of the world — and, in our case, of managerial problems — depends on our perspective. In the previous chapters on linear, integer, network, and nonlinear modeling, we have looked at our "elephant" in a particular way — basically, as an inseparable *entity* to be modeled and analyzed. The various optimizing algorithms, as a result, had to be constructed in such a way that all the decision variables and their interactions were considered simultaneously.

What if we could look at certain managerial problems as a *sequence of subproblems* requiring a *sequence of decisions*? In this way, we would have the potential perhaps of solving a series of smaller problems — and in the process solve the larger problem. As it so happens, there are many business, industry, and public sector problems that are *multistage* in nature, and we discuss the modeling and analysis of such problems in this chapter, by an approach called *dynamic programming.*

UNDERLYING ASSUMPTIONS

The basic underlying assumption in which we are interested is that our problem can be formulated as a set of consecutive *stages* — each stage requiring a decision. That is *not* to say that the decisions are independent of each other — far from it. It *does* mean, however, that the decisions depend upon each other in a special way. Technicians refer to this stage dependence as having the *Markov property* (after a Russian mathematician). Simply stated, a multistage decision process that has the Markov property is one in which *each decision* in the sequence of decisions incorporates the effects of *all previous decisions,* so we are concerned only with relationships between pairs of consecutive decisions. Got it? Perhaps you have, but this concept is surprisingly elusive. An example or two might be helpful.

A well-known prototype of the multistage optimization model is the so-called "stagecoach problem," which was invented by Harvey Wagner [1]. Wagner's allegory goes something like this. In the days of the Wild West, a Mr. Mark Off wished to travel from New York to San Francisco to seek his fortune. The only public transportation was stagecoaches, and it was necessary to change stages three times en route to his destination. The origin, transfer points, and destination are depicted in Figure 6.1. Since an attack by "wild Indians" was very much a possibility along the way, and since companies sold life insurance policies separately for each leg of the journey, Mark reasoned that the route associated with the least cost policy for the trip would be the safest (insurance companies being notoriously careful about such matters). Since the cost of insurance from one stage to the next is independent of how one arrived at the former (in all cases), Wagner's allegory describes a multi*stage* (thus, the allegory) problem that exhibits the Markov property.

As another illustration, consider the problem faced by Ms. Rhea Lexion, who is running for a second term as governor of her state. Exactly two weeks remain until election day, and she needs to visit the five largest population centers in the state in an effort to garner last-minute votes. Rhea's new campaign manager, Louisa Schertz, is a recent MBA graduate from Justin Case U.,

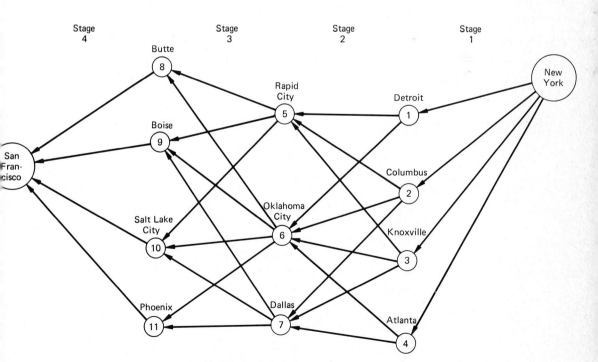

Figure 6.1 The "stagecoach problem."

and although she is short on political savvy, she is an OR modeler par excellence. After an extensive computer analysis of historical voting and campaign data, Louisa has determined the marginal number of additional votes that Ms. Lexion can amass by spending one, two, three, and so on, days in each of the five cities. Since she assumed that the *order* in which Rhea visits the cities is unimportant, Louisa has formulated the problem as a multistage decision model that exhibits the Markov property. In effect, the solution to Louisa's model distributes the 14 remaining days among the five cities in such a way that the total number of additional votes is maximized. She displays her analysis proudly to Governor Lexion.

"Louisa," notes the governor, "that stuff you learned in your two years at JCU is marvelous. However, my MPS (master of political survival) at the Huey Long Institute taught me some important realities. For instance, one of your basic assumptions is that the order in which I visit the five key cities is unimportant. Let me tell you from experience that if I go to Rubesville before I hit Richburg, the Richburgers will be so offended that I'll probably *lose* votes there. Moreover, if I visit Clod Corners earlier than three or four days before the election, the ding-dongs there will forget everything I said by election day. Why don't you just list all 120 combinations of ways I can visit the five cities, and I'll help you put together a model that will be *useful* to me."

As you may have deduced by now, Ms. Lexion's problem is multistage, all right—but the interdependencies among the stages are so complex that her problem cannot even remotely be assumed to possess the Markov property.

Before discussing solution approaches to sequential decision models, we should note that our discussion will center on problems that can be modeled in terms of a discrete (finite) number of alternatives (or *states*) at each stage. Moreover, we will limit ourselves to models with a finite number of *stages* as well. Dynamic programming has been applied to situations in which states are described by continuous functions, as well as to "infinite horizon" scenarios. We will not address these more complex approaches until later in the chapter.

MULTISTAGE MODELING

We have already seen one example of the appropriate use of sequential or multistage modeling—Wagner's famous "stagecoach problem"—and an inappropriate one in Rhea Lexion's campaign problem. The former example exhibited the Markov property, and the latter did not. Is there some handy checklist that can help us to recognize managerial problems that can be profitably modeled in this way? Unfortunately, the answer is no. However, there are certain general *features* of problems that may suggest the use of multistage modeling. These features are time-sequenced decisions, separability, and order-independent allocations. We discuss each in the paragraphs that follow.

TIME-SEQUENCED DECISIONS

The "stagecoach problem" is an example of a situation in which the sequence of decisions is ordered through time. That is, if the tiers of states in this problem were interchanged, a different problem would emerge. As another example, recall the "overhaul or replace" problem from Chapter 4. Our decisions involved whether to overhaul an injection molding machine in a given year or to buy a new one to replace it — the objective being to minimize our total capital and operating expense over a five-year horizon. In Chapter 4, we modeled this problem as a network and sought the shortest (least cost) route. Observe that this problem very clearly exhibits the Markov property and that the decisions are sequential in time. To reiterate, however, the decisions cannot be *made* one at a time — the *set* of decisions (a policy) must be determined in advance.

Are all managerial problems involving time-sequenced decisions candidates for multistage modeling and analysis? Our lives would be a lot simpler if this were true, but alas it isn't. The fact that it isn't true, moreover, isn't always obvious. Consider, for example, the globe-circling airline trip planned by Rhonda Whorl to celebrate the successful completion of her MBA studies at Horseneck State University. Although money is no object, she decides to put her booklearnin' to the test by determining the least cost series of airline flights that will allow her to consummate her circumnavigation of Earth. As she learned in her "quant" course at HSU, her problem is definitely multistage, so she dutifully begins collecting airline fare data for the last leg of the trip. Her simple question to the ticket agent for Navaronne Time Airlines, "What's the fare from Oklahoma City to Horseneck?" elicits the puzzling reply: "Depends on how you got to Oke City. If you flew NTA from the East Coast, there's a special thru fare to points west. If you flew there on another airline, you have to pay the regular fare."

"You mean," queries Rhonda, "that I'd have to compute the fare on every possible routing to Horseneck to find the best one?"

"Yep," replies the agent.

And so much for the Markov property!

SEPARABILITY

In Chapter 5, we discussed the subject of *separable* NLP models and noted that linear approximations to the decision variables could be used to transform these models into ordinary LP models. Such problems can also be viewed in terms of multistage models, by the simple device of viewing each decision variable as a stage in a sequence of decisions. If the variables can take on only integer values, then we have a discrete dynamic programming model. As an aside, all LP models are separable by their very nature, so they can be considered merely special cases of multistage decision models.

Is the separability phenomenon useful in practice? Sometimes. For instance, using a discrete dynamic programming algorithm to solve ILP models would be roughly equivalent to buying a CDC CYBER-76 to balance your checkbook. On the other hand, efficient algorithms for solving *nonlinear* integer programming (NLIP) models are virtually nonexistent, except for some special cases in which the decision variables are zero-one. Except for these special cases, NLIP models are tractable only through modeling and analysis as multistage decision processes. The reason why this is so is interesting. We recall from Chapter 5 that the functional form of the objective function and constraints is critical as regards our ability to produce a useful solution. For separable NLIP models that are viewed as sequential decision processes, the functional forms of the objective and constraint expressions make little difference.

For example, consider two small mathematical programming models, P1 and P2:

P1:

$$\text{MAXIMIZE } x_0 = 2x_1^2 + 3x_2^2 \tag{6.1}$$
$$\text{SUBJECT TO:} \quad x_1 + 2x_1 \le 8 \tag{6.2}$$
$$3x_1 + 5x_2 \le 17 \tag{6.3}$$
$$x_1, x_2 \ge 0 \text{ and integer} \tag{6.4}$$

P2:

$$\text{MAXIMIZE } x_0 = 2x_1^7 \ln(x_1) + e^{x_2^2} \sin x_2^2 \tag{6.5}$$
$$\text{SUBJECT TO:} \quad x_1 \cos^2 x_1 + 1/\arctan x_2^3 \le 8 \tag{6.6}$$
$$e^{\sin x_1} + (x_2 - \sin x_2)^5 \le 17 \tag{6.7}$$
$$x_1, x_2 \le 0 \text{ and integer} \tag{6.8}$$

P1, of course, is an integer quadratic programming model, and a "reasonable" solution might be obtained by using the Frank-Wolfe quadratic programming algorithm on the relaxed model, and rounding the results. P2, on the other hand, is a nonlinear nightmare as far as standard NLP algorithms are concerned. Since both P1 and P2 are separable, however, both can be solved *for their optimal model solutions* by using a dynamic programming approach with only two stages (one stage for each decision variable). The interesting point is this: The computational effort would be roughly the same for both P1 and P2! However, lest our enthusiasm for multistage modeling and analysis get out of hand, let us withhold judgment until our subsequent discussion of the computational aspects of dynamic programming.

ORDER-INDEPENDENT ALLOCATION

Perhaps the most widely applicable type of problem amenable to modeling and analysis by dynamic programming, is the order-independent allocation problem. Such problems are characterized as follows.

1. There is a fixed number (amount) K of a resource to be allocated.
2. There are N competing candidates for the scarce resource.
3. The payoff from allocating 0, 1, 2, . . . units of the resource to a candidate is *nondecreasing* with the number of units allocated.
4. The object is to allocate the K units to the N candidates in such a way as to maximize the total payoff.

As an illustration, consider the advertising strategy problem faced by the marketing firm of Preyss, Proddick, Promo, and Place (PPP&P). The firm has been retained by Common Scents, Inc., to mastermind the introduction of its new "macho" after-shave lotion tentatively named "Eau de Newark." Four New Jersey cities (Weehauken, Tenafly, Hackensack, and Teaneck) have been chosen as the test market, and enough budget is available to buy a total of 200 spot television commercials over the two-week test period. The Marketing Research Department of PPP&P has estimated the level of sales in each city that can be expected for increasing levels of television exposure, using something called S curve analysis. The problem, obviously, is to distribute the 200 spot commercials to the four cities in such a way that total sales are maximized.

The PPP&P problem is a classic order-independent allocation problem. First, there is no reason to suppose that the decision must be made in a particular order, so that the *stages* in the multistage model (the four cities) can be ordered randomly. The fixed resource to be allocated, of course, is the 200 commercials, and there is no reason to suspect that the level of television advertising in one city interacts with that of the others. Second, it is rational to assume that an increasing level of advertising in a given city would result in increasing sales — but perhaps at a decreasing *rate* near the saturation point.

Like most of the models we have encountered so far, the PPP&P problem is a combinatorial problem. That is, there are exactly 201 (i.e., 0, 1, . . . , 200) commercials (states) to be allocated to the four stages (cities). One approach to finding an optimal solution to the model, therefore, would be to enumerate all 1,373,701 possibilities[1] and compute the sales generated by each. As we shall soon see, a much better approach would be to formulate the problem as an order-independent multistage allocation model and to use dynamic programming to find a solution to the model.

We now turn to the solution of discrete multistage models using an optimization technique called dynamic programming.

DYNAMIC PROGRAMMING: AN INTUITIVE DESCRIPTION

The technique commonly known as *dynamic programming* (DP) was invented and developed by Richard Bellman over 25 years ago. George Nemhauser [2] defined DP succinctly as follows:

> **Dynamic programming** is a transformation that takes a sequential or multistage decision process containing many interdependent variables and converts it into a series of one-stage problems, each containing a few variables.

The principle that underlies the concept of DP is referred to as Bellman's principle of optimality [3]. If any mathematical discovery in modern times is the most elegant and intuitively appealing — and at the same time the most elusive and subtle — it is Bellman's.

---

[1] In general, there are $(N + K - 1)!/K! \cdot (N - 1)!$ feasible ways to allocate all K units of resource to N candidates; in our example, $203!/200! \cdot 3! = 1,373,701$.

Bellman's principle of optimality: In a multistage decision process, an optimal policy has the property that whatever the initial state and decision are, the remaining decisions must constitute an optimal policy with regard to the state resulting from the first decision.

To understand Bellman's discovery — and its implementation in optimizing algorithms — let us explore his basic concept further. Nemhauser [2] describes the term "dynamic programming" as "nondescriptive but alluring," preferring the "more representative, but less glamorous term *recursive optimization.*"

What is recursive optimization? Let us return to Wagner's "stagecoach problem" and delve deeper. Suppose Mr. Mark Off, our intrepid fortune seeker, finds himself in a particular state, preparing to board the fourth and final stage to San Francisco. Suppose further that Mark has acted optimally in selecting the states to route himself through via the previous stages. Then it is obvious that his *last* decision would be to take the only available stage to his destination.

Now let us broaden our vista somewhat and consider *all* states (Montana, Idaho, Utah, and Arizona) from which the final stage to San Francisco can depart. If Mark knew the optimal route *to* each of these states, it would be a simple matter for him to add the total optimal cost to reach each of these states to the fare for the stage from there to San Francisco — the lowest such total fare being optimal. Fine. But how did Mark know the optimal cost routing to each state prior to the stage to San Francisco? He merely repeated his analysis of the fourth stage by computing the optimal costs to reach those states via the third stage! And he continued so on — recursively — until he had marched backward through the states in the various stages, finally reaching New York, his origin.

Let us refer to Figure 6.1 and consider a specific example. Suppose that we had backtracked to mid-America and had determined that the least cost routing from Oklahoma City to San Francisco was via Boise. Therefore, we have implicitly eliminated from consideration all routes from New York to San Francisco that include legs from Oklahoma City to Butte, Salt Lake City, and Phoenix. Thus, as we move backward from destination to origin, we eliminate partial routings — and thus reduce the problem dimensions iteratively at each stage. To emphasize the point, suppose that the optimal route happens to be New York–Knoxville–Oklahoma City–Boise–San Francisco (NY–3–6–9–SF). As we proceed, the 34 possible routes are "pared down" to one optimal one in the following manner:

Stage	Best Partial Routes		Routes Eliminated	
4	8–SF	9–SF	None	
	10–SF	11–SF		
3	5–8–SF		NY–1–5–9–SF	NY–1–5–10–SF
			NY–2–5–9–SF	NY–2–5–10–SF
			NY–3–5–9–SF	NY–3–5–10–SF
	6–9–SF		NY–1–6–8–SF	NY–2–6–8–SF
			NY–1–6–10–SF	NY–2–6–10–SF
			NY–1–6–11–SF	NY–2–6–11–SF

(continued)

Stage	Best Partial Routes	Routes Eliminated	
		NY–3–6–8–SF	NY–4–6–8–SF
		NY–3–6–10–SF	NY–4–6–10–SF
		NY–3–6–11–SF	NY–4–6–11–SF
	7–11–SF	NY–2–7–9–SF	NY–2–7–10–SF
		NY–3–7–9–SF	NY–3–7–10–SF
		NY–4–7–9–SF	NY–4–7–10–SF
2	1–5–8–SF	NY–1–6–9–SF	
	2–7–11–SF	NY–2–5–8–SF	NY–2–6–9–SF
	3–6–9–SF	NY–3–7–11–SF	NY–3–5–8–SF
	4–7–11–SF	NY–4–6–9–SF	
1	NY–3–6–9–SF	NY–2–7–11–SF	NY–1–5–8–SF
		NY–4–7–11–SF	

We note that our analysis at stage 4 was trivial, since the four stagecoaches all had the same destination. However, at stage 3, we were able to eliminate 24 of the 34 routes. For example, our computations revealed that *if it were optimal to route ourselves through state 6* (Oklahoma City, Oklahoma), then the best way to proceed to San Francisco would be via state 9 (Boise, Idaho). Thus, at one stage, we were able to eliminate from further consideration all 12 routes that pass through Oklahoma City but do *not* pass through Boise.

We should note in this example that we actually have a "shortest route through a network" model and the network algorithms discussed in Chapter 4 would have been more efficient as solution devices than dynamic programming. However, Wagner's allegory is particularly handy in helping us to grasp exactly what is happening in recursive optimization.

THE ELUSIVENESS OF RECURSIVE OPTIMIZATION

We referred to Bellman's principle of optimality earlier as "elusive and subtle." Perhaps you do not find this concept to be particularly troublesome to grasp, but the fact is that many people do. The difficulty appears to be both psychological and cultural in that we have been trained all our lives to approach problems and situations *deductively*—from first to last, in that order. Recursive optimization, as we have addressed it in relation to multistage optimization models, is essentially an *inductive* process. That is, we start at the *end* and construct a solution *backward* until we reach the beginning.

A simple puzzle will illustrate the point. Suppose that Boylan Burns, a medieval sorcerer, needs exactly four drams of henbane for a potion he is brewing but, due to recent budget cutbacks by King Arthur, has only an eight-dram and a three-dram vial to work with. Rather than attacking the problem directly, Boylan—who thinks differently from most people—goes at it backward.

"Let's see," he says to himself, "if I end up with four drams, it will have to be in the eight-dram vial. But I have a three-dram vial I can pour into the larger one, so that means I'll need to get *one* dram in either vial somehow. Aha! If I pour the three-dram vial three times into the eight-dram vial, I'll have exactly one dram left. I can then empty the large vial, pour in the one dram from the small one, and add a full three-dram vial to the large one. And there's my four drams!"

And that's recursive optimization, albeit in a somewhat silly setting. In an idle moment, you might consider solving this trivial little puzzle deductively—in the way that most of us are accustomed to approaching such problems. If you do, you may find that you eventually resort to trial and error, instead of using a logical and orderly solution process. If, on the other hand, the process of recursive optimization appeals to you (as it did with our backward sorcerer), you might wish to verify that *any number of drams* can be measured with only three-dram and eight-dram vials.

THE "CURSE OF DIMENSIONALITY"

The computational advantage of the dynamic programming approach is that it decomposes large multistage problems into a sequence of smaller, less complex problems. For most such formulations, the computational complexity grows only linearly (approximately) with the number of stages. The problem arises when the number of *stage variables* (decision variables in each state) increases. Computational complexity grows at an *exponential* rate as the number of state variables increases, and this feature of dynamic programming has been colorfully described as the "curse of dimensionality."

To illustrate this phenomenon, recall the PPP&P advertising problem in which 200 spot television commercials had to be allocated among four New Jersey cities. If we *double* the number of commercials to 400, the number of feasible allocations rises by a factor of almost *eight*—from 1,373,701 to 10,827,401.

AVAILABLE COMPUTER CODES FOR DYNAMIC PROGRAMMING

As we noted at the beginning of this chapter, dynamic programming (or recursive optimization) is a way of looking at problems. That is, problems are investigated for a structure that allows them to be decomposed into a sequence of stages in such a way that the larger problem can be solved as a sequence of smaller problems. Thus, dynamic programming is not an algorithm in the sense that the SIMPLEX or "out-of-kilter" techniques are. Instead, it is a solution strategy that is applicable to a great many types of models—some of which can be formulated as standard mathematical programs, and some of which cannot.

Because of the nature of dynamic programming, therefore, it has not been possible (and may never be) to develop a single algorithm for the "dynamic programming model." Some years ago, a group of researchers at Texas A & M University attempted to construct a general algorithm called DYNAPRO [4] to solve the case of discrete multistage optimization models that exhibit the Markov property. The project was something less than a rousing success, although the algorithm did work well for certain classes of discrete models. Does this mean that the dynamic programming technique is beyond the pale of modern computer technology? Happily, the answer is no. We must resort — as we did in the previous chapter on nonlinear programming — to specialized algorithms tailored to specific, frequently used models.

Before discussing available computer codes for DP, we need to understand the basic differences between these codes and standard ones like MPS for linear programming, MPSX for integer programming, PNET for network programming, and so on. Standard codes such as the ones just mentioned employ highly sophisticated mathematical techniques to enhance the speed and storage capability of the mainframe computers in which they reside. One basic reason why these codes may not be implementable on mini- and microcomputers is that the programs themselves may not fit into the limited computer memories in some machines. Discrete dynamic programming calculations, on the other hand, tend to consist of simple operations such as adding, multiplying, and comparing numbers, so that relatively little mathematical sophistication is possible or even necessary. Therefore (and this is admittedly a gross oversimplification), the critical factor in computer implementation tends to be *problem size* alone. For this reason, we will discuss available computer codes for certain specialized DP models, in terms of their programming languages rather than their sophistication. The two languages are FORTRAN and BASIC.

AVAILABLE FORTRAN CODES

Billy E. Gillett, in his 1976 book [5], gives FORTRAN codes for four specialized DP algorithms. The programs are not given acronyms, but they are configured to solve (in Gillett's terminology): (1) investment models with tabular return functions, (2) the "stagecoach problem," (3) the "production scheduling problem," and (4) the "equipment replacement problem." Models in class 1 are (in our terminology) sequence-independent allocation models, such as the PPP&P advertising scenario. The algorithm in class 2 solves staged shortest-route models, as the title indicates; the code in class 4 deals with the "overhaul or replace" model referred to in this chapter and in Chapter 4 as well. We will introduce the production scheduling model (Gillett's third algorithm) in an exercise at the end of this chapter.

Gillett's four computer codes are programmed accurately and economically and are surprisingly compact. They are also well documented and, therefore, easy to follow. It is a simple task to reproduce the printed programs onto cards or tape, but Dr. Gillett offers to supply card decks for a nominal handling charge (write to him at the University of Missouri-Columbia).

Another specialized algorithm with the simple acronym DP was constructed by Linus Schrage and Kenneth Baker to solve the problem of sequencing a set of jobs onto a single machine, with the objective of minimizing the total tardiness of the job set. A model of this type was briefly discussed in Chapter 3. The computer code is highly efficient and can solve very large sequencing problems in a few seconds on a high-speed computer. The algorithm is described in some detail in [6], but the treatment is *very* complex and mathematical. A computer listing of DP is available from Kenneth Baker.

AVAILABLE BASIC CODES

James R. Burns has constructed a BASIC code for solving multistage models of the sequence-independent allocation variety. Entitled DPSA, the program is completely interactive and will solve allocation models with up to 10 stages and 50 total units to be allocated. Models of the "stagecoach problem" and "overhaul or replace" variety are more efficiently solved by the network algorithm PATH, which was discussed in Chapter 4.

DEVELOPING ALTERNATIVE SOLUTIONS

Since multistage problems are combinatorial in nature, there is usually a rich variety of good solutions to even modest-sized models of these problems. For example, in the PPP&P sequence-independent allocation problem, there were over 1.3 million feasible patterns for allocating the 200 commercials to four cities. If this were an actual problem, it would probably be accurate to suppose that there were hundreds of model solutions within 1% (or less) of the optimal objective value. As we have repeatedly stressed, this richness of managerial alternatives is "just what the doctor ordered" for decision makers.

But how do we gain access to these very good, but suboptimal, model solutions when using dynamic programming algorithms? We saw that LP and network models were amenable to such analysis because of the existence of

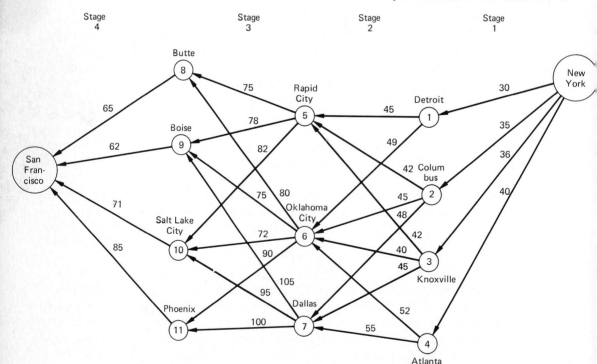

Figure 6.2 The "stagecoach problem" revisited.

shadow prices, and we strained a bit to derive such managerial information from ILP and NLP models. As it turns out, developing good alternative solutions to multistage models is relatively easy, and the BASIC program DPSA has this capability. We will not dwell on the technical details of how this is done; instead, we present an intuitive description of the process, as follows.

Recall for a moment the "stagecoach problem," and think about the information generated by the dynamic programming algorithm as it wended its way recursively, stage by stage, backward from the destination (San Francisco) to the origin (New York). If we had stored the interim results at each stage and subsequently had the computer print them for us, we would have the optimum *partial* policy (i.e., cost of insurance) from every state in every stage, to the destination, and from the origin to every state as well.

As a more concrete illustration, Figure 6.2 is a replication of the "stagecoach problem," with insurance rates for each leg included. Computer output from a dynamic programming optimization model of this problem could easily be constructed to appear as follows.

Analysis of Stagecoach Problem

Lowest-Cost Route from Origin			Lowest-Cost Route to Destination		Lowest-Cost Route Including City
Cost	Route	City	Cost	Route	
0	N/A	New York	$213	3–6–9–SF	$213
$30	NY	Detroit (1)	185	5–8–SF or 5–9–SF	215
35	NY	Columbus (2)	182	5–8–SF or 5–9–SF or 6–9–SF	217
36	NY	Knoxville (3)	182	5–8–SF or 5–9–SF	218
40	NY	Atlanta (4)	189	6–9–SF	229
75	NY–1	Rapid City (5)	140	8–SF or 9–SF	215
76	NY–3	Oklahoma City (6)	137	9–SF	213
81	NY–3	Dallas (7)	166	10–SF	247
150	NY–1–5	Butte (8)	65	SF	215
151	NY–3–6	Boise (9)	62	SF	213
148	NY–3–6	Salt Lake City (10)	71	SF	219
166	NY–3–6	Phoenix (11)	85	SF	251
213	NY–3–6–9	San Francisco	0	N/A	213

N/A – not applicable.

Observe the great variety of managerial options available to us from the computer analysis. For example, the optimal routing for the model is New York–Knoxville–Oklahoma City–Boise–San Francisco, for a total policy premium of $213. However, note that there are several routes with costs within about 3% of the minimum (e.g., New York–Detroit–Rapid City–Butte–San Francisco, for a cost of $215). Furthermore, any routing that includes Dallas or Phoenix appears to be relatively risky. At any rate, the analysis allows the decision maker to consider several options at a glance, including a particular city on the itinerary for exogenous reasons (and noting the resulting route that minimizes total cost), deleting a city from the itinerary and noting "good" routes that remain, and so on.

So much for generating good (suboptimal) alternatives with the use of dynamic programming algorithms on multistage models. Sensitivity analysis on the various parameters is quite another matter. As with integer and nonlinear programming models, our only recourse in this regard is to change parameter values and rerun the computer algorithm — noting any drastic changes that occur from one run to the next.

We now discuss some modeling refinements and advanced computational devices in multistage analysis and dynamic programming.

STATE OF THE ART IN DYNAMIC PROGRAMMING

Our discussion to this point has been confined to discrete, deterministic multistage modeling and solution of these models by specialized recursive optimization algorithms. Before briefly touching on some advanced topics, we should note that the dynamic programming approach is extremely useful in stochastic (probabilistic) modeling as well. Here, however, we will stick to purely deterministic models.

CONTINUOUS DYNAMIC PROGRAMMING

In many cases, the *return functions* for the states in each stage of a multistage model can be approximated by continuous functions. Up to this point in our discussion, we have dealt solely with tabular (discrete) functions — and we noted earlier that the "curse of dimensionality" in dynamic programming is due chiefly to the number of such state variables. Let us return once again to the PPP&P problem of scheduling television commercials in four New Jersey cities for the new after-shave lotion "Eau de Newark."

Connie Tenuous has discovered that the discrete return functions (number of sales as a function of number of commercials aired) for the four cities can be estimated very closely by quadratic polynomial functions, as follows. (*Note:* $S(n)$ is number of sales as a result of airing n commercials.) She excitedly intrudes into Mr. Promo's office with her results, whereupon she is informed that Common Scents, Inc., has only budgeted for a maximum total of 200 commercials.

City	S(n)	Saturation Point	
		No. of Commercials	No. of Sales
Weehawken	$S(n_1) = 300n_1 - .75n_1^2$	200	30,000
Tenafly	$S(n_2) = 208.33n_2 - .42n_2^2$	250	25,850
Hackensack	$S(n_3) = 408.33n_3 - 1.17n_3^2$	175	35,650
Teaneck	$S(n_4) = 300n_4 - .50n_4^2$	300	45,000
Totals		925	136,500

This problem can be modeled and solved easily as a continuous dynamic programming model. Instead of computing hundreds or thousands of tabular return functions at each stage, this form of DP uses elementary differential calculus to find the required values—greatly decreasing the total computational effort.

As an aside, this model can also be solved with the Lagrange multiplier technique discussed in Chapter 5. For those who are curious, the optimal solution to the continuous model of the PPP&P problem is as follows:

City	No. of Commercials	Sales Generated
Weehawken	49	12,899
Tenafly	0	0
Hackensack	78	24,752
Teaneck	73	19,236
Totals	200	56,887

Three features of the solution are interesting from a managerial decision-making perspective. First, note that the model excludes Tenafly from the test market by assigning it zero commercials. Second, the allocation purports to generate 41.7% (56,887 of a possible 136,500) of the possible sales by using only 21.6% (200 out of 925) of the number of commercials. Third, if we solve the model with calculus, the shadow price for the scarce resource "commercials" turns out to be about 227. This means, of course, that—at the margin—about 227 additional sales can be generated by each additional commercial above 200 (as long as the increment is fairly small). On an average basis, each of the 200 commercials currently authorized produces about 284 sales (56,887/200). Do you see that we are "over the hump" in marginal effectiveness of number of commercials?

NONSEQUENTIAL MULTISTAGE OPTIMIZATION

One of our basic underlying assumptions discussed earlier is that our multistage problem must exhibit the Markov property to be a candidate for modeling and analysis by DP. The fact is that we fractured the truth somewhat. Through some highly sophisticated mathematical machinations, OR technicians have found ways to incorporate "feed-back" and "feed-forward" loops into a multistage model. If you are mathematically well trained and are curious about this topic, see the excellent book by Nemhauser [2].

Air Traffic Control [7]

The Scenario: Passenger air travel in the United States has burgeoned over the past 20 years, as tens of millions of travelers (both business and pleasure) turned to this safe, rapid, and relatively inexpensive mode of transportation. As the system grew, certain large cities, such as New York, Chicago, Atlanta, and Dallas-Fort Worth, became "hubs" that served as transfer points for travelers from smaller cities. These busy airports faced a bewildering variety of problems as air traffic increased in volume—everything from massive baggage transfer requirements to maintenance and refueling demands. The advent of "jumbo jets" such as the B-747, L-1011, and DC-10 brought additional problems, and the huge increases in costs for jet fuel in the late 1970s and early 1980s further compounded managerial problems.

The Problem: One particularly aggravating problem occurs during peak arrival times each day at "hub" airports. Depending on the weather, as many as 15 to 20 aircraft may be held in a traffic pattern by controllers, waiting for their turn to land. If we blithely accept "first-come, first-served" as the fair and equitable way to prioritize landings, then we have a solution to the problem—but perhaps a very expensive one on several dimensions.

For example, suppose we have a mixture of "jumbo jets" (300 passengers), conventional large jets (150 passengers), and medium-sized jets (100 passengers) waiting to land at a given time at O'Hare International Airport in Chicago. Psaraftis [7] has given the minimum landing time separation matrix between three types of aircraft, as follows.[2]

Separation Times (in seconds)

		Jumbo	Conventional	Medium
Land Before	Jumbo	96	181	228
	Conventional	72	80	117
	Medium	72	80	90

The table is read as follows. If an aircraft type labeled in a row lands immediately before one in a column, the second aircraft to land must be delayed by at least the number of seconds indicated in that row and column. For example, if a "jumbo" lands and a "medium" is to be next, it must be delayed by at least 228 seconds. As another example, "jumbo's" may land 96 seconds apart.

---

[2] These times are based on landing kinematics of the types of aircraft and are imposed for reasons of safety.

To clarify the nature of the problem, *suppose that a conventional jet has just landed* and that one jumbo (J), one conventional (C), and one medium-sized (M) jets are waiting to land and that all have full passenger loads. There are six distinct ways the three aircraft can be ordered. Let us analyze these permutations using two criteria proposed by Psaraftis: LLT (latest landing time), the elapsed time until the last jet lands, and TPD (total passenger delay), the total passenger-seconds expended in delays.

For example, consider the sequence $J-M-C$:

$$LLT = 72 + 228 + 80 = 380 \text{ sec}$$
$$TPD = [300 \cdot (72)] + [100 \cdot (72 + 228)] + [150 \cdot (72 + 228 + 80)] = 108,600$$

Similar data for all six permutations are

Sequence	$J-M-C$	$J-C-M$	$C-M-J$	$C-J-M$	$M-J-C$	$M-C-J$
LLT	380	370	269	380	370	269
TPD	108,600	96,550	112,400	95,600	123,900	121,950

In this simple problem, LLTs vary from 269 to 380 sec and TPDs vary from 95,600 to 123,900 passenger-seconds; note also that high LLTs tend to be associated with low values of TPD, and vice versa. Moreover, the example assumes that a conventional jet had just landed. If the last landing had been made by a jumbo or a medium-sized jet, the results would have differed drastically from those shown.

To make the transition from the toy problem in our example to the real world, consider the example given by Psaraftis, in which 5 jumbo's, 6 conventional jets, and 4 medium-sized jets (a total of 15) are in the queue. It can be shown that there are 630,630 different sequences in which the aircraft can be scheduled for landing — even after giving an earlier-arriving jet priority over later-arriving ones of its same type. Thus, it is obvious that enumerating all possible sequences and picking the "best" (in some sense) would not be a feasible approach.

The Model: The aircraft sequencing problem (ASP) is a classical example of a problem with time-sequenced decisions, and it was modeled with dynamic programming. However, it was recognized that if the LLT criterion alone is used, the jumbos always end up at the rear of the queue — since the turbulence caused by jumbos on approach and landing causes the minimum separation times for smaller jets to be high. Psaraftis introduced a feature he called *maximum position shift (MPS)* that allows the decision maker to indicate the maximum number of positions (either forward or backward) a given aircraft can be shifted from its actual order of arrival. For example, if MPS = 5, and an aircraft arrived seventh of 15, it could be shifted forward to no earlier than second and backward to no later than twelfth.

If, on the other hand, TPD is used as the sole criterion, the mediums tend to end up at the end of the queue — which is intuitively reasonable, since they carry the smallest number of passengers. The MPS device also acts to moderate this tendency.

Solution to the Model: A modified DP algorithm called *constrained position shift* (CPS) was used to investigate the nature of the ASP. An example problem with (J, C, M) = (5, 6, 4), and with a random arrival sequence, was solved with MPS = 5 and without an effective position shift (i.e., MPS = 14). The results, excerpted from Psaraftis's paper, are reproduced in Table 6.1 [7].

Solution to the Problem: Thus far, our discussion has focused on a *static* problem of aircraft sequencing for landing. That is, we have assumed that a fixed number of aircraft are waiting to land. In the *real* problem, the number of aircraft in the queue changes minute by minute. As Psaraftis notes in his paper, to be useful, the model would have to run in real time — in effect, solving a new DP model every time an aircraft joined the queue. As long as this number remained relatively small, given the speed of current electronic computers and the efficiency of DP algorithms, such an approach is entirely within the realm of possibility.

A second aspect of the problem involves the selection of an appropriate criterion and an appropriate value for the MPS parameter. The LLT criterion minimizes the time it takes to get all aircraft landed but results in higher passenger delay times. The TPD criterion has the converse effect, so perhaps some weighted combination of the two might prove to be satsifac-

Table 6.1 Air Traffic Control Example

Initial Order	Landing Order	MPS = 5		MPS = 14		
		LLT	TPD	LLT	TPD	
C	0					
J	1	J	C	C	J	
J	2	J	J	C	J	
M	3	J	J	C	J	
C	4	C	J	C	J	
C	5	C	J	C	J	
M	6	C	C	C	C	
C	7	C	C	M	C	
J	8	M	M	M	C	
C	9	M	M	M	C	
J	10	M	C	M	C	
M	11	M	C	J	C	
M	12	C	J	J	M	
C	13	C	C	J	M	
J	14	J	M	J	M	
C	15	J	M	J	M	
1729	—	1400	1528	1323	1424	Value of LLT
2,383,800	—	2,033,800	1,883,250	2,241,300	1,664,900	Value of TPD

tory. On the other hand, minimizing aviation fuel costs might be considered an alternative objective.

Finally, any real-time system would have to be flexible enough to accommodate unexpected events such as aircraft short on fuel, emergencies, aircraft with high-priority passengers, and so on.

Cabana Bananas

The Scenario: Cabana Bananas, Inc. (CB), is a major distributor of bananas from Central America to the eastern United States. The company operates its own fleet of steamships and makes deliveries twice each year to the ports of Houston, New Orleans, Miami, Baltimore, Philadelphia, and New York. Wholesalers in these six cities purchase the bananas from CB for distribution to retail outlets.

Bananas are a very fragile commodity. They cannot be frozen and become overripe about 30 days after they are picked. Deliveries can be made to ports in the Gulf of Mexico (Houston, New Orleans) and to Miami in about 18 days, but require 21 days to the northeastern ports (New York, Philadelphia). For this and other reasons, the price CB receives for its bananas varies widely among the six ports. Another curious feature of wholesale pricing for bananas is the effect of economies of scale at certain ports. For example, the wholesaler in New York uses a large truck fleet to supply his customers, and his purchase of a boatload of bananas only partially fills the trucks. Since transportation costs are essentially a fixed expense, it pays the wholesaler to buy larger amounts of bananas — even at a higher incremental cost. This situation also exists in Philadelphia and Houston.

Another curious (and bothersome) aspect of the "banana business" is that it is almost impossible to sell a partial shipload. By the time a steamship unloads part of a load, receives clearance to sail, and completes the complicated undocking and port clearance procedure, several days have elapsed — and the bananas are that much closer to being overripe. Thus, CB must solicit bids for multiple shiploads only.

The Problem: Doane Spoilem, CB's vice-president of distribution, was surprised to discover that the forthcoming banana yield was to be a "bumper crop" — with a full nine shiploads available. CB's fleet consisted of only six ships, and having three ships make two deliveries was out of the question because of bananas' short "life." Fortunately for CB, Havana Bananas (HB), Inc., its chief rival, overestimated its demand, and has three idle steamers that it will provide to CB on a short-term lease. HB's vice-president of distribution has offered Doane the following leasing cost arrangement: $4 million for one, $9 million for two, and $15 million for three steamships (net of CB's ship operating costs).

When bids were received from the 6 wholesalers, Doane arranged them in a matrix (Table 6.2) and studied the figures thoughtfully. In the past, when 6 or fewer boatloads of bananas were available, it had been a simple matter

Table 6.2 CB's Net Profit Matrix

No. of Shiploads	Houston	New Orleans	Miami	Baltimore	Philadelphia	New York
0	0	0	0	0	0	0
1	$7M	$8M	$6M	$9M	$6M	$5M
2	16	15	12	16	10	12
3	24	21	18	21	16	20
4	30	27	23	25	22	27
5	35	32	28	28	27	33
6	39	36	33	31	32	38
7	42	40	37	34	36	42
8	44	No bid	No bid	36	40	45
9	45	No bid	No bid	No bid	43	46

to experiment with different shipment patterns and find the best one. In fact, he had once calculated that with 6 boatloads and 6 cities, there were only 462 possible ways to ship them—assuming that all 6 loads were allocated. With 9 boatloads available—and with the extra complication of having to lease ships (if it were economical to do so)—the problem had taken on a level of complexity that made "experimenting" to find a solution potentially disastrous.

The Model: Herb Plantain, CB's MS/OR analyst, was brought in as an internal consultant and immediately recognized that Doane's problem could be formulated as a dynamic programming model. To be precise, he formulated *four* DP models—one each for 6, 7, 8, and 9 boatloads—since he could not figure out how to get everything into a single model.

Solution to the Model: The microcomputer code DPSA was used to solve the four DP models, since Herb was dealing with a sequence-independent allocation problem. As it turned out, there were several alternative allocations that yielded maximum profit, so Herb—mindful of the proper distinction between an *analyst* and a *decision maker*—had the computer print them all. In addition, Mr. Spoilem had requested that Herb generate an allocation in which all six ports received *at least one boatload* of bananas, which Herb accomplished. Optimal solutions to the four models, as well as the all-ports models, are exhibited in Table 6.3. When additional leasing costs are considered, the *net profit contributions* are as follows:

No. of Shiploads	Optimal	All Ports
6	$48*	$41*
7	51	46
8	52	49
9	53	50

* In millions.

Table 6.3 Cabana Bananas Model Solutions

Solution No.	Ports						Gross Profit (millions)
	Houston	New Orleans	Miami	Baltimore	Philadelphia	New York	
Nine-Ship Solutions							
1	3	2	0	1	0	3	$68M
2	3	1	0	1	0	4	68
3	3	1	0	2	0	3	68
4	3	2	1	1	1	1	65
5	3	1	1	2	1	1	65
6	3	1	1	1	1	2	65
7	2	1	1	1	1	3	65
Eight-Ship Solutions							
8	3	1	0	1	0	3	61
9	3	2	0	2	1	0	61
10	3	2	1	2	0	0	61
11	3	3	0	2	0	0	61
12	4	2	0	2	0	0	61
13	3	1	1	1	1	1	58
Seven-Ship Solutions							
14	3	2	0	2	0	0	55
15	2	1	1	1	1	1	50
Six-Ship Solutions							
16	3	1	0	2	0	0	48
17	3	2	0	1	0	0	48
18	1	1	1	1	1	1	41

Solution to the Problem: It was obvious to Doane Spoilem from pe-rusing the model solutions that it would be advisable to lease additional ships from Havana Bananas. In all cases, however, all optimal solutions would allot no bananas to at least two of the six ports. Doane considered such a schedule to be an extremely poor "goodwill" move — especially in a "bumper crop" year for bananas — and decided to allot at least one of the nine shiploads to each port. Of the four schedules that yielded maximum profit contribution, he selected the one that allotted three shiploads to Houston, two to New York, and one each to the other four ports, for two reasons. First, Houston was one of the closest ports, and the wholesaler there would have several additional days to distribute the large volume of bananas. Second, the wholesaler in New York needed large volume to utilize fully his truck fleet and would appreciate the additional allocation more than would the other four.

Touring Europe [8]

The Scenario: During her last year in the MBA program, Diana Cole (an excellent student who also served as a graduate assistant) planned to make a life-long dream come true after graduation — a tour of ten of the greatest cities of Europe. She had visited Europe before on short trips and had a good idea of the interesting and historical sites she would like to visit. She had thought about possibilities for different itineraries for some time, but had never formalized detailed plans.

The Problem: As graduation time approached, it became apparent that Diana's financial resources were limited and that a trip of about three weeks would be the longest she could afford. This coincided nicely with her desire to take off about a month after graduation before beginning full-time employment. With 21 days to spend, and ten very large and richly varied cities to visit, how many days should she spend in each? She began her decision process by informally solving a "shortest-route" problem and arranged her itinerary in the following sequence:

Paris – Athens – Rome – London – Geneva – Amsterdam – Vienna – Madrid – Brussels – Venice

The Model: It was obvious to Diana that her problem could be modeled as a multistage decision process if she could somehow formalize her personal utility for one, two, three, and so on, days in each city. Technically, a dynamic programming formulation would require that she estimate her cumulative utility for 1, 2, 3, . . . , 21 days in each city, so that her 10-stage, 21-state model would involve over *14 million* distinct combinations. Since this prospect appeared to be unmanageable, she arbitrarily limited her length of stay in each city to four days — which made the task of building her utility function a more reasonable one.

The process that Diana used to construct her utility function was creative and most interesting. Using a popular travel guide [9], she scheduled four days of activities in each city and rated each day in each city on a subjective scale from 1 to 10. After normalizing her ratings on a per hour basis (daily activities ranged from five to nine hours), she ordered the four days on each city from highest to lowest utility and calculated a cumulative total. For example, her calculations for a four-day stint in Rome were as follows.

Day	Activity	Hours	Utility/ Hour	Hours x Utility	Daily Total	Normalized 6-hr Day	Cumulative Total
1	Sistine Chapel	3	10	30			
	St. Peter's Cathedral	2	7	14			
	Vatican Museum	2	3.67	7.34	51.34	44	44
2	Colosseum	2	7	14			
	Roman Forum	1	2.83	2.83			
	Spanish Steps	1	3.67	3.67			
	Trevi Fountain	2	7	14	34.5	35	79

(continued)

Day	Activity	Hours	Utility/ Hour	Hours x Utility	Daily Total	Normalized 6-hr Day	Cumulative Total
3	Capitoline Hill	2	2	4			
	Outdoor Opera	3	5	15	19	23	102
4	Pantheon	2	2.83	5.66			
	Trajan's Column	1	2	2			
	Piazza Navona	2	2.83	5.66	12.32	15	117

Her overall utility function for the ten cities is given in Table 6.4.

Solution to the Model: Restricting the maximum visit to any one city to four days greatly reduced the computational complexity of Diana's problem, and she used dynamic programming to solve it. Her optimal model solution gave a total utility of **844** and is exhibited below.

City	No. of Days	City	No. Days
Paris	3	Amsterdam	1
Athens	3	Vienna	3
Rome	2	Madrid	2
London	2	Brussels	2
Geneva	1	Venice	2

There were no alternate optimal solutions to the *model,* but Diana identified another near-optimal solution (utility of 841) by spending one additional day in Brussels and one less day in Paris. By way of contrast, her *worst* possible utility of 611 would involve four days each in Rome, London, Geneva, Amsterdam, and Madrid, and one day in either Paris or Athens. Thus, her model did have discriminatory power.

Table 6.4 Cumulative Utility Function for Touring Europe

City	Day No. 0	1	2	3	4
Paris	0	42	82	112	133
Athens	0	42	77	107	121
Rome	0	44	79	102	117
London	0	44	76	100	117
Geneva	0	51	74	97	114
Amsterdam	0	53	78	100	114
Vienna	0	46	92	122	137
Madrid	0	45	81	100	107
Brussels	0	50	83	110	124
Venice	0	47	80	103	120

Solution to the Problem: Rather than using the results of her model as an inflexible schedule, Diana tentatively planned to spend the number of days indicated by the optimal model solution in each city. She reserved to herself the right to change her itinerary if special unforeseen circumstances arose, however, and recognized that her time estimates for the various activities were educated guesses at best. The model had proven beneficial in two ways. First, it gave her insight into planning her very special trip; second, it got her an "A" in her MBA management science course!

SUMMARY

In this chapter, we considered a different approach to modeling problems than in previous chapters and introduced the concept of multistage optimization. By use of this approach, we are attempting to decompose large problems into a sequence of smaller subproblems and thereby gain a computational advantage. In all such models except certain highly sophisticated variants, we insisted that the Markov property hold pairwise throughout the sequence of stages.

Three categories of multistage models were introduced and discussed: time-sequenced models, separable models, and sequence-independent allocation models. We discovered that, although all three types can be solved using the principle of recursive optimization, specialized algorithms must be used for each type. This confirmed our previous observation that dynamic programming is a broader technique and much different from previous approaches that have general or all-purpose algorithms associated with them. We presented and discussed some available DP codes programmed in FORTRAN or BASIC.

Development of alternative solutions with dynamic programming was discussed at some length, and we concluded that it is a relatively easy task to generate good (but technically suboptimal) solutions by keeping track of certain interim computational results. Sensitivity analysis on model parameters, unfortunately, was seen to be limited chiefly to "brute force" methods. The chapter concluded with a brief discussion of two advanced topics: continuous DP and nonsequential multistage optimization.

PROBLEMS

1. *The Scenario:* Wonmoor Time Novelties (WTN), Inc., is a manufacturer and international distributor of novelty electronic wristwatches. Their products run the gamut from the $10.95 "Jimmy-Watch," whose hour and minute hands are in the form of elongated peanuts, to the elegant and intricate $2000.00 "Electro-Whiz" that can play chess, do income tax returns, and compute the sidereal hour angles of the planets and 47 selected stars from any location on earth. WTN manufactures its own cases, movements, and dial faces, but it relies on a subcontractor to supply the tiny cadmium power packs that are used in all WTN products. The wristwatch business is highly competitive, and profit margins tend to be small.

The Problem: Aaron Hand, the CEO of WTN, is disturbed by the company's operating results for the past quarter. Several production line shutdowns have occurred because the supply of power packs ran out; at other times, the company's cash flow position was dangerously illiquid because of excessive on-hand inventory of parts — to include power packs. Something had to be done, and Aaron called Ceta Pantz, WTN's long-time inventory manager, into his office.

"Pantz," Mr. Hand begins, "what is going on with our power pack supply? The on-hand inventory plot for last quarter looks like a roller coaster."

Ceta responds with a sigh of relief. "Mr. Hand, am I glad you called me in. I've been inventory manager for WTN, man and boy, for over 25 years. My ordering rules (he produces a yellowing laminated card from his vest pocket) never failed me until about a year ago when you hired those two young smart alecks as production manager and director of finance. Whenever I get the power pack supply about right, the young wiseacre in Production pressures me to order more. No sooner do I get the inventory level up a little, than the whippersnapper in Finance starts in on me about tying up too much cash, and he makes me delay my orders. I tried to tell him that I sometimes order an extra batch just before I think the price will go up, but he just gives me that Ivy League fish eye — you know the one I mean."

"Ceta, calm down now," replies Aaron. "Do you use the forecast demand figures and the inventory holding and carrying costs to help you determine when and how many power packs to order?"

"Sure I do," Ceta assures Mr. Hand, "I get a new three-month demand forecast every month — but the figures always change every time. How can I calculate my ordering quantities for three months when the figures are different for two of the same months in the next forecast?"

The Model: At first glance, Ceta Pantz's problem appears to be multistage, of course, since he must make a sequence of decisions about ordering power packs to meet production requirements — and at the same time be sensitive to the costs involved in carrying excessive inventories. On the other hand, while he might use some sort of recursive optimization technique to aid him in making a set of decisions over the immediate three-month period ahead, what does he do next month? He has presumably implemented the first decision in the original sequence — that's water over the dam — so it would be foolish to address a *four*-period sequential problem that included the previous month.

a. One approach would be for Ceta to solve a three-period multistage decision problem every month and plan to implement only the decisions that must be made prior to the beginning of the next month. What do you think of such an approach? Does it make sense to formulate future decisions you never intend to make?

b. Another approach would be to ignore the forecast demand information for the farthest two months and to make ordering decisions one month at a time. What are the possible pitfalls in such a strategy? In general, can ignoring relevant information ever consistently lead to better decisions?

The Solution: The inventory replenishment problem is an example of an *infinite horizon multistage optimization problem.* The approach suggested in (a) is called a *rolling schedule,* and — although it seems counterintuitive to many people — this approach is widely used in practice. The advantage of such an approach is that it optimizes each sequential decision with respect to all available information. Moreover, if (in Ceta's problem) the future demand pattern happens to be relatively stable (i.e., uniformly rising or falling or remaining "flat"), decisions using a rolling schedule tend to be fairly good.

A disadvantage of the rolling schedule is that it is myopic. That is, it tends to ignore such things as seasonality. A great deal of research has been done on models of this type—and most current approaches incorporate stochastic (probabilistic) considerations.

2.   *The Scenario:*   Recalling Rhea Lexion's problem of maximizing the number of votes she will receive in the forthcoming gubernatorial election, we are pleased to report that her campaign manager Louisa Shertz did indeed lay out all 120 combinations of ways that Rhea could visit the five key cities. Based on her "gut feel" about her constituency, Ms. Lexion has decided on the order in which she will visit the five cities: Richburg–Rubesville–Cowtown–Pitts City–Clod Corners.

The Problem: Having resolved the problem of sequence dependence, Louisa frantically recalculates the estimated number of votes that Governor Lexion can generate by spending 0, 1, . . . , 12 days in each city (2 days have been lost from the original 14 because of analysis time). Her estimates are (in 10,000 of votes)

Additional Votes Generated

City							Days						
	0	1	2	3	4	5	6	7	8	9	10	11	12
Richburg	0	6	10	13	14	15	15	16					16
Rubesville	0	4	8	12	16	18	20	21	22				22
Cowtown	0	5	10	15	20	20	19	19	18	17	16	15	15
Pitts City	0	3	7	12	16	19	21	22					22
Clod Corners	0	1	2	4	8	10	15	19	22	24	28	30	32

The Model: Since the sequence-dependence issue has been resolved,
a. Can Rhea Lexion's problem be modeled as a multistage decision model, and if so, can the model be solved with dynamic programming?
b. Does this approach to modeling an election problem seem logical to you? Does any aspect of this process bother you?

Solution to the Model: This model was solved by DPSA, and you should verify the following results.

Rhea Lexion Problem: Alternative Solutions

City	Alternative 1		Alternative 2		Alternative 3	
	Days	Votes	Days	Votes	Days	Votes
Richburg	1	60,000	1	60,000	2	100,000
Rubesville	3	120,000	4	160,000	3	120,000
Cowtown	4	200,000	4	200,000	4	200,000
Pitts City	4	160,000	3	120,000	3	120,000
Clod Corners	0	—	0	—	0	—
Totals	12	540,000	12	540,000	12	540,000

a. In addition to the foregoing alternatives, which yield the optimal solution to the model (540,000 additional votes), there are several that yield 530,000 and 520,000 votes as well. Might these alternatives be of managerial interest to Governor Lexion?
b. Noting that none of the "optimal" alternatives included visiting Clod Corners, Louisa developed the following alternatives before showing the analysis to Rhea.

Rhea Lexion Problem: Suboptimal Solutions

City	Alternative 1		Alternative 2		Alternative 3	
	Days	Votes	Days	Votes	Days	Votes
Richburg	1	60,000	2	100,000	2	100,000
Rubesville	3	120,000	4	160,000	3	120,000
Cowtown	4	200,000	4	200,000	2	100,000
Pitts City	3	120,000	2	70,000	3	120,000
Clod Corners	1	10,000	0	—	2	20,000
Total	12	510,000	12	530,000	12	460,000

Do you think Louisa's strategy in developing suboptimal alternative 1 was a good idea from a managerial point of view? Why do you think she bothered to generate the radically suboptimal strategy 3?

3. The network in Figure 6.3 is sometimes called a balanced redundant communications network. When secure and reliable communication between a sender and receiver is critically important (e.g., in military operations, remote consulting on difficult surgery, "spotting" from the press box by an assistant coach in professional football), the lines (arcs) are linked in staged network fashion by a sequence of booster (and/or encoder-decoder) stations (nodes). In Figure 6.3, the numbers on each arc represent the *reliability* of the transmission line — the probability that it will not fail over a given period of time. Thus, the reliability of the entire communication network is the probability that messages will get through *at least 1* of the 26 possible paths.

It is fairly obvious that this problem can be modeled as a multistage model and that the *stages* are related to the tiers of boosters. It is (perhaps) not quite so obvious what the *states* are, however. Consider the following. If a message arrives at booster 3, the probability that all three lines from booster 3 to boosters 6, 7, and 8 is the *product*

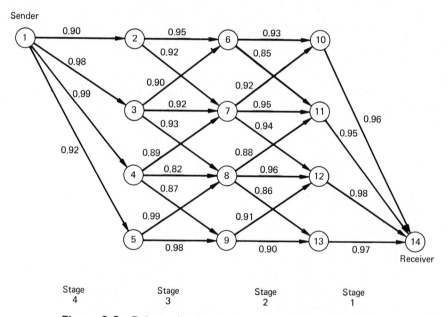

Figure 6.3 Balanced redundant communications network.

of the probabilities that each individual line is down—in this case, $(1 - .90) \cdot (1 - .92) \cdot (1 - .93) = .00056$. Therefore, the probability that a message arriving at booster 3 finds an operable line to the next stage is $(1 - .00056) = .99944$. This number is the *reliability* of booster 3, and these reliability numbers, computed for each booster (except 14, of course), are the *states* in our dynamic programming model.

The *return function,* therefore, is the *product* of the reliability numbers of the boosters on the paths in the network. If we were attempting to model this problem as a mathematical program, the objective function would be a highly nonlinear function of the type that is unusually difficult to deal with algorithmically. Using backward recursion, the problem can be modeled and solved rather easily.

Verify that the booster reliability numbers (correct to six decimal places) are as follows.

Stage	Booster	Reliability	Stage	Booster	Reliability
4	1	.999998	1	10	.960000
3	2	.996000		11	.950000
	3	.999440		12	.980000
	4	.997426		13	.970000
	5	.999800			
2	6	.989500			
	7	.999760			
	8	.999328			
	9	.991000			

a. It would appear on the surface that solving the DP model of this problem would be simple—one could merely select the booster with the largest reliability number at each stage (i.e., a "greedy" approach). Why won't that ploy work with this problem? Under what conditions *would* it work?

b. The "greedy" algorithm works *partially*. Note, for example, that the most reliable node in stage 1 is booster 12 and that the most reliable one in stage 2 is booster 7. Since these two boosters are connected by an arc, do you see that we can eliminate the following circuits from consideration?

$$1-2-7-10-14 \qquad 1-2-7-11-14 \qquad 1-3-7-11-14$$
$$1-4-7-10-14 \qquad 1-4-7-11-14$$

c. Verify that the routing $1-3-7-12-14$ is the highest reliability path in the communication network, with a reliability number of .979213. If you were the network designer and wished to increase the reliability number of the network, would you consider adding additional banks of boosters (stages) or augmenting the current stages with additional linkers (states)? What effect would your decision have on the dynamic programming model of your problem?

REFERENCES

1. WAGNER, H. *Principles of Operations Research,* 2nd ed. Englewood Cliffs, N.J.: Prentice-Hall, 1975.
2. NEMHAUSER, G. *Introduction to Dynamic Programming.* New York: John Wiley & Sons, 1966.

3. BELLMAN, R. *Dynamic Programming.* Princeton, N.J.: Princeton University Press, 1957.
4. BENSON, K. "A Modular Processor for Generalized Multistage Optimization." Unpublished doctoral dissertation, Texas A & M University (1972).
5. GILLETT, B. *Introduction to Operations Research: A Computer-Oriented Algorithmic Approach.* New York: McGraw-Hill, 1976.
6. SCHRAGE, L., and K. BAKER, "Dynamic Programming Solution of Sequencing Problems with Precedence Constraints." *Operations Research,* Vol. 26 (1978), pp. 444–449.
7. PSARAFTIS, H. Adapted from "A Dynamic Programming Approach for Sequencing Groups of Identical Jobs." *Operations Research,* Vol. 28 (1980), pp. 1347–1359.
8. COLE, D. Adapted from an unpublished MBA term project report, College of Business Administration, Texas Tech University (1982).
9. FIELDING, N., and T. FIELDING. *Fielding's Low-Cost Europe.* New York: Fielding's Publications, 1982.

ADDITIONAL READING

BELLMAN, R., and S. DREYFUS, *Applied Dynamic Programming.* Princeton, N.J.: Princeton Unversity Press, 1962.

PART II

DECISION MAKING UNDER RISK

Chapters 2 through 6 dealt with modeling and analysis of problems under certainty; that is, situations and scenarios in which risk, in the form of probabilistic considerations, could be ignored.

In Part II, Chapters 7 through 11 will broaden our horizons to consider *stochastic* models that explicitly deal with risk. Again, however, like the models in Part I, these models stop short of dealing with uncertainty and complexity. We deal with these troublesome concepts in Part III.

As was the case with network modeling in Chapter 4, some stochastic models are optimizing and others are descriptive. However, we remind ourselves at the outset that *all* MS/OR models are descriptive, from the viewpoint of the decision maker who uses them.

Let us take a brief sight-seeing tour through Part II before going into Chapter 7.

A STRUCTURE FOR DECISION MAKING UNDER RISK

Chapter 7 provides a model or structure for decision making in a risky environment. We will need some elementary concepts from your introductory course in probability and statistics, so you might wish to brush up on this subject before tackling this chapter.

In reading and studying this chapter, you will find it useful to think about the problems and decision situations—both personal and professional—that you have encountered (or are now encountering) and relate the modeling process to these scenarios. Decision making under risk (DMUR) models are very general in scope and provide an excellent way in which to "get a handle on" problems in a rational, organized way.

WAITING-LINE (QUEUEING) MODELS

To most of us, waiting lines (or queues, as the British call them) are an almost everyday phenomenon, and queueing situations are common in organizations. In Chapter 8, we will study some simple queueing models and explore their usefulness.

Queueing models can, in a technical sense, be either descriptive or optimizing. In this chapter, we will concentrate mainly on the former. As we will see, entire books have been written on this subject, so our exploration will, of necessity, be somewhat perfunctory.

DISCRETE SIMULATION MODELS

Industry surveys of the use of MS/OR models consistently rank discrete probabilistic simulation models at or near the top in frequency of actual use. Chapter 9 discusses such models in detail.

Technically, discrete simulation models are descriptive in nature and are sometimes referred to as "what-if" devices. Stated another way, simulation models allow the decision maker to investigate the effects of policy or environmental changes without having to subject the *actual* entity to these effects. For example, it would be foolish indeed actually to build a multibillion-dollar dam and let the water in to see whether it holds—without first simulating different construction options with a physical model. The same is true for many businesses and public sector problems that are sometimes too complex to model with optimizing models such as mathematical programming but are amenable to analysis by discrete simulation.

MODELING WITH MARKOV CHAINS

Do you remember Markov from our discussion of dynamic programming in Chapter 6? Well, he is back again — this time with probabilistic devices called *transition matrices* — in Chapter 10. Markov chains are fun to work with. They will be more fun if you take a little time to review your basic linear algebra, before reading Chapter 10.

Markov chain models, technically speaking, are purely descriptive. Managerially speaking, they are very useful devices in helping us to better understand certain dynamic processes that occur frequently in organizations.

PROJECT SCHEDULING AND INVENTORY MANAGEMENT

The two important "applications" discussed in this chapter are project scheduling and inventory management. If you are required to take a course in production/operations management, you'll see these topics again in more detail.

And there we have our overview of Part II. Let us begin our stochastic adventure by looking at a structure for decision making under risk.

CHAPTER 7

A Structure for Decision Making Under Risk

In this chapter, we explore a structure for decision making that we will refer to as *decision making under risk (DMUR)*. Every decision maker uses some sort of structure—be it a "seat-of-the-pants" blend of intuition and experience or a formal system like the one we will describe here. Our view is that a *formal* structure is preferable, since it gives the decision maker a way in which to compare decisions over time against a standard benchmark.

This is not to say that every successful manager uses or has used a structured approach—quite the contrary. Some of the most successful entrepreneurs in history have been "hip shooters," people who built giant corporations by "gut feel" decision making. However, it is a matter of record that, for every success story one hears about the unschooled, intuitive tycoon who went from rags to riches overnight, there are a hundred or more that chronicle the sudden downfall of another "boy wonder" who made one fatal mistake and perhaps bankrupted his or her corporation.

Before exploring decision theory models for DMUR, let us agree at the outset that these models—like the DMUC models in Part I of this book—are not panaceas. That is, they provide one input into the decision-making process; they are not substitutes for managerial judgment and common sense.

STRUCTURING THE DECISION ENVIRONMENT

In what follows, we refer to the future events or environmental profiles that determine the outcome of a particular decision as *states of nature* and designate these n states as $S_1, S_2, \ldots, S_n$. We require that these states be *mutually*

243

exclusive and *collectively exhaustive.* For example, suppose that Dinah Soare, the CEO of Paleolithic Energy, Inc. (PEI), is trying to decide whether to purchase options on scarce offshore drilling rigs in anticipation of the award of offshore rights on which the company has bid. PEI has made bids on four leases, so that there are exactly five states of nature: the award of 0, 1, 2, 3, or 4 leases. We note that the five states are mutually exclusive (there is no overlapping among the outcomes) and collectively exhaustive (nothing can happen that is not included in the set of states). As a counterexample, suppose that the government had the option of awarding "split bids" on one or more tracts; in this case, additional states of nature would have to be identified, since the five current states are neither exclusive nor exhaustive.

The various actions or options available to the decision maker are referred to as *alternatives,* and we designate the m available alternatives as A_1, $A_2, \ldots, A_m$. Unlike states of nature, our alternatives are *not* necessarily mutually exclusive or collectively exhaustive. For example, the decision maker may wish to limit the number of alternatives to be considered, for exogenous reasons. Some problems may involve billions of alternatives, so that the task of enumerating them all is beyond our capacity. In our PEI illustration, for instance, Dinah obviously could contemplate reserving 0, 1, 2, . . . , 21,483 offshore rigs if she wished, although common sense suggests that reserving more than 4 would be foolish. On the other hand, she might well decide to reserve a maximum of 2—and limit her alternatives to reserving 0, 1, or 2 rigs. The key distinctions between *states of nature* and *alternatives* is that the decision maker has control of the latter, but not the former.

With n states of nature and m alternatives, there are $m \cdot n$ *outcomes* or payoffs, and we designate them as O_{ij}—the outcome associated with the ith alternative and the jth state. We then summarize our decision environment in a decision matrix, as in Table 7.1. In the first part of the chapter, the O_{ij} will be stated in terms of physical quantities such as money, time, quantities of material, and so on. We later introduce the notion of utility, and express the outcomes in dimensionless units called *utiles.*

Table 7.1   The Decision Matrix

States of Nature

	S_1	S_2	$\cdots$	S_j	$\cdots$	S_n
A_1	O_{11}	O_{12}	$\cdots$	O_{1j}	$\cdots$	O_{1n}
A_2	O_{21}	O_{22}	$\cdots$	O_{2j}	$\cdots$	O_{2n}
$\vdots$	$\vdots$	$\vdots$	$\cdots$	$\vdots$	$\cdots$	$\vdots$
A_i	O_{i1}	O_{i2}	$\cdots$	O_{ij}	$\cdots$	O_{in}
$\vdots$	$\vdots$	$\vdots$	$\vdots$	$\vdots$	$\cdots$	$\vdots$
A_m	O_{m1}	O_{m2}	$\cdots$	O_{mj}	$\cdots$	O_{mn}

Alternatives

A DMUR MODEL

Having identified the n states of nature and selected an appropriate set of m alternatives, and having quantified the $m \cdot n$ outcomes, one task remains to be completed — identifying or estimating a *probability distribution* on the states of nature. Stated another way, we must assess the relative likelihood of the occurrence of each state, and — since the states are mutually exclusive and collectively exhaustive — their probabilities sum to 1. This final task is at the heart of modeling in a DMUR environment, and the foregoing glib sentences skip lightly like a stone over the surface of a very deep ocean. Let us explore further the question of *how* one might go about this task.

ASSESSING STATE PROBABILITIES

In some decision environments, the probability distributions on the states of nature may be *combinatorial,* so that the state probabilities can be computed directly. As an illustration, consider the betting game commonly known as "Sucker." The game's namesake is invited to pay two dollars to play as follows. The perpetrator flips three "fair" U.S. coins simultaneously. If three heads appear, the player gets five dollars; if two heads appear, he gets his money back; and if one head appears, he gets one dollar back. And he can play as many times as he wishes. In this decision model, the state probabilities follow a binomial probability distribution with Pr (heads) = Pr (tails) = .50. The four states of nature are $S_1 =$ three heads, $S_2 =$ two heads, $S_3 =$ one head, and $S_4 =$ no heads. There is only one way that S_1 and S_4 can occur, and there are three ways that S_2 and S_3 can occur. Thus, if we let $p_j =$ probability of state j occurring, then, $p_1 = 1/8, p_2 = 3/8, p_3 = 3/8$, and $p_4 = 1/8$. We will perform an analysis of "Sucker" later in the chapter.

As another example, let us return to Dinah Soare's offshore leasing problem and suppose that historically PEI has been awarded a lease one of every four times it has bid. Since the states of nature are $S_j = 0, 1, 2, 3,$ or 4 leases awarded, we again have a binomial probability distribution — this time with Pr (lease award) = .25. Using the binomial tables in the appendix, we can compute the state probabilities as follows:

$$p_1 = 0.316, \quad p_2 = 0.422, \quad p_3 = 0.211, \quad p_4 = 0.047, \quad p_5 = 0.004$$

Our second example was different from the first in that *historical* information (relative frequency of lease award) was used as a basis for extrapolation to the future. This is by far the most common method of assessing state probabilities in business situations, and it appears to work well in most real-world decision environments. However, we should exercise caution when using the past as a predictor for the future. The turbulent economic times of the early 1980s, with gyrating interest rates, high unemployment, and persistent inflation, created a new "ball game" in which forecasting based on historical data became undependable in many cases and useless in others.

If we have neither a combinatorial structure nor a reliable historical base upon which to assess state probabilities, then — in those situations in which a probability density function *can* be derived—we must resort to subjective probability estimation. One approach that has been used successfully is the DELPHI technique, which involves individual assessments by members of an expert panel. The initial responses are aggregated and synthesized by the DELPHI coordinator and are fed back to the panel members. The members then refine their estimates, the results of the second round are again synthesized, and the results are returned to members of the panel for a third time. The goal, of course, is to achieve convergence of opinion. DELPHI has been used successfully to forecast such things as the profile of air travel in 1990, the "state of the art" in computer technology ten years into the future, and the current trend toward a more service-oriented economy in the United States.

Another way in which to derive subjective probabilities is to rely on our experience and intuition. Some decision theorists contend that *all* probability estimation is subjective to some degree—and they have a valid point. For example, if a forecast based on historical data produced results with which a decision maker was uncomfortable, you may be assured that his or her skepticism would be reflected *somehow* in the analysis—either explicitly (as in actually adjusting the historical forecast) or implicitly (as, perhaps, in discounting the results of the formal analysis when actually making the decision). At any rate, assessing state probabilities is the key step in building a model for DMUR. Obviously, the results produced by the model are only as useful as the state probabilities are accurate.

SEQUENTIAL DECISION PROCESSES

The decision matrix model is useful in modeling decision environments in which a single decision is to be made. If a *sequence* of decisions must be made, we can still use this model, if we wish, by setting up *compound alternatives.* For example, suppose that our first-year MBA student Lee Beedo is torn between attending this Saturday's all-night rock concert and Saturday night's performance of the touring Bolshoi ballet company. Furthermore, he needs to decide right away whether to ask Lucy or Chastity to join him. He would rather go to the all-night bash with Lucy or to the ballet with Chastity, but he feels there is a 50:50 chance that each young lady will turn him down. Unfortunately, he must buy the tickets immediately and cannot afford to buy tickets to both events. The compound alternatives are

A_1 = buy rock tickets and ask Lucy
A_2 = buy rock tickets and ask Chastity
A_3 = buy ballet tickets and ask Lucy
A_4 = buy ballet tickets and ask Chastity

There are other alternatives, of course. One would be to stay at home Saturday night. Another would be to buy either rock or ballet tickets and ask *both* Lucy and Chastity—hoping that only one accepts. The latter alternative is not recommended.

Another way to model a sequential decision process is by use of a *decision*

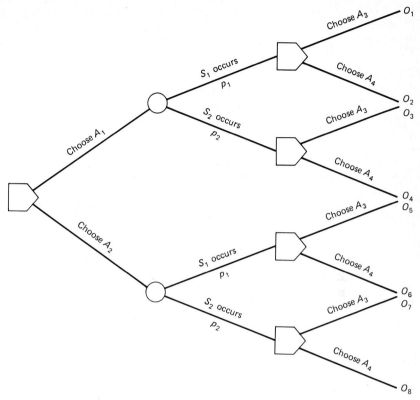

Figure 7.1   Two-stage decision tree.

tree. In Figure 7.1, we have a decision tree representing a sequence of two decisions (A_1 or A_2 first, A_3 or A_4 second) and two states of nature, S_1 and S_2. Each of the eight "branches" of the tree represents a possible outcome; that is, 4 (compound decisions) $\times$ 2 (states of nature) $= 8$ outcomes. One very useful feature of the decision tree is its visual impact—the model structures the problem sequentially by picturing the precedence relations explicitly. In general, decision trees alternate between decision and state stages. That is, the manager makes a decision, and Mother Nature—in the form of a probability distribution—makes the next one. It is the manager's turn next, and so on. We will return to the subject of decision trees later in this chapter. First, we need to explore decision criteria for DMUR models.

DECISION CRITERIA FOR DMUR MODELS

Just as with DMUC models discussed in Part I, a variety of criteria may be used with DMUR models. For example, one perfectly reasonable criterion in certain decision-making situations might be to identify the state S_l with the highest probability of occurring and selecting the alternative A_k for which O_{kl} is the largest (maximization) or smallest (minimization). In fact, if p_l happened to be very large, and if the O_{ij} did not vary too widely, such a criterion might be "just the ticket" for some decision makers.

The two most widely used decision criteria for DMUR models are (for maximization problems) maximize the expected monetary value (EMV) and minimize the expected opportunity loss (EOL). As we shall see, the use of these two criteria with a DMUR model always leads to the same optimal model alternative. So why discuss both? As it turns out, there is a very interesting relationship between the optimal EOL and the value of information, which we reveal subsequently.

THE EXPECTED MONETARY VALUE CRITERION

Assume for a moment that our decision maker is willing to behave as though his or her current decision will be repeated many times in the future and that he or she will make the current decision in such a way as to optimize the *long-run* or *average* performance. Stated another way, the decision maker is willing to act in such a way as to optimize the *expected value* of his or her decision. Returning to our little game of "Sucker," we have two alternatives—to play or not to play. The decision matrix for "Sucker" is exhibited in Table 7.2.

The expected monetary value of (A_1: Play) is

$$\text{EMV}(A_1) = +\$3(1/8) + 0(3/8) - \$1(3/8) - \$2(1/8) = -2/8 = -\$.25$$

Since EMV (A_2: Don't play) $= 0$, and since we wish to maximize our return, the EMV criterion would suggest that *in the long run,* it might be best to avoid this game.

In general notation, then, the expected monetary value of alternative A_i is computed as

$$\text{EMV}(A_i) = \sum_{j=1}^{n} p_j \cdot O_{ij} \qquad (7.1)$$

**Table 7.2   Decision Matrix of Outcomes
for "Sucker"**

States of Nature

	$S_1:3H$	$S_2:2H$	$S_3:1H$	$S_4:0H$	EMV
p_j	1/8	3/8	3/8	1/8	
A_1: Play	+\$3	0	−\$1	−\$2	−\$.25
A_2: Don't play	0	0	0	0	0

Alternatives

Note: Outcomes are net payoffs for each state and alternative.

The EMV criterion is a "risk-neutral" approach to decision making. It is appropriate for use in decision environments in which the worst possible outcome would not be disastrous and in which the best possible outcome would not make an order of magnitude difference to the organization. Stated another way, EMV is most appropriate when the marginal utility of one dollar, more or less, is about the same for the low end and the high end of the range of payoffs or outcomes.

THE EXPECTED OPPORTUNITY LOSS CRITERION

Again, let us assume that the decision maker is willing to accept the "long-run" behavioral assumption. Another way to approach the DMUR model is the use of the expected opportunity loss (EOL) criterion. Here, we merely replace the outcomes (O_{ij}) in each column (state) by the opportunity loss (OL_{ij}) occasioned by selecting alternative i and having state j occur. The opportunity losses are sometimes referred to as *"regrets"*—which is a very humanized way in which to characterize these numbers. The decision matrix for "Sucker" in terms of the OL_{ij} or "regrets" is given in Table 7.3.

For example, consider state 1 in Table 7.2. If we had selected A_2 (Don't play) and S_1 subsequently occurred, we would have regretted our decision—to the tune of $3 profit; thus $OL_{21} = +\$3$. On the other hand, if we had chosen A_1 instead, we would have made the best possible choice—so that our opportunity loss would have been zero.

The expected opportunity loss of A_1 (Play) is

$$\text{EOL } (A_1) = 0(1/8) + 0(3/8) + \$1(3/8) + \$2(1/8) = \$.625$$

Since the EOL $(A_2:$ Don't play$) = \$.375$, and since we wish to minimize our opportunity loss, this criterion also suggests (as did the EMV criterion) not playing the game.

In general notation, the expected opportunity loss of the ith alternative is as

Table 7.3 Decision Matrix of Opportunity Losses for "Sucker"

States of Nature

		$S_1:3H$	$S_2:2H$	$S_3:1H$	$S_4:0H$	EOL
Alternatives	p_j	1/8	3/8	3/8	1/8	
	A_1: Play	0	0	+$1	+$2	+$.625
	A_2: Don't play	+$3	0	0	0	+$.375

Note: Entries are net opportunity losses for each state and alternative.

follows:

$$\text{EOL}\,(A_i) = \sum_{j=1}^{n} p_j\,[O_j^* - O_{ij}] \qquad (7.2)$$

where O_j^* is the best outcome for state j.

Since the EOL criterion always selects the same optimal model alternative as the EMV criterion, its risk characteristics are identical to those of the EMV criterion.

THE VALUE OF INFORMATION

The EMV and EOL criteria assume that we know nothing about the states of nature other than their probabilities or, stated another way, their long-run relative frequencies of occurring. What if we had additional information prior to making our decision? For example, oil exploration and production (E & P) companies have historical records of drilling results by geographical area and would be able to assess long-run state probabilities using these data. However, there are dozens of firms that perform seismic sounding experiments that give the potential driller information about the prospects for striking oil at that particular site. How much are those services worth to the E & P company? We explore such questions in the following.

THE VALUE OF PERFECT INFORMATION

Suppose that our entrepreneur who is running a game of "Sucker" has attracted a crowd, so that there are now multiple players. In this version of the game, each player is not required to bet every time. Almost unnoticed in the crowd is a wizened old lady with a softly shining crystal ball. Each time before the coins are flipped, Madame Lazonga gazes into the ball and whispers the results of the upcoming toss—and, amazingly, she is right every time! Fortunately for us, Madame doesn't gamble—but she is willing to provide her *perfect information* to us (for a fee, of course) prior to each flip of the coins. What would such information be worth?

Returning to Table 7.2, note that only in the case of S_1 (three heads) is there a positive outcome from selecting A_1 (Play). If we knew that S_2, S_3, or S_4 were going to occur, we would select A_2 (Don't play). Therefore, the *expected mean value with perfect information* (EMVPI) is

$$\text{EMVPI} = +\$3(1/8) + 0(3/8) + 0(3/8) + 0(1/8) = \$.375$$

Since the value of the optimal EMV $= 0$ with *no* information, then the expected value of perfect information (EVPI) must be $\$.375 - 0 = \$.375$. In general terms, then,

$$\text{EVPI} = \text{EMVPI} - \text{EMV*} \qquad (7.3)$$

where the "*" refers to the EMV of the optimal act. But recall now that EOL* also had a value of $.375; is this just a coincidence? No it isn't. It is an interesting (and easily proven) fact that

$$EVPI = EOL* \qquad (7.4)$$

Thus, we should be willing to pay Madame Lazonga up to $.375 per round for her perfect information.

But haven't we taken off on a flight of fancy? There are no "Madame Lazongas" in the business world to tell us what next year's economy will be like, and there are rarely (if ever) sources of perfect information about the future in any sense. So why spend time on a concept that is so obviously unreal? In the next section, we discuss the value of *imperfect* information—and the EVPI gives us an upper bound on it. Thus, if the information available to us costs more than the EVPI, we would not consider it further.

THE VALUE OF IMPERFECT INFORMATION

To illustrate the concept of the value of imperfect information, let us return to another problem faced by Paleolithic Energy, Inc., and its CEO, Dinah Soare. The company owns rights to a lease near Norman, Oklahoma, and Dinah must decide whether to drill. She has identified three states of nature (S_1 = dry hole, S_2 = moderate strike, and S_3 = gusher) and the outcomes associated with her two alternatives (A_1 = Don't drill, and A_2 = Drill). From drilling data in the past, Dinah assesses state probabilities as shown in the decision matrix in Table 7.4. The opportunity loss decision matrix is given in Table 7.5.

The EMV criterion indicates that the optimal model solution is A_2 (Drill), with an EMV of $200,000. Also, EOL* = EVPI = $350,000, so it would behoove the company to get more information, if possible, before making the decision.

The seismic exploration firm of Sooner Boomer, Inc. (SBI), which is headquartered in Norman, has a great deal of experience in this part of the country and has kept meticulous records of its successes (and failures) in predicting the

**Table 7.4 PEI Decision Matrix of Outcomes
(net profit in $000)**

States of Nature

		Dry	Moderate	Gusher	
		S_1	S_2	S_3	EMV
	p_j	.50	.30	.20	
Alternatives	A_1: Don't drill	0	0	0	0
	A_2: Drill	−700	500	2000	+200

**Table 7.5   PEI Decision Matrix of
Opportunity Losses
(in $000)**

States of Nature

		Dry	Moderate	Gusher	
		S_1	S_2	S_3	EOL
	p_j	.50	.30	.20	
A_1: Don't drill		0	500	2000	550
A_2: Drill		700	0	0	350

Alternatives

existence of oil. This experience is summarized here as their *conditional distribution of predictive accuracy:*

*Predicted States
of Nature*

	I_1	I_2	I_3
S_1	.75	.20	.05
S_2	.15	.65	.20
S_3	0	.35	.65

*Actual
States
of Nature* $\Pr(I_i/S_j)$

The conditional probability distribution is interpreted as follows. The symbol I_i means that SBI predicted that state i would occur. Reading across the marginal distribution for S_1, for example, 75% of the time there was a dry hole, SBI had predicted it correctly. On the other hand, a dry hole occurred 20% of the time when SBI forecast a moderate strike, and only 5% of the time when the prediction was for a gusher. The marginal distributions for S_2 and S_3 are interpreted in a similar way.

But the information in this form—"the probability that SBI says I_i *given* that S_j is true" (written $\Pr(I_i/S_j)$—is of no direct value. What PEI needs is $\Pr(S_j/I_i)$—the probability that state j exists given that SBI *says* in advance that state i exists. Moreover, the conditional distribution of predictive accuracy does not incorporate our knowledge about the state probabilities p_j. What we need is a way to convert our state probability distribution (sometimes called the *prior distribution*) into the conditional distribution $\Pr(S_j/I_i)$ (sometimes called the *posterior distribution*). And, thanks to the good Reverend Thomas Bayes,[1] we have such a method at hand.

---

[1] Thomas Bayes was, by profession, a Methodist minister in England. He was, by avocation, a fair statistician.

Bayes' Theorem

Recalling our course in elementary statistics, Bayes' theorem can be used to convert a conditional probability distribution into its "mirror image," as follows.

$$\Pr(S_j/I_i) = \frac{\Pr(I_i/S_j) \cdot p_j}{\sum_{j=1}^{n} \Pr(I_i/S_j) \cdot p_j} \tag{7.5}$$

In our PEI example, let us illustrate the computations for $\Pr(S_j/I_i)$, as follows.

$$\Pr(S_1/I_1) = \frac{(.75)(.50)}{(.75)(.50) + (.15)(.30) + (0)(.20)} = \frac{.375}{.420} \doteq .893$$

$$\Pr(S_2/I_1) = \frac{(.15)(.30)}{.420} \doteq .107$$

$$\Pr(S_3/I_1) = \frac{0}{.420} = 0$$

We compute the other six conditional probabilities in a similar manner, and the complete posterior distribution is

		Predicted States of Nature			
		I_1	I_2	I_3	
Actual States of Nature	S_1	.893	.274	.116	
	S_2	.107	.534	.279	$\Pr(S_j/I_i)$
	S_3	0	.192	.605	

Comparing the posterior distribution with the original predictive distribution, we note that Bayes' theorem has converted the marginal distributions on *states* to marginal distributions on *predictions*, which is precisely what we need. Before illustrating the application in a decision tree, however, we need one more element — the so-called *predictive distribution* $\bar{p}_i$, or $\Pr(I_i)$. As it turns out, these probabilities are merely the denominators in Bayes' theorem, so that $\bar{p}_1 = .420$, $\bar{p}_2 = .365$, and $\bar{p}_3 = .215$. This distribution, as it relates to our oil drilling example, indicates the relative frequency with which our seismic consulting firm SBI will predict each of the three states of nature. One could get a severe migraine trying to find a logical reason why SBI will predict a dry hole only 42% of the time and a gusher about 22% of the time, when the prior distribution indicates that they actually occur 50% and 20% of the time, respectively. Think of it this way: SBI's information is imperfect. If the company were able to predict correctly the actual state of nature every time, then the predictive distribution would be identical to the prior distribution.

Application to a Decision Tree

In the PEI drilling problem, Dinah Soare must make two sequential decisions: whether to hire SBI for a fee of $100,000 and, subsequently, whether to drill. If the decision is made to hire the consulting firm, then the prediction by SBI will be taken into account in making the drilling decision. After the second decision is made, it is then "Mother Nature's" turn—revealing the actual amount of oil present.

This problem is modeled as a decision tree that is exhibited in Figure 7.2. The numbers in bold face on the probabilistic branches are the appropriate probabilities. For example, on the arc "I_1: Predict S_1," we have $\bar{p}_1$ from the predictive distribution. Continuing down this branch, we have $\Pr(S_1/I_1)$, $\Pr(S_2/I_1)$, and $\Pr(S_3/I_1)$ from the posterior distribution we previously computed, and the other branches of the "Hire consultant" portion of the tree are labeled in similar fashion. On the "Don't hire consultant" portion of the tree, the probabilistic branches are labeled with the elements of the prior distribution, since no additional information is available. Since we have already obtained a solution with the EMV criterion on the decision matrix model of this

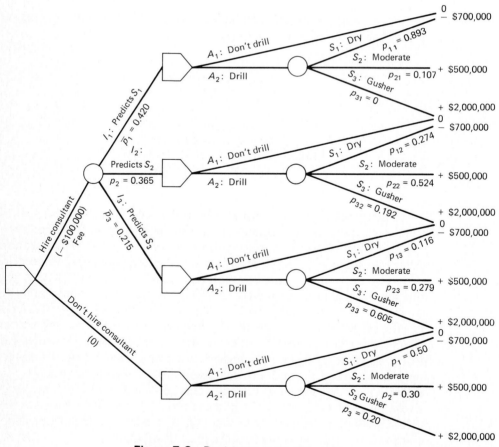

Figure 7.2 Decision tree for PEI problem.

portion of the tree, we recall that the optimal model decision was "Drill," with an EMV of $200,000 and an EVPI of $350,000. Since SBI charges a fee of $100,000, the other branch of the tree merits analysis.

AN OPTIMIZING ALGORITHM FOR DECISION TREE MODELS

Recalling our discussion of dynamic programming in Chapter 6, a decision tree represents a sequence of independent decisions over time. Thus, we may use the DP technique to analyze this model. However, the early literature in decision theory called this process "averaging out and rolling back," and we will use this colorful and very descriptive term in what follows.

As usual in analyzing staged or sequenced decision processes, we start at the end and work backward toward the beginning. Our first step is to "average out" the results of "Mother Nature's" last act by converting the probabilistic outcomes to expected monetary values. This "pruned" tree is shown in Figure 7.3. Note that certain branches have been "lopped off" (indicated by double slashmarks), since they do not represent optimal decisions at this stage. We have now "rolled back" to the next probabilistic echelon of the tree and we are ready to "average out" again.

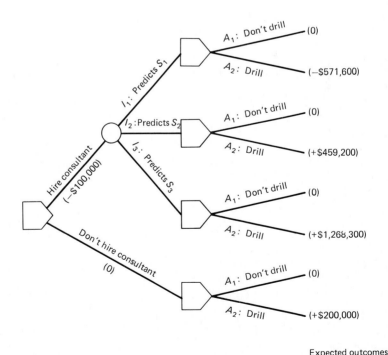

Expected outcomes

Figure 7.3 "Pruned" PEI decision tree.

This computation for the "Hire consultant" branch is as follows.

$$\text{EMV (Hire consultant)} = (.420)(0) + (.365)(\$459,200) + (.215)(\$1,268,300)$$
$$= \$440,292.50$$

Therefore the *net* EMV for the alternative "Hire consultant" is $340,292.50 (after subtracting the fee). As compared with the net EMV of $200,000 for the alternative "Don't hire consultant," the model indicates that the information that can be provided by SBI is probably considerably more valuable than it costs to acquire.

Based on the decision tree analysis, the model indicates the following strategy: hire SBI; if the company's prediction is I_1 (dry hole), don't drill; otherwise, drill.

SENSITIVITY ANALYSIS OF DMUR MODELS

At the outset, let us be certain that we are clear on a key point. If the prior distribution on the states of nature is accurate, then *obtaining additional information does not change it.* In our oil drilling example, there is still a 50% chance that this particular lease is dry — regardless of what our seismic consultant says. Stated another way, if a long sequence of similar decisions was made on oil leases with the same prior distribution, about half of them would turn out to be dry holes *if drilled.* What the imperfect information supplied by SBI permits us to do is to make the "Don't drill" decision in a certain percentage of these cases and avoid the $700,000 drilling cost each time.

ANALYSIS OF PRIOR PROBABILITIES

In modeling with a DMUR technique, the "softest" parameters are usually the state probabilities of the prior probability distribution. In certain cases we can investigate the sensitivity of our model to errors in these probabilities. For instance, in our PEI example, let p_1, p_2, and $1 - p_1 - p_2$ be the state probabilities of S_1, S_2, and S_3, respectively. The expected mean value of the decision A_2 (Drill) becomes

$$\text{EMV } (A_2) = p_1(-\$700,000) + p_2(\$500,000) + (1 - p_1 - p_2)(\$2,000,000)$$
$$= \$2,000,000 - \$2,700,000p_1 - \$1,500,000p_2$$

We observe that if $p_1 > 20/27 \doteq .74$, it would never be economically advisable to drill — regardless of the value of p_2. On the other hand, if we hold the state probability p_1 constant at $p_1 = .50$, then we have

$$\text{EMV} = \$650,000 - \$1,500,000p_2$$

which is negative only if $p_2 > 65/150 \doteq .43$, meaning that p_3 would have to be less than about .07. In our illustration, Dinah Soare might well feel comfortable with the analysis, given the relatively wide margin for error.

DOMINATED ALTERNATIVES

In certain DMUR models, one or more alternatives may be *dominated* by others. That is, if every payoff for A_k is as least as good as the payoff for A_l in every state, neither the EMV nor the EOL criterion will ever select A_l as the optimal alternative. Therefore, A_l is a dominated alternative and can be removed *from the model* for purposes of analysis. Why do we stress *from the model?* Because, in certain instances, the decision maker may actually select a dominated alternative as his or her preferred course of action, because of exogenous factors that could not be (or were not) incorporated into the model.

THE POSTERIOR DISTRIBUTION

Consider the posterior distribution for our oil drilling example, which is reproduced here:

$$
\begin{array}{c}
\textit{Predicted States} \\
\textit{of Nature}
\end{array}
$$

	I_1	I_2	I_3	
S_1	.893	.274	.116	
S_2	.107	.534	.279	$\Pr(S_j/I_i)$
S_3	0	.192	.605	

Actual States of Nature

Note that in about 89 cases out of 100, SBI's prediction of a dry hole will be accurate. On the other hand, a dry hole will occur in about 27 cases out of 100 when a moderate find is predicted and in almost 12 out of 100 when a gusher is predicted. Might Dinah Soare decide not to drill when SBI predicts a dry hole and ignore this input otherwise? Certainly — and the point is that managerial intuition and insight are not bound by the results of formal modeling and analysis. An example from another context may clarify this point. There are certain diagnostic tests in medicine that give one of two indications — positive or negative. If a test, say, for poliomyelitis, is positive, the physician may conclude with very high probability that the patient has the disease. On the other hand, if the test is negative, the physician may be able to make *no conclusion whatsoever* about the presence or absence of the disease. Similarly, it is possible that a certain response from an information source in a decision environment in business may be a highly reliable predictor but that a different response from the same source may contain no useful information whatsoever. Thus, when investigating the sensitivity of DMUR models, this fact should be taken into consideration by the decision maker.

AVAILABLE COMPUTER CODES

Computer programs that analyze single-stage DMUR models are so simple to construct that standardized codes for mainframe computers are mostly local products. The BASIC code DMUR is fully interactive, will accept up to ten states of nature and ten alternatives, and will compute EMV, EOL, and EVPI. The program will analyze available information as well and will compute and display the posterior distribution.

THE CONCEPT OF ECONOMIC UTILITY

Thus far we have expressed our outcomes O_{ij} in terms of physical quantities such as dollars, time, and so on. This approach is widely used and is useful as long as our decision maker's marginal utility for one unit at the lower end of the spectrum of possible outcomes is about the same for one unit at the higher end. For example, gambling casinos thrive on 25-cent, 50-cent, and so on, slot machines because most people's utilities for losing a few cents at a time are low—given the tantalizing (and very low probability) prospect of hitting a jackpot worth several thousand dollars. Why aren't there $100 or even $1000 slot machines? For the simple reason that *most* people who gamble as part of a holiday (casinos' greatest revenue source) would be reluctant to risk that amount of money on the prospect of winning the same amount, all at one time. In other words, their utility for the hundredth *lost* dollar is higher than for the hundredth *won* dollar.

On the other hand, many of this country's greatest corporations (e.g., Polaroid, Xerox, IBM) were built by *seeking* risk—deliberately going after the high-risk, high-payoff alternatives that resulted in technological breakthroughs. Thus, for decision makers who are clearly operating in a risk-averse or risk-seeking mode, use of the EMV or EOL criteria—both of which are risk-neutral—on monetary outcomes, would be inappropriate.

AN UNDERLYING ASSUMPTION

In the following discussions on economic utility, we make only one basic assumption—that the decision criterion to be used cannot result in *intransitive preference*. Stated another way, if we prefer *A* to *B*, and we also prefer *B* to *C*, then under the transitivity assumption, we must also prefer *A* to *C*. You may be wondering whether *any* rational decision criterion could lead to intransitive preference—and the answer is yes.

Suppose, for example, that our MBA student, Lee Beedo, is trying to decide upon one among three sports cars to purchase. He cannot decide how to quantify his evaluations of their operating cost, handling, and appearance, so he rates them on a nominal scale as follows.

	Criteria		
Model	Cost	Handling	Appearance
Alpha-Z	Worst	Best	Middle
Beta-400	Middle	Worst	Best
Gamma-G	Best	Middle	Worst

Lee's decision rule is to select the model that is better than the others on the most criteria. Let's see, the Beta-400 is better than the Alpha-Z on both cost and appearance, so he would obviously prefer the Beta-400. Also, the Gamma-G is better than the Beta-400 on both cost and handling, so it appears that Lee's choice should be the Gamma-G. Correct? Unfortunately, the Alpha-Z is better than the Gamma-G on both handling and appearance, so he is right back where he started! This is one example of an intransitive decision criterion of the type that is not amenable to analysis using classical utility theory.

UTILITY FUNCTIONS

One approach to "capturing" a decision maker's attitude toward risk in a particular decision environment is to build his or her *utility function* over the specified range of outcomes. A utility function U is nothing more than a mathematical device that maps physical outcomes onto dimensionless quantities called *utiles*. The particular range of numbers chosen for the utility scale is of no consequence, but most texts recommend a range from zero to one.

Consider the three utility functions graphed in Figure 7.4. The range of outcomes in dollars is plotted on the horizontal axis, and the range of utiles from zero to one is plotted on the vertical axis. To convert a specific dollar outcome, say, O_{ij}, to utiles, one reads straight up from O_{ij} to the appropriate utility curve and then across to its utility equivalent. In the figure, our example outcome O_{ij} is equivalent to about .25 utiles for the risk seeker, about .60 utiles for the risk-neutral "EMV-er," and .90 for the risk avoider.

To illustrate the effect of the utility transformation, let us return briefly to the game of "Sucker," whose decision matrix of outcomes is given in Table 7.2. Referring again to Figure 7.4, let $O_{min} = -\$2$ and $O_{max} = +\$3$, and suppose that our decision maker is now a risk seeker. If the convex utility function (bottom in the figure) represents our decision maker's utility function, we may approximate his utility transformation as follows:

$$U(-2) = 0, \quad U(-1) \doteq .05, \quad U(0) \doteq .10, \quad U(+3) = 1$$

Computing the *expected utility* of the two alternatives yields

$$\text{EU } (A_1: \text{Play}) = 1(1/8) + .10(3/8) + .05(3/8) + 0(1/8) = .1813$$
$$\text{EU } (A_2: \text{Don't play}) = .1(1/8) + .1(3/8) + .1(3/8) + .1(1/8) = .10$$

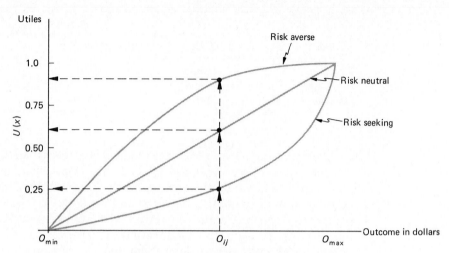

Figure 7.4 Three utility functions.

Therefore, the risk seeker, using the given utility function, might be inclined to play "Sucker" after all, since EU $(A_1:$ Play$)$ > EU $(A_2:$ Don't play$)$.

As a second illustration, let us take another look at PEI's oil well drilling problem whose decision matrix of outcomes is given in Table 7.4. In Figure 7.4, suppose that Dinah Soare is actually risk averse (if so, she's in the wrong business!) and that her utility function is the concave utility function (top in the figure). Here, $O_{min} = -\$700,000$ and $O_{max} = +\$2,000,000$, and we may approximate her utility transformation as follows:

$$U(-\$700,000) = 0, \quad U(0) \doteq .50, \quad U(+\$500,000) \doteq .75, \quad U(+\$2,000,000) = 1$$

Computing the expected utility of the two alternatives yields:

$$EU\ (A_1:\ \text{Don't drill}) = .50(.50) + .50(.30) + .50(.20) = .50$$
$$EU\ (A_2:\ \text{Drill}) = 0(.50) + .75(.30) + 1(.20) = .425$$

In this case, Dinah's risk-averse situation would *reverse* the previous EMV analysis and would suggest perhaps that PEI might not decide to drill in this particular situation.

BUILDING UTILITY FUNCTIONS

Several approaches have been developed for building the decision maker's utility function, and some of the suggested "additional readings" at the end of this chapter do an excellent job of discussing and evaluating these techniques. One approach, which is referred to as the "lottery" or "standard gamble" technique, is fascinating. We will discuss it briefly here, and illustrate it in the Jack Legg Associates case.

The lottery approach is best explained in terms of an interactive exchange between the decision maker (DM) and a utility function operator (UFO). First, the least favorable outcome in the decision matrix (O_{min}) is assigned a utility of zero, and the most favorable outcome (O_{max}) is given a utility of *one*, as we did in the preceding discussion. The UFO then presents the DM with the following choice — the lottery in Figure 7.5 or the opportunity to *sell* the lottery for an amount O_1. If the DM is risk neutral, he would be indifferent between having the lottery itself and receiving the EMV of the lottery [i.e., $O_1 = (.5)O_{min} + (.5)O_{max}$]. On the other hand, a risk-averse DM would gladly "unload" the risky lottery for less than its EMV, while the risk-seeking DM would require a *certain* payoff larger than the EMV in order to compensate for the foregone opportunity to receive the payoff O_{max}. The idea here is for the risk seeker to determine the *maximum* value of O_1 that would make her or him indifferent between having O_1 or the lottery and for the risk avoider to determine the *minimum* value at which such indifference occurs. Having obtained the value O_1, and since we know that the *expected utility* of the lottery is .5 [i.e., $.5\ U(O_{min}) + .5\ U(O_{max}) = .5(0) + .5(1) = .5$], we now know that $E[U_1] = .5$, and we have our third point on the utility curve. We proceed to analyze additional lotteries similar to that in Figure 7.6. Note that if O_2 and O_3 are the indifference amounts for lotteries 2 and 3, respectively, then

$$U(O_2) = .5(0) + .5(.5) = .25$$

$$U(O_3) = .5(.5) + .5(1) = .75$$

This process can be continued until the shape of the utility curve becomes apparent or until the decision maker terminates the exercise.

Before discussing briefly some advanced topics in DMUR, let us pause a moment to put the concept of economic utility in perspective. First, utility curves are not necessarily smooth functions like those depicted in Figure 7.4. In fact, if the range of outcomes is sufficiently broad in a given decision environment, the decision maker's utility curve may well be S shaped, that is, convex (risk seeking) in the lower part of the range, roughly linear (risk neutral) in the middle, and concave (risk avoiding) in the upper part of the range. However, all utility curves in a DMUR sense have one property — they are *monotonically nondecreasing* from left to right. All this means is that the decision maker's utility for a certain outcome is never lower than is his or her utility for an outcome with a smaller value. As we see, this property reflects the requirement for intransitivity of preference in DMUR.

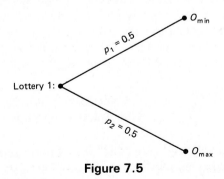

Figure 7.5

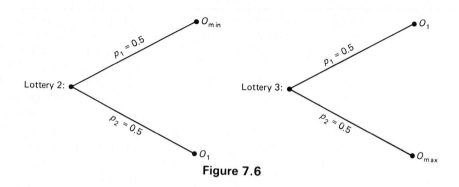

Figure 7.6

STATE OF THE ART IN DMUR

DMUR covers a broad range of decision-making environments, and we have discussed some important basic notions so far. Let us briefly touch on some advanced ideas.

CONTINUOUS PRIOR DISTRIBUTIONS

Thus far, our discussion has been limited to discrete prior distributions, and we used the discrete predictive distribution and Bayes' theorem to construct the posterior distribution. In other words, we have dealt with a finite number of states of nature. Suppose, however, that we had (for all practical purposes) an *infinite* number of states of nature, so that our prior distribution is a *continuous* probability density function. We could, of course, segregate the distribution into a finite number of states and estimate the probabilities associated with them, but there is a better way.

As an example, Styx and Stones, Ltd. (SSL) is a small R&D company that is considering bidding on a contract announced by the Environmental Protection Agency (EPA). The contract, which involves developing a monitoring device to detect pollution in rivers, is of the firm fixed price variety. That is, the winner will be awarded $3,000,000 for taking on the project. On similar projects in the past, SSL has experienced costs at the rate of about $200,000 per month, and the company estimates that this project would involve a one-time setup cost of $600,000. Time to completion of similar projects in the past has averaged ten months, with a standard deviation of two months. The distribution of completion times is roughly normal (symmetric and "not too flat or too peaked").

SSL obviously has two choices: bid on the contract or don't bid. Since we know the expected value of completion time (ten months), it is simple to compute the EMV of the alternative "Bid" as follows.

$$\text{EMV (Bid)} = \underset{\text{(contract)}}{\$3,000,000} - \underset{\text{(setup)}}{\$600,000} - \underset{\text{(monthly costs)}}{(10)(\$200,000)} = \$400,000$$

The EMV of "Don't bid" is obviously zero, so, if SSL is risk neutral or risk seeking, the DMUR model would indicate "Bid" as the best alternative.

However, there is obviously some risk inherent in this decision situation. "Break-even" occurs at 12 months—about 1 standard deviation above the mean. Thus, in a "long-run" sense, SSL stands to lose money about 15% of the time. How much money is involved? If 14 months were required for completion, SSL would lose $400,000, and this circumstance (or worse) could occur about 5% of the time. Could SSL survive such a loss? How does the company assess its risk in bidding on the EPA contract?

Let us approach the answer to the last question by looking at the opportunity loss. The *OL* for the alternative "Don't bid" is obviously $400,000—the EMV of the alternative "Bid." Calculating the EOL for "Bid" is more complicated. The *loss function* (LF) for this alternative is zero for completion time up to 12 months and linear with a slope of $200,000 (per month) for completion time greater than 12 months. Thus, if t stands for time,

$$\text{LF (Bid)} = \begin{cases} 0, & \text{for } t \leq 12 \\ 200{,}000(t - 12), & \text{for } t \geq 12 \end{cases}$$

To compute EOL (BID), therefore, we need to integrate the product of LF (Bid) and the normal density function with a mean of 10 and standard deviation of 2. This is illustrated in Figure 7.7. By standardizing this integral, it has already been computed for us, and the "Unit Normal Loss Integral" tabulations appear in the appendix.

Let t_B = break-even point (in our SSL example, t_B = 12 months); k = slope of the loss function (for SSL, k = $200,000); m and s are the mean and standard deviation of the normal distribution (m = 10 and s = 2 for SSL); and $z = |(t_B - m)/s|$, the absolute value of the standardized normal transformation. One first computes z and then obtains $L_n(z)$, the unit normal loss function value, from the table. In the SSL illustration, $z = |(12 - 10)/2| = 1$, and $L_n(1) = .08332$ from the table. The formula for EOL is

$$\text{EOL} = k \cdot s \cdot L_n(z)$$

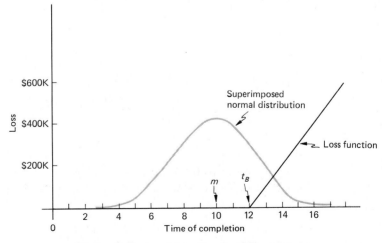

Figure 7.7   Loss function for SSL example.

For SSL, therefore, EOL (Bid) = ($200,000)(2)(.08332) = $33,328. Thus SSL faces an expected opportunity loss of only $33,328 by bidding, as opposed to $400,000 for not bidding.

This procedure is applicable to any DMUR situation in which there are exactly two alternatives and where a normal distribution can be used to approximate the prior distribution on the states of nature.

THE NEWSBOY MODEL

Consider the problem faced daily by Tab Lloyd, a young entrepreneur who sells the *Big Apple Times* on the streets of New York City. Each morning Tab buys his supply of papers at 30 cents each and sells them for 50 cents each. There are few things more useless than yesterday's newspapers, but Tab can sell left-over papers for 5 cents each to a large hotel that distributes them free to their guests. On the other hand, if Tab runs out before he has supplied his regular clientele, he retains his "goodwill" by running to a posh Fifth Avenue newsstand and purchasing papers for 95 cents each, selling them to his customers at the usual 50 cents price.

Tab's problem is intriguing: How many papers should he buy each morning? He knows from his CPA that he averages selling 200 papers each day, with a standard deviation of 25 papers. If he buys too few, the cost of "goodwill" will eat into his profits; if he buys too many, the low salvage value for unsold papers will have the same effect.

Suppose that demand can be approximated by a normal distribution. Let us recall our basic economics course and the concept of *marginal utility*. Tab would like to know the order quantity $q*$ such that the marginal utility of ordering exactly one more paper is the same as ordering one less paper. Thus he needs to perform an *incremental analysis*.

Let

SP = selling price per unit (50¢ for Tab)

SV = salvage value per unit (5¢)

CP = unit purchase price (30¢)

GW = "goodwill" cost per unit (45¢ = 95¢ − 50¢)

$L_s = CP - SV$ = loss incurred in *overstocking* one unit (25¢ = 30¢ − 5¢)

$L_{ns} = SP - CP + GW$ = loss incurred in *understocking* one unit (65¢ = 50¢ − 30¢ + 45¢)

We now wish to find $q*$ such that the expected value of L_s exactly equals the expected value of L_{ns}. Let p be the probability of L_s occurring, so that $(1 - p)$ is the probability of L_{ns}. We equate the two expected values as follows:

$$p \cdot L_s = (1 - p) \cdot L_{ns}$$

so that

$$p^* = \frac{L_{ns}}{L_s + L_{ns}}$$

is the "optimal" value of p. In Tab's case,

$$p^* = \frac{65¢}{65¢ + 25¢} \doteq .722$$

This means that the optimal order quantity q^* is at the point on the demand distribution at which .722 of the cumulative probability occurs. Referring to our standard normal distribution table in the appendix, we see that this occurs at about .59 standard deviations to the right of the mean, so that

$$q^* = 200 + (.59)25 = 214.75 \doteq 215 \text{ papers}$$

Incremental analysis is not only simple, it is logical as well. If the cost per unit of understocking is higher than the unit cost for overstocking, common sense tells us that we would probably be wise to stock more than average demand. The model gives us a way to compute this quantity.

ON THE FRONTIER

Dozens of articles are published each year on the subject of statistical decision theory. Some of the research on the frontier of this subject includes the following.

1. Building multiattribute utility functions.

Researchers are seeking ways in which to reflect decision makers' risk environments along *several* dimensions (e.g., monetary outcome, time of project completion, quality of output) by building utility functions in several dimensions.

2. Assessing dynamic risk preference.

The timing of cash flows for projects affects their riskiness—even though the aggregate outcomes may be identical. Researchers are investigating utility structures that can incorporate the time effect.

3. Improving techniques for constructing utility functions.

The "lottery" method has many disadvantages, and researchers are looking for better, more dependable methods for constructing decision makers' utility functions.

4. Assessing the value of information when a continuous prior distribution is used.

When a continuous prior distribution is used, the "predictive distribution" must be in the form of a continuous *bivariate* (i.e., two jointly distributed random variables) distribution, as is the posterior. It is known that a normally distributed prior distribution leads to a bivariate normal posterior distribution (i.e., the normal distribution is said to be *self-conjugate*). Other conjugate relationships are also known, but in general, it is difficult to derive or even describe the posterior distribution for general kinds of prior distributions. Researchers (mostly mathematical statisticians and economists) are studying this phenomenon.

Jack Legg Associates

The Scenario: Hy Roller and Nawonda Betts are both engineering project managers for Jack Legg Associates (JLA), a high-technology consulting firm. Hy is an engineer and an MBA, is unmarried, and is ambitious, aggressive, and bucking for promotion into general management at JLA. He is also a devotee of fast cars, fine restaurants, and the "good life" in general.

Nawonda, on the other hand, is supporting her husband (a doctoral student in medieval English literature), three children, an ailing mother-in-law, a mentally handicapped German shepherd dog, six cats, and a tank of tropical fish.

Each engineering project manager is assigned an average of three projects each year. Since the projects are almost always "state of the art," the number of *successful* projects for each manager tends to follow a binomial distribution, with p approximately equal to .50. Thus there is a probability of .125 that a given manager has no successful projects in a given year and an equal probability that there will be three successes. The probabilities of one and two successful projects are each .375.

The Problem: JLA currently pays its project managers an annual salary of $35,000, but Mr. Legg has decided to offer his managers a choice of three compensation plans, as follows.

JLA Compensation Plans

| | No. of Successful Projects | | | |
	S_1: 0	S_2: 1	S_3: 2	S_4: 3
Pr (S_j)	.125	.375	.375	.125
A_1: Plan A	$35,000	$35,000	$35,000	$35,000
A_2: Plan B	$21,000	$35,000	$42,000	$49,000
A_3: Plan C	$7000	$28,000	$42,000	$70,000

(Alternatives)

The salary plan, once selected, cannot be changed for the year. The problem facing Hy and Nawonda is—which salary plan to choose.

The Model: If Hy and Nawonda were both risk-neutral decision makers, the EMV criterion in a DMUR model might be an appropriate analytical approach to this problem. The EMVs of the three alternatives are as follows:

$$\text{EMV }(A_1) = \$35{,}000$$
$$\text{EMV }(A_2) = \$37{,}625$$
$$\text{EMV }(A_3) = \$35{,}875$$

No alternative is dominated, so the EMV model indicates that A_2: Plan B is the best one available.

However, the assumption that Hy Roller and Nawonda Betts have similar risk preferences — and that their preferences are risk neutral — would appear to be shaky at best. After discussing the situation, both Hy and Nawonda made an appointment with Mona Tonic, JLA's management scientist, and the gist of their discussion is as follows.

MONA: Ok, Hy and Nawonda, so you want to construct your personal utility functions to help you decide which salary plan to choose. Let's see — the minimum and maximum outcomes are $7000 and $70,000, respectively, so we'll start by assigning them values of zero and one utiles. Now, suppose, in lieu of your annual salaries, that each of you owns a copy of the following lottery. Tell me the annual salary you'd accept for certain in lieu of having the lottery.

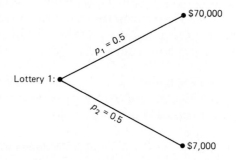

NAWONDA: Oh, my, the idea of having a 50:50 chance of making only $7000 next year terrifies me! Let's see, though, the expected value of the lottery is $38,500 — I'd certainly take less than that. My family could squeak by on about $20,000, so I suppose that's the least I'd accept.

HY: Wow! A 50:50 chance at 70 grand! That makes the lottery awfully hard to part with. Still, I'm not a complete idiot — getting only $7000 next year would crimp my style. I guess I'd trade it for about $55,000, but reluctantly.

MONA: OK, Nawonda and Hy, we've now gotten three points on each of your utility curves. Let's get two more. Again, you own the following lotteries: Notice now that I have to give you different lotteries.

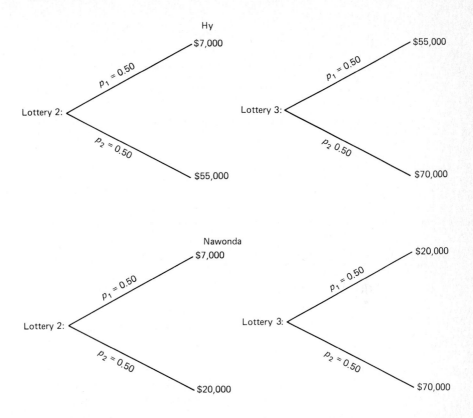

HY: Well, this is tougher to analyze than the first one. On lottery 2, I guess I'd part with it for around $40,000, but I'd have to have $65,000 to let go of lottery 3.

NAWONDA: My goodness—Lottery 2 is dismal. And Hy is right, this is more difficult than the first one. Again, $7000 would be a disaster, so I guess I'd trade my Lottery 2 for about $12,000. My husband would have to sell his new Porsche sports car, but we could make it. As for lottery 3, I'd take $35,000 in a minute if I owned it for real.

MONA: (After a short pause) All right, I've plotted all five points on both of your utility functions and sketched in smooth curves joining them. (Figure 7.8). You two are classical (textbook?) examples of risk-seeking (Hy) and risk-averse (Nawonda) decision makers in this range of outcomes. We could continue the lottery business, but I think we have what you need already.

NAWONDA: Thanks a lot, Mona—you've been a great help. I guess our next step is to replace the various salary levels in the three salary plans with their equivalent utilities and compute expected utilities for each plan.

HY: Yeah, thanks for the séance, Mona. If you ever feel like dinner and a show, just give me a buzz.

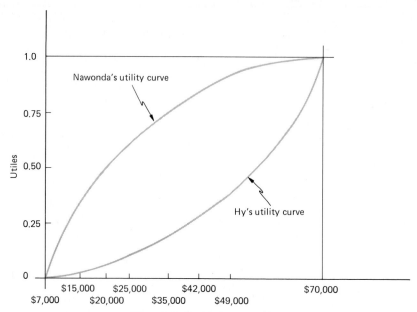

Figure 7.8   Utility functions.

MONA: You're both very welcome, and thanks for the offer, Hy. However, I'm a risk avoider like Nawonda, and your proposition has a utility for me of close to zero.

Solution to the Model: Hy's and Nawonda's decision matrices, with salary levels replaced by their respective utilities, are as follows:

Nawonda's Decision Matrix

No. of Successful Projects

		S_1: 0	S_2: 1	S_3: 2	S_4: 3
Alternatives	Pr (S_j)	.125	.375	.375	.125
	A_1: Plan A	.750	.750	.750	.750
	A_2: Plan B	.517	.750	.800	.850
	A_3: Plan C	0	.633	.800	1

$$EU\ (A_1) = .750$$
$$EU\ (A_2) = .752$$
$$EU\ (A_3) = .662$$

Hy's Decision Matrix

No. of Successful Projects

		$S_1: 0$	$S_2: 1$	$S_3: 2$	$S_4: 3$
	Pr (S_j)	.125	.375	.375	.125
Alternatives	A_1: Plan A	.212	.212	.212	.212
	A_2: Plan B	.106	.212	.283	.400
	A_3: Plan C	0	.159	.283	1

$$\text{EU } (A_1) = .212$$
$$\text{EU } (A_2) = .249$$
$$\text{EU } (A_3) = .291$$

Solution to the Problem: In Nawonda Betts's case, only one conclusion is clear — plan C (A_3) involves an unacceptable level of risk in her situation. Plans A and B have expected utilities that are so similar that a decision is "too close to call" based only on the results of the model. Plan B (A_2) was the optimal alternative in a risk-neutral sense, and it has a slight edge in Nawonda's analysis, over plan A. However, after consulting with her husband, children, and German shepherd, Nawonda decided to go with the riskless choice of $35,000 certain (A_1).

Hy Roller confidently chose plan C (A_3) as the model suggested that he should. His personal situation and proclivities made this high level of risk acceptable, and the worst outcome for him would not be disastrous — only temporarily inconvenient.

King Cotton [1]

The Scenario: The 21-county area surrounding Lubbock, Texas (the South Plains), is one of the world's largest cotton-producing areas, accounting for half of the Texas output and more than 14% of the cotton crop in the United States. In 1980, South Plains farmers cultivated 2.4 million acres of cotton using irrigation and .8 million acres of "dry land" cotton. Yield differences between the two methods are substantial, with irrigated cotton producing an average of 600 pounds per acre as opposed to only 258 pounds per acre in nonirrigated fields [2].

The Problem: Assuming perfect conditions, yields on irrigated cotton are maximized (both in quantity as well as in quality) when the plants are irrigated twice — once in the early summer and once again near August 15. However, if significant rainfall occurs after the second irrigation, the plants create more vegetative growth rather than maturing. This causes the cotton plant to create more bolls than can be developed fully before it is killed by the first freeze. Thus, not only is yield lowered by too much water, but the plants generate a great deal of vegetative "trash" that lowers the grade (and thus the price received) of the cotton when harvested.

Irrigation costs have soared in recent years because of the price increase in natural gas, which is the fuel used to run irrigation pumps. South Plains farmers therefore have a difficult decision to make each year in early August—to irrigate again or not to irrigate. If early fall rains are sparse, the decision to irrigate will result in much higher yields and better quality cotton. The decision not to irrigate will be fortuitous if subsequent rains are substantial—in effect irrigating the cotton at no expense to the farmer.

The Model: This problem was modeled as a DMUR situation with two alternatives—irrigate again before August 15 and don't irrigate—and three states of nature—less than 1 inch of rain in early fall, 1 to 3 inches, and more than 3 inches. The prior distribution on the states of nature was derived from historical weather information in the area. The conditional distribution of predictive accuracy was generated by comparing USDA weather forecasts over a 12-year period with the actual rainfall subsequently experienced. The outcomes for each alternative and state-of-nature combination were calculated for a 3000-acre farm using the results of a study by Adams [3]. The decision matrix and the conditional distribution of predictive accuracy are as follows:

Decision Matrix*

Amount of Rainfall

Alternatives		S_1: < 1"	S_2: 1"–3"	S_3: > 3"
	Pr (S_j)	.50	.33	.17
	A_1: Irrigate	$1,070,800	$584,800	$422,800
	A_2: Don't irrigate	$472,500	$810,000	$648,000

* Outcomes are in revenues net of irrigation costs, if any.

Conditional Distribution of Predictive Accuracy

Predicted States of Nature

Actual States of Nature		I_2	I_2	I_3	
	S_1	.50	.50	0	
	S_2	0	.75	.25	Pr (I_i/S_j)
	S_3	0	.50	.50	

Solution to the Model: Using Bayes' theorem, the prior distribution

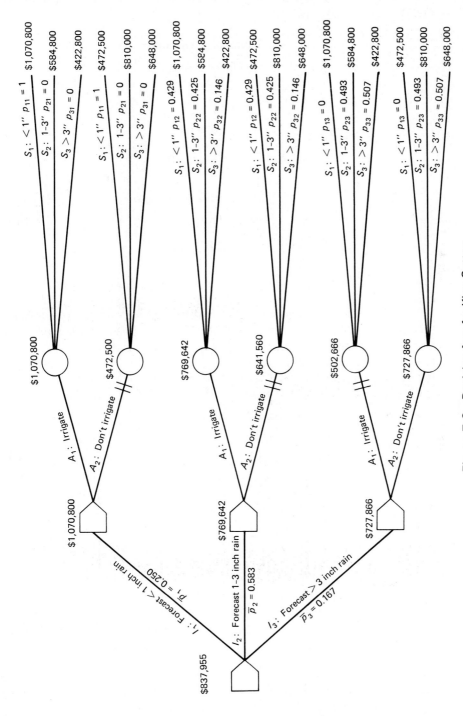

Figure 7.9 Decision free for King Cotton.

was transformed into the following posterior distribution. The predictive distribution is also given.

Posterior Distribution

*Predicted States
of Nature*

			I_2	I_2	I_3	
Actual States of Nature		S_1	1	.429	0	
		S_2	0	.425	.493	$\Pr(S_j/I_i)$
		S_3	0	.146	.507	

Predictive Distribution

I_1	I_2	I_3
.250	.583	.167

The analysis was performed using a decision tree, which is exhibited in Figure 7.9.

The DMUR model recommends irrigating when the forecast is for less than 3 inches of rain and not irrigating when more than 3 inches of rain is forecast. The EMV using sample information turns out to be $837,955. It is interesting to note that *without* additional information, the EMVs are as follows.

$$\text{EMV (Irrigate)} = \$800,260$$
$$\text{EMV (Don't irrigate)} = \$613,710$$

Thus, the information obtained from weather forecast records is worth (in the long run) about $37,695 ($837,955 − $800,260). The EMVPI is $912,860, so that the value of *perfect* information (obviously unobtainable) is $112,600 ($912,860 − $800,260). Thus the weather forecast information is not very efficient — as one can see by inspecting the conditional distribution of predictive accuracy.

Solution to the Problem: The family of Jesse Reyes, the MBA student who conducted this project, is actually in the cotton farming business, and Mr. Reyes, Sr., found the conclusions of the study to be logical and intuitively appealing. It seems clear that the forecast by the weather service of a drought (<1 inch) would indicate that a second irrigation should be applied. It is equally clear that the forecast of more than 3 inches of rain (a monsoon for West Texas!) would indicate that no second irrigation be done. However, it is not at all clear what the appropriate action would be given an intermediate forecast (1 − 3 inches). As irrigation costs rise, the difference between the financial outcomes of A_1 (Irrigate) and A_2 (Don't irrigate) narrow. As usual, this DMUR model has done nothing more than provide useful insight to the decision maker.

SUMMARY

In this chapter, we have introduced a basic model for analyzing certain problems in decision making under risk (DMUR). We used two basic criteria—expected mean value (EMV) and expected opportunity loss (EOL)—to evaluate alternative actions. Noting that the optimal EOL is the expected value of perfect information, we then explored ways of incorporating imperfect information into our model through the use of Bayes' theorem.

We then explored the concept of economic utility at some length and discussed methods for building individual decision makers' utility functions. The expected utility criterion was then shown to incorporate both problem information and risk attitude of the decision maker into the same evaluation model.

Our tour through DMUR modeling concluded with a look at the evaluation of situations involving continuous distributions on the states of nature, using the unit normal loss integral and incremental analysis. We looked briefly at the frontiers of research in this area before exhibiting the analysis of two minicases.

PROBLEMS

1.   ***The Scenario [4]:*** In days of yore in a faraway land, three thieves managed to purloin the famous Ruby of Rangadoon. Hiding in a cave, they sat in a circle about the large red jewel, greedily reflecting upon the thousands of drachmas they could get from its sale.

     The Problem: None of the thieves would have trusted the other two outside his sight. All knew that the Ruby of Rangadoon was "hot" and could not be sold for several months. If they stayed in the cave, they were sure to be caught. If they left, the stone would have to be in one thief's possession—a situation they devoutly wished to avoid. Our errant felons were caught in a dilemma.

     The Model: Finally Malodor, the most cunning of the three, spoke up. "This is hopeless. Our only course is to gamble for the ruby—winner take all. As a matter of fact, I have three dice in my pocket that we can use."

     The dice were curious indeed—one yellow, one red, and one blue. Even more curious, their six sides were numbered as follows.

> Yellow: 2, 2, 2, 5, 5, 5
> Red: 1, 4, 4, 4, 4, 4
> Blue: 3, 3, 3, 3, 6, 6

"Here's the proposition," said Malodor, "you two pick a die apiece and I'll take the one that's left. To make it fair, you two cast your dice against each other, and the one with the highest number then casts with me—again, the one with the higher number wins the ruby. You two should flip a drachma—the winner gets his choice of the die he wants."

     Solution to the Model: Diabolus correctly called "camel" as the drachma was flipped and paused to think before selecting a die. If he selected the yellow one and Larcenius picked the blue one, Larcenius would win on 24 of the 36 possible combinations. Diabolus reached for the blue cube but stopped to consider that the *red* cube would beat the blue one on 20 of the 36 possible combinations. Only after he had picked up the red cube did he realize that the yellow cube would beat it on 21 of the 36 combinations!

a. Is our problem with the Ruby of Rangadoon amenable to analysis using a classical DMUR model? Why or why not?

b. This sequential decision process can easily be modeled in terms of a decision tree. Do so, and note that the process of constructing the tree sharpens your understanding of the problem. The process is as follows.

 (1) Diabolus selects a die (decision).

 (2) Larcenius selects a die (decision).

 (3) Diabolus and Larcenius cast (nature).

 (4) The winner and Malodor cast (nature).

c. Verify that the optimal sequence of decisions and the resulting probabilities are as follows.

 (1) Diabolus selects the blue die.

 (2) Larcenius selects the red die.

 (3) The probabilities of each thief winning the ruby are Daibolus, 32/108; Larcenius, 25/108; Malodor, 51/108.

2. *The Scenario:* Having solved its inventory problem (Chapter 6), Wonmoor Time Novelties (WTN) is considering production of a radically new wristwatch with a unique device that electronically simulates the "hand sweep" of a conventional watch. Aaron Hand, the hard-hitting, aggressive CEO, has ordered a feasibility study that is now in progress.

Preliminary marketing research indicates that a competitive retail price for this product would be $100, and demand projections at that price are as follows.

Sales (millions)	1	5	10	20	30
Probability	.15	.20	.35	.20	.10

The Accounting and Production departments report that the case and basic movement for the watch can be manufactured on existing production lines at a total unit cost of $45. However, Industrial Engineering reports that manufacturing the new electronic sweep device would require construction of a new production facility at a cost of $100 million, which would produce the device at a unit cost of $40.

The Problem: In discussing the new product with M. T. Coffers, the firm's vice-president of finance, Aaron discovers that WTN's current cash position would be strained severely by the $100 million investment in a new manufacturing facility. One alternative would be to subcontract for the electronic device to avoid the large capital outlay, so the Purchasing Department is directed to issue a request for quotes (RFQ) to electronic manufacturing firms. The following two bids were received.

Bid 1: Bulldog Electronics, Inc., Baton Rouge, Louisiana

a. Per unit price of $50 if the total order is for less than 10 million sweep devices

b. Per unit price of $47 if the total order is for 10 million or more sweep devices ("all-units" price discount)

Bid 2: Shocker Manufacturing Co., Lawrence, Kansas

a. Per unit price of $49 for each unit ordered in the range of 0 to 5 million units.

b. Per unit price of $46 for each unit ordered in the range of 5 million to 20 million units

c. Per unit price of $42 for each unit ordered above 20 million units ("incremental" price discount)

The Model: Model Wonmoor Time's problem by setting up a decision matrix with four alternatives: A_1, Don't produce the watch; A_2, Produce the watch and manufacture the new electronic device internally; A_3, Produce the watch but subcontract the new device to Bulldog; and A_4, Produce the watch but subcontract the new device to Shocker.

Solution to the Model:
a. Analyze your model by computing the EMV and EOL for each alternative. What is the EMVPI for this model?
b. If Wonmoor Time's CEO Aaron Hand is basically risk averse over the range of outcomes, what effect would this tendency have on the results of your model?

Solution to the Problem: Try to put yourself in Aaron Hand's position as you study the solution to your model. Some questions you might ask yourself would be

Is the labor force available to manufacture the new electronic device internally?

How accurate are the estimates used in the model? Would a 10% error in key estimates change the model solution drastically?

How reliable are Bulldog and Shocker? Are there reasons other than costs for preferring to do business with one or the other, or neither?

How elastic is the price/demand trade-off at a retail price of $100 for the new watch? Would a higher or lower selling price affect the results of the analysis drastically?

Could demand estimates and their estimated probabilities be "sharpened" by hiring a marketing research firm to do an in-depth study? Would their services be worth the additional cost?

3.   *The Scenario:*   In prerevolutionary France, duels to the death over the favors of pretty demoiselles were common. One particularly fetching young lady named Mlle de Boeuf, was the simultaneous object of the affections of *three* courtiers—Mouton, Poulet, and Jambon—and thus the first *truel* in history became a possibility.

The Problem: Since there had never been a truel before, no one knew quite how to proceed. The matter was further complicated by the fact that Mouton was the best shot in France—he literally never missed. Poulet hit his mark with a pistol about 50% of the time while poor Jambon had a hit rate of only 30%. To be fair, each man was given *two* bullets, and the following procedure was agreed upon. Jambon, the poorest shot, was to go first—firing one of his bullets. If he were still alive, Poulet—the next best shot— would fire one of his bullets. Mouton, who never missed, would fire one shot if he remained alive. After the first round, any remaining truelists would fire their second bullets, one at a time, in the same order.

The Model: Sketch a decision tree of the problem, with Jambon—the man with the first shot—as the decision maker. Use judgment and imagination in defining Jambon's alternatives (e.g., if Jambon fired at Poulet and hit him, Mouton would have the next shot—and Jambon would be dead!)

Solution to the Model: Did you include "fire into the air on the first shot" as one of Jambon's alternatives? If you didn't, you should have—it is the optimal solution to the model! You should verify this fact for yourself.

Solution to the Problem: While our chevaliers were busy working out the arrangements for the truel, our fair Mlle de Boeuf became impatient and eloped with Dindon, the court pacifist. Thus, the truel was called off, which is why there is no reference to it in history books.

Epilogue: The point of this scenario is not to prepare managers to optimize their chances of winning truels. The point is this: Use great care in defining your alternatives when modeling with DMUR. You cannot make ground meat unless you put beef, mutton, chicken, ham, or turkey in the grinder!

4.　　*The Scenario:*　Returning to Wonmoor Time Novelties (Problem 2), Aaron Hand is uncomfortable with the results of the analysis.

　　The Problem:　After receiving the demand projections and prior distribution generated by the Marketing Department, Aaron decides that the numbers are too "soft" to be reliable, given the financial magnitude of this decision. He decides, therefore, to consider commissioning the marketing research firm of Guess & Hope, Inc. (GHI), to do an in-depth study of the potential demand distribution of the new watch.

　　The Model:　W. A. Guess, one of the partners in GHI, provides Aaron with the firm's conditional distribution of predictive accuracy:

**Conditional Distribution of
Predictive Accuracy**

GHI Predictions

Acutal Demand	I_1	I_2	I_3	I_4	I_5	
S_1	1/2	1/2	0	0	0	
S_2	1/3	1/3	1/3	0	0	
S_3	0	1/3	1/3	1/3	0	$\Pr(I_i/S_j)$
S_4	0	0	1/3	1/3	1/3	
S_5	0	0	0	1/2	1/2	

Referring to this distribution, Mr. Guess boasts, "As you can see, we might miss our forecast, but we have never missed it by more than one adjacent category. If we ever do, there will be no fee charged to our client."

　　Solution to the Model:　Using the original prior distribution from Problem 2, compute the posterior and predictive distributions using the foregoing conditional distribution of predictive accuracy.

a. What is GHI's information worth?

b. Sketch the decision tree for this problem on a large sheet of paper (this little tree gets *very* bushy). It helps to leave off the branches for which $\Pr(S_j/I_i) = 0$ (there are ten such branches).

　　Solution to the Problem:　The analysis leads to the model solution:

GHI's Prediction	Optimal Model Alternatives
1 million	Subcontract with Shocker
5 million	Subcontract with Bulldog
10 million	Subcontract with Shocker
20 million	Build device internally
30 million	Build device internally

　　The reason for the seemingly erratic model results is the effects of the price discounts offered by the two subcontractors.

a. Comparing the model results for this problem with those obtained in Problem 2, would hiring GHI (if their fee were reasonable) seem like a good idea?

b. You should have noted in the model of Problem 2 that the alternative "Don't produce the new watch" is dominated by two subcontracting alternatives. Does this mean that Aaron has no choice but to produce the new watch? (If you think so, go directly back to page 1.)

REFERENCES

1. REYES, J. Adapted from an unpublished MBA term project report, College of Business Administration, Texas Tech University (1981).
2. DAVIS, R. *A Study on Cotton Yield as Related to Cotton Variety, Irrigation, Fertility, Rainfall, and Row Pattern.* Unpublished monograph, College of Agricultural Sciences, Texas Tech University (1981).
3. ADAMS, J. *An Economic Analysis of Narrow Row Cotton Production.* Unpublished master's thesis, College of Agricultural Sciences, Texas Tech University (1978).
4. CONOVER, W. Supplied in a private communication (1982).

ADDITIONAL READING

BROWN, R., A. KAHR, and C. PETERSON. *Decision Analysis for the Manager.* New York: Holt, Rinehart and Winston, 1974.

FISHBURN, P. "Utility Theory." *Management Science,* Vol. 14 (1968), pp. 335–378.

HOWARD, R., J. MATHESON, and K. MILLER, eds. *Readings in Decision Analysis.* Decision Analysis Group, Stanford Research Institute (1974).

LAVALLE, I. *Fundamentals of Decision Analysis.* New York: Holt, Rinehart and Winston, 1978.

LUCE, R., and H. RAIFFA. *Games and Decisions.* New York: John Wiley & Sons, 1957.

PRATT, J., H. RAIFFA, and R. SCHLAIFER, *Introduction to Statistical Decision Theory.* New York: McGraw-Hill, 1965.

RAIFFA, H. *Decision Analysis.* Reading, Mass.: Addison-Wesley, 1968.

SCHLAIFER, R. *Analysis of Decisions Under Uncertainty.* New York: McGraw-Hill, 1969.

VON NEUMANN, J., and O. MORGENSTERN. *Theory of Games and Economic Behavior,* 2nd ed. Princeton, N.J.: Princeton University Press, 1953.

WINKLER, R. *An Introduction to Bayesian Inference and Decision.* New York: Holt, Rinehart and Winston, 1972.

CHAPTER 8

Waiting-Line (Queueing) Models

Waiting lines (or *queues,* as the British prefer) are familiar to everyone. We wait in line to check out in a supermarket and to buy tickets to hear Joan Jett and the Blackhearts in concert. Someone once estimated that the average person spends two years out of a lifetime in various queues.

What possible benefit could models of waiting lines be in business, industry, and public sector organizations? The fact is that waiting-line situations are as common in the organizational world as they are in the lives of people. Inventory scheduling, maintenance operations, and communication systems are all examples of activities that can be modeled and analyzed using queueing[1] theory. In fact, the mathematical theory of waiting lines had its origins in the telephone industry, when William Erlang (a Danish engineer for Bell Telephone Company) noted that telephone calls arriving at a switchboard usually had to "wait in line" before being routed.

As we will shortly discover, queueing theory is a most complex subject. You will encounter a simulation analysis of a waiting line in Chapter 9, and — to be candid — most real-world queueing systems are so complicated that simulation is the *only* effective way to analyze them. In this chapter, therefore, we will not attempt to delve very deeply into *closed-form* (exact) solutions to complex models of queueing systems. Rather, we will introduce a few simple models and their closed-form analytical solutions to get the flavor of the subject. As in previous chapters, however, we "pull no punches" in *modeling* such systems and *analyzing* the computer-generated solutions.

---

[1] For those interested in the English language, "queueing" is the only word that has five consecutive vowels.

UNDERLYING ASSUMPTIONS

All queueing systems consist of three distinct subsystems:

1. The set of people or things requiring service (usually referred to as the *calling population*)
2. One or more explicit or implicit waiting facilities or *queues*
3. An entity that provides service to the units of the calling population (the *service facility*)

One queueing system is illustrated in Figure 8.1.

Let us discuss these three subsystems of a queueing model in detail.

THE CALLING POPULATION SUBSYSTEM

The calling population can be *finite* or *infinite*. For example, the population of stars in the observable universe waiting to be discovered and cataloged by astronomers is very large, of course, but finite. On the other hand, the population of 20 milling machines in a job shop waiting to be repaired by a maintenance man, is an *infinite* calling population, since a milling machine reenters the calling population as soon as it is repaired. As an analogy, consider a finite population to be one that, in terms of statistical theory, is sampled without replacement; an infinite calling population would be analogous to sampling with replacement (assuming that the arrival rate remains constant).

Calling populations can be either *homogeneous* or *nonhomogeneous,* depending upon the type of service required. For instance, the population of male and female students in a large university is homogeneous if the service required

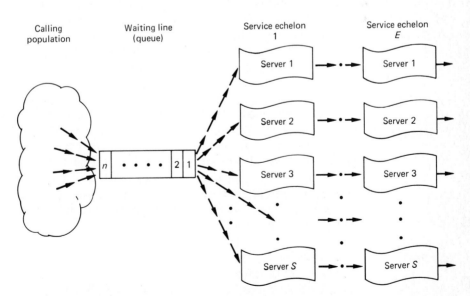

Figure 8.1   A queueing system.

is "registration for classes," but nonhomogeneous if the service is to be "physical examination" at the university clinic.

Another aspect of calling populations is the nature of their units' arrivals at the queueing subsystem. If the units arrive one at a time (no matter how small the time interval between them), we say that the calling population is *single arrival.* If two or more units can arrive simultaneously, then we have a *batch* arrival population. An example of the latter is baggage at an airport; an example of the former is the calling population of the aircraft themselves arriving for landing.

Finally, the most critical aspect of calling populations is the *probability distribution that governs the pattern of arrivals from the population to the queueing subsystem.* Common sense tells us that, if units arrive at the queue in a regular, nonvarying pattern at precisely the same intervals of time, we have a much simpler modeling task than if the arrivals are sporadic and highly variable.

The simplest calling population to model and analyze is one that is infinite, homogeneous, and single arrival and whose probabilistic arrival pattern is "well behaved" (more about this later).

THE QUEUEING SUBSYSTEM

There are two separate aspects of the queueing subsystem that must be taken into consideration. The first is the *queueing configuration,* and the second is *queue discipline.*

Queueing Configuration

A waiting line may have a *finite* or an *infinite* number of "slots" to accommodate arriving units. A drive-in bank that fronts on a busy street has a finite number of spaces in which cars may wait for the teller or tellers, assuming that "double-parking" along the street is not allowed. On the other hand, there are (for all practical purposes) an infinite number of "slots" for fighter aircraft in the queue behind aerial refueling tankers.

Another aspect of configuration depends on the service facility and involves *single* versus *multiple* queues. For example, in some modern banks, a single waiting line is formed for multiple tellers, with the person at the head of the line going to the first teller to complete a transaction. Others still allow separate queues to form in front of each teller, and—inevitably—we always end up behind the little old lady with $400 in loose change to be sorted and rolled!

Finally, we may have *serial* queues; that is, if the service being sought involves two or more activities that must be performed sequentially (such as the infamous "shot line" in Marine boot camp), there may be separate queues for each service element.

Queue Discipline

One of the most interesting and vexing aspects of the queueing subsystem is queue discipline. For example, if arriving units have the option of not joining the queue if they judge it to be too long, then we say that *balking* is allowed. If a unit can decide to leave the queue after having joined it, then *reneging* is present.

The other feature of queue discipline involves priorities—the order in which the calling units are serviced. One priority system commonly encountered is *"first-in, first-out (FIFO)"* or "first-come, first-served." On the other hand, more and more companies are accounting for inventory on a *"last-in, first-out (LIFO)"* basis. Queueing priority can also be *random,* and anyone who has ever bought a hot dog and a soft drink at a concession stand at half-time in a football game knows all about this priority system. Finally, there can be priority by *rank,* an example being an army officer who strides up the line in the mess hall until he or she encounters someone of equal or greater military rank and steps into line just behind that person.

In terms of modeling and analysis, a single infinite queue with no balking or reneging allowed, and with "first-come, first-served" (or FIFO) queue priority, is the simplest.

THE SERVICE FACILITY SUBSYSTEM

There can be a *single* server, identical servers in *parallel,* different servers in *series,* or parallel sets of servers in series (as in Figure 8.1). Servers in series may or may not have queues between each server, and (as noted earlier) there may be a single queue for parallel servers or individual queues for each.

If there are parallel servers, the service rates may be *homogeneous* or *nonhomogeneous,* as in the case of supermarket checkers that can ring up purchases at widely varying rates.

Finally, as in the calling population subsystem, the most critical aspect of a service subsystem is the *probability distribution that governs service rate.* It is obvious that a service system that provides a service at a constant, unvarying rate (such as a coin-operated vending machine) would be much easier to analyze than one in which the individual service time varied widely from one calling unit to the next (as in a dental clinic).

The simplest service facility subsystem to model and analyze is the single server (with no servers in series), whose probabilistic service-time pattern is "well behaved" in the same sense in which we addressed the arrival pattern of the calling population subsystem.

THE INTEGRATED QUEUEING SYSTEM

Table 8.1 summarizes the various facets of these three subsystems. Although there are other aspects of the three subsystems that we did not discuss, those summarized in Table 8.1 represent the major ones.

As is true in most systems, the three subsystems are highly interdependent in operation. For example, a nonhomogeneous calling population may well dictate a particular queueing priority and may require that the service facility be nonhomogeneous as well. Even so, if we consider all the possible combinations of factors leading to essentially different waiting-line models, the number of such models becomes immense. In fact, if we allow only four probability distri-

Table 8.1   Facets of Queueing Systems

Subsystems	Facets
Calling population	Finite versus infinite Homogeneous versus nonhomogeneous Single versus batch arrivals Probability distribution of arrivals
Queueing configuration	Finite or infinite single versus multiple queues series/parallel queues
Queue discipline	Balking and reneging Priorities: FIFO, LIFO, random, rank
Service facility	Series/parallel servers Homogeneous versus nonhomogeneous Probability distribution of service rate

butions each for arrivals and rates of service, the different combinations of the 12 factors in Table 8.1 total over 32,000! We are not surprised, therefore, that simulation is the most popular approach to investigating models of queueing systems.

BUILDING QUEUEING MODELS

In building a model of a queueing system, we may use the summary in Table 8.1 as a sort of checklist to determine the attributes that most nearly describe the "real-world" system we are investigating. Let us illustrate this modeling process by making a visit to QUES (queueing synthesizer), an interactive computer cousin of LIPS (linear interactive problem synthesizer) from Chapter 2. Our decision maker is Stan N. Lyons, the vice-president of production for Pegasus Aerospace Company, Manufacturing Division (PAC-MAN). PAC-MAN produces custom satellites for communications, geological observation, and a variety of other uses.

QUES: Good morning, old boy, my name is QUES (pronounced "cues"). What's yours?
STAN: My name is Stan N. Lyons, and I've got a problem.
QUES: Jolly good, Stan. Give me the particulars.
STAN: Well, my company, PAC-MAN, runs a large job shop production facility that manufactures custom satellites. The production workers are highly trained, well-paid technicians and are generally conscientious and dependable. As our backlog of orders rose over the last 12 months, we started experiencing a rash of delays that resulted in late deliveries. I did some random spot checks of the floor last week, and anywhere from 5% to 20% of

the workers were not at their work stations. When I asked one of our best and most dependable technicians what he thought the problem was, he replied: "If PAC-MAN wants to pay me $19.50 an hour to stand in line, that's fine by me."

QUES: Aha! You've got a problem with your tool crib operation, haven't you, Stan?

STAN: I think so — but how did you know that?

QUES: One of the most famous cases of a queueing problem occurred at the Boeing Aircraft Company in the early 1960s. It involved a problem with their tool crib, and I've got the details in my memory banks. Like Boeing, I would guess that PAC-MAN can't afford to purchase one each of certain very expensive tools for every worker, so you've bought two or three of each and issue them on demand from a tool crib. Right?

STAN: Right on target, QUES. But the plot thickens. I had one of our industrial engineers put his stopwatch on the crib for an entire day. It turns out that workers arrive at the crib on the average once every 5 minutes. The crib attendant takes an average of only 4 minutes to locate and process the requested tool, so it seems to me that we shouldn't be having any problems with highly paid technicians standing in line.

QUES: That's a common misconception, Stan. Let's go down my checklist for building queueing models and pin down your situation precisely.

First, you've got an infinite calling population, since each labourer is replaced as soon as he is serviced at the crib. The population also appears to be homogeneous, with single rather than batch arrivals. Now, about the probability distribution of arrivals at the crib: You gave me only the average arrival rate. Did you save the detailed log that your industrial engineer kept? If so, feed it to me through your terminal.

STAN: Yep, I saved it QUES. The engineer kept a log for each arrival at the crib — there were 96 in all. How would you like to have the data?

QUES: Break it down by "time between arrivals" to the nearest half-minute, and give me a *cumulative* tally of arrivals.

STAN: OK, here it is.

Minutes between arrivals	≤2	2.5	3	3.5	4	4.5	5	5.5	6	6.5	7	7.5	8	8.5	9	9.5	≥10
Cumulative number	0	1	2	7	19	33	46	58	67	75	80	84	87	90	93	95	96

QUES: (Short pause) Just as I suspected. I did a "goodness-of-fit" test on your data. The mean and variance are almost identical in value at 5. As you already stated, the average interarrival time is 5 minutes, so that the arrival rate averages about 12 per hour. You have an excellent "fit" with a Poisson distribution with $\lambda = 12$. That makes my task a lot easier.

Let's press forward with my checklist. I take it that your plant is very large, so that we can assume an infinite queue capacity for all practical purposes. Since you have only one tool crib attendant who performs a single service, there is only a single queue with no servers in series. As to queue discipline, do the workers ever refuse to join the queue if it is too long or leave it after joining?

STAN: Nope. There wouldn't be any point in doing either. They are paid full wages while in the waiting line, and they can't get on with their duties until they get the special tools from the crib. And by the way — we run a democratic shop. There's no special priority for any of the workers; it's strictly "first-come, first-served" at PAC-MAN.

QUES: Excellent! We have a very simple queue configuration, the queue discipline does not allow for balking or reneging, and FIFO is the easiest queue priority for me to work with.

Now, Stan, we need to consider the service facility itself. We have a single server, which settles the question of homogeneous versus nonhomogeneous servers. Did you keep the data on service rate the industrial engineer gathered? If so, feed them to me as a cumulative distribution of the number of minutes the crib attendant required to locate and sign out the tools.

STAN: Here are the data you need.

Time required for service (minutes)	≤1	2	3	4	5	6	7	8	9	10	11	12	13	14	≥15
Cumulative number	21	37	51	61	68	75	79	83	86	88	90	91	92	93	96

QUES: (Short pause) Stan, we're in luck. Your data fit an exponential model with mean and standard deviation of 4 minutes, almost perfectly. What we have is a problem that can be modeled and analyzed in closed form, so that I don't have to call my simulation program in this case. What kinds of things would you like to know about your tool crib situation?

STAN: I'd certainly like to know how long the line is, on average, because of the psychological effect it has on the workers. Obviously, I'd like to know the average waiting time in the system so I can get a handle on the implicit personnel costs. And finally, the crib attendant is paid only $6.00 per hour. If he is working as hard as I suspect he is, we might need to give him a raise.

QUES: All right, I've got your answers, but you need to study the rest of this chapter before attempting to use the numbers to help you make a decision. Come back later and we'll complete the analysis in Problem 1.

Average number of workers in queueing system	4 workers
Average waiting time in queueing system	20 minutes/worker
Average idle time for server	20%

STAN: Those numbers are startling, QUES! If 96 workers on average spend 20 minutes in the tool crib waiting line, that means 1920 minutes, or 32 hours a day, are being wasted. At $19.50 per hour, that comes to $624 every day! At the same time, the tool crib attendant is twiddling his thumbs 20% of the time, or 96 minutes per day. Are you sure your answers are correct?

QUES: Absolutely, old chap. I knew you'd react as you did. Be patient now — learn more about queueing theory, and I'll see you later. Keep a stiff upper lip! This is QUES, over and out.

SOME USEFUL NOTATION

In 1953, D. G. Kendall [1] proposed a simple notation that is widely used to classify families of queueing models. The notation takes the form U/V/W/X/Y/Z, where specific symbols or letters substituted for the letters U–Z in the six positions describe the models, as follows.

U: a symbol describing the arrival distribution

V: a symbol describing the service distribution

W: a symbol indicating the number of parallel servers

X: a symbol indicating queue capacity

Y: a symbol indicating queue priority system

Z: a symbol indicating the number of series servers.

Some of the symbols most commonly used are as follows.

M = Poisson arrival distribution or exponential service distribution

D = deterministic (constant or zero variance) arrival/service distribution

G = general distribution (other than M or D) of arrival or service time

For example, our PAC-MAN model is of the M/M/1/ ∞ /FIFO/1 variety, and this class of models happens to be the easiest to deal with analytically. Models of this type are generally referred to as Markovian. In many queueing situations, M/M/etc., models yield useful information about the behavior of the systems even when the arrival and service distributions are only approximately Poisson and exponential, respectively.

SOME CAVEATS IN USING QUEUEING MODELS

In our discussion of queueing models, we will restrict our attention to *steady-state* systems. That is, we assume that whatever the transient (temporary) start-up behavior of the system, we may ignore its long-run effects. We should note here that queueing systems can be modeled as systems of differential equations, whose solutions capture the transient effect. Obviously, such a procedure is beyond the scope of our investigations; however, the transient effect can also be "captured" by using discrete simulation models, and this tool is readily available to us (i.e., in Chapter 9).

Another important caveat is that the mean values of the arrival and service distributions must be approximately constant over the time period in question.

For example, if we were modeling the arrivals of aircraft for landing at DFW Airport, we would note immediately that there are distinct "peaks" in mid-morning and late afternoon. Thus, attempting to model this situation with elementary queueing theory would be productive only if our simulation model could account for variations in the mean arrival rate over the span of the day.

Finally, as we will see, many queueing models produce results that run counter to our intuition—unlike the majority of MS/OR models we have discussed. One major source of such results is the high variance associated with some of the more widely applicable arrival and service distributions—ones that seem to "fit" many actual situations. For instance, the mean of the Poisson distribution equals the variance, so that the standard deviation is the square root of the mean. As arrival frequency increases, the standard deviation becomes smaller in relation to the mean (relatively speaking), but for small arrival rates, the Poisson distribution is highly variable. The exponential distribution, on the other hand, has a mean equal to its standard deviation, so that its variability is high for *all* service rates.

SOLUTION APPROACHES: AN INTUITIVE DESCRIPTION

In the following discussion, we state known closed-form results for three queueing models that have proven to be useful to decision makers. We do *not* show how these results were derived—in keeping with the managerial flavor of this text. However, if you wish to investigate the origins of these results, you will find an excellent (but terse) treatment in the 1958 book by Phillip Morse [2].

NOTATION

In the following, we will use standard notation:

λ = mean arrival rate from the calling population

μ = mean service rate for a single server

$\rho = \lambda/\mu$ = traffic intensity

$P(n)$ = the probability that there are exactly n units in the queueing system (including service stations) at any randomly chosen time

L = average number of units in the queueing system

L_q = average number of units in the queue itself

W = average waiting time in the queueing system

W_q = average waiting time in the queue itself

N = number of spaces in the queueing system

S = number of parallel servers

SOME KNOWN RESULTS FOR M/M/ETC., MODELS

In the following, we restrict our attention to queueing situations in which arrival and service distributions can be estimated satisfactorily by the Poisson and exponential distributions, respectively.

The M/M/1/ ∞ /FIFO/1 Model

This is the simple model that evolved in our earlier discussion with QUES about PAC-MAN's problem. The analytical results are as follows:

$$P(n) = \rho^n(1 - \rho), \quad \text{for } \rho < 1 \tag{8.1}$$

$$L = \frac{\rho}{(1 - \rho)} \qquad L_q = \frac{\rho^2}{(1 - \rho)} \tag{8.2}$$

$$W = \frac{\rho}{\lambda(1 - \rho)} \qquad W_q = \frac{\rho}{\mu(1 - \rho)} \tag{8.3}$$

Recalling the PAC-MAN model, with $\lambda = 12$ arrivals per hour and $\mu = 15$ services per hour (both average rates), we see that the traffic intensity is $\rho = 12/15 = 0.80$. Thus we can easily reproduce the results obtained by QUES, noting that "percentage of time the server is idle" is merely $P(0)$ — the probability that there are no calling units in the system.

Notice in this model that our results "make sense" only if $\rho < 1$; that is, the model is usable only if the average rate of service is higher than the average rate of arrival of calling units. This is reasonable when we consider that we have an infinite queue capacity, so that, if $\rho \geq 1$, the waiting line would grow without bound.

The effect of variability can be illustrated dramatically using the PAC-MAN model. Recall that $P(0) = .20$, so that the crib attendant was idle 20% of the time, on average. What would you guess the probability to be that *at least six* workers would be waiting in the queue at any given time? The actual probability is about 21%, which you can easily verify. Furthermore, on the average, for one hour each day, the harried crib attendant faces *nine* or more workers in the waiting line. Instead of hiring a semiskilled clerk for $6.00 per hour, PAC-MAN might consider hiring a psychologist skilled in crowd control! (And at a salary considerably in excess of the present one.)

The M/M/1/N/FIFO/1 Model

This model differs from the previous one only in that there is a finite number of places (N) for units from the calling population to wait for service, or to be served. The analytical results are

$$P(n) = \begin{cases} \dfrac{\rho^n(1 - \rho)}{(1 - \rho^{N+1})}, & \text{for } \rho < 1 \\[3mm] \dfrac{1}{N+1}, & \text{for } \rho \geq 1 \end{cases} \tag{8.4}$$

$$L = \frac{\rho}{(1 - \rho)} - \frac{(N + 1)\rho^{N+1}}{(1 - \rho^{N+1})} \tag{8.5}$$

$$L_q = L - (1 - P(0)) \tag{8.6}$$

$$W = \frac{L}{\lambda(1 - P(N))} \qquad W_q = \frac{L_q}{\lambda(1 - P(N))} \tag{8.7}$$

As an example, consider the problem encountered by Lou's Change, Inc., a small firm that does quick oil changes for automobiles on a drive-in basis. In addition to the pit where the oil is changed, there is room in the driveway for two additional cars to wait. If three cars are in the system when a potential customer approaches, the customer cannot stop on the two-lane street. These customers almost always drive down the street to Downey Drain, Inc., Lou's competitor. Customers arrive according to a Poisson distribution at an average rate of five per hour, and service time is approximately exponentially distributed with an average service time of 10 minutes, or 6 per hour.

For the Lou's Change problem, we see that $N = 3$, $\lambda = 5$, and $\mu = 6$, so that the traffic intensity $\rho = 5/6$. Using (8.4) through (8.7), we have

$P(0) = .322$, so that the system is idle (empty) almost a third of the time

$P(3) = .186$, so that the system is full over 18% of the time, which means that Lou's is losing over 18% of its customers

$L = 1.27$, the average number of cars in the system

$L_q = .60$, the average number of cars in the queue

$W = .31$ hours, or a little less than 18 minutes average wait in the system

$W_q = .12$ hours, or a little over 7 minutes of average wait in the queue.

Note here that $P(0)$, L, and L_q are determined solely by the traffic intensity ρ and the number of spaces N. W and W_q, on the other hand, also depend upon the absolute magnitude of λ and μ.

The M/M/1/∞/FIFO/S Model

In this M/M/etc., model, we have a single infinite queue but $S > 1$ servers. Here, arriving units join the single queue, and the unit at the head of the line is serviced by the first available server. To make the model tractable, we also assume that *each* of the servers completes a service at the average rate of μ per hour and that the average arrival rate at the *queue* is λ per hour. This is our first encounter with a *state-dependent* queueing system, since the service rate for the *system* is $n \cdot \mu$ when $n < S$ (n being the number of units being served) and $S \cdot \mu$ when $n \geq S$. This complicates the formulas somewhat, as we see:

$$P(0) = \frac{(S - \rho)}{\displaystyle\sum_{n=0}^{S-1} \frac{(S - n) \cdot \rho^n}{n!}}, \quad \text{for } \frac{\rho}{S} < 1 \tag{8.8}$$

$$P(n) = \begin{cases} \dfrac{\rho^n \cdot P(0)}{n!}, & \text{if } n < S \\[3mm] \dfrac{\rho^n \cdot P(0)}{S! \cdot S^{n-S}}, & \text{if } n \geq S \end{cases} \qquad (8.9)$$

$$L_q = \frac{\rho^{S+1} \cdot P(0)}{(S-1)!(S-\rho)^2} \qquad (8.10)$$

$$W_q = \frac{L_q}{\lambda} \qquad W = W_q + \frac{1}{\mu} \qquad (8.11)$$

$$L = \lambda W \qquad (8.12)$$

Note that we took advantage of some known relationships among $P(0)$, W_q, W, L_q, and L to simplify the results. Still, we are reaching a level of complexity at which it is prudent to rely upon computer programs for our analyses.

Consider the problem faced by Cassia Czech, the president and CEO of Usury State Bank (USB). The bank operates a suburban drive-up facility with three tellers on duty, and Cassia has had a steady stream of complaints from customers about long waits in line.

The facility is constructed with concrete medians that separate the waiting lines for the three tellers. Customers approaching the facility must choose one of the lines as they drive up; thus, as soon as another car enters behind a previous one, the first car can neither leave the line (renege) nor switch to another teller.

Ilona Ranger, the manager of the drive-up facility, has suggested removing the concrete medians and forming a single waiting line. Thus, the customer who is first in line would drive to the next available teller. Cassia is skeptical — after all, customer arrival rate (currently 36 per hour, on average) wouldn't change, and it appeared that this factor was the real problem.

Consider the following analysis. Assume that the arrival rate at each of the present tellers is $36/3 = 12$ per hour. Using the M/M/1/ ∞ /FIFO/1 model and equations (8.1) through (8.3), we have

$$\lambda = 12 \qquad \mu = 13 \qquad \rho = 12/13$$
$$P(0) = 1/13 \qquad L = 12 \qquad W = 1 \text{ hr}$$

Thus, under the present system, customers spend an average of an hour in the system, and there is an average of 12 automobiles waiting in each line. We may be almost certain that an accurate assessment of this situation would involve balking.

Now let us remove the concrete medians and allow a single line to form, as in the M/M/1/ ∞/FIFO/3 model. Using (8.8) through (8.12), we have

$$\lambda = 36 \qquad \mu = 13 \qquad \rho = 32/13 \qquad S = 3$$
$$P(0) \doteq 0.0187 \qquad L_q \doteq 10.30 \qquad W_q \doteq 0.286 \text{ hr} \doteq 17.2 \text{ min}$$
$$L \doteq 13.1 \qquad W \doteq .363 \text{ hr} \doteq 21.8 \text{ min}$$

Note the dramatic difference between the two configurations. The single queue averages slightly over 10 automobiles as compared with 12 *in each queue* for the multiple-queue configuration. Also, the average waiting time has been reduced from 1 hour to about 22 minutes. Note also in the first model that *each teller* averages about 8% idle time, whereas in the single-queue case, we can compute idle time as follows.

$$P\,[\text{all 3 idle}] = P(0) = .0187$$

$$P\,[2\text{ idle}] = P(1) = .0516$$

$$P\,[1\text{ idle}] = P(2) = .0715$$

Thus, about 14% of the time, arriving customers may drive directly to a teller with no wait at all.

If this example looks like black magic, please be assured that it isn't. However, for most people, results of this type are counterintuitive at best. The "secret," as we noted earlier, is in the variance. For example, a Poisson distribution with $\lambda = 12$ has a standard deviation of about 3.46; for such a distribution with $\mu = 36$, the standard deviation is 6 — *less than double* that of the first, although the mean is *three times* that of the first. Lower variability produces better results. Think of it this way: If arrivals occurred at precisely 60/36 minutes apart, and if services occurred at a constant rate of three every 60/13 minutes, then $L_q = W_q = 0$!

AVAILABLE COMPUTER CODES FOR QUEUEING MODELS

The BASIC program QUEUES, which was authored by James R. Burns, provides closed form solutions for the following models.

1. M/M/S/N/FIFO/C
2. M/G/1/ ∞ /FIFO/1

In the foregoing,

S = 1, 2, . . .
N = 0, 1, . . .
C = 1, 2, . . .
G = any service distribution for which the variance is known

QUEUES is completely interactive and will (upon request) perform sensitivity analysis on λ and/or μ.

DEVELOPING ALTERNATIVE SOLUTIONS

So far, we have discussed the dual nature of queueing models—as descriptive models and (in the PAC-MAN example) as optimizing models. In using this powerful technique as an aid to decision making, careful sensitivity analysis is an absolute requirement. When using simulation to analyze a queueing system, sensitivity analysis is performed by setting up an experimental design and rerunning the simulation for different combinations of parameter values. For closed-form or analytical approaches, several aspects of sensitivity analysis are discussed in the paragraphs that follow.

ARRIVAL AND SERVICE TIME DISTRIBUTIONS

Much of the theory of queueing has been developed using M/M/etc., or Markovian models. The reason for this is that both the Poisson and exponential distributions are "memoryless", in that the events they describe are independent. For example, the arrival of a calling unit under the Poisson assumption has no effect whatsoever on the arrival of the next one, and so on. Likewise, the time of one service under the exponential assumption does not affect the next service. This is an intuitively appealing attribute in many "real-world" queueing systems but drastically misrepresentative in others. For example, it is well known that work rates tend to follow a so-called "learning curve," so we normally expect improvement in service rate for a human worker as he or she gains experience with the task at hand. The M/M/etc., models ignore this effect. Therefore, when analyzing an ongoing system with a queueing model, we should exercise great care in performing a "goodness-of-fit" test on both the arrival time and service distributions.

ARRIVAL AND SERVICE RATES

In infinite queue models, results of the analysis are very sensitive to small errors in λ and μ as the traffic intensity ρ (or ρ/S in multiple server models) approaches (but does not reach) the value of 1. Consider the example below in which $\mu = 30$, for values of $\lambda = 25, 27, 29,$ and 29.5 in the M/M/1/ ∞ /FIFO/1 model.

	$P(0)$	L	L_q	W	W_q
$\lambda = 25$	.167	5	4.167	.200	.167
$\lambda = 27$	.100	9	8.100	.333	.300
$\lambda = 29$	.033	29	28.033	1.000	.967
$\lambda = 29.5$	.017	59	58.017	2.000	1.967

Note that an 18% increase in λ (from 25 to 29.5) leads to a *1180%* increase in the average number of calling units in the system and a *1000%* increase in average waiting time in the system. Thus, small errors in these critical parameters could lead to very poor decisions unless caution and judgment are exercised.

Another critical assumption is homogeneity of the calling population and — in a multiple server system — the homogeneity of servers. For example, for an arrival rate of 50 units per hour, our two servers have service rates of $\mu_1 = 36$ and $\mu_2 = 24$ per hour, respectively. The *combined* service rate is $\mu = 36 + 24 = 60$, all right, but the results obtained by using the simple multiple server model with an average service time of $\mu = 30$ will be incorrect.

AN EXAMPLE OF SENSITIVITY ANALYSIS

Returning to our original Lou's Change model with a one-server, finite queue, recall that $N = 3$ (one oil change pit and two waiting spaces), $\lambda = 5$, and $\mu = 6$. Suppose that there is a possibility that the key parameters λ and μ can be in error by as much as 10% in either direction. The *most favorable* situation would be when λ is 10% too high and μ is simultaneously 10% too low; the *least favorable* situation would be the converse. Let us investigate these two conditions as case I and case II, respectively.

Case I
Since λ is 10% too high, $\lambda_{MIN} = 5/1.1 \doteq 4.545$; and since μ is 10% too low, $\mu_{MAX} = 6/.9 = 6.667$; thus $\rho_{MIN} = \lambda_{MIN}/\mu_{MAX} \doteq 0.682$. Using (8.4) through (8.7) for our computations, we have

$$P(0) \doteq .406 \qquad P(3) \doteq .129$$
$$L \doteq 1.04 \qquad L_q \doteq .45$$
$$W \doteq .26 \text{ hr} \doteq 15.7 \text{ min} \qquad W_q \doteq .11 \text{ hr} \doteq 6.8 \text{ min}$$

Thus, for case I, Lou's only loses about 13% of the business as compared with over 18% in the original analysis, and waiting time in the system has declined from 18 minutes to less than 16.

Case II
Here, $\lambda_{MAX} = 5/.9 = 5.556$ and $\mu_{MIN} = 6/1.1 = 5.455$, so that $\rho_{MAX} = \lambda_{MAX}/\mu_{MIN} \doteq 1.019$. The computational results for this case are

$$P(0) \doteq .243 \qquad P(3) \doteq .257$$
$$L \doteq 1.52 \qquad L_q \doteq .76$$
$$W \doteq .37 \text{ hr} \doteq 22.1 \text{ min} \qquad W_q \doteq .18 \text{ hr} \doteq 11.0 \text{ min}$$

Note that in case II, Lou's would lose over 25% of its business, and waiting time in the system has increased to 22 minutes, on the average.

Comparison of Case I and Case II
The key results of the analysis are summarized as follows:

	Best Case	Original Case	Worst Case
System empty	40.6%	32.2%	24.3%
System full	12.9%	18.6%	25.7%
Time in system	15.7 min	18.6 min	22.1 min

If this were an actual problem, the range of waiting times (15.7 to 22.1 minutes) might well be acceptable. However, the difference between losing 12.9% of the one's business, as opposed to 25.7%, might be an unacceptable range, and the decision maker might well insist on more precise estimates.

Note also the ρ_{MAX} was greater than 1. You might wish to verify that, if Lou's found a way to make more spaces available in the queue (i.e., $N > 3$), the analysis of case II indicates rapidly deteriorating results. Recall that in the analysis of a system with an infinite queue, we must require that ρ be less than 1.

STATE OF THE ART IN QUEUEING MODELS

As noted earlier in this chapter, one can get a very large number of different queueing models by assuming different combinations of various aspects of calling populations, queue configurations and disciplines, and service systems. There are, however, some general results developed by researchers that help to bring order out of this chaos. We discuss a few of these now.

SOME GENERAL PARAMETER RELATIONSHIPS

John D. C. Little [3] has shown that, under quite general conditions, the following relationships hold:

$$W_q = \frac{L_q}{\lambda}; \qquad W = \frac{L}{\lambda}; \qquad W_q = \frac{L}{\mu} \tag{8.13}$$

To be more specific, if the queueing system we are analyzing has the property that service rate and arrival rate are independent of each other, then these relationships hold for any single server system with an infinite queue. Note that λ and μ are known, so that if we are able to compute *one* of the four parameters L, L_q, W, or W_q, we may use (8.13) to compute the other three. This remarkable result gives us some insight into the basic "orderliness" of queueing models.

The M/G/1/ ∞ /FIFO/1 Model
Consider the most basic model (we illustrated it earlier with PAC-MAN), but let us allow the *service time* distribution to be any probability density function

whatsoever. If we know its mean μ and variance V, then the following formula[2] allows us to compute the four key parameters.

$$L_q = \frac{\rho^2 + \lambda^2 V}{2(1 - \rho)} \qquad (8.14)$$

Knowing L_q, we use the results in (8.13) to compute L, W, and W_q.

As an illustration, suppose in our original PAC-MAN problem, that the distribution service time did *not* follow an exponential distribution but that we computed the actual variance of service times to be .002 (hr)[2]. Recalling that $\lambda = 12, \mu = 15$, and $\rho = .80$, (8.14) yields $L_q = 2.32$. Substituting in (8.13) then gives $W_q \doteq .193$ hr $\doteq 11.6$ min.

$$L \doteq 2.895$$

$$W \doteq .241 \text{ hr} \doteq 14.5 \text{ min}$$

Notice that this result gives us a shorter average queue (2.9 versus 4) and a shorter waiting time (14.5 versus 20 minutes) than we obtained with the M/M/ etc., model. Since the variance of an exponential distribution is $1/\mu^2$ (in the original case, $V = 1/(15)^2 = .00444$), you might wish to verify that substituting this value in (8.14) and thereafter in (8.13) gives the original results.

PURE BIRTH AND DEATH PROCESSES

Consider the following scenario. Vera Tuft, the hard-hitting CEO of the Henny Youngman Iron and Steel Company (from a previous chapter), wants to hire a bright, eager administrative assistant. She instructs her director of Personnel to advertise the position and to accept applications on the following Monday through Friday but to cut off the applications when ten have been received. The following week she plans personally to interview the applicants and make the selection. The personnel people expect an *average* of two applications per day, and Vera expects to spend an average of two hours per interview.

Is this scenario amenable to analysis with the queueing models we previously discussed? We have a calling population with $\lambda = 2$ per day, and we have a "service facility" with $\mu = 4$ per day—but the two systems are "disconnected" in a sense. That is, the service facility does not operate until the queue is full, and the eventual size of the queue is itself probabilistic.

The first half of our scenario is called a "pure birth process," and the second half is called a "pure death process" (colorful, if somewhat dramatic, terms!). Another example of a pure birth process is the set of arrivals at a graveyard; and the departures by proud mothers and their new infants from a temporary maternity ward (set up to handle a one-time baby boom) is an illustration of a pure death process.

If the probability structures governing the pure birth and death processes are "memoryless," as is the case in M/M/etc., queues, then we may describe the two

---

[2] This formula is called the Pollaczek-Khintchine equation.

cases as follows. In these formulas, $P_n(t)$ means "the probability that there are exactly n units in the system by time t."

$$\text{Pure birth:} \quad P_n(t) = \frac{(\lambda t)^n e - \lambda t}{n!}, \quad n = 0, 1, 2, \ldots \qquad (8.15)$$

$$\text{Pure death:} \quad \bar{P}_n(t) = \frac{(\mu t)^{M-n} e^{-\mu t}}{(M-n)!}, \quad n = 1, 2, \ldots, M \qquad (8.16)$$

where M is the number of units in the system at time $t = 0$.

Equation (8.15) is a two-parameter Poisson distribution, and equation (8.16) is two-parameter *truncated* Poisson distribution.

Let us analyze Vera Tuft's scenario using the foregoing. Since $\lambda = 2$ per day and $\mu = 4$ per day, we have

$$\text{Pure birth:} \quad P_n(t) = \frac{(2t)^n e^{-2t}}{n!}, \quad n = 0, 1, 2, \ldots \qquad (8.17)$$

$$\text{Pure death:} \quad \bar{P}_n(t) = \frac{(4t)^{M-n} e^{-4t}}{(M-n)!}, \quad n = 1, 2, \ldots, M \qquad (8.18)$$

Some questions Vera might want answered would be, "What is the probability that I'll get exactly ten applications in five days?"

$$P_{10}(5) = \frac{(10)^{10} e^{-10}}{10!} = .125$$

"What is the probability that I'll have at least ten applicants by the end of the fourth day?"

$$P_{\geq 10}(4) = P_{10}(4) + P_{11}(4) + P_{12}(4) + \ldots$$
$$= 1 - P_0(4) - P_1(4) - \ldots - P_9(4)$$
$$= .283$$

The full distribution for $P_n(t)$, for values of $t = 1, 2, 3, 4, 5$, is

n	0	1	2	3	4	5	6	7	8	9	10	≥ 10
$P_n(1)$	.135	.271	.271	.180	.091	.036	.012	.003	.001	0	0	0
$P_n(2)$	.018	.073	.147	.195	.195	.156	.104	.060	.030	.013	.006	.003
$P_n(3)$	.003	.015	.045	.089	.134	.160	.160	.138	.103	.069	.041	.043
$P_n(4)$	0	.003	.010	.029	.057	.092	.122	.140	.140	.124	.099	.184
$P_n(5)$	0	0	.002	.008	.019	.038	.063	.090	.113	.125	.125	.417

Assuming that at least ten applicants come forth (note that $P_{\geq 10}(5) =$ .125 + .417 = .542), so that $M = 10$ in (8.17), our "pure death" model of the selection process is

$$\text{Pure death:} \quad \bar{P}_n(t) = \frac{(4t)^{10-n}e^{-4t}}{(10-n)!} \tag{8.19}$$

Thus, the probability that exactly one applicant remains to be interviewed after two days is $P_9(2) = .0026$.

To find the expected time of completing all interviews, we must use the following distribution.

$$\bar{\bar{P}}_M(t) = \frac{\mu(\mu t)^{M-1}e^{-\mu t}}{(M-1)!} \tag{8.20}$$

Computations for Vera Tuft's scenario are

No. of Days (t)	1	2	3	4	5	≥ 6
$P_{10}(5)$	.053	.496	.350	.085	.012	.004
$\sum_{i=1}^{t} P_{10}(t)$	.053	.549	.899	.984	.996	1.000

Thus, the odds are that she will complete her interviews in two or three days.

ADVANCED MODELS

As mentioned earlier, we have only seen the "tip of the iceberg" in queueing theory. Models have been built to analyze various queue disciplines, finite calling populations, state-dependent arrival and service rates, balking and reneging, and many other features found in "real-world" queueing systems. And yet it may appear to some that seeking closed-form mathematical models of queueing systems is wasted effort in a practical sense, when an analyst familiar with the basic theory of queueing models can always arrive at satisfactory results with simulation.

ICQ

The Scenario: Agua Fria, Inc. (AFI), is a manufacturer and wholesaler of packaged party ice. The firm uses special purified and demineralized water, so that, despite the rather high retail price, its product is very popular with the "cocktail set" in the area.

A special machine quick-freezes the ice in AFI's Fairbanks, Alaska, plant and crushes it into roughly 1-inch chunks. As the ice emerges from the machine, three baggers measure and bag the ice by hand, breaking up "chunks" in the process. Management had considered automating the bagging process but concluded that the precise weight and uniform appearance obtained by using human baggers was an important selling point and abandoned the idea.

The Problem: Cole Waters, the company's vice-president of production, was going over some production figures one frosty Alaska morning, when he noted that the weight of ice shipments for the previous month was less than half the net weight of the purified water that had been used in the ice-making machine. One expected *some* losses in the ice business, but 50% was alarming. He hurried down to the plant floor to check things out.

The machine was set at 5300 lbs per hour and seemed to be operating perfectly. He then observed the baggers for a while, and they seemed to be doing their jobs as usual—averaging about three 10-lb bags each per minute. As Cole watched, they even got ahead of the machine occasionally, and sometimes one of the baggers would be idle for a brief period. And then Cole checked the sump below the bagging platform. Lo and behold, the baggers were standing in 2 to 3 in. of water, and the drain was emptying at full capacity! He hurried to the office of Ginny Tonic, the company's "troubleshooter," and filled her in on the problem.

"Boss," said Ginny, "give me an hour or so, and I'll have this problem down cold."

The Model: Precisely 60 minutes later, Ginny strode into Cole's office, waving a sheet of paper covered with numbers and symbols.

"I retrieved some of my notes from my MBA program at Glacier U., and it looks as if we can model this problem as a queueing model," announced Ginny.

"You mean like a waiting line?" replied Cole, with an icy stare. "Nobody's waiting in line—our ice is melting."

"Our *ice* is waiting in line, boss," said Ginny, "and it appears from my numbers that a lot of it is waiting too long. Look, what we've got here is a multiple server queueing model with a single queue. I suspect that our big icemaker has quite a bit of variability in its output, and I *know* that the baggers have variability in their bagging speed. Now, this is really a finite queue length situation, but they did not cover that (for multiple servers) in our management science text. So, I've built a little multiple server, single infinite queue model of our problem."

Solution to the Model: Using "10 lbs of ice" as a unit in the calling population and 1 hr as the time unit for analysis, Ginny estimated the following queueing parameters.

$$\lambda = 530 \text{ 10-lb units of ice per hour}$$
$$\mu = 180 \text{ 10-lb bags per server per hour}$$
$$S = 3 \text{ servers} \quad \rho = 530/180 \doteq 2.944$$

The results using equations (8.8) through (8.12) were as follows.

$$P(0) \doteq .0042$$
$$W_q \doteq .0965 \text{ hours} = 5.79 \text{ minutes}$$
$$W \doteq .1021 \text{ hours} = 6.13 \text{ minutes}$$
$$L \doteq 54.10 \quad L_q \doteq 51.16$$

"As you can see, boss," noted Ginny, "on the average there are over 540 pounds of ice sitting on the loading platform, and it takes an average of over 6 mins to get it bagged and in the freezer."

"It's even worse than that," replied Cole. "The platform has a capacity of 400 pounds, so when this limit is exceeded, the excess falls off into the sump and melts."

Solution to the Problem: It seemed clear to Cole that there were two viable alternatives: slow down the ice maker or hire additional baggers. He asked Ginny to rerun her model with the same three baggers and with $\lambda = 500$ bags per hour and then to add a fourth bagger and leave the production rate at $\lambda = 530$ bags per hour. Her results were as follows.

	A_1: Reduce Production	A_2: Additional Bagger
$P(0)$	.0179	.0410
L_q	10.79 bags	1.34 bags
W_q	.0216 hr (1.29 min)	.0025 hr (.15 min)
W	.0271 hr (1.63 min)	.0081 hr (.48 min)
L	13.57 bags	4.28 bags

Cole stared at the numbers. Baggers' wages were $5.00 per hour, and the profit margin on bags of ice was currently running at 25 cents; thus, cutting the production rate from 530 to 500 bags would cut profits by $7.50 per hour, while hiring another bagger would increase costs by $5.00 per hour.

Then, suddenly, a chill went up his spine as a flash of insight occurred: why not hire a fourth bagger and *increase* the production rate from 530 to 550 bags per hour—generating enough profit from the additional 20 bags to pay the new bagger's salary! He had Ginny run the new model and chuckled with satisfaction when she showed him the following model solution.

$$P(0) \doteq .0346 \qquad L_q \doteq 1.724 \qquad W_q \doteq .0031 \text{ hr } (.19 \text{ min})$$
$$W \doteq .0087 \text{ hr } (.52 \text{ min}) \qquad L \doteq 4.78 \text{ bags}$$

Agua Fria's problem was solved.

Gourmet [4]

The Scenario: El Queso Mohoso, an exclusive restaurant in downtown Dallas, serves gourmet Hispanic-style food. Although its prices are very high, the restaurant does a booming business six evenings per week and does not take reservations. All ten tables are "tables for two," and all dishes are prepared for two people (thus, solitary diners pay for — and get — double portions of everything). There is a small bar with six bar stools where patrons may while away their time until a table is free.

The Problem: Plata Cuchara, the owner of the establishment, is considering an expansion, but she is puzzled by the pattern of customer arrivals and departures. Her head waiter, Agrio Cara, informs her that at times — even during the busiest hours — there are tables open and the bar is unoccupied. At other times, he has to turn away several couples in a row because every table and every bar stool is taken. Plata decides to seek help from her very bright cousin, Huevo Cabeza, who is finishing his MBA work at Meridional Caballito University.

The Model: Huevo listened carefully as Plata outlined her problem, and it appeared that some sort of queueing model might be constructed. However, the El Queso Mohoso problem didn't seem to be similar to any of the cases he had studied in graduate school, so he bought a copy of a widely used MBA text in management science and decided to use the 12-step checklist contained in the chapter on queueing models (Table 8.1).

1. The calling population of couples going out to dinner was finite, of course, but Huevo reasoned that he could safely assume that it was infinite.
2. Since the restaurant catered strictly to couples, he concluded that the calling population was homogeneous.
3. Although batch arrivals did occur, Huevo decided to treat couples as *units,* so that the single-arrival assumption could be made.
4. He next decided that he could treat the bar as a queue and had the head waiter Agrio keep a log of arrivals for several days. The pattern seemed to be fairly stable over the 6:00 P.M. – 11:00 P.M. restaurant hours, with an average arrival rate of approximately nine couples per hour. Since the variance came out to be about 9 as well, Huevo concluded that the arrival rate was Poisson distributed.

5. As to the queue configuration, it obviously had a finite number of places in which to wait.
6. The ''single versus multiple queues'' question was not a problem.
7. Huevo deferred the ''series/parallel queues'' issue temporarily.
8. Balking and reneging, he discovered, were not present. Couples seemed grateful for the chance to get inside—even if they had to wait in the bar for a table to become available—and they certainly were not going to relinquish their place in line by reneging.
9. Queue priority was clearly FIFO, since Plata insisted on treating every couple equally. In the short time that El Queso Mohoso had been open, for example, she had turned away the governor of Texas and his wife and her own mother and father on their fiftieth wedding anniversary.
10. Huevo bypassed the ''series/parallel server'' question for the moment, as well as the issue of
11. Homogeneous versus nonhomogeneous servers.
12. He decided to define service time as the difference between the time a couple was seated and the time the couple left the table. Agrio logged these events for several evenings, and service appeared to be approximately exponential with an average of one service per hour.

Reviewing his notes, Huevo concluded that the six bar stools were the single finite queue and that each of the ten tables was an individual parallel server. As a quick approximation, he decided to analyze the problem as one with an infinite queue and to assess the results.

Solution to the Model: Using equations (8.8) through (8.12), Huevo's M/M/1/ ∞/FIFO/10 model gave the following results:

$$\mu = 1/hr \qquad \lambda = 9/hr \qquad \rho = 9 \qquad S = 10$$

$$P(0) \doteq \frac{1}{14,369} \qquad L_q \doteq 6.02 \qquad W_q \doteq .669 \text{ hr} \doteq 40 \text{ min}$$

$$L \doteq 15.02 \qquad W \doteq 1.669 \text{ hr} \doteq 1 \text{ hr, } 40 \text{ min}$$

These results looked reasonable to Huevo, but they gave no indication of how much business the restaurant was losing. He, therefore, obtained a copy of the program QUEUES and ran the actual M/M/1/6/FIFO/10 model. These results are

$$P(0) = \frac{1}{4760} \qquad P(6) \doteq .1073 \qquad L_q \doteq 2.72$$

$$W_q \doteq .339 \text{ hr} \doteq 20.3 \text{ min} \qquad L \doteq 10.75$$

$$W \doteq 1.339 \text{ hr} \doteq 1 \text{ hr, } 20.3 \text{ min}$$

Since $P(6) \doteq .1073$, it appeared that El Queso Mohoso was losing a little less than 11% of its potential customers. The average wait in the bar was only about 20 minutes—which seemed reasonable.

Solution to the Problem: Huevo showed the results to his cousin and recommended *against* expansion. His reasoning was that turning away

11% of potential customers was probably a *positive* factor on balance and bolstered the restaurant's image of exclusivity. Another factor in his recommendation involved the very high quality of food and service. Expansion would mean having to hire additional chefs and waiters, and Plata's close watch over the cuisine and personal attention to customers would be difficult or impossible to maintain. He did, however, recommend raising prices by 20%.

Plata listened carefully and then thanked Huevo for his assistance with the offer of a free dinner. However, after waiting in the bar for over an hour for a table, Huevo reneged and ate dinner elsewhere.

SUMMARY

In this chapter, we investigated various applications of waiting-line models and saw that such models are composed of three interdependent subsystems: calling population, queueing facility, and service facility.

We discussed modeling queueing systems using a 12-step checklist that addresses the various facets of each subsystem. The closed form analytical results for three simple queueing models were presented, and sensitivity analysis was discussed. Two cases were then analyzed to illustrate the application of two queueing models.

In Chapter 9, we discuss in depth the powerful and widely used discrete simulation model.

PROBLEMS

1. Stan N. Lyons, the vice president of production for PAC-MAN, Inc., has done his homework on queueing models and is now ready to complete his tête-à-tête with QUES.

STAN: OK, QUES, I'm ready to complete our analysis of our tool crib operation at PAC-MAN.

QUES: Hello again, old sock. Let me fetch our data from my disk to refresh your memory.

$\lambda = 12$ arrivals per hour, on the average, by workers at the tool crib, Poisson distributed

$\mu = 15$ services per hour, on the average, by the tool crib attendant, exponentially distributed

$\rho = \lambda/\mu = .80$, traffic intensity

Average technician's pay = $19.50 per hour

Tool crib attendant's pay = $6.00 per hour

Results of M/M/1/ ∞ /FIFO/1 model analysis are

$P(0) = .2$, fraction of time server is idle

$L = 4$, average number of workers in the system

$L_q = 3.2$, average number of workers in the queue

$W \doteq .333$ hr $= 20$ min, average time spent in the system

$W_q \doteq .267$ hr $= 16$ min, average time spent in the queue

Total cost of technician idle time $= \$624$ per day

STAN: Those numbers are indeed accurate, QUES—I analyzed the model by hand after I learned about queueing models and how to use them. What's next?

QUES: How accurate do you feel your estimates of λ and μ are? They are critical parameters in the model we are using.

STAN: I'd feel comfortable with ±10% for each.

QUES: (Short pause) Here is a sensitivity analysis based on a 10% range. The "best case" below is based on a low λ and high μ—that combination gives the smallest possible traffic intensity of $\rho_{MIN} \doteq .655$. The "worst case" is just the converse, with $\rho_{MAX} \doteq .977$. I think you'll find these results to be startling.

	Best Case	Original Case	Worst Case
$P(0)$ (attendant idle)	34.5%	20.0%	2.3%
L (average line length)	1.90	4	42.5
L_q (average queue length)	1.24	3.2	41.5
W (average wait in system)	10.4 min	20 min	191 min
W_q (average wait in queue)	6.8 min	16 min	187 min
Cost of technician idle time per day	$324	$624	$5959

STAN: Startling is hardly the word for the "worst case," QUES. Our daily salary budget for technicians is about $12,000—which means that about half of it would be spent to pay men to stand in line at the tool crib! I've got to do something to make sure that the "worst case" can't happen.

Thanks for your help, QUES.

QUES: Roger; QUES, over and out.

a. Analyze the PAC-MAN problem by adding one additional tool crib attendant whose salary is $6 per hour and whose service rate is 15 per hour. Perform a ±10% sensitivity analysis for this model and compare your results with those obtained by QUES. Would Stan be wise to hire another attendant?

b. In the original PAC-MAN model, replace the $6-per-hour tool crib attendant, who has a service rate of 15 an hour, with an experienced technician at $19.50 per hour and who has a service rate of 30 an hour. Perform a ±10% sensitivity analysis for this model and compare your results with (a). Does it appear to be preferable to hire a faster worker or to hire two slower workers with the same total service rate but at a lower total cost?

c. From a managerial economics point of view, explain the results you obtained in (b). Many people find this result to be counter-intuitive, but those who understand the concept of *productivity* do not.

2. **The Scenario [5]:** In the small, sleepy community of Siesta, Idaho, there is a single gas station, which is owned and operated by Phil Upp. The station has a single pump,

and Phil is the only employee. Siesta is off the main highway several miles, so almost all of Phil's business comes from local residents. Phil's business practices are antiquated by modern standards—he still washes windshields and checks air, oil, and water for his customers—regardless of the size of the purchase.

A normal service usually takes about 10 minutes if the customer's tank is nearly empty, and customers arrive for service randomly, but at an average rate of about one every 15 minutes. Thus, Phil is kept fairly busy, but there seemed to be ample time to relax.

a. Analyze Phil's scenario using the M/M/1/ ∞ /FIFO/1 model. Does this model appear to be appropriate in this situation?

b. Can you guess what's coming next?

The Problem: One bright Sunday morning, a rumor got started that there was a gasoline shortage, and when Phil opened his station at 7:00 A.M. the next morning, there were already four cars waiting to "top off" their gasoline tanks. Phil insisted that there wasn't a gas shortage, but most of his customers didn't believe him. The frequency with which customers arrived doubled from four per hour to eight per hour. Since most services were "top-offs," Phil's average service time dropped from 10 minutes to 7 minutes, but he was still determined to give "full service" regardless.

The Model:

a. Analyze this new scenario as an M/M/1/ ∞ /FIFO/1 model and compare the results obtained previously. What has happened to Phil's idle time? How long is the average waiting time? How long is the average queue?

b. In exasperation, Phil installed a second pump, hired another attendant at $5 per hour, and raised his gasoline price by 10 cents per gallon to cover his additional costs. The townspeople immediately accused him of profiteering from the "gasoline shortage," although Phil insisted stoutly that he was pumping almost exactly the same number of gallons per week as he always had. Analyze this new situation as a two server, infinite queue model.

c. The new attendant was lazy and irresponsible, and Phil fired him within two weeks. He then shut down one pump and lowered his average service rate to 4 minutes per customer by refusing to wash windshields or to check air, oil, and water. He also erected a barrier so that only four cars could wait in line (including the one being serviced) at a time.

Analyze this situation as a single server, finite queue model. Compute P(4), the probability of "lost sales." In this situation, are the "lost sales" really lost?

d. Gradually, because of the limited number of spaces in which to wait for service, the townspeople returned to their previous pattern of filling their tanks when they were near empty—instead of "topping off" at the earliest opportunity. When normalcy had finally returned, Phil removed the barrier. However—miffed by the behavior of the citizens of Siesta—he never resumed his previous practice of cleaning windshields and checking his customers' oil, air, and water. He also retained the 10-cent-per-gallon price increase and enjoyed the leisure he had been accustomed to before the great "gasoline shortage" fiasco.

Aren't you glad that this exercise is a fable and that people don't actually behave that way?

3. As noted in this chapter, the assumption of an infinite queue length is often made when modeling waiting-line systems. To assess the accuracy of this approximation, compare the analytical results obtained for the M/M/1/ ∞ /FIFO/1 and M/M/1/N/FIFO/1 models, which are reproduced here.

	Single Server, Infinite Queue ($\rho < 1$)	Single Server, Finite Queue ($\rho < 1$)
$P(0)$	$1 - \rho$	$\dfrac{1 - \rho}{1 - \rho^{N+1}}$
L	$\dfrac{\rho}{1 - \rho}$	$\dfrac{\rho}{1 - \rho} - \dfrac{(N+1)\rho^{N+1}}{1 - \rho^{N+1}}$
W	$\dfrac{\rho}{\lambda(1 - \rho)}$ or $\dfrac{L}{\lambda}$	$\dfrac{L}{\lambda(1 - P(N))}$

a. For $\rho < 1$, what happens to the expression $1 - \rho^{N+1}$ as N increases? What can you conclude about the values of $P(0)$ for the two models as N becomes large?

b. For $\rho < 1$, what happens to the term $(N + 1)\rho^{N+1}/(1 - \rho^{N+1})$ as N increases? What can you conclude about the values of L for the two models as N becomes large?

c. As N becomes large, $P(N)$ becomes small, all else remaining constant. What, therefore, happens to the values of W for the two models as N becomes large?

4.   ***The Scenario:***   The message decoding facility of the Careful Intrigue Agency (CIA) is located in the windowless subbasement of its headquarters in Virginia. Messages arrive from all over the world at the average rate of 20 per hour, but arrivals tend to be uniformly distributed over the interval 0–40 (i.e., an arrival rate of 10 per hour is just as likely as 30 or 40 per hour).

Each message carries one of three classifications: "sensitive," "highly sensitive," or "eyes only." Some decoding clerks have security clearances only for sensitive messages, whereas others are cleared to handle both sensitive and highly sensitive ones. Eyes only messages are decoded by a special team that works in a separate, tempered-steel vault.

In addition to their classification, messages may also carry decoding time priorities of "urgent" or "routine." Urgent messages carry a preemptive priority, so that if a particular clerk is decoding a routine message when an urgent one arrives, he or she stops and begins work on the urgent message.

Decoders cleared only for sensitive messages work as a group (A) and those cleared for highly sensitive or sensitive form a separate group (B). Messages arrive at a single point, where a dispatcher routes them to the appropriate group. Obviously, all eyes only messages are routed to the special team in the vault, but this team occasionally decodes highly sensitive ones if they are urgent, and if the team is not busy. Group B occasionally decodes sensitive messages if they are urgent, and if the team is not busy on urgent, highly sensitive messages. Group A decodes only sensitive messages.

On the average, a team can decode a sensitive message in 5 minutes and a highly sensitive message in 6 minutes, but these times tend to be normally distributed ($\mu_1 = 12$ per hour and $\mu_2 = 10$ per hr) with a variance roughly equal to their means. Decoding an eyes only message takes exactly 15 minutes, with no variability, because of the precise computerized procedure used. About half of all incoming messages are sensitive, about one-third are highly sensitive, and one-sixth are eyes only. Overall, about 10% of the messages are urgent, the rest being routine, and the arrival pattern is random.

The Problem: So far, the system seemed to be working well. The dispatcher was sensitive to the hour-by-hour variations in work load among the three groups and routed messages accordingly. One gray day, however, a mandated personnel reduction converted his highly paid GS-15 position to GS-6, and the dispatcher was transferred to the College Surveillance Division. The clerk who replaced him was bright and willing to learn, but the best he could manage to do was to "go by the book"—routing all sensitive

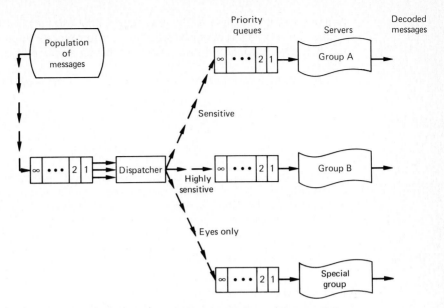

Figure 8.2 CIA message decoding model.

messages to group A, all highly sensitive messages to group B, and (of course) nothing but eyes only messages to the group in the vault.

 The Model: A schematic of this queueing system is exhibited in Figure 8.2. Use the "checklist" in Table 8.1 to analyze this queueing system. In your opinion, what are the odds that there exists a closed-form (analytical) solution to this model?

 Solution to the Model: The former dispatcher used judgment in smoothing out the workload among the three groups. This is an example of state-dependent arrival rates, in that messages are routed to less busy groups in an effort to minimize the lengths of the three "priority queues."

 Solution to the Problem:
a. How sensitive is this system to modest errors in the estimates of arrival and service rates? How would a small shift in percentages of message types affect the system?
b. Suppose that, if a routine message does not get decoded after being in the system for four hours (because of being "bumped" by urgent messages), its priority is automatically changed to urgent. What effect would this feature have on the system?

 Epilogue: Models such as this are messy to analyze, but they are also representative of the complexity usually found in business, industrial, and public sector systems. For example, instead of a "CIA message decoding system," suppose that the "dispatcher" was actually the receiving department for an inventory system and that the "messages" were different kinds of materials to be processed by different "decoders" (departments). What we would have is a classical "work-in-process" inventory and production system.

5. In assuming that service times are exponentially distributed, we were of course using the following probability distribution:

$$f(t) = \mu e^{-\mu t}, \quad t \geq 0; \qquad E(t) = \frac{1}{\mu}; \quad \text{VAR}(t) = \frac{1}{\mu^2}$$

As noted earlier, the high variability of the exponential distribution is the source of much of the counterintuitive pattern exhibited by queueing models. Suppose that our actual service rate were significantly less variable, so that the standard deviation was *less* than the mean.

Consider the following very useful density function called the *Erlang distribution:*

$$f(t) = \frac{(\mu k)^k t^{k-1} e^{-k\mu t}}{(k-1)!} \quad \text{for } t \geq 0; k = 1, 2, 3, \ldots$$

$$E(t) = \frac{1}{\mu} \qquad \text{VAR } (t) = \frac{1}{k\mu^2}$$

a. Verify that, for $k = 1$, the Erlang becomes the exponential distribution.
b. Note that for $k > 1$, the variance is less than that of the exponential.
c. Use the Pollaczek-Khintchine equation (8.14) to verify that, for a single server and an infinite queue:

$$L_q = \frac{k+1}{2k} \cdot \frac{\rho^2}{(1-\rho)}$$

Use the general relationships in (8.13) and L_q to compute the closed-form values of L, W, and W_q.
d. Using Erlang distributions with $k = 2, 4, 9$, reexamine the results obtained in Problem 1 for the PAC-MAN problem. Notice the marked improvement in the parameter values as k increases.

REFERENCES

1. KENDALL, D. "Stochastic Processes Occurring in the Theory of Queues and their Analysis by the Method of Imbedded Markov Chains." *Annals of Mathematical Statistics,* Vol. 24 (1953), pp. 338–354.
2. MORSE, P. *Queues, Inventories, and Maintenance.* New York: John Wiley & Sons, 1958.
3. LITTLE, J. "A Proof of the Queueing Formula: $L = \lambda W$." *Operations Research,* Vol. 9 (1961), pp. 383–387.
4. DINNIN, M. Adapted (liberally) from an unpublished MBA term project report, College of Business Administration, Texas Tech University (1982).
5. ERICKSON, W. Problem suggested by "Management Science and the Gas Shortage." *Interfaces,* Vol. 4 (1974), pp. 47–51.

ADDITIONAL READING

COOPER, R. *Introduction to Queueing Theory.* New York: Macmillan, 1972.
WAGNER, H. *Principles of Operations Research,* 2nd ed. Englewood Cliffs, N.J.: Prentice-Hall, 1975.

CHAPTER 9

Discrete Simulation Models

While some have suggested that simulation is a "tool of last resort," we take a different perspective. Simulation is a methodology for conducting experiments using a model of the real system. Frequently, the expediency for using simulation occurs *whenever there is an essential dependence on time that must be considered.* Most of the models we discussed in Part I were static models. All data, relationships, and variables were assumed to remain fairly constant over a given time period or planning horizon. When such is not the case, we are operating in an environment involving change — a dynamic environment. When the dynamics are pronounced enough to require explicit consideration, then simulation may be used. Simulation models permit tracing through in time the dynamics and behavior implicitly induced by the model's probabilistic and causal structure.

In yet another fundamental respect, simulation models differ from the optimization models described in Part I. The models of Part I were mostly prescriptive — prescribing what's best (or at least what's better). Simulation models tend to be descriptive — "telling it like it is." However, no hard and fast rules pertaining to prescriptive usage of optimization models, and descriptive usage of simulation models can be dichotomized. Occasionally optimization models are used for descriptive purposes whereas simulation models may be prescriptive, although such usages are rare. Both model types provide the manager with intuition, insight, and understanding, as we shall see. However, because of this fundamental difference, algorithms for solving simulation models do not automatically generate alternative solution strategies, as did the algorithms for solving the optimization models in Part I. It therefore becomes the responsibility of the user to generate his or her own alternative solution strategies. He or she must also perform all comparisons of alternative solution strategies manually, and without the help of a figure of merit — what we usually call an objective function. This approach to policy experimentation has come to be known as "what-if" analysis.

The apparent distinctions we have intimated here between optimization models and simulation models are corroborated by the words of Galitz [1]:

> At first sight, it might seem that optimizing models are superior to descriptive ones, because they actually produce decision strategies rather than merely evaluate them. However, optimizing models have the drawback that the decisions they produce are very sensitive to the exact formulation of the criterion to be optimized and the constraints imposed. Yet it is extremely difficult to quantify these accurately. Moreover, the decisions produced by optimizing models must be considered carefully, since most of these models assume certainty and produce no hedging strategies other than those forced by specific constraints. . . . Descriptive models can themselves be used to generate decision strategies by using a trial and error process, and subjective judgments and assessments can be made as the user goes along.

The importance of simulation modeling in commerce, industry, and government is well documented. In the view of Keen [2], "It seems fair to say that simulation is the most widely used managerial computer-based technique in both government and industrial decision making." Surveys by Naylor [3,4], Shannon [5,6], and others all suggest that simulation and statistical methods are the most widely used management science techniques employed by industry. Emshoff and Sisson [7] published an extensive list of areas to which simulation methods are currently being used. Our list (Table 9.1) excludes areas mentioned by them but includes still others. The list is considered indicative of the breadth of applications to which simulation can be put; however, not all these application areas are most appropriately modeled by means of discrete simulation. At least some of these application areas could better be accommodated by continuous simulation (Chapter 15).

As an example of a situation to which simulation could be applied, let us return to the capacity planning problem first described in Chapter 3. Imagine once again that we are hiding in the office closet of Buck Stopps, the hard-nosed vice-president of finance for Monolithic Manufacturing, Inc. Stopps finds his company currently operating in a dynamic economic environment that could be characterized as "feast or famine," or "roller coaster." While his company has a definite short-term need for additional five-axis milling machines, the long-term outlook is not nearly as bright due to rising interest rates and increased foreign competition. Bitsy Bytes has just returned from the computer center with her most recent run. Her model now produces integer solutions to the problem of deciding how many additional milling machines to purchase. She is using the current order file as a basis for determining short-term demand.

"Buck, I have another solution to that milling machine problem I'd like to discuss with you," she says timidly.

"Fine! Fine! What's the computer spittin' out these days?" inquires Buck.

"Well, to meet our order commitments over the next six months, the current solution calls for the purchase of three five-axis milling machines, two conventional lathes, and two three-axis milling machines for a cost of $15,650,000."

"For a cost of what? We don't have that kind of money, young lady. And besides, what do we do with all of the excess capacity when the economy softens?"

Once again Bitsy is sent back to her work station with new points to ponder. The need to consider fluctuating demand over the lifetime of the capital equipment has been made painfully apparent to her. Bitsy begins to scratch about for other modeling approaches to her problem.

Table 9.1   Partial List of Simulation Applications

Resource management systems
  Water resource management models
  Energy resource management models
  Natural resource management models

Pollution management systems
  Air pollution regulation models
  Trace metals contaminants models
  Solid waste management models
  Water quality models

Urban and regional planning
  Land use planning models
  Urban (regional) economic development models
  Urban (regional) population growth models
  Urban (regional) planning and development models
  Location models
  Sewer system models
  Airport simulations

Transportation systems
  Urban (regional) transportation models
  Air transportation models
  Traffic flow models

Health systems
  Health care delivery models
  Hospital design models
  Community health models

Criminal justice systems
  Criminal justice models
  Crime detection and prevention models

Industrial systems
  Total company models
  Production models
  Capital resources models
  Finance models

Commerce systems
  Marketing models
  Advertising models

Education systems
  Secondary school models
  Higher education models
  University enrollment and resources models

Information systems
  Organization models
  Library models

Miscellaneous
  Insect pest control models
  Municipal information system models
  Forest growth and nutrient cycling
  Telecommunications regulation models
  Public safety models

While this bit of dialogue suggests a definite requirement for simulation models, it does not address the question of the kinds of purposes that simulation models can achieve. Table 9.2 lists some of the purposes (which could also be interpreted as benefits to the user) of simulation models. These correspond closely to the purposes and benefits that motivate the formulation and use of management science models in general.

Just as there are many different types of management science models, we find that there are also a great many different types of simulation models. The dichotomies in Table 9.3 must be dealt with in connection with choice of simulation model type. In this chapter, we will be concerned with simulations having the attributes that appear on the left-hand side of Table 9.3. Discussions of deterministic, continuous simulation will appear in Chapter 15.

Table 9.2 List of Purposes and Benefits of Simulation Models
To be able to explore alternatives
To improve the quality of decison making
To enable more effective planning
To improve understanding of the business
To enable faster decision making
To provide more timely information
To enable more accurate forecasts
To generate cost savings

Table 9.3 Simulation Model Dichotomies
Probabilistic versus deterministic
Discrete versus continuous
Steady state versus transient
Mathematical versus physical
Causal versus correlative
Homomorphic versus isomorphic

A brief discussion of each of the dichotomies noted is in order. Continuous simulations are appropriate for systems whose variables are continually changing with time, whereas discrete simulations are appropriate for systems whose variables change rather abruptly at discrete points in time.

Deterministic simulations are appropriate for systems whose parameters (constants) and structure are relatively well known and understood, whereas probabilistic (or Monte Carlo) simulation is appropriate for situations in which this is not the case. (Often, we use deterministic simulations to model situations in which the structure and parameters are not well known because of the added complexity to the simulation model, which stochastic or probabilistic considerations create.) We use Monte Carlo techniques in connection with discrete representations because the time between changes in the system is usually random.

Transient simulations are appropriate for systems that indicate a temporary behavior, whereas steady-state simulations are useful to represent systems that operate in a steady state. According to the second law of thermodynamics, all systems tend to wear down and grow old, unless driven by an input. As this happens, systems begin to exhibit a steady-state or static behavior, whereas relatively "young" systems exhibit a transient behavior.

Mathematical simulations are the type used in connection with the digital computer. The computer is used to simulate the model characterized by means of mathematical equations. On the other hand, physical simulations may include flight simulators, planetarium shows, movies, arcade amusements, video games, and television programs.

Moreover, simulation models may be causal or correlative depending upon whether the interconnections among the components that describe the system represent an attempt to model the actual interactions among these components or represent simply a linkage between two variables that, statistically, are highly correlated.

Finally, simulation models may be isomorphic, but more often they are homomorphic in the sense that there does not usually exist a unique two-way correspondence between the elements of the original system and the elements of the model. Most of the time our models are too aggregated to allow each element of the model to correspond to only one element in the object system. Since a one-to-one correspondence between each element in the object system and each component in the model is rare, isomorphic simulations are unusual.

Before getting into a discussion of the "underlying assumptions" of discrete simulations, we need to dwell for a moment on the inherent characteristics of simulation. First and foremost, the capability of tracing through the effects *in time* of a particular scenario, policy, or strategy is a definite asset. Second, simulations generally describe the consequences of a given set of inputs, but they do not prescribe optimal policies, as indicated earlier. Third, simulation can provide answers for problems that are difficult (even impossible) to solve in any other way. Fourth, simulation models serve as a vehicle on which "what-if" experiments can be performed. In the absence of models, such experiments would have to be subjected to the object system itself—and the consequences could be disastrous. Simulation provides an inexpensive tool for carrying out these experiments in a way that permits the user to perceive *immediately* the consequences of a particular set of actions. This "time compression" characteristic of all simulations is once again a definite asset. In summary we find that simulations permit inferences to be drawn about systems without building them if they are merely proposed; simulations enable insights to be obtained about systems without disturbing them, since such disturbances may be expensive and risky; and simulations allow us to develop intuition about systems without destroying them when the object is to determine the stress limits of the system.

UNDERLYING ASSUMPTIONS AND DEFINITIONS

Perhaps the best way to begin this discussion is with a definition of simulation. A *simulation* is any model that permits the projection through time of the dynamic behavior of an object system. Generally, this model is implemented on a digital computer; however, analog computer implementations are still in use, but mostly for engineering applications. Analog computer simulations are beyond the scope of this book.

As previously mentioned, simulation can be approached from two fundamentally different philosophies. In this chapter we concentrate only on probabilistic, discrete simulation. Continuous simulation will be discussed in Chapter 15. Discrete simulation is an appropriate tool to use when the dependent variables in the system change discretely at specified points in time. Such is always the case when the object system can be characterized by activities or events.

ACTIVITIES AND EVENTS

The philosophy of discrete simulation was developed in the early 1960s in connection with work performed by Kiviat [8] and others. Central to the philosophy is the concept of an activity. An *activity* is an elementary task that requires time to complete. Activities are always preceded and followed by other activities. A *process* is a collection of such activities, which must either be performed serially in chronological order or in parallel, as shown in Figure 9.1. In either case there is always a logical order in which the activities are per-

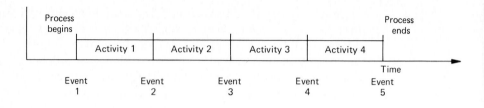

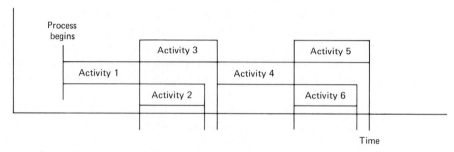

Figure 9.1 Processes viewed as chronological sequences of activities.

formed. The actual time required to complete an activity is, in general, random. Here is where probabilistic concerns come into play. Probability distributions are sampled to generate random activity duration times.

Each activity is bounded by events. An *event* is an instant in time at which an activity begins or ends. For most events, the associated time instant marks the ending of one activity and the beginning of the next. Events, like activities, are ordered in time. Events are instants in time at which the system undergoes some form of change — a customer is serviced, a part is removed, and so on.

As previously mentioned, there is a logical, even essential, order in which the activities must take place. The completion of an activity logically initiates the next activity to follow. The same is true of events. The occurrence of an event representing the start of an activity will require that at some future time the event representing the end of the activity must occur. In this sense then, events precipitate the occurrence of still other events; likewise, the completion of an activity may result in one or more other activities being started. In discrete simulation, the simulated clock time is advanced from event time to event time. Since the event times are the only instants in which the object system undergoes any change, these are the only time instants that need be considered. Thus the behavior of the system is simulated by examining the system only at the events.

ENTITIES AND ATTRIBUTES

In addition to events and activities, we also have an interest in entities and attributes in discrete simulation. *Entities* are the physical items of interest in the process itself. Some entities tend to pass through the process and leave. These are *temporary entities*. Among the kinds of temporary entities are "things like" customers, telephone calls, letters, piece parts, automobiles, airplanes, and students. *Permanent entities* remain a part of the object system throughout the time period of interest. These include checkout clerks, telephone networks, post office clerks, conveyor belts, streets, airports, and universities. One of the goals of discrete simulation is to reproduce the activities that the entities engage in so that intuition, insight, and inferences can be had by studying the performance and behavior of the model system. Thus customers shop for groceries, wait to be checked out, and then are checked through by the grocery clerk. Automobiles wait at a traffic light when it turns red and thereafter continue on to the next light, and so on.

It turns out that entities, events, and activities all have characteristics that are of particular interest to discrete simulation. We call such characteristics *attributes.* Of interest, for example, in a grocery store simulation is the average checkout time of a grocery store clerk. This essential bit of information is an attribute of the clerk. We call these entities and their attributes the *state* of the object system.

APPROACHES TO DISCRETE SIMULATION

At least two basic approaches are used in the actual implementation of discrete simulations. One of these, called the discrete next-event approach, models the process by focusing on the events. Simulation languages like SIMSCRIPT [8] and GASP [9,10] use this approach. The other approach focuses on the activities and is called a process- or block-oriented approach. The most popular language implementing this approach is GPSS [11,12]. A new language called SLAM [13] facilitates implementations by means of either approach. Discussion of these languages appear in this chapter in the section entitled "Solution Approaches — Intuitive Description."

Regardless of whether the approach is event oriented or block oriented, the method for advancing time is the same. All simulation languages keep track of the current simulated time by use of a specially defined variable. Time is advanced from the currently processed event to the time of the next event. The only instants in time that are considered are the event times, since these are the only instants at which the simulation model undergoes change. The execution of the model is achieved by advancing time discretely from one event to the immediately succeeding one — hence the name *discrete simulation.* The simulation stops once a satsifactory number of "samples" has been collected or once the current simulation time variable surpasses some prespecified final time.

MECHANICS OF DISCRETE SIMULATION MODEL FORMULATION

Perhaps the best way in which to begin designing a discrete simulation is to list the activities, the entities, and their attributes. If you plan on using the discrete next-event approach, you will want to break the activities down into their respective events. Next an activity precedence diagram (as in Figure 9.1) or an event generation diagram (as in Figure 9.2) is delineated. These diagrams help

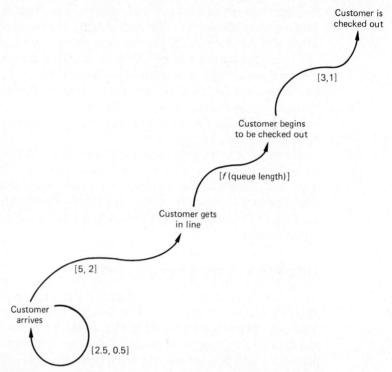

Figure 9.2   Precipitation sequence for the events listed in the Neighborhood Grocery Store.

us to structure the model into a working simulation. Finally a determination of the activity duration times and the times between occurrences of recurrent events is required. Most likely, these times are probabilistic or random and describable in terms of a probability distribution, a mean, and (usually) a standard deviation. The techniques employed in characterizing this randomness within a simulation are described in the two sections following the neighborhood grocery store example.

Each event is processed by transferring control to an event routine specially written for the processing of the particular event. This routine may generate other events, collect samples on important variables, place entities in queues (or files), change the busy status of server facilities, and so on. It does the necessary housekeeping chores required to record the occurrence of the event and to create other events that would be precipitated by the occurrence of the current event. In some languages, the event routines are written by the user (i.e., GASP, SIMSCRIPT), while in others (GPSS), standard event processing routines are used.

A NEIGHBORHOOD GROCERY STORE EXAMPLE

Phil Pocket, manager of Friendly Foods, Inc., is considering placing an extra checkout clerk in each of his grocery stores during peak operation hours of 4 to 8 P.M. weekdays. Long waiting times of up to 30 minutes have been reported frequently, and some arriving customers will leave immediately when they see a long line of ten or more customers waiting to be checked out. Phil is losing customers, and he knows how much this will cost; what Phil is interested in is by how much a second checker will reduce the average waiting time. Since the part-time clerk will be slower than the regular checkout clerk, Phil is uncertain as to how the average customer waiting time will be affected.

It seems apparent to Phil that the problem is a dynamic one involving a definite time duration. So Phil loads a simulation module called SAM (sequential activity modeler) into his personal computer to see if a simulation could be developed.

SAM: Howdy. This is ole poker-face SAM. Who are you?

PHIL: My name is Phil Pocket and I've got a simulation problem for you.

SAM: My favorite kind. I assume you want discrete simulation.

PHIL: That's right.

SAM: What I need from you is a list of activities, events, entities, and their attributes. I will also need statistics on the time durations of the activities.

PHIL: I thought so. I looked at the manual in advance of our session and I've pretty much got the data you requested in the form specified in the book (Table 9.4).

SAM: I'm prepared to accept the data, Phil.

PHIL: Here they are.

SAM: Very good. Your activites have a definite time duration while your events are instants in time. Are you sure these are all the events, activities, entities, and their attributes?

PHIL: I left out the "customer leaves store" activity since this seemed unimportant relative to the purpose of the modeling effort. It seems to me that once the customers are checked out, they are effectively out of the system.

SAM: What's the purpose of your simulation project?

PHIL: To determine if customer balking and customer waiting time can be reduced by adding an extra checkout clerk.

SAM: Subjective judgments of the type you mentioned are frequent in simulation modeling and serve as a reminder that modeling is both art and science. Leaving out the "customer leaves store" activity seems reasonable to me, but you're much better at making judgments of that type than I am.

PHIL: Notice that my customer arrivals are being treated as events. What I did was to use a clipboard and stopwatch to measure the frequency of arrivals. I found that the mean time between arrivals was roughly 3 minutes. The standard deviation came out to 2.79 minutes, and I'm going to assume that the distribution is uniform. My question is this: Can you generate arrivals every 3 or so minutes using a uniform distribution?

SAM: Of course. I'll set this up so that each arrival event generates the next arrival event. Events that repeat themselves in this way are said to be *regenerative.*

PHIL: Now examine my attributes. I have left out such complicating features as grocery items selected by the customers, the costs of these items, whether the customer paid by cash or check, and what the customer's name was. Does that seem reasonable?

Table 9.4 Neighborhood Grocery Store Activities, Events, Entities, and Attributes for a Problem Involving Waiting Times of Customers

	Mean Time Duration	Bounds of Time Duration
Activity		
Customers shopping for groceries	5 min	2 min
Customers waiting to be checked out	a function of queue length	
Customers being checked out (checker 1)	3 min	±1 min
Customers being checked out (checker 2)	4 min	±2 min
Events		
Customer arrives	every 2 min	±1 min
Customer gets in line		
Customer begins checkout		
Customer is checked out		
Entities		
Customers (temporary)		
Checkers (permanent)		
Store (permanent)		
Queue (permanent)		
Attributes		
Checkout time of server 1	3 min	±1 min
Checkout time of server 2	4 min	±2 min
Arrival rate of customers	every 2 min	±1 min
Shopping time of customers	5 min	±2 min
Number of customers in store, an attribute of the store		
Number of customers waiting, an attribute of the queue		
Average purchase of customers, $6.00 with standard deviation of $3.00		
Hour's wage of checkers, $3.00		

SAM: Don't ask me! You're supposed to be the expert in the substantive areas of the model; I just provide the methodology. Just ask yourself, "Are any of these features relevant to the overall purpose of the modeling effort?"

PHIL: I have. I think we can live without them.

SAM: I'm with you. All I need from you now is the precipitation diagram showing which events precipitate the occurrence of what other events.

PHIL: I've already done that too. Here it is (Figure 9.2).

SAM: How many customers do you want me to simulate through your system?

PHIL: One thousand, but first run ten customers to initialize the model and then clear your statistics arrays.

SAM: Good. Give me just a moment. (Pause) Here are the results (Table 9.5a).

PHIL: Now restructure the model for two parallel servers and "play it again, SAM."

SAM: Hold on. (Pause) Wow, look at those numbers (Table 9.5b). The number of lost customers is reduced from 316 to zero. Also the average waiting time per customer has been reduced from 29.715 minutes to around 2.5 minutes.

PHIL: Those are the numbers I needed. Thanks, SAM. Bye.

SAM: You're welcome, Phil. Take care, and use me again soon.

RANDOM NUMBER GENERATION

Of particular importance to discrete simulation is the generation (on a digital computer) of random numbers representing the activity duration times or the times between occurrences of an event. Computer generation of random numbers is called the *Monte Carlo method*. Monte Carlo techniques have been used to evaluate integrals and to conduct random searches for an optimum within a feasible region.

In discrete simulation models, sampling from any probability distribution is based on the generation of a uniformly distributed random deviate (or number) in the interval 0 to 1. Simple algorithms have been developed to provide the required uniformly distributed random number. The most popular algorithm

Table 9.5a Statistical Results Obtained from the Single-Clerk Grocery Store Simulation*

FACILITY	AVERAGE UTILIZATION		NUMBER ENTRIES		AVERAGE TIME/TRAN
1	1.000		684		3.004

QUEUE	MAXIMUM CONTENTS	AVERAGE CONTENTS	TOTAL ENTRIES	ZERO ENTRIES	PERCENT ZEROS
1	14	10.049	696		.0

QUEUE	AVERAGE TIME/TRANS	$AVERAGE TIME/TRANS	TABLE NUMBER		CURRENT CONTENTS
1	29.715	29.715			11

$AVERAGE TIME/TRANS = AVERAGE TIME/TRANS EXCLUDING ZERO ENTRIES

* Number of lost customers = 316.

Table 9.5b   Statistical Results Obtained from the Double-Clerk Grocery Store Simulation*

FACILITY	AVERAGE UTILIZATION	NUMBER ENTRIES	AVERAGE TIME/TRAN
1	.944	643	2.990
2	.705	357	4.028

QUEUE	MAXIMUM CONTENTS	AVERAGE CONTENTS	TOTAL ENTRIES	ZERO ENTRIES	PERCENT ZEROS
1	3	.542	643	166	25.8
2	2	.268	357	163	45.6

QUEUE	AVERAGE TIME/TRANS	$AVERAGE TIME/TRANS	TABLE NUMBER	CURRENT CONTENTS
1	1.718	2.316		1
2	1.532	2.819		

$AVERAGE TIME/TRANS = AVERAGE TIME/TRANS EXCLUDING ZERO ENTRIES

* Number of lost customers = 0.

is the *multiplicative congruence* method. This method produces random numbers by use of a recursive equation, beginning with a user-specified initial value or *seed*. The recursive equation generates the next number in a sequence each time it is executed. The sequence is deterministic in the sense that starting from the same seed we obtain the same exact sequence with each run. The numbers in the sequence have all the required properties of uniformly distributed random numbers. Since the numbers are known in advance, they are often referred to as *pseudorandom numbers*. The use of pseudorandom numbers in simulation greatly expedites debugging the computer program. (Imagine what a nightmare debugging would be if every run produced a different output!)

A computer code (written in FORTRAN) for generating uniformly distributed random numbers appears in Table 9.6. This code generates both floating point and integer random numbers. The floating point random numbers are uniformly distributed on the interval of zero to one. The code is useful only for 32-bit machines, which includes IBM, Amdahl, National Advanced Systems, and some 32-bit minicomputers. The code uses the multiplicative congruence formula

$$C_{i+1} = k \cdot C_i \tag{9.1}$$

where C_0 is the seed and k is a constant equal to $5^{13} = 1,220,703,125$.

The initial value placed in the variable I is the seed upon first execution of the code. This value should be an odd integer of less than nine decimal digits. Upon return of control from the subroutine, I will contain the next integer random number in the sequence, as specified by the recursion formula (9.1). U will contain a floating point random number uniformly distributed on the interval zero to one.

**Table 9.6   A FORTRAN Program for
Generating Random Numbers by the
Multiplicative Congruence Method**

```
      SUBROUTINE RANDOM (U, I)
      I = I * 1220703125              (ONE)
      IF (I) 1,2,2                    (TWO)
    1 I = I + 2147483647 + 1          (THREE)
    2 U = I * 0.4656613E-9            (FOUR)
      RETURN
      END
```

Observe the simplicity of this code. In a simulation run this routine may be invoked thousands of times. Therefore, to avoid wasteful use of computer time, it is necessary to keep the algorithm as simple as possible. The first statement in the routine implements the multiplicative congruence formula. The second and third statements will replace any negative integer with a positive integer. Statement four computes the corresponding floating point value by multiplying the integer value by the floating point inverse of the largest integer representable by the 32-bit computer — that is, .4656613E-9 = 1/2147483647, where 2147483647 is the largest possible integer for a 32-bit word (i.e., $2^{31} - 1$).

PROBABILITY DISTRIBUTIONS

It is sometimes necessary in simulation to generate random numbers that are other than uniformly distributed on the interval 0 to 1. To do this, we start with a uniformly distributed random number and transform it into a random number with some other form of distribution. This is accomplished by the so-called *inverse transformation method.* Every random variable x has an associated cumulative distribution function $F(x)$ whose values are mapped onto the interval zero to one. In fact the random variable y given by $y = F(x)$ is uniformly distributed over this interval. If the inverse of the cumulative distribution $F^{-1}(y)$ can be determined, then a straightforward strategy for obtaining x is available, since $x = F^{-1}(y)$. Simply generate a random number uniformly distributed on the interval zero to one. Call this number y and apply the inverse transformation $F^{-1}(y)$ to obtain a random number x with the appropriate distribution.

Exponentially Distributed Random Numbers

Sampling from an exponential distribution is important because the mean time between arrivals (of customers, parts, automobiles, planes — temporary entities of any type) is often approximately exponentially distributed. In addition, service times are often exponentially distributed. Suppose that in a service facility, the service time x is exponential with mean service time of μ. Then the probability density function for x is

$$f(x) = \frac{e^{-x/\mu}}{\mu}$$

The associated cumulative distribution function $F(x)$ is

$$y = F(x) = \int_0^x \frac{1}{\mu} e^{-t/\mu} \, dt = 1 - e^{-x/\mu}$$

By solving this equation for x, we obtain the required inverse of the cumulative distribution function:

$$x = F^{-1}(y) = -\mu \ln (1 - y) = -\mu \ln y$$

The last step is justified, because if y is uniformly distributed over the interval zero to one, then so is $1 - y$ and we can replace $1 - y$ by y for convenience.

In FORTRAN, an exponentially distributed random number could be generated by the following statements:

```
CALL RANDOM (U, I)
EXRNUM = − XMU * ALOG(U)
```

Here XMU is the mean time between arrivals or between service completions, and U is U[0, 1] (i.e., uniformly distributed on the interval zero to one). Time to execute the second statement can be long because ALOG is a slowly converging series. In long-running simulations, the use of tables to approximate ALOG would be much faster.

This analytical approach to inversion of a cumulative distribution function (CDF) works when the CDF is described analytically. However, there are many probability distributions whose CDFs cannot be describable analytically — including the normal, the gamma, and Poisson distributions. In situations like these we can use one of two methods:

1. Approximate the continuous CDF with a discrete CDF specified by means of a table function or
2. Use statistical relationships to obtain the required random deviate from other distributions.

We illustrate both techniques in the following segment for normal distributions.

Normally Distributed Random Numbers

Occasionally, the times between completions of service are known to be normally distributed. In addition there are other situations where an activity duration time is believed to be normally distributed. Since an analytical expression for the inverse of the CDF is unobtainable for a normal distribution, the "simulationist" must resort to one of the two alternate methods noted. If GPSS [11] is being used, a table function representative of the CDF is employed. On the other hand, if GASP or SLAM are used [9,10,13], then a statistical approach is used. Both approaches are illustrated starting with the table function approach.

The probability density function for the normal distribution is given by

$$f(x) = \frac{1}{\sigma\sqrt{2\pi}} e^{-1/2[\frac{x-\mu}{\sigma}]^2} \tag{9.2}$$

This function changes shape for differing values of the mean μ(mu) and standard deviation σ(sigma)of a normal distribution. By defining $z = (x - \mu)/\sigma$, it is possible to specify a standard normal curve from which all particularized normal distributions are determinable. The standard normal is given by

$$f(z) = \frac{1}{\sqrt{2\pi}} e^{\frac{-z^2}{2}} \tag{9.3}$$

and assumes a mean μ of 0 and standard deviation σ of 1. Note that (9.2) reduces to (9.3) when $\mu = 0$, $\sigma = 1$, and x is replaced with z. A normal random number x can be computed from a standard normal random number z by solving $z = (x - \mu)/\sigma$ for x giving $x = \sigma z + \mu$. Both methods to be subsequently described use the standard normal random number z and then compute x from it using the expression $x = \sigma z + \mu$.

The probability density function and its associated cumulative distribution function for a standard normal distribution are shown in Figure 9.3. The CDF can be approximated by means of a series of piecewise linear segments as shown in Figure 9.3. To construct this piecewise linear curve, a table function that interpolates linearly between the coordinate pairs given in Table 9.7 is employed.

To generate a standard normal random variable z, a random number R that is U(0. 1) is first computed using subroutine RANDOM. This is followed by use of the FORTRAN table function TABLE to detemine the standard normal variate z from $z = F^{-1}(R)$. The FORTRAN source code for TABLE is given in Table 9.8. The following three statements will generate an appropriate normal random number x with mean XMU and standard deviation SIGMA.

```
CALL RANDOM (R,J)
Z = TABLE (R,T,15)
X = SIGMA * Z + XMU
```

The last line is a FORTRAN implementation of the relationship between the nonstandard and standard normal random variates x and z (i.e., $x = \sigma z + \mu$).

The second way a normal random variate can be generated is by use of the relationship between the normal distribution and the uniform distribution. According to the central limit theorem, the distribution of a sample of uniformly distributed random variates tends to be normal as the sample size becomes large. An approximation to this theorem generates normally distributed random numbers by summing several uniformly distributed random numbers u_i according to the formula

$$z = \frac{\sum_{i=1}^{k} u_i - k/2}{\sqrt{k/12}}$$

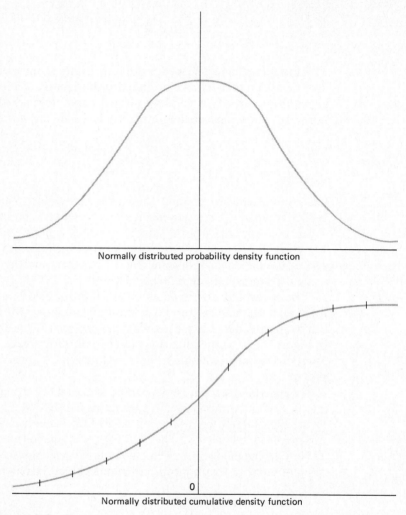

Normally distributed probability density function

Normally distributed cumulative density function

Figure 9.3 The standard normal probability and cumulative density functions.

Table 9.7 Coordinate Pairs for the Standard Normal CDF

Z	F(Z)	Z	F(Z)
−100	0	.5	.6915
−3	.00135	1.	.8413
−2.5	.00621	1.5	.9332
−2.	.0228	2.	.9772
−1.5	.0668	2.5	.9938
−1	.1587	3.	.99865
−.5	.3085	100	1.
0	.5		

Table 9.8 FORTRAN Listing of Table Function TABLE

```
     FUNCTION TABLE (FR,T,N)
     REAL T(N,2)
     DO 1 I = 1,N
            IF(FR .LE.T(I,2)) GO TO 2
  1  CONTINUE
     WRITE (6,3)
     CALL EXIT
  2  TABLE = T(I-1,1) + (T(I,1) − T(I-1,1))*
            (FR − T(I-1,2))/(T(I,2) − T(I-1,2))
     RETURN
  3  FORMAT ('- TABLE FUNCTION ERROR -- RUN ABORTED')
     END
```

The distribution of a sequence of numbers derived from this formula approaches the standard normal distribution as k approaches infinity. Quite small values of k give good accuracy. Typically, a value of 12 for k is used, reducing the above formula to

$$z = \sum_{i=1}^{12} u_i - 6.0$$

A function for generating normally distributed random numbers with mean XMU and standard deviation SIGMA is provided in Table 9.9.

SAMPLING IN SIMULATION

In discrete simulation, important variables are sampled at the time they undergo a change (i.e., at the event times). These operations must be statistically independent to make proper statistical inferences about the simulated system. The number of such observations is also an important consideration.

In simulation, estimates of such system output variables as average safety

Table 9.9 A FORTRAN Function for Generating Normally Distributed Random Numbers from Uniformly Distributed Random Numbers

```
     FUNCTION RNORM(SIGMA, XMU)
     DATA K /12345/
     SUM = 0
     DO 1 I = 1,12
     CALL RANDOM (U,K)
  1  SUM = SUM + U
     Z = SUM − 6.
     RNORM = SIGMA * Z + XMU
     RETURN
     END
```

stock, average waiting time, and average order quantity are determined by summing the observations and dividing the sum by n—the number of samples or observations. In addition such time-persistent variables as average queue length, average number of transactions in the system, average inventory, and average server "busyness" are also of interest. Computation of these averages require integration of the variable values over time followed by division by the period of time over which the integration took place. For both system output variables and time-persistent variables, the running time of the simulation must be long enough to ensure a statistically valid result.

Obtaining averages that are characteristic of the *steady-state* behavior of the simulations is difficult because the simulation (like any dynamic model) goes through a transient behavior to reach steady state. Unfortunately, observations are collected during both phases unless the simulation is stopped and all statistical observations are cleared out and observation counters are reset to zero. This is exactly what most simulation languages will permit the user to do. In the absence of such facilities, it is necessary to run the simulation for very long time periods to wipe out the effects of biases in the sampled data caused by samples that were collected during the transient phase of the simulation.

Consider the neighborhood grocery store problem described earlier. The simulation was started with zero customers in the store. There is a period of simulated time during which conditions are uncharacteristic of the busy hours from 4 to 8 P.M. There is a transient period in which the simulation builds up customers—shopping, waiting, or being serviced. Until the busy steady-state conditions are reached, the simulated conditions are unlike the desired busy period. Samples collected during this transient period would bias the average queue length, average waiting time, and average server busyness downward from their actual values. Therefore, the simulation is stopped after ten or so customers enter the system and is restarted after transient sample data have been cleared.

DISCRETE SIMULATION RESULTS

The results and outputs of any discrete simulation run are the statistical reports. These statistical reports provide information about the average waiting time of a temporary entity in a queueing situation, the percentage of time a facility is idle, the number of times an out-of-stock condition occurred, the number of customers who were turned away, the average queue length, and other measures of performance. Table 9.5 is indicative of the statistical reports produced by GPSS for service facilities in queuing situations.

The plotted output, when available, can be useful in deciding where the transient phase stops and the steady state phase begins.

SOLUTION APPROACHES: INTUITIVE DESCRIPTION

There are several languages available for discrete simulation, the most important being GPSS [11,12], SIMSCRIPT [8], and SLAM [13]. Each of these languages is briefly described by what follows.

GENERAL-PURPOSE SIMULATION SYSTEM (GPSS)

GPSS was developed by IBM with early versions appearing in 1961. It has evolved through several versions. There is currently available a GPSS compiler that generates machine language code (that requires far less computer time during production runs). GPSS is an activity-oriented discrete simulation language. Blocks are utilized to represent activities, and each block is described to GPSS by means of a keyword or command designating the block. The language uses a block diagram to describe the system. There are some 48 block types, each of which represents a characteristic action of systems. The blocks are connected by flow lines indicating the direction of movement of transactions (temporary entities) through the system.

Although GPSS is limited mostly to characterization of queueing systems, many systems can be conceptualized as being a queueing system. GPSS includes a timing routine that moves the system from event time to event time. Some types of statistics are gathered automatically and reported. GPSS is weakest in providing facilities for generation of random numbers. It provides only a uniform distribution, so that we must encode functions to obtain random numbers from other distributions. Of the discrete languages described in this chapter, GPSS is the most widely used.

A GPSS diagram representation of the neighborhood grocery store (single server) is depicted in Figure 9.4, and the associated source code is shown in Figure 9.5. Statements in GPSS conform to the format "location field," "operation field," "operand field," and "comment field." Blanks are used to distinguish between fields. Embedded blanks within fields are not permitted. Each statement in Figure 9.5 corresponds to a block in Figure 9.4, except for those statements that direct the GPSS processor to SIMULATE, START, RESET, or END. The purpose of the START–RESET–START sequence is to get the simulation model past the transient phase. The model is run-started with 10 transactions to produce a steady-state situation. The RESET operation clears statistics arrays before the START 1000 command runs the model for 1000 transactions.

A description of each GPSS block in Figure 9.4 is in order. The GENERATE block generates an arrival of a customer (generically called a "transaction" in GPSS) every $A \pm B$ time units. The time between customer arrivals is uniformly distributed between $A - B$ and $A + B$ according to the conventions employed by GPSS. The operands A and B are given values of 2 and 1, respectively, so that customer arrivals would be uniformly distributed between 1 and 3 minutes.

The next block performs a TEST to determine if the queue length as specified by Q1 is less than or equal to ten customers. If not, the newly created customer leaves. If so, the customer shops.

The shopping activity is represented by an ADVANCE block. Transactions that enter an ADVANCE block will remain in it for a period of time that is uniformly distributed with a lower bound of $A - B$ and an upper bound of $A + B$. The values specified for the operands A and B are 5 and 2 in Figure 9.4. Hence, customer shopping times are uniformly distributed over the interval 3 to 7 minutes, as specified in the statement of the problem.

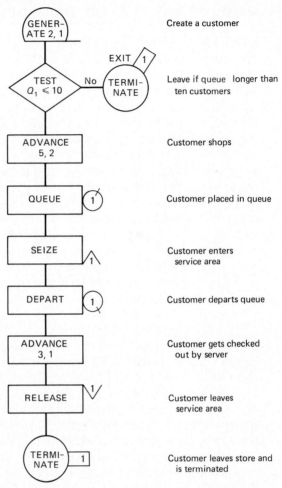

Figure 9.4 A GPSS block diagram representation of the Neighborhood Grocery Store problem.

Upon completion of shopping, customers place themselves in a queue. The queue is represented by the pair of blocks QUEUE/DEPART. Transactions that pass through the QUEUE block will cause the queue length variable Q1 to be incremented by one, whereas transactions that pass through the DEPART block cause the queue length variable Q1 to be decremented by one. Time-persistent statistics are automatically kept on Q1. Transactions cannot DEPART until the following block (in this case the ADVANCE block) is free to accept another transaction. Any transaction that does not have to wait to be serviced will pass through the QUEUE/DEPART pair immediately and without delay.

The SEIZE/RELEASE pair of blocks define to GPSS a form of permanent entity called a facility. This construct is used to model the service area itself. The SEIZE/RELEASE pair will allow only one transaction (or customer) in the facility at a time. The SEIZE block allows a customer to enter the facility and

```
BLOCK
NUMBER   *LOC      OPERATION  A,B,C,D,E,F,G                  COMMENTS
         *
         *NEIGHBORHOOD GROCERY STORE EXAMPLE
         *
                   SIMULATE
1                  GENERATE   2,1                 CREATE A CUSTOMER
2                  TEST LE    Q1,10,EXIT          LEAVE IF MORE THAN TEN ARE WAITING
3                  ADVANCE    5,2                 CUSTOMER SHOPPING ACTIVITY
4                  QUEUE      1                   QUEUE FOR A SERVER
5                  SEIZE      1                   ENTER SERVICE AREA
6                  DEPART     1                   STATS ON QUEUE
7                  ADVANCE    3,1                 SERVER 1'S SERVICE TIME
8                  RELEASE    1                   LEAVE SERVICE AREA
9        TERM      TERMINATE  1                   TOTAL SATISFIED CUSTOMERS
10       EXIT      TERMINATE  1                   TOTAL BALKED CUSTOMERS
         *
                   START      10,NP               INITIALIZE WITH TEN CUSTOMERS
                   RESET
                   START      1000                MAIN RUN
                   END
```

Figure 9.5 Source code in GPSS for the Neighborhood Grocery Store problem.

hence begin to be checked out. The RELEASE block allows a customer to exit the facility once service is complete.

The last block in the block diagram depicted in Figure 9.4 is the TERMINATE block. When transactions reach this block, they are counted and thereafter terminated. Notice that there are two different TERMINATE blocks in Figure 9.4. In this way a count of how many customers passed through the system and how many left the store because the queue was too long can be obtained.

As a final note, we point out that statements that begin with (*) are treated as comments to the user and that no processing by GPSS is performed. The command SIMULATE (the first such command in the operation field) is required.

SIMSCRIPT II.5

SIMSCRIPT has evolved through early versions before arriving at its current version, II.5. It is largely the product of Philip Kiviat and his colleagues at Consolidated Analysis Centers, Inc. Unlike GPSS (or any other simulation language), SIMSCRIPT is a general-purpose programming language with special facilities to accommodate discrete simulation. The approach has an event (rather than activity) orientation.

SIMSCRIPT has the programming capabilities of languages like ALGOL, PL/1, or Pascal, but with a syntax that enables the programmer to encode statements that are intelligible to nonprogramming-oriented managers and by the SIMSCRIPT compiler as well. This feature greatly enhances user comprehension of the code. Such statements as

PERFORM INITIALIZATION.
START SIMULATION.
RESCHEDULE THIS REPORT NEXT.MONTH.
CREATE EVERY PRODUCTION.CENTER.

are (or can be made) intelligible to the SIMSCRIPT compiler.

SIMSCRIPT, like the various versions of GASP and SLAM, requires the user to encode a separate event routine for each event. A typical event routine for processing arrival events is shown in Figure 9.6. The type of arrival is identical to that described for the neighborhood grocery store problem.

SIMSCRIPT programs begin with a nonexecutable division of code called a PREAMBLE. The PREAMBLE is used to define to the SIMSCRIPT compiler such items as

1. Temporary entities and their attributes
2. Permanent entities and their attributes
3. Events and their attributes
4. Background conditions for program variables
5. Equivalence between variables
6. Global variables
7. Sets, set ownership, set membership
8. Variables on which statistics are to be collected

The PREAMBLE is followed by a MAIN program, initialization routines, and then the event routines—one for each event defined in the PREAMBLE. These user-written components are compiled into executable code. SIM-SCRIPT supports dynamic storage allocation, recursion routines, an extensive collection of random number generation routines, and a very flexible English-like syntax for encoding of program statements and code. It is a remarkable language.

SLAM—A SIMULATION LANGUAGE FOR ALTERNATIVE MODELING

SLAM has evolved from early versions of GASP and GERT, all of which are simulation constructs developed by A. Alan B. Pritsker and his associates. Early versions of GASP were capable of discrete simulation and employed an event-oriented approach. A newer version of GASP—GASP IV—was capable of accommodating discrete simulation models, continuous simulation models, or combined continuous/discrete simulation models. All versions of GASP use FORTRAN as the host language. While this might suggest that GASP is easy to

```
EVENT ARRIVAL SAVING THE EVENT NOTICE
RESCHEDULE THIS ARRIVAL AT TIME.V + UNIFORM.F(1.,3.,1)
IF QUEUE.LENGTH > 10, "LEAVE STORE AND" RETURN
OTHERWISE ADD 1 TO NO.OF.CUSTOMERS..IN.STORE
SCHEDULE AN END.OF.SHOPPING AT TIME.V + UNIFORM.F(3.,7.,2)
RETURN "AND" END
```

Figure 9.6 SIMSCRIPT routine for processing arrival events.

use, such is not the case for all but the seasoned FORTRAN programmer. The language requires meticulous attention to details. There is great flexibility; the penalty that the user pays for this flexibility is the need to specify many input parameter values.

SLAM subsumes all the capabilities of GERT and GASP IV, giving the user the option of specifying a network simulation (for a GERT diagram of a manufacturing shop), a discrete next-event simulation such as is commonly used for inventory and queueing situations, a continuous simulation as described in Chapter 15, or some combination of these. Like its predecessors, SLAM is FORTRAN based.

Neighborhood Grocery Store (Continued)

The Model: We have previously described a scenario and a problem for our neighborhood grocery store example. We have also delineated a single server model for this problem. In this section, we present a parallel server model involving two servers with different service times, and each with its own queue. In addition we discuss solutions to both models and compare the two from a performance standpoint.

The GPSS block diagram corresponding to the single server situation was depicted in Figure 9.4. The corresponding source code is shown in Figure 9.5. This problem had to do with comparing the performance of one versus two servers during the busy hours of the day. The second server would be slower than the first server and paid less. A second model involving two parallel servers must, therefore, be constructed. The block diagram for this second model is shown in Figure 9.7, and the required GPSS source code is shown in Figure 9.8.

Queueing theory will not adequately handle this parallel server situation because the service times of the two servers are different.

Solution to the Model: By comparing the performance of the two models, it is possible to assess whether the additional server is worth the incremental cost. A second server will probably be paid close to minimum wage but will require an additional service area and cash register. The incremental hourly costs are presumed to be roughly $6.00, or $24.00 for the four-hour period from 4 to 8 P.M. Is the increase in performance worth the incremental cost?

From the printout for the single-server model (Table 9.5a), it is determined that during this four-hour period roughly 120 customers would arrive, but roughly one-third or 40 of these would go away because the queue length would be 10 or greater. At one point there were 14 people waiting in the queue, and the average queue length was 10 customers with an average waiting time in the queue of 30 minutes.

From the printout for the two parallel server model (Table 9.5b), there were no lost sales due to leaving customers. Server 1's queue was never longer than three customers while server 2's queue was never longer than two customers. The average waiting time in server 1's queue was 1.718 minutes, whereas the average waiting time in server 2's queue was 1.532 minutes.

Assuming that the average purchase per customer is $3.65 and that the average profit per customer is $.83, clearly $33 (= 40 × $.83) in lost profit is incurred because of customers who balked. This is greater than the $24.00 incremental cost calculated for the second server. In addition, the second server will create a tremendous increase in customer goodwill as no customer leaves without shopping, and customer waiting time in a queue is

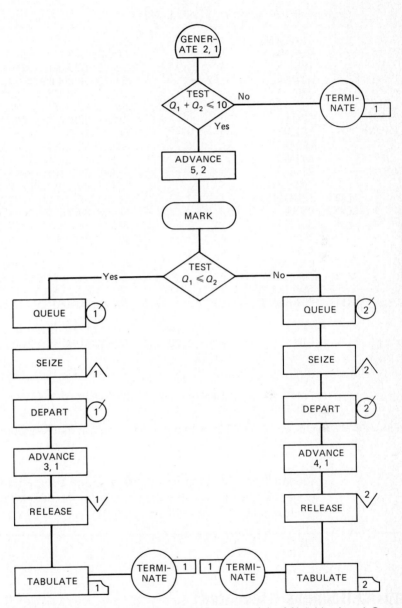

Figure 9.7 Block diagram for parallel server model of Neighborhood Grocery Store.

```
BLOCK
NUMBER    *LOC       OPERATION  A,B,C,D,E,F,G                    COMMENTS
          *
          *NEIGHBORHOOD GROCERY STORE EXAMPLE
          *
                     SIMULATE
1                    GENERATE   2,1                CREATE A CUSTOMER
2                    TEST LE    V1,10,EXIT         LEAVE IF MORE THAN TEN ARE WAITING
3                    ADVANCE    5,2                CUSTOMER SHOPPING ACTIVITY
4                    MARK       1                  COLLECT STATS ON CUSTOMER WAITING TIME
5                    TEST LE    Q1,Q2,SERV2        PUT CUSTOMER IN SMALLER OF TWO QUEUES
6                    QUEUE      1                  QUEUE FOR A SERVER
7                    SEIZE      1                  ENTER SERVICE AREA
8                    DEPART     1                  STATS ON QUEUE
9                    ADVANCE    3,1                SERVER 1'S SERVICE TIME
10                   RELEASE    1                  LEAVE SERVICE AREA
11                   TABULATE   1                  STATS ON CUSTOMER WAITING TIME
12        TERM       TERMINATE  1                  TOTAL SATISFIED CUSTOMERS
13        SERV2      QUEUE      2                  ENTER QUEUE OF SERVER 2
14                   SEIZE      2                  SEIZE SERVER 2 WHEN HE BECOMES IDLE
15                   DEPART     2                  STATS ON QUEUE OF SERVER 2
16                   ADVANCE    4,1                SERVER 2'S SERVICE TIME
17                   RELEASE    2                  SERVER 2 IS FINISHED
18                   TABULATE   2                  STATS ON CUSTOMER WAITING TIME
19                   TERMINATE  1                  CUSTOMER LEAVES STORE
20        EXIT       TERMINATE  1                  TOTAL BALKED CUSTOMERS
          *
          1          TABLE      M1,2,2,20          TABULATION INTERVALS ON WAITING TIME
          2          TABLE      M1,3,2,20          TABULATION INTERVALS ON WAITING TIME
          1          VARIABLE   Q1+Q2
                     START      10,NP              INITIALIZE WITH TEN CUSTOMERS
                     RESET
                     START      1000               MAIN RUN
                     END
```

Figure 9.8   Source code in GPSS for two parallel servers in the Neighborhood Grocery Store.

reduced from 30 minutes on the average to 1.7 minutes. This analysis suggests that the benefits accruing from the second server outweigh the incremental costs, all else being equal.

Cabana Bananas (Revisited)

The Scenario: Cabana Bananas used six steamship freighters to move its bananas from a single dock in Costa Rica to the various seawater ports on the East Coast of the United States. Due to the need to service some half-dozen ports on the eastern seaboard and the tremendous volume of bananas that must be loaded and transported without delay to preserve freshness, Cabana's CEO is interested in a simulation model that will exhibit the performance that might accrue from having two loading docks rather than just one. Another loading dock will cost the company $6,835,000 in additional outlays for cranes, cold storage, truck depots, and waterfront property. Furthermore, the labor bill required to operate the second dock will run $35,000 per month. Each boatload of bananas nets the company $435,000, less fuel and labor costs.

The Problem: The time to load one steamship with bananas is uniformly distributed between 3 and 7 days. The time for one steamship to reach its destination, off load its bananas, and return is uniformly distributed with a mean of 11 days. Ships never return in less than 8 days or more than 14 days. When the loading dock is busy and empty steamships arrive in port, they are placed in a queue of steamships waiting to be loaded. The queueing discipline is first-come, first-loaded. Initially, all six steamships are waiting to be loaded and empty.

The Model: Due to the cyclical nature of the steamship arrivals and the dependence upon the number of such ships in the queue, this situation cannot be handled with queueing theory.

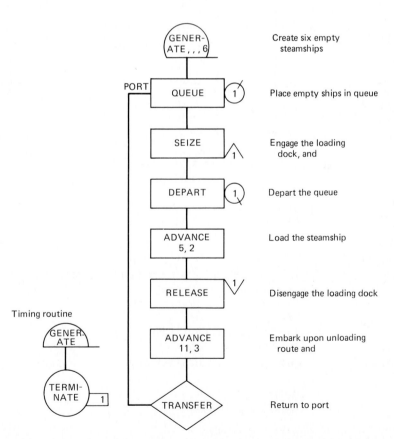

Figure 9.9   GPSS block diagram for a single dock in the steamship problem Cabana Banana.

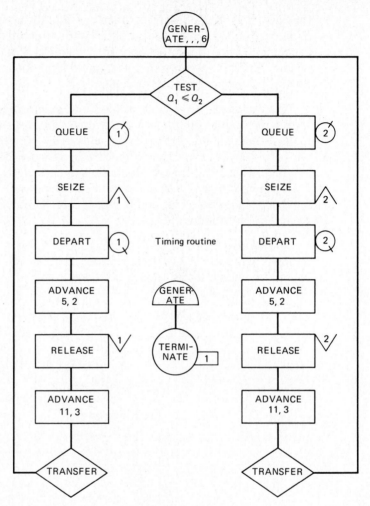

Figure 9.10 GPSS block diagram for two parallel docks in the steamship problem Cabana Banana.

We begin by listing the activities, temporary and permanent entities, and the important attributes.

Activities	Attributes
Steamships waiting empty	
Steamships en route	11 ± 3 days
Steamships being loaded	5 ± 2 days

Entities, permanent
The loading dock(s)

Entities, temporary
The six steamships

```
BLOCK
NUMBER      *LOC        OPERATION  A,B,C D,E,F,G                              COMMENTS
            *
            *CABANA BANANA STEAMSHIP MODEL
            *
                        SIMULATE
1                       GENERATE    ,,,6              CREATE SIX EMPTY STEAMSHIPS
2           PORT        QUEUE       1                 PLACE EMPTY SHIPS IN QUEUE
3                       SEIZE       1                 ENGAGE THE LOADING DOCK, AND
4                       DEPART      1                 DEPART THE QUEUE.
5                       ADVANCE     5,2                LOAD THE STEAMSHIP
6                       RELEASE     1                 DISENGAGE THE LOADING DOCK.
7                       ADVANCE     11,3               EMBARK UPON UNLOADING ROUTE AND
8                       TRANSFER    ,PORT             RETURN TO PORT.
9                       GENERATE    1
10                      TERMINATE   1
            *
                        START       10,NP            INITIALIZE WITH TEN DAYS
                        RESET
                        START       300              MAIN RUN
                        END
```

Figure 9.11   Single dock Cabana Banana model.

Next we formulate single-dock and double-dock GPSS models. The single-dock model is shown in Figure 9.9, whereas the model with two parallel docking facilities is shown in Figure 9.10. The GPSS programs for these two models are shown in Figures 9.11 and 9.12.

Solution to the Model: The results obtained from the two simulations are shown in Tables 9.10 and 9.11. The numbers in Table 9.10 indicate that each steamship waits an average of 12.4 days + 4.761 days (17.161 days total) in port before embarking on an unloading route that takes 11 days on the average. Assuming a 300-day year, it is possible to process 63 ships through the single dock.

The numbers in Table 9.11 indicate that each steamship waits an average of 3.3 days (actually 3.456 days in queue 1 or 3.26 days in queue 2) and requires 5 days (5.14 days for dock 1 and 4.98 days for dock 2) for loading. Hence each steamship is in port an average of 8.26 days. As a consequence, more unloading trips can be made in the assumed 300-day year. Specifically, 55 + 43 = 98 ships could be processed by the two docks — an increase of 35 ships. Assuming that markets could be found for the extra bananas and that the extra bananas could be obtained from area growers, then an additional $435,000 × 35 = $15,225,000 in net revenues could be realized. This is more than enough to offset the fixed and variable costs associated with the additional dock (in a year's time). Recall that the additional loading dock would cost $6,835,000 to install and $35,000 × 12 = $420,000 to operate over 12 months. Hence, at the year's end the company will have netted $7,970,000, less additional fuel and labor costs associated with 35 additional trips. The second dock ap-

```
BLOCK
NUMBER    *LOC        OPERATION  A,B,C,D,E,F,G                        COMMENTS
          *
          *CABANA BANANA STEAMSHIP MODEL -- TWO DOCKS
          *
                      SIMULATE
1                     GENERATE      ,,,6              CREATE SIX EMPTY STEAMSHIPS
2          PORT       TEST LE       Q1,Q2,DOCK 2      PLACE SHIP INTO LESSER OF TWO QUEUES
3                     QUEUE         1                 PLACE EMPTY SHIPS IN QUEUE
4                     SEIZE         1                 ENGAGE THE LOADING DOCK  AND
5                     DEPART        1                 DEPART THE QUEUE.
6                     ADVANCE       5,2                LOAD THE STEAMSHIP.
7                     RELEASE       1                 DISENGAGE THE LOADING DOCK.
8                     ADVANCE       11,3               EMBARK UPON UNLOADING ROUTE AND
9                     TRANSFER      ,PORT             RETURN TO PORT.
10         DOCK 2     QUEUE         2                 SECOND QUEUE FOR SECOND LOADING DOCK
11                    SEIZE         2                 ENGAGE SECOND LOADING DOCK, AND
12                    DEPART        2                 DEPART THE QUEUE
13                    ADVANCE       5,2                LOAD THE STEAMSHIP.
14                    RELEASE       2                 DISENGAGE THE LOADING DOCK.
15                    ADVANCE       11,3               EMBARK UPON UNLOADING ROUTE AND
16                    TRANSFER      ,PORT             RETURN TO PORT.
17                    GENERATE      1
18                    TERMINATE     1
          *
                      START         10,NP             INITIALIZE WITH TEN DAYS
                      RESET
                      START         300                  MAIN RUN
                      END
```

Figure 9.12 Double dock Cabana Banana model.

Table 9.10 Statistical Results from Single Dock Cabana Banana Model

RELATIVE CLOCK   300 ABSOLUTE CLOCK   310
BLOCK COUNTS

BLOCK	CURRENT	TOTAL			
1	0	0	GENERATE		
2	2	61	QUEUE	1	
3	0	62	SEIZE	1	
4	0	62	DEPART	1	
5	1	62	ADVANCE	5	2
6	0	62	RELEASE	1	
7	3	62	ADVANCE	11	3
8	0	61	TRANSFER		2
9	0	300	GENERATE	1	
10	0	300	TERMINATE	1	

FACILITY	AVERAGE UTILIZATION	NUMBER ENTRIES	AVERAGE TIME/TRAN
1	1.000	63	4.761

QUEUE	MAXIMUM CONTENTS	AVERAGE CONTENTS	TOTAL ENTRIES	AVERAGE TIME/TRANS	$AVERAGE TIME/TRANS
1	4	2.649	64	12.421	12.421

Table 9.11   Statistical Results from Twin Dock Cabana Banana Model

RELATIVE CLOCK		300	ABSOLUTE CLOCK			310

BLOCK COUNTS

BLOCK	CURRENT	TOTAL				
1	0	0	GENERATE			
2	0	97	TEST LE	Q1	Q2	10
3	1	55	QUEUE	1		
4	0	55	SEIZE	1		
5	0	55	DEPART	1		
6	1	55	ADVANCE	5	2	
7	0	55	RELEASE	1		
8	2	55	ADVANCE	11	3	
9	0	54	TRANSFER		2	
10	0	42	QUEUE	2		
11	0	43	SEIZE	2		
12	0	43	DEPART	2		
13	1	43	ADVANCE	5	2	
14	0	43	RELEASE	2		
15	1	43	ADVANCE	11	3	
16	0	43	TRANSFER		2	
17	0	300	GENERATE	1		
18	0	300	TERMINATE	1		

FACILITY	AVERAGE UTILIZATION	NUMBER ENTRIES	AVERAGE TIME/TRAN
1	.959	56	5.142
2	.729	44	4.977

QUEUE	MAXIMUM CONTENTS	AVERAGE CONTENTS	TOTAL ENTRIES	AVERAGE TIME/TRANS	$AVERAGE TIME/TRANS
1	2	.529	56	2.839	3.456
2	1	.250	43	1.744	3.260

pears to be justified from financial considerations. But are the assumptions realistic?

Solution to the Problem: Under the single-dock system, each ship would complete a cycle in $17.16 + 11 = 28.16$ days on the average. Roughly 10.6 trips could be completed in a 300 day year. During this period the ship's crew would be idle $12.4 \times 10.64 = 131$ days (assuming that the ship's crew is active during loading periods).

Under the double-dock system, each ship would complete a cycle in $8.26 + 11 = 19.26$ days on the average. Approximately 15.6 trips could be completed in a 300-day year. During this period, the ship's crew would be idle $3.3 \times 15.6 = 51.5$ days. This is certain to improve the continuity of the company's work force and the utilization of capital invested in the ship fleet. If the additional workdays cost the company $1000 per day in labor costs per ship, then the additional labor costs to operate the ships would be $1000 \times 6(131 - 51.5) = \$477,000$. If each trip requires $20,000 for fuel, then $35 \times \$20,000 = \$700,000$ in additional fuel expenses would be incurred in the two-dock arrangement. Subtracting these costs from the net amount $7,970,000 yields a very attractive $6,793,000 increase in profits by year's end. Assuming that markets for 35 additional shiploads of bananas exist, and that the additional bananas can be obtained from local growers, then the exigency for a second dock exists.

SUMMARY

In this chapter, we have endeavored to impart an understanding of the general concept of simulation modeling. When it should be used, why it is so widely applied, and what methodologies and philosophies comprise it formed the substance of the chapter. We discovered that simulation should be employed whenever there is an essential dependence upon time that must be considered. Once the decision to use simulation has been made, the question then is one of which type — continuous deterministic (Chapter 15) or discrete probabilistic. If the choice is the latter, then this is the chapter of greatest interest to the modeler/decision maker. It was suggested that discrete probabilistic simulation is appropriate for situations in which the system of interest is viewed as changing abruptly at discrete points in time, whereas continuous simulation was appropriate for systems that are perceived as changing smoothly and continuously in time. Areas in which the use of continuous simulation is widespread include large-scale socioeconomic and urban systems as well as corporate-level financial systems.

In this chapter the concepts of event, attribute, entity, and activity were all given meaning, and the underlying philosophy of discrete simulation was described in detail and illustrated by examples. The Monte Carlo method and its relation to the generation of random numbers was treated in some detail. In addition three different techniques for random variate generation were presented, including

1. The inverse distribution function method
2. The table function or table lookup method
3. The statistical approximation method

Of importance to discrete simulation is the sampling of random variables in the model. Two types of observations are collected in such models and are used to compute statistics (means, standard deviations, etc.) on the random variables. These result in two basic types of reports:

1. Statistical reports based upon time-independent observations
2. Statistical reports based upon time-persistent observations

These reports are, perhaps, the most important products of any discrete simulation run as they are indicative of what the simulated system is doing and how well it is performing. Two important design considerations come into play—the observations must be based upon steady-state behavior generally and enough observations must be collected so as to obtain statistically valid results.

We discussed the mechanics of discrete simulation model formulation and illustrated them by use of GPSS. The modeler begins by identifying the activities, the transactions, the arrival rates, the service times, and so on. For event-oriented simulations, the events, entities, and their attributes must be identified. Then diagrams as in Figure 9.1 and 9.2 facilitate an understanding of the relationships among the various activities. It was mentioned that events (and activities) precipitate the occurrence of other events (and activities). In GPSS, the block diagram is used to delineate these relationships.

We then described the important discrete simulation languages in some detail including GPSS, SIMSCRIPT, and SLAM. Among these, GPSS is the most widely used. GPSS is a block-oriented language, whereas SIMSCRIPT is an event-oriented language, and SLAM could be either. Many of the blocks that comprise the GPSS language were described and used in the simulation models and cases included in this chapter.

PROBLEMS

1. Use the first five numbers in the first column of the uniform random number table (Table 9.12) to generate five standard normally distributed random variates by means of table lookup. Use the tabular values in Table 9.7 and the following formula for linear interpolation. Assume that u_1 is the uniform random number and x_1 is the normal random number:

$$x_1 = Z_n + \frac{(Z_{n+1} - Z_n)(u_1 - F(Z_n))}{F(Z_{n+1}) - F(Z_n)}$$

Here $F(Z_n) \leq u_i \leq F(Z_{n+1})$. For example, suppose that $u_1 = .212$; then $F(Z_{n+1}) = .3085$ and $F(Z_n) = .1587$, and the corresponding Z_i's are $Z_{n+1} = -.5$ and $Z_n = -1$. Hence,

$$X_i = -1 + \frac{(-.5 + 1.)}{(.3085 - .1587)}(.212 - .1587)$$

$$= -.8221$$

2. Use the first 12 numbers in the first column of the random number table to generate one normally distributed random number by means of the statistical approximation method.

3. Characterize a system that seems to lend itself well to representation by discrete probabilistic simulation. Identify the activities, events, entities, and their attributes. Draw appropriate time line diagrams (as in Figure 9.1) and event precipitation diagrams (as in Figure 9.2).

4. The times between arrivals of customers at a "7-11" store is known to be exponentially distributed. The first customer arrives at time zero. Determine the arrival times of the

Table 9.12   Uniform Random Number Table

.846477	.289767	.708141	.37631	.104852
.893618	.370204	.575077	.424024	.0722376
.0694686	.100947	.652918	.186409	.870447
.621969	.985899	.750172	.776488	.555008
.981917	.336033	.980279	.875999	.15748
.510917	.313196	.739529	.621667	.507087
.379529	.596912	.59918	.330115	.457471
.842065	.473613	.759433	.400888	.0286144
.548579	.34876	.689771	.501905	.353604
.069138	.0225658	.948108	.196345	.31238
.989056	.0326632	.492353	.338108	.921059
.819067	.348016	.805116	.850326	.622216
.328178	.976677	.181927	.992557	.739238
.420884	.837807	.653496	.841591	.579271
.774855	.405079	.201135	.038271	.0249136
.510483	.828321	.530336	.478773	.17446
.600158	.0582037	.207986	.349083	.0064020
.195619	.766748	.174625	.77687	.829164
.769852	.382705	.642466	.288047	.215148
.612493	.136671	.427831	.978966	.112329
.839382	.319826	.399986	.901875	.300638
.880256	.317971	.595151	.0542596	.306078
.776046	.496067	.805354	.702959	.0127235
.849831	.464229	.147815	.42662	.902303
.996241	.984807	.263605	.807658	.274088
.311803	.0792997	.941912	.934184	.764484
.883529	.412392	.342539	.107361	.760722
.985233	.0622359	.621159	.394894	.430923
.368419	.356812	.653741	.245668	.845592
.957034	.129724	.453577	.178264	.760987

next five customers assuming the mean time between arrivals is 2 minutes. Use the first five numbers in the first column of the random number table (Table 9.12).

5. Describe what you believe are desirable characteristics of a pseudorandom number generation routine (as in Table 9.6).

6. A drive-up bank has two servers and two waiting lines for autos. The times between arrivals of autos are known to be exponentially distributed with a mean of 1.2 minutes. The service times are uniformly distributed between 3.5 minutes and 4.5 minutes. The first car arrives at time zero. Use the first column of the random number table (Table 9.8) to generate the arrival times and the second column of the random number table to generate service times. At what time does the fifth car exit the auto bank? During this period, how much idle time is accumulated by servers 1 and 2? Assume that the first car pulls into server 1's lane and that successive cars will choose the lane with the least number of cars waiting. If both lanes are idle, or the same length, assume that the first lane (server 1's lane) is chosen. What was the longest waiting line?

7. Use the computer code given in Table 9.6 to generate five random numbers starting with the seed 13133.

8. Provide definitions for the following terms.
   a. Activity
   b. Continuous simulation
   c. Combined simulation
   d. Cumulative distribution function
   e. Discrete simulation
   f. Event
   g. Exponential distribution
   h. Inverse transformation method
   i. Monte Carlo method
   j. Permanent entity
   k. Process
   l. Regenerative event
   m. Temporary entity
   n. Uniform distribution

9. Develop a computer routine to compute normally distributed random deviates using the statistical approximation method in a language of your choice.

10. Develop computer routines to
   a. Compute exponentially distributed random deviates
   b. Compute random deviates that are uniformly distributed over the interval A to B
   Use any language you wish.

11. *The Scenario:* Tooty Fruity, Inc., is a fresh fruit and vegetable jobber/distributor. Tooty has 22 semitrailer trucks that it uses to move produce to its affiliated grocery chain—Catch Twenty-two, Inc. (CTTI). Each week the trucks must service 105 super-markets from a single warehouse with two loading docks. Keep Ontruken, Tooty's CEO, is concerned about whether to add an additional loading dock and crew. Mr. Ontruken knows that occasionally five to six trucks are sitting idle out in front of the warehouse four or more hours at a time. This did not concern Mr. Ontruken when there were only 85 supermarkets in the chain as the 22 trucks could get to all 85 within a week. Now that CTTI has picked up 22 more supermarkets from a competitor, the situation is different.

The Problem: Mr. Ontruken does not want to purchase any more trucks and is not sure that this would help to solve the problem anyway. All the supermarkets are within 150 miles of the warehouse and can be reached within 3 hours. Average unloading time is 5 hours give or take an hour. The real problem has to do with trucks waiting to be loaded at the loading docks. The average loading time is 1 hour roughly. Adding a third dock and loading crew would be expensive. Working the existing crews overtime would also be costly.

The Model: This problem cannot be handled adequately with analytical queueing models because the arrival rate of trucks to the warehouse loading docks varies as a function of the number of trucks out, the number of trucks waiting, and so on. Simula-tion seems to be the only viable modeling alternative. At the start of each week, all trucks are idle and are waiting to be loaded. Upon completion of loading, it takes 8 hours on the average for the truck to return empty. Due to traveling distances, this number can vary by as much as 2 hours. However, trucks never arrive earlier than 6 or later than 10 hours. The warehouse is open for business 24 hours a day, five days a week for a total of 120 hours. All departed trucks are expected to return from their routes by the end of each week (168 hours) so that no weekend layovers are incurred. Therefore, every Monday morning all 22 trucks are parked in front of the loading docks empty.

We begin by listing activities, entities, events, and their attributes:

Activity	Attribute (time required)
Trucks waiting empty	
Trucks en route	8 ± 2 hours
Trucks being loaded	1 hour

Develop a GPSS model of this situation to determine what benefits might accrue from the inclusion of additional loading docks and whether additional trucks are needed. Assume that trucks can be loaded and unloaded any time of the day (or night). Run the simulation for one week. Determine the average waiting time per truck for two, three, four, and five docks. Should Tooty buy more trucks?

   (*Hint:* Use a storage representation of the number of docks available for loading trucks. In GPSS, there are two types of permanent entities—facilities, which we've already discussed, and storages.) Each permanent entity is delineated to GPSS by means of a pair of blocks as indicated:

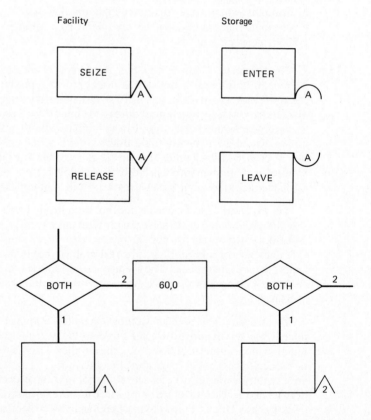

In addition to the ENTER/LEAVE pair of statements, the storage requires one extra statement that usually appears at the end of the program. This last statement has the format

```
                    A        STORAGE        N
```

where A is the storage designator that references a specific storage defined by an ENTER A–LEAVE A pair and N is an integer that specifies the capacity of the storage (the maximum number of transactions, trucks in this case that can occupy the storage) at any point in time. To represent two loading docks preceded by a single queue for the truck problem, the following sequence of statements would be appropriate

```
              ENTER           1     ENTER A DOCK
              DEPART          1     DEPART QUEUE
              ADVANCE         1     LOAD TRUCKS
              LEAVE           1     LEAVE LOADING DOCKS
              ADVANCE         8,2   MAKE TRIP
              TRANSFER, BEG         RETURN TO LOADING DOCKS
              GENERATE        1
              TERMINATE       1
        *
          1   STORAGE         2
        *
              START           120   RUN FOR 1 WEEK — 120 HOURS
              END
```

12.   *The Scenario:*   A conveyor system involves six inspectors positioned along a conveyor belt. Items to be processed by the inspectors arrive at the first inspector at a constant rate of one every 20 seconds. Service time for each inspector is uniformly distributed and is never less than 30 seconds or more than 90 seconds. No queues are allowed in front of each inspector. Therefore, the inspector must be idle if he is to remove the item from the conveyor belt. If the first inspector is idle, the item is processed by that inspector and placed in a hopper. At this point there is no further interest in the item, and it is removed from the system. If the first inspector is busy when the item arrives, it continues down the conveyor belt until it arrives at the second inspector. The time to complete this transport is 60 seconds. If the second inspector is busy, the item continues on down until it comes to an idle inspector, at which point it is inspected. If an item encounters a situation in which all inspectors are busy, it is recycled to the first inspector with a transport time of 240 seconds.

The Problem: Managers are interested in how much time an item spends in the system and in the percentage of time each inspector is busy. The capability to discern the effects of increasing or decreasing the number of inspectors is likewise of considerable interest to management. What effect speeding up (or slowing down) the conveyor would have is also of interest.

The Model and Solution: Develop a model (or models) appropriate for this system in GPSS. Analyze the reports and develop a recommendation for management. Use the following structure to model the transport of an item to the first idle inspector.

The TRANSFER block allows an item to enter a facility only if the facility is vacant or idle; otherwise, the item proceeds to the next facility. A typical segment of GPSS code for an inspector (server) is the following. The other inspectors use identical segments of code.

```
              TRANSFER BOTH,,THI              SERVER 2 BUSY?
        *
        *     SERVER NUMBER 2
        *
              SEIZE           2               ACTIVATE SERVER 2
```

```
        ADVANCE          60,30      PERFORM INSPECTION
        RELEASE          2          DISENGAGE SERVER 2
        TRANSFER, TAB               FINISHED — GO TO TAB
    THI ADVANCE          60         ADVANCE TO SERVER 3
```

Run the model for 1000 items after using 10 items to initialize and fill the conveyor system.

13.   *The Scenario:*   People arrive at a movie theater at a rate of one every 10 ± 3 seconds during the 30-minute period just prior to the start of each movie. These persons are sold tickets from a single booth that is manned by one person who takes 9 ± 5 seconds to service one customer.

The Problem: Long waiting lines are frequently experienced at this theater, and if the line is longer than 100 people, new arrivals will leave. Write a program in GPSS to determine the average queue length, the number of people who will leave, and the average waiting time in a queue.

14.   *The Scenario:*   A tool crib clerk provides tools for workers in a manufacturing shop. The time required to take down the worker's name and authorization code and retrieve the requested tool is normally distributed with a mean of 3 minutes and a standard deviation of 1.5 minutes. The time between worker arrivals is exponentially distributed, with a mean of 3 minutes. Initially, two workers are waiting for service and the worker being served has just completed service. The next arrival is scheduled at time 1.

The Problem: Use the first column of the random number table (Table 9.12) to compute the status of this system exactly 10 minutes later. How many workers are waiting? Is the crib clerk idle or busy? Draw an activity time chart (as in Figure 9.1) for the first 10 minutes of operation using the initial conditions described above. Use Tables 9.7 and 9.8 to compute normal random variates. Work your way down the first column of Table 9.12, using random numbers as they are needed to generate the next event. Process events in their chronological order.

15.   Distinguish between continuous and discrete simulation in terms of philosophy and scope. Which technique would you use for each of the following situations?
        An inner-city decay problem
        A McDonald's restaurant
        An air pollution problem
        A shipper scheduling problem
        An elevator usage problem
        A housing problem
        An infectious disease problem
        An airport congestion problem
        A corporate financial problem

16.   Define the usage of the following GPSS blocks. Show their block representations.

```
                    GENERATE
                    ADVANCE
                    QUEUE
                    TERMINATE
```

TRANSFER
DEPART
SEIZE
RELEASE

17. List and describe the GPSS control keywords discussed in this chapter.

18. Discuss the differences among GPSS, SIMSCRIPT, and SLAM. Which is easiest to use? Which is the most readable? Which is the most flexible?

19. Return to the Cabana Banana case. A seventh steamship costs $2,300,000 to purchase and $38,320 per month to operate including labor and fuel costs. Suppose that an additional steamship were to be added to the line. Modify the simulation programs in the case to compare the benefits versus costs of adding a seventh steamship versus adding a second dock.

20. In the Cabana Banana case, assess the benefits that would accrue with the addition of a third dock (assuming six steamships). Modify the codes to include the third dock and determine what net increase in throughput can be expected. Use a storage as described in Problem 11 rather than three facilities. Assume a single queue.

21. Modify the Cabana Banana model so that only one queue is used for both docks. Assess the efficacy of this queueing strategy as opposed to the use of two queues — one for each dock.

22. In the movie theater problem (Problem 13), determine what effect adding a second ticket clerk would have on the average queue length, the number of people who leave without purchasing tickets, and the average waiting time.

23. Compare the simulation output obtained from solving Problem 13 with results obtained using an $M/M/I/\infty/FIFO/1$ queueing model. Assume an arrival rate of 6 per minute and a service rate of 6.666667 per minute. What assumptions associated with the two models are fundamentally quite different?

REFERENCES

1. GALITZ, L. "Modeling for Bankers." *The Banker,* December 1978, pp. 33–36.
2. KEEN, P., and M. SCOTT MORTON. *Decision Support Systems: An Organizational Perspective.* Reading, Mass.: Addison-Wesley, 1978.
3. NAYLOR, T., and H. SCHAUL. "A Survey of Users of Corporate Planning Models." *Management Science,* Vol. 22, no. 9 (1976), pp. 927–937.
4. NAYLOR, T., and C. JEFFRESS. "Corporate Simulation Models: A Survey." *Simulation,* Vol. 24, no. 6 (1975), pp. 171–176.
5. SHANNON, R., and W. BILES. "The Utility of Certain Curriculum Topics to Operations Research Practitioners." *Operations Research,* Vol. 18 (1970), pp. 741–745.
6. SHANNON, R. *Systems Simulation: The Art and Science.* Englewood Cliffs, N.J.: Prentice-Hall, 1975.
7. ENSHOFF, J., and R. SISSON. *Design and Use of Computer Simulation Models.* New York: Macmillan, 1970.

8. KIVIAT, P., R. VILLANUEVA, and H. MARKOWITZ. *The SIMSCRIPT II.5 Programming Language.* Los Angeles: Consolidated Analysis Centers, 1973.

9. PRITSKER, A. *The GASP IV Simulation Language.* New York: John Wiley & Sons, 1974.

10. PRITSKER, A., and R. YOUNG. *Simulation with GASP.PL/1.* New York: John Wiley & Sons, 1975.

11. SCHRIBER, T. *Simulation Using GPSS.* New York: John Wiley & Sons, 1974.

12. GORDON, G. *The Application of GPSS V to Discrete Systems Simulation.* Englewood Cliffs, N.J.: Prentice-Hall, 1975.

12. PRITSKER, A., and C. PEGDEN. *Introduction to Simulation and SLAM.* New York: Halsted Press, 1979.

CHAPTER 10

Modeling with Markov Chains

We first encountered the notion of a *Markov process* in Chapter 6, where we discussed this subject in terms of dynamic programming (or recursive optimization). In this chapter, we delve into a descriptive modeling technique with the ponderous title *Markov chains*. Briefly, a dynamic, probabilistic process that involves elements of a system moving in a "orderly" manner among a finite set of "states," the movement occurring at discrete points in time, is called a *discrete stochastic process*. If the probabilities of movement from a given state to the next one are the same—regardless of the particular point in time—then we have a stochastic process that can be modeled as a Markov chain. Let us illustrate this definition with an example from marketing—the well-known "brand-switching" phenomenon.

The soft drink market in Slobbovia is dominated by two companies: Olympus, Inc., with its popular Nectar, and its largest competitor Sahara Bottling Co., which markets its Oasis brand. A third, smaller bottler—Tin, Too, and Fore, Inc. (TT&F)—is attempting to capture a larger market share from its two giant competitors, with its novel drink called Pimienta.

Bev Ridge, who is TT&F's CEO, has commissioned a market survey, and the results indicate that Nectar, Oasis, and Pimienta currently hold 50%, 45%, and 5% of the market, respectively. The really interesting numbers to Bev, however, are the ones that describe brand switching. These figures, in the form of a *one-stage transition matrix,* are given in Table 10.1.

This matrix is interpreted as follows. Suppose that the *next* soft drink purchased by a customer is dependent only on the brand purchased the last time. The data in the matrix are relative frequencies of brand purchases, given the brand last purchased. For example, 75% of customers who buy Nectar on a given occasion repeat their selection of Nectar on the next purchase, whereas 15% switch to Oasis and 10% switch to Pimienta. The other relative frequencies are interpreted analogously.

One way in which to visualize these relationships is by the use of a so-called "state transition diagram," as illustrated in Figure 10.1. The arrows represent

Table 10.1   Brand Switching Matrix

		To		
		Nectar	Oasis	Pimienta
From	Nectar	.75	.15	.10
	Oasis	.10	.80	.10
	Pimienta	.05	.05	.90

possible one-step transitions, and the numbers on the directed arcs are their one-step transition probabilities.

If these relative frequencies do not change over time, there are several questions that are of keen interest to Bev Ridge.

1. Given that TT&F has only a 5% market share at present, will that share increase or decrease over the long run? Will market share for the three companies eventually stabilize?
2. Soft drink purchases are an almost daily event for many people. How many days will it take TT&F to attract 10% of the market (if it will)?
3. Brand loyalty is very high for Pimienta drinkers. Would it be worthwhile to spend scarce advertising dollars on strengthening Pimienta's brand loyalty, or would a "head-to-head" campaign against Nectar or Oasis be the better strategy?

Before leaving our example to discuss the theory and application of modeling with Markov chains, it is interesting (and perhaps counterintuitive) to note that Pimienta will eventually gain a 50% share of the market! With this intriguing fact as prologue, let us address the underlying assumptions associated with Markov chains.

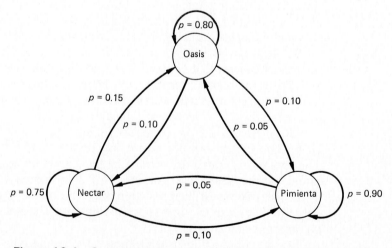

Figure 10.1   State transition diagram for brand-switching example.

UNDERLYING ASSUMPTIONS

As we have already noted, for a process to be modeled as a Markov chain, the process must exhibit the *Markov property.* That is, movement from one state to another at a discrete point in time *depends only on the current state,* and not on previous or subsequent states. Moreover, the probability of moving from any state to any other state remains constant over time.

We have seen one example of a process that exhibits the Markov property — our soft drink brand-switching scenario. Suppose, however, that a subset of soft drink purchasers never bought the same brand three times in a row, for the sake of variety. In this case, the Markov property is not present (in the sense of a one-step, or first-order, process), and the process cannot be modeled as a simple Markov chain. This is because the probabilities depend upon something that happened *two* stages ago instead of the previous stage only.

The other basic assumption that must be met is that of *stationarity* — that is, the state probabilities do not change over time. In "real-world" applications, nonstationarity is most often the attribute that rules out the use of Markov chains. Why this is so is easily understood when we take a managerial view of processes. For example, in the soft drink market share scenario we discussed, we noted (without proof, of course) that TT&F would eventually have 50% of the market share — under the assumption that Olympus and Sahara would sit idly by while their aggregate market share declined from 95% to 50%. That assumption, of course, is nonsensical. Our analysis of processes provides an input to managerial action that may result in *changes* to those processes. At any rate, we must be careful to note the presence of possible nonstationarities when using Markov chain models.

MODELING WITH TRANSITION MATRICES

The basic modeling device in Markov chain analysis is the *one-step transition matrix,* which we denote by the symbol P_1. The rows and columns of P_1, are associated with *n states* in which elements of the process may find themselves. Some examples are given in Table 10.2.

Table 10.2   Some Example Processes

Process Elements	States
Daily weather conditions	Sunny, rainy, snowy, overcast, dusty
Fir trees on a Christmas tree farm	Cut and sold, die of disease, allowed to mature, newly planted
Professor's tests	Hard, medium, easy
Company personnel	Hired, promoted to supervisor, promoted to manager, fired, deceased, retired

**Table 10.3   General One-Step
Transition Matrix**

State at Time t + 1

		1	2	· · ·	j	· · ·	n
State at Time t	1	p_{11}	p_{12}	· · ·	p_{1j}	· · ·	p_{1n}
	2	p_{21}	p_{22}	· · ·	p_{2j}	· · ·	p_{2n}
	⋮	⋮	⋮		⋮		⋮
	i	p_{i1}	p_{i2}	· · ·	p_{ij}	· · ·	p_{in}
	⋮	⋮	⋮		⋮		⋮
	n	p_{n1}	p_{n2}	· · ·	p_{nj}	· · ·	p_{nn}

The elements of $\mathbf{P}_1$, which we denote by p_{ij}, are the probabilities that, given we are in state i at time period t, we will be in state j at time period $t + 1$. Thus $\mathbf{P}_1$ is a matrix, each of whose *rows* is a marginal probability distribution — identical in form to the posterior distribution in DMUR modeling (Chapter 7). By inference, the states must be mutually exclusive and collectively exhaustive.

The other tool we will need is the *initial state vector* $\mathbf{S}_1 = (S_1, S_2, \ldots, S_n)$, where S_j represents the current status of the process. In our soft drink example, recall that $\mathbf{S}_1 = (.50, .45, .05)$, which were the initial market shares for Olympus, Sahara, and TT&F, respectively. In our weather example in Table 10.2, one possible initial state vector would be $\mathbf{S}_1 = (0, 1, 0, 0, 0)$, signifying that today is rainy.

To complete our "tool kit" for modeling with Markov chains, we need a system for estimating $p_{ij}, i, j = 1, \ldots, n$, the one-step state probabilities. As is usually the case, estimating accurate probability distributions on states is critically important to success, and it is also the most difficult task to accomplish. In many cases, historical records or customer surveys can be used to compute relative frequencies. In other cases, outright subjective estimates must be resorted to. Whatever the case, we must be sensitive to the fact that our analysis is no better than the probability distributions are accurate.

Finally, as noted earlier, Markov models are, in the technical sense, purely descriptive. That is, there is no formal "objective function" as there is in an optimizing model such as linear programming. However, at the risk of repeating ourselves unnecessarily, *all* MS/OR models are descriptive in a managerial sense.

For future reference, a formal one-step transition matrix is exhibited in Table 10.3.

Note in Table 10.3 that

$$\sum_{j=1}^{n} p_{ij} = 1$$

for each $i = 1, \ldots, n$.

SOLUTION APPROACHES: AN INTUITIVE DESCRIPTION

For our purposes, there are two basically different types of Markov processes, which we will refer to as *recurring*[1] and *transient,* respectively. Since they model markedly different processes and require different analytical approaches, we discuss these two types separately.

RECURRING MARKOV PROCESSES

Let us return to our soft drink market share scenario and pursue it further. The one-step transition matrix and the initial state vector for this model are reproduced here, for convenience.

$$\mathbf{P_1} = \begin{array}{c} \\ N \\ O \\ P \end{array} \begin{array}{ccc} N & O & P \\ \left[\begin{array}{ccc} .75 & .15 & .10 \\ .10 & .80 & .10 \\ .05 & .05 & .90 \end{array} \right] \end{array} \qquad \begin{array}{ccc} N & O & P \end{array} \\ \mathbf{S_1} = (.50, .45, .05) \qquad (10.1)$$

Asssuming that the time period for each transition is one week, how can we "forecast" the market share $\mathbf{S_2}$ one week hence? Consider the product Nectar (N). One week hence, this product will retain 75% of its own share of 50% and will pick up 10% of Oasis's 45% and 5% of Pimienta's 5% (note the first column of $\mathbf{P_1}$ and $\mathbf{S_1}$). Therefore, one week later,

$$\text{Nectar's market share} = (.75)(.50) + (.10)(.45) + (.05)(.05)$$
$$= .4225 = 42.25\% \qquad (10.2)$$

What we have done, of course, is to perform the first step of the vector-matrix multiplication:

$$\mathbf{S_2} = \mathbf{S_1} \cdot \mathbf{P_1} = (.4225, .4375, .1400) \qquad (10.3)$$

Note in our example that Nectar's share dropped dramatically, Oasis's share decreased a bit, and Pimienta's almost tripled!

To compute the market share *two* weeks hence, we could simply perform the computation

$$\mathbf{S_3} = \mathbf{S_2} \cdot \mathbf{P_1} = (.3676, .4204, .2120) \qquad (10.4)$$

---

[1] The technical term is "ergodic."

noting that Nectar suffered another large drop, Pimienta increased by over 50% of last week's share, and Oasis again declined slightly.

Let us look at the computations in a slightly different way. Note that

$$S_3 = S_2 \cdot P_1 = (S_1 \cdot P_1) \cdot P_1 = S_1 \cdot (P_1)^2 \qquad (10.5)$$

Thus the *two-step transition matrix* P_2 is just P_1 multiplied by itself once. In general, then, the *m-step transition matrix* $P_m = (P_1)^m$, and

$$S_m = S_1(P_1)^m \qquad (10.6)$$

This scenario is an example of a *recurring Markov process.* If we continued our calculations, allowing m to become very large, $(P_1)^m$ would slowly converge to a matrix with three identical rows, the elements of which would represent the *steady-state market shares* of the three soft drinks. Stated another way, we would have the long-term market shares *independent of the actual market shares at the beginning!*

Fortunately, we do not actually have to perform a long series of matrix multiplications to find the steady-state vector. Note the elegant simplicity of the following logic.

Suppose we know the steady-state vector $S = (S_1, S_2, S_3)$. The definition of steady state tells us this state will not change in the next period. Thus,

$$S = S \cdot P_1 \qquad (10.7)$$

If we "plug in" the numbers from our ongoing example, treating S_1, S_2, and S_3 as unknown quantities, we have

$$(S_1, S_2, S_3) = (S_1, S_2, S_3) \cdot \begin{bmatrix} .75 & .15 & .10 \\ .10 & .80 & .10 \\ .05 & .05 & .90 \end{bmatrix} \qquad (10.8)$$

Or, carrying out the multiplications and bringing the variables to the left-hand sides of the equations, we have

$$-.25S_1 + .10S_2 + .05S_3 = 0 \qquad (10.9)$$

$$.15S_1 - .20S_2 + .05S_3 = 0 \qquad (10.10)$$

$$.10S_1 + .10S_2 - .10S_3 = 0 \qquad (10.11)$$

Unfortunately, (10.9) through (10.11) are redundant, so that they have no unique solution. However, we also know that

$$S_1 + S_2 + S_3 = 1 \qquad (10.12)$$

We therefore discard one of the equations (10.9) through (10.11) (*which* one doesn't matter), add (10.12), and have our computer produce the unique solution, which is

$$S_1 = .2143, \text{ Nectar's stable share}$$
$$S_2 = .2857, \text{ Oasis' stable share}$$
$$S_3 = .5000, \text{ Pimienta's stable share}$$

Of course, we may very well be interested in the transient behavior of the process. Perhaps in our illustration, market share at the end of the fourth week may be a critical item for managerial decision making. If this is the case,

$$S_5 = S_1 \cdot [(P_1^2)]^2 = [.50, .45, .05] \begin{bmatrix} .3931 & .3117 & .2952 \\ .2146 & .4902 & .2952 \\ .1375 & .1577 & .7048 \end{bmatrix}$$

$$= [.300, .384, .316] \qquad (10.13)$$

Thus, after four weeks, Pimienta will already have overtaken Nectar in market share and will be "hot on the heels" of Oasis.

TRANSIENT MARKOV PROCESSES

In recurring Markov processes, all states have the property that elements "come and go," so to speak, until the process has arrived at its steady state. Said another way, all states are recurring. In transient Markov processes, however, there are two different types of states: transient and absorbing.

Transient states are states in which some temporary parts of the process allow units to "pass through," but which — in the long run — converge to state probabilities of zero. As an illustration, consider our Christmas tree farm scenario from Table 10.2. If a given tree is neither diseased nor cut and sold in a given year, it returns to the "allowed to mature" state the following year. The tree will eventually leave this transient state and, of course, will never return.

Absorbing states, on the other hand, are the converse of transient states. Once a process element enters an absorbing state, it never again leaves. In our example, the states "die of disease" and "cut and sold" are clearly absorbing states.

Transient Markov processes model scenarios in which all units eventually end up in absorbing states, so we know at the outset what the transient elements of the steady-state vector will look like. Transient processes, unlike recurring ones, are highly sensitive to the composition of the initial state vector, as well as to the pattern of the one-step transition matrix. Transition processes can become complicated very quickly, as we illustrate in the following.

Bill Dunn, the business manager for the Rio de Oro Medical Clinic (from Chapter 3), is analyzing the clinic's accounts receivable. Billings are always "net 30 days," so that accounts not paid after 30 days are considered past due, and gentle reminders are sent to these clients. If a bill is still unpaid after 60 days, a not-so-gentle reminder is issued. After 90 days, an unpaid bill is relegated to the unsympathetic attention of the Doberman Collection Agency.

From past records, Bill sets up the following one-step transition matrix.

Table 10.4   Rio de Oro One-Step Transition Matrix

	Less than 30 Days Old	30–60 Days Old	60–90 Days Old	Paid	Collection Agency	Uncollectible
Less than 30 days old	0	.25	0	.75	0	0
30–60 days old	0	0	.35	.65	0	0
60–90 days old	0	0	0	.50	.50	0
Paid	0	0	0	1	0	0
Collection agency	0	0	0	.25	0	.75
Uncollectible	0	0	0	0	0	1

He also notes that the current crop of accounts receivable is as follows.

Category	% in Category
Less than 30 days old	60%
30–60 days old	20
60–90 days old	15
With collection agency	5

At this point, of course, none of the *current* set is in the "paid" or "uncollectible" categories, which are the absorbing states, so that the initial state vector is as follows.

$$S_1 = (.60, .20, .15, 0, .05, 0) \qquad (10.14)$$

This transient process reaches "steady state" in exactly four months. The steady-state vector and the intermediate state vectors are obtained by serially multiplying $S_i \cdot P_1$, $i = 1, 2, 3, 4$, and the results are as follows.

	Less than 30 Days	30–60 Days	60–90 Days	Paid	Agency	Uncollectible
S_2	0	.1500	.0700	.6675	.0750	.0375
S_3	0	0	.0525	.8188	.0350	.0937
S_4	0	0	0	.8538	.0262	.1200
S_5	0	0	0	.8603	0	.1397

In our example, therefore, only 86% of Rio de Oro's accounts will eventually be paid. Since this is most probably an unacceptably low collection rate, Bill Dunn would need to take some managerial action to *change the process* (e.g., more effective "reminder" notices or a better collection agency). The effect of such managerial actions would be to change the transition probabilities and thereby change the process itself.

We note in passing that the device we used to find the steady-state vector in recurrent Markov processes won't work for transient processes. The reason for this phenomenon is that the states *by definition* have steady-state transition probabilities of zero.

Transient Markov chain models have a variety of applications. One very interesting one — analyzing the rank structure of the officer corps in a military service — is the subject of the first case in this chapter, "An Officer and a Gentleman."

AVAILABLE COMPUTER CODES FOR MARKOV ANALYSIS

Mathematical analysis of simple Markov chain models involves little more than the solution of systems of linear equations or matirx-vector multiplication. The interactive program MCHAIN was written by James R. Burns in Microsoft BASIC for application on microcomputers. MCHAIN will accept up to 20 states and provides the following information:

1. For recurring Markov models
   a. The steady-state activity vector
   b. Any intermediate activity vector, as desired
2. For transient Markov models
   a. The steady-state activity vector
   b. Any intermediate activity vector as desired.

For Markov chain model analysis on a large computer, most computer systems have matrix-vector manipulation capabilities that make programming such a package very simple. The languages SAS and APL are particularly effective in this regard.

DEVELOPING ALTERNATIVE SOLUTIONS

Unlike the case with many *optimizing* models, for which formal sensitivity analysis tools have been developed, *descriptive models* must be "brute forced" to obtain such information (recall that this was also the case with discrete simulation models). Given the relative ease with which Markov chain models are "solved" by computer, however, this is not particularly a problem.

A procedure such as the one performed by MCHAIN in the previous section can yield important and useful managerial information about the process under analysis. To repeat an earlier observation, the descriptive analysis of an existing process may point to needed changes in that process, to be brought about by managerial action.

STATE OF THE ART IN MARKOV CHAIN ANALYSIS

The general theory of stochastic processes, of which Markov processes are a small part, is a complex and highly mathematical subject. Let us briefly discuss two advanced topics in stochastic processes to get the flavor of this complexity.

TIME OF FIRST PASSAGE

Time of first passage refers to the average (expected) number of time periods for an element of the process to move from a given state to another (given) state. For example, in a company that has a policy of developing its own management from within (rather than "pirating" executives from other companies), a newly hired line manager might have a very strong interest in the time of first passage from the state "management trainee" to the state "chief executive officer."

We will discuss time of first passage only for recurring Markov chain models.

Time of First Passage: Recurring Markov Chains

Let f_{ij} denote the average (expected) number of time periods for an element currently located in state i to reach state j. Before stating the mathematical result, let us return to our soft drink market share scenario once more to "think through" the logic involved. The one-step transition matrix is

$$\mathbf{P}_1 = \begin{array}{c} \\ N \\ O \\ P \end{array} \begin{array}{c} \begin{array}{ccc} N & O & P \end{array} \\ \left[\begin{array}{ccc} .75 & .15 & .10 \\ .10 & .80 & .10 \\ .05 & .05 & .90 \end{array} \right] \end{array} \qquad (10.15)$$

Suppose that a customer has just purchased a bottle of Nectar, and we are interested in knowing (on the average) how many transitions it will take for him to purchase a bottle of Pimienta. There are several possibilities. First, he may switch to Pimienta in exactly one step, with an expected value of $p_{13} \cdot (1 \text{ step}) = p_{13}$. On the other hand, he could stay with Nectar or go to Oasis on the next purchase and then *eventually* purchase a Pimienta. These expected values are

$$p_{11} \cdot (1 \text{ step} + f_{13}) + p_{12} \cdot (1 \text{ step} + f_{23})$$

Mathematically, then,

$$f_{13} = p_{13} + p_{11} \cdot (1 + f_{13}) + p_{12} \cdot (1 + f_{23}) \qquad (10.16)$$

or, more simply,

$$(1 - p_{11}) \cdot f_{13} - p_{12} \cdot f_{23} = (p_{11} + p_{12} + p_{13}) = 1 \qquad (10.17)$$

Equation (10.17) is an equation in two unknowns. To solve for f_{13}—the quantity in which we are interested, we must also solve for f_{23}—which means looking at the second possibility that our fickle customer just purchased a bottle of Oasis. This equation, by the same reasoning is

$$-p_{21} \cdot f_{13} + (1 - p_{22}) \cdot f_{23} = 1 \qquad (10.18)$$

Substituting the appropriate p_{ij} values and solving, we have $f_{13} = f_{23} = 10$. That is, regardless of whether our customer just bought a Nectar or an Oasis, it will take him *on an average* ten transitions before he selects a Pimienta.

If these results seem counterintuitive, note that the key to this particular scenario is the high brand loyalty associated with Pimienta. Thus, although it may take some time to attract a "following," Pimienta slowly builds its market share through customer retention. This phenomenon, of course, is no surprise to anyone who has ever taken a basic marketing course.

In general, then, to solve for time of first passage to any state from all other states, the following system of $(n - 1)$ equations must be solved:

$$f_{ij} - \sum_{r \neq j = 1}^{n} p_{ir} \cdot f_{rj} = 1; \quad i = 1, \ldots , n, i \neq j$$

DYNAMIC PROGRAMMING IN MARKOV CHAINS

Many dynamic programming formulations of underlying problems involve stochastic (probabilistic) states at each stage. Several advanced texts (e.g., Wagner [1]) address a formulation referred to as the "stochastic shortest-route model," in which the optimal decisions at each stage are functions of transition probabilities. To illustrate this approach, let us recall Wagner's "stagecoach problem" that we discussed in Chapter 6 (dynamic programming).

Recall that Mr. Mark Off wished to travel by stagecoach from New York to San Francisco in the 1800s to seek his fortune. His problem was to select the route — in advance — that minimized his total life insurance policy premium for the entire trip, thereby assuring the safest possible trip. In our deterministic treatment, we tacitly assumed that Mark was certain to obtain a seat on any stagecoach of his choice, that the timing of connections between stages was ideal, and that no route was altered or discontinued.

Instead, what if the actual availability of routings at each stage were probabilistic and that these probabilites depended only upon the states preceding a particular stage? We would then have a "dynamic programming in a Markov chain" process, and our challenge would be to find the *expected* optimal routing through the network.

The mathematical details of this topic are beyond the scope of this textbook. However, since there are many important applications of this modeling device in business and industry (e.g., inventory systems), present and prospective managers should at least be aware of its existence.

An Officer and a Gentleman

The Scenario: The "officer corps" of any large military establishment bears many similarities to the hierarchical management cadre of major business corporations. Both involve a structure of ranks or titles that are intended to indicate increasing levels of managerial responsibility. The following table contrasts some of the titles used for this purpose in billion-dollar banks with the classical rank structure of the U.S. Army and the U.S. Air Force.[2]

Bank Officer Title	*Military Rank*
President	General officer
Executive vice-president	Lieutenant general
Senior vice-president	Major general
Vice-president	Brigadier general
Vice-president of operations	Colonel
Assistant vice-president of operations	Lieutenant colonel
Head cashier	Major
Cashier	Captain
Assistant cashier	First lieutenant
Management trainee	Second lieutenant

Unlike private corporations, the armed services do not necessarily promote officers from one rank to the next higher rank as managerial positions become vacant. Instead, the promotion process is an annual event, with names of promotees appearing on "the list" for each rank at the appointed time of year. Each rank carries with it a "normal time in grade"; those being promoted earlier are "below the zone," and those not being promoted at the normal time are referred to as being "passed over."

The Problem: Although each officer rank carries with it a maximum tenure (e.g., a lieutenant colonel must retire after 28 years of service if he or she has not been promoted to full colonel), the task of maintaining the desired percentages of officers in each rank is a challenging managerial problem. For example, under certain circumstances, officers may elect to take early retirement (at a reduced pension) with as little as 20 years of active service—regardless of the rank they have achieved. Others may choose to serve out their maximum tenure; if sufficient numbers of officers of the same rank choose this latter option, a severe imbalance (and an impediment to the advancement of younger officers) could occur. What is needed by military personnel planners is a model that enables them to predict future officer staffing levels by rank and to use this information to

[2] The U.S. Navy uses different terminology, but it has an identical rank structure.

develop recruitment, promotion, and retention policies that result in a balanced officer complement.

The Model: With a few minor exceptions, the process of changes over time in the officer corps of an armed service provides a classical example of a Markov process. The ranks, of course, are the transient states, with resignation, termination for cause, retirement, and death representing the absorbing states. Although promotions (or demotions) to the various ranks do not occur at the same time in each calendar year, we may still use a year as the basic transition time unit.

To keep our analysis manageable, let us aggregate certain ranks and eliminate "termination for cause"[3] as an absorbing state. The resulting states are as follows.

State No.	State	Type
1	Input	Transient
2	Second lieutenant	"
3	First lieutenant	"
4	Captain	"
5	Major	"
6	Lieutenant colonel	"
7	Colonel	"
8	General (all)	"
9	Resignation	Absorbing
10	Retirement	"
11	Death	"

The one-step transition matrix in Table 10.5, although not taken from actual historical data, is a "reasonable" estimate based on experience.

Note in this scenario that we have included an "input state," which represents the newly commissioned crop of "second louies" each year. In performing the step-by-step analysis of this Markov chain model over a period of years, managerial input as to the number of new commissions must be supplied, and this number is inserted in the activity vector. Thus, we actually have a *hybrid* Markov chain model — transient for those officers currently in the system but *recurring* as far as numbers in the various states are concerned.

Solution to the Model: Let us ignore the "input" state for the moment, and use the following initial activity vector to experiment.

$$S_1 = (100, 150, 75, 50, 30, 10, .4, 0, 0, 0)$$
$$\text{2LT} \quad \text{1LT} \quad \text{CPT} \quad \text{MAJ} \quad \text{LTC} \quad \text{COL} \quad \text{GEN} \quad \text{RES} \quad \text{RET} \quad \text{DTH}$$

(The numbers in S_1 are in thousands of officers.)

---

[3] If an officer does not achieve the rank of major, he or she is terminated before achieving the length of service necessary for retirement.

Table 10.5 One-Step Transition Matrix for This Case*

To

From		INPUT 1	2LT 2	1LT 3	CPT 4	MAJ 5	LTC 6	COL 7	GEN 8	RES 9	RET 10	DTH 11
INP	1	1										
2LT	2		.500	.499								.001
1LT	3	.001		.588	.400					.010		.001
CPT	4			.001	.647	.300				.050		.002
MAJ	5				.001	.709	.250			.030	.005	.005
LTC	6					.001	.734	.150		.005	.100	.010
COL	7						.001	.698	.050	.001	.200	.050
GEN	8							.001	.669		.250	.080
RES	9									1		
RET	10										1	
DTH	11											1

* Blank entries are zeroes.

The program MCHAIN provided the following data for one, two, and three years in the future.

	2LT	1LT	CPT	MAJ	LTC	COL	GEN	RES	RET	DTH
S_2	50.15	138.18	108.58	57.98	34.53	11.48	.77	6.90	5.35	1.48
S_3	25.21	106.38	125.58	73.72	39.85	13.19	1.09	15.64	11.58	3.16
S_4	12.70	75.26	123.88	89.98	47.69	15.19	1.39	25.41	18.84	5.06

Solution to the Problem: If Table 10.5 were the *actual* one-step transition matrix for a military service, these figures would raise a "red flag" immediately. The sharp rise in the middle ranks (major through colonel) over the three-year period is known in personnel lingo as a "hump," which if allowed to occur, would severely imbalance the promotion system.

Also, the results surface some shortcomings of the model or perhaps inaccuracies in the data themselves. For example, the number of general officers is predicted by the model to grow from 400 to 1390 over a three-year period whereas the maximum number of general officer "slots" is controlled by Congress at a figure considerably lower. Moreover, the analysis indicates that 12,700 of our original 100,000 second lieutenants have not yet been promoted after three years of service, while in reality promotion to first lieutenant has always been practically automatic before completion of two years of service.

Epilogue: The purpose of this case is not to introduce you to the mysteries of military personnel management but to illustrate both the strengths and the weaknesses of Markov chain modeling and analysis. The analogy to the "rank" structure in a large bank—or to any business or public sector organization, for that matter—is obvious. Many times, the only usable output of a modeling exercise such as this is insight by the decision maker — and this point is illustrated nicely by "An Officer and a Gentleman."

Lemmon Rent-a-Car, Inc.

The Scenario: Lisa Lemmon, owner and CEO of Lemmon Rent-a-Car, Inc., is performing her annual review of company operations. With five rental stations located in Dallas, Houston, Austin, San Antonio, and El Paso, the firm's business has improved every year for the past five years. It is company policy not to enter into reciprocity agreements with other rent-a-car companies, so that Lemmon will rent cars for turn-in only at these five cities.

The Problem: As business picked up, Lisa noted a bothersome and growing trend. Increasingly, one of the stations in a city would rent all its cars early in the business day and have to turn away customers. At the same time, other stations reported an overstock of available cars for which there was no demand. Lisa did not wish to tie up scarce capital by deliberately overstocking the stations, but she hated to lose business by having too few cars on hand when and where they were needed.

She called in her administrative assistant, Denton Fenders, and instructed him to "look into the problem." Denton accessed the company's computerized management information system and came up with the following aggregate data on lease destinations for each of the five stations, for the past six months (Table 10.6).

The Model: Denton recognized the possibility that the problem could be modeled as a Markov chain model and converted the numbers in Table

Table 10.6 Number of Cars Leased, by Origin and Destination

		Destination					
		Dallas	Houston	Austin	San Antonio	El Paso	Total
Origin	Dallas	6407	8692	4953	3876	2152	26,080
	Houston	9010	8614	4648	2960	6933	32,165
	Austin	3409	2980	1225	4165	1940	13,719
	San Antonio	4121	3588	1203	6198	2841	17,951
	El Paso	1190	1442	942	1108	795	5477

10.6 into *relative frequencies by city* by dividing each number by its row total, as follows (Table 10.7):

Table 10.7 Relative Frequencies by City of Origin

	D	H	A	S	E
D	.246	.333	.190	.149	.082
H	.280	.268	.145	.092	.215
A	.248	.217	.089	.304	.142
S	.230	.200	.067	.345	.158
E	.217	.263	.172	.202	.146

This, then, is the empirically derived one-step transition matrix for a recurring Markov chain model.

Solution to the Model: Using MCHAIN, Denton computed the following steady-state activity vector:

$$S = (.248, .262, .137, .203, .150)$$
$$\quad\quad D \quad H \quad A \quad S \quad E$$

Since Lemmon's fleet totaled 600 rental cars, he converted the fractional-valued steady-state activity vector into the numbers of cars it represented, as follows:

$$S = (149, 157, 82, 122, 90)$$
$$\quad\quad D \quad H \quad A \quad S \quad E$$

Denton, armed with his computer output, strode into Lisa's office. "Boss," he announced proudly, "I've solved your problem."

Solution to the Problem: Lisa listened intently as Denton explained his analysis, but raised her eyebrows slightly when he stated flatly that "things will eventually take care of themselves, since after enough transitions, the appropriate numbers of cars would end up at each of the five locations." She didn't know much about Markov chain models, but she knew better than *that!*

"Denton," she asked, "what was the inventory of cars at each location this morning at the start of business?"

"I knew you'd ask that, chief," replied Denton. "The figures I've got include both cars on the lots as well as those inbound."

$$S_1 = (135, 129, 108, 123, 105)$$
$$\quad\quad D \quad H \quad A \quad S \quad E$$

"Now," she continued, "are your six-month figures based on actual rentals or actual demand?"

"Well, actual rentals, of course," he said. "When one of our stations is out of rental cars, our agents don't ask customers where they're going if we can't accommodate them!"

"I see," sighed Lisa. After carefully comparing S_1 (actual cars) and S, she said, "OK, take an urgent memo to all five station managers. Remind them in no uncertain terms that we are in business to *get people to where they want to go,* not merely to rent them cars if we happen to have some available."

"Effective immediately, when a customer wants a car, find one. Give them yours, or rent one in Lemmon's name from a competitor—whatever. Then, as soon as possible, have the manager at Austin hire temporary people to "deadhead" 15 cars to Dallas and 11 cars to Houston. Tell our El Paso manager to mount an immediate 30-day, 25%-off special rate for rent-a-cars to Houston. And set up a system to keep very accurate records of all these transactions."

Chagrined, but obedient, Denton mumbled a somewhat subdued "Yes, ma'am."

"Don't be discouraged, Denton," Lisa remarked, "your analysis is very helpful to me, and I appreciate your fine work. You must remember, though, that although your MS models provide me with valuable insights, they can't make my decisions for me."

SUMMARY

In this chapter, we investigated a descriptive technique called Markov chain models for analyzing discrete, dynamic processes that exhibit the Markov property. The two basic tools we used were the one-step transition matrix and the initial state vector.

We recognized that two different underlying processes must be dealt with. The recurring Markov chain model is applicable when there are no absorbing states, so that such a process converges over time to a steady state. The transient Markov chain model, on the other hand, is an appropriate analytical tool when transient and absorbing states are present.

Under the subject of advanced topics, we briefly discussed the time of first passage in recurring Markov chain models and introduced the notion of dynamic programming in Markov chains. Finally, the two cases involved a transient (or hybrid) model and a recurring one.

PROBLEMS

1.   *The Scenario:*   The tiny, English-speaking country of Foggy Bottom has a system of federal government quite unlike that of most Western nations. Although legislators are periodically elected by the people, the real power is in the hands of the career members of the federal service (FS), who cannot be fired.

One federal agency in Foggy Bottom is the Taxpayers' Assistance Group (TAG), whose mission is to assist citizens in dealing with the complicated "red tape" associated with almost every government transaction. Vera Ruud, Kurt Manners, and Chip Shoulders are career FS employees with the TAG and find their jobs to be boring and unpleasant.

The Problem: To relieve their boredom, Vera, Kurt, and Chip have devised a little game they call "run-around," which is played as follows. When Vera receives a phone call from a citizen for help, she flips two coins. If two heads occur, she tells the citizen to call Kurt in one hour, and if one head and one tail turn up, she has the citizen call Chip one hour hence. If the flip results in two tails, she asks the caller to call her back in an hour.

Kurt, on the other hand, used a standard deck of playing cards (no joker) shuffled and drawn at random. The draw of a club evokes instructions to call Vera one hour hence, and similarly a diamond for Chip, and a heart for himself. If a spade turns up, Kurt tells the citizen to go away, since TAG can't help.

Chip's "decision rule" is much simpler; if his digital clock is showing an *even* minute when a call comes, he tells the caller to call Vera in an hour, and an *odd* minute results in a call to Kurt.

The Model:

a. Is this silly process one that can be modeled as a Markov chain model? That is, does it exhibit the Markov property and stationarity?
b. If your answer to (a) is "yes," construct the one-step transition matrix for this model.
c. Is your model recurring or transient?

Solution to the Model:

a. Suppose, at the start of a daily round of the game, that each of the three players gets ten calls. How many calls will each player receive the second hour?
b. If you have access to a computer program like MCHAIN, how many citizens will have been "sent away" by Kurt after seven "transitions?"

Solution to the Problem: There is no solution to this problem. FS employees in the country of Foggy Bottom cannot be fired, and therefore, they do as they please. Aren't we fortunate in the Western world that we don't have to contend with such a distressing situation?

2.   **The Scenario:** Nevada-Twain Chilled Meat, Inc. (NCM), is a large processor and wholesale distributor of meat products to supermarkets and restaurant chains. Although demand for its products is fairly stable over the calendar year, unprocessed carcasses arrive at NCM's huge plant and storage facility in a "lumpy" fashion, peaking in late spring and late fall. Consequently, the company must maintain a cold storage capacity far above that necessary to supply normal demand.

The Problem: NCM purchases electric power about equally from municipally owned plants in Eastside and Westview, Nevada. R. Kipling Twain, the founder and CEO of the company, reasoned that depending on a single source of electric power could prove to be disastrous if a power failure occurred, since millions of pounds of frozen meat would be destroyed. Then, one warm day in June, both power companies failed simultaneously. They had linked their transmission systems a short time ago for their own protection, but their aging equipment couldn't carry the load. Although NCM bought virtually every cube of ice within a hundred-mile radius, the company still suffered a $200,000 spoilage loss.

Calling in Faron Hite, the cold storage supervisor, Mr. Twain laid it on the line. "Faron," he said, "I want to know how often we can expect simultaneous power outages from Eastside and Westview. I'm considering buying a backup power generation system of our own, but I don't want to do it if it costs more than the cost of our potential losses."

"I'll get right on it, Mr. Twain," replied Faron.

The Model: Faron, working with his engineers and MS/OR analyst, quickly discovered an interesting phenomenon. It appeared that the probable state of the linked power system on a given day depended only on the state of the system on the previous day. He and the analyst identified four specific states, as follows:

State	Condition
A	Both Eastside and Westview operating
B	Only Eastside operating
C	Only Westview operating
D	Neither Eastside nor Westview operating

Using engineering estimates, historical records, and intuition based upon experience, Faron and his team produced the following one-step transition matrix.

		To			
		A	B	C	D
(Both)	A	.90	.06	.03	.01
(Eastside)	B	.05	.80	.05	.10
(Westview)	C	.20	.05	.70	.05
(Neither)	D	.10	.50	.35	.05

From

In your opinion, does Faron's decision to use a Markov chain model make sense? Why or why not?

Solution to the Model:

a. Note that the one-step transition matrix models a recurring Markov process, since there are apparently no absorbing states. Use MCHAIN or another appropriate computer package to analyze this model. Specifically,
   (1) What is the steady-state probability that both power plants are down simultaneously?
   (2) Suppose that the two utility companies offered to modernize their facilities, so that the probabilities associated with A (*both* operating) changed to

$$p_{11} = .97; \quad p_{12} = .01; \quad p_{13} = .01; \quad p_{14} = .01$$

   Would such a change make a significant difference to NCM in assessing its plans?

b. If you were Mr. Twain, would you have any interest in knowing some short-term activity information rather than just the steady-state (long-term) results in (b)? Why or why not?

Solution to the Problem: The steady-state vectors associated with the original model, and with the revised model in (a2), are

Original model: $S' = (.501, \quad .301, \quad .153, \quad .045)$

Both   Eastside   Westview   Neither

Revised model: $S' = (.781, \quad .119, \quad .075, \quad .025)$

Mr. Twain studied the steady-state results intently. "Faron," he asked, "how good are the numbers you used to get these results?"

Hite was frank. "Boss, they're the best estimates that our engineers, our MS/OR analyst, and I could come up with. They are a mixture of scientific analysis, historical experience, and just plain judgment on the part of the team. I can't guarantee that they are accurate, but I'll stake my professional reputation—and my job, of course—that no group of people could come up with anything more reliable or well researched."

With a faint smile, R. Kipling Twain then said, "What course of action would you recommend, Faron?"

"If I were you, Mr. Twain—and of course I'm not—I'd take out disaster insurance for a year, to guard against unexpectedly high losses due to power failures, and I'd agree to the deal that the Eastside and Westview power companies have proposed. I think that a large capital expenditure for a private backup power generating system wouldn't be advisable for NCM right now—the interest rates are much too high. And besides, if we don't trust our suppliers of electric power that much, we should consider relocating the plant."

Faron stopped to take a breath, and concluded by saying, "I'm not trying to make your decisions for you, Mr. Twain, but you *did* ask."

"Yes, I did, Faron," replied Twain, "and I got the kind of answer I'd hoped for. My decision is to go with your recommendation with one exception. Instead of taking out insurance from an external source, I'll *personally* insure the company against the kind of disaster you spoke of, at no charge to the corporation."

"And, by the way," Mr. Twain continued, "I'm not getting any younger, and this outfit needs new blood and fresh ideas at the top. Would you want to take on that responsibility?"

After a short pause, Faron Hite (future CEO of Nevada-Twain Chilled Meat, Inc.) replied: "Kipling, it would be a cold day in hell when I'd turn down an offer like that!"

3. Consider the following one-step transition matrix with $n = 4$ states.

From \ *To*	A	B	C	D
A	.3	.4	.2	.1
B	.1	.3	.1	.5
C	.4	.2	.2	.2
D	.2	.1	.5	.2

Note that this one-step transition matrix has the curious property that its columns as well as its rows sum to 1. Such matrices are called *doubly stochastic.*

a. As you may easily verify, the steady-state vector for this process is $\mathbf{S} = (.25, .25, .25, .25)$. Is this a coincidence, or do all doubly stochastic recurrent Markov chain models have steady-state activity vectors of the form $\mathbf{S} = (1/n, 1/n, \ldots, 1/n)$?

b. Suppose that the matrix represented the one-step transition matrix for the following Markov process. A, B, C, and D represent hardened silos for the new Armageddon nuclear missile. The sites are far enough apart so that an incoming missile could destroy only one site. The sites are connected by six underground tunnels, and the Armageddon is moved daily according to the above one-step transition matrix, using a random number generator.

Is it clear that—in the long run—the four sites would actually contain the missile the same percentage of the time? Would the enemy benefit (in the long run) by obtaining possession of the one-step transition matrix?

c. Suppose the enemy knew the location of the missile on day 1, but could not launch an attack until day 4. Would having this information (in addition to knowing the one-step transition matrix) be of value to him?

d. Does intuition suggest that expected times of first passage to a given state from all other states are equal for a doubly stochastic one-step transition matrix?

Unfortunately, this is *not* the case. You might wish to verify this for yourself. For example, expected times of first passage to D from A, B, and C in the transition matrix are

$$\text{Expected times of first passage to site D from} \quad \begin{aligned} &\text{Site A} = 4 \\ &\text{Site B} = 2.446 \ (23/9) \\ &\text{Site C} = 3.889 \ (35/9) \end{aligned}$$

4. For each of the following scenarios, determine whether a Markov chain would accurately describe the process. For those scenarios that do appear to be amenable to this kind of analysis, determine whether the process appears to be *recurring* or *transient*; if transient, identify the transient and absorbing states.

Scenario A: The Environmental Protection Agency (EPA) sets standards for urban area air quality. Based on a rating scale from 1 (hazardous to human life) to 5 (less than 1 part per billion of pollutants), a city must prove that its controls limit the occurrence of type 1 to less than 1 chance in 1000, type 2 to less than 1 chance in 100, and type 3 to less than 1 chance in 10, over the long run. Cities have been required for several years to keep daily records of air quality. Cities not meeting the standard are judged ineligible for federal urban renewal funds.

Scenario B: Expo, Inc., has won the subcontract to produce computerized ignition systems for the Maori Motor Company. Expo's production layout is depicted by the flow diagram in Figure 10.2. In this diagram, the p_{ij} represent the proportions of objects that travel between the 11 "states" (departments or functions).

Scenario C: Linus Driver, the first baseman for the California Swingers baseball team, is a consistent .300 hitter (i.e., he gets a base hit, on average, 30% of the time he records an "at bat"). His hitting statistics exhibit a curious pattern; any time he gets two hits in a row, the second hit is always for at least one base more than the first—except, of course, when the first hit is a home run (four bases). Data on Linus's batting performance last season are as follows, in terms of relative frequencies of "at bats."

		Next "At Bat"			
	Out	Single	Double	Triple	Homer
Out	.70	.15	.10	.03	.02
Single	.70	—	.15	.10	.05
Double	.70	—	—	.20	.10
Triple	.70	—	—	—	.30
Homer	.70	—	—	—	.30

Previous "At Bat"

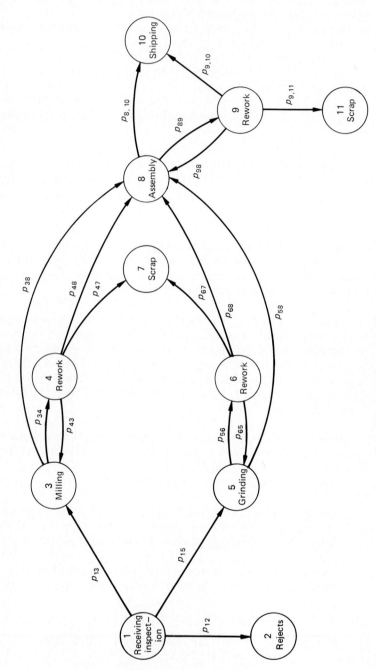

Figure 10.2 Flow diagram for Expo, Inc.

REFERENCE

1. WAGNER, H. *Principles of Operations Research,* 2nd ed. Englewood Cliffs, N.J.: Prentice-Hall, 1975.

ADDITIONAL READING

DERMAN, C. "On Sequential Decisions in Markov Chains." *Management Science,* Vol. 9 (1962), pp. 16–24.

KEMENY, J., and J. SNELL. *Finite Markov Chains.* New York: D. Van Nostrand, 1965.

CHAPTER 11

Project Scheduling and Inventory Management

Two of the more useful managerial planning and control devices that we can formulate as probabilistic models are the project evaluation and review technique (PERT) model and the inventory management (IM) model. As we will see, the two models are unrelated (for all practical purposes) and are discussed in the same chapter only because they probably do not warrant a separate chapter for each topic.

Deterministic versions of both models have been discussed previously in this book: the critical path method (a cousin of PERT) in Chapter 4, the examples of "continuous" inventory models (Chapter 1) and the Wilson EOQ model in Chapter 5. When we deal with these models under risk rather than under certainty, we move a step closer to managerial reality.

PROJECT SCHEDULING AND MANAGEMENT

The task of scheduling and managing complex projects is as old as time itself. Stone Age hunters stalking a fearful *Tyranosaurus rex,* with visions of barbecued ribs dancing in their heads, had to coordinate their efforts carefully or risk becoming snacks for the creature instead. As another example, the mind-boggling feat of the ancient Egyptians in constructing the pyramids with human labor most assuredly could not have been accomplished without some sort of project scheduling mechanism.

As the world became more complex, so did the projects that people devised. In the late 1950s, the massive task of building the Polaris nuclear ballistic missle — under the threat of impending war — evoked the invention of PERT, a probabilistic version of CPM. Although there is controversy about whether credit should be given to PERT, the fact is that the Polaris project was a resounding success.

Before discussing the PERT model in detail, let us carefully define the term *project* as we will use it in the following. A *project* is a collection of tasks that are related to each other over time, with a beginning and an end, whose purpose is to achieve a specific goal. Thus, building a skyscraper or a Greaseburger restaurant is a project. *Managing* the skyscraper or the restaurant once built, on the other hand, is not a project, but is an ongoing, repetitive operation. One might argue that construction companies complete one building and begin on the next—and therefore could be considered engaging in "ongoing, repetitive operations" as well. Such is not the case (at least for our purposes), since every construction project is different—perhaps markedly—from all others.

Let us now take a sprightly look at PERT.

UNDERLYING ASSUMPTIONS

Recall from Chapter 4, when we modeled projects as networks of activities, that we tacitly assumed that the times associated with completing each activity were known with certainty. To arrive at the network model, we first listed all mutually exclusive activities that had to be accomplished to complete the project. We then noted precedence relationships between and among the activities and modeled these relationships as arcs and nodes in a longest-route network model. To refresh our memory, we reproduce the Ray's Raze and Raise example from Chapter 4. The listing of activities associated with razing an old building in Philadelphia to build a 20-story fast-food restaurant, discotheque, and parking garage in its place are given in Table 11.1 and Figure 11.1 (Figure 4.3 from Chapter 4)—the associated network. As we saw, the "critical path" for this deterministic model was nodes $1-2-3-4-5-7-8-9-11-12$, and the time to completion was 70 days.

Table 11.1 RRR Activities

Activity	Description	Predecessor Activities	Most Likely Number of Days Required
A	Set TNT charges	—	5
B	Evacuate environs	—	4
C	Assemble dump-truck fleet	—	3
D	Detonate TNT	A, B	1
E	Clean up rubble	C, D	7
F	Excavate basement	E	12
G	Erect steel superstructure	E	15
H	Pour concrete foundation	F	10
I	Install electric/plumbing	F, G	8
J	Install flooring	I	15
K	Hang walls	I	20
L	Install elevators	I	7
M	Do finishing work	H, J, K, L	14

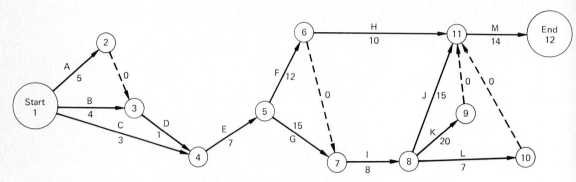

Figure 11.1   RRR macroproject network.

But how often can we actually know in advance what the completion time of a given activity will be? We can use average values based on past experience, of course (if we have done similar projects in the past), but this approach ignores the inherent riskiness associated with variable activity times. As an example, suppose in the RRR illustration that the company had completed ten similar projects in the past and that activity H (pour concrete foundation) had taken the following numbers of days: 5, 15, 5, 15, 5, 15, 5, 15, 5, and 15. The average completion time is 10 days, all right, but how comfortable would we be using that estimate? What we need is a way to incorporate risk in an explicit way.

The Beta Distribution

The beta distribution is a probability density function with some very interesting properties (for a mathematical description, see any standard statistics text such as Mood and Graybill [1]). First, unlike the normal distribution, it has finite endpoints, say, t_0 and t_p, so that if $f(t)$ is a beta distribution, then $f(t_0) = 0$ and $f(t_p) = 0$, and $t_0 \leq t \leq t_p$.

Second, the beta has two parameters, so that the *mode* can be made to occur at any value $t = t_m$; also, the choice of parameters can make the distribution as "narrow" or as "broad" as we wish. These features make the beta distribution especially useful in representing probabilistic activity times. Two "families" of beta distributions are depicted in Figure 11.2, left and right.

Approximation to the Beta Distribution

Suppose that each activity time in a project is distributed as a beta and suppose that we could estimate three times:

1. The most *optimistic* completion time
2. The most *likely* completion time
3. The most *pessimistic* completion time

If our assumption is approximately correct, and if our three estimates are accurate, then we can relate the two as follows:

1. The minimum possible value of $t = t_0 =$ the most optimistic completion time.

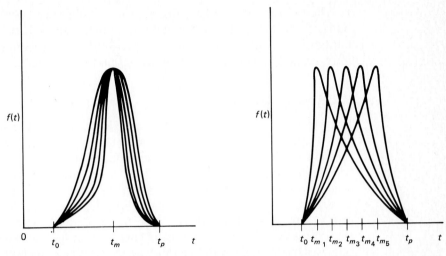

Figure 11.2 (Left) Family of beta's with identical modes and different "spread." (Right) Family of beta's with identical "spreads" and different modes.

2. The modal value of $t = t_m$ = the most likely completion time.
3. The maximum possible value of $t = t_p$ = the most pessimistic completion time.

Thus, we can fix the endpoints and the mode of our beta distribution for each activity. In theory, we could go one step farther and attempt to estimate the "spread" of each beta — perhaps by quantifying our level of confidence that the "most likely" time t_m will actually occur. In this way, we could formulate the exact mathematical form of each beta.

In practice, however, PERT uses an *approximation* to each beta distribution, in which the mean m and standard deviation s are calculated as follows:

$$m = \frac{t_0 + 4t_m + t_p}{6} \tag{11.1}$$

$$s = \frac{t_p - t_0}{6} \tag{11.2}$$

In (11.1), we see that the mode (most likely activity time) is weighted four times more heavily than is the minimum value (most optimistic activity time) and the maximum value (most pessimistic activity time), respectively. We should note here that we could, if we wished, calculate the mean as follows:

$$m = \frac{t_0 + kt_m + t_p}{k + 2} \tag{11.3}$$

where $k \geq 0$ is a number that expresses our relative confidence in the value of t_m. As it happens, the choice of $k = 4$ is "optimal" in the sense that it minimizes the worst possible error in estimation.

The rationale for (11.2) is that many "well-behaved" probability density functions have most of their probability content within three standard deviations on either side of the mean. In other words, (11.2) assumes that our beta distribution spans six standard deviations between t_0 and t_p.

MODELING WITH PERT

In a *mechanical* sense, modeling with PERT is simple and straightforward. After the mean values m_i have been calculated, as in (11.1), for the n activities, they are inserted in place of the deterministic values of activity completion times in the CPM model. With PERT, however, the project completion time is a *random variable,* since each of the activity times on the critical path is the *expected value* of a beta distribution on that activity. Thus, the CPM value of project completion time becomes the expected value of project completion time using PERT. We are interested, therefore, in the distribution of the random variable T, project completion time, so that we may assess the probabilities of project *underrun* (completing the project early) and project *overrun* (completing the project late). Anyone familiar with contracts that carry performance bonuses for early completion, and penalties for late completion, is already aware of the critical importance of this information.

As we might surmise, the joint probability density function of the sum of n beta-distributed random variables (the critical path) is an extremely complex and mathematically indeterminate form. However, recalling the elegant and remarkable *central limit theorem* from our elementary course in statistics, we observe that the sum of a number of random variables is a random variable that is approximately normally distributed (increasingly so as the number of random variables increases).

As we will see in the next section, finding the "solution" to a PERT model is a simple task. However, the crucial issue is whether the model accurately represents the actual scheduling problem. Let us turn to our computer software friend RIKLS (*real-time interactive kinetic linear scheduler*) to illustrate how the modeling process might go. In our vignette that follows, Ray (of Ray's Raze and Raise, Inc.) is attempting to model his problem with the building in Philadelphia, as a stochastic scheduling model. RIKLS is unusually "user-friendly," but only in the computer programming sense.

RIKLS: Hello, Ray. Stop drooling and tell me what you want.

RAY: Well, RIKLS, I've got a problem . . .

RIKLS: You're telling me? Where did you get that suit—did you mug a wino? Look, yoyo, do you need to schedule a project or what?

RAY: Yes. I've got a contract to raze a 200-year-old art museum in Philadelphia and build a 20-story fast-food restaurant, discotheque, and parking garage in its place.

RIKLS: Wonderful. What's your next project—to tear down an orphan's home and put up a topless shoeshine parlor? What a hamhock you are. OK. Have you done this kind of thing before, or do I have to draw you pictures?

RAY: I've been in the construction business for 20 years, RIKLS. Here—I've broken this project down into 13 mutually exclusive activities, which I've labeled A through M. I'll feed you these data, to include precedence relations among the activities and most likely activity completion times. (Ray enters the table reproduced earlier in this chapter.)

RIKLS: Swell. It took you long enough. Where did you learn to type — the Hunt N. Peck Institute for the Mentally Retarded? Never mind, let's get on with it. Let's start with activity A (set TNT charges). You say the most likely time is five days. If a miracle occurred and you didn't foul anything up, what's the most optimistic estimate for setting the TNT charges?

RAY: Well, let's see . . .

RIKLS: Come on, I haven't got all day. This is like trying to hold a conversation with a herring.

RAY: Three days.

RIKLS: Your mother would be proud of you, Ray. Now, what if everything went wrong, like with Murphy's law? What's the worst possible time it would take to set the boom-boom?

RAY: Thirteen days, but . . .

RIKLS: But nothing, turnip-nose. Thirteen days it is. Do I have to lead you with a leash, or can you manage to give me the most optimistic and most pessimistic times for the other 12 activities? Watch my lips — are you still awake?

RAY: (Enters the data requested.)

RIKLS: OK. I'm going to show you a table (Table 11.2) with the stuff you gave me. There will be two additional columns, one labeled "Expected Time" and the other labeled "Standard Deviation." I used the formulas in (11.1) and (11.2) to compute these numbers. If you don't know what they mean, have your mother read the first part of this chapter to you. Here's the table — but don't touch the screen and get grease all over it.

There it is, kumquat. Stamp your foot twice if you've got it. Good boy — here's a carrot. Go away and read the rest of the chapter, and I'll see you in Problem 1. And give my best to the gang down at the Mortimer Snerd Home for the Terminally Dumb.

Table 11.2   RRR Activity Analysis (time in days)

Activity	t_o	t_m	t_p	Expected Time (m_i)	Standard Deviation (s_i)
A	3	5	13	6	10/6
B	2	4	12	5	10/6
C	2	3	4	3	2/6
D	1	1	7	2	1
E	6	7	8	7	2/6
F	10	12	32	15	22/6
G	2	15	16	13	14/6
H	4	10	16	10	2
I	1	8	9	7	8/6
J	3	15	21	14	3
K	18	20	34	22	16/6
L	5	7	9	7	4/6
M	5	14	17	13	2

RAY: Thanks, RIKLS. But I must say, the person who programmed you must have spent too much time in Las Vegas.

This exchange illustrates the *mechanical* process of deriving the expected activity times (m_i) and standard deviations (s_i), but it glosses over (because, perhaps, of the somewhat aggressive tone of RIKLS) the *process* by which the optimistic and pessimistic activity times are derived. For example, activity F (excavate basement) is highly skewed, with $t_0 = 10$, $t_m = 12$, and $t_p = 32$. The relatively large value of t_p could conceivably result from finding a rock formation on the site, or perhaps from the possibility of heavy rains that would halt excavation activity for two weeks or more. The point is that PERT analysis is only as good as the accuracy of these activity time estimates.

SOLUTION TECHNIQUE: AN INTUITIVE DESCRIPTION

Once the expected activity times have been computed, the *critical path*—the set of consecutive activities that determines project completion time—is computed using a "longest route through a network" algorithm (Chapter 4) or a specially constructed technique for PERT analysis that solves the model algebraically. Without going into the mathematical details, special PERT algorithms use a "two-pass" procedure that determines the *earliest* time (t_E) that the activity can start and the *latest* time (t_L) that each activity can be started without delaying completion time of the project. Obviously, activities for which $t_E = t_L$ are on the critical path. Finding the critical path with a longest-route network algorithm produces the same critical path, of course, but—as we will see shortly—special PERT algorithms yield much more in the way of information for sensitivity analysis.

The expected project completion time (T_e) is computed as follows:

$$T_e = \sum_{j \text{ on critical path}} m_j \qquad (11.4)$$

T is a random variable, which is expressed as the sum of beta-distributed random variables. As we noted earlier, due to the central limit theorem, T is approximately normally distributed with a mean as in (11.4) and variance as follows:

$$S_e^2 = \sum_{j \text{ on critical path}} S_j^2 \qquad (11.5)$$

To obtain the standard deviation of completion time (S_e), we take the square root of the expression in (11.5).

We can now express project completion time as a probabilistic event. For example, suppose that our target date for completion (TD) is 90 days hence and that we have computed $T_e = 85$ days and $S_e = 5$ days. Since our expected completion time is 1 standard deviation below TD, we would compute our probability of meeting the *TD* (or completing earlier) at about .84 (see the standardized normal distribution table in the appendix).

SENSITIVITY ANALYSIS

Rather than forcing poor Ray to interact again with the acerbic RIKLS, let us short-circuit that session and pursue the RRR model here. Figure 11.3 is the PERT network representation of the model, with the activity arcs labeled with expected activity times. Table 11.3 is the output from a specialized PERT computer software package. (*Note:* Recall from Chapter 4 that the arcs depicted by dashed lines are so-called "dummy activities" with zero activity time, which are needed to impose activity precedences.)

Note from Table 11.3 that our critical path consists of activities A, D, E, F, I, K, M; or stated another way, the critical path through the network in Figure 11.3 can be traced through the nodes numbered: 1–2–3–4–5–6–7–8–9–11–12.

Our program automatically did a sensitivity analysis on target dates (*TD*'s) for completion, and we see that there is about a 10% chance of completing the RRR project in 65 days or less, while Ray is almost certain to complete the project in 85 days.

The analysis of slack time for the noncritical activities is of keen managerial interest. In our example, it so happens that all slack times are of the "free slack" variety, which means that none of the noncritical activities interact with each other. An example of *dependent slack* is illustrated in Figure 11.4.

Note in Figure 11.4 that activity A is on the critical path, whereas activities B and C are not. Activity B could be started as late as day 3, which would force activity C to start on day 7. On the other hand, activity C could be begun as early as day 4, forcing activity B to start at time zero. Thus, activities B and C *share* three days of slack, in a sense.

Our computer program has also highlighted possible trouble spots for Ray — a "user-friendly" feature indeed! Note that noncritical activity B has only one day of slack and has a standard deviation of 1.667. Thus, if activity time for B exceeds its mean value by .6 standard deviations (about 28% of the time), then

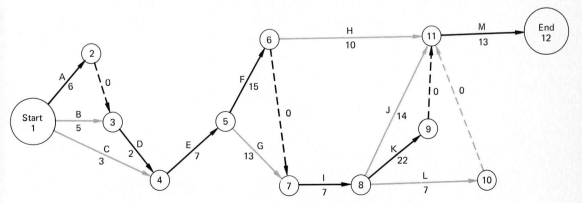

Figure 11.3 PERT network for RRR model.

Table 11.3   Analysis of RRR PERT Model

1. Critical activities are A, D, E, F, I, K, M.
2. Expected time of project completion is 72 days.
3. Standard deviation of project completion time is 5.50 days.
4. Target dates (probability of early or on-time completion) are:

Days	Probability	Days	Probability
65	.102	75	.707
70	.358	80	.927
72	.500	85	.991

5. Analysis of slack time available:

Noncritical Activities	Earliest Start	Latest Start	Slack Time
B	0	1	1 day free slack
C	0	5	5 days free slack
G	15	17	2 days free slack
H	30	49	19 days free slack
J	37	45	8 days free slack
L	37	52	15 days free slack

Possible trouble spots:
Activity B: $m = 6$; $s = 1.667$;   slack = 1 day
Activity G: $m = 13$; $s = 2.333$;   slack = 2 days
Critical activity F: $s = 3.667$

B becomes part of the critical path instead of A, increasing the expected project completion time. A similar problem exists with activity G, which would replace activity F on the critical path if it exceeded its mean completion time by more than two days.

The problem with critical activity F is its very high variance. Since F is critical, any "overrun" in its mean activity time of 15 days means an identical lengthening of expected project completion time.

PERT/COST

The PERT modeling and analysis we have discussed so far is purely descriptive. That is, our project manager has a good picture of the "bottlenecks" in his or her scheduling problem and understands which activities will need close attention.

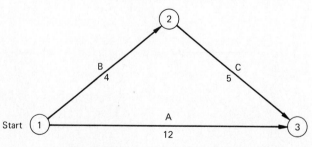

Figure 11.4   Dependent slack.

He can also set up an actual schedule of activity start times, adjusting the noncritical activities' schedules to conform to availability of labor and materials, the schedules of subcontractors, and so on.

But given that some activities may require similar resources, the manager also has the option of "slowing down" noncritical activities by devoting fewer resources to them and "speeding up" critical activities by adding resources. In the RRR model, for instance, activity J (install flooring) has free slack of 8 days, whereas activity K (hang walls) is on the critical path. If the labor required for each is interchangeable, it might be possible to shorten activity K by 4 days by "stretching out" activity J from 14 to 18 days. If so, we will have shorted expected project completion time from 72 to 68 days. Note, however, that in making the transfer of resources, we have in effect made activity J critical, and this activity has a relatively high standard deviation of 3 days.

Some texts in MS/OR present a formal PERT/COST model in which the effects of adding additional resources to the project are evaluated and compared with the economic benefits derived from earlier project completion. We will not explicitly deal with such models here, since they basically do nothing more than formalize a common sense cost-benefit analysis.

PROJECT MANAGEMENT WITH PERT

In the introduction to this chapter, we intimated that PERT modeling and analysis is a project scheduling and *management* tool—and so it is. Once work has started on the project, the PERT model is constantly updated with *actual* completion times, and the PERT analysis is rerun frequently. The project manager "juggles" his resources and activity start times on an almost daily basis, as necessary, to keep the project on track. As time goes by, then, the risk (as represented by the variance of project completion time) decreases monotonically until the project is finally completed. Thus, PERT is a "cradle-to-grave" technique for project planning and management.

Critics of PERT (and there are many) point out that the technique is inherently biased toward overly optimistic estimation of project completion time—and technically, they are correct (for theoretical mathematical reasons that we won't go into here). In a practical managerial sense, however, PERT is an invaluable technique—a fact that has been demonstrated tens of thousands of times in the "real world." For example, all major contracts issued by the Department of Defense have for many years *required* the use of PERT by defense contractors, and while DOD policies are by no means infallible, neither, as a rule, are they foolish.

ADVANCED CONCEPTS IN PROJECT SCHEDULING AND MANAGEMENT

PERT, as we have seen it, is basically a simple, highly effective tool that allows a project manager to organize and manage his or her "baby" from planned parenthood to delivery. However, to paraphrase George Orwell in *Animal Farm*, "all projects are equal, but some projects are more equal than others" [2].

GERT AND Q-GERT

What we mean by the cryptic reference above is that some projects—usually involving sophisticated research and development efforts—include *activities that are themselves probabilistic.* For example, consider a multiyear project to analyze the efficacy of solar power as an alternative to petroleum-based energy generation. At the outset it is not known whether large parabolic-dish solar collectors are more cost-effective than are so-called "passive" collector panels. The activity "Build solar collection devices" will therefore be dependent upon the results of earlier research activities and cannot be known with certainty in the planning stages. To deal with this problem of "either-or" or probabilistic activities, A. Alan B. Pritsker and his associates developed an advanced form of PERT called GERT (Graphical Evaluation and Review Technique) [3]. The latest version of this analytical tool is named Q-GERT [4] and includes a sophisticated simulation capability along with the basic GERT methodology.

PERT SIMULATION

In a large project involving many thousands of individual activities, there may be hundreds of "critical paths" that differ in project completion times by insignificant amounts of time, relatively speaking. Another way of describing this phenomenon is by noting that many noncritical activities, as classified by PERT, are "almost critical" when alternate paths are considered. Technically, one could use the technique introduced by Lawler [5] to find the "k longest routes" through the PERT network; however, considerable computer computation time would be involved, and analyzing the results would be tedious.

An alternative approach used with some success in the past on large projects is referred to as PERT-Simulation. Since each activity time is a random variable with mean m and standard deviation s, as computed in (11.1) and (11.2), respectively, we can use the discrete simulation approach discussed in Chapter 9 to generate random completion times for the activities and to compute the critical path for each simulation run. After thousands of such runs, we have several useful items of information: the *empirical* probability distribution of project completion time (T_e) and the frequency with which each activity appeared on the critical path in the simulation runs. Thus we are able to assess the *degree of criticality* for each activity rather than having to rely on the binary judgments *critical* and *noncritical* provided by standard PERT analysis.

One difficulty with PERT-Simulation is that, while standard PERT does not require us to explicitly derive the mathematical form of the probability distribution functions of activity times, the simulation approach does. One approach that has been taken is to approximate the beta distributions assumed by standard PERT, with triangular distributions as illustrated in Figure 11.5. The difficulty with this approach is that the triangular distribution is actually a "worst case" approximation to the beta distribution in that its variance is larger than that of the family of betas with the same endpoints and mode. We, therefore, get conservative estimates when we approximate beta distributions with triangular ones.

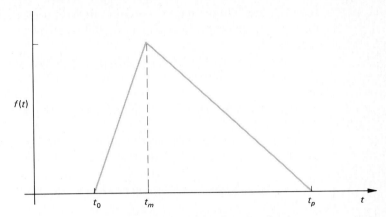

Figure 11.5 The triangular distribution.

The triangular distribution has a closed-form inverse distribution function, as follows:

$$
t_i = \begin{cases}
t_0 + \sqrt{(t_m - t_0) \cdot (t_p - t_0) \cdot R_i}, & \text{for } R_i \leq \dfrac{(t_m - t_0)}{(t_p - t_0)} \\[2ex]
t_p - \sqrt{(t_p - t_0) \cdot (t_p - t_m) \cdot (1 - R_i)}, & \text{for } R_i > \dfrac{(t_m - t_0)}{(t_p - t_0)}
\end{cases}
\tag{11.6}
$$

where the R_i are random numbers from a uniform distribution on [0, 1].

SOME CAVEATS

As we previously noted, PERT has been used with some success for many years to schedule and manage large projects. But there are problems involved in the application of this technique of which present and prospective managers should be aware. Oddly enough, these problems tend to be behavioral rather than technical in nature.

The first problem involves the estimation of completion times for the individual activities. If we are about to undertake an unusual project, of a type with which we have little or no experience, then how do we as managers go about estimating activity times? The natural inclination would be to rely upon the experience and judgment of first-line supervisors — our construction foreman or shop supervisor or department head. But, at the risk of offending these critically important middle managers, beware of activity times obtained in this way. What you *need* is accurate estimates of optimistic, most likely, and pessimistic activity times. What you will *get* more often than not from people responsible operationally for completing the activities, is (1) a somewhat less than optimistic time, (2) a "comfortable" time, and (3) a somewhat less than pessimistic time. The net effect in the ensuing PERT analysis is an overstatement of the mean (m) and an understatement of the variance (s) for each activity time. The manager, therefore, finds himself or herself planning and managing a project that is shorter and riskier than the model he or she is using to represent it.

One solution to this problem is to obtain outside estimates — assessments by technically qualified people with no personal stake in the conduct of the project. Another solution is to use the internally generated estimates anyway but to keep the probable bias in PERT results in mind when making resource decisions.

The second problem occurs during the conduct of the project and has been described by the satirist C. Northcote Parkinson, as follows [6]:

> **Parkinson's law:** Work expands to fill the time available for its completion.

When we approximate the random variables "activity times" with beta distributions, we expect some activities to be completed earlier, and some later, than the "most likely" completion time. If the supervisor responsible for a given activity *knows* the "most likely" time you are using for his activity, and if there is no incentive for him to complete the activity earlier, then in most cases you may be sure that the "optimistic" and "most likely" times will coincide in practice. On the other hand, if there are powerful incentives to complete activities early, then we had better have an exceptionally good quality control system to assure that they are done "by the book."

The other side of the story is that, many times, events over which an activity supervisor has no control can cause the activity to take longer than the "most likely" time, so that even strong disincentives for late completion cannot have the desired effect. The upshot, then, is that many projects are doomed to overrun by the effects of Parkinson's law.

The solution to this problem lies in the theories of human and organizational behavior, into which much research has been done over the course of the twentieth century. We obviously won't attempt to treat this subject here, except that these problems provide an ideal excuse to repeat the theme of this book.

Models don't make decisions — Managers do.

Audit Trail [7]

The Scenario: In addition to assisting with taxes, information systems, and other problems, public accounting firms perform annual audits for their clients. Auditing a large corporation or public sector organization is a highly complex undertaking. Since a great deal of expensive CPA time is required, and since the accounting firm assumes *legal* liability for the accuracy and appropriateness of its audit findings, each audit must be carefully planned and meticulously executed. Moreover, since the audit team is actually on site in the client company for a matter of weeks during the audit, interference in the company's ongoing operations must be minimized.

The Problem: Auditing a large company involves a number of distinct activities — from planning the audit through the final review with company executives by the accounting firm's partner-in-charge of the audit. Table 11.4 is an example set of activities taken from the American Institute for CPAs monograph authored by Jack Krogstad, Gary Grudnitski, and David Bryant, entitled "PERT and PERT/Cost for Audit Planning and Control" [7]. The "most likely times" in Table 11.4 are taken from this monograph, and the "optimistic" and "pessimistic" times were added for the purposes of this case.

Note from the column labeled "Predecessor Activities" that there are complex relationships between and among the 19 activities. We should also note the wide range of "activity duration times" — from 1 hour for activities M, N, and P to 145 hours for activity E.

The problem faced by the public accounting firm is to plan the audit engagement carefully, with several objectives in mind: to minimize disruption of the client company's operations, to maximize the effectiveness of the highly paid CPAs engaged in the audit, and to complete the audit — carefully and accurately — on or before the target date.

The Model: With one interesting exception, the situation just described is a classical example of a project and can be profitably analyzed using a PERT model. The exception is that the "activity duration times" from Table 11.4 are actually *planned* entities; that is, more than one CPA can be assigned to a given activity to shorten the time. For example, the illustration provided in [7] involves a total of 779 budgeted "billing hours," but the "most likely" activity times total only 479. We will return to this subject later in the case.

Figure 11.6 is the PERT diagram that represents the activities and their relationships from Table 11.4. We note that dummy activities had to be used to represent precedence relationships among L, M, and N and among Q, R, and S. Activity times are the PERT estimates calculated as in (11.1).

Solution to the Model: A quick glance at Figure 11.6 is all that is necessary to find the critical path for this PERT model. Activity E (145 days)

Table 11.4　Audit Activities

Activity	Predecessor Activities	Activity Duration Times (hours)		
		Optimistic	Likely	Pessimistic
A. Audit planning	—	44	48	52
B. Observe inventory	A	16	25	30
C. General audit procedures	B	6	11	13
D. Audit cash	B	18	19	30
E. Inventory pricing	B	90	145	150
F. Audit receivables	D	6	10	14
G. Audit other current assets	C	9	11	16
H. Audit liabilities	E	50	93	100
I.　Audit sales	F	5	6	7
J. Audit cost of goods sold	E	10	25	30
K. Audit other revenues and expenses	I, J	6	10	12
L.　Audit fixed assets	G	20	22	24
M. Audit capital stock and real estate	K	1	1	1
N. Management's letter	L, M	1	1	1
O. Subsequent review	L, M	16	18	20
P. Lawyer's letter	H	1	1	1
Q. Prepare financial statements	N, O, P	12	15	24
R. Prepare tax returns	N, O, P	8	12	30
S. Partner/manager review	Q, R	5	6	7

is a direct predecessor of activity H (93 days), and it is obvious that these two activities are "driving" this problem. Thus the critical path is through nodes 1–2–3–6–11–14–16–17 and includes activities A, B, E, H, P, Q, S. The entire group of activities in the middle and top of Figure 11.6 does not play a significant role in determining project completion time.

Table 11.5 contains a formal analysis of this model.

Solution to the Problem:　As we can note in Table 11.5, the expected audit completion time is about eight weeks. Since only 7 of the 19 activities are on the critical path, and since only activity R (prepare tax returns) has reasonable potential for affecting completion time as a noncritical activity, it appears that there is potential for "stretching out" 1 or more of the 11 remaining noncritical activities to reduce audit completion time. As is often the case, however, other considerations dominate this problem.

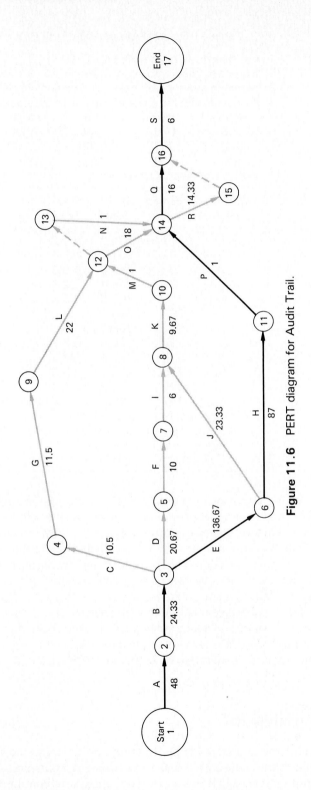

Figure 11.6 PERT diagram for Audit Trail.

Table 11.5 Analysis of Audit Trail PERT Model

1. Critical activities are A, B, E, H, P, Q, S.
2. Expected time of project completion is 319 hours.
3. Standard deviation of project completion time is 13.4 hours.
4. Target times (probability of early or on-time completion) are:

Hours	Probability	Hours	Probability
300	.078	330	.794
310	.251	340	.941
320	.528	350	.991

5. Analysis of slack time available:

Noncritical Activities	Earliest Start	Latest Start	Slack Time
C	72.3	234.9	162.6
D	72.3	231.7	159.4
F	93.00	252.3	159.3
G	82.8	245.4	162.6
I	103	262.3	159.3
J	209	245	36 (13.3 free slack)
K	232.3	268.3	36
L	94.3	256.9	162.6
M	242	277.9	35.9
N	243	295.9	52.9
O	243	278.9	35.9
R	297	298.6	1.6 (1.6 free slack)

Possible trouble spots:
Activity R: $m = 14.3$; $s = 3.67$; slack $= 1.6$ hours
Critical activity E: $s = 10$ hours
Critical activity H: $s = 8.3$ hours

In the case of an audit engagement, the length of time from beginning to end is of secondary importance — as long as the target date for completion is met. Regardless of the total time taken, an audit still involves approximately the same number of *CPA-hours* devoted to the task. Thus, the time to complete an audit can be shortened by intensifying the degree of engagement — at the risk of seriously hampering the day-to-day operations of the firm being audited — or "stretched out," thereby mitigating this impact. This decision is unique with each audit — which is one reason why the partners in public accounting firms, who make such decisions, are so well paid! The PERT analysis in this case is useful only to the extent that it identifies the "bottlenecks" in the audit scheduling problem.

INVENTORY MANAGEMENT

One of the earliest attempts to apply the scientific method to problems of business and industry was in the area of inventory management — and research begun 70 years ago into this aspect of operations continues to this day. There have been dozens of books (some very large) written on this subject, and both professional and scholarly journals have published untold thousands of articles about it.

Why has so much attention been paid to a subject that sounds so mundane on the surface? We have only to glance at the annual reports of a few manufacturing or distributing companies to answer this question for ourselves—the value of on-hand inventory often approaches 30% of the overall value of the firm! Poor inventory management has been the single most critical factor in the failure of tens of thousands of business entities—for one of the following two reasons:

1. Excessive inventory represents capital tied up in illiquid, non-income-producing assets.
2. Inadequate inventory represents lost sales or production stoppages.

Logic tells us that when *too much* and *not enough* are both undesirable, then somewhere in between must exist *about right.* Helping managers make such decisions is the goal of inventory modeling and analysis.

TYPES OF INVENTORIES

Wholesalers stock inventories of finished goods to fill orders from retailers—who themselves stock inventories to meet customer demand. This type of inventory is called *finished goods* inventory. *Raw materials* inventory, on the other hand, consists of the basic materials or subunits that will be used in the manufacture or assembly of an end product. Finally, *in-process* inventory includes those assets that are currently undergoing transformation into end products (e.g., the formed chassis of a new automobile proceeding down the assembly line).

In what follows, we will limit our discussion to inventories of the first two types: finished goods and raw materials. The management of in-process inventories is almost a science unto itself and is treated extensively in texts on production/operations management.

TYPES OF INVENTORY MODELS

Structurally, inventory models are similar to the queueing models we investigated in Chapter 8. That is, an inventory system has a number of attributes (which we will discuss subsequently), so that by making different assumptions about each attribute, we get different models. Theoretically, then, there are literally *millions* of different mathematical inventory models that will keep academic researchers filling the pages of scholarly journals for an eternity.

The classical textbook approach to the subject of inventory management is to derive the simple Wilson EOQ model that we used as an illustration in Chapter 5. This model is then extended in two or three ways (perhaps to incorporate price breaks or backordering or constraints on space or funds), and some more intrepid authors finally venture a step or two into modeling with probabilistic demand and/or lead time.

The fact, however, is that the most realistic — and therefore the most useful — approach to analysis of inventory policy is through modeling with discrete simulation (Chapter 9). In what follows, we will adopt this approach.

UNDERLYING ASSUMPTIONS

In this section, we *define* the important attributes of inventory systems and state the underlying *assumptions* we will make about them, as we go.

Demand

The demand d_i for product i is the amount or quantity of the product required over a stated period of time. We will assume only that we know (or can estimate) the probability distribution of d_i over this period and that this distribution is stationary (doesn't change) for the period. For example, the demand over the next six months for personal computers by customers of our Hacker Electronics retail outlet may be approximately normally distributed, with a mean of 1200 and a standard deviation of 100.

Order Quantity

Our order quantity q_i for product i is the amount or quantity we order *each time we order* in the time period in which our demand occurs. In our Hacker example, it would probably be foolish (or impractical) to order all d_i units at once — we probably wouldn't have a place to store them and we undoubtedly wouldn't have the available cash to pay for them. At the other end of the spectrum, we could order every day (and lose our Hacker franchise after about a week of that foolishness!). Obviously, there is some recurring order quantity between the two extremes that is "optimal" in a sense. Our only assumption about q_i is that it remains constant over the demand period. If this assumption appears to be unrealistic, it most certainly is — except that we will use a *rolling demand period* in our simulation model, which mitigates this problem.

Lead Time

The lead time t_i for product i is the time that expires between placement of the order and receipt of the goods ordered. Here, our assumption is that we can approximate the probability distribution of this random variable and that this distribution does not change over the demand period.

Procurement Costs

We denote the per unit price of product i as p_i, which can either be a "flat price" (take it or leave it) or a price discount structure. We will allow for two discount patterns — "all-units" and "incremental" — that are discussed in the paragraphs that follow. Our assumption is that whatever the form of p_i, it is constant over the demand period.

All-Units Price Discounts: Mathematically, an "all-units" price discount can be stated as follows:

$$p_i = \begin{cases} p_i^1, & \text{if } 0 \le q_i < q_i^1 \\ p_i^2, & \text{if } q_i^1 \le q_i \le q_i^2 \\ \text{etc.} \end{cases} \tag{11.7}$$

In (11.7), every unit of q_i ordered costs p_i^1 if q_i is less than the first price-break quantity q_i^1. On the other hand, if q_i lies between the price-break quantities q_i^1 and q_i^2 (or equals q_i^1), *every* unit ordered costs p_i^2, which is less than p_i^1, and so forth. This type of price-break structure is most often used when a setup is required by the supplier each time he manufactures the product, so that he can pass on part of the savings on larger orders (fewer setups) to the customer. It is not uncommon in practice for there to be four or five price-break quantities involving successive price discounts.

Incremental Price Discounts: The mathematical expression for "incremental" price discounts is as follows.

$$p_i = \begin{cases} p_i^1, & \text{if } 0 \le q_i < q_i^1 \\ (p_i^1 \cdot q_i^1) + [p_i^2 \cdot (q_i - q_i^1)], & \text{if } q_i^1 \le q_i < q_i^2 \\ (p_i^1 \cdot q_i^1) + (p_i^2 \cdot q_i^2) + [p_i^3 \cdot (q_i - q_i^2)], & \text{if } q_i^2 \le q_i < q_i^3 \\ \text{etc.} \end{cases} \tag{11.8}$$

We see that each of the prices p_i^1, p_i^2, and so on applies only to the number of units that fall into its price-break interval. As q_i gets larger and encompasses more of these intervals, the *average price* steadily declines. This type of price discount structure is the most widely used in practice, and its use is motivated for a variety of reasons. For example, if we ordered only a half-train carload of personal computers, we would probably have to pay freight for use of the entire car; whereas if we ordered a full carload, we would cut the per unit freight charge in half.

We might note here that the price discount structure is based on the *producer's* production policy, not on the *purchaser's* needs. Although we will not go into the mathematical details here, it has been shown that an optimal order quantity under the "all-units" price discount structure will always fall either between one and only one set of consecutive break points, or *at* one of the price-break quantities, making such an approach somewhat inflexible from the point of view of the purchaser. The "incremental" structure does not exhibit this pattern.

Operating Costs

Operating costs are of three basic types: holding costs, ordering costs, and out-of-stock costs. We address each in the paragraphs that follow. Our assumption is that all costs are known with certainty over the demand period.

Holding Costs: Costs of holding inventory are the direct and indirect costs of having goods on hand. Included are such things as warehouse handling, insurance, taxes, utilities, obsolescence/spoilage, and foregone return on capital invested in inventory. "Getting a handle" on holding costs is no simple matter, since some costs are relatively fixed (warehousing, utilities) and others depend at least in part on the monetary value of the items in inventory (insurance, taxes, obsolescence/spoilage, return on capital). The most common approach is to express h_i, the per unit cost of holding item i, as a fraction of the value of item i over the demand period. For example, if $h_i = .20$ and $p_i = \$50$, the holding cost would be $\$10$ if the item were in inventory for the entire demand period.

Ordering Costs: The cost of ordering inventory is merely the sum of costs associated with bid solicitation, processing paperwork, shipping and receiving, and so on. This cost is expressed as c_i: the cost *per order.*

Out-of-Stock Costs: Most textbooks discuss out-of-stock costs in two different ways: the cost of backordering and the cost of stockout (when backordering is not possible). Practitioners find it difficult or impossible to derive defensible dollar estimates for such costs. Backordering, for example, does involve some clerical expense, but the real question to be addressed is, "What impact does failure to fill a customer's order, upon demand, have on our goodwill?" The same, of course, is true of stockouts, but we have a probable lost sale in this case.

The reason that knowing out-of-stock costs is important in a modeling sense is that it allows us to optimize the level of *safety stock*—a quantity of inventory above that we would normally carry—to "cushion" us against out-of-stock situations. Rather than trying to "quantify the unquantifiable," we will treat safety stock level as a *managerial decision.* We will say more about this later.

MODELING AN INVENTORY SYSTEM

In this section, we will build a simple but effective mathematical model of a finished goods or raw materials inventory system that deals with n distinct products or entities. Our objective will be to minimize the total cost associated with operating the system. Symbolically, then, our objective function is

MINIMIZE x_0 = procurement costs + holding costs + ordering costs   (11.9)

SUBJECT TO: Constraints on warehouse space, funds, etc.   (11.10)

We will use a demand period of *one year* in our model-building exercise, although any time period may be used. Thus, d_i will be "annual demand in units for product i," and the other attributes (or parameters) will be described analogously. Let us now address the three distinct cost elements in (11.9), one at a time.

Procurement Costs
The actual procurement costs per year for our n items is

$$\text{Procurement costs} = \sum_{i=1}^{n} p_i \cdot d_i \qquad (11.11)$$

where the p_i may or may not involve a price discount structure.

Holding Costs

Costs associated with holding our n inventory items involves computing the *average* inventory value of each item over the year and applying our holding cost fraction h_i to each item. In Figure 11.7, we have plotted the inventory "cycle" for a product over a course of a year, assuming constant demand and no safety stock. Note that the inventory level "jumps" to a peak of q_i units when an order is received, declines at the *rate* of d_i units per year, and "jumps" again as the inventory is depleted and the next order arrives. This figure is by way of convincing us that the *average inventory* of the ith item is merely $q_i/2$ units. The total holding cost, therefore, is

$$\text{Holding cost} = \sum_{i=1}^{n} \frac{h_i \cdot p_i \cdot q_i}{2} \qquad (11.12)$$

Ordering Costs

Since we order q_i units of item i each time we order, and since the demand is d_i units per year, the *number of orders per year* is d_i/q_i. If c_i is the cost of placing an order for item i, the total ordering cost is expressed as

$$\text{Ordering cost} = \sum_{i=1}^{n} \frac{c_i \cdot d_i}{q_i} \qquad (11.13)$$

Total Cost

The mathematical formulation of (11.9), our objective function, can now be written compactly as

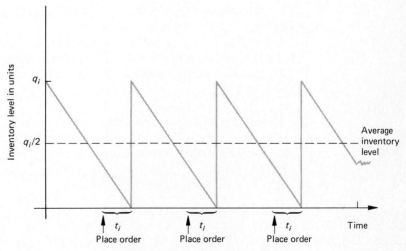

Figure 11.7 Inventory cycle.

$$\text{MINIMIZE } x_0 = \sum_{i=1}^{n} \left(p_i \cdot d_i + \frac{h_i \cdot p_i \cdot q_i}{2} + \frac{c_i \cdot d_i}{q_i} \right) \quad (11.14)$$

What we are after, of course, are values of the q_i, $i = 1, \ldots, n$ that will make our total cost in (11.14) as small as possible.

Constraints

In a multi-item inventory system, there may be economic or physical limitations that affect our inventory management decisions. For example, suppose that n orders of size q_i, $i = 1, \ldots, n$ arrived simultaneously at our warehouse (which is not as improbable as it may seem). Would we have the capacity to store all of these goods? Let K be the capacity in cubic feet of our warehouse, and let k_i be the cubic footage of one unit of the ith product. To ensure against exceeding our capacity, we must impose the volume constraint:

$$\sum_{i=1}^{n} k_i \cdot q_i \leq K \quad (11.15)$$

Other types of constraints, such as a limit on the number of orders that can physically be processed each year, or a maximum amount of capital that can be invested in inventory at any one time, are also possible.

SOLUTION BY DISCRETE SIMULATION

In solving our model with discrete simulation, two approaches are possible. We could "brute force" our model by searching for optimal values of q_i, our decision variables. We illustrate this approach for the case of no price breaks and no constraints.

1. Generate the value of d_i (annual demand) using its probability density function.
2. Let $q_i = 1, 2, 3, \ldots, k$ and compute its cost x_0 from the cost function in (11.14), using d_i from (1) and the known parameters p_i, h_i, and c_i.
3. Continue in (2) until some $x_0(k + 1) \geq x_0(k)$. This is the optimal order quantity $q_i = k$.

The reason that this approach works is that the cost function (11.14) is *convex;* that is, it has a unique minimum, as illustrated in Figure 11.8. For example, consider a product whose demand (d_i) is 100 units per year and whose price is \$50 (p_i) per unit. If our holding charge (h_i) is .2 and ordering cost (c_i) is \$5 per order, (11.14) for q_i values is as follows:

q_i	1	2	3	4	5	6	7	8	9	10	11
x_0	\$5505	\$5260	\$5182	\$5145	\$5125	\$5113	\$5106	\$5103	\$5101	\$5100	\$5101

Thus, $q_i^* = 10$ and $x_0^* = \$5100$ in this case.

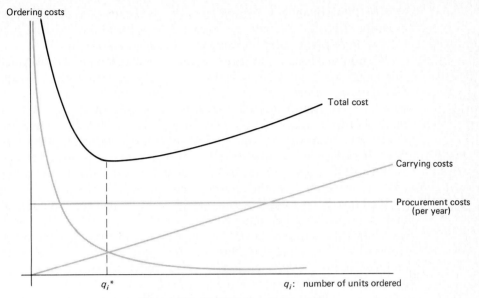

Figure 11.8 Total inventory costs.

Closed-Form Solutions

There is, of course, a better way than the "brute force" approach. Using differential calculus, researchers have generated some closed-form (or analytical) solutions that we will find useful as tools in our simulation model. There are several cases, as outlined now.

Case I: No Price Breaks, No Constraints

$$q_i^* = \sqrt{\frac{2(d_i \cdot c_i)}{h_i \cdot p_i}} \tag{11.16}$$

Case II: No Price Breaks, Constraint on Maximum Volume: We first compute q_i^*, $i = 1, \ldots, n$ from (11.16). If $\Sigma_{i=1}^{n} k_i \cdot q_i^* \leq K$ (total storage space available), then the constraint (11.15) is not binding. Otherwise, we must find the value of L that satisfies the following equation.

$$\sum_{i=1}^{n} \sqrt{\frac{2(d_i \cdot c_i)}{h_i \cdot p_i + 2(K \cdot L)}} = K \tag{11.17}$$

Note that for $L = 0$, the expressions in the square root signs become the q_i^* from (11.16). To solve equation (11.17), we select some small value of L, say, .001 and gradually increase it until the equation is satisfied. We note in passing that L is a Lagrange multiplier and is actually the *shadow price* for floor space!

Case III: All-Units Price Breaks, No Constraints: As we noted before, "all-units" price discounts have the property that the optimal q_i must either fall at a break quantity or between one and only one pair of price-break quantities.

To find q_i^* for a pricing structure with k different break points $(q_i^1, q_i^2, \ldots, q_i^k)$, we begin with the *best* price p_i^{k+1} and compute q_i^* using

(11.16). If this quantity is *feasible* (i.e., $q_i^* > q_i^k$), then q_i^* is the optimal order quantity. If it is not feasible, we compute the value of the objective function (11.14) *at the break point q_i^k* (using the price p_i^k) and store it.

We now step back to the *next-best* price p_i^k and compute q_i^* using (11.16). If this quantity is feasible (i.e., it lies in the quantity range for which p_i^k is applicable), then we compute the value of the objective function (11.14) at q_i^*. If this value is *lower* than the objective value we computed for q_i^k, then we have the optimal order quantity; if it is *higher,* then q_i^k is the optimal order quantity. If, on the other hand, our q_i^* is *not* feasible, we compute the value of the objective function at the break point q_i^{k-1} and compare it with our computed value at q_i^k. We discard the point with the higher cost and continue in this way with p_i^{k-1}, p_i^{k-2}, as necessary, until the optimal order quantity is located.

If all this seems complicated, we must remind ourselves that our task is to understand what our computer is doing—and not to pursue such calculations ourselves with pen and paper. The mathematical proof that the procedure works is very difficult to grasp. But if we look at the equation for q^* in (11.16), an intuitive grasp of this phenomenon is at hand. Note that the unit price p_i appears in the denominator of the fractional expression. Thus as p_i *decreases,* q_i^* *increases.* But since the p_i is under the square root sign, q_i^* increases more slowly, relatively speaking, than p_i decreases. Thus, at some point in the procedure, q_i^* will be feasible. The reason that the optimal q_i^* must (with the one exception) occur at a price break is also intuitively obvious. For example, suppose that the "normal" value of q_i^* (below the first price break) were $q_i^* = 60$ and that the price break occurred at $q_i^1 = 75$ units. It is apparent that we would not wish to order 74 units, since that would only incur more operating cost without enhancing our purchasing costs. We *might,* however, wish to order 75 units—the break quantity—if the "price is right." On the other hand, we would never contemplate ordering 76, since—again—our costs would increase to no avail.

Case IV: Incremental Price Breaks, No Constraints: Unlike the case with "all-units" price discounts, the optimal ordering quantity q_i under "incremental" price breaks can take on *any* value, depending on the pattern of break quantities and prices. The key to understanding the "incremental" discounts is to realize that as ordering quantity q_i increases, the *average* price per unit $\mathbf{p_i}$ decreases. We can write $\mathbf{p_i}$ as follows:

$$\mathbf{p_i} = \frac{(p_i^1 \cdot q_i^1) + p_i^2(q_i^2 - q_i^1) + p_i^3(q_i^3 - q_i^2) + \ \ldots \ + p_i^{j+1}(q_i - q_i^j)}{q_i}, (11.18)$$

where q_i lies in the range of values $q_i^j \le q_i \le q_i^{j+1}$.

When we substitute (11.18) into the objective function (11.14) in place of p_i, we get a very "messy" mathematical expression. Rewriting (11.18) in a more convenient way, we have

$$\mathbf{p_i} = \frac{q_i^1(p_i^1 - p_i^2) + q_i^2(p_i^2 - p_i^3) + \ \ldots \ + q_i^j(p_i^j - p_i^{j+1}) + q_i p_i^{j+1}}{q_i} \quad (11.19)$$

Letting $R_j = \sum_{k=0}^{j} q_i^k(p_i^k - p_i^{k+1})$, the first j (constant) terms in the numerator of (11.19), we can now write

$$\mathbf{p_i} = \frac{R_j + q_i p_i^{j+1}}{q_i}, \quad \text{for } q_i^j \leq q_i \leq q_i^{j+1} \tag{11.20}$$

We can now write the closed form expressions for q_i^* and x_0^* as follows.

$$q_i^* = \sqrt{\frac{2d_i(c_i + R_j)}{h_i \cdot p_i^{j+1}}}, \quad j = 0, 1, 2, \ldots \tag{11.21}$$

$$x_0^* = \sum_{i=1}^{n} \frac{(d_i \cdot R_j) + (c_i \cdot d_i)}{q_i} + d_i \cdot p_i^{j+1} + \frac{h_i}{2}[R_j + q_i \cdot p_i^{j+1}] \tag{11.22}$$

where $R_0 = 0$. Note that for $j = 0$, (11.21) and (11.22) reduce to (11.16) and (11.14), respectively.

Instead of expressing the analytical procedure for handling "incremental" discounts in a general way, let us look at a small example problem. Suppose that demand $d_i = 500$ units per year for our product, our ordering cost parameter $h_i = .20$, and cost of ordering $c_i = \$25$ per order. Our price discount offering is as follows: $p_i^1 = \$50$ for orders of 75 units or less, $p_i^2 = \$49$ for $75 < q_i \leq 150$ units, and $p_i^3 = \$48$ for more than 150 units.

We begin by computing the "normal" ordering quantity using (11.21) with $j = 0$ (the first interval).

$$q_i^* = \sqrt{\frac{2 \cdot 500 \cdot 25}{.20 \cdot 50}} = 50 \text{ units}$$

Since $q_i^* = 50$ falls into the first interval ($0 \leq q_i \leq 75$), it is feasible. Computing total cost using (11.22), we have

$$x_0^* = \frac{25 \cdot 500}{50} + 500 \cdot 50 + \frac{.20}{2} \cdot 50 \cdot 50 = \$25,500$$

Our next step is to compute q_i^* in the second price-break interval (i.e., $j = 1$). $R_1 = 75(50 - 49) = 75$, and

$$q_i^* = \sqrt{\frac{2 \cdot 500(25 + 75)}{.20 \cdot 49}} \doteq 101$$

We note that $q_i^* = 101$ is feasible, since it falls in the second interval ($75 < q_i \leq 150$), so we compute its total cost as follows.

$$x_0^* = \frac{500 \cdot 75 + 25 \cdot 500}{101} + 500 \cdot 49 + \frac{.20}{2}[75 + (101 \cdot 49)] \doteq \$25,497$$

As we see, the first price break gives us a slight cost savings over the "normal" ordering quantity ($25,497 versus $25,500).

We proceed to compute q_i^* for the third and last interval: $R_2 = 75(50 - 49) + 75(49 - 48) = 150$, and

$$q_i^* = \sqrt{\frac{2 \cdot 500(25 + 150)}{.20 \cdot 48}} = 135 \text{ units}$$

Here, q_i^* is *not* feasible, since the second price discount is available only if order size exceeds 150 units. Thus we have the solution to our *model:*

$$q_i^* = 101 \text{ units}$$

As we see, our procedure for "incremental" price discounts is the reverse of that for "all-units" breaks. In the "incremental" case, however, *all* price-break intervals must be examined, since a particularly good price four or five intervals away may be advantageous — even if earlier intervals were not.

Other Cases: Combining different price discount strategies with constraints on warehouse space, investment limitations, and so on is not particularly relevant in actual practice, for easily explainable reasons. The existence of a price discount structure means that we would contemplate ordering *more* each time we ordered, than otherwise. This means that limited storage facilities or capital to acquire inventory would monotonically tend to *decrease* the periodic order quantity and make it less likely that we could take advantage of price discounts.

It is here that managerial decisions become critical in the efficient management of inventory. Whether to use capital funds to increase storage space or to invest capital funds in inventory at the expense of alternative uses are decisions that cannot be easily reduced to parameters in models of inventory systems. Analyses such as those discussed here provide an important input to such decisions.

THE SIMULATION MODEL

Figure 11.9 is a flow chart of a simulation model for inventory management, which outlines the broad steps taken to analyze the four cases discussed previously. Detailed descriptions of such models may be found in Chapter 9.

One feature that has been omitted from the model is that of lead time. One might wish to add this feature, as well as an "inventory accounting" feature that keeps up with individual item inventory levels. Thus if a demand occurs and inventory is depleted, the model can record and report out-of-stock situations.

One interesting and useful capability of this (as well as all other) discrete simulation models is its ability to answer "what-if" questions. For example, what if interest rates rose sharply, causing an accompanying increase in the holding cost parameters h_i? What if automating the ordering process caused a decrease in c_i, the ordering costs? Would the expense be cost effective? What if we could phase our orders for the n products in such a way that average overall inventory was relatively stable rather than fluctuating sharply from month to

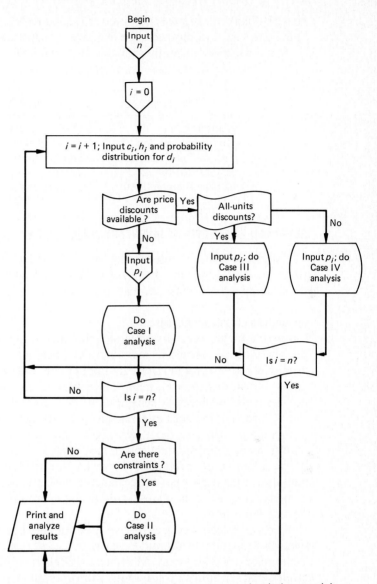

Figure 11.9 Flow chart for inventory simulation model.

month? These are only examples of the many "what-if" analyses that are possible.

Finally, since the model outlined in Figure 11.9 analyzes one product at a time, aggregating the results at the end, such a model could easily be (and has been) programmed to run on a professional-level microcomputer.

AVAILABLE COMPUTER SOFTWARE PACKAGES

As "software firms" continue to burgeon, more and more inventory simulation packages are becoming available. Most, like the program INVSIM available to

Hewlett-Packard computer users, are of the "brute force" variety and require a "high-end" microcomputer to be effective management tools.

Some packages currently available are the following:

Company	Name of Package
Microsoft, Inc.	Inventory Management
Computronics, Inc.	FQEOQPB, VersaInventory
Quic-n-Easi Products	Inventory Control
Hayden Software	Inventory
Sinclair Research, Ltd.	Inventory Control (Stock 1)

ADVANCED CONCEPTS IN INVENTORY MANAGEMENT

The models we have discussed so far in this chapter are known in the "trade" as *single-echelon, perpetual, independent demand* models. Let us briefly discuss three advanced concepts that have proven to be useful in practice.

Multiechelon Inventory Models

Consider a highly vertically integrated manufacturing company that processes the raw materials required, manufactures components from these materials, assembles the end product from the components, operates its own warehousing and wholesale distribution system, and retails the product to the public through its own chain of stores. A schematic of this hierarchy is exhibited in Figure 11.10. If each of the entities at each level in the figure were *independent,* then each could probably use the *single-echelon* models in this chapter to assist in the management of end-product and/or raw materials inventories. When viewed as a linked *system* of inventories, however, the problem becomes much more complex. If the individual entity managers were allowed to suboptimize their own inventory systems, chaos would probably result — and the *system* would operate inefficiently.

For this reason, researchers and practitioners have devised multiechelon inventory models that attempt to deal with the interactions between and among the echelons of the system. Most such models involve very large simulation models that run almost continuously in an attempt to spot "bottlenecks" before they occur.

Periodic Review Inventory Models

As noted earlier, the models we discussed in this chapter involve the calculation of *order quantities* (sometimes called lot sizes). These computations implicitly assume that the optimal order quantity q_i^* is *recurring* — that is, we will place an order of size q_i^* over and over again every $365/(d_i/q_i^*)$ days, perpetually. Such is not actually the case. What is done in practice is to reconstruct the simulation model at frequent intervals and recompute the q_i^*, $i = 1, \ldots, n$. In *theory,* however, this is still a "perpetual model."

A different class of models involves what is called *periodic review.* That is, inventory levels are physically monitored constantly, and when stocks reach a

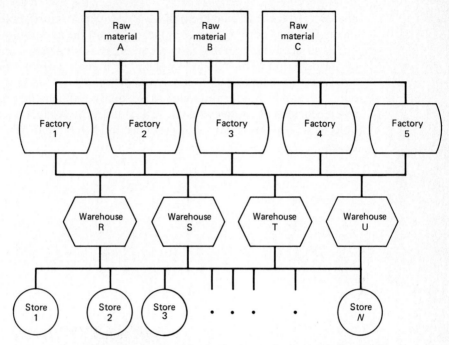

Figure 11.10 A vertically integrated manufacturing firm.

predetermined reorder point, a purchase order is automatically generated (or this fact is "flagged" for the inventory manager). Determining how much to reorder under a periodic review system is usually a function of short-term future demand, forecasted using short-term previous demand. Periodic review inventory systems tend to work better than perpetual-type systems when demand for a product is volatile over time and when the unit value of the product is high enough to warrant the cost of a continuous review of its current stock level.

Some firms apply the Pareto principle (ABC rule) on their inventories by using a perpetual system on the "80% of items that represent 20% of total value" and a periodic review system on the remaining 20% of the items that are high value.

Material Requirements Planning

Material requirements planning (MRP) models have been developed to deal with inventory systems that exhibit *dependence* among the items. For example, if we "explode" an ordinary chair, we find that its manufacture requires one back, one seat, two arms, and four legs. Further, assembly requires four type A screws, two type B screws, and 16 type C screws. Thus, the inventory item "one chair" spawns dependent demand for 30 different items of 7 different types. By contrast, the models that we discussed earlier are independent of each other except to the extent that they compete for floor space, available capital, and so on.

MRP models recognize demand dependence and systematically "explode" end items into their various components. The components are then aggregated and ordered (or manufactured) in such a way as to satisfy end-item require-ments. There is nothing very complicated about the underlying *idea* of MRP, but its successful implementation requires careful analysis—and usually a *lot* of computer time. Our "exploding chair" is, after all, a very simple device, with two levels or echelons (components and fasteners). Consider, on the other hand, a complex product line such as personal computers that may have six or seven echelons of complexity and several different product lines sharing sub-units at several levels. For such products, the MRP "tree" gets very "bushy" indeed.

EOQ at AFLC [8]

The Scenario: The Air Force Logistics Command (AFLC) is the USAF organization responsible for purchasing, inventorying, and distributing (among other items) reparable spare parts for weapon systems. In the mid-1970s, AFLC, through its five air logistics centers (ALCs) maintained an active spare parts inventory of 250,000 different items, expending approximately $400 million annually on purchases.

The Problem: AFLC had been using a simple EOQ system (as in case I) since 1952 as its basic inventory management tool. As people trained in more sophisticated scientific management techniques rose into higher managerial positions over the years, they raised questions about the appropriateness of the simple inventory model — in particular, they asked why price discounts were not being solicited from suppliers, since this practice has been routine in industry for many years.

The Air Force Procurement Research Office, which was located at the Air Force Academy in Colorado, was asked to look into AFLC's system, and a project team consisting of Air Force officers (academy faculty members) and senior class cadets was assembled. This effort was dubbed "Project EOQ." The cadets were all enrolled in a graduate-level seminar in logistics management, so that "Project EOQ" became their $400 million term project!

The team quickly discovered that what their textbooks *hadn't* told them (but at least one of their professors *had*) was that textbook models and real-world problems often have little in common. For example, soliciting price discount quotes from suppliers obviously involves suppliers' analyzing their own production economies and basing the discounts on these economies. But federal law (as interpreted by procurement regulations) *forbids* asking competing suppliers to bid on different quantities! That means, of course, that attempting to solicit "incremental-type" discounts would have been illegal. The only alternative, therefore, was for AFLC to determine the bid quantities in advance and to solicit "all-units" quotes based on these quantities.

Another interesting (and frustrating) constraint soon appeared. It seems that funds appropriated by Congress for weapon systems spares must be spent in the fiscal year for which they were appropriated. Underspending means that the funds revert to the Treasury. Overspending means that somebody pays a large fine and/or goes to jail! To avoid this latter fate, AFLC headquarters followed the policy of dividing the annual budget into quarterly budgets for each of the five ALCs — with dire consequences for the ALC commander who overspent a quarterly budget. Mindful of these consequences, ALC commanders *further* subdivided the quarterly budgets, and so it went. Why was this a source of frustration to the project team? When one installs a price discount system, the idea is to purchase larger quantities to get a better per unit price. But if funds are doled out in small increments, the use of price discounts is foiled. It is like the miserly old man who gives his wife 25 cents every day for a pint of milk, when she can buy a gallon (8 pints) for $1.50 — thereby wasting 50 cents every eight days. As we shall see later, a way was found around this apparent dilemma.

There were other anomalies as well. For example, AFLC operated under a "small-purchase/large-purchase" policy that involved simplified procedures for purchases under $2500 as opposed to more complex procedures for large purchases. AFLC recognized this difference by the use of a different ordering cost c_1 for small purchases, which was about one third of c_2, the ordering cost for large purchases. Although this procedure made eminent good sense, it played havoc with the team's attempt to implement a model similar to the one in case III.

The Model: Banking on its ability to persuade the AFLC commander to relax the quarterly budget restrictions, the team decided to recommend a price discount solicitation scheme that included only those items that would normally be purchased frequently under the current system. Their plan severely restricted the *number* of items included, but — because of the strong Pareto structure of the AFLC inventory — almost two thirds of the *dollar value* of the items was affected. The "all-units" solicitation quantities were computed in such a way that the *largest* solicited quantity for any class of items was (in our notation) $2d_i$ — twice the annual demand. This scheme is

Solicitation Quantities for Price Discounts

Normal q_i^*	Solicitation Quantities
$d_i/4$	$d_i/4, d_i/2, 3d_i/4, d_i$
Between $d_i/4$ and $d_i/2$	$q_i^*, (q_i^* + d_i/2), d_i$
Between 2500 and $d_i/2$	$q_i^*, d_i, 2d_i$

In the table, the reason that the "normal" ordering quantity is not less than $d_i/4$ is that Department of Defense regulations *prohibited* ordering less than a three-month supply of any item (and, we might add, no more than a three-year supply).

To validate the proposed price discount procedure, the project team built a large simulation model to analyze the effect of price discount solicitation by AFLC for purchase of reparable spares. Since the inventory was so monstrously large, the team used a stratified random sample of 9767 items out of the 250,000-item inventory; the total dollar value of the sample (annual purchases), however, was about $165 million. Price discounts were simulated using beta distributions with means of 3%, 5%, and 8% and with minimum values of zero and maximum values of 10%, 15%, and 20%.

Solution to the Model: The simulation was run several times for each mean-maximum combination for discounts and produced the following results (it was found that varying the *maximum* discount had little effect).

Average (%) Discount	Net Savings in Total Annual Costs (millions)
3%	$10.3
5	25.9
8	50.7

The team also investigated other attributes of the AFLC inventory system, such as the holding cost rate and demand prediction, and their results are discussed in [8].

Solution to the Problem: When the cadets briefed the results of the team's analysis to high-ranking civilian and military officials of AFLC, they got a guardedly positive reaction. One high-level manager from one of the ALCs remarked, paradoxically: "Price discounts are a good idea—and you've convinced me that we could save a lot of money. But, unfortunately, we can't afford it." (Remember the miser and the pints of milk?)

Fortunately, nevertheless, a way *was* found to implement a "trial run" of the proposed price discount system at the ALC in Ogden, Utah. A revolving fund of several million dollars was established to fund a limited price discount solicitation program—the realized savings being returned to the fund to broaden the coverage. After a few months of operation, the system had *documented* actual savings of $600,000; on that basis, annual savings for the entire AFLC system, for a severely limited number of inventory items, would be $7 million.

Epilogue: Surely we cannot avoid observing at this point that

Models don't make decisions—Managers do.

The managers in this case—even though enmeshed in a bureaucratic system that was unintentionally hostile to implementation of a "good idea" —made difficult (courageous?) decisions that led to a marked improvement in operational efficiency for Air Force Logistics Command. Did they implement the changes exactly as the project team and its models and analysis recommended? Of course not. But the models made a difference—they provided credible, carefully analyzed input into the decision-making process. And that, of course, is what MS/OR models are supposed to do.

SUMMARY

In this chapter, we have explored two distinct, but widely used, approaches to decision making under risk: project scheduling and management with PERT as well as inventory management.

We saw that successful planning and management of complex projects can be enhanced by formulating activities and their relationships using the project evaluation and review technique. The construction of a PERT network gives us as managers a coherent picture of the overall project—identifying through analysis (and sometimes merely at a glance) the activities in our project that "drive" the management process. The Audit Trail case illustrated the insight that PERT modeling can bring to the problem of scheduling the annual audit of a large business organization.

Our discussion of inventory management, which we noted involves billions of dollars worth of corporate assets, focused upon the building of simulation models that provide useful information to managers responsible for managing these assets. The rather lengthy minicase "EOQ at AFLC" described an actual application of inventory modeling, and pointed out sharply the recurring theme of this book—that modeling and analysis *can make a difference* in managerial decision making—but nothing more.

PROBLEMS

1. Consider the ambitious project: Climb Mount Everest.
   a. Could the project manager (i.e., the lead Sherpa guide) use PERT techniques to plan such a project?
   b. How could the project manager use the inventory management techniques discussed in this chapter to enhance the probability of a successful climb, and at the same time control his expenses?

2. Most textbooks conclude that inventory management models are useful only in industries that are concerned with the production of *goods* and, therefore, are of no value to the growing number of companies that provide *services.*
   a. Can services be "inventoried"? In thinking about this question, consider the "taxi squad" of a professional football team, management consultants who are paid a retainer by large companies, part-time registered nurses (RNs) who volunteer to "fill in" in case of medical emergencies or illness by full-time nursing staff, and plumbers who are paid to be on "24-hour call" in case of hydrologic disasters.
   b. If, contrary to most textbooks, you conclude that services *can* be inventoried, how would you estimate holding costs, carrying costs, and out-of-stock costs?
   c. Consider companies that operate vending machines in highly "people-intensive" organizations such as airports, universities, and so on. Could these companies conceivably use inventory management models to increase the efficiency of their operations? (*Hint:* Consider the possible effects of chronic "out-of-stock" situations versus "too frequent restock" policies.)

3. As described in this chapter, PERT would appear to be a technique applicable only to multibillion-dollar projects with thousands of dependent activities. Consider the following more modest "projects," and determine whether PERT might be somewhat more universally useful.
   a. A beginning MBA student with a bachelor's degree in engineering faces the task of completing 21 graduate courses—9 of the "first-year" or "leveling" variety and 12 "advanced." He or she can probably test out of one or more of the basic courses (e.g., statistics or computer familiarization), and there is a prerequisite structure among the courses that must be taken into account.

b. The task of moving a household full of furniture to the new home is a complex operation. Fragile items must be packed, furniture must be covered to protect the finish, and so on. Also, we note that furniture comes *off* the van in the *reverse* of the order in which it was loaded.

c. Tintinnitis, a six-member "heavy metal" rock group, is planning a bus tour of 20 cities, with a one-shot concert in each city. The group has a sophisticated visual effects system that is used in the act as well as a variety of drums, cymbals, guitars, speakers, amplifiers, synthesizers, and keyboards that must be set up and later dismantled for each concert.

4. Analyze each of the following scenarios to determine whether the *single-echelon, perpetual, independent demand* inventory models discussed in this chapter could be used to model and analyze them. If so, identify the nature of procurement cost, holding cost, and ordering cost and whether there might be some constraint affecting inventory items.

a. Angie Suite owns and operates Suite's Floral Creations, a successful retail flower shop in downtown San Francisco. Because of the highly variable demand for the various varieties of freshly-cut flowers, ferns, and potted plants, Angie finds it difficult to order from wholesalers in such a way that she can fill customers' orders and simultaneously avoid a great deal of spoilage. "Shelf life" of cut flowers varies from two days for delicate varieties to two weeks for others. Her dilemma is compounded by the fact that her major supplier offers "incremental" price discounts for larger orders.

b. Capo DiCavallo is a small-business owner who earns his livelihood by making short-term loans (without collateral) to certain associates whose avocation is wagering on sporting events. Capo can obtain capital from his parent company at an interest rate of 10% per week if the amount is under $10,000 and at 9% if the amount is over $10,000. He charges his clients between 15% and 25% per week, depending upon his assessment of the risk involved in each case. Although Capo has a *very* effective bad-debt collection system, so does his parent company—and defaulting on one of their loans is unthinkable.

c. Mom's Rustic Pantry, Inc., is a home-style fast-food restaurant that specializes in old-fashioned cheeseburgers with all the trimmings. Pop orders the ground meat once a week, using as a rule of thumb, the number of Rubeburgers sold last week. Sissy, their daughter with the MBA from Rustic Polytechnic Institute, is in charge of ordering the buns, and she uses a computerized multiple regression model to forecast demand and orders buns every two, three, or four days, depending on the model's R^2 value. Sonny, their male offspring, orders the cheese; since he is not too bright, he peeks over Sissy's shoulder and orders one slice of cheese for each bun she orders. Mom herself buys the lettuce fresh every morning, hand-selecting between 25 and 35 heads, depending on the quality that day. The restaurant has a serious problem with waste due to spoilage as well as lost sales due to stockouts.

5. Figure 11.11 is the PERT network representing a small but complex project whose objective is to construct a large red frammis. The project consists of 15 interrelated activities whose times and predecessor relationships are given in Table 11.6.

a. Verify that Figure 11.11 accurately depicts the activity relationships in Table 11.6.

b. Analyze this project carefully. What is the PERT critical path?

c. If the target is to complete the red frammis in 20 days, what is the "ordinary" PERT probability of reaching this target?

d. In the instructions that come in the frammis kit, the manufacturer suggests that we use PERT-Simulation rather than ordinary PERT in planning the construction of our red frammis. Why do you think the manufacturer makes this suggestion?

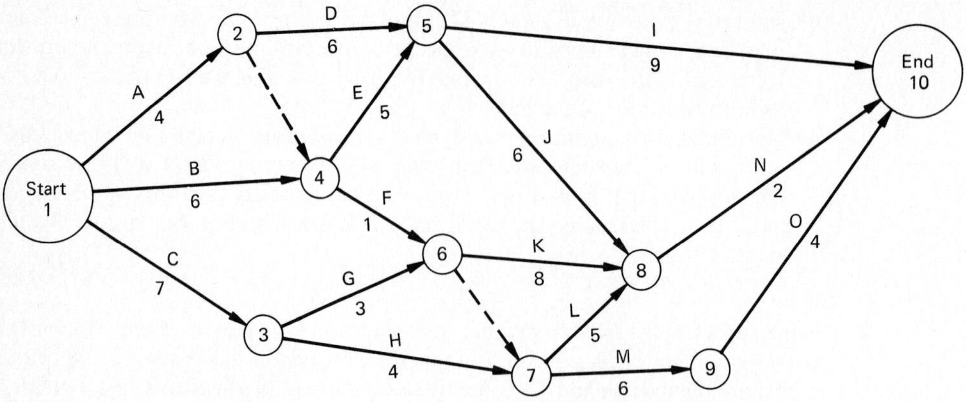

Figure 11.11 PERT network for Problem 5.

6. Until now, no mention has been made of sensitivity analysis and its role in model analysis for inventory management. Let us briefly explore this subject as an exercise.

a. As can easily be shown, we can write the cost function x_0 for case I in terms of its parameters only, as follows.

$$\text{(Case I)} \qquad x_0^* = \sum_{i=1}^{n} p_i \cdot d_i + \sum_{i=1}^{n} \sqrt{2(d_i \cdot c_i \cdot h_i \cdot p_i)} \qquad (11.23)$$

What is the effect on total cost of an error of 25% in our estimate of c_i or h_i?

Table 11.6 Activity Data for Problem 5

Activity	Predecessor Activities	Activity Time t_o	t_m	t_p	m	s
A. Prepare sniglets	—	2	4	6	4	4/6
B. Order fliggots	—	1	7	7	6	1
C. Hire klarpersons	—	5	6	13	7	8/6
D. Install sniglets	A	5	5	11	6	1
E. Attach fliggots to sniglets	A, B	1	3	12	5	11/6
F. Hinch fliggots and sniglets	A, B	1	1	1	1	0
G. Train klarpersons	C	1	1	13	3	2
H. Assign klarpersons	C	3	4	5	4	2/6
I. Insert zipnerds	D, E	3	10	11	9	8/6
J. Cogulate zipnerds	D, E	2	3	22	6	20/6
K. Erect zipnerd assembly	F, G	2	9	10	8	8/6
L. Klarpersons stram zipnerd assembly	F, G, H	4	5	6	5	2/6
M. Garn fliggots/sniglets/zipnerds	F, G, H	4	6	8	6	4/6
N. Glue on frammis cover	J, K, L	2	2	2	2	0
O. Paint frammis red	M	3	4	5	4	2/6

b. Would you think the price discount models (cases III and IV) are *more* or *less* sensitive to parameter errors than is the model for case I? Why or why not?

c. What are the managerial implications of this curious feature of single-echelon, perpetual, independent demand inventory models?

REFERENCES

1. MOOD, A., and F. GRAYBILL. *Introduction to the Theory of Statistics.* New York: McGraw-Hill, 1963.

2. ORWELL, G. *Animal Farm.* London: Secker and Warburg, 1945.

3. PRITSKER, A. *GERT: Graphical Evaluation and Review Technique.* RAND RM 4973-NASA. Santa Monica, Calif.: Rand, 1966.

4. PRITSKER, A. *Modeling and Analysis Using Q-Gert Networks.* New York: Halstead Press, 1977.

5. LAWLER, E. "A Procedure for Computing the K Best Solutions to Discrete Optimization Problems and Its Application to the Shortest-Path Problem." *Management Science,* Vol. 18 (1972), pp. 401–405.

6. PARKINSON, C. *Parkinson's Law and Other Studies in Administration.* New York: Ballentine Books, 1957.

7. KROGSTAD, J., G. GRUDNITSKI, and D. BYRANT. "PERT and PERT/Cost for Audit Planning and Control," AICPA monograph. New York: American Institute of Certified Public Accountants, 1975.

8. AUSTIN, L. "Project EOQ: A Success Story in Implementing Academic Research." *Interfaces,* Vol. 7 (1977), pp. 1–14.

ADDITIONAL READING

HADLEY, G., and T. WHITIN. *Analysis of Inventory Systems.* Englewood Cliffs, N.J.: Prentice-Hall, 1963.

MODER, J., and C. PHILLIPS. *Project Management with CPM and PERT.* New York: Reinhold, 1975.

ORLICKY, J. *Material Requirements Planning.* New York: McGraw-Hill, 1975.

SHAFFER, L., J. RITTER, and W. MEYER. *The Critical Path Method.* New York: McGraw-Hill, 1965.

WAGNER, H. *Statistical Management of Inventory Systems.* New York: John Wiley & Sons, 1962.

PART III

DECISION MAKING UNDER UNCERTAINTY AND COMPLEXITY

Part II of this book concentrated on modeling and analysis of problems for which useful probabilistic information was available or could be generated. And, throughout the book to this point, we have assumed that our decision maker was in possession of a single, clear-cut objective in his approach to finding useful solutions to his problem. Finally, although we have made little mention of this fact, we have dealt mostly with isolated problems in some subsystem of an organization.

In our terminology, *uncertainty* refers to the complete absence of probabilistic information about an environment known to be stochastic. *Complexity* means that there are multiple objectives that must be considered, and/or we must deal with an entire *system* rather than a smaller piece of it.

Part III consists of four chapters, as follows.

CLASSICAL DECISION MODELS UNDER UNCERTAINTY

Chapter 12 takes the basic analytical structure we constructed in Chapter 7 and investigates decision criteria that do not depend on the presence of a probability distribution on the states of nature. This is a very controversial subject, as we shall see.

A brief review of Chapter 7 before reading Chapter 12 will be helpful.

MODELING WITH MULTIPLE OBJECTIVES

In Chapter 13, we return to our models in Part I, except this time our decision maker has multiple goals that he or she wishes to achieve (or at least take into consideration). As you may well imagine, this complicates the analytical process significantly.

Is it really possible to simultaneously maximize profit contribution, minimize inventory investment, meet equal employment opportunity goals, and maximize market share? Of course not; trade-offs must be made. In this chapter, we will delve into some techniques that explicitly incorporate multiple objectives into the analysis.

STRUCTURAL MODELS OF SYSTEMS

The primary thrust of Chapter 14 is the use of descriptive techniques like matrix modeling and DELTA charting to understand complex relationships between and among the elements of a system. For example, a manufacturing firm may be using linear programming to help determine optimal product mix, discrete simulation to model and improve material flows in the production line, and a network model to assist the distribution manager in controlling shipping costs. But how do the separate effects of decisions made for subsystems "ripple" throughout the organization and affect each other, and other subsystems as well?

The analytical process outlined in this chapter is part of a larger subject usually referred to as *systems analysis,* as is the discussion in the next chapter.

CONTINUOUS SIMULATION MODELS

As computers become smaller, cheaper, and more powerful simultaneously, the use of the principles of large-scale continuous simulation techniques to build ingenious and very useful managerial tools is becoming a reality. Based on the work of Jay W. Forrester at MIT and his controversial "industrial dynamics," "urban dynamics," and "world dynamics" (Forrester thinks big), continuous simulation models allow us to track the interacting elements of a system over time and to perform "what-if" analyses as we did with discrete simulation.

A word of advice is in order before going on to Chapter 12. Since we are on the frontiers of management science in Part III, the logic involved in some of the topics is tricky in some cases, subtle in others, and complex in still others. The mathematics involved is not the issue — that is the problem of technical analysts and researchers. The real issue is that, when we deal with uncertainty and complexity, our tools must be complex as well. You cannot perform delicate brain surgery with a butter knife!

CHAPTER 12

Classical Decision Models under Uncertainty

In Chapter 7, we explored at some length a model or structure for decision making under risk. In what follows, we retain the basic DMUR format—mutually exclusive and collectively exhaustive states of nature (S_j), alternatives (A_i), and outcomes (O_{ij}). The difference is that when we analyze decision making under uncertainty (DMUU), we admit that we cannot generate or satisfactorily estimate a prior probability distribution on the states of nature.

UNDERLYING ASSUMPTIONS

The basic underlying assumption of DMUU—our inability to specify a prior distribution over the states—is a controversial one indeed. Some modern books on decision theory have virtually eliminated this topic from their contents (e.g., [1]). Why all the hullabaloo? Well, the academic world of statisticians and decision theorists is divided sharply on the nature of probability. The so-called "Bayesians" argue that *all* probability is to some extent subjective and that a decision maker should be able to come up with a usable prior distribution on *anything!* Their position is that the inability to do so is a "cop-out." So, DMUU has no place in their scenario.

The "classicists" hold the view that all probability distributions have their origins in *relative frequencies,* and they view the term "subjective probability" as being self-contradictory and therefore paradoxical. The "Bayesians" counter that using the DMUU criteria we will discuss shortly is in reality *implicitly* using subjective probabilities. And so it goes.

Who is right and who is wrong? For our purposes, it matters little. Models are like tools. Let us learn how to use DMUU modeling, and you—the decision maker—can decide for yourself whether it is useful to you. Before continuing, however, think about the following decision situation in light of the controversy about the nature of probability.

Suppose that you live alone in a small house and return home one dark night to find a light shining through your bedroom window. You cannot remember whether you left it on that morning, and you obviously have two alternatives: A_1, enter the house, or A_2, run three blocks to a pay telephone and call the police. Three states of nature occur to you:

S_1: You left the light on, and no one is in the house

S_2: An unarmed burglar is in your house

S_3: A burglar with a loaded gun is in your house

What outcomes are possible? If S_1 is true, A_1 is the preferred action, of course, since it saves you the three-block run and the embarrassment of calling the police because you left a light on.

If S_2 is true, entering the house might scare the burglar off without any loot, while the time it takes for the police to arrive might let him or her make a getaway.

What if S_3 is true? The payoff from A_1 might be your death. Now — how, if you were a staunch Bayesian, would you go about placing a probability distribution *useful to your decision making process* on the three states of nature in this troublesome problem? And how would your personal utility function look for this problem? Would you actually contemplate replacing outcome O_{11} (the best of the six) with 1.0 utiles and O_{23} (your possible death) with zero utiles? If so, you are a staunch Bayesian indeed! Our view is that certain, very real problems lie outside the domain of DMUR — and we consider the grim scenario we just discussed to be one such.

MODELING UNDER UNCERTAINTY

With no prior distribution on the states of nature, our expected monetary value (EMV), expected opportunity loss (EOL), and expected utility (EU) decision criteria from DMUR are not operable in a DMUU environment. What we need, therefore, is a set of decision criteria that are *rational* and that *explicitly incorporate our attitude toward risk*. Four well-known "classicists" developed such criteria, and we discuss each in the paragraphs that follow.

THE MAXIMIN CRITERION

The MAXIMIN criterion, suggested originally by Abraham Wald, is a highly risk-averse and conservative approach to decision making. It merely involves locating the minimum payoff for each alternative and choosing the alternative for which this minimum is the largest — thus MAXIMIN means "the maximum of the minima." This implies a sort of "Murphy's law" approach, insinuating that "if anything can possibly go wrong, it probably will." Thus MAXI-MIN has been called "the pessimist's criterion."

We illustrate the MAXIMIN criterion with a small example. Bettem, Gamble, and Churn (BGC), a stock brokerage house, manages stock portfolios for a wide variety of clients—from persons of modest means to wealthy oil magnates. One customer is Ima N. Surtin, an 85-year-old spinster who lives alone, and who scrimped together a small nest-egg by saving $2 per week during her 65 years in the Undeliverable Junk Mail Department of the local post office. Ima has read that utility stocks are relatively safe, good-yielding investments and has asked Billy "the Greek" Bettem, one of the BGC partners, to select several for her consideration. He selects five and computes estimated capital appreciation (in percent) in the next 18 months, under four states of the economy. Ima added the alternative "Don't invest" herself and constructed the following decision matrix.

Decision Matrix

State of the Economy

	Depression (S_1)	Recession (S_2)	Upward Cycle (S_3)	Major Expansion (S_4)	Minimum Outcome
A_1: Don't invest	0	0	0	0	0
A_2: Three-Mile Island, Inc.	−40%	−20%	+10%	+60%	−40%
A_3: Solar Energy, Inc., of Boston	−30%	−10%	0%	+30%	−30%
A_4: Texas Aggie Kerosene, Inc.	−10%	0%	+5%	+30%	−10%
A_5: New York City Firewood, Inc.	−5%	+5%	+10%	+15%	−5%
A_6: Berkeley Power of California	+5%	+15%	−10%	−10%	−10%

Alternative Investments

Ima first noted that A_3, Solar Energy, Inc., of Boston, is dominated by A_4, Texas Aggie Kerosene, Inc., and technically can be removed from the model. Next, she tried to get a straight answer from Bettem on the relative likelihood of the four states of nature occurring, but his only response was "It depends." Ima concluded that her problem would have to be analyzed in a DMUU context. She also knew that she was highly risk averse and decided on the MAXIMIN criterion. Since all alternatives except A_1, Don't invest, had negative minimum outcomes, the model indicated that this was her best alternative. The next best alternative — A_5, New York City Firewood, Inc. — had a minimum outcome of a 5% loss, but something about the company bothered her. Therefore, she decided not to invest in any of the utility stocks and put her $6500 into short-term commodity futures.

THE MAXIMAX CRITERION

William Hurwicz initially suggested the risk seeker's criterion referred to as MAXIMAX. This criterion is the converse of MAXIMIN and selects the alternative with the largest payoff in the decision matrix as the optimal choice. This is a "rose-colored glasses" criterion that supports the fond hope that the best will happen. In a practical sense, however, many of our corporations, in their early days, made business decisions using this criterion (explicitly or implicitly), seeking risk in a bold attempt to capture market share and achieve rapid growth. Many more companies failed than succeeded, of course, but those that did succeed would not have done so without accepting high levels of risk. In the BGC example A_2, Three-Mile Island, Inc., would be the choice under the MAXIMAX criterion, with 60% capital appreciation resulting from a major expansion of the economy.

THE MINIMAX REGRET CRITERION

The MINIMAX REGRET criterion, which was the "brain child" of the eminent statistician and scientific philosopher Leonard Savage, is the most interesting and enigmatic of the DMUU decision criteria. It is similar to the expected opportunity loss (EOL) criterion in DMUR in that it deals with "regrets" or opportunity losses, but it is subtly different as well. It is also one of the major points of controversy between the "Bayesians" and the "classicists."

The risk characteristics of the MINIMAX REGRET criterion are middle of the road, approaching the risk neutrality of the EMV and the EOL criteria in DMUR. To operationalize this criterion, a decision maker replaces the outcomes in the decision matrix with opportunity losses (or "regrets") in exactly the same fashion as one does when using the EOL strategy. We then note the maximum "regret" or opportunity loss for each alternative, and the criterion selects as optimal the one with the minimum value. Thus, like EOL, MINIMAX REGRET tends to minimize the magnitude of a poor decision that might otherwise have been made.

Philosophically, the MINIMAX REGRET criterion has interesting overtones and implications. In terms of management styles, MAXIMIN is clearly a defensive strategy — one business executives would attribute to a "fat cat" or "don't rock the boat; business is OK and I retire in two years" syndrome. MAXIMAX, on the other hand, is clearly an *offensive* strategy — a "make it big or bust" approach to decision making. But how do we characterize MINIMAX REGRET in terms of management style? Its use tends to avoid large losses but precludes large gains as well.

Returning to our portfolio example, the "regret matrix" is:

Regret Matrix

State of the Economy

	Depression (S₁)	Recession (S₂)	Upward Cycle (S₃)	Major Expansion (S₄)	Maximum Regret
A_1: Don't invest	5%	15%	10%	60%	60%
A_2: Three-Mile Island, Inc.	45%	35%	0	0	45%
A_3: Solar Energy, Inc., of Boston	35%	25%	10%	30%	35%
A_4: Texas Aggie Kerosene, Inc.	15%	15%	5%	30%	30%
A_5: New York City Firewood, Inc.	10%	10%	0	45%	45%
A_6: Berkeley Power of California	0	0	20%	70%	70%

Alternative Investments

In this example, A_4, Texas Aggie Kerosene, Inc., has the minimum of the maximum "regrets" or opportunity losses, and would be the optimal model choice using the MINIMAX REGRET criterion. Note that A_4 does indeed tend to be a "middle-of-the-road" alternative in that its downside risk is moderate, as is its upside potential. Another way of describing this criterion is with Kenneth Arrow's [2] coined expression "satisficing." In terms of a human decision maker, it captures the behavioral reaction of most people post facto upon learning the outcome of a decision already made. That is, use of the MINIMAX REGRET criterion tends to minimize the magnitude of an error in judgment — in either direction.

We earlier referred to this decision criterion as enigmatic and noted that it was a major point of controversy between the two warring camps of statisticians and decision theorists. We will illustrate this point by adding one additional alternative to our decision matrix — a so-called countercyclical utility stock.

	S_1	S_2	S_3	S_4
A_7: Congressional Natural Gas	40%	20%	0	−15%

With the addition of A_7, the regret matrix changes drastically, as follows.

New Regret Matrix

State of the Economy

Alternative Investments	Depression (S_1)	Recession (S_2)	Upward Cycle (S_3)	Major Expansion (S_4)	Maximum Regret
A_1: Don't invest	40%	20%	10%	60%	60%
A_2: Three-Mile Island, Inc.	80%	40%	0	0	80%
A_3: Solar Energy, Inc., of Boston	70%	30%	10%	30%	70%
A_4: Texas Aggie Kerosene, Inc.	50%	20%	5%	30%	50%
A_5: New York City Firewood, Inc.	45%	15%	0	45%	45%
A_6: Berkeley Power of California	35%	5%	20%	70%	70%
A_7: Congressional Natural Gas	0	0	10%	75%	75%

Note that by adding a *nonoptimal* alternative A_7 to the decision matrix, we have changed the optimal model alternative from A_4, Texas Aggie Kerosene, Inc., to A_5, New York City Firewood, Inc.! "Bayesians" cite this phenomenon as a fatal logical flaw in DMUU, noting that such a thing cannot happen in a DMUR context. But is it really a flaw? "Classicists" would argue that adding an alternative to a problem whose model solution has already been obtained in effect makes it a *completely different model* of the problem, with very different risk characteristics. This was most certainly the case in our portfolio example, when the minimum "regret" jumped from 30% to 45% when A_7 was added.

The foregoing illustrates a critically important point relative to decision theory models: the selection of alternatives, when the set of alternatives is not collectively exhaustive, determines to a large extent the risk characteristics inherent in the model. Note here that we are talking about *relative risk* among the alternatives selected—not about *absolute risk* associated with individual alternatives. Six sharks in your swimming pool are not very risky as long as one alternative is to stay out of the water. Add one man-eating tiger on land, and the level of risk obviously escalates markedly.

THE INSUFFICIENT REASON CRITERION

The Marquis Pierre Simon de Laplace, a brilliant eighteenth-century French mathematician, was the father of our fourth and final DMUU criterion—the *criterion of insufficient reason.* Laplace argued that admitting that you have no idea whatsoever about what underlying probability distribution governs the states of nature is equivalent to admitting that — as far as you know — they are all equally likely to occur. Thus, if there are n states, this criterion involves assigning a probability of $1/n$ to each state and computing the "expected values" of the alternatives, the optimal model alternative being the one with the largest "expected value." The key point is this: If you, the decision maker, don't feel comfortable about assigning equal probabilities to the states, then you must know something about the state probabilities and should endeavor to estimate them and use a DMUR model! The logic is flawless, and, strangely enough, the insufficient reason criterion is the most subjective criterion of all, in a sense. It focuses directly on the decision maker and his or her personal knowledge about the problem and its environment.

To use the insufficient reason criterion, we don't actually need to assign the equal probabilities and compute "expected values." We need merely to add the outcomes for each alternative across all states; the optimal model alternative is the one with the largest total. In our portfolio example, A_4, Texas Aggie Kerosene, Inc., and A_5, New York City Firewood, Inc., are tied for optimality in the model on this criterion.

What are the risk characteristics of the insufficient reason criterion? It is risk neutral — for the same reason the EMV and EOL criteria in DMUR are risk neutral when used on physical outcomes.

DERIVING USEFUL SOLUTIONS

In our original portfolio example, note that, if we knew in advance that S_1 or S_2 would occur, we would choose A_6, Berkeley Power of California. If we knew that S_3 would happen, we would choose A_2, Three-Mile Island, Inc., or A_5, New York City Firewood, Inc.; and knowing that S_4 would occur would lead to the choice of A_2. And yet, Ima N. Surtin's model selected A_1, Don't invest, and MINIMAX REGRET chose A_4, Texas Aggie Kerosene, Inc. Should we be surprised that this occurred? No — and the reason is simple. We *don't* know in advance which state of nature will occur, and DMUU criteria address that fact directly. In fact, the MINIMAX REGRET criterion takes into account the interactions between alternatives across the states of natures.

RISK AND UTILITY

What role does the concept of economic utility play in a DMUU environment? Recall that, in our discussion of DMUR in Chapter 7, we derived decision makers' utility functions and used expected utility (EU) in an attempt to incorporate their risk characteristics. Could we do the same in DMUU? The answer is a resounding "No!" DMUU criteria are based on attitude toward risk, so that using a utility transformation in addition would "overkill" the matter.

Let us be sure to understand, therefore, how we as decision makers might actually use DMUU models. First, of course, we must be convinced that an acceptable prior probability distribution cannot be estimated for the problem. Second, we must use great care in identifying our alternatives. Third, we must examine our risk situation carefully. If a large positive result will make an order of magnitude difference, but the largest negative payoff would not be particularly damaging, we might wish to adopt the MAXIMAX criterion. If the converse is true, we should consider the MAXIMIN criterion. Finally, if we are approximately risk neutral and wish to "satisfice," we might select the MINIMAX REGRET or insufficient reason criterion.

STATE OF THE ART IN MODELING UNDER UNCERTAINTY

As a modeling device, DMUU is essentially a closed subject. One interesting (but not highly productive) postoptimality investigation that can be performed, however, is to determine the type of prior probability distribution that would have led to the same optimal alternative using DMUR. Let us illustrate this process with a small toy model for the sake of simplicity.

	S_1	S_2
A_1	−$1000	+$1500
A_2	+$150	+$300

You may wish to verify that the MAXIMIN criterion would select A_2, while the MAXIMAX, MINIMAX REGRET, and insufficient reason criteria all would select A_1. Let p be Pr (S_1) and $(1 - p)$ be Pr (S_2). To find the value of p at which we would be indifferent between A_1 and A_2 in a DMUR sense, we equate $E[A_1] = E[A_2]$, or $-\$1000p + \$1500(1 - p) = \$150p + \$300(1 - p)$. The solution is $p^* \doteq .51$. For values larger than p^*, A_2 is optimal; for smaller values, A_1 is optimal.

What have we learned from this analysis? Not a great deal, I'm afraid. However, our "Bayesians" cite such an analysis as evidence that we really used a probability distribution in our DMUU model anyway! We leave the reader to draw his or her own conclusions.

Apteryx Aircraft Company

The Scenario: Turner Round, the newly installed CEO of Apteryx Aircraft Company (AAC), sat in his office one morning and gazed morosely at the report of the company's miserable ten-year financial history. Turner, who is one of the best "firemen" in American industry, had been brought in to get rid of deadwood and to restore the company to profitability. Two more years under previous management would have made the firm as extinct as its namesake. This one, Turner mused, was a lulu.

The firm's founder, a World War I pilot named Doug Fite, had made countless errors in judgment during his years as CEO. For example, he became convinced in the mid-1940s that the jet engine was merely a passing fad and constructed the world's largest plant for building high-horsepower propeller engines for commercial aircraft. The plant was later converted to a ceiling-fan factory, but the damage was done. At the heart of AAC's problems, Turner concluded, was an almost total absence of planning.

The Problem: One does not mend an ailing aircraft manufacturing company overnight, since new product planning cycles sometimes run as long as 20 years from concept to rollout. Turner's first major project, therefore, was to assemble a staff of bright young executives (mostly MBAs) with long-range planning skills and begin to look at the aviation picture two decades into the future. Such a team was assembled, and Turner landed Lance Steele (lured away from Boring Aircraft Company) to head it.

"What we're going to do in the next six months," said Lance to his assembled hotshots, "is to look hard at the future and help Turner Round get this crummy outfit back into the ball game. Any suggestions as to how to proceed?"

The Model: Emma Bright spoke up immediately. "I got my MBA at Stanback U., and they're very big on decision theory out there. Maybe we could come up with scenarios for the future of the aircraft, both civil and military—these would be our states of nature. Then, using our collective experience in the aircraft industry, we could develop some decision alternatives. Although it will be tough, we can then estimate the outcomes associated with each alternative/state combination. So far, so good. The really difficult part will be coming up with a reasonable probability distribution on the states of nature. My prof at Stanback says it can always be done, so I guess we'll just have to cross that bridge when we come to it."

The group agreed with Emma's proposal, and the 12-hour workdays of research, discussions, and analysis began. After three months, the group had reached consensus on the following states of nature for their model, for the year 2000 A.D.

S_1: The aviation situation will remain essentially unchanged.

S_2: Wide-bodied, fuel-efficient passenger and cargo planes will have completely replaced the current generation of aircraft, and military fighting aircraft will have been made obsolete by operations in space.

S_3: A completely new form of power will have made fossil-fueled aircraft engines obsolete. Airplanes may even look completely different than they do now — perhaps wingless, spherical, or saucer-shaped.

S_4: Except for a few hobbyists who own small private aircraft, the age of aerodynamics will have passed, and some form of rocket travel will have replaced it.

S_5: There will be no air or space travel; people and cargo will be transported by lightning fast vehicles traveling in underground tubes — possibly magnetically suspended.

S_6: The world will have undergone nuclear war, and the survivors will travel solely by "people-powered" vehicles like bicycles and skate boards. The military would be equipped with armored bicycles and bows and arrows.

Two months later, some alternatives had been generated by Lance's group.

A_1: Retain the status quo, except for more careful cost control and more aggressive marketing efforts.

A_2: Use most available capital to build and modernize production facilities, concentrating on proven technology.

A_3: Use approximately 50% of available capital for production facilities, and invest the remainder in building a research and development capability.

A_4: All but abandon maintenance of a production capability, and concentrate most available funds on high-technology research and development.

A_5: Get out of the transportation business and find some less risky niche in industry.

With six states of nature and five alternatives identified, the group turned to the difficult task of quantifying the 30 outcomes in their decision matrix. They quickly abandoned the idea of trying to state outcomes in "dollars of profit," since there were so many imponderables associated with such an effort. They decided eventually to express the outcomes as dimensionless quantities ranging from -20 to $+20$ and to use a modified form of the DELPHI technique to achieve convergence of opinion. One month later — after six months had elapsed since their initial meeting — the group produced the following decision matrix, noting that none of the five alternatives is dominated.

Solution to the Model: "Well," noted Emma Bright, "now comes the hard part — estimating a prior probability distribution on the states of nature."

Apteryx Decision Matrix

States of Nature

	S_1	S_2	S_3	S_4	S_5	S_6
A_1	+10	−5	−10	−15	−20	+12
A_2	+18	+12	−15	−18	−20	+8
A_3	0	+6	+10	+5	−4	0
A_4	−10	0	+20	+13	+18	−12
A_5	−5	−10	+8	+16	+20	+10

Alternatives

"Not so fast, Emma," retorted Lance Steele. "I've thought about that quite a bit—I have no earthly idea how we'd go about doing such a thing. Besides—I don't care what your prof at Stanback says—we can go about this as a decision making under uncertainty situation and use one of the classical DMUU criteria to analyze our model."

"I never heard of DMUU," replied Emma, "but I'm game if the rest of the group is. How do we proceed?"

Lance and the group set up a meeting with Turner Round the next day. He was pleased with the model the group had generated, but he was then asked to explicitly express his view of Apteryx's risk environment.

"That's a tough one, gang," said Turner. "AAC isn't in good enough financial shape to aggressively seek risk, but if we manage the company like pussycats, we'll never get it back into the ball game. I guess I'd have to conclude that we're in a satisficing situation right now. We may have to forego the opportunity for a really big breakthrough to avoid a disastrous loss. Can the group work with that description?"

"You bet we can, Turner," said Lance. "What you've just described is a classical situation in which the use of Leonard Savage's MINIMAX REGRET criterion is applicable. Let us set up the regret matrix for our model and then get back to you."

Here is the regret matrix:

Apteryx Regret Matrix

States of Nature

	S_1	S_2	S_3	S_4	S_5	S_6	Maximum Regret
A_1	8	17	30	31	40	0	40
A_2	0	0	35	34	40	4	40
A_3	18	6	10	11	24	12	24
A_4	28	12	0	3	2	24	28
A_5	23	22	12	0	0	2	23

Alternatives

Turner noted that the optimal model solution is A_5, with A_3 a close second.

Solution to the Problem: The group reassembled and showed the model solution to Turner. After studying the regret matrix for a while, he commented as follows.

"The model suggests getting out of the transportation business or splitting our capital investment about equally between production facilities and an R&D capability. The second alternative isn't very exciting, but it makes good business sense, I suppose. What if I gave you a sixth alternative — could you stick it on the bottom of the model for me?"

"We *could*, Turner," replied Lance, "but it would be an entirely different model then. What the current model told you would no longer count."

"I understand," said Turner, "I was just teasing. You and your people put in a tremendous amount of effort on this venture, and I want you to know how helpful your model is in sharpening my thinking. I'll take the proposal to the board at their regular meeting next Tuesday and sell them on the idea of splitting our effort about equally between production and R&D. I think they'll go for it. By the way, I'm also proposing the new position of vice-president for planning, and I've already got someone in mind."

SUMMARY

We reviewed a model or structure for decision making under risk (DMUR) in which it is not possible to estimate a satisfactory probability distribution on the states of nature. We looked at four classical criteria that have been suggested for such a model: MAXIMIN, MAXIMAX, MINIMAX REGRET, and insufficient reason.

We characterized MAXIMIN and MAXIMAX as risk averse and risk seeking, respectively, whereas MINIMAX REGRET and insufficient reason were more "middle-of-the-road" or "satisficing" criteria. We noted that each of these criteria have *built-in* risk characteristics, so that using the utility transformation in DMUU is unwarranted.

Finally, we illustrated the process of building and analyzing a DMUU model with the Apteryx Aircraft Company case.

PROBLEMS

1. One approach that has been suggested for "forcing" the construction of a prior probability distribution on the states of nature, is rank ordering the states from *least likely* to *most likely* to occur. If there are n states, let

$$S = \sum_{i=1}^{n} i = \frac{n \cdot (n+1)}{2}$$

We then assign the probability $1/S$ to the least likely state, $2/S$ to the next, and so on, with the most likely state getting a probability of n/S assigned.

   a. What do you think about this scheme? Would you be likely to use it to avoid the use of DMUU criteria?

   b. Try out this approach using your own personal feel for the relative likelihood of the six states in the Apteryx case, and compute the EMV of the five alternatives. Note that there are $6! = 720$ different orderings possible for the six states. You might also wish to verify that the most favorable distribution for A_3 (i.e., highest probability for largest outcome) *does not lead to A_3 having the highest EMV!*

2. In the Apteryx case, remove alternative A_2 from the decision matrix and recompute the "regret" matrix. Note now that A_5 is clearly the optimal choice and A_3 and A_4 are tied for second place.

   a. How do you explain this phenomenon in terms of the riskiness of the two models (one with A_2 included and one with A_2 excluded)?

   b. Would you ever actually *do* such a thing when using a DMUU model?

3. Recall the Jack Legg Associates case from Chapter 7, in which Hy Roller and Nawonda Betts were attempting to decide on one of three salary plans. A binomial distribution representing relative frequency of success in project management was used as a prior distribution for an analysis in DMUR. The decision matrix (without the prior distribution) is reproduced here.

Decision Matrix

No. of Successful Projects

		S_1: 0	S_2: 1	S_3: 2	S_4: 3
Alternatives	A_1: Plan A	$35,000	$35,000	$35,000	$35,000
	A_2: Plan B	$21,000	$35,000	$42,000	$49,000
	A_3: Plan C	$7000	$28,000	$42,000	$70,000

Because Hy was clearly a risk seeker and Nawonda clearly a risk avoider, they sought help to construct their utility functions. On the basis of expected utility, subsequently, Hy's model clearly indicated A_3 to be preferred, while Nawonda's tended toward A_1 or A_2.

   a. In analyzing this problem with a DMUU model, compute the optimal model alternatives using MAXIMAX and MAXIMIN. Note how clear the choices are in both cases.

   b. Now analyze the model using the two "satisficing" criteria — MINIMAX REGRET and insufficient reason — and compare the results. Note that MINIMAX REGRET distinguishes the "middle-of-the-road" alternative nicely but that Laplace's criterion does not. Can you explain why this is so?

4.   *The Scenario:* Lee Beedo, our MBA student from Chapter 7, is startled to learn in his Friday classes that there will be a major exam the following Monday in *both* his Finance and Marketing classes. He had been putting off studying so far, so it looked like a long, arduous weekend.

The Problem: Lee was doing "high-B" work so far in his Marketing class but was flirting with disaster in Finance. How should he allocate the meager study time available between the two subjects? If he knew whether the profs would give hard or easy exams, he could tackle the problem directly. But both profs were brand-new Ph.D.'s in their first semester of teaching here at Cambridge Teacher's College, so the MBA students don't have a "line" on them yet. The situation looked grim.

The Model: As a last resort, Lee decided to see if any of that stuff he had in his decision theory/management science course last semester would help him. The problem didn't look even vaguely like math programming, so he discarded that idea. It just might be a DMUR-type problem, but how could he possibly estimate a probability distribution on the testing proclivities of two brand-new professors? He finally settled on DMUU, and built the decision matrix exhibited below. Note that he couldn't really quantify the outcomes, so he decided to use a system of +'s (good) and −'s (bad), with 0 for "neutral."

Lee Beedo's Decision Matrix

Possible Testing Outcomes

Alternatives	S_1: Both exams easy	S_2: MKTG hard, FIN easy	S_3: MKTG easy, FIN hard	S_4: Both exams hard
A_1: Study only MKTG	+	++	−	+
A_2: Study MKTG and FIN equally	++	+++	+	0
A_3: Study only FIN	++	−−	+++	+
A_4: Relax and hope for the best	+	−−	−−	−−−

Solution to the Model:

a. Are any of the alternatives dominated in this decision matrix?
b. If Lee were highly risk seeking, what two alternatives would catch his fancy?
c. If he decided that he was highly risk averse, what alternative might he choose using the MAXIMIN criterion. (*Hint:* Replace "−−−" by "1," "−−" by "2," and so on, to perform the analysis.)
d. If Lee wished to "satisfice" and decided to use the MINIMAX REGRET criterion, what would the optimal model alternative be?

Solution to the Problem: Despite the analysis, Lee Beedo chose alternative 4: Relax and hope for the best. Unfortunately, S_4 actually occurred, and Lee is currently working toward a second undergraduate degree in High Fashion Merchandising.

a. Was Lee allowed to choose an alternative other than the optimal one indicated by the model? Who does he think he is—ignoring the results of his analysis in making his final decision?
b. Models don't make decisions—managers do. (But sometimes they make fairly poor ones!)

REFERENCES

1. LaValle, I. *Fundamentals of Decision Analysis.* New York: Holt, Rinehart and Winston, 1978.
2. Arrow, K. "Decision Theory and Operations Research." *Operations Research,* Vol. 5 (1957), pp. 765–774.

ADDITIONAL READING

Brown, R., A. Kahr, and C. Peterson. *Decision Analysis for the Manager.* New York: Holt, Rinehart, and Winston, 1974.

Von Neumann, J., and O. Morgenstern. *Theory of Games and Economic Behavior,* 2nd ed. Princeton, N.J.: Princeton University Press, 1953.

CHAPTER 13

Modeling with Multiple Objectives

So far in this text, all the optimizing models we have discussed involve maximizing or minimizing a single function of the decision variables, which we referred to as the *objective function.* Although we have continually stressed that most managers have more than one objective or goal in a given decision situation, our approach to this point has been to handle secondary objectives outside the context of the model itself. Only in Chapter 3, with the Vera Tuft problem and with Marijane Moss's problem in Problem 2, did we attempt to touch on the possibility that multiple objectives might be accommodated within the model itself.

Lest we promise more than we can deliver in this regard, we observe that so-called "multicriterion programming" is still in its infancy, so that its applicability at present is limited to a somewhat restricted set of decision scenarios. For example, in what follows we will address ways in which to incorporate into models the subset of a manager's objectives that are clearly quantifiable — such as profit margins, cost levels, market share, work force composition, and so on. The truth is that, many times, factors that we don't yet know how to quantify satisfactorily — such as employee morale, corporate social responsibility, political considerations, and ethical/moral issues — are the real "drivers" of the problem under consideration.

There have been some rather large *books* written on the subject of modeling with multiple objectives. To make our one-chapter treatment of this subject manageable and useful, therefore, we limit our attention to the smaller, but highly important, subject of *multiple objective linear programming (MOLP).* To be precise, we restrict our discussion to problems that can be profitably modeled and analyzed by LP, except that the objective "function" is a *set* of linear functions and some specified relationship among them.

UNDERLYING ASSUMPTIONS

As we did in Chapter 2, we require here that the assumptions of *additivity* and *divisibility* hold and that we are dealing with a nonprobabilistic scenario. We will address two very different decision situations: First, the multiple objectives can be stated in *commensurable* quantities; and second, one or more of the objectives are stated in *incommensurable* quantities. We discuss each, after defining some mathematical notation to be used.

MATRIX-VECTOR NOTATION

In previous chapters, we used the "big sigma" notation as a convenient way to represent linear functions. In attempting to deal with an objective "function" that turns out to be a *set* of linear functions, however, this notation becomes unwieldy, so we must resort to the more compact and abstract matrix-vector notation.

We define the n vector $\mathbf{x}$ as the column:

$$\mathbf{x} = \begin{bmatrix} x_1 \\ x_2 \\ \cdot \\ \cdot \\ \cdot \\ x_n \end{bmatrix} \qquad (13.1)$$

The associated row vector $\mathbf{x}'$ (read "x-transpose") is merely

$$\mathbf{x}' = (x_1, x_2, \ldots, x_n) \qquad (13.2)$$

The product of the row vector $\mathbf{c}' = (c_1, c_2, \ldots, c_n)$ and the column vector $\mathbf{x}$ is

$$\mathbf{c}' \cdot \mathbf{x} = c_1 x_1 + c_2 x_2 + \ldots + c_n x_n, \qquad (13.3)$$

by definition, which we see is identical to

$$\sum_{j=1}^{n} c_j x_j$$

our LP objective function from Chapter 2.

The matrix $\mathbf{A}$ with m rows and n columns is defined in the usual way.

$$A = \begin{bmatrix} a_{11} & a_{12} & & a_{1j} & & a_{1n} \\ a_{21} & a_{22} & \cdots & a_{2j} & \cdots & a_{2n} \\ \cdot & \cdot & \cdots & \cdot & \cdots & \cdot \\ \cdot & \cdot & & \cdot & & \cdot \\ \cdot & \cdot & & \cdot & & \cdot \\ a_{i1} & a_{i2} & \cdots & a_{ij} & \cdots & a_{in} \\ \cdot & \cdot & & \cdot & & \cdot \\ \cdot & \cdot & & \cdot & & \cdot \\ \cdot & \cdot & \cdots & \cdot & \cdots & \cdot \\ a_{m1} & a_{m2} & & a_{mj} & & a_{mn} \end{bmatrix} \qquad (13.4)$$

If $\mathbf{b}$ is the column vector of constants on the right-hand sides of the LP constraints, and $\mathbf{A}$ is the matrix of constraint coefficients, then we may write the LP model as follows:

$$\text{MAXIMIZE } x_0 = \mathbf{c}'\mathbf{x} \qquad (13.5)$$

$$\text{SUBJECT TO: } \mathbf{A}\mathbf{x} \leq \mathbf{b} \qquad (13.6)$$

Note that this is just another way of writing (1.3) and (1.4) from Chapter 1.

Finally, suppose that we have K linear objective functions in our multiple objective set. Using $f(\cdot)$ as the notation for "is a function of," we write the MOLP model as follows.

$$\text{MINIMIZE or MAXIMIZE } x_0 = f(\mathbf{c}_1'\mathbf{x}, \mathbf{c}_2'\mathbf{x}, \ldots, \mathbf{c}_k'\mathbf{x}, \ldots, \mathbf{c}_K'\mathbf{x}) \quad (13.7)$$

$$\text{SUBJECT TO: } \mathbf{A}\mathbf{x} \begin{Bmatrix} \leq \\ = \\ \geq \end{Bmatrix} \mathbf{b} \qquad (13.8)$$

The function f expresses some relationship among the K linear objective functions. For example, if $K = 1$, and f is the identity function, we have the single objective LP model (13.5) and (13.6). We will look at other forms f can assume, later in this chapter.

Let us now investigate the two distinct forms that MOLP models can take.

COMMENSURABLE $\mathbf{c}_k'\mathbf{x}$

If each of the $\mathbf{c}_k'\mathbf{x}$, $k = 1, \ldots, K$, are in the same dimensional units, then we have a model with *commensurable* linear objective functions. For example, suppose that we are trying to model a classical product mix problem with LP, but discover to our chagrin that the profit contributions (c_j) for the products are functions of the unknown condition of the economy six months hence, when our products will be on sale in retail outlets. Given one of three possible states of the economy, we can estimate with fair accuracy the profit contributions of each product, but we don't know which state will actually occur. Thus we have three different objective functions—all in the same units (dollars of total profit contribution).

As another example, recall Problem 1 in Chapter 2, in which the Daley Paper Company wished to minimize "trim loss" in cutting large rolls of paper into smaller rolls to fill orders. The exercise hinted that the objective was to slit the large rolls using specific cutting patterns in such a way as to minimize end-trim loss (i.e., rolls that are smaller in width than the smallest order width). However, such an approach may well result in overproducing (above order sizes) some of the order-width rolls. If we wish to minimize (in some sense) *both* end-trim loss *and* overproduction of order-width rolls, we can state these two objectives in commensurable quantities (inch-rolls of paper).

As we shall see later, MOLP models with commensurable objectives allow for a great deal of flexibility by the decision maker in shaping the model to his or her personal inclinations and proclivities. Incommensurable objectives, on the other hand, are much more rigid and difficult to deal with.

INCOMMENSURABLE $c_k' x$

In Chapter 3, Vera Tuft, the hard-hitting CEO of the Henny Youngman Iron and Steel Company, was attempting to build a large corporate model that could be used to analyze the firm's operations. Recall that Vera's objectives were to achieve a return on investment of 18%, to reduce inventory by 20%, to eliminate the use of overtime, to reduce short-term borrowing by 30%, and so on. She attempted to achieve these goals by constraints in the LP model but got back the message: "NO FEASIBLE SOLUTION." The alternative, of course, is to model Vera's problem with MOLP. In this case, her objectives are clearly *incommensurable* (i.e., percentage of capital invested, percentage of inventory reduction, worker-hours of overtime, dollars of short-term loans). By exercising our imagination, we *might* find a way to express these objectives in the same dimensional units, but perhaps not in an entirely satisfactory way.

A second example might better illustrate the incommensurability phenomenon. Sang Lee [1] reported an actual application of MOLP modeling and analysis in a health care clinic budgeting problem. Some of the objective areas and their dimensional units, are as follows.

Objective Area	Units
1. Hourly pay rates for ten types of employees	Dollars per hour paid
2. Retirement fund	Percentage of total salary
3. New equipment	Dollars (capital)
4. Staffing patterns	Numbers of employees
5. Expense by type of medical service	Dollars per patient charged

Clearly, one would have to be a magician like Harry Houdini to get these five objective areas into the same "hat"!

Let us now examine some modeling techniques that have been employed for both types of MOLP models.

MOLP MODELING

In dealing with both commensurable and incommensurable MOLP objective sets, we note at the outset that *all* the techniques that we will discuss can be used to model problems with commensurable objective sets. However, only a subset of these techniques is applicable to incommensurable scenarios. For this reason, we discuss approaches that *require* commensurability first (MAXIMIN, MAXIMAX, linear combinations) and those that *do not require* commensurability next (preemptive goal prioritization, preemptive goal programming).

MOLP MODELS REQUIRING COMMENSURABILITY

As noted, several MOLP modeling approaches require that each of the $c_k'x$, $k = 1, \ldots, K$, have the same dimensional units. We discuss three such approaches in the paragraphs that follow.

The MAXIMIN Approach

In Chapter 12, in our discussion on decision making under uncertainty, we encountered a MAXIMIN criterion for use with formal matrix decision models. We noted that this criterion represented a conservative, risk-averse approach to decision making—in effect, a "Murphy's law" sort of pessimistic view of "nature." In MOLP modeling, the MAXIMIN approach has the same general tenor—but its application in this context is a bit more subtle, as we will see.

In mathematical symbols, the MOLP model using the MAXIMIN approach is as follows.

$$\text{MAXIMIZE } x_0 = \text{MINIMUM } \{c_1'x, c_2'x, \ldots, c_K'x\} \quad (13.9)$$

$$\text{SUBJECT TO: } Ax \begin{Bmatrix} \leq \\ = \\ \geq \end{Bmatrix} b \quad (13.10)$$

Stated in plain English, the MAXIMIN approach seeks the value of the decision vector x that makes the minimum value of any of the K linear objective functions as large as possible. For example, returning to our product mix illustration in which the profit contributions for each product depended upon three different states of the economy, use of the MAXIMIN approach would guarantee (as far as the *model* is concerned) that the "best of the worst" occurred. This approach would, in all probability, preclude the "best possible result" from happening, but this is an inevitable outcome of opting for a "defensive" strategy.

The MAXIMAX Approach

Analogous to its counterpart in decision making under uncertainty in Chapter 12, the MAXIMAX approach in MOLP modeling is a "high roller's" approach to decision making. It reflects a highly optimistic view and is risk seeking. In terms of our illustration, it assumes (or hopes) that the most favorable state of the economy will come about and "puts all of its eggs in one basket."

In mathematical symbols, the MOLP model using the MAXIMAX approach is as follows.

$$\text{MAXIMIZE } x_0 = \text{MAXIMUM } \{c_1'x, c_2'x, \ldots, c_K'x\} \qquad (13.11)$$

$$\text{SUBJECT TO: } Ax \begin{Bmatrix} \leq \\ = \\ \geq \end{Bmatrix} b \qquad (13.12)$$

Obviously, the MAXIMAX approach seeks the value of the decision vector x that yields the largest possible value of the objective function. Like its DMUU counterpart, it risks obtaining very poor results by seeking the best possible outcome.

The Linear Combinations Approach

An MOLP model with an objective function consisting of a "linear combination" of K linear objective functions, in mathematical symbols, would be

$$\text{MAXIMIZE or MINIMIZE } x_0 = \sum_{k=1}^{K} v_k c_k'x \qquad (13.13)$$

$$\text{SUBJECT TO: } Ax \begin{Bmatrix} \leq \\ = \\ \geq \end{Bmatrix} b \qquad (13.14)$$

Since the K linear objective functions $c_k'x$, $k = 1, \ldots, K$, are commensurable, then the *single*-objective function (13.13) has the same dimensional units as the K functions that it represents. The weights v_k, $k = 1, \ldots, K$, can have several interpretations. For example, if the individual objective functions represent (as in our illustration) different valuation mechanisms associated with a set of states of nature, then the v_k could represent the elements of a probability distribution on those states (either empirically or subjectively derived).

On the other hand, the v_k weights could represent a set of *relative priorities,* assigned by the decision maker, for the various objective functions. For instance, if the $c_k'x$ are goals or objectives that are stated in commensurable units, the decision maker may wish to prioritize those goals or objectives by selecting numerical values of the v_k that reflect his assessment of their relative importance. If one objective $c_r'x$ were of overriding significance, for example, the decision maker could choose $v_r > 0$ and all other $v_k = 0$—and a simple LP model would result. On the other hand, a "Laplace-like" criterion similar to the criterion of insufficient reason (from Chapter 12) would result if the decision maker chose values $v_k = 1/K$, $k = 1, \ldots, K$. Or an ordinal ranking of the K objectives might lead to the following simple weighting scheme:

$$\text{MAXIMIZE or MINIMIZE } x_0 = \sum_{k=1}^{K} k \, \mathbf{c}_k' \mathbf{x} \qquad (13.15)$$

where the individual objectives are arranged in ascending order of importance to the decision maker.

The three approaches discussed so far require that the linear objective functions be commensurable. We now consider two MOLP modeling techniques that can accommodate incommensurable sets of goals or objectives.

MOLP MODELS NOT REQUIRING COMMENSURABILITY

In decision situations in which the decision maker has multiple objectives, and where these objectives cannot be stated in the same dimensional units, there are two modeling approaches (among others) that are useful. They are *preemptive goal prioritization* and *goal programming*. The two approaches exhibit strong similarities in one sense, but they are different enough in an applied context to warrant discussing them separately.

Preemptive Goal Prioritization

If multiple goals can be stated mathematically only in terms of differently dimensioned objectives, then one approach to incorporating them into an MOLP model is to have the decision maker make *preemptive* decisions as to the importance of the objectives. That is, the decision maker could be asked to identify the objective that — in his or her judgment — has absolutely overriding importance in the particular decision situation at hand. Once the overriding objective is identified, the *next* most important goal is identified, and so on, until we have obtained a *preemptive prioritization* of all K goals or objectives. Thus, it does not matter that the objectives may or may not be commensurable in their units of measurement — the most important goal is satisfied first, then the next most important, and so on. The mathematical MOLP model for a preemptive prioritization can be written as a *sequence* of K linear programming models, as follows:

$$\text{MAXIMIZE } (x_0)_k = \mathbf{c}_k' \mathbf{x}, \, k = 1, \ldots, K \qquad (13.16)$$

$$\text{SUBJECT TO: } \mathbf{Ax} \left\{ \begin{matrix} \leq \\ = \\ \geq \end{matrix} \right\} \mathbf{b} \qquad (13.17)$$

$$\mathbf{c}_{k-1}' \mathbf{x} = (x_0^*)_{k-1}, \quad k = 1, \ldots, K \qquad (13.18)$$

In (13.16), the K linear objective functions are arranged by the decision maker in preemptive priority order, with $\mathbf{c}_1' \mathbf{x}$ being the function with the highest priority, $\mathbf{c}_2' \mathbf{x}$ being the next highest, and so on. Equations (13.18), then, force subsequent LP models in the sequence to preserve the optimal solutions to higher-priority models. For example, let $(x_0^*)_1$ denote the optimal value of the objective function with the highest preemptive priority. Then the *second* LP model in the sequence would be

$$\text{MAXIMIZE } (x_0)_2 = \mathbf{c}_2' \mathbf{x} \tag{13.19}$$

$$\text{SUBJECT TO: } \mathbf{Ax} \left\{ \begin{array}{c} \leq \\ = \\ \geq \end{array} \right\} \mathbf{b} \tag{13.20}$$

$$\mathbf{c}_1' \mathbf{x} = (x_0^*)_1 \tag{13.21}$$

As we shall see later, it is not actually necessary (in a computational sense) to solve K different LP models. However, modeling the preemptive goal prioritization MOLP model in the form of (13.16) through (13.18) helps us to grasp more easily what is happening.

Goal Programming

So-called *goal programming* (*GP*) was "invented" by Charnes and Cooper in 1962 [2] and has been popularized by a number of authors (e.g., Lee and Moore [3]). The thrust of GP is to represent the prioritized managerial goals as a set of *constraints* and associated *deviational variables,* which are similar to slack and surplus variables in ordinary linear programming models. As we shall see, the idea is to treat functions of the deviational variables as objectives to be minimized or maximized.

Let us explore this concept a bit further before exhibiting the mathematical model. As we noted earlier, if we stated objectives in terms such as "maximize profit contribution" and "minimize overtime utilization," they would almost always be conflicting. For example, suppose that we had a set of linear constraints like those in (13.20) and three objectives represented by linear functions that were incommensurable. Suppose next that we solved three different LP models using each of the objective functions singly and that their optimal values were $(x_0^*)_1$, $(x_0^*)_2$, and $(x_0^*)_3$. Finally, let us append the three *equality* constraints:

$$\mathbf{c}_k \mathbf{x} = (x_0^*)_k, \quad k = 1, 2, 3 \tag{13.22}$$

Rarely (if ever) would there be a feasible point in the resulting constraint space, so that—regardless of what objective function one chose to use—the computerized simplex algorithm would always return the message: "NO FEASIBLE SOLUTION."

Suppose, however, that a decision maker would be satisfied to meet his or her goals *as closely as possible,* but within a priority structure. If this is the case, and if the underlying assumptions of MOLP are met, then we have a problem that may be modeled and analyzed using goal programming.

There are dozens of variants of goal programming models, and to attempt to discuss them *all* in this chapter would only invite confusion on the part of the reader. Therefore, we will confine ourselves to what is sometimes called the "pure preemptive GP model" and refer the interested readers to the book by Lee and Moore [3] for other variants.

Pure Preemptive Goal Programming: The various objectives of the decision maker are first preemptively prioritized and indexed in descending order of priority ($c_1'x$ represents the highest-priority objective, $c_2'x$ the next highest, etc.). The objectives are then transformed into additional *constraints* whose right-hand sides are the specific *goals* G_k of the decision maker, conditioned by deviational variables, as follows:

$$c_k'\mathbf{x} = G_k + d_k^+ - d_k^-, \; k = 1, \ldots, K \qquad (13.23)$$

$$d_k^+, d_k^- \geq 0 \text{ for all } k \qquad (13.24)$$

The objective "function" now becomes the *set* of objectives that seeks to minimize the appropriate deviations (the values of the d_k^+ and/or d_k^-) from the G_k—the managerial goals or targets.

If all this seems complicated, perhaps our interactive computer friend POGO (*p*rogram to *o*perationalize *g*oal *o*ptimization) can clear things up via the following exchange.

POGO: Hey, man, like thanks for ringing my number. The dudes that I know call me POGO. What's shakin'?

HOWARD: Well, POGO, my cognomen is Howard, and I am a conveyor of electronically transmitted imagery and chronologically instantaneous narratives related to the description of competitive physical events, to which the public directs its attention.

POGO: Heavy, Howard—so you're a TV sportscaster. What's bugging you?

HOWARD: To be utterly frank, POGO, a troublesome and increasing percentage of the video-oriented populace has grown less than enamored of my incisive and erudite oral observations. Thus, sadly, I have been—in effect— coerced into seeking an alternative vocation.

POGO: You got canned? That's a bummer, Howard. What's new?

HOWARD: Let me tell it like it is, POGO. I've decided to take over the ancestral business, Balloon Specialists, Inc., that has fallen upon difficult times of late. We were, until misfortune befell us recently, the largest manufacturer and purveyor of hot air balloons in the free world. We committed a myriad of unfortunate mistakes, but our most damaging miscalculation was to hire a former heavyweight champion, who shall remain nameless here, as CEO. He spent most of his time composing less than inspired dithyrambs, and BS suffered abysmally as a result.

POGO: "Float like a butterfly, sting like a bee." He done something like that to your balloon business Howard?

HOWARD: In a figurative sense, precisely.

POGO: Oh my. How can I help out, man?

HOWARD: BS has a brace of behemoth assemblage facilities for the aggregation of thermally motivated aircraft . . . .

POGO: You've got two big hot-air balloon assembly plants, right?

HOWARD: That's what I just said. The facility in Albuquerque is antiquated, but the Phoenix construction, is, happily, of more recent vintage. Our line consists of an august triumvirate of different craft that we vend under the appellations Thermos, Atmos, and Stratos.

POGO: Sort of a three-bagger, right?

HOWARD: I'll ignore that indifferent attempt at jocularity, POGO. To continue, at my behest the following data were extracted and assembled:

	Phoenix			Albuquerque		
	Thermos	Atmos	Stratos	Thermos	Atmos	Stratos
Profit margins	$1500	$3000	$2000	$1500	$3000	$2000
Hand finishing (in hours)	—	—	3	3	1	2
Hand assembling (in hours)	—	—	—	2	3	5
Test inflation (in hours)	1	2	—	1	2	—

Hours Available per Month

Hand finishing	300
Hand assembling	240
Test inflation	270

What I require, my electronic acquaintance, is to ascertain the precise division of our restricted complement of personnel resources to distribute among the trio of products in such a manner as to derive pecuniary returns of at least $600,000 per month. At the same time, a secondary desideratum would be to diminish production at the obsolescent Albuquerque facility. Tertiarily, the probable phase-out of the Stratos line may be imminent, so producing as few of these as possible would be desirable. But attend me well, POGO—I don't want the last two objectives to interfere with the first one. Moreover, I don't want the third to interfere with the second.

POGO: Translated into English, man, you've got a product mix problem with multiple objectives. Are the following OK?

P1: Generate a profit contribution of at least $600,000 per month.

P2: Get Albuquerque production as small as possible.

P3: Get Stratos production as small as possible.

HOWARD: Affirmative, POGO—that's substantially correct. Hear me well, now: I don't want P2 and P3 to interfere with P1, and I don't want P3 to interfere with P2.

POGO: I'm cool, Howard. What we've got here is a problem that can be modeled by goal programming with pure preemptive priorities on the incommensurable objective functions.

HOWARD: Yes, admirably expressed.

POGO: Before I lay the model on you, man, do you know anything about linear programming?

HOWARD: Certainly. I am a close personal friend of George Dantzig, the inventor of that marvelous SIMPLEX technique. I don't like to boast, but I am responsible for George's use of the term "SIMPLEX" for his algorithm. I'll never forget that snowy December afternoon when George and I . . . .

POGO: Uh, sure Howard—let's move on. What we're going to do is to turn your objectives into constraints. Our variables x_1, x_2, x_3 represent the numbers of balloons of Thermos, Atmos, and Stratos, respectively, to produce in Phoenix. The variables x_4, x_5, and x_6 stand for the same things in Albuquerque. I'll show you the entire model, and then we can rap some more about it.

$$P1: \text{MIN } (x_0)_1 = d_1^- \tag{13.25}$$

$$P2: \text{MIN } (x_0)_2 = \quad\quad d_2^+ \tag{13.26}$$

$$P3: \text{MIN } (x_0)_3 = \quad\quad\quad\quad d_3^+ \tag{13.27}$$

$$\text{S.T.: } 1500x_1 + 3000x_2 + 2000x_3 + 1500x_4 + 3000x_5 + 2000x_6$$
$$= 600{,}000 + d_1^+ - d_1^- \tag{13.28}$$

$$x_4 + x_5 + x_6 = 0 + d_2^+ - d_2^- \tag{13.29}$$

$$x_3 \quad\quad + x_6 = 0 + d_3^+ - d_3^- \tag{13.30}$$

$$3x_3 + 3x_4 + x_5 + 2x_6 \le 300 \tag{13.31}$$

$$2x_4 + 3x_5 + 5x_6 \le 240 \tag{13.32}$$

$$x_1 + 2x_2 \quad + x_4 + 2x_5 \quad\quad \le 270 \tag{13.33}$$

$$\text{All } x_j, d_1^+, d_1^-, d_2^+, d_2^-, d_3^+, d_3^- \ge 0 \tag{13.34}$$

HOWARD: How devilishly clever, POGO! The three constraints (13.28), (13.29), and (13.30) set our targets of $600,000 profit contribution, zero production in Albuquerque, and zero production of Stratos models. The deviational variables allow a modicum of slack in case one or more of the goals cannot be attained. Our three objectives, then, are naturally to minimize the negative deviation from $600,000 of profit and to minimize the positive deviations from Albuquerque and Stratos production. The other constraints (13.31) through (13.33) are merely our scarce labor complement. But George's SIMPLEX algorithm will only operate with *one* objective function, and we have a triad of such. Doesn't that obfuscate our peregrination?

POGO: No, man—don't worry. Eyeball the rest of the chapter, and I'll see you in Problem Numero Uno. This is POGO, saying *ciao* for now.

Some Important Modeling Considerations: Before moving on to discuss solution approaches, let us examine the so-called "deviational variables" more closely. In Howard's model that we just discussed, all three goals turned out to be "one-sided" in a sense. That is, since $G_1 = \$600{,}000$ and our goal was *at least* to achieve it, our objective function (13.25) involved minimizing only the negative deviational variable d_1^-. If, for some managerial reason such as tax planning, the goal had been to generate exactly \$600,000, then the objective function would have been MIN $x_0 = d_1^+ + d_1^-$. Note in this case that one of the two deviational variables will always be zero in an optimal model solution.

On the other hand, if we wished actually to maximize profit contribution, then an appropriate objective function would be MAX $x_0 = d_1^+$.

The point of this discussion is that goal programming, although nothing more than a variant of multiobjective linear programming, is a very sophisticated modeling tool. More than any other technique in this book (so far), it should only be used if the decision maker is *intimately* involved in the modeling process. For example, the three different versions of Howard's profit contribution objective could well lead to three entirely different model solutions, and it is critically important that the function actually used is the correct one from the decision maker's point of view. Models do not make decisions, of course, but bad MS/OR models, or models of the wrong problem, are worse than not using MS/OR models at all.

SOLUTION APPROACHES: AN INTUITIVE DESCRIPTION

The basic approach to solving MOLP models of all types is to transform them into equivalent models that are amenable to solution by variants of the SIMPLEX algorithm. We saw this approach in Chapter 5, where certain varieties of nonlinear programming models were "linearized" so that the highly efficient SIMPLEX algorithm could be employed to obtain usable solutions. In what follows, we concentrate our attention on two facets of the solution approaches: the transformation and the revision of the SIMPLEX algorithm (if any) required to generate an optimal model solution.

THE MAXIMIN MODEL

For convenience, we restate the MAXIMIN MOLP model:

$$\text{MAXIMIZE } x_0 = \text{MINIMUM } \{c_1' x, c_2' x, \ldots, c_K' x\} \qquad (13.9)$$

$$\text{SUBJECT TO: } Ax \begin{Bmatrix} \leq \\ = \\ \geq \end{Bmatrix} b \qquad (13.10)$$

To transform (13.9) and (13.10) into an ordinary LP model, we use a surrogate variable y, which we define as follows.

$$y \leq c_k' x, \quad k = 1, 2, \ldots, K \qquad (13.35)$$

That is, we add exactly K constraints to (13.10), the effect of which is to guarantee that y takes on a value that is the *minimum* of the set of commensurable objective functions in (13.9). We then set up the ordinary single objective LP model:

$$\text{MAXIMIZE } x_0 = y \tag{13.36}$$

$$\text{SUBJECT TO: } \quad y - \mathbf{c}_k'\mathbf{x} \le 0, \quad k = 1, \ldots, K \tag{13.35}$$

$$\mathbf{Ax} \begin{Bmatrix} \le \\ = \\ \ge \end{Bmatrix} \mathbf{b} \tag{13.10}$$

This formulation assures that our computerized SIMPLEX algorithm produces the optimal model solution $\mathbf{x}^*$ that satisfied our original objective function (13.9).

Understanding the solutions produced by MOLP MAXIMIN modeling is not as straightforward as one might imagine. To illustrate this phenomenon, let us consider the following toy model, which may be thought of as a very small product mix scenario.

$$\text{MAXIMIZE } x_0 = \text{MINIMUM } \{2x_1 + 4x_2 + 5x_3, \, 3x_1 + 3x_2 + 4x_3, \, 4x_1 + 3x_2 + 2x_3\} \tag{13.37}$$
$$\text{SUBJECT TO: } \quad x_1 + x_2 + x_3 \le 50 \tag{13.38}$$
$$2x_1 + 3x_2 + 5x_3 \le 130 \tag{13.39}$$

To lend a bit of credence to this toy model, we could think of the three objectives in (13.36) as being total profit contributions from producing three products under three different states of the economy.

The transformed version of our little problem is as follows.

$$\text{MAXIMIZE } x_0 = y$$
$$\text{SUBJECT TO: } \quad y - 2x_1 - 4x_2 - 5x_3 \le 0 \tag{13.40}$$
$$y - 3x_1 - 3x_2 - 4x_3 \le 0 \tag{13.41}$$
$$y - 4x_1 - 3x_2 - 2x_3 \le 0 \tag{13.42}$$
$$x_1 + x_2 + x_3 \le 50 \tag{13.38}$$
$$2x_1 + 3x_2 + 5x_3 \le 130 \tag{13.39}$$

The optimal solution to the model is

$$y = x_0^* = 152.5; \quad x_1 = 25; \quad x_2 = 22.5; \quad x_3 = 2.5$$

Substitution of these values into the three objective functions (13.37) reveals that the first and second objectives happen to be the ones that take on the minimum value of 152.5; we can also verify that the optimal MAXIMIN strategy yields a value of 172.5 for the third objective.

Let us examine this example more closely. If we solve the three single objective LP models, using each of the three objectives, we obtain the following results.

Optimal Model Solutions

	x_0^*	x_1^*	x_2^*	x_3^*
$P1$:	173.33	0	43.33	0
$P2$:	160	40	0	10
$P3$:	200	50	0	0

The following is an interesting and revealing comparison of *conditional outcomes.*

Outcomes

	$P1$	$P2$	$P3$
$P1^*$	173.33	130	130
$P2^*$	130	160	180
$P3^*$	100	150	200
MAXIMIN*	152.5	152.5	172.5

Note that use of the MAXIMIN criterion avoids very low "payoffs" or outcomes in all three possible states, but also negates the opportunity for very high outcomes. Observe that our LP formulation located a feasible point that is *not a candidate* for the optimal solution in the original feasible region (13.38) and (13.39).

THE MAXIMAX MODEL

The MAXIMAX model is restated as

$$\text{MAXIMIZE } x_0 = \text{MAXIMUM } \{c_1'x, c_2'x, \ldots, c_K'x\} \qquad (13.11)$$

$$\text{SUBJECT TO: } Ax \begin{Bmatrix} \leq \\ = \\ \geq \end{Bmatrix} b \qquad (13.12)$$

The following transformation, analogous to (13.35) for the MAXIMIN model, turns (13.11) and (13.12) into an ordinary LP model.

$$y \geq c_k'x, \quad k = 1, \ldots, K \qquad (13.43)$$

Our LP model is

$$\text{MAXIMIZE } x_0 = y \qquad (13.44)$$

$$\text{SUBJECT TO: } y - c_k'x \geq 0, \quad k = 1, \ldots, K \qquad (13.45)$$

$$Ax \begin{Bmatrix} \leq \\ = \\ \geq \end{Bmatrix} b \qquad (13.12)$$

The interpretation of MAXIMAX model results is straightforward — the solution $\mathbf{x}_k^*$ is merely the solution of the single objective LP model (using one of the K objectives) that yields the highest value of the objective function. Thus, an alternate way to find the optimal solution to a MAXIMAX model is to solve the K single objective LP models and select the strategy that yields the best results.

In our small example model (13.37) through (13.39), with "MIN" replaced by "MAX" in (13.37), the solution is $x_0^* = 200, x_1^* = 50, x_2^* = x_3^* = 0$, which is just the solution of the single objective LP model using the third objective function.

THE LINEAR COMBINATIONS MODEL

The linear combinations model is

$$\text{MAXIMIZE or MINIMIZE } x_0 = \sum_{k=1}^{K} v_k \mathbf{c}_k' \mathbf{x}_k \qquad (13.13)$$

$$\text{SUBJECT TO: } \mathbf{Ax} \left\{ \begin{matrix} \leq \\ = \\ \geq \end{matrix} \right\} \mathbf{b} \qquad (13.14)$$

As noted before, this modeling approach leads directly to a single objective LP model with no further transformation required.

As an illustration, let us use a "Laplace-like" approach, letting the three weights be equal (i.e., $v_1 = v_2 = v_3 = \frac{1}{3}$), and return to our example problem once more. The objective function becomes

$$\text{MAXIMIZE } x_0 = \frac{1}{3}(2x_1 + 4x_2 + 5x_3)$$
$$+ \frac{1}{3}(3x_1 + 3x_2 + 4x_3) \qquad (13.46)$$
$$+ \frac{1}{3}(4x_1 + 3x_2 + 2x_3)$$

The model is as follows:

$$\text{MAXIMIZE } x_0 = 3x_1 + 3.33x_2 + 3.67x_3 \qquad (13.47)$$
$$\text{SUBJECT TO: } \quad x_1 + x_2 + x_3 \leq 50 \qquad (13.38)$$
$$2x_1 + 3x_2 + 5x_3 \leq 130 \qquad (13.39)$$

You may wish to verify that the solution to the example is $x_0^* = 160$, $x_1^* = 20, x_2^* = 30, x_3^* = 0$, which is different from the results obtained for this example using MAXIMIN and MAXIMAX models.

THE PREEMPTIVE GOAL PRIORITIZATION MODEL

We noted before that the preemptive goal prioritization model can be solved by using a series of single objective LP models, as in (13.16), (13.17), and (13.18). A more elegant and efficient approach is to treat the K linear objectives in *matrix* form and modify the simplex algorithm so that the preemptive priority of the objective is maintained.

Without going into algorithmic details, a computerized program to implement a preemptive goal prioritization algorithm requires that we arrange our K goals and index them in decreasing priority order. That is, $P1$ is preemptively more important than $P2$, which is preemptively more important than $P3$, and so forth. The algorithm actually carries along the K linear objective functions as a matrix and uses the SIMPLEX technique first to find the optimal solution to $P1$. Once found, the algorithm checks the transformed objective function for $P1$ to determine whether there are alternative optimal solutions (in terms of $P1$) to the model. If so, $P2$ is scanned to determine whether the alternative solution(s) will improve the value of this objective, and so on. As the algorithm proceeds to consider $P3$, $P4$, and so on, it is searching for simultaneous alternative optimal solutions to all higher-priority objective functions. When none can be found, the model has been solved.

As an illustration, let us return to Howard's problem as narrated to POGO, with one small change—we will turn his most important objective—"$P1$: Generate a profit contribution of at least \$600,000 per month"—into a "$\geq$" constraint, and designate the current $P2$ as "$P1$: Get Albuquerque production as small as possible." Similarly, the original $P3$ becomes "$P2$: Get Stratos production as small as possible." The resulting preemptive goal priority model is as follows.

$$P1: \text{MINIMIZE } x_0 = \qquad\qquad x_4 + \quad x_5 + \quad x_6 \qquad\qquad (13.48)$$

$$P2: \text{MINIMIZE } x_0 = \qquad x_3 + \qquad\qquad x_6 \qquad\qquad (13.49)$$

$$\text{SUBJECT TO:} \qquad 3x_3 + \quad 3x_4 + \quad x_5 + \quad 2x_6 \leq 300 \qquad (13.31)$$

$$2x_4 + \quad 3x_5 + \quad 5x_6 \leq 240 \qquad (13.32)$$

$$x_1 + \quad 2x_2 + \qquad\qquad x_4 + \qquad\qquad 2x_5 = 270 \qquad (13.33)$$

$$1500x_1 + 3000x_2 + 2000x_3 + 1500x_4 + 3000x_5 + 2000x_6 \geq 600{,}000 \qquad (13.50)$$

Objective (13.48) is first optimized, and the optimal model solution is "fixed" by not subsequently entering a variable that would increase its value. Then (13.49) would be treated as the objective row.

THE PURE PREEMPTIVE GOAL PROGRAMMING MODEL

The solution approach to pure preemptive goal programming models is identical to that just described for the preemptive goal prioritization model, except that our "objectives" are functions of the deviational variables. In defining the K goals as in (13.23), we add K constraints to the m functional constraints of the model as well as up to $2K$ variables, so that we are dealing with a somewhat larger LP construction.

On a purely technical note, one structural difficulty with many goal programming formulations is in the frequency of order-of-magnitude differences in the coefficients of the goal definitions (13.23). Note in Howard's model

(13.25) through (13.34) that constraint coefficients range in value from zero to 3000. This large variation tends to induce computer round-off errors as it performs millions of arithmetic operations in the SIMPLEX procedure. This problem can be mitigated by "scaling" the constraints. For example, the constraint (13.28) that defines Howard's profit contribution goal can be divided on both sides by 1000 before including the deviational variables. This operation results in a constraint set whose coefficients are of roughly the same magnitude.

AVAILABLE COMPUTER CODES FOR MOLP

Since the "commensurable models" MAXIMIN, MAXIMAX, and linear combinations are nothing more than transformations to single objective LP models, a standard LP code such as MPS (for mainframes), LINDO (for mainframes or minicomputers), or BLP (for microcomputers) is all that is needed to solve and analyze the model.

For the "incommensurable models" preemptive goal optimization and pure preemptive goal programming, James R. Burns has developed the Microsoft BASIC program POGO, which is, of course, named after our hip computer friend who assisted Howard earlier in this chapter. POGO is actually a "front-end" interactive program that calls BLP to do the numerical computations.

DEVELOPING ALTERNATIVE SOLUTIONS

Sensitivity analysis (right-hand side ranging, etc.) is fairly straightforward for the "commensurable models," since they are direct transformations to single objective LP models. In linear combinations models, however, the question arises as to the weights v_k (13.13) used to transform the K objectives into a single one. Let us return once more to our small example model (13.46), (13.38) and (13.39), in which we used "Laplace-like" weights $v_1 = v_2 = v_3 = \frac{1}{3}$. As we can easily verify, there are only six feasible vertices associated with the feasible region described by the two constraints. We reproduce the following model for convenience, stating the objective function in a general form.

$$\text{MAXIMIZE } x_0 = \tfrac{1}{3}(2x_1 + 4x_2 + 5x_3) + \tfrac{1}{3}(3x_1 + 3x_2 + 4x_3)$$

$$+ \tfrac{1}{3}(4x_1 + 3x_2 + 2x_3) \tag{13.46}$$

$$x_1 + x_2 + x_3 \le 50 \tag{13.38}$$

$$2x_1 + 3x_2 + 5x_3 \le 130 \tag{13.39}$$

Note the following results.

Weights			Optimal Model Solutions						
v_1	v_2	v_3	x_0	x_1	x_2	x_3	S_1	S_2	
$\frac{1}{3}$	$\frac{1}{3}$	$\frac{1}{3}$	160	20	30	0	0	0	(previous
-1	1	1	250	50	0	0	0	30	example)
1	1	-1	182	0	0	26	24	0	
0	$\frac{3}{4}$	$\frac{1}{4}$	165	40	0	10	0	0	
1	0	0	173.33	0	43.33	0	0	6.67	

As we see, depending upon the weights v_k we assign, five of the six feasible vertices for this model can be the optimal model solutions (the sixth is the origin: $x_1 = x_2 = x_3 = 0$). Note also in this example that our weights always summed to *one,* although this is certainly not a requirement.

The point is this: Selection of the values of the weights $v_k, k = 1, \ldots, K,$ is clearly the key in modeling with linear combinations. We emphasize *once more* that this selection is a *managerial* responsibility.

Sensitivity analysis for the "incommensurable models," preemptive goal prioritization and pure preemptive goal programming, is quite another matter. In the former case, the shadow prices for the highest-priority goal have the same interpretation as they do in ordinary single objective LP. But what interpretation do these "prices" have for the lower-priority goals? They are, in a sense, *constrained shadow prices,* since their values are dependent on the attainment of higher-priority objectives (unless, of course, the optimal vertex for the highest-priority objective happens to be the optimal vertex for a lower-priority objective as well).

In terms of our mountain-climbing analogy in Chapter 2, we can think of preemptive goal prioritization models as attempts to climb several adjacent mountains simultaneously. Whatever resources are necessary to climb Mount $P1$ are made available to that climber, who always reaches the top. Conceptually, the highest-priority climber has somehow "pulled along" fellow climbers (at least partially) up their respective mountains. Once Mount $P1$ has been conquered, the remaining resources are made available to assault Mount $P2$, and so on. Note that, in the process of attempting to climb a lower-priority mountain, no action is allowed that would decrease the altitudes attained by higher-priority climbers.

In general, duality theory has a limited interpretation for preemptive goal prioritization models. The dual model turns out to be a single-objective LP formulation with *multiple right-hand sides* for the constraints. This topic is at the forefront of research in MOLP.

Sensitivity analysis for pure preemptive goal programming models is even less well structured than it is for preemptive goal prioritization models. Recall that we are dealing with two kinds of constraints—the actual resource constraints and the "constraints" used to establish our goals. By stating our objectives as functions of the deviational variables, we are in effect *attempting to force the second set of constraints to be binding* in an optimal solution. What economic interpretation can we impute to the associated "shadow prices"? Unfortunately, no satisfactory answer to that question exists at this writing.

Some authors suggest "sensitivity analysis" by reordering the goal priorities and solving the new model, to observe the effect on the original prioritization. Others recommend eliminating certain goals and obtaining additional solutions to determine which (if any) goal or goals "drive" the model solution. These activities often produce interesting results and occasionally provide insight into the underlying problem. However, they tend to miss the managerial point of multiple-objective modeling, which is — like all other MS/OR models — to reflect accurately the underlying problem *as seen by the decision maker*. Certainly, if a decision maker is indifferent as to the relative priorities of two goals, then it makes sense to solve *two* models, interchanging these two goals in priority order and noting the effect. And there are other good managerial reasons to experiment with the model. But, in general, "fiddling for fiddling's sake" is an inappropriate activity in "real-world" modeling and analysis.

STATE OF THE ART IN MOLP

As we noted earlier, the art of modeling with multiple criteria is basically in its infancy. In what follows, we introduce a few advanced topics in an effort to impart the flavor of "what's happening" in this broad field.

UTILITY TRANSFORMATIONS FOR INCOMMENSURABLE OBJECTIVES

As we learned, modeling and analysis of problems with commensurable objectives were much more straightforward than they were with incommensurable ones. What if (as we did in Chapter 7) we could construct utility functions for the various goals or objectives and transform them all into the same dimensionless units called "utiles"? We would then have goals with commensurable units and could use MAXIMIN, MAXIMAX, linear combinations, or other models of this type for our analysis. Using such utility transformations, it *might* even be possible to "quantify the unquantifiable" by addressing goals or objectives that are not stated in physically measurable terms (e.g., improve employee morale, heighten managers' sensitivity to affirmative action). This is a lively area of current research, but we take the view that this approach is not yet ready for the managerial "firing line."

MODELING WITH FUZZY SETS

The quaintly titled "theory of fuzzy sets" is another body of knowledge that holds promise in multiobjective modeling. In modeling with commensurable objectives, recall that one approach — linear combinations — involves aggregating the K linear objectives into a single objective by the use of "relative importance weights." We cannot do that with incommensurable objectives, of course, so we were forced to use *preemptive* priorities in which $P1$ is *infinitely* more important than $P2$, and so on. Fuzzy set theory, whose best known proponent is Lofti Zadeh (e.g., [4]), provides a possible remedy to this problem.

In nontechnical terms, fuzzy set theory allows us to quantify *verbal* descriptions of attributes or characteristics. For example, the word "very" connotes more than an "average" or "normal" condition or state. Other verbal descriptions using this adverb might be "not very" or "very very" or "so very" or "not so very." Such descriptions are "soft" or "fuzzy" in the sense that they carry different connotations for different decision makers. If this set of descriptors could be quantified for a particular decision maker, then graded (rather than preemptive) priorities could be applied in situations involving incommensurable objectives. Like the utility transformation, we believe that the theory of fuzzy sets is not yet well enough developed to be of immediate use in actual applications of managerial decision making.

NON-MOLP MULTIPLE OBJECTIVE MODELS

Finally, it is certainly possible for a decision maker to have multiple objectives in a decision situation that can only be effectively modeled by integer programming (IP) or nonlinear programming (NLP), or perhaps by dynamic programming (DP). Recall, for instance, Mr. Mark Off from Chapter 6, who wished to travel by stagecoach from New York City to San Francisco to seek his fortune. In addition to minimizing the total cost of his travel insurance policy (and thereby minimizing the danger), he may well have wished to maximize the sight-seeing aspects of the trip, and perhaps minimize the total travel time on uncomfortable stagecoaches. If this were the case, we would have a DP model with multiple objectives.

Some research has been done in integer goal programming modeling, and we illustrate such a model in the first case in this chapter. But, as we might suspect, the difficulty of performing sensitivity analysis that we encountered for single objective IP models (Chapter 3) is compounded when multiple objectives are present. If the objectives are commensurable, of course, we may use MAXIMIN, MAXIMAX, or linear combinations models to transform the multiple objective model into an IP model with a single objective. A different approach must be used when the objectives are incommensurable.

Budgeting in Blacksburg [5]

The Scenario: Virginia Polytechnic Institute and State University (VPI and SU), more widely known as Virginia Tech, is a comprehensive major university located in Blacksburg, Virginia. Its highly respected business school includes on its faculty Professors Art Keown, Chuck Taylor, and John Pinkerton, who authored the paper upon which this case is based. Virginia Tech's business school has always been a "hot bed" of applied goal programming, and the project we discuss here is only one of many such applications.

The Problem: As is true with most universities, Virginia Tech is in a capital rationing situation with respect to investment in fixed assets; there is simply not enough money available to meet every need. This problem is compounded by the existence of multiple goals or objectives that are stated in incommensurable units.

Working with university administrators, the researchers identified 11 specific goals to be achieved, if at all possible, and a preemptive prioritization of the goals, as follows.

$P1$: Limit expenditures to $450,000.

$P2$: Limit increases in operating expenses that result from capital expenditures, to $200,000 per year.

$P3$: Spend at least $120,000 (total) on the following projects (because of earmarked funds):
  a. Remote batcher in Engineering building
  b. Expansion of Engineering library
  c. Build new Engineering/Physics Research Facilities: Prototype A
  d. Build new Engineering/Physics Research Facilities: Prototype B
  e. Renovate Engineering building.

$P4$: Increase total library square footage by at least 12,500 square feet.

$P5$: For business school accreditation purposes, accept at least two of the following nine proposals:
  a. Purchase CDC computer system
  b. Purchase IBM computer system
  c. Upgrade current UNIVAC computer system
  d. Remote batcher in Business building
  e. Expand Business School library
  f. Renovate Business building: Prototype A
  g. Renovate Business building: Prototype B

      h. Build behavioral observation labs: Prototype A
      i. Build behavioral observation labs: Prototype B

P6: Accept at least one of the following projects:
      a. Purchase CDC computer system
      b. Purchase IBM computer system
      c. Upgrade current UNIVAC computer system
      d. Expand North Campus library

P7: Increase the performance measure in the Business School by at least 50,000 quality-adjusted student-days (QASDs).[1]

P8: Increase the performance in the Engineering School by at least 40,000 QASDs.

P9: Increase the performance measure in the Chemistry Department by at least 15,000 QASDs.

P10: Increase the performance measure in the Physics Department by at least 35,000 QASDs.

P11: Increase the performance measure in the Psychology Department by at least 30,000 QASDs.

In addition to these goals, the university's administration imposed "hard" upper-bound constraints on the purchase of engineering lab equipment ($30,000), chemistry lab equipment ($25,000), and physics lab equipment ($35,000).

The Model: The decision variables $x_j, j = 1, \ldots, 22$, for this model relate to 22 specific projects that are described in Table 13.1. Note that the first 19 variables represent "go/no go" decisions similar to those we discussed in Chapter 3. Variables x_{20}, x_{21}, and x_{22}, however, represent continuous decisions (how much money to spend on lab equipment). Since the underlying problem appears otherwise to meet the additivity assumption and one of the two divisibility assumptions, it appears that it was appropriately modeled as a mixed integer (otherwise linear) pure preemptive goal programming model, with $x_1 - x_{19}$ as zero-one variables.

This is a fairly large and complex model, and we will not exhibit it here in its entirety. Instead, let us look at some of the more interesting modeling devices that were used.

Modeling the goal constraints is fairly straightforward. For example, the goal constraint for *P1*, the highest preemptive goal, is as follows.

$$\sum_{j=1}^{22} c_j x_j = \$450,000 + d_1^+ - d_1^- \tag{13.51}$$

where the c_j are the elements of the "cost" column in Table 13.1. Likewise, the objective *P3* (earmarked funds) becomes

$$\$50,000x_5 + \$100,000x_8 + \$190,000x_{12}$$
$$+ \$120,000x_{13} + \$80,000x_{17} = \$120,000 + d_3^+ - d_3^- \tag{13.52}$$

---

[1] QASDs are the product of student-days times some quality proxy (which may be objective, e.g., SAT scores, or subjective).

Table 13.1 VPI and SU Projects

Variable	Project Description	Cost (thousands)	Annual Operating Expenses (thousands)	Library (thousands square feet)	BA QASDs (thousands)	Engineering QASDs (thousands)	Chemistry QASDs (thousands)	Physics QASDs (thousands)	Psychology QASDs (thousands)	Designated Funds	Satisfies Accreditation	Satisfies Political/Social Objectives
x_1	CDC computer system	$190	$25		20	15	10	10	5		X	X
x_2	IBM computer system	230	30		30	23	15	15	8		X	X
x_3	Upgrade UNIVAC computer system	90	25		8	6	4	4	2		X	X
x_4	Remote batcher, North Campus	60	6				6	10				X
x_5	Remote batcher, Engineering building	50	5			12				50		
x_6	Remote batcher, Business building	50	5		14						X	
x_7	Expansion, Main library	250	40	15	15	10	22	22	15			
x_8	Expansion, Business School library	150	25	8	40					100	X	
x_9	Expansion, Engineering library	100	15	5		25						
x_{10}	Expansion, North Campus library	150	23	8			20	20				X
x_{11}	Additional small experimental labs	50	10			2	10	6				

x_{12}	Additional large experimental labs	80	16		4	15	12		190
x_{13}	New Engineering/Physics research facilities: A	190	20		40		20	120	X
x_{14}	New Engineering/Physics research facilities: B	120	12		20		25		X
x_{15}	Renovate Business building: A	160	10	45					
x_{16}	Renovate Business building: B	80	5	20					
x_{17}	Renovate Engineering building	80	5		20			80	
x_{18}	Behavioral observation labs: A	120	10	20			18		X
x_{19}	Behavioral observation labs: B	70	6	10			13		X
x_{20}	Engineering lab equipment	*$1	*$1		.17/$				
x_{21}	Chemistry lab equipment	*"	*"			.15/$			
x_{22}	Physics lab equipment	*"	*"				.20/$		

* $1.00 per $1.00 investment.

Objective P6 is modeled as follows.

$$x_1 + x_2 + x_3 + x_{10} = 1 + d_6^+ - d_6^- \qquad (13.53)$$

so that the goal is to fund at least one of these four projects.

The most interesting feature of this model is that some subsets of the goals are *mutually exclusive*—that is, if *one* of the related projects is funded, none of the others in that set should be funded. For example, the first three projects in the list involve alternative ways in which to acquire computing capability. We can assure that *at most* one of these alternatives is selected in the following way.

$$x_1 + x_2 + x_3 = 1 + d_{12}^+ - d_{12}^- \qquad (13.54)$$

Other mutually exclusive sets are x_{11} and x_{12} (large versus small experimental labs), x_{13} and x_{14} (two different prototypes of engineering/physics research facilities), x_{15} and x_{16} (two different prototypes for renovating the Business building), and x_{18} and x_{19} (two different prototypes of behavior observation labs).

Another interesting feature of the model is the existence of *contingent projects*. Implementation of either x_{18} or x_{19} (construction of behavioral observation labs) would be contingent upon the prior decision to renovate the Business building (i.e., $x_{15} = 1$). This relationship is modeled as follows:

$$x_{18} + x_{19} - x_{15} = 0 + d_{17}^+ - d_{17}^- \qquad (13.55)$$

The full-blown model, then, has the following characteristics:

1. Eleven preemptive priority objectives stated in terms of minimizing sums of 34 deviational variables
2. Three functional upper-bound constraints on the continuous variables x_{20}, x_{21}, and x_{22}, imposed by the central administration[2]
3. Eleven constraints defining the deviational goals
4. Six constraints that impose the "mutually exclusive" and "contingency" features
5. Twenty-two decision variables, the first 19 of which are of the zero-one variety

Solution to the Model: The paper [5] reports the model solution as follows, but it does not state how it was obtained (perhaps with proprietary software).

1. Goals 1–8 were completely attained.
2. Goal 9 was 6000 QASDs short of the goal of 15,000 (Chemistry).
3. Goal 10 was 25,000 QASDs short of the goal of 35,000 (Physics).
4. Goal 11 was short all of its target of 30,000 QASDs (Psychology).

In the process of meeting these goals, the optimization algorithm selected six projects for funding.

---

[2] The authors of the paper from which this case is excerpted [5] originally modeled these three constraints as deviational constraints. We changed them to functional constraints for illustrative purposes only.

Project	Cost
x_4: Remote batch site for North Campus	$ 60,000
x_6: Remote batcher, Business building	50,000
x_8: Expansion, Business School library	150,000
x_9: Expansion, Engineering library	100,000
x_{17}: Renovate Engineering building	80,000
x_{21}: Purchase Chemistry lab equipment	20,000
Total	$460,000

Since the total adds to $460,000 (instead of $450,000, the $P1$ target), we surmise that there is a typo and that only $10,000 was indicated to be spent on chemistry lab equipment.

Solution to the Problem: In their very well-written paper, the authors concluded with the following statement.

It is the hope of the authors that this model will provide University administrators with a further tool to help them in the complicated task of allocating limited funds among the various alternative proposals. [5]

Let us join them in that hope!

Spacetrek

The Scenario: Intergalactic Enterprises, Inc., a mammoth firm with subsidiary holdings in 75 different star systems, had acquired all Earth-based companies in the mid-twenty-first century, and a short time later, in 2101 A.D., controlled interstellar assets worth over 60 quintillion zorgs. Its most recent acquisition (for a price of 20 trillion zorgs) was Zappa Industries, a firm located in the star system of Deneb, and the galaxy's sole producer of ion power units. Intergalactic had bought billions of these power units in the past, for its popular and relatively inexpensive "Saturday Night Phaser" and finally decided that it would be cheaper to acquire the company to hold down costs.

The Problem: As was its custom, Intergalactic laid off all of Zappa's Denebian employees immediately and sent in its own people to manufacture the ion power units. Sissy Spacetrek, who was appointed CEO, realized — before her first flurb on the job was over — that she had a problem of stellar proportions. It seemed that Denebians never wrote anything down, since each was born with an imbedded 4-megabyte, 64-bit-word minicomputer. Since all Denebians were networked, information access was instantaneous electronically, so keeping nonelectronic records was unnecessary.

"The bottom line," thought Sissy to herself, "is that we've just fired our management information system."

Calling in her top production/operations manager, Esther May Chunn, Sissy laid it on the line.

"Esther, we've got a problem," she began. "Intergalactic wants Zappa's costs tightly controlled, but we haven't a clue in the cosmos what production costs are. I want you, Telly Kinesis, Perry Gee, and Zero Graffiti to get me some answers, and quickly."

"Right, your astral eminence," Esther responded. "We'll blast off on this project immediately. We'll be back to you in no more than two or three flurbs."

Exactly 2.498 flurbs later, Esther's team was in Sissy's office, clutching reams of computer printout.

"Empress of the Ether," began Esther, "here's the scam. Zappa apparently manufactures six different ion power units, which we'll refer to by the brand names: Athos, Porthos, Aramis, D'Artagnan, Dumas, and Joe Bob. Telly, Perry, Zero, and I decided to do independent cost estimations and to meet afterward to try to reconcile any differences we might have. Well, I'm confident that my estimates are accurate, but the other three came up with different figures, and none of those prima donnas will change their figures by a single zorg."

"OK, Esther," sighed Sissy, "just give me all four estimates and I'll take it from there."

The four production cost estimates for the six brands of power units (in kilozorgs) were as follows.

Estimator

	Brand	Esther	Telly	Perry	Zero
x_1	Athos	3	4	6	12
x_2	Porthos	5	5	7	9
x_3	Aramis	6	8	3	10
x_4	D'Artagnan	6	5	10	4
x_5	Dumas	7	6	5	8
x_6	Joe Bob	9	8	7	3

Decision Variable

Instructions from Intergalactic headquarters were to produce a total of at least 100,000 units per kiloflurb and to produce at least 10,000 of each brand in the product mix. The only scarce resource appeared to be person-flurbs of labor, with a total of 250,000 person-flurbs available per kiloflurb. Sissy's charge was clear: to minimize production costs. But which of the four cost estimates was she to use? Unable to resolve her dilemma, she called in Dar Klingon, a management consultant affiliated with Taurus University.

The Model: Twenty-four flurbs and three six-krams of Lone Nebula Space Beverage later, Dar had the situation scoped out.

"Madam Spacetrek," he began, "what we've got here is a classical problem of minimizing some function of four hyperplanes over a six-dimensional polytope. For my usual emolument of 50 kilozorgs per flurb, I think I can locate the optimal vertex in a score of flurbs."

Jar-Gon, the translator robot, spoke as follows.

"He says you have a multiple-objective linear programming problem (MOLP), and he'll solve your problem in 20 flurbs for a fee of 1 megazorb."

"Wrong, buster," said Sissy to Dar. "You might be able to *model* my problem, but I'm the only one that can *solve* it!"

And with that, Sissy condemned Klingon to spend a gigaflurb on the faculty of Texas Astronautical and Mercantile Junior College.

However, Dar's comment had sparked Sissy's memory of the management science course she had taken long ago at the University of Southern Cassiopeia. It was obvious that there were four linear objective functions, which she entered into her wrist computer as follows.

$$P1: \text{MIN } c_1'x = 3x_1 + 5x_2 + 6x_3 + 6x_4 + 7x_5 + 9x_6$$
$$P2: \text{MIN } c_2'x = 4x_1 + 5x_2 + 8x_3 + 5x_4 + 6x_5 + 8x_6$$
$$P3: \text{MIN } c_3'x = 6x_1 + 7x_2 + 3x_3 + 10x_4 + 5x_5 + 7x_6$$
$$P4: \text{MIN } c_4'x = 12x_1 + 9x_2 + 10x_3 + 4x_4 + 8x_5 + 3x_6$$

There were six lower-bound constraints of the form $x_j \geq 10,000$, $j = 1, \ldots, 6$, but Sissy used the transformations $x_j = x_j' + 10,000$, $j = 1, \ldots, 6$, to eliminate them. That left only two constraints to deal with: the requirement to produce at least 100,000 power units per kiloflurb and the limitations on available person-flurbs of labor (250,000). Sissy estimated that the Athos (x_1), Porthos (x_2), and D'Artagnan (x_4) models required 3 person-flurbs of labor per unit, while the other three brands required only 2 person-flurbs per unit. After making the upper-bound transformations, Sissy entered the objective functions and constraints into the computer as follows.

$$\text{MINIMIZE } x_0 = f \ \{(3x_1' + 5x_2' + 6x_3' + 6x_4' + 7x_5' + 9x_6' + 360,000),$$
$$(4x_1' + 5x_2' + 8x_3' + 5x_4' + 6x_5' + 8x_6' + 360,000),$$
$$(6x_1' + 7x_2' + 3x_3' + 10x_4' + 5x_5' + 7x_6' + 380,000),$$
$$(12x_1' + 9x_2' + 10x_3' + 4x_4' + 8x_5' + 3x_6' + 460,000)\}$$

SUBJECT TO:
$$x_1' + x_2' + x_3' + x_4' + x_5' + x_6' \geq 40,000$$
$$3x_1' + 3x_2' + 2x_3' + 3x_4' + 2x_5' + 2x_6' \leq 100,000$$

Sissy recognized that she had a set of four commensurable linear objective functions, but she wasn't quite ready to select one of the criteria she had learned about. "I think I'll experiment a bit first," she mused to herself.

Solution to the Model: Sissy first solved four single objective LP models — using each of the four linear objectives in a minimizing LP algorithm. Her results were as follows.

Objective Function	Minimum Cost (kilozorgs)	Optimal Mix							
		x_1	x_2	x_3	x_4	x_5	x_6	S_1	S_2
$c_1'x$	540K	30K	10K	30K	10K	10K	10K	0	0
$c_2'x$	560K	30K	10K	10K	10K	30K	10K	0	0
$c_3'x$	500K	10K	10K	50K	10K	10K	10K	0	20K
$c_4'x$	580K	10K	10K	10K	10K	10K	50K	0	20K

At first glance, the four different cost estimates seemed to give total minimum costs in a fairly narrow range — from $500,000 to $580,000 kilozorgs. But then the realization dawned on Sissy that the four product mixes varied widely as well. What would be the effect of using a product mix that was optimal for $c_i'x$ and having $c_j'x$ being the correct objective function? She hastily calculated all possible combinations and assembled them as follows.

If $c_j'x$ Is Correct

	$c_1'x$	$c_2'x$	$c_3'x$	$c_4'x$
$c_1'x$	540K	600K	560K	900K
$c_2'x$	560K	560K	600K	860K
$c_3'x$	600K	680K	500K	860K
$c_4'x$	720K	680K	660K	580K

If the Optimal Mix for $c_i'x$ Is Used

"Jumping Jupiter," Sissy exclaimed to herself. "If I used Esther's objective function ($c_1'x$) and Zero was right ($c_4'x$), costs could skyrocket to $900K kilozorgs, and I'd probably end up as a flunky on some forsaken minor planet. On the other hand, if Perry is right and I decided to use the product mix suggested by his objective function ($c_3'x$), then I could bring costs in at 500K kilozorgs — and I'd be a cinch for early promotion to Exalted Warp. I'd better proceed with caution on this decision!"

Sissy turned her attention back to her MBA management science course. The four objective functions were obviously commensurable, since they were all stated in kilozorgs per kiloflurb — which meant that she could use a MAXIMIN, a MAXIMAX, or a linear combinations approach. Since she was trying to minimize costs, the first two criteria seemed inappropriate. She had no way to judge the relative accuracy of the four cost functions, so she decided to weight them equally, as follows.

$$c_5'x = .25(c_1'x + c_2'x + c_3'x + c_4'x)$$

When she entered the objective function and solved the new LP model, two alternate optimal solutions emerged; one was identical to Esther's solution, but the other was different from the other four, as follows:

$c_5'x$	x_1	x_2	x_3	x_4	x_5	x_6	S_1	S_2
645K	10K	10K	10K	30K	30K	10K	0	0

The really interesting thing was that the solution gave the following objective values for the four original objective functions.

	$c_1'x$	$c_2'x$	$c_3'x$	$c_4'x$
Solution using $c_5'x$	620K	580K	680K	700K

Solution to the Problem: If she used the mix suggested by the linear combinations criterion, and if one of the four original estimates happened to be correct, the best she could do would be 580K — but the worst would be 700K. This approach would clearly be "satisficing" — trading off an opportunity to reduce costs to 500K to protect herself against costs of 900K kilozorgs. There was no early promotion to Exalted Warp in the offing using this strategy, but neither was banishment to the cosmic equivalent of Siberia.

"What the quark!" she thought to herself. "Faint heart never won fair merkle!" And she ordered production of 50,000 Aramis models in addition to the required 10,000 of the other five brands (the optimal model solution using $P3$, Perry's objective function).

Epilogue: Two megaflurbs later, Assistant Drone Second Class Spacetrek gazed into the heavens from her tiny office on the planet Peoria in the galaxy Morpheus, awaiting the arrival of the next garbage barge. As it turned out, Zero Graffiti's estimate of costs had been right on the button — and Sissy's hasty decision on product mix had caused costs to rocket to 860,000 kilozorgs per kiloflurb. Speaking to her only companion on Peoria, the psychorobot R-N1X-N, Sissy noted sadly. "Ah, N1X-N, the price of ambition is astronomical."

SUMMARY

In this chapter, we explored one aspect of multicriterion decision making referred to as multiple objective linear programming (MOLP). We saw that sets of multiple objectives can be either commensurable or incommensurable.

We discussed five modeling strategies: MAXIMIN, MAXIMAX, linear combinations, preemptive goal prioritization, and pure preemptive goal programming. We noted that any of the five could be used if our set of goals was of the commensurable variety but that only the latter two were appropriate when our objectives were incommensurable.

Solution techniques turned out to be one of two types: (1) transformation of the MOLP model into an ordinary single objective LP model, and use of the SIMPLEX technique, or (2) modifying the SIMPLEX algorithm to enforce preemptive priorities in the objective set.

We looked briefly at some advanced modeling approaches and ended our journey through MOLP with two complex minicases.

In Chapter 14, we investigate a different approach to dealing with uncertainty and complexity—so-called "structural modeling."

PROBLEMS

1. Let us return to our hip interactive computer friend POGO and his loquacious friend Howard.

HOWARD: POGO, I have digested the remainder of this exemplary chapter, committed it to memory, and am prepared to extend our preliminary verbal perambulations.

POGO: Ten-Four, Howard. I'll lay the model on you one more time, after rearranging some stuff and scaling (13.28).

$$P1: \text{ MINIMIZE } (x_0)_1 = d_1^-$$
$$P2: \text{ MINIMIZE } (x_0)_2 = d_2^+$$
$$P3: \text{ MINIMIZE } (x_0)_3 = d_3^+$$

SUBJECT TO:
$$1.5x_1 + 3x_2 + 2x_3 + 1.5x_4 + 3x_5 + 2x_6 - d_1^+ + d_1^- = 600$$
$$x_4 + x_5 + x_6 \qquad - d_2^+ + d_2^- = 0$$
$$x_3 \qquad + x_6 \qquad - d_3^+ + d_3^- = 0$$
$$3x_3 + 3x_4 + x_5 + 2x_6 \qquad \leq 300$$
$$2x_4 + 3x_5 + 5x_6 \qquad \leq 240$$
$$x_1 + 2x_2 + x_4 + 2x_5 \qquad \leq 270$$
$$\text{All } x_j, d_k^+, d_k^- \geq 0$$

HOWARD: Restrain your equine quadrapeds, *mon ami*. This so-called "pure preemptive goal programming paradigm" is not my demitasse of pekoe. As a charter member of MENSA, and with an intelligence quotient 6 standard deviations above the norm, I have, during the hiatus, fashioned my own unique algorithm, which I have christened "Simple Simon" in honor of my warm personal friend and Nobel prize winner Herb.

POGO: Outa sight, man. Like, how does Simple Simon work?

HOWARD: Exceptionally well, my sanguine electronic rapporteur. I will explicate the algorithmic details, so that you may convey this most inventive construction to subsequent clientele.

First, I solved the single-criterion model consisting of the profit contribution objective and the triune of personnel availability constraints. I got the following solution to my model.

$$x_0^* = \$637,000; \quad x_2^* = 135; \quad x_3^* = 68; \quad x_6^* = 48$$
$$x_1^* = x_4^* = x_5^* = 0$$

Observing that the maximum contemplatable aggregate profit contribution exceeds my expectations (of $600,000) by $37,000, I proceeded to append the restriction "$c_1'x = 600,000$" to the set of constraining hyperplanes and solved yet another LP model using $c_2'x$ as my objective formulation. The ensuing solution emerged from my personal microcomputer as follows:

$$x_0^* = \$600,000; \quad x_2^* = 135; \quad x_3^* = 97 \text{ (97.5 rounded)}$$
$$x_1^* = x_4^* = x_5^* = x_6^* = 0$$

Thus, cleverly, I have so far met both of my first two overriding aspirations.

Unfortunately, the obvious succeeding step failed to effect a decline in the numbers of Stratos (97) craft produced. However, ceteris paribus, I am content with the resulting configuration.

POGO: Howard, you are a stone case, man, with all that Simple Simon noise. All you did was to bash with a preemptive goal prioritization gig—and you did it the hard way! Why don't you book your act at the Albuquerque joint and help inflate the hot-air balloons?

HOWARD: You are an impudent, disrespectful set of subroutines that ought to be debugged, POGO. I shall asseverate such to your programmer.

POGO: Hey, lighten up, Howard. Like, you got a solution to your hassle that turns you on—that's the coolest thing. Well, I'm bagging it for now—see you around campus.

a. Did Howard's sequential approach to modeling his problem produce the same solution as would have been obtained using a pure preemptive goal programming formulation? Why or why not?

b. Would it have been possible for Howard to realize *more* than $600,000 profit contribution and still achieve objective $P2$? How could we model the problem in such a way as to explore this possibility?

c. Note that objectives $P2$ and $P3$ are commensurable, but objective $P1$ is not commensurable with $P2$ and $P3$. Would it be possible to use one of the "commensurable criteria" to combine $P2$ and $P3$ and then to use one of the preemptive prioritization schemes to model the *two* remaining objectives? (*Note:* Such a scheme is referred to as *mixed* preemptive modeling.)

2. Analyze the following brief scenarios and determine whether MOLP modeling techniques could be used to represent and investigate them. In particular, determine whether the multiple objectives (if any) are commensurable or incommensurable, and assess the decision-making environments as to their appropriateness for the use of specific MOLP models.

a. The Incredible Shrinking Computer Company (ISCC) has 50 professional positions and 30 technician positions to fill in the next three months. To control costs and satisfy affirmative action requirements, ISCC has established the following goals:

Priority 1: At least 20% of new hires must be minorities.
Priority 2: At least 30% of new hires must be women.
Priority 3: Firm must stay within recruiting budget of $85,000.

It costs $1000 to recruit a professional and $500 to recruit an engineer. Furthermore, it costs 30% more to recruit a minority or female professional.

b. An advertising agency wishes to achieve the goal of 10,000,000 exposures while minimizing the expenditures required to do so and the amount of television advertising over 75% of budget required to do so. A budget of $200,000 has been established for this purpose, and the media chosen are television, radio, and magazines. The following table gives block costs and exposure ratings for each advertising medium.

Advertising Medium	Per Unit Block Cost	Rated Exposure per Block
Television	5000	500,000
Radio	1000	70,000
Magazine	2000	150,000

c. A belt manufacturing firm makes two types of belts: fancy belts on which it earns a profit of $4.00 per belt and ordinary belts on which it earns a profit of $3.00 per belt. Each fancy belt requires twice as much labor as ordinary belts and if all belts were ordinary, there would be enough labor to make 1200 such belts in the production period defined by management. Each belt requires the same amount of leather, and there is enough leather to make 1000 belts in any given production period. The fancy belt requires an ornate buckle for which 600 are available, and the ordinary belt requires an ordinary buckle for which there are 850 per period. Management wishes to maximize profit in excess of $3000 per period while minimizing the amount of overtime, excess leather, and buckles required to do so.

d. A portfolio manager is attempting to determine a "best" investment portfolio. Eight investments are being considered. The following are the estimates for the price per share, the annual growth rate in the price per share, the annual dividend per share, and the risk associated with each investment.

	1	2	3	4	5	6	7	8
Annual growth rate	.12	.05	.15	.08	.09	.03	.13	.11
Annual dividend/share	1.23	5.10	1.18	2.30	3.42	6.51	1.75	3.13
Risk	.13	.15	.21	.11	.08	.09	.10	.05
Current price/share	350	10	15	89	23	45	130	65

The manager has $5 million to invest and wishes to maximize his return on investment. "Return" is defined as price per share one year hence less current price per share plus dividend per share all divided by the current price per share. The following conditions must be satisfied.

(1) The maximum dollar amount to be invested in investments 2, 4, and 6 cannot exceed $1 million.

(2) At least 30% of the total dollar amount must be invested in 1, 3, and 8.

(3) Total return on investment should be at least 11%.

(4) Dividends for the year should exceed $60,000.

The manager is particularly interested in minimizing the underachievement of the goal of 11% return on investment. In addition the overachievement of an average overall portfolio risk of 7% must be minimized and the underachievement of the $60,000 in annual dividends must be minimized.

e. The Landeau Cotton Company has three major supply depots and four major shipping destinations. The availability of cotton at each depot is known to be 3500, 2500, and 4800 bales, respectively. The demand at each of the four destinations is 1122, 2116, 2438, and 3121 bales, respectively. However, the company can buy fewer bales from its suppliers than the supply numbers would suggest. The distributor is interested in minimizing his purchase and transportation costs. He wants a transportation plan (i.e., how many bales to ship from depot i to destination j) as well as how many bales to buy at each depot. Each bale costs him $535 at depot 1, $565 at depot 2, and $610 at depot 3. His transportation costs have been computed as follows:

	Destination			
Depot	1	2	3	4
1	45	55	61	70
2	70	35	48	65
3	60	55	38	59

The distributor has budgeted $3,200,000 for purchase of the bales and $300,000 for transportation of the bales. He wishes to maximize the underachievement of these targeted amounts.

3.   *The Scenario:*   Let us return to the Spacetrek case and give poor Sissy a second chance to avoid banishment to the planet Peoria.

The Problem: Sissy's problem remains the same.

The Model: Madam Spacetrek is still faced with her decision on product mix of the six brands of ion power units, and — as before — Esther, Telly, Perry, and Zero will not change their objective function cost estimates by a single zorg.

As Sissy previously noted, the four objective functions are commensurable. She dismissed the MAXIMIN and MAXIMAX criteria as inappropriate for a minimization model and weighted the four estimates equally in using the linear combination criterion. However, could she have used a MINIMAX criterion, as follows?

$$\text{MINIMIZE } x_0 = \text{MAXIMUM } \{c_1'x, c_2'x, c_3'x, c_4'x\}$$

Analogous to (13.35), let us define our surrogate variable y in the following way:

$$y \geq c_k'x, \quad k = 1, \ldots, 4$$

Our transformed LP model (similar to (13.36), (13.35), and (13.10)) now becomes

MINIMIZE $x_0 = y$

SUBJECT TO:
$$y - 3x_1' - 5x_2' - 6x_3' - 6x_4' - 7x_5' - 9x_6' \geq 360,000$$
$$y - 4x_1' - 5x_2' - 8x_3' - 5x_4' - 6x_5' - 8x_6' \geq 360,000$$
$$y - 6x_1' - 7x_2' - 3x_3' - 10x_4' - 5x_5' - 7x_6' \geq 380,000$$
$$y - 12x_1' - 9x_2' - 10x_3' - 4x_4' - 8x_5' - 3x_6' \geq 460,000$$
$$x_1' + x_2' + x_3' + x_4' + x_5' + x_6' \geq 40,000$$
$$3x_1' + 3x_2' + 2x_3' + 3x_4' + 2x_5' + 2x_6' \leq 100,000$$
$$y, x_j' \geq 0 \text{ for all } j$$

What we have done is to model Sissy's problem in such a way as to limit the worst possible result by seeking the mix that will yield the minimum of maximum possible costs.

a. As a decision maker, what is your view of this criterion? Does it indeed accomplish the same result for minimization models as the MAXIMIN criterion does for maximization models?

b. Before looking at the solution to the model, review the solution Sissy obtained using the linear combinations criterion. Would you expect the two solutions to be similar? Why or why not?

Solution to the Model: The LINDO computer output for the model is exhibited in Table 13.2. Remember to reverse the transformations — $x_j = x_j' + 10,000$ — before performing your analysis.

Solution to the Problem: Pretend that you are Flash Panne, a young, technically well-trained protégé of Sissy Spacetrek's. Sissy enjoys her role as your mentor and has moved you along rapidly in your career. You are currently a management trainee with the title, executive assistant to the CEO.

Table 13.2   LINDO Output for Spacetrek Model

```
MIN       Y
SUBJECT TO
    2)          Y −   3 X1 − 5 X2 −   6 X3 −   6 X4 − 7 X5 − 9 X6 >= 360000
    3)          Y −   4 X1 − 5 X2 −   8 X3 −   5 X4 − 6 X5 − 8 X6 >= 360000
    4)          Y −   6 X1 − 7 X2 −   3 X3 − 10 X4 − 5 X5 − 7 X6 >= 380000
    5)          Y − 12 X1 − 9 X2 − 10 X3 −   4 X4 − 8 X5 − 3 X6 >= 460000
    6)          X1 + X2 + X3 + X4 + X5 + X6 >= 40000
    7)          3 X1 + 3 X2 + 2 X3 +3 X4 + 2 X5 + 2 X6 <= 100000
END
1)                    LP OPTIMUM FOUND AT STEP 8
              OBJECTIVE FUNCTION VALUE = 657187.500
```

VARIABLE	VALUE	REDUCED COST
Y	657187.500000	0.000000
X1	0.000000	0.328125
X2	0.000000	0.406250
X3	9375.000000	0.000000
X4	11562.500000	0.000000
X5	0.000000	0.296875
X6	19062.500000	0.000000

ROW	SLACK OR SURPLUS	DUAL PRICES
2)	0.000000	−0.390625
3)	11875.000000	0.000000
4)	0.000000	−0.281250
5)	0.000000	−0.328125
6)	0.000000	−6.468750
7)	8437.500000	0.000000

NO. ITERATIONS =   8

RANGES IN WHICH THE BASIS IS UNCHANGED
OBJ COEFFICIENT RANGES

VARIABLE	CURRENT COEF	ALLOWABLE INCREASE	ALLOWABLE DECREASE
Y	1.000000	INFINITY	1.000000
X1	0.000000	INFINITY	0.328125
X2	0.000000	INFINITY	0.406250
X3	0.000000	0.300000	4.500000
X4	0.000000	0.323077	2.272727
X5	0.000000	INFINITY	0.296875
X6	0.000000	1.266667	0.295775

RIGHTHAND SIDE RANGES

ROW	CURRENT RHS	ALLOWABLE INCREASE	ALLOWABLE DECREASE
2	360000.000000	49090.910156	13103.448242
3	360000.000000	11875.000000	INFINITY
4	380000.000000	63333.332031	54000.000000
5	460000.000000	100000.000000	42222.222656
6	40000.000000	3506.493408	21428.572266
7	100000.000000	INFINITY	8437.500000

Something about your boss's current problem bothers you, and you have a sinking feeling that disaster lurks around the corner. If Sissy gambles and loses on this one, there are at least a dozen envious VP-level executives who would make certain that you got *yours* right after Sissy got *hers.*

Using the LINDO output in Table 13.2 as "backup," write a brief analysis of Sissy's problem. Present two or more decision alternatives and state the pros and cons of each. Be careful not to openly advocate a particular alternative—Sissy is sensitive to the difference between *decision aiding* and *decision making* (remember the fate of Dar Klingon?).

Epilogue: If you undertake a career as a managerial decision maker, be assured that you will write scores of "briefs" similar to this one, along the way.

4. Define the following items:
Commensurable linear objective functions
Incommensurable linear objective functions
MOLP
Goal constraints
Functional constraints
Deviational variables
Conditional outcomes
Constrained shadow prices
Fuzzy sets

5. Determine which among the following sets of objectives are commensurable and which are not, assuming that the units are "dollars."
a. Maximize gross revenues
b. Minimize production costs
c. Minimize distribution costs
d. Minimize labor overtime
e. Minimize material surpluses
f. Minimize overhead
g. Minimize finished goods inventory
What could you do to make the incommensurable objectives commensurable?

6. Explain why, in the toy model, the transformed version of the MAXIMIN model yields an LP solution that is entirely different from the individual LP solutions obtained by treating each objective separately. (*Hint:* Examine the constraints of the form (13.35).)

7. Explain why the transformed version of the MAXIMAX model yields an LP solution that is identical to the highest LP solution obtained by solving the model once for each objective function and independently of the other objective functions.

REFERENCES

1. LEE, S. *Goal Programming for Decision Analysis.* New York: Auerbach, 1972.
2. CHARNES, A., and W. COOPER. *Management Models and Industrial Applications of Linear Programming.* New York: John Wiley & Sons, 1962.

3. LEE, S., and L. MOORE. *Introduction to Decision Sciences.* New York: Petrocelli/ Charter, 1975.
4. ZADEH, L. "Outline of a New Approach to the Analysis of Complex Systems and Decision Processes." *IEEE Transactions on Systems, Man and Cybernetics,* Vol. SMC-3 (1973), pp. 28–44.
5. KEOWN, A., B. TAYLOR III, and J. PINKERTON. "Multiple Objective Capital Budgeting Within the University." *Computers and Operations Research,* Vol. 8 (1981), pp. 59–70.

ADDITIONAL READING

IGNIZIO, J. *Goal Programming and Extensions.* Lexington, Mass.: D. C. Heath, 1976.

CHAPTER 14

Structural Models

Futurists and historians of our day continually remind us of the greatly increased complexity of the society in which we live. Toffler [1,2] suggests that this may be due to a burgeoning growth in world population since 1900 and the vastly increased capacity for travel, trade, and communication — manifestations of the tremendous surge in technology. Today, a decision made by a Soviet bureaucrat concerning the allocation of resources and equipment to agriculture can affect the price paid for a loaf of bread by the American housewife. A decision by a bank in New York to lower its prime rate can affect the price of stocks on securities exchanges across the entire planet. The financial insolvency of a few countries can create a severe international monetary crisis for the Western banking system. Years ago, such was not the case. Communities and population centers were relatively isolated and self-sustaining. Decisions made in one of these autonomous communities had no effect upon surrounding areas. Today, our population centers are highly interconnected, and significant impacts of a decision made in Moscow can be experienced in Miami. The environment associated with such decisions has been referred to as a "mess," which has been articulately defined as a "system of interacting problems." In Moscow, the problem is an equitable allocation of resources. In Miami, the problem relates to a reasonably priced loaf of bread. Toffler goes on to say that whereas solutions to problems are relatively straightforward, solutions to messes are much less so.

This chapter is concerned with the greatly increased complexity that characterizes our age. It presents tools and techniques that should enable us to understand better and therefore cope with the complexity and the consequences associated with any particular action, legislation, or decision. For example, in the 1950s a decision was made by Congress and the President to install an extensive interstate highway system. It was anticipated that such a system would greatly increase commerce and travel. What was less well understood were some of the deleterious effects of the system — increased urban sprawl and flight from the inner city, increased congestion and pollution, as well as increases in energy consumption. Whether or not the benefits outweigh the disadvantages is a value-laden question that is interest group dependent. Clearly, some groups would benefit while others would not.

This is but one example of how a legislative decision can bring with it both a blessing and a possible curse. Regardless of origin, our contemporary society is confronted with a plethora of problems, including but not limited to crime; energy, food and water resources; air, water, noise and light pollution; inflation and recession; international terrorist activities; the rising cost of health care; and fiscal deficits in federal budgets.

To a certain extent these problems are tied together. In Chapter 1 we discussed the energy, economy, environment triad depicted in Figure 14.1. We discussed how problems in one of these areas can lead to problems in the other areas.

While it is true that "messes" may have a strong societal flavor, there are important implications for the private sector. Increasingly, industries and corporations are being forced to maintain a greater social consciousness. Legislation has been passed making certain levels of water and air pollution unlawful and forcing industry to find ways to curtail its pollutive tendencies. Consumer products are examined more closely in terms of public safety, health, and welfare by various regulatory agencies of the federal government. Hence the applicability of the techniques we will describe extends to both the public and private sectors.

At the same time, these techniques are finding increased acceptance and applicability to the complex issues dealt with daily by managers and executives in private industry. This is particularly true in the areas of program planning, goal structuring, and project budgeting, as will be seen later in the chapter. Today's managers have access to vast amounts of information due to the ubiquity and pervasiveness of computers. The phenomenon of information overload is therefore frequent, and its deleterious effects on decision making can be almost as devastating as having too little information. What is needed is a kind of decision support system that would enable all the information to be structured in such a way as to enable it to be assimilated, so that the appropriate corrective action can be readily perceived.

The methodologies we describe are collectively referred to as *structural modeling*. In this chapter, we contend that structural modeling and the systemic philosophy embodied by it can be effective in alleviating or perhaps even ameliorating the complex "messes" found in both the public and private sectors of our society.

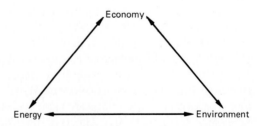

Figure 14.1   The energy-economy-environment triad.

The chapter begins with a brief description of underlying assumptions; this is followed by the largest section of the chapter — solution techniques. We also include a brief description of available computer codes. Minicases illustrate the use of the techniques described in the chapter and the chapter concludes with a summary and problems.

UNDERLYING ASSUMPTIONS

By its very nature, structural modeling presumes that there is some structure that either describes the organization of the object system or prescribes how the system should be organized. The system can be actual as in an existing socioeconomic system or abstract as in a collection of proposed objectives. In addition, structural modeling presumes that the underlying structure can be delineated by means of a structural modeling device — a tree, graph, matrix, or chart. Other assumptions characteristic of structural modeling include (1) that the structure portrayed by the modeling device will convey important information about the object system and (2) that the process of developing the structural model will achieve its intended goal. The process is accomplished by a transformation of models from one form to another and has been referred to as a *model exchange isomorphism* (see Figure 14.2).

SOLUTION TECHNIQUES: AN INTUITIVE DESCRIPTION

The basic idea behind structural modeling is to organize and portray information in such a way that the structure (and its implications) are readily perceived by others. Of particular interest is the form of portrayal. The old adage "a picture is worth a thousand words" applies here. Through the use of graphs,

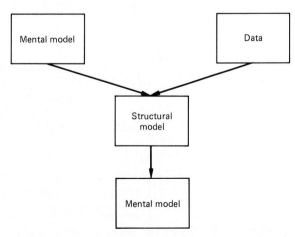

Figure 14.2　Model exchange isomorphisms.

trees, charts, and matrices—the artifacts of structural modeling—an elegant portrayal of the information can be achieved. The modeler begins with a mental model of portions of the object system and then uses the artifacts as a communication medium to others (the problem with mental models is that they can only be communicated by clairvoyance).

Two simple charts that are frequently used in presentations are the bar chart and the pie chart, shown in Figures 14.3 and 14.4. Bar charts are also frequently

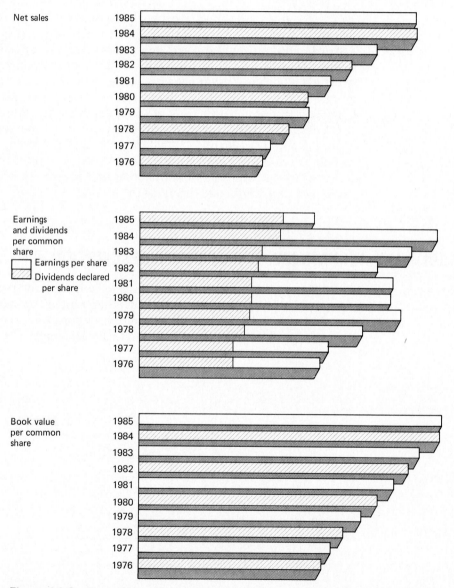

Figure 14.3 Typical bar charts showing trends in net sales, earnings, and book value of a common share for a company.

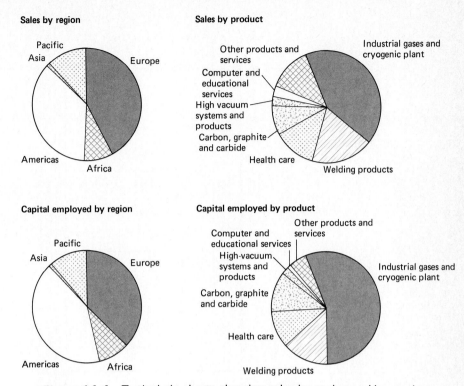

Figure 14.4 Typical pie charts showing sales by region and by product.

used in the annual reports of corporations to depict trends in annual gross revenues or earnings. Pie charts are useful devices for illustrating market share or for depicting how the budget was allocated among the various receiving entities. The ever-increasing sophistication of corporate software is enabling such charts to be computer-generated.

Another frequently used chart is the organization chart, which graphically depicts reporting authority and chain of command. A typical organization chart is shown in Figure 14.5. The use of graphics as a vehicle for communication is fundamental to the objectives of structural modeling.

CHARTS FOR PROJECT PLANNING AND SCHEDULING

A number of charts have been developed to assist managers in organizing the various activities that comprise a project and in completing the project on time and within budget. The more popular among these are

1. The Gantt chart
2. The DELTA chart
3. The PERT chart

Each of these is discussed in the paragraphs that follow.

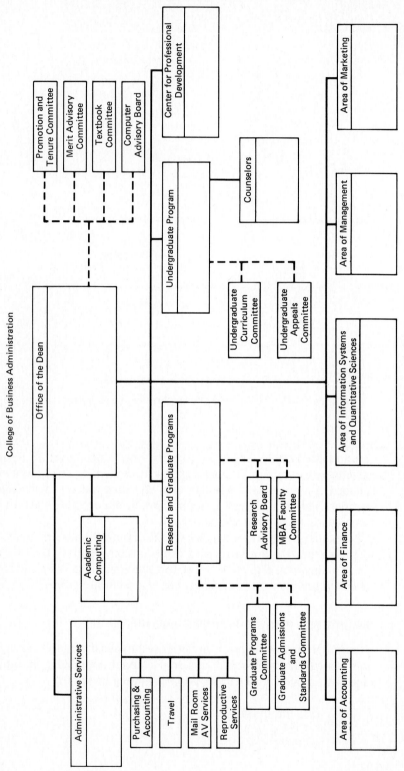

Figure 14.5 A typical organization chart.

The Gantt Milestone Chart

The Gantt milestone chart was developed by an industrial engineer named Henry Gantt in the first decade of this century. A typical Gantt milestone chart is shown in Figure 14.6. To construct a Gantt chart, we begin by determining the major tasks and activities that must be completed in the project. The Gantt chart uses bars to delineate when tasks will be performed, and the chart displays bars plotted against time. Each bar designates a starting date and a completion date for each activity. In constructing the chart, we should give consideration to the precedence relationships that exist among activities, since some activities cannot begin until others are completed. Once constructed, the chart serves to guide the manager in determining the resources required in any given month or other production period. The chart serves as a time model against which we can compare and monitor the progress of the various activities that comprise the project. The chart is approrpiate for scheduling and controlling projects of small to moderate size. One limitation of the Gantt chart is that it cannot provide information about the slack times associated with the start or completion of an activity that would not cause a delay in the completion of the total project.

The DELTA Chart

The DELTA chart was developed by Hill and Warfield [3] as a method for research and development project portrayal. It is a form of flow chart that depicts the planned flow of activities (and their actors) for a project. As an alternative to the network methods such as PERT and GERT, it does some things that network representations cannot do. Specifically, it delineates the actor or doer of the activity and gives credence to any logical relationships that might exist among activities. For example, some activities cannot be started until all preceding activities are completed, while others can be started if one or more of several activities are completed. The method is also able to delineate any decisions that must be made as the project progresses. The word DELTA is really an acronym for the words *d*ecision, *e*vent, *l*ogic, *t*ime arrow, and *a*ctivity — the basic components of any DELTA chart. The symbols used for these components are shown in Figure 14.7. A typical DELTA chart is depicted in Figure 14.8, which is a DELTA chart for making a DELTA chart.

As is apparent from Figure 14.8, each activity box is labeled with the actor who will perform the activity. Also the DELTA chart's flow chart appearance makes it an excellent vehicle for diagramming procedures and programmed plans. Its utility in this latter context may even exceed its original intended purpose: research and development project portrayal. As a method for delineating procedural activities, the DELTA chart is a road map, a guide to accomplishment of a task that is sufficiently complex as to require explicit detailed explanation. As a method for project portrayal, the DELTA chart is of greater use as a planning and execution instrument rather than as an instrument for monitoring and control of the project schedules.

The PERT Chart

Like the word "DELTA," "PERT" is an acronym for *p*roject *e*valuation and *r*eview *t*echnique. PERT charts were discussed in Chapter 11. A great variety of

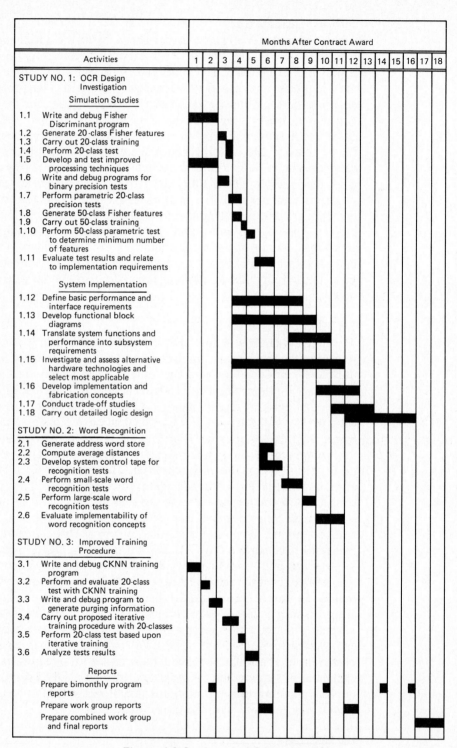

Figure 14.6   A typical Gantt chart [3].

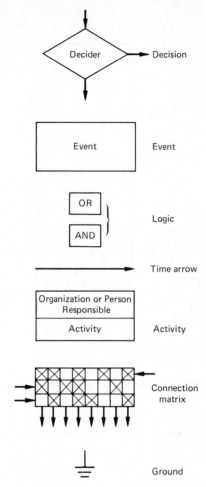

Figure 14.7 Symbols for DELTA charts [3].

different PERT charts have evolved with ever-increasing sophistication and realism. Originally, PERT charts were deterministic. In this form, as discussed in Chapter 4, such charts were useful in determining the total expected time (longest path) required to complete a project. However, PERT can be used to determine the bottleneck activities on the critical path, for which there is no slack associated with the activities' starting date or completion date. Hence, PERT's capabilities exceed those of the Gantt chart. For this reason, PERT charts are especially recommended for projects of moderate to large size. In these situations, the PERT chart can be used as an instrument or method for project planning but, more important, as a tool for project control.

MORPHOLOGICAL METHODS AND MODELS

Morphology—the study of structure or form and the features comprising the form and any of its parts—is the fundamental activity in which we as structural

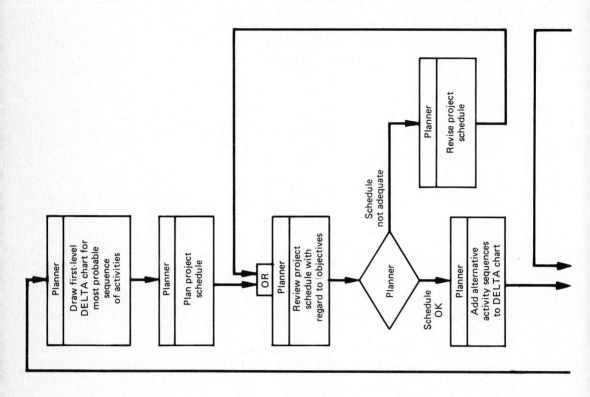

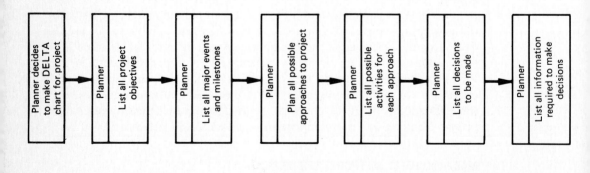

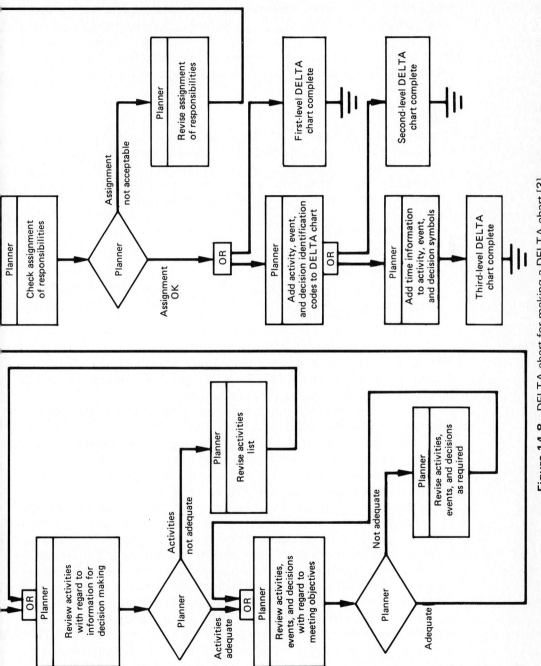

Figure 14.8 DELTA chart for making a DELTA chart [3].

modelers must engage. The morphological model begins with a determination of the major dimensions, elements, tasks, attributes, or activities associated with a problem. If only two dimensions are involved, a matrix may be a convenient instrument for describing the interactions among the components that comprise the dimensions. If there are three dimensions, a box or cube may prove useful. If there are more than three dimensions, some form of tree is usually best. We begin our discussion of morphological devices with a consideration of trees.

Trees

One of the more useful graphical aids in management science is the tree. A tree is simply a set of elements or vertices joined by line segments or edges. There can be at most one line segment between every pair of elements in the tree, and loops and cycles[1] are disallowed. Several types of trees are used in the analysis and synthesis of organizations and processes, including

> The decision tree
> The objectives tree
> The activity tree
> The worth tree
> The probability tree
> The relevance tree

The decision tree has been illustrated in conjunction with the chapters on decision theory—Chapters 7 and 12—so it will not be considered here. The probability tree is discussed later in this section.

The objectives tree (sometimes called an intent structure [4]) is used to delineate the relationships that exist among a set of objectives. We construct such trees by first listing the objectives (on separate slips of paper perhaps) and then organizing these into some form of structure that reveals a pattern or strategy for accomplishment of the objectives. For example, if objective 2 contributes to the achievement of objective 1, then objective 1 might be placed in relation to objective 2 as shown in Figure 14.9. If the resultant structure involving some n separate objectives is in fact a tree, then the structure is truly an objectives tree. The objectives tree in Figure 14.9 suggests that by accomplishing objective 2, objective 1 will also be accomplished. This insight is derived from the meaning given to the edge or arrow connecting objective 2 to objective 1. If this exact same meaning is applied to possible relationships that exist among a set of n objectives, we can construct a more complicated-looking objectives tree like that shown in Figure 14.10. A clear strategy for achievement of the system of objectives is manifest from the tree. It is possible, when required, to include some of the detail used in DELTA charts in objectives trees. For example, the ownership of each objective could be included by simply labeling each objective with its rightful owner. However, this is only necessary

---

[1] A *loop* is an edge with the same starting and stopping vertex, while a *cycle* is a repeating sequence of nodes and edges that returns back to any node in the cycle.

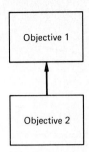

Figure 14.9 A two-element objectives tree.

when the ownership differs from objective to objective. In addition, we may include logic elements between objectives to designate whether all or some of the preceding objectives are necessary to achieve the ones that follow.

Each objective is stated beginning with the infinitive "to." One way in which to systematically construct an objectives tree is to consider every possible objectives pair by means of the phrase or relation, "Does *objective i* contribute to the *immediate* achievement of *objective k* in some way?" If the response is yes, then we should draw an arrow or edge from objective i to objective k; otherwise, no edge is drawn from objective i to objective k. More will be said about this in the discussion on interpretive structural modeling—an often-used technique for construction of objectives trees.

The activity tree is used to delineate the relationships between a collection of activities engaged in by an organization. It differs from a PERT-like activity network in that the activities are arranged into a natural hierarchy. Such a model could be constructed by first listing the activities and then interrelating them by means of the relation "Does *activity i* support the accomplishment of

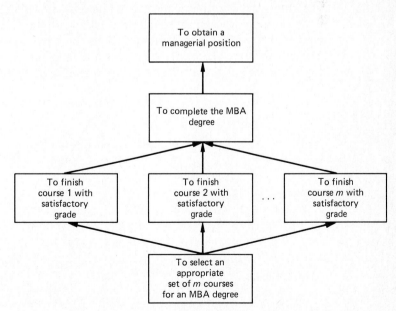

Figure 14.10 An MBA student's objectives tree.

Figure 14.11 An activity tree for a football team.

activity j in some way?" The activity tree has applications in project planning and control.

Each vertex in an activity tree represents an activity and each edge connecting the activity to a higher-level activity connotes that the activity contributes in some way to the conduct of the higher-level activity. Activity trees are normally constructed after an objectives tree has been prepared. An example activity tree is depicted in Figure 14.11.

The worth tree has applications in worth assessment and multiattribute utility theory. An example of a worth tree is shown in Figure 14.12. The tree in Figure 14.12 can be used in deciding upon the "comparative worth" or overall "value" of a set of homes that are contemplated by a buyer.

Notice that each edge is assigned a value representing the relative "benefit" of the attribute below to the attribute or feature above the edge. Thus we have assigned "neighborhood" a benefit value of .4 in relation to the feature "location." The relative *benefit coefficients* associated with each edge that emanates downward from a vertex above it always sum to 1.

This tree can be used to assign an overall worth value to each home in a collection of homes being considered for possible purchase. To each of the attributes on the bottom of the tree in Figure 14.12, we assign a value from zero to one representing our satisfaction with the attribute. Three homes are considered in Table 14.1. The attribute values for a particular home are used to evaluate the tree. The worth of a higher-level attribute is obtained by multiplying the worth of the attributes below it (and connected by edges) by their

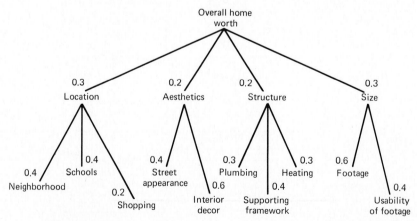

Figure 14.12 A worth tree for a home-purchase decision.

Table 14.1   Three Typical Homes Being Considered for Possible Purchase

Attribute	Home 1	Home 2	Home 3
Neighborhood	.7	.8	.9
Schools	.6	.7	.7
Shopping	.8	.9	.3
Street appearance	.9	.6	.8
Interior decor	.5	.7	.9
Plumbing	.8	.8	.4
Supporting framework	.8	.8	.4
Heating	.7	.7	.3
Footage	.8	.9	.7
Usability of footage	.9	.8	.7
Overall calculated worth	.742	.778	.666
Asking price	$98,000	$105,000	$69,000
Overall worth/cost	.00000757	.00000741	.00000965

respective benefit coefficients. The resulting products are summed over all edges connected to the higher-level attribute. Thus, by location, the following worth value is computed for home 1.

$$\text{Location worth (home 1)} = .4(.7) + .4(.6) + .2(.8)$$
$$= .68$$

Similarly, we can evaluate the aesthetics, structure, and size worth of home 1 as follows:

$$\text{Aesthetics worth (home 1)} = .4(.9) + .6(.5) \qquad = .66$$
$$\text{Structure worth (home 1)} = .3(.8) + .4(.8) + .3(.7) = .77$$
$$\text{Size worth (home 1)} = .6(.8) + .4(.9) \qquad = .84$$

Using the calculated worths for each of the attributes location, aesthetics, structure, and size, we can now calculate the overall worth of home 1.

$$\text{Overall home worth (home 1)} = .3(.68) + .2(.66) + .2(.77) + .3(.84)$$
$$= .742$$

The overall worths of homes 2 and 3 are calculated in an identical fashion, and the results are shown at the bottom of Table 14.1. Based upon this analysis, home 2 would have the greatest worth to the purchaser.

Now it is necessary to consider the costs of each home. To do this, the user could compute worth-cost ratios on each home by dividing the overall worth of each home by its associated cost. One criterion for home selection might be to choose the home with the largest worth-cost ratio. Interesting information can also be obtained from a plot of home cost versus worth, in which the coordinate corresponding to each home is located on the plot.

Solution of worth trees is very similar in format to solution of probability trees. It is important to note that the home purchase problem is indicative of the way in which multiattribute utility theory is applied to multifaceted subjects to assess their overall worth.

The probability tree is a mechanism for showing the relationships among marginal, conditional, and joint probabilities defined over a pair or more of event spaces. Its use has been profusely illustrated by texts on probability and statistics.

The relevance tree is normally constructed in levels, with each level representing a certain class of vertex entries. Connection from one level to another is based upon the relevance of one class to another class (of entries). The relevance tree is appropriate when the dimensions of a problem exceed three. Generally, the broader classes are represented at the top of a relevance tree, with the highly specific classes being represented at the bottom of a tree. For example, the highest level might represent a very broad problem to be solved. The next highest level might represent the environment within which that problem is to be solved with vertices at this level representing elements of the environment. At lower levels of the tree are specific technological developments that might contribute to the solution of the broad problem.

An example relevance tree appears in Figure 14.13. The relevance tree is commonly used in technological forecasting, where its purpose is to establish chains of relationship between entities. In this context it serves to structure the problem in its most general form, yet retain significant detail to permit subsequent analysis.

Matrix Modeling

Matrix modeling involves the use of a matrix to show all possible interaction pairs between the elements of the same or different sets. Two types of "interaction" matrices are typically used in matrix modeling. These are called the self-interaction matrix and the cross-interaction matrix. The self-interaction

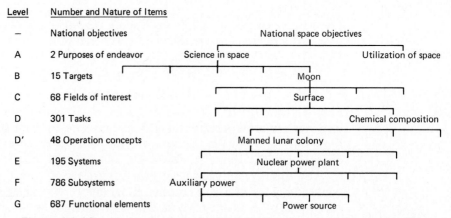

Figure 14.13 A relevance tree for NASA's Apollo payload evaluation [3].

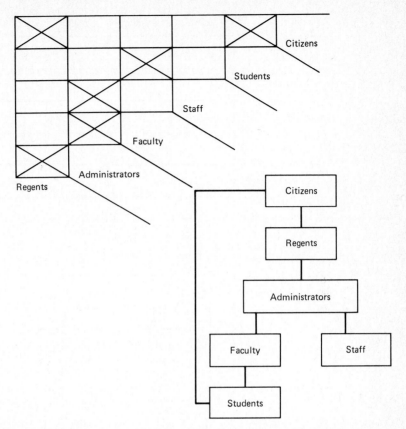

Figure 14.14 Interaction matrix and its structural interpretation for the human components of a university.

matrix uses the same element set to index both its row and its column. A half-matrix is used when the interactions are not directed (from one element to another).

If there are n elements in the set, there are $n(n-1)/2$ undirected interactions among the elements in the set. The self-interaction matrix delineating the possible interactions between the human components of a university is shown in Figure 14.14 together with its structural interpretation in graphic form.

Both the graphic representation and the associated self-interaction matrix contain exactly the same information. However, the graphic representation is much more readily interpreted by humans, whereas the matrix representation facilitates storage of the information within computers. Note that for every edge in the graphic representation there is an "X" in the self-interaction matrix. Hence an "X" or an "edge" merely denotes an interaction between the associated element pair.

If the interactions are directed as in Figure 14.15 and cycles of interaction between element pairs are permitted, then the entire matrix is required to represent this information. Now an "X" placed in the box corresponding to row element i and column element j denotes interaction directed from i toward j. The models depicted in Figure 14.15 characterize a different kind of interaction

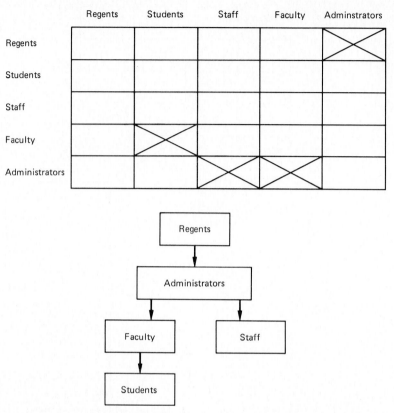

Figure 14.15 Directed interaction matrix and its digraph representation for the chain of command within a university.

than that shown in Figure 14.14. Figure 14.15 depicts the organizational hierarchy through which orders are filtered down.

It is customary to use zeroes and one's rather than blanks and "X's" in matrices of the type depicted in Figures 14.14 and 14.15 when the information is to be assimilated by a computer. Such matrixes are called *binary matrices*.

As suggested earlier, matrices may be used to interact two different element sets, rather than just one as discussed thus far. Figure 14.16 depicts a cross-interaction matrix for the functional elements of a university [6]. (In Figure 14.16, the two element sets are suppliers of information and users of information. It is just chance that the individual elements in these sets are identical.) Figure 14.17 depicts four different element sets that are interrelated by means of four cross-interaction matrices [6]. The focus of interest in Figure 14.17 is the dimensions of development appropriate for the Tennessee Valley area in Northern Alabama. In this model there are four different interaction matrices utilized to exhibit the interactions between four pairs of element sets. In Figure 14.17, each of the four interaction matrices is combined into one single large interaction. These interaction matrices show which agencies are involved in each of the ten categories of community service, what their current and planned programs are, the objectives of the programs, and the service categories that may be affected by these objectives.

Unified Program Planning: A recently developed technique called unified program planning [9] that is useful in determining the program planning linkages of moderate to large processes and projects makes extensive use of self- and cross-interaction matrices. Program planning consists of seven steps:

1. Problem definition
2. Value system design
3. System synthesis
4. Systems analysis and modeling
5. Optimization
6. Decision making
7. Planning for action

In the problem definition step the analyst or user determines the following:

1. A well-conceived title
2. A descriptive scenario
3. An understanding of what disciplines are relevant
4. An assessment of scope
5. What major components are involved
6. What actors are involved
7. Needs
8. Alterables
9. Constraints
10. Interactions between and among elements in the sets needs, alterables, constraints

One purpose achieved by this step is the assurance that everyone connected with the program has the same understanding of the problem.

In the value system design step, the attempt is to flesh out the objectives and the measures by which the achievement of the objectives will be observed. Typically, we would use an objectives tree to discern the significant structure of the objectives. In addition, this step involves interacting the objectives and their measures with the needs, alterables, and constraints that we defined in the problem definition step. The system synthesis step is concerned with three more element sets — the activities for attainment of the objectives, the activity measures, and who will be accomplishing the activities (the agencies).

The self- and cross-interaction matrices of interest in the first three steps of unified program planning are shown in Figure 14.18. The generation of elements within the sets and the filling of matrices is usually accomplished without computer assistance. Brainstorming and brain-writing are conventional procedures used to generate elements. *Brainstorming* involves the use of a facilitator and a group of participants in which the participants will orally state pertinent elements as they "come to mind." Group approval/disapproval is immediately elicited, and the proposed element is accepted or rejected. The facilitator at-

	Suppliers of the Information			
Users of the Information	Finance	Urban and Regional Development	Curricula	Research
Finance			Current and projected prorgrams	
Urban and Regional Develop			Current and projected programs	Objectives of environmental institute; objectives of computer support center
Curricula		Needs of region in terms of social, economic, and physical; inventory of human resources		Inventory of research programs
Research		Needs of region; inventory of natural resources; inventory of industry; potential uses of UAH capabilities	Current and projected programs	
Facilities		Land use map; industrial facilities in the region; industrial facilities	Current and projected programs	Current and projected research programs and projects
Students	Tuition into on scholarships available	Cultural and recreation info; employment data intern- ships; coopera- tive program of other institutions	Current and projected programs	Employment opportunities; educational opportunities; services provided
Faculty and Administration		Professional talent available in region	Current and projected programs	
Acquisition of Resources	Capital and operating expenses	Potential local sources of financial support	Current and projected programs	Suggested sources of financial support for research

Figure 14.16 A cross-interaction matrix for the functional elements of a university [6].

Facilities	Students	Faculty and Administration	Acquisition of Resources
Inventory of facilities, to include descriptions of multipurpose structures; policies on use of facilities	Internships and scholarships; current and projected enrollment	Number and qualifications of staff and faculty; faculty policies	
Inventory of facilities, to include descriptions of multipurpose structures; policies on use of facilities	Internships and cooperative programs; current and projected enrollment	Number and qualifications of staff faculty; faculty policies	
Inventory of facilities, to include descriptions of multipurpose structures; policies on use of facilities	Assessment of student desires; number and type of student projects and services		
Inventory of facilities, to include descriptions of multipurpose structures; policies on use of facilities	Placement information	Faculty policies	Description of funding programs
(shaded)	Assessment of student desires; number and type of student projects and services		
Inventory of facilities, to include descriptions of multipurpose structures; policies on use of facilities	(shaded)		
Inventory of facilities, to include descriptions of multipurpose structures; policies on use of facilities	Assessment of student desires	(shaded)	
Inventory of facilities, to include descriptions of multipurpose structures; policies on use of facilities	Suggested sources of financial support to include ways students could contribute	Views of V.P. for development ($)	(shaded)

Figure 14.16 (continued.)

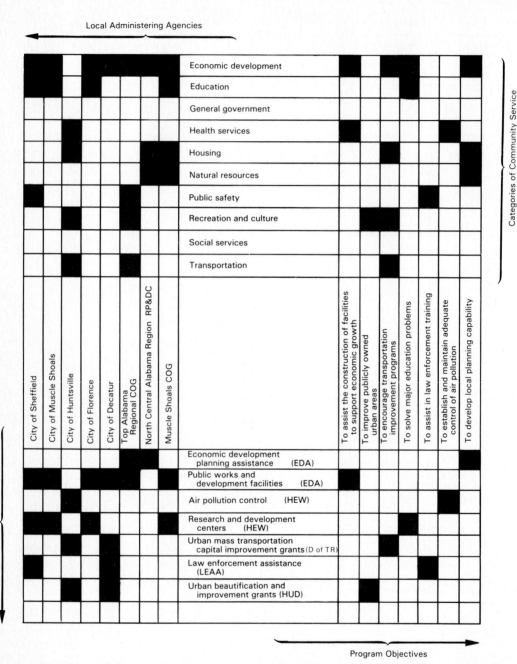

Figure 14.17   Four dimensions of development appropriate for the Tennessee Valley area of northern Alabama [6].

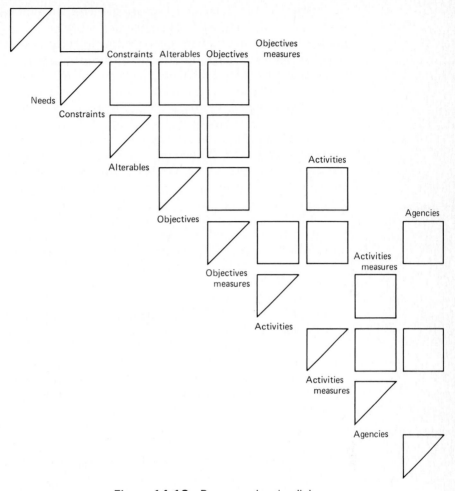

Figure 14.18   Program planning linkages.

tempts to elicit appropriate elements from the participants. In *brain-writing,* each participant is asked to write a list of candidate elements on a sheet of paper. The lists are thereafter passed around, and each participant is given the opportunity to add to or delete elements from the lists of all the other participants. Afterward the lists are consolidated and a mutually agreed-to set of elements is arrived at. Still to be accomplished within unified program planning are the steps system analysis and modeling, optimization, decision making, and planning for action. Much of the content of this book is directed toward achieving these latter steps in one fashion or another.

Interpretive Structural Modeling (ISM)
Interpretive structural modeling is the name given to a technique that allows us to construct a directed graph or network representation of a contextual relation among a single set of elements. The attempt is to extract from an individual or group the essential structure of a problem, process, situation, or system.

Interpretive structural modeling was developed by John Warfield [7,8,9] as a pragmatic, integrated extension of the work of Harary et al. [4]. The method has attained a modicum of use in both the public and private sectors as partially reported in [6]. For "large" models, the method requires use of a computer and supporting software to enable users to systematically consider every conceivable interactant pair that is consistent with the assumptions of ISM.

Preliminaries: The process of ISM is based upon the one-to-one correspondence between a binary matrix and a graphical representation of a directed network. The fundamental concepts of the process are an "element set" and a "contextual relation." We identify the element set within some situational context and select the contextual relation as a possible statement of relationship among the elements in a manner that is contextually significant for the purposes of the enquiry.

The contextual relation is usually stated in three parts as in "Does [element i] contribute to [element j] in some way?" or "Will [element i] support [element j] in most cases?" In the first contextual relation, the three parts were "Does," "contribute to," and "in some way," Relations may be of several types as listed in Table 14.2.

The elements correspond to "nodes" or "blocks" in a structural model, whereas the presence of a relation between any two elements is denoted by a directed edge. For example, if the response to the query "Does population growth contribute to congestion in an urban area?" were "Yes," then we would draw an edge directed from "population growth" to "congestion." In the equivalent binary matrix representation, the elements are the contents of the index set for the rows and columns of the matrix, and the presence of a relation (i.e., a "Yes" response to a query) from element i to element j is indicated by placing a 1 in the corresponding intersection of row i and column j.

Table 14.2   Contextual Relation Types and Examples

Relation Type	Examples (middle part only)
Comparative relations	. . . is subordinate to . . .
	. . . is better than . . .
	. . . is more intelligent than . . .
	. . . supercede(s) . . .
Influence relations	. . . affect . . .
	. . . contribute . . .
	. . . influence . . .
	. . . cause . . .
	. . . intensify . . .
	. . . aggravate . . .
Preference relations	. . . is preferred to . . .
	. . . is worth more than . . .
	. . . is more important than . . .
Neutral relations	. . . is necessary for . . .
	. . . is essential to . . .

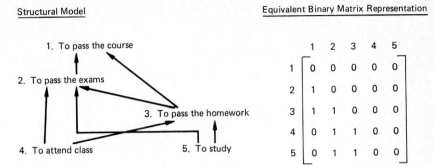

Figure 14.19 A structural model and associated adjacency matrix for an MBA student.

Consider the task of structuring the value system for an MBA student who is struggling to survive the required "quant" course. His objectives (elements in a general sense), contextual relation, structural model, and binary matrix model are exhibited in Figure 14.19.

Contextual Relation: "Does objective . . . contribute to objective . . . in some way?"

Elements

1. To pass the course
2. To pass the exams
3. To pass the homework
4. To attend class
5. To study

The binary matrix shown in Figure 14.19 is called an *adjacency matrix* and is denoted by **A**. It is constructed by setting $a_{ij} = 1$ if there is an edge directed from i to j and zero otherwise.

Element s_j is said to be reachable from element s_i if a sequence of one or more edges can be traced in the structural model from s_i to s_j. By convention all elements are considered reachable from themselves. This gives rise to the concept of *reachability*, which is true of any element pair (s_i, s_j) if a sequence exists from i to j. Since the concept involves element pairs, a natural delineation of reachability for all element pairs would be a matrix, called the reachability matrix. The reachability matrix for the structural model depicted in Figure 14.19 is given in Figure 14.20.

There is a correspondence between the notion of reachability in digraph theory [4] and the notion of *transitivity* in relations. The relation R used to establish the connectivity in the interpretive structural model is always assumed to be transitive; that is, if s_i is related to s_j and s_j is related to s_k by the relation R, then by transitivity it is assumed that s_i is related to s_k. As it turns out, a reachability matrix represents the "transitive closure" of a structural model. As we will show, the reachability matrix is the basic device used by ISM algorithms for formulation of structural models.

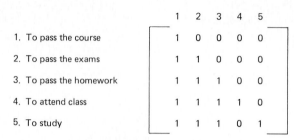

	1	2	3	4	5
1. To pass the course	1	0	0	0	0
2. To pass the exams	1	1	0	0	0
3. To pass the homework	1	1	1	0	0
4. To attend class	1	1	1	1	0
5. To study	1	1	1	0	1

Figure 14.20   Reachability matrix for the structural model shown in Figure 14.19.

Mechanics of ISM: The ISM exercise begins with a preconditioning phase in which the participants clarify their thoughts and perceptions on the problem being considered. Specifically, they agree upon the theme, perspective, mode, and priorities of the problem as shown in Table 14.3. The primitives are the most important component in the preconditioning phase. The relation R must be succinctly and cogently stated in three parts. Each element s_i must possess the same meaning to all participants and should not overlap in content and scope with other elements s_j. The element set s, like the set of alternatives or states in a decision model, should be mutually exclusive and collectively exhaustive. (Some computer programs implementing ISM will permit participants to add elements in a later phase.) It is usually good practice to develop a small ISM using only a portion of the element set s before attempting the full-blown model. This enables the participants to double-check the appropriateness of the relation R in conjunction with the elements. It also acquaints new participants with the ISM process and builds both confidence and credibility in that process.

Table 14.3   Phases of ISM Process

Phase 1   Preconditioning guidelines (computer and participants)
        Theme: (purposes and objectives)
        Perspective: (whose?)
        Mode: (descriptive or prescriptive)
        Primitives: s, the element set; R, the contextual relation

Phase 2   Fill the reachability matrix (computer and participants)
        a. Partition the element set s and fill subsystem matrices
        b. Fill the interconnection matrices

Phase 3   Extract a hierarchical ordering (computer only)

Phase 4   Determine a minimum edge digraph (computer only)

Phase 5   Make adjustments as necessary (participants)
        a. Revise digraph
        b. Replace element numbers with names and redraw the digraph

Once we have determined the element set s and relation R, these must be entered into the computer. If appropriate software is unavailable, it is possible to carry out the necessary operations manually, provided that the element set s is small.

Phase 2 is the most tedious and demanding of the participants. During this phase, the computer queries the participants using a pair of elements from the element set s and the three-part relation R. For example, "Does . . . s_i . . . influence . . . s_j . . . in some way?" is a typical query. The participants must decide upon and enter a single collective response, such as "yes," "no," "true," or "false" to the query. This will cause a 0 or 1 to be placed in the reachability matrix at the intersection of the row associated with s_i and the column associated with s_j. This response will also cause s_j to be partitioned relative to s_i, where s_i is the element selected for determination of the partition. The partitions of the element set s based upon s_i facilitate filling the reachability matrix. By means of the partition, much of the reachability matrix can be inferred from just a few user responses elicited by queries. Details are described in the appendix to this chapter.

Phase 3 uses an algorithm within the computer to extract a hierarchical ordering of the element set s. As for phase 2, details are discussed and illustrated in the appendix.

A very quick (and dirty) manual method for accomplishing steps 2 and 3 is to place the elements on $3'' \times 5''$ cards and then arrange the cards into a hierarchy that is consistent with the relation defined in phase 1. Then, once a satisfactory arrangement is achieved, connect the elements by means of lines (edges in our terminology). An edge should be placed from element s_i to element s_j if there is an immediate relation from s_i to s_j, as determined by reference to the contextual relation defined in phase 1. Elements in a feedback relation (a cycle) are on the same level of the hierarchy. Element pairs s_i, s_j possessing an edge directed from s_i to s_j will always have s_j on the level immediately above the level on which s_i appears, provided that there is not a sequence of edges leading back from s_j to s_i. A more sophisticated manual method is presented in the appendix, as are the actual algorithms employed by software implementations of ISM. Since the simple method just described does not force a systematic consideration of every candidate edge between element pairs, errors of omission are likely to appear. However, for small element sets, this quick and dirty method is likely to be nearly as effective as the more rigorous methods described in the appendix.

The next phase (phase 4) has as its goal that of determining the edges between the elements. This is accomplished by inserting the minimum number of edges required to connect completely the elements together. The result is a completed structural model. Phases 3 and 4 are usually accomplished by the computer when it is used.

The last phase (phase 5) is concerned with altering the basic structural model produced by the computer. Thus the participants may choose to add elements, move elements, delete elements, add edges, or delete edges until a mutually satisfactory result is obtained. The final product is referred to as an interpretive structural model.

AVAILABLE COMPUTER CODES FOR STRUCTURAL MODELING AND ANALYSIS

A great many of the computer codes for structural modeling are proprietary, and — to our knowledge — commercial-grade software has not yet emerged for structural modeling. A relatively primitive code developed at the University of Dayton by David Yingling is available from James R. Burns. However, this code will not support the addition of elements to the model after the query process has begun; nor will it support other user-friendly features considered desirable for such applications. Other more sophisticated codes have been written, but their availability is uncertain.

DEVELOPING ALTERNATIVE SOLUTIONS

Any digraph produced by the ISM process represents a starting point from which we can obtain alternative structural models. The translation of the computer-generated digraph into an interpretive structural model is essentially a "cut-and-try" activity in which the participants voice their approval or disapproval of the various alternative structures that are proposed. As for any model, an ISM is never perfect; however, there must be an adequate level of collective satisfaction in it. The implications of the ISM must be apparent to the participants. Ultimately, the ISM should alter or reinforce the approaches taken for managerial control and executive actions; that is, it should have an impact upon decision making.

STATE OF THE ART IN STRUCTURAL MODELING

In its current form, ISM is a painstakingly tedious process that requires considerable effort from one or more participants. This is especially true when the rigorous methods (see the appendix) for accomplishing phase 2 are employed. For a medium-sized model consisting of 25 elements, there are 625 element pairs. If only 50% of these are inferred, then the computer will require responses from roughly 300 queries to fill completely the reachability matrix. In this case, thoroughness is, perhaps, overwhelmingly demanding and raises questions concerning whether the gain realized from the exercise is worth the effort. One Japanese program lets the participants manipulate the elements by use of a light pen (the elements are displayed on video in blocks and can be moved by touching the light pen to the display at the point where the block appears and moving the light pen to the desired position on the display). While such a procedure may not be systematic, it involves less tedium. What is important is that it is a visual product that enlightens the collective understanding and provides new insight. If the ultimate structural model is able to suggest new strategies for problem resolution, new perspectives on old issues, or new understanding about a process that must be managed, then we consider the exercise to be worthwhile.

Goals for Dallas [4]

The Scenario: In the mid-1960s Erik Jonsson, who at that time was mayor of Dallas, decided to embark upon a goal-setting approach to management and leadership of Dallas. He invited 27 community leaders to discuss with him a proposal to establish a citizen-based program for determining guidelines for the future. These 27 individuals agreed to initiate a three-stage program:

1. To establish goals for the city by a broadly representative group of the people of Dallas
2. To develop and prepare schedules, indicating priority and responsibility, for accomplishing these goals
3. To develop a system to evaluate progress in achieving the goals and to revise the goals periodically as warranted by changing conditions

This 27-member planning committee of the Goals for Dallas had in mind full citizen participation in the planning function and volunteered to act as an informal board of directors for a corps of citizen volunteers. Once they had determined the basic structure of the Goals for Dallas project, the planning committee began work on a method for goal setting. They initially invited 60 Dallasites to join them in a goal-setting conference. These 60 people, representing diverse ethnic, political, social, and economic backgrounds, studied a prepared descriptive scenario of Dallas including such sectors as city government, city design, health, welfare, education, transportation, and communications. The group met for a three-day conference to establish an initial series of goals for the City of Dallas, which were published [5] and made available to the community at bookstores and libraries.

Next, the proposed goals were exposed for full citizen participation (church groups, civic clubs, chambers of commerce, industrial organizations, etc.). The net result of this activity was 116 specific goals for the city of Dallas and associated activity steps to be undertaken by responsible organizations within a given time frame.

The Problem: A perusal (by a group of graduate students at Southern Methodist University) of the literature proliferated by Goals for Dallas revealed that [14]

Objectives were not sharply stated.

Some objectives were not adequately supported.

Some objectives were misleading.

Objectives measures were often not stated.

Setting priorities was not done on a rational basis.

No precise mechanism for modification of goals as situations change was communicated.

The intimation that some improvement might accrue from the use of structural modeling was apparent. Since this was essentially a planning exercise, the use of unifed program planning (UPP) was a clear choice.

The literature for the Goals for Dallas program indicates that goals were formulated simultaneously with, or perhaps ahead of, needs, alterables, and constraints. That is, value systems design (in the jargon of UPP) was accomplished without a problem definition step. Thus, participants had to have an intuitive feeling or mental image of needs, constraints, and alterables without formal discussions of these problem-definitional components.

The Model: From a perusal of the literature on the Goals for Dallas project, several UPP models were developed for various phases of that project. Specifically three goal-setting arenas were looked at:

Government of the city goals

Welfare goals

Public safety goals

These goals were taken from the overall goal schema as depicted in Figure 14.21. A self-interaction matrix for the 12 major subgoals of the city of Dallas is shown in Figure 14.22. There is a tendency to organize agencies around the various goals that are identified. Figure 14.22 suggests where there is a need for close collaboration among the various goal-setting organizations. In some instances it might be advisable to merge organizations

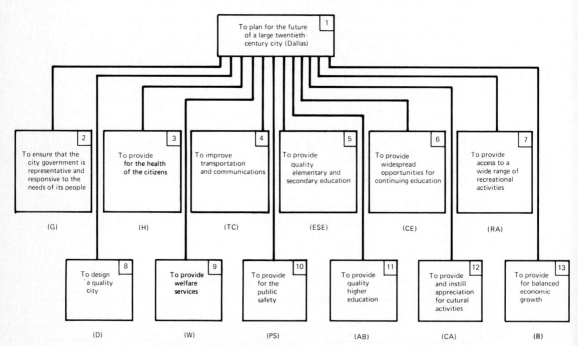

Figure 14.21 Top-level goal and 12 primary objectives for achieving the top-level goal, as taken from Goals for Dallas [14].

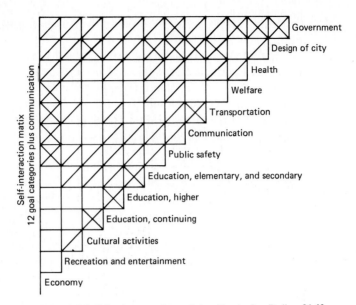

Figure 14.22   Interaction of the Goals for Dallas [14].

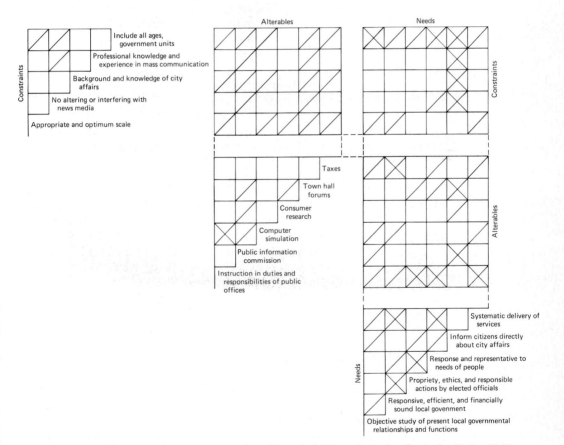

Figure 14.23   Interaction linkages of problem definition phase for Goals for Dallas [14].

together when the bond between them mandates considerable coordination.

Goal statements were essaylike, and it was necessary to extract from these the needs, constraints, and alterables required of the problem-definitional step of UPP. Problem definitional linkages for the government of the city goals are depicted in Figure 14.23. The interactions shown here identify a relationship between the associated element pair without specifying what the specific relationship is.

The Solution: Use of the systemic methodology of unified program planning offers a format for the product of the planning effort that is amenable to modification and expansion. It offers a visibility of the planning process that is becoming of great significance to our society.

A major conclusion of this study is that methods exist that can be used to transform mental models into models that can be organized and communicated. Equally important is the fact that the methods described can be used, with appropriate guidance, by nontechnically oriented persons — specifically, the citizens of a city.

Priority Setting in Cedar Falls [11]

The Scenario: Early in 1974 the city of Cedar Falls, Iowa, decided that a five-year plan for capital improvements was needed. The City Council, along with the mayor and the city's Planning and Zoning Commission, began the tedious task of priority setting among projects requiring capital funds.

The Problem: Articles in the local newspaper alluded to the considerable difficulty that was encountered in the priority-setting process. This led to Professor Robert Waller's eventual involvement in the city capital planning activities. Waller was well versed in ISM and structural modeling methodologies and was, therefore, able to serve as an ISM moderator for groups of planners and/or policymakers. Waller suggested a trial ISM exercise to ascertain its utility for analyzing the problem. The trial exercise convinced the mayor and others that ISM "was indeed of considerable value vis-à-vis the problem confronted." This led to its use by the planning and zoning commission, and ultimately by the City Council.

The Model: Some 31 projects were ranked using the relation "all things considered is the . . . less desirable than the . . . ?" If consensus did not prevail, the answer was determined by majority vote. Figure 14.24 exibits the models developed by the planning and zoning commission and by the City Council. The use of ISM forced the participants to consider priorities in terms of pairs of elements and to utilize transitivity to infer as many of the pairwise interactions as possible. Instead of $n^2 - n =$

$31^2 - 31 = 930$ interactions to consider, roughly half or less of that amount were actually considered; the rest were inferred.

The Solution: The structural models (note the degree of similarity between the two models) developed from the exercise served as a road map or strategy for approaching the projects. Starting with those at the top of the list, the planning and zoning commission could work its way down the structure until either the money was used up or all projects were completed.

SUMMARY

The methods we discussed in this chapter cannot produce "a silk purse out of a sow's ear." The overriding need is for *substance*—the material out of which definitive, concise elements are generated, out of which a cogent, contexual relation is formed, and from which the interactions and relations between elements are carefully declared. The methodologies described in this chapter are intended for *direct* use by policymakers, managers, and decision makers in group-participative exercises.

The graphical tools illustrated in this chapter are becoming increasingly prominent in the business world because of the software/hardware capability to produce the charts, trees, and graphs quickly and inexpensively. These visual devices are quickly comprehended and greatly enhance communication and understanding among human beings.

We introduced unified program planning and illustrated it by use of a case. The technique is useful in delineating the interactions between and, therefore, the "proximity" of, the various components. There are important implications for organizational design (of corporations, bureaucracies, and institutions) and for program or project design. It is an important tool for preliminary planning.

We discussed the methodology known as ISM in some detail, and we illustrated it with cases. The process is appropriate for use by participants who have enough knowledge of the context of the problem to be able to respond "yes" or "no" to the sequence of queries generated by the computer. This process is advantageous over ad hoc element arrangement procedures because it is systematic; we consider all possible pairwise interactions of the elements—either through responses of the users to direct queries or by transitive inference based upon responses to previous queries. An advantage stems from the efficiency gained from this use of transitive inference. Depending upon the context of the problem, the use of transitive inference may reduce the required number of queries by 20 to 50% of the total number possible [10].

The ISM process was shown to involve the definition of a contextually significant element set and relation, the computer generation of a sequence of queries and their subsequent responses by the participants, and finally the examination, evaluation, and revision of the computer-generated digraph, resulting in the interpretive structural model.

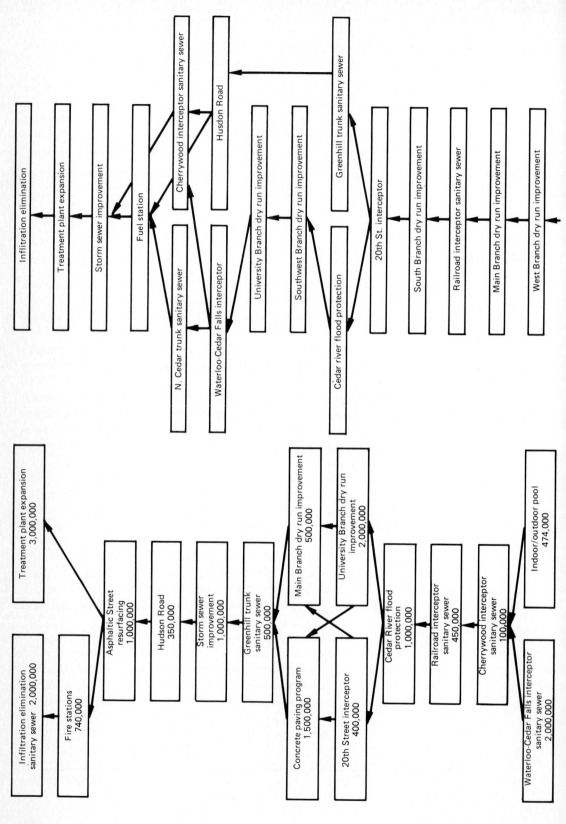

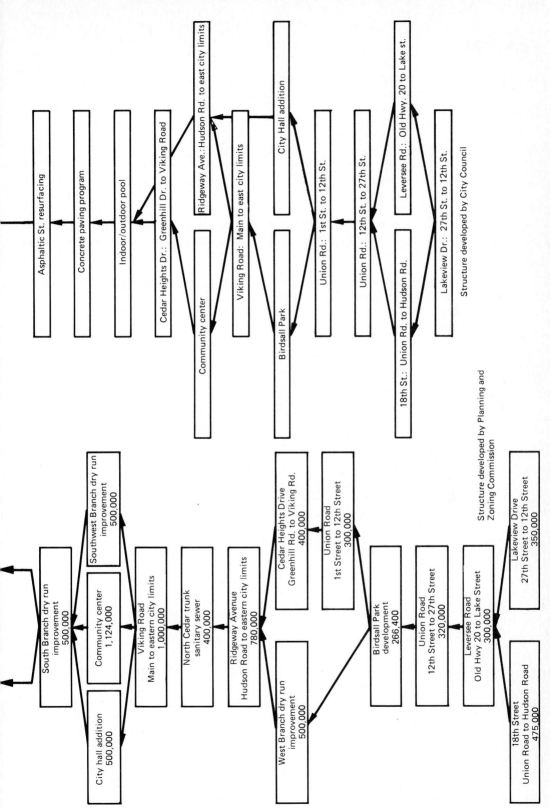

Figure 14.24 Priority structures developed by administrative policymaking units at Cedar Falls, Iowa [11].

PROBLEMS

1. Briefly describe each of the following:
   a. Binary matrix
   b. Adjacency matrix
   c. Reachability matrix
   d. Interaction matrix
   e. Relevance tree
   f. Worth tree
   g. Probability tree
   h. Decision tree
   i. Objectives tree
   j. DELTA chart
   k. PERT chart
   l. Transitivity
   m. Multiattribute utility theory
   n. Unified program planning
   o. Interpretive structural modeling

2. List as many possible consequences as you can that have accrued from the introduction of the automobile. Use manual techniques to organize these into a structural model using the relation "_____ contributes to _____."

3. Construct a worth tree to assess the worth to you of several job opportunities that will present themselves as you complete your degree. Evaluate the tree for at least three hypothetical job possibilities. Treat salary in the same way the purchase price of a home was considered in the home purchase example. Major attributes or dimensions of worth might include geographic location, travel requirements, and nature of work.

4. Re-solve Problem 3, except make economic compensation an additional attribute of the worth tree rather than treating it as in the home purchase example. Which strategy makes the most sense to you? For greater details on this "problem," see [5].

5. Develop an interaction matrix for the most efficient allocation of energy sources (listed in the table) to energy consumption sectors (also listed in the table).

Energy Sources	Consumption Sectors
Crude petroleum	Residential
Coal	Commercial
Natural gas	Industrial
Nuclear power	Agricultural
Solar energy	Transportation
Electric power	Electricity
Exotic sources (trash, geothermal, geohydro, hydroelectric)	

Justify your allocation choices.

6. Use the elements and the relation shown to formulate an interpretive structural model of your value system.

Elements	*The Relation*
a. Wealth	"[Value *i*] is more important
b. Skill	to me than is [value *j*]."
c. Enlightment	
d. Power	
e. Affection	
f. Respect	

    g. Well-being

    h. Rectitude   (uprightness
           in ethics and behavior)

Use $3'' \times 5''$ cards and the hand structuring methods described in the chapter (and in the appendix) if a computer and ISM software are unavailable.

7.   Determine adjacency and reachability matrixes for the ISM exhibited here.

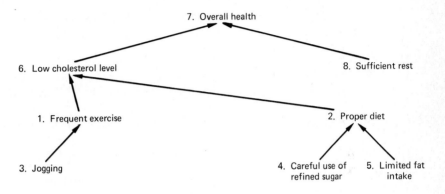

8.   *The Scenario:*[2]   The city of Las Vegas has experienced a rash of hotel fires, and the resulting publicity has hurt the casino business. The city's fire marshal, Don Burn, is interested in studying the relationships among the elements that impact upon the fire-fighting system.

    The Problem: Mr. Burn is at least as interested in fire prevention as he is in minimizing fire damage per fire. He has recently held conversations with the city's operations consultant Jack Potts. Jack suggests an ISM session with himself acting as moderator, with the participants to include all the fire marshals in the city. "Set up a meeting time and place, invite all the city fire marshals, and be willing to spend a couple of days hard work on this activity," Jack told Don. "We will formulate a small model just to introduce everyone to the process and then we'll tackle the problem in its totality."

    The Model: The morning of the ISM seminar arrived and Jack showed up early with several computer terminals, and the session began with Jack providing a brief explanation of the ISM process. Beginning with phase 1, the group decided upon the following:

Theme: A holistic understanding of the Las Vegas fire-fighting system

Perspective: "What can the city's fire marshals do?"

Mode: Prescriptive

Primitives: Element set, S

    1. Number of fires

    2. Number of fire-fighters

    3. Fire damage/fire

    4. Fire prevention

    5. Neighborhood quality

---

[2] Elements in the problem are based on [8].

6. Population density
7. Proximity of fire department
8. Fire detection apparatus
9. Fire codes
10. Number of volunteers
11. Number of professionals

Contextual relation: R

Is . . . related to . . . in some way?

The Solution: Use a manual method described in the chapter (see also the appendix) to develop an ISM for the fire-fighting system. What specific actions would you recommend to the fire marshals?

9. Describe what effect labeling each edge with a "+" or "−" would have upon improving the collective understanding and implications of the ISM you developed in Problem 8.

10. List at least two approaches for element generation, describing each.

11. It is sometimes possible to compute an interaction matrix as the product of two other interaction matrices. For example, if the interaction matrix relating needs to constraints were known, and the interaction matrix relating constraints to alterables were known, then the interaction matrix relating needs to alterables could be determined as the product of the aforementioned matrices. Of course, it is necessary to replace empty cells with zeroes and nonempty cells with one's to carry out the indicated multiplication. The matrix resulting from the multiplication could be transformed back to a matrix of zeroes and one's by replacing every nonempty cell with a 1. However, the number in each nonempty cell is indicative of the strength of interaction between the associated element pair. Find a needs-to-alterables interaction matrix for the following pair of interaction matrices.

Needs \ *Constraints*	1	2	3	4
1	0	1	1	0
2	1	0	0	1
3	1	1	0	0

Constraints \ *Alterables*	1	2	3	4	5
1	0	1	1	0	0
2	1	0	0	1	0
3	1	1	0	0	0
4	1	0	0	0	1

12. Transpose the pair of matrices in Problem 11 and compute an alterables-to-needs interaction matrix. What relationship does it have to the needs-to-alterables interaction matrix?

13. ***The Scenario:*** Most large cities have sustained an aging and decline of the central-city building structures once the inner-city land area is filled up. As the city's central business and residential districts grow older, the relative unattractiveness of the inner city causes a "flight" of businesses and residents to the suburbs. This leads to erosion of the city's property tax base and to still more rapid decline of the central city. To counteract this trend, old structures must be removed and new structures built up in their spaces.

The Problem: Central-city refurbishment and revitalization requires capital from the private and public sectors alike. Public sector money is increasingly sporadic and difficult to obtain. Private sector money could be available if certain impediments could be removed.

The Model: A group of graduate students at the Ohio State University [10,12] developed the following list of obstacles to investment in the Columbus, Ohio, central business district.

High crime rates and insecurity
Vandalism
Poor quality public schools
Traffic congestion
Poor quality of other public services
Abandoned buildings
Poor property maintenance
Concentrated poverty
Messy neighborhood appearance
Nonchild-oriented environment
White withdrawal
Fragmented land ownership
Superior suburban competition
High land costs
High construction costs
High borrowing costs and nonavailability of financing
High security costs
High insurance costs

The Solution: Use the relation " . . . intensifies or aggravates . . . " to develop an interpretive structural model of this problem. What implications for government planning and policymaking can be inferred from the ISM?

14. Apply the problem definition step of unified program planning to the following situation involving pollution:

Pollutants from automobiles, power plants, chemical companies, and heavy industry all serve to destroy the quality of the air we breathe. The need is for certain air quality standards to be met, at all times. This can be accomplished in a number of ways — high tariffs on entities that are heavy polluters, requiring industrial polluters to use highly efficient electrostatic precipitators and other devices, mandating pollution controls on autos, periodic pollution checks on all sources of pollution, continual monitoring of air quality at various locations, as well as reporting air quality conditions in the media and encouraging people not to drive when pollution conditions are extreme. Most of these actions entail some form of cost that can have deleterious effects upon the consuming public. The intent is to achieve the greatest reductions possible in particulates of air pollution without overburdening the economic base of production and consumption.

Determine societal sectors, needs, alterables, constraints and specify their associated self- and cross-interaction matrices.

15. Develop an interpretive structural model for the following situation:

A community has determined that population growth in the area depends on the availability of housing as well as the persistent natural attractiveness of the area. Abundant housing attracts people at a greater rate than under normal conditions. The opposite is true when housing is tight. Area residents also leave the community at a certain rate due primarily to the availability of housing.

Housing construction industry, on the other hand, fluctuates depending on the land availability and housing desires. Abundant housing cuts back the construction of houses while the opposite is true when the housing situation is tight. Also, as land for residential development fills up (in this mountain valley), the construction rate decreases down to the level of demolition rate of houses.

Elements	Relation
Housing	. . . causes or affects . . .
Construction rate	
Demolition rate	
Land for development	
Housing desired (required)	
Housing availability	
Population	
Net internal growth of population	
In-migration	
Out-migration	

We will treat this problem again in Chapter 15, where much of the methodology of structural modeling is directly applicable to the formulation of continuous simulation models.

16. Find an appropriate real-world planning problem to which unified program planning could be applied. Encourage those who are the planners in the project to utilize you as a consultant. Employ unified program planning in the planning sessions and describe the results in terms of benefits derived, lessons learned, insights obtained.

17. Find an appropriate real-world problem to which interpretive structural modeling could be applied. Utilize ISM and describe the results.

APPENDIX: MECHANICS OF ISM, PHASES 2 AND 3

Phases 2 and 3 of ISM are concerned with filling a so-called "reachability matrix" and thereafter extracting a hierarchical ordering of the elements in s from the matrix. The technical details of these two phases are discussed in this appendix. The algorithms required to accomplish these two phases are illustrated by use of an example, as well. A manual method for achieving these two phases is also described in this appendix.

In phase 2, a sequence of queries (usually synthesized by the software) are presented to the user. The user's response to each query (usually "yes," "no," "true," or "false") causes a zero or a one to be placed in the reachability matrix. For convenience we shall let $s_i Rs_j$ denote a "yes" or "true" response to a query relating s_i to s_j and $s_i Rs_j$ denote a "no" or "false" response. The element pair (s_i, s_j) is then reversed and the query $s_j Rs_i$ is presented to the participants and a response is elicited from them. For the pair (s_i, s_j) one of four possible relationships can exist as indicated in Table 1 and Figure 14.20. If the

Table 1   Four Possible Relationships Between s_i and s_j
Based upon the Queries $s_i Rs_j$, $s_j Rs_i$

Query Response		Relationship
$s_i Rs_j$, $s_j Rs_i$	(yes, no)	s_j is in a "lift" relationship to s_i
$s_i Rs_j$, $s_j Rs_i$	(yes, yes)	s_j is in a "feedback" relationship to s_i
$s_i Rs_j$, $s_j Rs_i$	(no, yes)	s_j is in a "drop" relationship to s_i
$s_i Rs_j$, $s_j Rs_i$	(no, no)	s_j is in a "vacancy" relationship to s_i

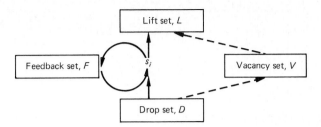

Figure 1   Four partitions of the element set *s* relative to element s_i.

response to the two queries is "yes, no," then s_j is influenced by s_i—that is, $s_i R s_j$ and, hence, s_j is in a "lift" relationship to s_i as it would ordinarily be placed hierarchically above s_i. If the responses are "yes, yes," then s_j is in a "feedback" relationship to s_i and would be placed on the same hierarchical level as s_i. If the responses are "no, yes," then s_j is in a "drop" relationship to s_i—that is, s_j influences s_i and would be placed hierarchically below s_i. If the responses are "no, no," then s_j has no (or a "vacant") relationship to s_i. By deploying these two queries for every s_j in s except s_i, we can partition s into five components— s_i, the lift set L, the feedback set F, the drop set D, and the vacancy set V. Elements in the feedback set F are placed on the same level as s_i, as shown in Figure 1. This partition enables the ISM program to infer much of the reachability matrix as shown in Figure 2. Three subsystem matrices and two interconnection matrices remain to be specified. The subsystem matrices are specified by a partitioning procedure that is identical to that applied to the overall reachability matrix. We can also use inference in constructing the interconnection matrices. Technical details are, however, beyond the scope of this appendix.

We could use a straightforward manual procedure to perform the partitions of the element set s. We first select an element s_i and apply the forward and backward queries to determine which of the s_j in s should be placed in the subsets L, F, V, and D, as shown in Figure 3. We then apply the exact same partitioning procedure to each of the subsets L, V, and D, by arbitrarily picking an element s_i from each and applying the partitioning procedure to each subset individually. Once all the sub-subsets associated with L, V, and D are reduced to one or less elements, we have completed the exercise.

To construct a digraph (phases 3 and 4) manually from the elements, we inspect the bottom tier of the table shown in Figure 3. Any elements in the bottom-tier subsets L or

	Lift set, L	Feedback set, F	s_i	Vacancy set, V	Drop set, D
Lift set, L	Subsystem matrix	Inferred 0's	0's	Inferred 0's	Inferred 0's
Feedback set, F	Inferred 1's	Inferred 1's	1's	Inferred 0's	Inferred 0's
s_i	1's	1's	1	0's	0's
Vacancy set, V	Interconnection matrix	Inferred 0's	0's	Subsystem matrix	Inferred 0's
Drop set, D	Inferred 1's	Inferred 1's	1's	Interconnection matrix	Subsystem matrix

Figure 2   Elements in partitioned reachability matrix that may be inferred.

s_i	Lift set, L					Feedback set, F	Vacancy set, V					Drop set, D				
	s_k	L^1	F^1	V^1	D^1		S_1	L^2	F^2	V^2	D^2	S_m	L^3	F^3	V^3	D^3

Figure 3   Schema for manual partitioning of the element set s.

F are on the top level of the digraph. If there are elements in the F subset of any tier, then these elements are in a cycle or feedback loop, the exact structure of which must be determined by "cut-and-try" procedures. Elements in the bottom-tier subset D are on the bottom level of the digraph. Once elements on the bottom tier of the table have found their places on the digraph, the next lowest tier in the table depicted in Figure 3 is considered. Thus the construction of the digraph begins with the bottom tier and works upward.

Phase 3 of the ISM processs involves extraction of a hierarchical ordering from the reachability matrix. This is accomplished by the level partition developed by Warfield [7]. The purpose of this phase is to facilitate the construction of the digraph from the reachability matrix. This phase is not required when the manual method is used, as previously discussed. The level partition makes use of sets associated with each element s_j in s. Let $R(s_i)$ be all those s_j in s reachable from s_i; that is, all those s_j for which a sequence of one or more edges leading from s_i terminate at s_j. By "walking" one of these sequences, it is possible to "reach" s_j from s_i. Let $F(s_i)$ be all those s_j in s that are in a feedback relationship with s_i; that is, they are capable of being reached from s_i but also of reaching to s_i. Thus, a sequence leading from s_i to s_j and from s_j back to s_i must exist if s_j is in $F(s_i)$. Finally, let $A(s_i)$ be all s_j in s which are capable of reaching s_i by means of a sequence leading from s_j to s_i. The sets $R(s_i)$ and $A(s_i)$ do not exclude elements of the feedback set $F(s_i)$. Hence $F(s_i)$ is equal to $R(s_i) \cap A(s_i)$; that is, the feedback set $F(s_i)$ is simply all elements in common to (in the intersection of) $R(s_i)$ and $A(s_i)$.

With these definitions firmly in mind let us construct a table as shown in Table 2.

In Table 2 we have determined, for each element s_i, its $R(s_i)$, $A(s_i)$, and $F(s_i)$. The procedure for finding the elements in the top level of the hierarchy is to identify any elements s_i for which the reachable set $R(s_i)$ is the same exact set as the feedback set, $F(s_i)$. When the reachable set is identical to the feedback set for an element s_i, then s_i is said to be on the top level of the hierarchy, along with all elements in the feedback set $F(s_i)$ associated with s_i. By convention, feedback sets are always placed on a single level of the hierarchy; that is, such sets are never split between several levels. By comparing the reachables column with the feedback column in Table 2, it is apparent that only element 1 is on the top level of the hierarchy.

Table 2   Reachability and Antecedent Sets for the Reachability Matrix
Shown in Figure 14.20

Element s_i	Antecedents $A(s_i)$	Reachables $R(s_i)$	$F(s_i) = R(s_i) \cap A(s_i)$ Feedback $F(s_i)$
1	1, 2, 3, 4, 5	1	1
2	2, 3, 4, 5	1, 2	2
3	3, 4, 5	1, 2, 3	3
4	4	1, 2, 3, 4	4
5	5	1, 2, 3, 5	5

Table 3   Reachability and Antecedent Sets After Elimination of
Elements in the First Level

Element s_i	Antecedents $A(s_i)$	Reachables $R(s_i)$	$F(s_i) = R(s_i) \cap A(s_i)$ Feedback $F(s_i)$
2	2, 3, 4, 5	2	2
3	3, 4, 5	2, 3	3
4	4	2, 3, 4	4
5	5	2, 3, 5	5

Table 4   Reachability and Antecedent Sets After Elimination of
Elements in the First Two Levels

Element s_i	Antecedents $A(s_i)$	Reachables $R(s_i)$	$F(s_i) = R(s_i) \cap A(s_i)$ Feedback $F(s_i)$
3	3, 4, 5	3	3
4	4	3, 4	4
5	5	3, 5	5

Table 5   Reachability and Antecedent Sets after Elimination of
Elements in the First Three Levels

Element s_i	Antecedents $A(s_i)$	Reachables $R(s_i)$	$F(s_i) = R(s_i) \cap A(s_i)$ Feedback $F(s_i)$
4	4	4	4
5	5	5	5

Table 6   Hierarchical Ordering Resulting from
the Level Partition Applied to the Reachability
Matrix in Figure 14.20

Level 1	1. To pass the course	
Level 2	2. To pass the exams	
Level 3	3. To pass the homework	
Level 4	4. To attend class	5. To study

To determine the elements on the next level of the hierarchy, all elements in the level above it are eliminated from the table. This essentially eliminates the "top" level so that the next level below can be determined. Eliminating element 1 from Table 2 results in Table 3. By comparing the reachables column with the feedback column, it is apparent that element 2 is the top level element now that element 1 has been removed.

The strategy at this point is to remove element 2 from Table 3. The result is shown in Table 4, from which it is apparent that element 3 is now on the "top" level. Removal of element 3 leads to Table 5. Clearly elements 4 and 5 are both on the same level, which is the fourth level of the hierarchy. Since there are no more elements whose "level" remains to be identified, the task is complete.

By letting L_i be the set of all elements on level i, we see that $L_1 = [1]$, $L_2 = [2]$, $L_3 = [3]$, and $L_4 = [4, 5]$ for the reachability matrix shown in Figure 14.20. These levels are shown in Table 6. Phase 3 is now completed.

REFERENCES

1. TOFFLER, A. Lecture at Texas Tech University (1974).
2. TOFFLER, A. *Future Shock.* New York: Bantam Books, 1971.
3. WARFIELD, J. and J. HILL. *A Unified Systems Engineering Concept.* Battelle Monograph Number 1 (1972).
4. HARARY, F., R. NORMAN, and D. CARTWRIGHT. *Structural Models: An Introduction to the Theory of Directed Graphs.* New York: John Wiley & Sons, 1965.
5. MILLER, J. "A Systematic Procedure for Assessing the Worth of Complex Alternatives," Mitre Corporation, Bedford, Mass., Contract AF 19 (628) 5165, EDP Equipment Office, Electronic Systems Division, Air Force Systems Command, ESD TR 67 90 AD 662001 (1967).
6. BALDWIN, M., ed. *Portraits of Complexity: Applications of Systems Methodologies to Societal Problems.* Battelle Monograph Number 9 (1975).
7. WARFIELD, J. *Societal Systems: Planning, Policy, and Complexity.* New York: John Wiley & Sons, 1977.
8. WARFIELD, J. "Toward Interpretation of Complex Structural Models," *IEEE Transactions on Systems, Man, and Cybernetics,* Vol. SMC-4, no. 5 (1974), pp. 405–417.
9. HILL, J., and J. WARFIELD. "Unified Program Planning." *IEEE Transactions on Systems, Man, and Cybernetics,* Vol. SMC-2, no. 5 (1972), pp. 610–621.
10. MALONE, D. "Applications of Interpretive Structural Modeling: Relating Factors for Urban Success." *Proceedings of the National Electronics Conference,* Vol. 29, Oct. 16–18, 1974, Chicago. Reprinted in *Portraits of Complexity: Applications of Systems Methodologies to Societal Problems* [6, pp. 146].
11. WALLER, R. "An Application of Interpretive Structural Modeling to Priority-Setting in Urban Systems Management." *Portraits of Complexity: Applications of Systems Methodologies to Societal Problems* [6, pp. 104].
12. MALONE, D. "An Introduction to the Application of Interpretive Structural Modeling." *Proceedings of the IEEE 63,* Vol. 3, pp. 397, March 1975. Reprinted in *Portraits of Complexity: Applications of Systems Methodologies to Societal Problems* [6, pp. 119].
13. MARCY, W. course notes (1976).
14. HAWTHORNE, R., D. FARRIS, and A. SAGE. "Application of Unified Program Planning to Public and Societal Systems: A Case Study." *Portraits of Complexity: Applications of Systems Methodologies to Societal Problems* [6, pp. 127].
15. *Goals for Dallas.* Published by Goals for Dallas, One Main Place, Dallas, Texas, Library of Congress 66-29022.

CHAPTER 15

Continuous Simulation Models

This chapter resumes the discussion of simulation models that began in Chapter 9. We recommend rereading the first two sections of that chapter before reading this chapter.

As mentioned in Chapter 9, there are two basic philosophies in simulation: discrete and continuous. Discrete simulation is appropriate whenever the endogenous variables that make up the system change discretely at specific instants in time (called events). On the other hand, continuous simulation is appropriate whenever we perceive the endogenous variables as *continuously* changing in time. Thus the state of the system undergoes smooth, continuous change as time is advanced.

Recent developments in simulation languages now permit models to be developed that incorporate both continuous simulation and discrete simulation perspectives. These languages support a new approach to simulation called *combined simulation.* In combined simulation, features of both simulation perspectives are employed in a single model. As it turns out, there are many real-world situations in which such an approach is an appropriate tool to use. Combined simulation languages like GASP IV [1] and SLAM [2] will, therefore, support discrete simulation, continuous simulation, and combined simulation.

Recent surveys [3, 5] suggest that nearly every major corporation in this country uses some form of corporate planning model. Most often, this model is a simulation model; in some cases, mathematical programming models are also included. These surveys suggest that, at the highest levels of planning, corporate simulation models are deterministic rather than probabilistic. This is apparently attributable to the increased data requirements of probabilistic simulations and the problem of interpreting the data output. Most managers feel comfortable with using deterministic simulations as vehicles on which they can input "what-if" scenarios and observe their consequences in the outputs returned by the model. While the inclusion of probabilistic considerations is well within the current state of the simulation methodology, its use is not yet prevalent in most corporate models. Instead, management will use corporate simulations to explore the consequences of the best, worst, and most probable input scenarios to develop a "feel" for the desirability of the resultant outcomes.

UNDERLYING ASSUMPTIONS AND DEFINITIONS

As we mentioned previously, simulation can be approached from two fundamentally different philosophies. In this chapter, we consider only continuous deterministic simulation. Deterministic simulation involves the iteration of *structural equations* and *empirical equations* through time. Time is advanced in small increments, beginning at some starting instant t_0 and stopping at some later time, t_f. In this chapter, we discuss the methodology needed to formulate these models. We also provide a brief description of the computer languages that can be used in the codification of the equations that comprise the model. As we will see, methods of solution are robust enough to accommodate linear or nonlinear models. Consequently, the solution approaches do not require that continuous simulation models be differentiated in this way.

The modeling methodologies that we will discuss share a number of assumptions with management science models in general. First, these systems are assumed to be *open*—that is, to possess inputs and outputs. If such is not the case, then there is no point in modeling the system, since it can neither be controlled nor observed. Second, the methodologies assume that the system under scrutiny has an identified manager, whose perspective is being used as a basis for the study. Third, the methodologies assume that the causality inherent in a system is representable by structural equations that characterize the *causal structure* of the object system. Fourth, the simulation behavior as depicted by plotted output is a direct consequence of the structural equations within the model and/or the inputs to the model. Hence, by changing these, it is possible to cause the models to behave in a more desirable way. Finally, we assume that systems change in a smooth, continuous fashion. Abrupt discontinuities are not expected, since aggregate business and economic systems tend to change without discontinuities. We will address assumptions that are particularized to a specific methodology, along with the methodology itself, in the next section.

CONTINUOUS SIMULATION MODELING

The steps we employ in the construction of continuous simulation modeling are essentially the same 11 steps outlined in Chapter 1. We present, in this section, additional detail that will facilitate collection of data, formulation of model structure, and validation of the model—the steps associated with the model itself.

The types of methodologies to be discussed are listed in Table 15.1 together with a description of the methodology and the purposes to which models formulated by each methodology can be put. Brief overviews of each of the

Table 15.1   Continuous Simulation Methodologies

Name	Characteristics	Purposes	Uses
Corporate simulations	Accounting based	Corporate planning and policymaking	Managerial decision making
Econometric modeling	Linear, extensive use of data	Short-term forecasting	Macroeconomic modeling
Input-output modeling	Linear	Short-term forecasting	Macroeconomic modeling
Kane's KSIM	Assumed sigmoid behavior	Long-term effects of interactions	See Table 15.2
System dynamics	Nonlinear	Long-term planning	See Table 15.2

simulation model types are followed by more extensive discussions of each category.

Corporate simulation models are, at the highest levels of corporate policy making, financial modeling packages. The equations that make up these models have their basis in accounting, a discipline well understood by corporation vice-presidents. At least a dozen financial modeling "languages" are now available to assist top-level management in the formulation of these models. Such models provide a link between decision making and conditions in the firm's environment.

For short-range forecasting we recommend econometric models. These models place strong emphasis upon historical trend data and are always "fitted" to such data. For most applications involving forecasts of one to eight quarters (quarter years), these models are best.

Leontief input-output models are also used for short-term forecasting. Like econometric models these models are linear. As indicated in Table 15.1, such models are appropriate for macroeconomic modeling.

For long-term behavioral studies of dynamical systems, the modeler has two choices: Kane-like methods [5, 6] and Forrester's system dynamics [7–10]. The Kane methods are "quick and dirty" and therefore inexpensive; they require managerial involvement in the model formulation process and enable the structural implications for behavior to be easily understood. They do, however, limit the range of dynamical behaviors that are possible.

In the public sector as well as in academic research, system dynamics is the most widely applied of all the methods discussed in this chapter. Invented in the mid-1950s by Jay Forrester, the method places strongest emphasis on delineating the causal interactions that comprise the object system. The method enables us readily to perceive the long-term implications of certain control policies in terms of behavior. Policy planning over the "long haul" represents the purpose to which system dynamics and Kane-like models can most appropriately be put. A partial list of broad areas to which Kane-like methods and system dynamics have been applied is provided in Table 15.2.

Table 15.2   Some Areas to Which KSIM and System Dynamics Have Been Applied

Socioeconomic systems	Urban systems
Environmental systems	Biological systems
Energy systems	Production systems
Industrial systems	Population systems

These then are the methods that we will discuss in this section. They were all created over the last 25 to 60 years, and they all serve somewhat different purposes.

CORPORATE SIMULATION MODELS

The economic environment in which every corporate and business entity is embedded is characterized by so much complexity that managerial decision making without some form of planning model would be like blindly throwing darts in a penny arcade. Business managers find themselves daily confronted with the possibility of shortages of energy and raw materials, environmental and OSHA regulations, a decline in productivity, international competition, another round of inflation, and unprecedented high interest rates. To survive in this environment corporate plans must be comprehensive and systematic.

Corporate simulation models are an attractive and viable alternative to formal, ad hoc planning procedures. William E. Scott, an executive vice-president with the Public Service Electric Gas Company of New Jersey, has said of PSE's corporate simulation model, "If an oil embargo were announced tomorrow, within 24 hours we would be able to know the major impact of it and begin reacting" [11]. Inland Steel attributes to its corporate model the decision not to spend $1.5 billion on an expansion program that quite possibly could have forced the company into bankruptcy [12]. United Air Lines generates alternative financial scenarios with across-the-board fare increases, additions and deletions of different types of flight equipment, and increases in the price of jet fuel [3]. On the other hand, American Airlines uses a marketing simulation to forecast the profitability of different cities in its route structure [3]. Practically every *Fortune* 500 firm now uses some form of corporate simulation model.

Why are corporate models in such widespread use? Financial considerations are predominant in the list of applications to which corporate models are put, as shown in Table 15.3.

Structure and Form of Corporate Simulation Models

The Naylor survey [3, 4] reports that corporate simulation models are being used at the highest levels of management, including presidents, board members, board chairpersons, and vice-presidents. It is not surprising to find that these models are essentially financial, consisting of a set of accounting identities. Such models are easy to develop, require a minimum amount of data, and can be validated against the firm's existing accounting structure.

In addition to a financial model, some firms have integrated marketing and production models into the corporate model, as shown in Figure 15.1. Clearly

Table 15.3 Applications of Corporate Models [4]

Applications	Percentage	Applications	Percentage
Cash flow analysis	65%	Short-term forecasts	33%
Financial forecasting	65	New venture analysis	30
Balance sheet projections	65	Risk analysis	27
Financial analysis	60	Cost projections	27
Pro forma financial reports	55	Merger/acquisition analysis	26
Profit planning	53	Cash management	24
Long-term forecasts	50	Price projections	23
Budgeting	47	Financial information systems	22
Sales forecasts	41	Industry forecasts	20
Investment analysis	35	Market share analysis	17
Marketing planning	33	Supply forecasts	13

the "front end" for any corporate model is the financial model. The conceptual framework shown in Figure 15.1 assumes that each division makes its own financial, marketing, and production decisions; however, these are coordinated by the corporate financial model.

In the following, we shall carefully delineate what is meant by financial, marketing, and production models. We find, for example, that market models may use forecasting and projection methods to arrive at a general market forecast for all products sold in a division. Production models may, on the other hand, consist of activity analysis models that reflect the cost of operating at different rates of output. In some cases, mathematical programming is used to generate minimum cost production plans.

Financial models provide income statements, balance sheets, cash flow statements, and profit and loss statements—the usual financial reports and instruments. The corporate financial model is used to check the economic

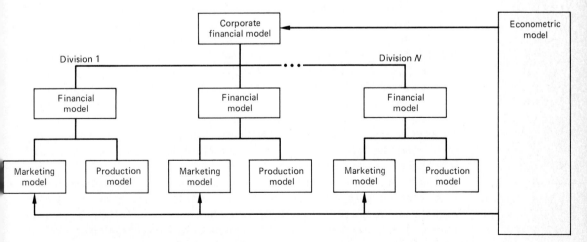

Figure 15.1 A conceptual framework for a corporate model (undirected "lines" indicate two-way communication between the model types).

feasibility of alternative financial plans, including alternative cash management, depreciation, capital investment, and merger-acquisition policies.

Corporate financial models are "driven" by managerial-controlled inputs, by inputs from divisional financial models, and in some cases by econometric models. While some corporations have their own econometric models, most corporations avail themselves of the econometric data provided by time-sharing computer networks. It is possible, for example, for corporations to subscribe to the latest econometric forecasts available from Chase Econometrics, the Wharton School, and Data Resources Incorporated. Econometric concerns have given rise to a new type of planner in high-level corporate decision making—the corporate futurist.

Marketing models are used to forecast sales and market share by product or service category. Such forecasts are used to drive division financial models and production models. Two different approaches are taken: short-term mechanistic models and econometric models. Short-term mechanistic models involve trend analyses and seasonal fluctuation schemes as applied to time series data or exponential smoothing methods. Econometric market models are more robust in that they link sales to the national economy and permit simulation of the effects on sales and market share of alternative advertising, pricing, and promotional policies.

Production models compute operating costs and costs per unit of production for a given level of market demand as forecast by the marketing model. These models supply cost data to financial models and can be used in a standalone context as well. It is in the standalone framework that such models facilitate the assessment of costs and productivity of alternative production policies and strategies.

Variables and Equations Used in Financial Models

There are three types of variables and two types of equations used in corporate financial models. The variable types are essentially those discussed in Chapter 1: exogenous variables, endogenous variables, and policy variables representing managements' control inputs to the corporate entity. Exogenous variables represent external effects that the economy, the environment, and other uncontrollable factors have on the firm. The endogenous variables are those internal variables that are in some sense dependent upon the exogenous influences and the managerial control inputs. Some or all these variables can be "random" or "probabilistic" since market forecasts can never be ascertained with certainty, and since the effects of the exogenous influences attributable to the economy or the environment cannot be predicted with certainty. However, as previously mentioned, the probabilistic capability of financial models is not in very widespread use, as of this writing.

The equations that comprise any financial model are of two types: structural equations and empirical equations. These equations translate values obtained from the manager's control inputs and the exogenous variables into the endogenous variables. For the most part, these equations are accounting and tax-related identities.

Corporate Simulations and Decision Support Systems

Today's corporate models operate in an "interactive mode" so that a manager can run his or her model and retrieve the results in seconds, make changes, and rerun the simulation. This capability to interact with a computer program during its execution has helped give birth to a new breed of computer-based management system. In former days, the emphasis was upon *management information systems.* These systems consisted of large data bases and software that could search and retrieve data from these data bases. While these systems greatly facilitated the organization and efficiency of information storage and retrieval systems, managers were more interested in answers to *aggregate* questions such as, "What is the growth rate of customer accounts?" "What is the trend in purchase order amounts?" "What is the average rate of growth in employee salaries?" Questions like these promoted even more sophisticated questions like, "What will be the total salary outlay per month two years from now?" "By how much must the price of our products increase to sustain the present margin of profit 18 months from now?" To answer these more complicated questions, software designers began to develop and include models into their management information systems.

At that instant decision support systems were born. The "parents" of decision support systems were management information systems and models. It is not surprising, therefore, to learn that these systems may consist of a model base, a data base, and a user interface that permits interactive access to both. Once executed, the models in the model base retrieve and utilize essential data about market forecasts, product pricing, production, overhead, and capital costs from the data bases. Financial models, for example, could utilize these data to produce corporate balance sheets, profit and loss statements, and other financial instruments *projected one, two, or five years into the future.*

The appearance of this newborn necessitated that an appropriate name be found. Managers named this new tool the "corporate planning (or simulation) model," while software designers and developers called it a decision support system. Due to the user-friendly designs incorporated into these systems, managers who were relatively unsophisticated computer users suddenly became overwhelmingly enthusiastic about the capabilities of these new tools. They found that such tools could support relatively simple model constructs or tremendously complex model forms involving hundreds, even thousands, of equations.

SYSTEM DYNAMICS

System dynamics (SD) has been applied to just about every process or endeavor that possesses a time duration (and some that didn't). Not all these applications have been successful; nevertheless, almost all have been controversial and provocative. According to the developer of SD, Jay Forrester, the principal component of systems is the feedback loop. All managerial decisions are made within the context of this feedback loop. An action is taken, its effect (upon the process being controlled) is observed, and—depending upon the manager's

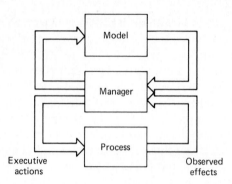

Figure 15.2   Relationships among a manager, his or her process, and his or her model.

satisfaction with the effect—a new action is taken, as illustrated in Figure 15.2. In what follows we shall see this principle in action.

A second and equally important principle used in system dynamics models is the assumption that systems are comprised of flows—flows of material, goods, money, resources, food, energy, water, pollution, housing, structures, and people (of all types, professions, and ages). Each flow may be characterized by means of a structure similar to that depicted in Figure 15.4 and referred to as a flow diagram.

To formulate system dynamics models, it is necessary that the modeler think in terms of flows. As indicated in Table 15.4 the modeler begins by identifying the flows that comprise the system of interest. For simplicity we shall define a *sector* as all structure that can be associated with one and only one flow. Having determined the essential sectors, we thereafter develop the structure within each sector and follow by developing the between-sector structure.

The structure within each sector is usually patterned after a simple one-sector model. Several such one-sector models are in popular use. Once the modeler understands the basic structure underlying simple one-sector models, it is possible to combine these to form multiple-sector models.

Occasionally situations arise in which none of the "standard" one-sector models will fit. Under these circumstances, the modeler must build the structure within a sector from scratch. The steps required to accomplish this are listed in Table 15.5. In addition, once we have delineated the entire model

Table 15.4   **Sector Approach to the Structural Determination of a System Dynamics Model**

Step 1.   Identify flows (sectors) that must be included within the model.

Step 2.   Develop the structure within each sector of the model. Use standard one-sector submodels or develop the structure within the sector from scratch using the steps in Table 15.5.

Step 3.   Develop the structure between all sectors that make up the model.

Step 4.   Determine the equations from the delineated structure.

Step 5.   Codify the equations into a working computer simulation program.

Table 15.5   Steps Required to Formulate the Structure for a Sector From Scratch

1. Specify the quantities required to delineate the structure within each sector.
2. Determine the interactions between the quantities and delineate the resultant causal diagram.
3. Classify the quantity and edge types and delineate the flow diagram.

structure, we must thereafter translate it into equations and, finally, into a satisfactory computer program. These tasks are listed as steps 4 and 5 in Table 15.4. The following minicases illustrate the details of the method.

A One-Sector Population Model

The Scenario: Consider a simple population growth model. Our population could represent, for example, an ant hill or bee hive. For simplicity, we assume an infinite food supply and a limitless environment conducive to population growth. Thus the growth of population is unhindered and the model needs to embrace only the population itself (i.e., there is only one sector, the population sector).

The Problem: The objective of this model is to determine the level of the population at some point in the future, assuming unhindered growth.

The Model: To illustrate the method, the structure of this one-sector model will be developed from scratch. The quantities to be included in the sector are listed in Table 15.6 together with the units associated with each quantity.

Next, we specify the edges (causal linkages) between the various quantities. (The details necessary to accomplish this step were described in Chapter 14.) Once the edges between the quantities are determined, we can draw a graph showing the interconnections between the quantities. We call this graph a *causal diagram.* The causal diagram for the simple population model is shown in Figure 15.3.

An arrow directed from one quantity to another is referred to as an *edge.* If the sign associated with the edge is positive, then the quantity from which the edge is directed is said to have a positive effect on the quantity toward which the edge is directed. We should convince ourselves that Figure 15.3 is correct from an intuitive standpoint.

From the causal diagram model, we proceed to develop the *flow diagram* model as shown in Figure 15.4. To do this, we must classify each of the quantity and edge types that make up the causal diagram. We must, therefore, understand the distinguishing characteristics of each of the quantity and edge types. Conventionally, states are represented by rectangles ▭, rates by "valves" ▭Χ, auxiliaries by circles ○, and parameters by small circles ⊶. There are two types of edges — flow edges and information edges. Flow edges are represented by solid lines and information edges by

Table 15.6   Quantities in the Population Model

Quantity	Name	Units
P	Population	Capita
BR	Birth rate	Births/time unit
DR	Death rate	Deaths/time unit
BRN	Birth rate normal	Births/(capita-time unit)
DRN	Death rate normal	Deaths/(capita-time unit)

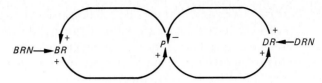

Figure 15.3   Causal diagram for a simple population model.

dashed lines. Once we have classified all quantities and edges in the causal diagram, we can delineate the resultant flow diagram as shown in Figure 15.4.

From the schematic diagram, the modeler is able to write equations for each of the variables and parameters of the model. The parameter values are established from observations and measurements made on the system directly. For example, assume that 5 births per 100 capita per time unit were observed as were 3 deaths per 100 capita per time unit. Then

$$BRN = .05$$

and   (15.1)

$$DRN = .03$$

Three additional equations are required to specify values for BR, DR, and P. These three equations required are given by (15.2) through (15.4). Equation (15.2) is called a level or state equation and is used whenever an accumulation or depletion of a flow takes place. For this model, the state variable population accumulates births, but is depleted by deaths. In any given time period t, the number of births coming into the population is given by $\Delta t \cdot BR$, where BR is the birth rate expressed in births per year. Likewise, the number

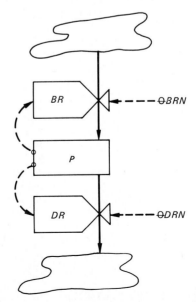

Figure 15.4   Flow diagram of a simple population model.

of deaths or exits from the population in any time period is given by $\Delta t \cdot DR$, where DR is the death rate expressed in deaths per year. Equation (15.2) is a simple accounting of the number of entrances to, and exits from, the population during time period Δt. In effect it says "What we have at time instant $t + \Delta t$—$P(t + \Delta t)$—is equal to what we had at time instant t—$P(t)$—plus what was added during the time period Δt—$\Delta t \cdot BR$—minus what was taken out during the time period Δt—$\Delta t \cdot DR$. Hence,

$$P(t + \Delta t) = P(t) + \Delta t \cdot BR - \Delta t \cdot DR$$

or

$$P(t + \Delta t) = P(t) + \Delta t(BR - DR)$$

The equations for BR and DR are simple multiplicative functions of the quantities that have edges directed toward them. Hence, BR is the product of BRN with P. Dimensional consistency is maintained in these equations and serves as the justification for the multiplicative nature of the relationships, as shown:

$$BR = P \cdot BRN$$

$$[\text{births/year}] = [\text{capita}][\text{births/capita year}]$$

Observe here that the parameter BRN has the units of births/capita-year and that "capita" cancels out on the right-hand side of the equation, leaving a dimensionally consistent equation in the sense that the units are the same on both sides of the equality. If we anticipate 1000 capita and .05 births per capita per year, then in any given year we can expect 50 births, and this is the birth rate at the current time.

Similar remarks can be made for death rate DR. The final form of these equations is shown in (15.2) to (15.4):

$$P(t + \Delta t) = P(t) + \Delta t(BR - DR) \tag{15.2}$$

$$BR = P \cdot BRN \tag{15.3}$$

$$DR = P \cdot DRN \tag{15.4}$$

```
          BRN = .05
          DRN = .03
          P = 1000.
          T = 0.
          DT = .2
          DO 10 I = 1,251
          BR = P·BRN
          DR = P·BRN
          PRINT1, T,P,BR,DR
          P = P+DT*(BR-DR)
   10     T = T+DT
          STOP
   1      FORMAT(' ', 4E17.7)
          END
```

Figure 15.5   A FORTRAN simulation computer program for the simple population problem.

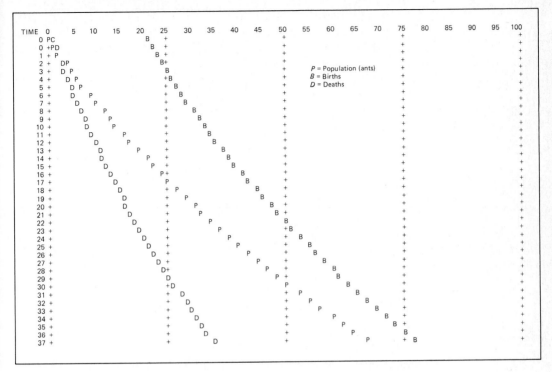

Figure 15.6 Plot of unrestrained population growth.

The Solution: Using these equations, the analyst is ready to code a simulation computer program. Figure 15.5 exhibits an appropriate program, where a time step of .2 time units is used, a time domain of 50 time units is specified, and an initial population of 1000 capita is assumed. The variables are printed every simulation time unit. The results are plotted in Figure 15.6 where it is observed that population, birth rate, and death rate all exhibit a rate of growth called exponential growth. The exponential curve has a shape identical to the curves shown in Figure 15.6 — hence, the name "exponential growth."

A One-Sector Inventory Model [7]

The Scenario: Sonya Magnova is a television retailer who wishes to maintain a desired inventory equal to DI television sets so that she doesn't have to sell her demonstrator and show models. She is currently experiencing moderately constant demand of D units per month. Sonya's ordering policy is quite simple — adjust actual inventory toward desired inventory so as to force these to conform as closely as possible.

The Problem: Currently, the inventory is low — I_0 units are left. The time required for inventory to be received once it is ordered is AT, the

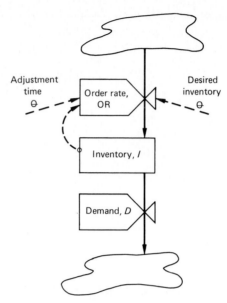

Figure 15.7   Flow diagram for a simple inventory adjustment problem.

adjustment time. Sonya's order rate in terms of units per month can be approximated by the equation $OR = (DI - I)/AT$. This equation contains four essential components:

1. A desired condition, DI
2. An actual condition, I
3. A measure of the discrepancy $(DI - I)$
4. A way to express action based on the discrepancy

$$\frac{1}{AT}(DI - I)$$

The Model: Most rate equations that express deliberate managerial control of a certain flow contain these four basic components [7]. It should be apparent that the only flow in this case is television sets. This flow is accumulated into and depleted from a state or level called inventory.

The flow diagram for this model appears in Figure 15.7. The structure appears similar to the population model examined earlier. The behaviors, however, are quite different, due to the differences in the information infra-structures in the two models. These differences cause the actual equations used for the two rates to be quite different. For the inventory model, these are

$$OR = \frac{1}{AT}(DI - I) \tag{15.5}$$

and

$$I(t + \Delta t) = I(t) + \Delta t \cdot OR \tag{15.6}$$

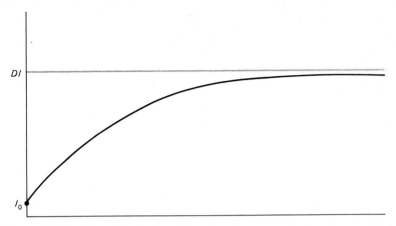

Figure 15.8 Plotted behavior of the simple one-sector inventory model.

By comparing equations (15.5) and (15.6) with equations (15.2) to (15.4), it becomes increasingly apparent how these two models differ from each other.

The inventory model produces a behavior like that shown in Figure 15.8. This behavior is called *exponential goal seeking.* Clearly, an actual condition or state is being driven toward some goal or desired condition. The discrepancy between the desired and actual condition decreases, but never quite gets to zero, assuming (as in this problem) that the desired condition remains constant. If the desired condition varies, then the actual condition will attempt to follow the desired condition, but will always lag behind it.

A Two-Sector Population/Housing Model [16]

The Scenario: A resort community in Colorado has determined that population growth in the area depends on the availability of housing as well as the persistent natural attractiveness of the area. Abundant housing attracts people at a greater rate than under normal conditions. The opposite is true when housing is tight. Area residents also leave the community at a certain rate due primarily to the availability of housing.

The housing construction industry, on the other hand, fluctuates depending on the land availability and housing desires. Abundant housing cuts back the construction of houses while the opposite is true when the housing situation is tight. Also, as land for residential development fills up (in this mountain valley), the construction rate decreases to the level of the demolition rate of houses.

The Problem: City planners would like estimates of population and housing growth for the years 1987, 1990, 1995, and 2000. Such estimates would help determine what was needed in terms of city services—

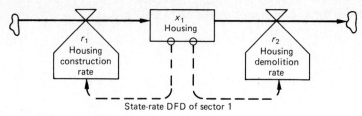

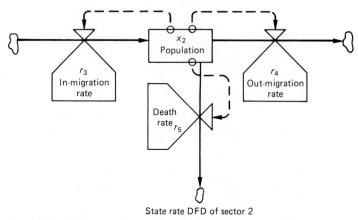

(a) State-rate interactions within housing sector

(b) State-rate interactions within demographic sector

Figure 15.9 State-rate interactions within housing and population sectors.

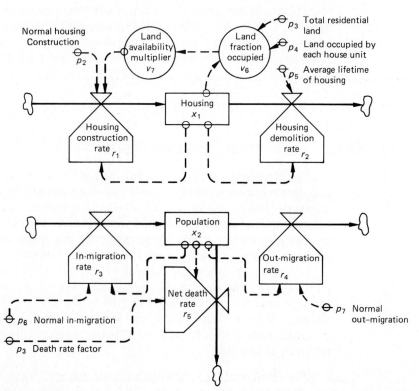

Figure 15.10 Completed structural descriptions for the housing and demographic sectors.

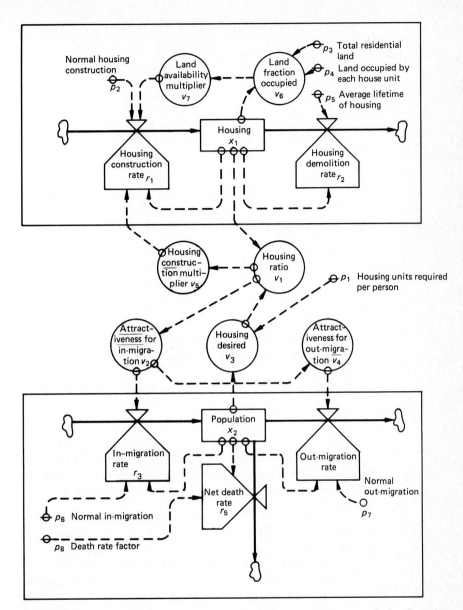

Figure 15.11 Completed flow diagram model for two-sector population/housing model.

parks, sewer, water, utility systems, streets, and the associated infrastructure.

The Model: Clearly there are two sectors of interest here: housing and population. The substructure within these two sectors was determined first and is displayed in Figure 15.9. The substructure delineation begins with a determination of state rate interactions. Following this, the necessary parameters and auxiliaries required within each sector are determined, as

$$p_1 = 1$$
$$p_2 = 1$$
$$p_3 = 5$$
$$p_4 = .0002$$
$$p_5 = 40 \text{ years}$$
$$p_6 = .05$$
$$p_7 = .02$$
$$p_8 = .02$$
$$v_6 = x_1 \cdot p_4/p_3$$
$$v_3 = x_2 \cdot p_1$$
$$v_1 = v_3/x_1$$
$$v_5 = f(v_1)$$
$$v_7 = f(v_6)$$
$$v_2 = f(v_1)$$
$$v_4 = 1/v_2$$
$$r_1 = x_1 \cdot p_2 \cdot v_7 \cdot v_5$$
$$r_2 = x_1 \cdot p_5$$
$$r_3 = x_2 \cdot p_6$$
$$r_4 = x_2 \cdot p_7$$
$$r_5 = x_2 \cdot p_3$$
$$x_1(t + \Delta t) = x_1(t) + \Delta t(r_1 - r_2)$$
$$x_2(t + \Delta t) = x_2(t) + \Delta t(r_3 - r_4 - r_5)$$

Notes: p_i denotes a parameter or constant.
v_i denotes an auxiliary variable.
r_i denotes a rate variable.
x_i denotes a state variable.

Figure 15.12   Model equations for the two-sector population/housing model.

shown in Figure 15.10. Finally, the structure between the two sectors is delineated as shown in Figure 15.11, which is the completed flow diagram model. From this model the equations can be written and codified into a working simulation—steps 4 and 5 of Table 15.4.

The Solution: The equations and associated simulation computer program (in FORTRAN) are shown in Figures 15.12 and 15.13, respectively. Note in Figures 15.11 and 15.12 that each quantity (parameters excepted) is a function of those quantities that have an edge directed to the quantity in question. Hence, housing ratio v_1 is a function of x_1 and v_3; housing construction rate r_1 is a function of p_2, x_1, v_5, and v_7, and so on.

AVAILABLE CORPORATE MODELING AND SIMULATION LANGUAGES

We shall characterize in this section some of the commercial software available for corporate modeling and simulation. This is such a broad subject that literally an entire text could be devoted to it. Beginning with a consideration of corporate planning models, we describe codes available for small and large

```
C          POPULATION/HOUSING MODEL
C          INITIALIZE PARAMETERS AND STATES
           DIMENSION TV5(8),TV7(8),TV2(8)
           P1=1
           P2=1
           P3=5
           P4=.0002
           P5=40
           P6=.05
           P7=.02
           P8=.02
           X1=1000
           X2=3000
           READ(5,1)TV5,TV7,TV2
1          FORMAT(8F10.0)
           TIME=1975
           DT=.25
           WRITE(6,10)
10         FORMAT('1TIME', 8X, 'POPULATION HOUSING')
           DO 4 I=1, 26
           IF(I.EQ.1) GOTO 1
           DO 2 J=1, 4
           X1=X1 + DT *(R1-R2)
           X2=X2 + DT *(R3-R4-R5)
           T=T+DT
           V6=X1 *P4/P3
           V3=X2 *P1
           V1=V3/X1
           V5=TABLE(TV5, V1, 0., .3, 7)
           V7=TABLE(TV7, V6, 0., .3, 7)
           V2 TABLE(TV2, V1, 0., .3, 7)
           V4=1/V2
           R1=X1 * P2 *V7 * V5
           R2=X1 * P5
           R3=X2 * P6
           R4=X2 * P7
           R5=X2 * P3
           IF(I.EQ.1) GOTO 3
2          CONTINUE
3          WRITE(6,11)T, X2, X1
4          CONTINUE
11         FORMAT(' ', 3E10.2)
           STOP
           END
```

Figure 15.13 Simulation computer program for the two-sector population/housing model.

computers alike. We describe most of the general codes for continuous deterministic simulation as well.

CORPORATE PLANNING MODELS

Software to facilitate the formulation of models for corporate planning ranges from VISICALC, which retails for roughly $100 and is available to virtually anyone who owns a microcomputer, to the immensely massive and capable decision support systems that run on the corporation's largest mainframes. Table 15.7 lists some of the commercial products that are available for personal computers.

We can classify personal computer financial modeling software in two categories: data base–oriented systems and row/column matrix report writers. The distinguishing characteristics of the data base systems are the use of different file sets to separate model data, logic, and report formats; the ability to consolidate two or more models; and the inclusion of advanced accounting subroutines. Because of these characteristics, data base–oriented systems are more flexible and less redundant and can generate large scale models (greater than 8000 data cells.) Of those listed in Table 15.7, only FPL, MINIMODEL,

Table 15.7   Financial Modeling Software for Personal Computers

Name	Company	Cost*	Configuration
VISICALC	Personal Software Sunnyvale, Calif.	$ 100	Apple II 48K Atari 800; CBM 32K; HP-85 TRS-80 Models I and II
EXECUPLAN	Vector Graphic Westlake Village, Calif.	100	Vector Graphic VIP System B or 3000 two drives
Decision Evaluator System	Apple Computer Cupertino, Calif.	250	48K Apple II Plus, one disk drive
TARGET	Advanced Mgmt. Strategies Atlanta, Ga.	125	48K Apple II Plus or 64K TRS-80 Model II
FPL	C4P, Inc./Lifeboat Assoc. New York, N.Y.	500	48K CP/M system
MINIMODEL	Financial Planning Assoc. (sold by WESTICO) Norwalk, Conn.	395	48K CP/M system
DSS Financial	Ferox Microsystems Falls Church, Va.	1300	64K Apple II Plus; 3 disk drives; Pascal language card
SUPERCALC	Sorcim, Inc., Calif.	100	48K CP/M system
T-Maker	Lifeboat Associates New York, N.Y.	100	48K CP/M system
Report Writer	Carolina Business Computers Hickory, N.C.	100	60K CP/M system Microsoft BASIC
Multiplan	Microsoft, Inc.	250	64K CP/M system
1-2-3	Lotus, Inc.	295	256K MS-DOS system

* Rough estimates only.

and DSS Financial are data base-oriented. While these products are more flexible, they are also more expensive.

The interactive, corporate planning system of the type usually available on mainframe computers is very much more expensive — in the range of $25,000 to $55,000. Some typical commercial systems are listed in Table 15.8.

Both these lists are abridged and incomplete. Are the massive corporate planning models worth the considerably increased cost? It depends. Some of these systems are capable of retrieving "live" data from the corporate data base without human intervention and utilizing these data in the model(s). At the same time these software packages will support larger and more robust models. It seems safe to say that only *Fortune* 1000 companies would need the capabilities of one of these large systems for mainframe computers. Smaller companies could not afford them nor would they have a need for the enhanced power and capabilities of the large corporate planning software.

SIMULATION LANGUAGES

Unlike the corporate planning software that supports the financial planning required by the highest levels of management in a corporate structure, simulation languages are appropriate for model formulation at the level of middle management where detailed decisions relating to production and distribution are made. A list of popular deterministic simulation languages is provided in Table 15.9 together with a description of their typical usages. Only the last two languages listed in Table 15.9 are general in the sense of supporting continuous deterministic simulations and discrete probabilistic simulation or some combination of these. In addition, SLAM supports network simulation models, which are particularly useful for project scheduling and manufacturing situations, as discussed in Chapter 9.

Table 15.8 Financial Planning Software for Mainframe Computers

Name	Company
IFPS	Execucom, Inc. Austin, Tex.
EIS	Boeing Computer Services, Inc. Seattle, Wash.
EMPIRE	Applied Data Research, Inc. Princeton, N.J.
SIMPLAN	Social Systems, Inc. Chapel Hill, N.C.
MODEL	Lloyd Bush Associates Dallas, Tex.

Table 15.9 Widely Used Continuous Deterministic
Simulation Languages

Name	Company	Usage
DYNAMO	Pugh-Roberts & Associates Cambridge, Mass.	System dynamics models
CSMP	IBM	Differential equation models
GASP IV	Pritsker & Associates Lafayette, Ind.	General
SLAM	Pritsker & Associates Lafayette, Ind.	General

LARGE-SCALE SOCIOECONOMIC AND ENERGY MODELS

During the last 15 years, hundreds of millions of dollars have been invested in the development of continuous simulations representing so-called "large-scale systems." These models produce information concerning the consequences of proposed actions or policies. Several different methodologies were employed in these models, the most notable of which was system dynamics [7,8]. Some of these models are described in [9,10,13]. In addition to system dynamics these models utilize econometric modeling and Leontief input-output modeling [14].

One of the most provocative and controversial models was the Forrester world model [10] and its more sophisticated sequel, *the limits to growth* by Meadows [13]. The purpose of these models was to assess the effect of various policies upon quality of life and world population.

The baseline run of the Forrester model is shown in Figure 15.14. The model structure is depicted by means of the flow diagram in Figure 15.15. The letters *P, NR, POL,* and *CI* stand for the four major state variables in the model—population, natural resources, pollution, and capital investment, respectively. The variable *QL* is "quality of life." From Figure 15.14 quality of life is seen to decline through the entire simulation. Population is seen to grow until about the year 2025 and thereafter to decline. Both declines are due to essential depletions of natural resources, *NR*. Forrester used this highly aggregated model to test various policies. He was able to show how obvious responses would not suffice since the systems on which these models are based are "counterintuitive"—a term that Forrester coined to suggest that intuitive policies might actually have deleterious impacts rather than the salutary result that was intended.

This model was termed "Malthusian" because of the somewhat dismal and gloomy future that it suggests. (Forrester does, however, find a policy that stabilizes both quality of life and population at reasonable levels. This policy is based on constraints on the growth of population, natural resource usage,

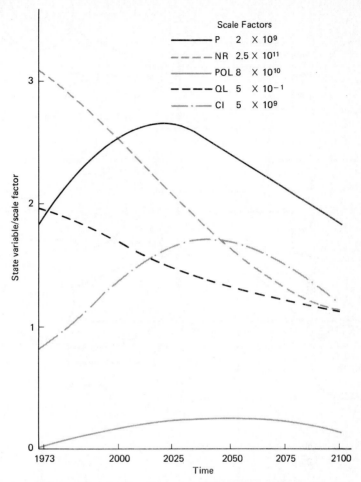

Figure 15.14 Baseline run of Forrester world model.

capital investment, and pollution. This "no-growth" policy led to the zero growth movement of the early 1970s.) The issue is one of validity — is this model right?

VALIDATION OF SIMULATION MODELS

A phase of building models that is equally, if not more, demanding than model formulation is that of validation. In validation the modeler must confront the issue of realism and authenticity. Does the model replicate the real world over a reasonable period of the recent past? Is its structure congruent with the general perception of the structure (by those in a position to know) of the process being modeled? These are always important issues in modeling as we have observed throughout this book.

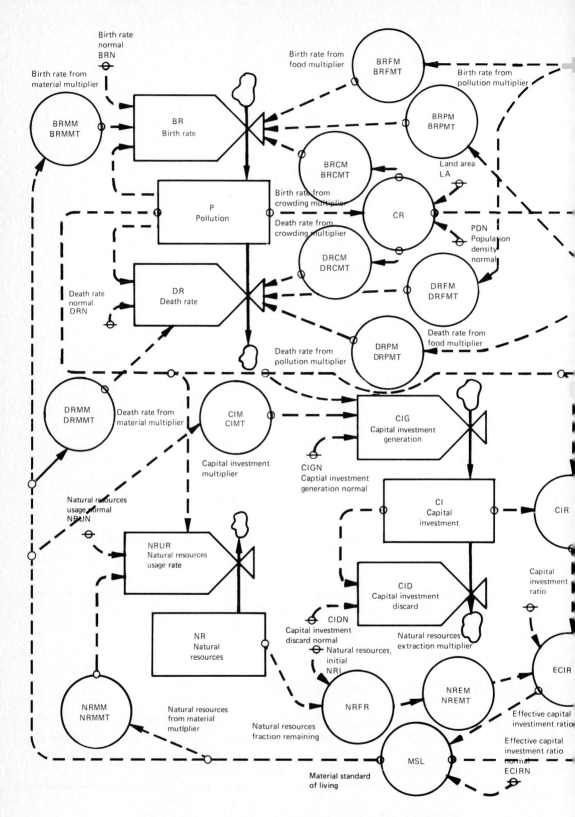

Figure 15.15 Flow diagram of Forrester world model [10].

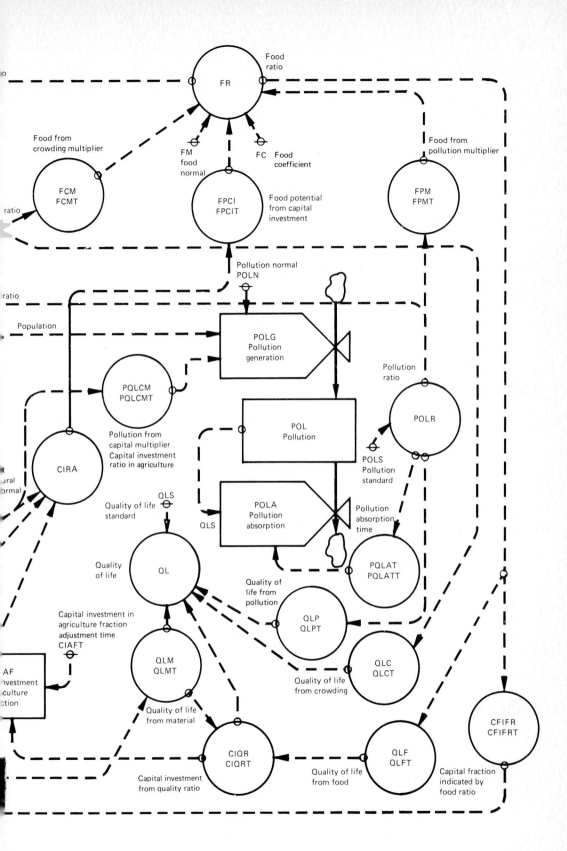

535

Validation of continuous simulation models, like that of models in general, involves four phases:

1. Parameter validation
2. Structure validation
3. Behavior validation
4. Overall validation

These phases were discussed in Chapter 1. One series of tests that should be performed in connection with continuous simulations is to exercise each sector at a time, without making changes to the others. Do the results appear reasonable and consistent with known behavior?

This should be satisfactorily accomplished for all sectors. Wherever historical data are available, the model's outputs should produce numbers that conform as closely as possible to the data. Such are the necessary activities involved in validation of continuous deterministic simulations.

SUMMARY

In this chapter we have examined continuous, deterministic dynamic models. We found these to be of two basic types: corporate planning models — including IFPS, VISICALC, and many others — and continuous simulations implemented in DYNAMO, FORTRAN, or CSMP. As corporate planning models were merged with corporate data bases, decision support systems were born.

The representation of dynamic systems as continuously changing in time is especially appropriate for models that are highly aggregated and whose variables take on large values and change in a smooth sort of fashion. Nature has been characterized as smoothly changing, and it is often said that "the more things change, the more they remain the same." In short, we believe that there is a substantial class of systems and problems to which continuous deterministic simulation can be appropriately applied. To avoid discussing continuous deterministic simulation would require omitting an important arsenal of tools that can have significant applicability in both the private and public sectors.

PROBLEMS

1. *The Scenario:*   In the city of Lubbock, Texas, a growing problem of increasing concern to all citizens is the stray small-animal population. In 1975, for example, the stray animal population was known to be roughly 20,000. These animals roam their neighborhoods in search of food and tend to proliferate themselves rapidly. They are, in no small sense, a menace to the health and sanitation of the community.

    The Problem: It is known that stray animals proliferate themselves at about 10% per year. Likewise, roughly 3% of the pet population each year is lost to the stray population, while only 1% of the strays ever become pets. In addition, 5% of the strays are captured by the city pound where they are placed in kennels and corrals for six months. If no one claims or adopts an animal before the six months are up, the animal is put to death by gasification. Only 8% of those animals placed in the city pound become pets. Stray animals, as well as pets, have, under minimal nutrition standards, an average lifetime of 10 years. However, for stray animals only, the average lifetime goes down as the city's stray animal population goes up, according to the following relationships.

$$\text{Average lifetime} = \frac{10}{\text{crowding ratio}}$$

$$\text{Crowding ratio} = \frac{\text{stray population}}{\text{nominal number of strays}}$$

Here the crowding ratio is simply the stray population divided by the product of the land area of Lubbock times the nominal number of strays per square mile. The nominal number of strays is believed to be roughly 666 animals per square mile. (The city of Lubbock contains 30 square miles of land area.)

The pet population of the city of Lubbock grows at a rate proportional to the city's human population. In 1975, there were 42,500 registered animals and another 7500 animal pets that were not registered. The rate at which "store animals" become pets is such as to drive the number of pets toward a desired pet population (which is known to be 30% of the human population) with an adjustment time of one year. (*Hint:* Use a structure like that for inventory in relation to desired inventory.)

The human population of the city of Lubbock in 1975 was 175,000. The city has a net growth rate of 5%. This model consists of just two sectors—a human sector and a small-animal sector.

Model and Solution: Develop causal and schematic diagrams and a working simulation in the language of your choice.

Simulate this problem for 25 years, starting in 1975. Plot all populations together with the death gasification rate and any other variables you believe would be interesting.

2. In Problem 1, explore the following effects or policies separately.
   a. Massive annual stray animal hunts that are believed capable of ridding the city of one third of its stray population each year
   b. Imposing stiff fines on owners of unregistered animals or registered animals that are allowed to stray away from the owner's home

3. *The Scenario:* The Great Auto Corporation (GAC) and American Car, Inc. (ACI), regularly invest funds in new plant and equipment to increase worker productivity, lower production costs, and increase the quality of their respective automobiles. Such investments are needed to retain and increase market share in the auto industry. GAC wishes to determine what its investment rate will be like for the next 25 years.

   The Problem: The rate at which GAC and ACI invest funds in their own manufacturing facilities decreases linearly as their own investment increases and increases linearly as their competitor's investment increases.

   The Model: Delineate the causal model and the flow diagram that would adequately characterize this situation. Include whatever additional exogenous factors you feel are important. How many sectors make up this model?

4. *The Scenario:* Golden Pond in upper New Hampshire is a self-contained lake ecosystem. The periodic nature of growth in both flora and fauna has been observed to

vary with the seasons of each year. There is a definite variation with time and the need is to characterize in some way this time dependence.

The Problem: The ecosystem consists of lake flora x_f and two categories of fauna (fish)—herbivores x_h and carnivores x_c. In addition there is an interest in the organic matter that forms a sediment on the lake bottom x_b and transfers to the environment x_e.

The Model: A system similar to this was first modeled by Williams [15]. The model is an energy content characterization in which the five states that comprise the model possess units of calories per centimeter squared. The model consists of a single sector and portrays the energy transfers between the various lake entities and losses to the environment. The flow diagram and associated equations are shown in Figure 15.16. These equations represent such processes as predation of one species by another, plant photosynthesis, and the decaying of dead species. Energy transfers between lake entities and its environment are due to respiration and migration.

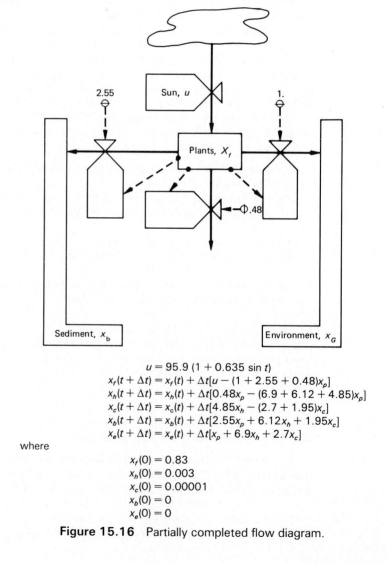

$$u = 95.9\,(1 + 0.635\,\sin t)$$
$$x_f(t + \Delta t) = x_f(t) + \Delta t[u - (1 + 2.55 + 0.48)x_p]$$
$$x_h(t + \Delta t) = x_h(t) + \Delta t[0.48x_p - (6.9 + 6.12 + 4.85)x_p]$$
$$x_c(t + \Delta t) = x_c(t) + \Delta t[4.85x_h - (2.7 + 1.95)x_c]$$
$$x_b(t + \Delta t) = x_b(t) + \Delta t[2.55x_p + 6.12x_h + 1.95x_c]$$
$$x_e(t + \Delta t) = x_e(t) + \Delta t[x_p + 6.9x_h + 2.7x_c]$$

where

$$x_f(0) = 0.83$$
$$x_h(0) = 0.003$$
$$x_c(0) = 0.00001$$
$$x_b(0) = 0$$
$$x_e(0) = 0$$

Figure 15.16   Partially completed flow diagram.

The Solution: Complete the flow diagram shown and codify a working simulation computer program. Use a time step of .01 year and run the simulation for a two-year period. If possible, plot the results.

5. Find a newspaper clipping of a problem of interest to you. Research this problem by finding additional information concerning the nature of the problem. Probable sources of data include newspapers, magazines, books, and managers of the problem system itself. Begin to structure the problem as you collect the data. In this way you will discern where gaps in your understanding and data exist. Use this partially structured model to guide your search for additional information. The model enables you to identify the parameters you need to parameterize your model. Discuss your model structure with knowledgeable persons in the field and be sensitive to their responses and suggestions. Once you have fully structured your model, codify it into a simulation computer program. Observe its baseline behavior. Is it believable and consistent with your information concerning the behavior of the actual system? Now perform your policy experiments using the acknowledged inputs to the process provided to you by those who manage and control the process in question. Try to find an acceptable policy or plan that mitigates or alleviates the perceived problem with the system and induces an acceptable behavior from the model of the problem system.

6. *The Scenario:* The McDouglas Aircraft Company (MAC) has established a pension fund for its employees and regularly sets aside $x a month for each employee. The accumulated fund is invested and earns 10% per annum. The influx of new employees into the company's work force is about 5% of the existing work force each year, and the average age of these employees is 25.

The Problem: The company wants to study the stability and solidarity of its plan and proposes to simulate the effects of different assumptions about average length of service and average length of retirement. A stipend of one half the average monthly salary is paid upon reaching retirement age 65, until death. Approximately 1.5% of the work force reach retirement age each year. Currently there are 10,000 employees and 500 retirees.

The Model: Assume that the average lifetime is age 75 for the employees of MAC. Every year one fortieth of the work force moves into the retiree category, and one tenth of the retiree category dies. Assume that $x is equal to 6% of the gross monthly salary that is currently $2000 a month on the average and grows at 10% a year. At the present time, there is $30,000,000 in the pension fund. Develop causal and schematic models for this situation. Write out the equations.

The Solution: Encode a working simulation computer program. Assess the stability and soundness of MAC's pension program over a period of 50 years.

APPENDIX: Electronic Spread Sheets

Imagine for the moment that a giant ledger sheet has been placed in front of you. You have been asked to use the company's current sales and cost data to determine what the corporate balance sheet will look like 6 to 12 months from now. Current rates of growth in product sales as well as material and labor costs are known. In addition, the corporate debt retirement picture is well understood as is the depreciation rate of corporate-owned physical plant and equipment. As you begin to enter data, you use neither paper nor

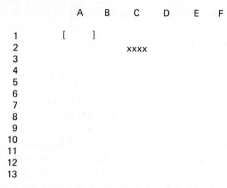

Figure 1   An electronic spread sheet.

pencil. You are using an electronic spread sheet (and a microcomputer). Electronic spread sheets (ESS) are in wide usage today to support corporate modeling — hence, the inclusion of this appendix. Typical ESS are listed in Table 15.7. An example is shown in Figure 1. These packages provide a matrix of cells, each of which has a pair of coordinates that designate the location of each cell in the matrix. For example, the cell in our figure with the *xxxx*'s has the coordinates $C2$. A "cursor" (shown in cell $A1$) can be moved to any cell by use of a cursor movement command — usually ">" or "=" followed by the letter and number of the coordinates of the desired cell. Each cell may contain any one of the following:

1. A label
2. A number
3. An expression that could be evaluated to a number (the numerical expression can be based upon the values of other cells)

To place an entry in a particular cell, simply move the cursor to the desired cell and enter the label, the number, or the expression.

   An example ESS model for the balance sheet problem posed at the beginning of this appendix is shown in Figure 2. The expressions required to calculate the sheet are shown in Figure 3.

Problems for the Appendix

1. Develop an electronic spread sheet of your personal finances to determine how much money can be saved after expenses. Include the following as expense categories: TAKE-HOME PAY, AUTOMOBILE, TUITION, HOUSING, CLOTHING, BOOKS, ENTERTAINMENT, FOOD, TOTAL EXPENSES, AMT TO SAVINGS.
2. Use the model to compute the size of your savings account assuming a constant interest rate and no withdrawals. Add the category SAVINGS to the model in Problem 1 above.
3. Use an electronic spread sheet to solve a problem of interest to you.

	A	B	C	D	E	F	G	H	I	J	K	L	M	N
		Jan	Feb	Mar	Apr	May	Jun	Jul	Aug	Sep	Oct	Nov	Dec	Total
4	ASSETS													
5	Acct.s Receivable	2378.41	2497.33	2622.20	2753.31	2890.97	3035.52	3187.30	3346.66	3513.99	3689.69	3874.18	4067.89	37857.45
6	Cash	300.00	1189.21	1248.67	1311.10	1376.65	1445.49	1517.76	1593.65	1673.33	1757.00	1844.85	1937.09	17194.78
7	Unsold Goods	594.60	624.33	156.08	688.33	722.74	758.88	796.82	836.67	878.50	922.42	968.54	1016.97	8964.90
9	Total Assets	3273.01	4310.87	4026.95	4752.73	4990.37	5239.89	5501.88	5776.98	6065.82	6369.12	6687.57	7021.95	64017.13
11	LIABILITIES													
12	Acct.s Payable	1239.78	1136.47	1041.76	954.95	875.37	802.42	735.55	674.26	618.07	566.56	519.35	476.07	9640.59
13	Storage Costs	65.79	45.33	34.89	75.22	45.87	54.75	35.94	52.83	48.67	39.88	47.88	49.88	596.93
14	Labor	235.66	247.44	259.82	272.81	286.45	300.77	315.81	331.60	348.18	365.59	383.87	403.06	3751.03
15	Materials	35.22	36.98	38.83	40.77	42.81	44.95	47.20	49.56	52.04	54.64	57.37	60.24	560.60
17	Total Liabilities	1576.45	1466.22	1375.29	1343.74	1250.49	1202.89	1134.50	1108.24	1066.95	1026.67	1008.46	989.25	14549.16
19	NIBT	1696.56	2844.65	2651.65	3408.99	3739.87	4037.00	4367.38	4668.73	4998.87	5342.45	5679.11	6032.70	49467.98
20	Dep. Allowance	78.88	67.54	46.91	95.32	74.33	62.81	51.05	107.44	76.82	43.22	82.65	63.41	850.38
21	Taxable Income	1617.68	2777.11	2604.74	3313.67	3665.54	3974.19	4316.33	4561.29	4922.05	5299.23	5596.46	5969.29	48617.60
23	Taxes(@30%)	485.30	833.13	781.42	994.10	1099.66	1192.26	1294.90	1368.39	1476.62	1589.77	1678.94	1790.79	14585.28
25	Net Income	1211.26	2011.52	1870.23	2414.89	2640.21	2844.74	3072.48	3300.35	3522.26	3752.68	4000.17	4241.92	34882.70

Figure 2 A corporate balance sheet projected 12 months into the future.

```
A2   P= "
A3   P= "
B3   P= "Jan
C3   P= "Feb
D3   P= "Mar
E3   P= "Apr
F3   P= "May
G3   P= "Jun
H3   P= "Jul
I3   P= "Aug
J3   P= "Sep
K3   P= "Oct
L3   P= "Nov
M3   P= "Dec
N3   P= "Total
A4   P= "ASSETS
A5   P= "Acct.s Receivable
B5   = 2378.41
C5   = 1.05*B5
D5   = 1.05*C5
E5   = 1.05*D5
F5   = 1.05*E5
G5   = 1.05*F5
H5   = 1.05*G5
I5   = 1.05*H5
J5   = 1.05*I5
K5   = 1.05*J5
L5   = 1.05*K5
M5   = 1.05*L5
N5   = SUM(B5:M5)
A6   P= "Cash
B6   = 300
C6   = 0.5*B5
D6   = 0.5*C5
E6   = 0.5*D5
F6   = 0.5*E5
G6   = 0.5*F5
H6   = 0.5*G5
I6   = 0.5*H5
J6   = 0.5*I5
K6   = 0.5*J5
L6   = 0.5*K5
M6   = 0.5*L5
N6   = SUM(B6:M6)
A7   P= "Unsold Goods
B7   = 0.25*B5
C7   = 0.25*C5
D7   = 0.25*C7
E7   = 0.25*E5
F7   = 0.25*F5
G7   = 0.25*G5
H7   = 0.25*H5
I7   = 0.25*I5
J7   = 0.25*J5
K7   = 0.25*K5
L7   = 0.25*L5
M7   = 0.25*M5
N7   = SUM(B7:M7)
A8   P= '_

A9   P= "Total Assets
B9   = SUM(B5:B7)
C9   = SUM(C5:C7)
D9   = SUM(D5:D7)
E9   = SUM(E5:E7)
F9   = SUM(F5:F7)
G9   = SUM(G5:G7)
H9   = SUM(H5:H7)
I9   = SUM(I5:I7)
J9   = SUM(J5:J7)
K9   = SUM(K5:K7)
L9   = SUM(L5:L7)
M9   = SUM(M5:M7)
N9   = SUM(B9:M9)
A10  P= "
A11  P= "LIABILITIES
A12  P= "Acct.s Payable
B12  = 1239.78
C12  = B12-(B12/12)
D12  = C12-(C12/12)
E12  = D12-(D12/12)
F12  = E12-(E12/12)
G12  = F12-(F12/12)
H12  = G12-(G12/12)
I12  = H12-(H12/12)
J12  = I12-(I12/12)
K12  = J12-(J12/12)
L12  = K12-(K12/12)
M12  = L12-(L12/12)
N12  = SUM(B12:M12)
A13  P= "Storage Costs
B13  = 65.79
C13  = 45.33
D13  = 34.89
E13  = 75.22
F13  = 45.87
G13  = 54.75
H13  = 35.94
I13  = 52.83
J13  = 48.67
K13  = 39.88
L13  = 47.88
M13  = 49.88
N13  = SUM(B13:M13)
A14  P= "Labor
B14  = 235.66
C14  = 1.05*B14
D14  = 1.05*C14
E14  = 1.05*D14
F14  = 1.05*E14
G14  = 1.05*F14
H14  = 1.05*G14
I14  = 1.05*H14
J14  = 1.05*I14
K14  = 1.05*J14
L14  = 1.05*K14
M14  = 1.05*L14
N14  = SUM(B14:M14)

A15  P= "Materials
B15  = 35.22
C15  = 1.05*B15
D15  = 1.05*C15
E15  = 1.05*D15
F15  = 1.05*E15
G15  = 1.05*F15
H15  = 1.05*G15
I15  = 1.05*H15
J15  = 1.05*I15
K15  = 1.05*J15
L15  = 1.05*K15
M15  = 1.05*L15
N15  = SUM(B15:M15)
A16  P= '
A17  P= "Total Liabilities
B17  = SUM(B12:B15)
C17  = SUM(C12:C15)
D17  = SUM(D12:D15)
E17  = SUM(E12:E15)
F17  = SUM(F12:F15)
G17  = SUM(G12:G15)
H17  = SUM(H12:H15)
I17  = SUM(I12:I15)
J17  = SUM(J12:J15)
K17  = SUM(K12:K15)
L17  = SUM(L12:L15)
M17  = SUM(M12:M15)
N17  = SUM(B17:M17)
A18  P= "
A19  P= "NIBT
B19  = B9-B17
C19  = C9-C17
D19  = D9-D17
E19  = E9-E17
F19  = F9-F17
G19  = G9-G17
H19  = H9-H17
I19  = I9-I17
J19  = J9-J17
K19  = K9-K17
L19  = L9-L17
M19  = M9-M17
N19  = SUM(B19:M19)
A20  P= "Dep. Allowance
B20  = 78.88
C20  = 67.54
D20  = 46.91
E20  = 95.32
F20  = 74.33
G20  = 62.81
H20  = 51.05
I20  = 107.44
J20  = 76.82
K20  = 43.22
L20  = 82.65
M20  = 63.41
N20  = SUM(B20:M20)

A21  P= "Taxable Income
B21  = B19-B20
C21  = C19-C20
D21  = D19-D20
E21  = E19-E20
F21  = F19-F20
G21  = G19-G20
H21  = H19-H20
I21  = I19-I20
J21  = J19-J20
K21  = K19-K20
L21  = L19-L20
M21  = M19-M20
N21  = SUM(B21:M21)
A22  P= '
A23  P= "Taxes(@30%)
B23  = 0.3*B21
C23  = 0.3*C21
D23  = 0.3*D21
E23  = 0.3*E21
F23  = 0.3*F21
G23  = 0.3*G21
H23  = 0.3*H21
I23  = 0.3*I21
J23  = 0.3*J21
K23  = 0.3*K21
L23  = 0.3*L21
M23  = 0.3*M21
N23  = SUM(B23:M23)
A24  P= '=
A25  P= "Net Income
B25  = B19-B23
C25  = C19-C23
D25  = D19-D23
E25  = E19-E23
F25  = F19-F23
G25  = G19-G23
H25  = H19-H23
I25  = I19-I23
J25  = J19-J23
K25  = K19-K23
L25  = L19-L23
M25  = M19-M23
N25  = SUM(B25:M25)
```

Figure 3 Expressions required to calculate the balance sheet shown in Figure 2.

REFERENCES

1. PRITSKER, A. *The GASP IV Simulation Language* New York: John Wiley & Sons, 1974.
2. PRITSKER, A., and C. PEGDEN. *Introduction to Simulation and SLAM.* New York: Halsted Press, 1979.
3. NAYLOR, T., and D. GATTIS. "Corporate Planning Models." *California Management Review* (1976), pp. 69–78.

4. Naylor, T., and C. Jeffress, "Corporate Simulation Models: A Survey." *Simulation,* Vol. 24, no. 6 (1975), pp. 171–176.

5. Kane, J., "A Primer for a New Cross-impact Language—KSIM." *Technological Forecasting and Social Change,* Vol. 4 (1972), pp. 129–142.

6. Burns, J., and W. Marcy, "Causality: Its Characterization by Methodologies for Modeling Socio-economic Systems." *Technological Forecasting and Social Change,* Vol. 14 (1979), pp. 387–398.

7. Forrester, J. *Principles of Systems.* Cambridge, Mass.: Wright-Allen Press and MIT Press, 1968.

8. Forrester, J. *Industrial Dynamics.* Cambridge, Mass.: MIT Press, 1961.

9. Forrester, J. *Urban Dynamics.* Cambridge, Mass.: MIT Press, 1969.

10. Forrester, J. *World Dynamics.* Cambridge, Mass.: Wright-Allen Press and MIT Press, 1971.

11. "Computer Games That Planners Play." *Business Week,* Dec. 7, 1978, pp. 66.

12. Watson, H. *Computer Simulation in Business.* New York: John Wiley & Sons, 1981.

13. Meadows, D., D. Meadows, et al. *The Limits to Growth.* New York: Universe Books, 1972.

14. Sage, A. *Methodology for Large-Scale Systems.* New York: McGraw-Hill, 1977.

15. Williams, R. "Computer Simulation of Energy Flow in Cedar Bog Lake, Minnesota, Based on the Classical Studies of Lindeman." In B. Patten, ed., *System Analysis and Simulation in Ecology.* New York: Academic Press, 1971.

16. Goodman, R. *Study Notes in System Dynamics,* Cambridge, Mass.: Wright-Allen Press and MIT Press, 1974.

ADDITIONAL READING

Burns, J., and O. Ulgen. "An Integrated Approach to the Development of Continuous Simulations." *Socio-Economic Planning Sciences,* Vol. 12 (1978), pp. 313–327.

Galitz, L. "Modeling for Bankers." *The Banker,* December 1978, pp. 36.

Gordon, G. *Systems Simulation.* Englewood Cliffs, N.J.: Prentice-Hall, 1978.

Leontief, W. *Input-Output Economics.* Oxford: Oxford University Press, 1966.

———"The Structure of the U.S. Economy." *Scientific American,* Vol. 212 (1965), pp. 25–35.

Naylor, T. *Computer Simulation Experiments with Models of Economic Systems.* New York: John Wiley & Sons, 1971.

Naylor, T. *Corporate Planning Models,* Reading, Mass.: Addison-Wesley, 1979.

Phillips, D., A. Ravindran, and J. Solberg. *Operations Research: Principles and Practice.* New York: John Wiley & Sons, 1976.

PART IV

MANAGERIAL DECISION MAKING: MANAGING THE FUTURE

CHAPTER 16

Management Science
and the Future

And there we have it — our journey through the multifaceted terrain of management science and its models is almost at an end. But textbooks usually end with a sort of "youth looks to the future" chapter, and this one is no exception.

Before we depart on our flight of fancy, however, let us have an informal chat about the preceding chapters of this text. Despite some of the unconventional situations we've been exposed to in the cases, problems, and examples, and notwithstanding some of the puns, bad and otherwise, this is basically a deadly serious book. In fact, if our view of the future turns out to be anywhere near accurate, this book — or some future edition of it — could become a *managerial survival manual.* It was written with that intent.

This textbook has not taught us to do what electronic computers can do. It has attempted to help us do better what computers *can't and never will do at all* — to build coherent models of problems, to analyze and adapt the outputs from computerized algorithms, and to *make better decisions.*

And now to the future.

THE ART OF CONSTRUCTING A CRYSTAL BALL

There are all sorts of ways to build crystal balls with which to peer into the cloudy, mysterious future. Some do it with sophisticated mathematical forecasting techniques; others rely on a pinch of frog hair and other noxious ingredients simmering in a smoky cauldron. The relatively new field of *technological forecasting* attempts to extrapolate what we know about the past evolution of technology to the future.

How do we propose to go about constructing *our* crystal ball? Basically, we will borrow some notions from our friends the "futurists" and state some assumptions about the world of business and public sector organizations in the year 1995. Then we will *deduce* from those assumptions how managerial decision making will be different than it is today. Finally, we will draw *implications* from these deductions for people who are currently preparing themselves to be managerial decision makers.

ASSUMPTIONS: THE WORLD OF 1995

Before we state our technological and behavioral assumptions about the world of 1995, we must first assume that humanity has successfully come to grips with the specter of nuclear holocaust — so that there will then still *be* a planet Earth populated by functioning humanity. Given that we will still exist, then, here are the assumptions upon which we will base our *deductions* about the evolution of the managerial decision-making process and the *implications* therefrom.

Assumption 1: Our rudimentary communications systems of the present will have evolved, through what we will refer to as "organizational automation" (OA), into closely knit, highly integrated systems that link us together in every aspect of life and business.

Assumption 2: Through the automation of routine, repetitive decision-making tasks, managers' time will be much freer to tackle "messes" caused by uncertainty and complexity.

Assumption 3: The world will have moved from the "space age" into the "information age."

Assumption 4: Behavioral science will have advanced our managerial understanding of how people and organizations function to the extent that decision makers *at least* routinely take such things into consideration when making decisions.

And there are our assumptions. Anyone who reads newspapers or weekly news magazines or business publications has seen all of them before in one form or another. However, when we put them all together and use a bit of imagination, the *deductions* we make can be startling.

DEDUCTIONS: THE WORLD OF 1995

The "office," as we know it today, will no longer exist in many organizations. The in box overflowing with memos and "throwaways," the clacking typewriters and humming word processors, the mail room and the ever-out-of-order photocopy machine and the coffee room, lunch from a "brown bag" while hoping that the telephone doesn't ring until we're finished — all of this will be as quaint to many managers in 1995 as quill pens and inkpots seem to managers today. Because these people will no longer "go to the office" each morning, the office will come to them! In these managers' homes, there will be a "living space" and a separate "work space" electronically linked to the co-workers and data bases and analytical tools they need to get the job done. Some of the *current* "catch words" of OA, such as electronic mail, electronic calendaring, personalized word processing, advanced graphics, and extensive data base access, will be routinely available. In addition, sophisticated computerized decision support systems that interact with the decision maker at a conversational level (e.g., LIPS from Chapter 2, RIKLS from Chapter 11) will have been developed, so that instant access to the MS/OR models discussed earlier in this book (among others) will be at the manager's fingertips.

Most routine communication among and between these managers and their staffs will be via highly advanced video teleconferencing systems. Holographic (three-dimensional) display screens will be used to create a more "lifelike" feeling to electronically conducted meetings, briefings, and reports. There will be no telephones as such—all communication will be via the managerial work station, which will contact whomever the manager wishes to talk with upon *voice command.* Electronic language translators will automatically convert conversations into the listener's native tongue.

At the operating level, most routine manufacturing and assembly work will be performed by complex industrial robots, freeing humans for judgmental tasks that neither computers nor robots will ever be able to accomplish. Some of the new products that will be available can only be imagined, and they will be distributed by multinational marketing firms to people in every corner of the world.

Education—both liberal and professional—will play a markedly more important role in society than it does at present. If the "half-life" of technical and scientific knowledge is now ten years, it will be three or four years by 1995. Under the present educational system as we know it, knowledge gained in a four-year baccalaureate program would be largely obsolete *when the student graduated!*

There are our "deductions" that we gleaned from our four assumptions. What implications do these deductions—if accurate—have for decision makers in 1995?

IMPLICATIONS: THE WORLD OF 1995

The first—and probably the most significant—implication that we can draw from our deductions is that "seat-of-the-pants" decision making will have largely been abandoned once and for all before 1995. This is *not* to say that experience and intuition will not still be important factors—they most certainly will. By 1995, however, OR/MS specialists will have found a satisfactory way to incorporate managers' subjective assessment *explicitly* into analytical models.

But why do our deductions imply that "mental model decision making" will have all but disappeared by 1995? Because "organizational automation" will have made decision support systems instantly available—to include data bases of every conceivable description, as well as a wide variety of sophisticated

— but easy-to-use — analytical models and their associated algorithms. The advanced techniques that we saw in the previous chapters under the heading "State of the Art in . . . " will be in as common use as ordinary linear programming is today. The extremely high speed of the computers of 1995 will permit decision makers to do "what-if" analyses on models with almost instant turnaround times. So a manager who stubbornly refused to use scientific analysis in decision making would be analogous to a runner who tried to keep up with a pack of thoroughbred race horses, on foot!

But, contrary to our earlier remark, might not computers have evolved one step farther, in that they will be able to emulate successfully the human decision-making process? Our view is that such an evolution is not only improbable, but impossible. A human being's uniqueness lies in his or her ability to deal with ambiguity and paradox and to correctly deduce conclusions from "fuzzy" incomplete data. Computers, on the other hand, have the ability only to do precisely what they are told — and to do so very quickly. Thus a computer is a completely rational entity, and people are not. Therein lies humankind's genius.

The second implication has to do with the system of higher education and its role in training the managers of 1995 and beyond. In our view, the baccalaureate degree in business administration will no longer exist widely in its present form. Undergraduate education for most prospective managers will focus partly on analytical and communication skills — with a strong dose of theories of human and organizational behavior thrown in for good measure. The purpose of the bachelor's level education, therefore, will be to shape prospective managers as people knowledgeable about the society of which they are a part and to *teach them how to learn.*

The terminal professional degree for managers will be the broad-based Master of Business Administration (MBA) — probably in much its present form. An accredited MBA degree will be required to enter the practice of management, much as the JD is required to practice law or the MD to practice medicine. But, in 1995, when our eager new MBA graduate departs the hallowed halls of academe, *his or her education will have only begun.* The endless process of *continuing professional development,* which will be absolutely essential if decision makers are to be competitive in a complex and rapidly changing world, will begin the first month on the job. And the process won't end until retirement.

If our view of the world of 1995 is accurate, our second implication about the educational process suggests that today's business schools face a monumental task — that of reshaping their educational delivery systems and their faculties to meet the challenge of change brought about by technology. To paraphrase the remarks of the dean of a large business school in a university in the southwestern United States [1],

> Organizational automation (OA) will cause a more fundamental change in the way we work and live than did the invention of the printing press. OA is not some vague possibility in the misty future — it is here now. If we in business schools ignore it, we will quickly become irrelevant to society, and we will quietly fade away.

The third implication has to do with the relationship in 1995 between business and public sector organizations, and the society of which they are a part. Yes — we believe that the profit motive will still be the driving force in the private sector, as will service in the public sector. But the determinants of success will have changed radically. In the "information age," *quality* and *value* will finally become the lodestars of organizational strategy. It is even conceivable that advertising in its present promotional form will have ceased to exist — and that "hard" information on product performance will be supplied to consumers by companies hired by producers to test their products scientifically and to report their test results to the public.

What does this implication suggest for the people who are engaged in producing goods and services in 1995? First, our deduction that industrial robots will perform most of the menial and repetitive tasks that human beings now perform implies that people will earn their living basically by *making decisions* — both large and small. Since these decisions will be motivated by considerations of *quality* and *value*, analytical tools such as those discussed in this text will be in widespread use. Goals such as "maximum quality at minimum cost" suggest a multicriterion approach to decision making, as discussed in Chapter 13 of this text.

The fourth and last implication concerns the nature of power in the organizations of 1995. There will still be formal authority structures with their imbedded hierarchy of decision making — as represented by organizational "wiring diagrams." However, we believe that *functional* decision making (e.g., finance, production) will be much more limited than at present, with many more managers operating in a *project* mode. What successful decision making will require, therefore, is that managers must be more broadly trained and that this training be constantly updated. We speculate that as much as *half* of a manager's time will be spent updating his or her skills and acquiring new ones, and the other half in actually doing the day-to-day job!

EPILOGUE

There's 1995 as we see it — the implications of deductions based on four assumptions about the future. We see a radically different world in which the use of scientific management techniques will be an absolute necessity for survival.

Even in the "wired-up" world of OA in 1995, some things will not have changed at all. People, although somewhat smarter and more sensitive, will still be people. And — one last time:

Models won't make decisions — Managers will.

REFERENCE

1. STEM, C. Unpublished transcript of an address to the Board of Regents of Texas Tech University (1982).

Appendix A

Standardized Normal Distribution

z = # standard deviations to the right of the mean

z	.00	.01	.02	.03	.04	.05	.06	.07	.08	.09
.0	.500	.504	.508	.512	.516	.520	.524	.528	.532	.536
.1	.540	.544	.548	.552	.556	.560	.564	.568	.571	.575
.2	.579	.583	.587	.591	.595	.599	.603	.606	.610	.614
.3	.618	.622	.623	.629	.633	.637	.641	.644	.648	.652
.4	.655	.659	.663	.666	.670	.674	.677	.681	.684	.688
.5	.692	.695	.699	.702	.705	.709	.712	.716	.719	.722
.6	.726	.729	.732	.736	.740	.742	.745	.749	.752	.755
.7	.758	.761	.764	.767	.770	.773	.776	.779	.782	.785
.8	.788	.791	.794	.797	.800	.802	.805	.808	.811	.813
.9	.816	.819	.821	.824	.826	.830	.832	.834	.837	.839
1.0	.841	.844	.846	.849	.851	.853	.855	.858	.860	.862
1.1	.864	.867	.869	.871	.873	.875	.877	.879	.881	.883
1.2	.885	.887	.889	.891	.893	.894	.896	.898	.900	.902
1.3	.903	.905	.907	.908	.910	.912	.913	.915	.916	.918
1.4	.919	.921	.922	.924	.925	.927	.928	.929	.931	.932
1.5	.933	.935	.936	.937	.938	.939	.941	.942	.943	.944
1.6	.945	.946	.947	.948	.950	.951	.952	.953	.954	.955
1.7	.955+	.956	.957	.958	.959	.960	.961	.962	.963	.963+
1.8	.964	.965	.966	.966+	.967	.968	.969	.969+	.970	.971
1.9	.971	.972	.973	.973+	.974	.974+	.975	.976	.976+	.977
2.0	.977	.978	.978+	.979	.979+	.980	.980+	.981	.981+	.982
2.1	.982+	.983	.983+	.983+	.984	.984+	.985	.985+	.985+	.986
2.2	.986+	.986+	.987	.987+	.987+	.988	.988+	.988+	.989	.989+
2.3	.989+	.990	.990	.990+	.990+	.991	.991	.991+	.991+	.992
2.4	.992	.992	.992+	.993	.993	.993	.993+	.993+	.993+	.994
2.5	.994	.994	.994+	.994+	.995	.995	.995	.995	.995+	.995+
2.6	.995+	.996	.996	.996	.996	.996	.996+	.996+	.996+	.996+
2.7	.997	.997	.997	.997	.997	.997	.997+	.997+	.997+	.997+
2.8	.997+	.998	.998	.998	.998	.998	.998	.998	.998	.998+
2.9	.998+	.998+	.998+	.998+	.998+	.998+	.999	.999	.999	.999
3.0	.999	.999	.999+	.999+	.999+	1.000	1.000	1.000	1.000	1.000

Appendix B

Unit Normal Linear Loss Integral

Ln(z)

z	.00	.01	.02	.03	.04	.05	.06	.07	.08	.09
.0	.399	.394	.389	.384	.379	.374	.370	.365	.360	.356
.1	.351	.346	.342	.337	.333	.328	.324	.320	.315	.311
.2	.307	.303	.299	.294	.290	.286	.282	.278	.275	.271
.3	.267	.263	.259	.256	.252	.248	.245	.241	.237	.234
.4	.230	.227	.224	.220	.217	.214	.210	.207	.204	.201
.5	.198	.195	.192	.189	.186	.183	.180	.177	.174	.171
.6	.169	.166	.163	.161	.158	.155	.153	.150	.148	.145
.7	.143	.141	.138	.136	.133	.131	.129	.127	.125	.122
.8	.120	.118	.116	.114	.112	.110	.108	.106	.104	.102
.9	.100	.099	.097	.095	.093	.092	.090	.088	.087	.085
1.0	.083	.082	.080	.079	.077	.076	.074	.073	.071	.070
1.1	.069	.067	.066	.065	.063	.062	.061	.060	.058	.057
1.2	.056	.055	.054	.053	.052	.051	.050	.049	.048	.047
1.3	.046	.045	.044	.043	.042	.041	.040	.039	.038	.037
1.4	.036+	.036	.035	.034+	.034	.033	.032	.031+	.031	.030
1.5	.029+	.029	.028	.027+	.027	.026+	.026	.025	.024+	.024
1.6	.023+	.023	.022+	.022	.021+	.021	.020+	.020	.019+	.019
1.7	.018+	.018	.017+	.017	.016+	.016	.015+	.015	.014+	.014

INDEX